Hotchkiss

Hotchkiss

A Chronicle of an American School

BY ERNEST KOLOWRAT

WITH CONTRIBUTIONS FROM

STEPHEN BIRMINGHAM

C.D.B. BRYAN, AND

JOHN HERSEY

New Amsterdam

Kolowrat, Ernest.

  Hotchkiss : a chronicle of an American school / by Ernest Kolowrat with contributions from Stephen Birmingham, C.D.B. Bryan & John Hersey.

    p. cm.

  Includes index.

  ISBN 1-56131-058-1

  1. Hotchkiss School – History.   I. Title.

LD7501.L35K65   1992

373.746'1 – dc20   92-413

        CIP

Photo Credits: Sven Martson, cover; Robert F. Haiko, pages 65, 468, 523, 554–5; Gabriel A. Cooney, pages 506, 526, 550; Dwight B. Foster, page 302; endleaves, Kelsey-Kennard. Other photos and illustrations courtesy of Hotchkiss School archives.

Mary Meehan Finney

"She would often emerge
from the headmaster's office
on an errand into the main
corridor bristling with boys.
Her presence sent a message
direct to the boys' hearts –
its power muted and refined
by its innocence and purity."
    –Robert V. Massey, Jr. '24

To the Hotchkiss School Staff

Far too often unheralded in the past, their

obliging devotion has been integral to the

school's functioning – whether in caring

for the buildings and grounds, preparing

the daily fare, providing medical care,

keeping the accounts straight, or carrying

out the myriad secretarial and other

service tasks. Symbolic of this role has

been the forty-year service of Mary

Meehan Finney as secretary to four

headmasters, whose burdens she lightened

immeasurably. At ninety-four, she

continues to reside not far from the school

where she first went to work as a young

woman.

Thank you, Mary Finney; thank you one

and all of the Hotchkiss staff.

Contents

First graduating class of the Hotchkiss School

Excerpt from Articles of Association

New Haven, Connecticut, July 7, 1891

Amended on July 17, 1974, at board of trustees

meeting to read ". . . for the preparation of

young men and women for a college or

university course."

What Made Maria Do It?

BY STEPHEN BIRMINGHAM '46

I t is the smells of the school that I remember best: the sour smell of the oil they rubbed the desks with; the classroom smell of chalk dust and old maps; the smell of fuller's earth scattered in wide arcs along the corridors, ahead of the pushbrooms that formed fat kittens out of the dirt tracked in daily by some three hundred pairs of feet; the smell of a master's unlighted pipe; the smell that would periodically drift through the school late in the morning to tell us that we were going to have corned beef and cabbage for lunch; the steamy, chlorinated smell of the indoor pool; the smell of the gym, which was a mixture of wintergreen oil and sneakers.

There are sounds too – the noise of showers running; the whack of a hockey stick against the puck; the sound of a springboard – which instantly bring back the whole flavor of school days to me, along with the random pictures, etched on my brain with such clarity and poignancy at the time that I can still see a play of sunlight on the ivy of a certain wall; an avenue of moonlight across the frozen lake; the small, pointed handwriting of the headmaster ("The following boys will please see me"); the molasses-colored varnish on my window sill; the thickening layer of stamps and address stickers on the laundry case I mailed home each week.

I am talking here, of course, of the days when Hotchkiss was still an all-male affair. But there was nonetheless a strong female presence at the school. Her portrait hung on the dining room wall, and her eyes seemed to follow you as you moved about the room. She was not a young woman when her portrait was painted. She appeared to have

1

been somewhat past middle age. There was nothing motherly about her face, however, nor was there anything to suggest that she had ever been pretty. Her jawline was strong and firm. Hers was a no-nonsense New England nose. Her wide-spaced eyes were alert and intelligent but wore a somewhat startled look. Just a trace of an almost forced-seeming smile hovered about her rather thin lips. Her expression, I used to think, was that of a well-brought-up woman who has just been told a tasteless joke.

She was, I knew, Mrs. Maria Bissell Hotchkiss, the school's principal benefactress, without whose money there would have been no Hotchkiss School. Then why, I used to wonder, did the school's official portrait of her not depict her looking more pleased with herself?

As a student at Hotchkiss, I developed a theory about this somber woman. She was, we had been told, the widow of the man who had not exactly invented but had somehow perfected the machine gun – a claim to fame that always struck me as something of an oxymoron. And so it was my naive assumption that Maria (and I am certain that she pronounced it Mar-EYE-ah, as my Yankee grandmother did) had established an elite school for boys in order to atone in some measure for the many promising young male lives that her husband's invention, or perfection, had mowed down during the course of various wars. That accounted for the odd expression on her face. It was an expression of guilt over being the recipient of bloodstained money.

That, it turns out, is not too far from the truth. Maria Hotchkiss had good reasons to feel guilty. So, in fact, did her husband. But that is as far as it goes, and lethal weapons were not the issue. The issues were far more human ones, and the story of how Hotchkiss came into being turns out to be a tale of an unhappy marriage; of a wife's refusal to be a proper nineteenth-century wife, while at the same time refusing to consent to a divorce; of an inevitable other woman; of a bigamous marriage involving forged documents; of a child born out of legal wedlock, and that child's early death – enough betrayals and plot twists, along with cliffhangers and unanswered questions, to inspire a revival of "Dallas" – and, finally, of the influence of a charismatic New England educator on an iron-willed farmer's daughter who was searching, a bit haphazardly, for a worthy cause.

Maria Harrison Bissell was born in 1827 in Salisbury, Connecticut, and grew up there on Tory Hill. There had been prominent Bissells in Litchfield County since the eighteenth century, and Harrison cousins in Ohio – in what was once Connecticut's Western Reserve – had already produced one and, in Maria's lifetime, would produce a second U.S. president. But Maria's father was a thrifty, though impecunious farmer.

In the early nineteenth century, if a young woman was not deemed marriageable by the time she reached eighteen, and if her family was not rich, she faced severely limited career choices. The two most available options were to become a schoolteacher – or a prostitute. Well-bred young women, naturally, were expected to choose the less lucrative of these professions. It seems likely that Maria's family foresaw spinsterhood for her because, after finishing high school, she was sent "away" to Amenia Academy, some ten miles distant across the New York State line. She returned, a year later, to become a schoolmistress at the same little red schoolhouse (still standing today as a private residence on what is now Route 112 in Salisbury) that she had attended as a child. Her salary was $4.50 a month. On this, she was expected to live at home with her parents and make do.

Then, in 1850, when Maria was twenty-three, her knight in shining armor appeared, or so it must have seemed to this girl of slender means. His name was Benjamin Berkeley Hotchkiss – Berk, to his friends – one year her senior, born in Watertown, Connecticut, but moved at the age of three to nearby Sharon, where his father ran a moderately successful hardware manufacturing business. Berk Hotchkiss proposed marriage, and Maria accepted him.

With Berk and his father, Asahel Hotchkiss, in the family business was Berk's older brother, Andrew. Though Andrew Hotchkiss was severely handicapped – he had been born without legs and pushed himself about in a handcart – he was something of an inventive genius, particularly in the field of military hardware. The firm was already busily patenting, manufacturing, and marketing Andrew Hotchkiss's inventions. He developed the Hotchkiss rifle field gun, two of which were later mounted on the grounds of Les Invalides, Napoleon's tomb in Paris. He also developed the Hotchkiss shot and shell. Other Hotchkiss contributions to modern warfare were cannon projectiles, percussion fuses, cannon rifling, metallic cartridge cases, a five-barreled machine gun, and a magazine rifle patent that was sold to Winchester Repeating Arms.

Maria's husband would later contribute inventions of his own but would always modestly insist that he could not have done so without the inspiration of his older brother. At the time of his marriage to Maria, Berk Hotchkiss, a hail-fellow, gregarious sort, from all reports, who made friends easily, was essentially the company's salesman.

The Civil War, which would create a number of fortunes in America, was not far off. Andrew Hotchkiss would not live to hear of the first shots fired on Fort Sumter, but he had evidently sensed that they were coming. Before he died, he urged his father and his brother to "keep on with the target practice," just in case munitions should be needed, as indeed they would be. In fact, rumors have persisted that during the North-South conflict, the Hotchkiss factories sold arms, ordnance supplies, and ammunition to both the Union and the Confederate armies. If true, the Hotchkisses were not the only American company that found dealing with both sides profitable. And, true or not, the Hotchkisses were nonetheless able to boast, by the war's end, that they had produced more projectiles for the Civil War than all other American munitions manufacturers combined. Thousands killed!

Meanwhile, Berk's and Maria's marriage was already in serious trouble. For one thing, their union was still childless. In those days, a barren marriage was an embarrassment, if not a disgrace, to a man and deeply painful to a woman since the situation was generally assumed to be her fault. There is evidence that both Berk and his father had rebuked Maria for her failure to produce, in particular, a son to carry on the family business. Furthermore, Maria was proving to be a failure to Berk in perhaps an even more important area. At the time, wives of successful men were expected to devote themselves to the comfort and adornment of their husbands' lives. As a man rose in the world, financially and socially, his wife was supposed to serve as his perfect, charming hostess, ever at his side, ready to gather the ladies into the drawing room after dinner while the gentlemen repaired to the library for brandy and cigars. But while genial Berk Hotchkiss found himself moving into higher and higher business and social circles and dealing, in his arms business, even with international heads of state, Maria dragged her heels. She either spitefully refused or was constitutionally unable to take part in a high society sort of life. When her husband traveled to Europe, Maria remained behind in Connecticut.

Years later, after Berk Hotchkiss's death, when the thin tissue of deceptions Berk had woven about his life began to unravel, the old *New York Herald* devoted nearly a full page to the Hotchkiss scandal. The *Herald*, it should be remembered, was never famed for editorial integrity, particularly when it felt it had a hot story. And so, though the bare bones of the *Herald*'s story may be correct, some of the interpretations and analyses by the (presumably male) reporter may be open to question.

According to the *Herald*, Maria was clearly to blame for the disintegration of her marriage. Quoting an anonymous "lifelong friend" of Berk Hotchkiss's, Berk "tried to induce her to take her proper place at the head of his establishment when he was constantly receiving people of note, but she was not adapted to shine in social life. It was patent to everyone that such affiliations were utterly beyond her." If true, Berk Hotchkiss would have felt doubly betrayed by his wife. She had failed to produce an heir, and she wouldn't help him entertain his customers.

Meanwhile, Berk Hotchkiss was about to do some betraying of his own. "He absolutely needed," this same lifelong friend continued, "someone in the relation of a wife who was able to keep up and push ahead his social and political acquaintance."

By the beginning of the Civil War, it seemed that such a woman already existed in Berk Hotchkiss's life. She was a certain Miss Cunningham of New York — no record of her first name has been uncovered – and there is evidence that she first worked for him as his secretary. Soon, however, Miss Cunningham was accompanying him on his travels and acting as his hostess.

Back in Connecticut, of course, where Maria continued her spinsterish existence, the rumormongers had another word for this woman "in the relation of a wife." Berk Hotchkiss had taken a mistress and was begging his wife for a divorce, which she refused to give him. One can only imagine the pitying looks that poor Maria was forced to endure from her friends and neighbors in the little New England town.

Then, in 1867, there was more shocking news. Berk Hotchkiss, with Miss Cunningham in tow, had moved permanently to Paris. There, perhaps outraged at Maria's refusal to divorce him, Berk Hotchkiss decided to marry Miss Cunningham anyway. They were married in a French civil ceremony, and the young woman who for the next eighteen years would style herself Mrs. Benjamin Berkeley Hotchkiss was apparently shown some faked documents indicating that her husband was free of other marital entanglements in America. "Some legal chicanery was indulged in," the friend told the *Herald*, "and through some lawyer he secured a make-believe set of divorce papers that were shown her. Don't for a moment suppose that she had a shadow of a suspicion that she bore any other relation to him than that of legal wife. We didn't blame him either, though of course it was wrong. He had a deep affection for her, and she was in every way calculated to enhance his prospects."

Maria Hotchkiss must certainly have known that her husband had a new romantic interest. Whether she knew, at the time, that he had become a bigamist is unclear.

The second Mrs. Hotchkiss was apparently able to do everything that Maria would not or could not do for Berk. Though she was, like Maria, no beauty, "the fame of the splendor of her receptions rang through the Continent," gushed the same ubiquitous and verbose lifelong friend. "It was her engaging manner, her clever *bon mots*, a naturally winning disposition and her ready tact that made her the diplomatist she was. She almost held the politicians of Europe in her hands, and when she had finished with them the Hotchkiss gun was generally adopted by that nation." The former Miss Cunningham also gave Berk Hotchkiss an heir, albeit a daughter, who died at the age of nine. His daughter's death was said to have left him brokenhearted.

In France, Berk set about making himself a second fortune. During the last days of the Franco-Prussian War, he had noticed certain short-comings in the French *mitrailleuse*, or machine gun. The weapon op-erated well from ground installations but was next to useless when mounted on the deck of a warship, where the motion of the ship's deck made the gun difficult to aim with accuracy. Using a complex system of gimbals, Hotchkiss began designing what he called a revolving can-non for maritime warfare, and soon he was sinking most of his com-pany's Civil War profits into perfecting this device.

The revolving cannon was the biggest gamble in Hotchkiss's invent-ing and manufacturing career, and for a while it looked as though he had failed. In 1873, Berk was described as being "in straightened [*sic*] circumstances," and four years later the firm's profits from the cannon amounted to less than one thousand francs. But in 1878, the French minister of marine began ordering the revolving cannon and soon was buying it in large numbers. Other countries, including the United States, followed suit, and within a few years the Hotchkiss firm's prof-its on this weapon alone were nearly seven million francs.

This all came abruptly to an end on Valentine's Day, 1885, when Benjamin Berkeley Hotchkiss was stricken with what was described as an apoplectic stroke and was dead at the age of fifty-nine. That he left no will was surely no accident. As a bigamist, he must have known that a deceased man cannot have two legal widows. He had apparently tried to think of some way to take care of wife number two. "A year or so before he died," the *Herald*'s privileged source claimed, "he told me that he would give a million dollars if he could so smooth things out that when he was gone she would be in a position that he would have her." Surely some way could have been devised to make a bequest to her. Instead, he seems to have taken the cowardly route and made no bequests at all. Let others handle this mess, he seemed to have decided.

And quite a mess it was. If it was on his death that Maria Hotchkiss discovered her husband's marital shenanigans, that discovery may partly account for the peculiar expression on Maria's face in the school's portrait. Months of international and probably very secret legal negotiations followed, for it was not until more than three years later, in April 1888, that the *Herald* published its scandalous story, and skeletons began tumbling out of closets. And more time would pass before the matter of Berk Hotchkiss's estate was settled.

The estate was estimated at $12 million, including shares of some very profitable companies. According to U.S. laws, under which the estate was probated, half was to go to Berk's aged father in Sharon and half to his legal widow, Maria. The former Miss Cunningham, faced with the double whammy that her marriage had been a fraud and that she had been left penniless to boot, must have been understandably bitter. When she continued to fight for some share of the estate, according to the *New York Times*, "the heirs bought her off by paying a large sum." Not so, said the lifelong friend in the *Herald*. The former Miss Cunningham received nothing. Had her child by Berk Hotchkiss lived, of course, it might have been quite different. And so, in the *Herald*'s words, "a broken-hearted woman, self-exiled from the society that once not only admired but loved her, [she] drags out a cheerless existence in the secluded corners of the earth." Which sounds like a reporter's tear-jerky way of saying that no one knows what became of the woman who was once the toast of the Continent.

It is improbable that Maria Hotchkiss received fully a half of that estimated $12 million estate, and if so, the actual estate probably fell far short of the estimate. Based on circumstantial evidence and the impressions left by some of Berk's widow's longer-lived friends, $1 or $2 million seems to be a more likely sum. Still, that would translate in today's money to between $15 and $30 million – making Maria one of the richest women in Connecticut. Let's permit her a moment or two of quiet gloating – that her husband's shabby treatment of her, based on what he perceived as her shabby treatment of him, had had this full-circle outcome. The bird – his money – had come home to roost. All at once the long-suffering abandoned wife found herself being viewed with new interest and respect by her formerly patronizing neighbors.

In 1889, four years after Benjamin Hotchkiss's death, Andrew Carnegie published an article in the *North American Review* titled, simply, "Wealth." The first duty of the person of wealth, Carnegie wrote, was "to set an example of modest, unostentatious living, shunning display or extravagance; to provide moderately for the legitimate wants of those dependent on him; and after doing so to consider all surplus revenues which came to him simply as trust funds, which he is called upon to administer, and strictly bound as a matter of duty to administer in the manner . . . best calculated to produce the most beneficial results for the community."

Carnegie's treatise, and the so-called Gospel of Wealth it detailed, had a profound effect on the collective psyches of America's rich people, most of whom had not been rich for very long. Up to then, few American millionaires had been troubled by anything as bothersome as a social conscience. In fact, most rich people had assumed that wealth came as a *reward* for virtue, not the other way around. That the rich should be expected, much less obligated, to contribute anything at all was a new and thrilling, if also somewhat frightening, idea. On the one hand, it offered the rich a way to star in the roles of Lords and Ladies Bountiful, to see their names emblazoned forever on the façades of hospitals, libraries, orphanages, and museums. On the other hand, it also made them sitting ducks for solicitations from all sorts of Worthy Causes to which, it was argued, it was their *Christian Duty* to contribute. Whether or not Mr. Carnegie's thesis had any effect on the Widow Hotchkiss's thinking, it is impossible to say, but it was about this time that Maria began considering ways to distribute at least some of her windfall for the common weal.

Needless to say, she was besieged with helpful suggestions for ways in which she and her money could part company. The Sharon *Bobolink* suggested editorially that a new hospital might be a fitting memorial for her late husband. Though Maria was not particularly interested in memorializing Benjamin, she did have some ideas of her own. One of her late husband's many patents had been for a macadamlike street-paving material. Also on the Hotchkiss drawing boards were plans for an automobile. Looking about at the rutted country roads of Salisbury and neighboring Sharon, she decided that she would personally pay to have all the streets of both towns macadamized. Pavements would be her legacy to that corner of her native county.

Apparently the two communities reacted with a certain amount of dismay to this unusual offer. Neither community possessed the equipment or the manpower to maintain paved streets, and there was a certain amount of civic huffing and puffing over Mrs. Hotchkiss's proposal. The idea died a-borning.

Did someone then suggest to Maria that, as a former schoolteacher, a more appropriate gift from her might be in the field of education, rather than highway construction? No one knows, but Maria's next thought was to establish a school for children who were feebleminded, the noneuphemistic term of that more straightforward era. A number of her late husband's factories in Connecticut and New York had employed children in menial tasks on the assembly line. If the feeble-minded could be trained in certain trades and taught to perform rote chores, Maria would be educating a useful labor force.

At this point, with Maria's thoughts turning toward the idea of a school, the redoubtable Timothy Dwight, president of Yale, entered the picture. Dwight was a commanding figure of his era, described by a contemporary as the unofficial Congregational Pope of New England. His grandfather, another Timothy Dwight, had been president of Yale during the American Revolution, and *his* grandfather had been the legendary Jonathan Edwards, whose descendants have included no fewer than thirteen college presidents, three of Yale alone. On the distaff side, through the daughters of Jonathan Edwards and his wife, have descended other American men of eminence, including two presidents, Grant and Cleveland, and Supreme Court Chief Justice Morrison Waite. With this pantheon of ancestors and cousins arrayed about him, few people disputed the ideas of Timothy Dwight, especially when this tall, black-frocked Yankee patrician deigned to appear in person, as he did when he came to reason with Maria Hotchkiss. And Timothy Dwight's idea for this wealthy widow was to finance a school that would prepare young men for college – for Yale, to be precise.

But still Maria seemed unconvinced. Her Yankee disposition was not to be easily impressed. When she learned that Dwight had a private boys school in mind, she also reputedly protested that she did not want to build "a school for the pampered sons of rich gentlemen." A free high school or an academy was more in line with her ideals. Not until the Yale president assured her that deserving boys from the surrounding communities would receive free tuition did Maria finally relent – and agree to provide the wherewithal to establish the school.

This "second marriage" for Maria Hotchkiss would prove to be no happier than her first, as readers of Ernest Kolowrat's history will discover in detail. She undoubtedly had never been properly apprised of the final cost of the school bearing her name. She soon had reason to think of herself as a beleaguered female being bled by money-thirsty males, while her advice on financial management of the school was repeatedly spurned. And her youthful beneficiaries could never quite feel at ease with this elderly crusty lady who refused to learn to be a hostess. From time to time, she invited Hotchkiss boys to her house for buttermilk and ginger cookies, which they dutifully downed before departing as soon as was politely possible.

Maria Hotchkiss spent much of her last years in New York, where she kept a permanent suite at the Plaza Hotel.* During her periodic forays to Lakeville, she would stay not in the modest farmhouse on Tory Hill where she had been born, but at the Farnam Tavern – a favorite spot of Hotchkiss boys, where they would sneak an occasional beer. She died in New York in 1901, at the age of seventy-four. With good reason, one supposes, she chose not to repose beside her faithless husband in Sharon. Instead, she lies, with her Bissell relatives, in the Town Hill Cemetery in Lakeville, a few steps from the Hotchkiss head-

---

*Not the Trumpish Plaza that New Yorkers know today, but a much more modest Plaza that occupied the site prior to 1907.

master's house. Sooner or later during their years at the school, most students will wander to gaze at the conspicuous obelisk marking the spot.

Maria's school has flourished, and this book tells how, with inevitable ups and downs, it has managed to do so for a hundred years, taking on a life of its own, quite independent of Maria.

Maria didn't get her way, exactly, but the streets of Salisbury and Sharon got paved anyway.

Fair Hotchkiss!

Kicked Out

BY C. D. B. BRYAN '54

My favorite spot at Hotchkiss was Taylor Field, the hilltop playing field across from Monahan Gym that served as the scene of my sole triumph at the school – athletic or otherwise. It took place my lower mid year during a baseball game for the club championship. My mother had come up, the only visit I can recall either of my parents making to any of the four boarding schools I attended.

I was Taylor's catcher, notorious for my two-bounce peg to second that never once caught a base-stealing runner. That special afternoon it was the last half of the ninth inning; the bases were loaded, the game was tied, and there were two out. Our coach, the beloved George Norton Stone, must have been desperate; if he'd had any alternative, he certainly would have replaced me at bat.

As I watched the first called strike pass me by, I could hear my teammates chanting, "Get a hit! Get a hit!" And I did! A blooping single that dropped like a water balloon behind the second baseman's head. The winning run scored; the championship was ours. Afterward, my mother told me that my teammates had been shouting not "Get *a* hit," but "Get hit!" so that I would have been given an automatic pass to first base.

The following spring, I was not playing baseball anymore. I was clearing brush, building bridges, cutting trails, sentenced to the woods squad for having possessed an electric coffeepot; confined for my infraction to a category called super-sequestration special disciplinary action group. And later, at the end of that spring term, when for some reason I panicked and flunked four out of five of my final exams, I further condemned myself to attending the Hotchkiss summer school.

At seventeen, I was already a smoker. June through August was the only time during which I could safely smoke, and I chafed with impatience at the summer school rules. As a result, near the end of that session, I lit up a Lucky Strike in direct defiance of the no smoking restriction and walked smoking it into Mr. Stone's rooms. He looked as stricken by what I had done as by what he knew he must do. "Well, you might as well finish it," he said.

At the end of that summer I was, as they put it, "asked not to return." I spent my final year of boarding school at nearby Berkshire, where the conversation at the seniors' table my first night was, as I recall, which school we had attended the year before.

Twenty-four years later, as I drove my thirteen-year-old son St. George to Hotchkiss to begin his prep year, we passed by Taylor Field awash in the morning light; it was so lovely a shade of lime green it took my breath away.

I turned to my son sitting beside me. "Did I ever tell you about the baseball game I played in for the club championship on this field?" I asked.

"Only about a million times," he said.

I don't think it's all that odd that I wanted my son to attend a school from which I had been expelled. Externally, the Hotchkiss I attended in the early 1950s was, with the exception of young women, pretty much the same as the Hotchkiss of the late seventies and early eighties. More important, many of the same faculty members were still there, among them the two men by whom I had been most influenced throughout my schooling: George Norton Stone and Robert Hawkins.

I had enrolled my son hoping he would find at Hotchkiss something of the academic excitement and generosity of spirit that had meant so much to me. And, yes, I hoped that the school might improve his chances of getting into the college of his choice. But I think most of all I hoped Saint would harvest at Hotchkiss a few enduring friendships, a keen appreciation of the elegance of education, and the sort of memories of a very special time and a very special faculty in a very special place that have warmed me all these years.

I had come to Hotchkiss in midterm after being expelled from the Episcopal High School in Virginia for cheating on a Latin exam. I had waited distraught and disgraced while my parents desperately searched for a school that would take me in. And when my mother asked me, "What would you think of going to Hotchkiss?" I could reply only, "It's a funny name for a school."

I was interviewed by the Duke, and although I can't say we warmed to each other, he must have decided I was worth a second chance. Hotchkiss would take me, he said, but I would have to slip back a year. There was no room in Buehler with the other preps; I was placed on the second floor of McChesney, a little white clapboarded building miles, it seemed, from the center of things. There was only one other student in McChesney at that time, an older boy: Griffith Rose.

Putting me in McChesney with Rose was like putting a Viennese Choir Boy in with Oscar Wilde. I will never forget turning around that first afternoon while unpacking to discover Rose lounging against my door, wearing a fabulously soiled silk bathrobe. He was holding a Russian cigarette – one of those black ones with about half an inch of tobacco at the end of four inches of cardboard filter tip – and as he stood, head tilted back to inspect me, he exhaled twin, delicious streams of smoke from his nose.

"What are you doing here?" he asked.

"Unpacking," I said.

"No, no," he said, airily dismissing my answer with a wave of his hand. "I mean what are you doing *here*, at *Hotchkiss?*"

"I didn't have much choice," I told him. "I just got expelled from my former school."

"You were *expelled?*" he asked, his face breaking into a delighted grin. "For what?"

"Cheating," I mumbled ashamedly.

"My God," Rose laughed, "you mean they actually expelled you for *that?*"

I nodded.

"What a bunch of assholes," Rose said. "Care for a cigarette and some Lapsang Souchong?"

Rose and I got along fine.

The fall of my lower mid year I was on George Stone's corridor in Coy. I'm not sure he ever understood, despite my efforts to articulate it during subsequent years, how much I appreciated all the kindness he and Jodie, his wife, showed me. I don't mean to suggest they had singled me out in any particular way; they were good to us all. But somehow, they intuitively knew when a boy needed to be invited in for a cup of tea and a soft voice, when a boy had had enough of pretending to be grown up. Somehow they recognized and nurtured our individuality despite our trying so hard to look alike: six Brooks Brothers button-down shirts, three white, three blue; two pairs of gray flannels and three pairs of khaki trousers; one hand-me-down brown herringbone Harris tweed jacket; one new blue blazer; a half-dozen ties, four striped regimentals, one paisley, one black knit; two pairs of cotton pajamas; one ancient hand-me-down flannel bathrobe; one pair of Bass Weejun loafers; one pair white Keds. I even wore my hair cut short and plastered to one side just like the guys from Grosse Pointe. On them it looked good. I was skinny, already six feet tall, with a long, reedy neck and narrow head. I resembled a giant insect with a crewcut.

I passed through Hotchkiss like a Chinese dinner. I'm not in any of the class pictures. I appear in only one *Mischianza*, the 1953, in the photo of the curiously spelled "Syncapators," our Dixieland band. I played banjo, Peter Duchin the piano, and the great Roz Rudd was on trombone. Even at that age they looked like musicians; I looked like a praying mantis clutching my banjo like a twig.

When I think about Hotchkiss, I think about the faculty: George Van Santvoord sighing, "I would simply say here is a boy who has done a terribly silly thing," when he was about to announce some wretch's punishment. I think about Thomas Price Stearns, who looked like what he had been: a Marine Corps sergeant. "Butch" we called him – though, God knows, never to his face. "All the way down, boy!" he would bellow during pushups at P. T. He wore tweed jackets as bristly as his beard. And there was wiry, doe-eyed Lou Connick, who was rumored to have been with the CIA. And of course, Charles Garside, Jr., of the jaw-jut, the high standards, the trilling laugh, the dramatic flair for teaching. Garside had gone from Exeter directly into the navy for the Second World War and then returned to attend Princeton. I wish I'd known him well enough to ask what that had been like.

My favorite English teacher was "The Hawk" – a nickname having less to do with Robert Hawkins's name, I always thought, than his ability to swoop down on the hapless student who was unprepared. I'm not sure that Hotchkiss graduates aren't the only Americans who know how to use a semicolon properly. The Hawk was responsible for that and more; he was the first to make me appreciate how precise and eloquent our English language is.

And there was tall, red-haired George Norton Stone, who taught me Math III-g and said, "Bryan, you're an *idiot* in math! I suggest you complete this course, fulfill your math requirement, and never *ever* come near a numeral again." He was right; my wife does our book-keeping. My God, the number of blackboard erasers and pieces of chalk he whizzed by my ears! "If you don't pay attention, I'm going to be all over you like a tent!" I loved that man – and Jodie, too.

Jodie Stone, who, like George, must have been over six feet tall, had the most beautiful legs of any woman I have ever seen – not, I hasten to add, that she ever showed them to me! George had in his rooms at Coy a mesmerizing photograph of Jodie sitting on a large rock before a tumbling stream. I suppose Jodie was in her very early twenties at the time. She was wearing shorts and a white shirt with the sleeves rolled up. Either her shorts were small to begin with or, in her efforts to keep herself from sliding down the rock, they had ridden up her thighs; but she is sitting sideways to the camera, facing to the left, her bare legs in profile. Her right knee is raised, the foot braced against the steep slope of the rock; the left leg, the leg closest to the camera, is straight, the toes pointed to dip into the icy water. She and George had just met; she is laughing happily; there is a thermos jug behind her, and in the bottom right corner of the photo what might be the tip of George's thumb. I don't think I saw any of that those evenings I was invited for tea in the Stones' apartment in Coy Hall. In those days, when I sneaked a glance at that photograph, all I could focus on were those long, perfectly shaped showgirl legs! They would have made a Vegas chorine green with envy!

I never forgot that photograph; and several years ago, just after George's death, I drove up to Hotchkiss to see Jodie, to take her out to lunch. After a certain amount of hemming and hawing, I finally worked up enough nerve to blurt out how that photograph had seared its way into my memory. A couple of days later, to my astonishment, it arrived in the mail. When I looked at that photograph again, for the first time in – what, almost forty years? – I was surprised to see I had not romanticized it all. It is still a photograph of a young woman with the most beautiful legs I have ever seen!

Well, not only did I never see Jodie Stone's legs, I never saw *any* girl's legs during those years. When I think back on how unnatural our lives were in our all-male boarding schools, how cloistered in mind and body we lived, I am surprised we survived intact. I recall the rare prom I attended, palms damp with anxiety, and the even rarer joint glee club concert – why else would so many boys want to sing? – with girls as nervous and jittery as we. In those days I never had a girl friend, much less a girlfriend, and I went to proms and concerts alone. But, then again, I suppose there was not much demand among the girls at Farmington or Miss Hall's for a boy who looked like he'd be most comfortable on a twig.

What did we boys do among ourselves? We pied each other's beds, we removed the hinge-pins from each other's bedroom door so that it fell on whoever opened it. We replaced each other's bureau drawers upside down; removed and hid each other's light bulbs; turned radiators up full; taped the brass tips of Scripto automatic pencils to shaving cream cans to shoot a spray a dozen yards. In the showers we snapped wet towels at each other's naked posteriors; gave each other "noogies": knuckle-punches to the biceps. We rolled wastebaskets and raced turtles down the hallways. And because we had read the newly published *Catcher in the Rye*, we railed against the "phonies" all about. But most of all, we went to classes together, took tests together, played sports together, ate in the dining hall together, studied together in study hall. In effect, what we did was *grow up* together. Many of my best friends at Hotchkiss I saw again at Yale. They are good friends still. We are the "old farts" now at the reunions.

I'm sorry I was kicked out of Hotchkiss. I suppose they had to do it; I had, after all, broken some major rules – major to them, at any rate, and major at that time. It all seems kind of silly now. "Daddy, what did you get kicked out of Hotchkiss for?"

"For having an electric coffeepot and smoking a Lucky Strike."

I can just hear what Griffith Rose would have to say about that!

The old dining hall

Part One

1   The Duke's Way:

A Memoir

E ver experience that piercing moment when another person seems to glance to the very core of you? When you feel stripped of all pretense, your armor penetrated, and your heart read in a way it has never been before?

This is what happened to me in the final days as a senior at Hotchkiss. What made my exposure all the more distressing was that it took place under the eyes of the one person at the school whom I especially admired and liked – George Van Santvoord, or the Duke, as the headmaster was universally referred to out of his earshot.

The best way to understand the Duke is within the context of some of that era's traditions and rules. Then as today the school motto was *Moniti Meliora Sequamur*, "Having been admonished, let us follow better ways." To make the process seem voluntary, the words *advised* or *instructed* were often substituted for *admonished* in the Blue Book of rules. There was a strong presumption that the school's guidance should lead beyond the mere correcting of errors to something positively good, such as becoming chairman of the Ford Motor Company, founding *Time* magazine, or being elected governor of New Jersey. Of course, if this benevolent paternalism failed to work, there was a system of graduated punishments. The most immediate and effective of these was having to spend two hours on Saturday night in study hall. This punishment could be imposed on the spot, by any member of the faculty, for such offenses as chronic inattention in class or casual disregard of authority. Saturday night was your free evening of the week, and study hall meant missing the movie in the auditorium. For graver offenses, such as sneaking out after lights, the faculty could vote censure or sequestration. Short of expulsion, sequestration was the most extreme punishment that could be imposed. It meant total banishment from social life for six weeks, which included having to move from your dorm to old Main or to the top floor of the headmaster's house; spending your free time in study hall, and, instead of athletics, running the triangle, a scenic but torturous five-mile course around and beyond the school grounds. Such exercise was supplemented, in my time, by servitude on the woods squad.

The woods squad was the personal creation of the Duke. Working alongside the headmaster for two hours each day was considered the most arduous part of the sequestration ordeal. It was not the task of keeping the hiking trails clear in the school's extensive forests that was so demanding. It was the Duke himself. Looking fit in his wash khakis and checkered wool shirt, the sixty-year-old white-haired headmaster was the hardest worker on the squad – and an exhausting conversationalist. He was rumored to be among the few people who understood, and could make others understand, Einstein's theory of relativity. And the Duke's reputation for brilliance was not restricted to the educational world. Important figures in industry and government often sought his commonsense advice. He was reputed to have been a confidant of Franklin Roosevelt; during the Truman years, when I was there, word had it that Harry S occasionally consulted the Duke by phone.

On the woods squad, the Duke would puff calmly on his pipe while wielding a saw or an axe and draw the sequestered students into discussions which they were hoping to avoid. He would insist on debating seemingly ridiculous topics. Should Mickey Mouse be allowed to have a driver's license? Should Lake Wononscopomuc be stocked with freshwater sharks? Wouldn't it be better to make golf a ten-hole or a twenty-hole game? Why nine or eighteen? "Those are pretty strange numbers, don't you think?" the Duke might suggest to a boy held captive on the other end of a handsaw, halfway through a heavy log. "I know if I were Ralph Vogel or someone else on the golf team, I would certainly want to keep my score in round numbers. Maybe we should consult the mathematics department. Find out what Dr. Renny and Mr. Hale have to say."

And so it would continue. There was no way a student could win in debating the Duke. No matter which side you happened to choose, the Duke would automatically take the opposite tack. Sometimes he would sucker you in, pretending he was agreeing, only to end up demolishing his own arguments, until you did not have the vaguest idea where you stood. No wonder that by the end of the day, most of the boys on the woods squad would be done in. The Duke, looking like the ruler of some domain, would not even be breathing hard.

Of course, every now and then one of the students would see the light. Almost overnight, the woods squad would become no longer something to be dreaded, a painful bore, the worst part of being sequestered – but something he was inexplicably looking forward to. It might even turn into the brightest point of the day, infusing everything with new meaning and clarity. Some of the boys preferred to keep such newfound enthusiasm to themselves; a bit embarrassed, as if by an unexpected conversion to a faith they had previously scorned. But eventually, when their punishment was over and they were free to return to the normal life of the school, they might quietly request to remain permanently with the woods squad and the Duke.

Though never a member of the woods squad through sequestration or otherwise, I too felt a special bond with the Duke. For one thing, I was at Hotchkiss thanks entirely to the Duke. He had personally taken me in, purely on faith, without reference to any faculty committee or board. As a prep, I had been one of the scrawniest members of our class, and many of the big wheels often pretended I did not exist. Yet the Duke invariably treated me as if I were every bit as important as they.

The Duke seemed altogether pleased with my progress during the four years under his tutelage. Though I had scaled no academic peaks, what impressed him most was how I had built myself up physically and had earned the respect of my peers. This visible evolution was, to the Duke, a likely sign of a deeper, spiritual growth – especially in the absence of any evidence to the contrary. In one of the last reports home, he had written that I was becoming the sort of well-rounded person who would one day make him, and the school, proud.

Then, just a few days before graduation, disaster struck.

It happened during breakfast at the headmaster's table. I was sitting right next to the Duke at the head of his long table for thirteen. Most of the students were reluctant to sit near the Duke. They were afraid he would not let them eat in peace and would prod them into debating some of his favorite topics. They would crowd around the dining room entrance until the last moment before the doors officially closed, hoping that a few of the more obliging types would fill the chairs nearest him.

I considered it an honor to sit next to the Duke. Besides everything he had done for me in the past, his glowing recommendation was undoubtedly the reason I had been granted a nearly full scholarship at Yale. Moreover, I truly enjoyed the Duke's incessant banter and his inexhaustible ability to carry on about whatever subject anyone might raise.

This particular meal started off with a discussion of *How Hot Is Hell?* "Don't tell me you don't know," the Duke chided the half-dozen students sitting on either side of him, when his query resulted in a round of exasperated groans. "At one time or another, I've heard just about every one of you complain it was 'hot as hell.' Surely you knew what you meant! Or are you in the habit of saying things you don't mean, or worse, don't even know what you mean?" The Duke took a sip of his orange juice and then pretended to share the students' exasperation. "I cannot understand why all of you refuse to tell me how hot hell is. It's really terribly frustrating not to know. I'm asking simply because I'm curious. It's your expression, not mine. I never use

The Duke

it. I can't use it, because I don't know how hot hell is. And not one of you is prepared to tell me. That's not very generous, is it? I don't even know whether they use centigrade or Fahrenheit in hell. Now, what do you think? Dan? Robert? Bill? Richard?''

Without getting a really satisfactory answer from any one of the students sleepily sipping their juice, the Duke launched into a far simpler question: *How Far Is a Stone's Throw?* Here, he managed to evoke a couple of weak retorts and, after making his point, lapsed into a momentary silence to concentrate on ladling out the hot cereal and passing it down the table.

The silence would undoubtedly have lasted only a few seconds before the Duke introduced another of his typical subjects. But for some
reason I thought this an ideal opportunity to interject a topic of my
own, one that I knew to be of considerable interest. It involved two of
the school's senior math teachers, Dr. Renny and Mr. Hale. That they
were not the best of friends was no secret. They had even been known
to thrust subtle barbs at each other in front of their respective students
in class. Rumor had it that this hostility was not merely a matter of
professional jealousy, but dated back to the time Dr. Renny had supposedly flunked Mr. Hale's son on a final exam in math.

"Is it true what they say," I asked the boy sitting across the table
from me, "that Dr. Renny flunked Mr. Hale's son in math?" I was not
expecting an answer from the boy. How would he know? This had
happened years ago. But certainly the Duke knew, and he would au-
thoritatively settle the question once and for all.

I was still looking across the table at that boy, when I had the strange
feeling that something had gone terribly wrong. I heard the Duke
pause, arresting the motion that was about to fill the next cereal bowl. I
had the sense of his putting the bowl down deliberately. Then I heard
him say quietly, but with the hurt incredulity of someone who has just
been slapped by a trusted friend, "What a malicious thing to say!"

I turned in time to see a tense, quizzical smile dissolve into a scowl of
great severity. The Duke's forehead became imbued with a tinge of
pink, and the little shock of white on top of his head seemed to quiver
ominously. His eyes, reflecting the dark clouds suddenly gathering
within, transfixed me with a look of moral outrage. "That's just the
sort of poisonous rumormongering we can do without!"

I was in shock, as if lightning and hail had struck, both at once. No
wonder some of the Duke's detractors had compared his anger to the
wrath of God.

"I was only trying to find out if it's true," I said defensively. "Everybody says it's so."

"Everybody?" Again, that tense, quizzical smile. The fact that the
Duke had not resumed ladling out the cereal added to the gravity of his
words. "What kind of talk is that? Who is *everybody*? There are three

hundred and sixty-five students in the school. Do they all say it? There are another thirty-five masters and staff. How about them?" There was no trace of humor in the Duke's voice. He glowered at me, defying me to name my source.

And naturally, under the circumstances, I could not think of anyone, except perhaps Dr. Renny himself, who had often implied as much in class. But my better judgment told me that would have been exactly the wrong thing to say.

"Well, there is simply no excuse for this sort of thing," the Duke said, as he resumed ladling. "All it does is create ill will and undermine the spirit of the school. In the long run, it's the same sort of thing that causes wars." The Duke paused to give me a prolonged, sorrowful look. It was hard to believe; yet, I sensed a distinct accusation in his face. It seemed as if he were making me personally responsible for starting some future world war – as if my indiscreet remark about Dr. Renny and Mr. Hale would resonate throughout the world and bring about a calamity on a global scale.

And he was not done yet. For the rest of the meal, the Duke carried on in a similar vein – while I ate the hot cereal and then the soft-boiled egg and toast, and even until I had finished my milk. Fortunately, I was no longer the direct target of his words. I sensed he did not want to embarrass me unnecessarily in front of the other boys. He was now lecturing the whole table on character flaws, how we must all be on guard against them because we were all susceptible, and how they must be nipped in the bud – preferably sooner, while they were a barely visible seed. Of course, for all the boys except me this was a welcome respite from the Duke's normal routine. They were not expected to respond and could eat in relative peace.

I was the first to finish breakfast. I wanted to put an end to this nightmare as quickly as I could.

"May I be excused, sir?" I now asked the Duke. This was a mere formality which every student went through with the master-in-charge.

"No, you may *not* be excused!" the Duke replied firmly.

It was the first time in four years that I had been denied permission to leave. I noticed several other students glancing at me, as if to say they were glad they did not happen to be in my shoes but it served me right for always trying – in the parlance of the day – to suck up to the Duke.

I sat there like a hockey player in the penalty box, wondering how long before I would be released. The Duke waited, now uncharacteristically silent, until everyone at the table had left. The rest of the huge dining hall had also emptied, except for the few students assigned to sweeping the floors and washing the tables in preparation for the next meal. "I'm frightfully disappointed," the Duke said gently, a touch of sorrow in his voice. "You've always had such exemplary school spirit. I was always so pleased how you had developed since we first took you in. Now, after four years, to find this strange streak within you – it really is quite disturbing."

The Duke reached into his pocket to take out a pipe. He had no intention of lighting it, but just wanted to hold it in his hand. Even though he seemed determined in this inquisition, there was no vengeance in his voice, no righteous desire for retribution. At times, he seemed almost embarrassed and pained.

"Frankly, I'm concerned what else might be lurking deep within you," he resumed after a pause. "What *does* go on in that head of yours? I was always sure I knew pretty well. Not the details. But whatever it was, I had no doubt it was something good and honorable. But now? Maybe you can tell me."

I sat there with a feverish glaze in my eyes, the sound of my heart thumping in my brain. I wanted to tell the Duke that I was still the same good old boy he had always known. Maybe in all of my enthusiasm, I *did* talk a little too much about people and their traits when they were not around. The Duke *was* right about that. And if *that* were a fault, I would watch myself. But otherwise, I was a pretty good guy.

The Duke's voice interrupted what must, by now, have become a blank stare. "These little things are like icebergs. Only the tip usually shows. What you don't see can be deadly. It can bring a lot of ships down, including your own. How can I be sure it isn't going to happen to you? How can I be sure there aren't all sorts of other things submerged within you, waiting to breach the surface?" The Duke looked at me intently, and I averted my eyes. "You're the last person from whom I would have expected something like this. It's a bad attitude to take with you, no matter where you go. It simply is not something that a gentleman would do."

Be a gentleman! That was the only rule, the Duke always liked to say, that the school truly had. It was a cardinal rule, and I had apparently broken it. I wanted to slither under the table and somehow disappear. It was surely the worst moment of my life – and yet it was all so completely silly! The fact was, I had only been repeating what I had heard dozens of times from others. The Duke knew about the rumor concerning Dr. Renny and Mr. Hale, just as he knew how hot *hot as hell* really was. Right now, I could have told him, if I thought he still cared. I was feeling the heat. But why pick on me? Every student had probably done something far worse during his four years at the school – I included. Maybe my classmates who did not want to sit next to the Duke were right. At the other end of the table, I would never have been overheard. Why this now, after I had gotten along so well with the Duke and he had thought so much of me? And only days before graduation!

Meekly, I followed the Duke out of the deserted dining hall, hoping I would be able to bolt on the other side of the doors. But as the Duke reached the threshold, he paused to wait for me, as if he had read my mind. He took me by the arm, as was his habit with students to whom he had something of vital importance to impart, and started to walk me down the corridor.

"To be a gentleman, to be a person of character – that is the most important thing we can teach you." The Duke's voice was gentle and fatherly. "I wish all of this had happened two years ago. Or even when you first came to us. We would have had a chance really to work with you, to help you. Now, I'm afraid you will have to do it pretty much on your own. You're going to be pretty much on your own at Yale. I think you will find that for the rest of your life you're going to be pretty much on your own. Unless you're ready, this can be dangerous. You have to have the proper armor."

We were near the Duke's office now. Other students were passing us in the busy corridor, getting ready for classes or rushing off to the infirmary to have their noses sprayed and throats swabbed by Doc Wieler and be excused from morning chapel. I was desperately hoping the Duke would be done with his sermonizing and let me go.

He opened the door to his office and then once more put his hand on my arm in what was apparently a parting gesture. "I don't want you pushing all of this out of your head," he said somberly. "I want you to think about it." And he was gone.

Walking down the busy corridor, I felt as if I had been cast into an unhappy trance. That I should so unjustly fall in the Duke's estimation! Suddenly, I was gripped by a terrible thought. What if the Duke would not let me graduate? Was that the meaning of his parting remark? Maybe he would give me only a certificate instead of a diploma. That is what happened to students who did not pass all their courses. Obviously, I had failed in the Duke's estimation, which was far more serious than failing any course. Nor was it something like being caught out of your room after lights, for which you could be censured or sequestered. My only censure had been for carelessly dropping a pipe wrench out of my window and almost beaning Butch Stearns, who was the toughest teacher at the school. The Duke had publicly made light of that incident, much to Mr. Stearns's dismay. But this was hardly a joking matter for the Duke. It was an overall failure of the worst sort.

I was beginning to succumb to my fears, suspecting that the Duke would indeed not let me graduate. And I soon had evidence that made me still more anxious. In my mailbox the following day was a note in the Duke's unmistakably careful script. He went on at length about character; how we must always be on guard that we do and say only those things that are truly worthy of us – regardless of whether anybody finds out or we get caught – which I saw as a pointed reference to my eleventh-hour gaffe. "We owe it to others," the Duke wrote, "to do what is right. And, above all, we owe it to ourselves. For only then can we live with ourselves in peace."

By now, I had reconciled myself to my fate. No, the Duke would not let me graduate. Would that mean I would lose my scholarship at Yale and have to find another place to go? It would hardly be the same, not going to Yale, and I would have to lower my expectations as to what life might hold in store. Still, if the Duke would only stop hounding me! He was like some crab that had locked onto me and would not let go. The Duke seemed at the point of obsession, almost irrational about the whole thing. As if he had nothing to do in these last days of school! Twice more before graduation he called me into his office to give me similar talks. And twice more I was to find in my mailbox those detailed, handwritten notes in the precise, formal script I had only so recently come to dread.

Then it was time to graduate. My parents had come up for the ceremonies, as well as my two brothers and two sisters. They were sitting there in the school chapel with all the other parents and friends, having no idea how I was sweating it out. I had never been so nervous now that my name was about to be called.

And then I heard it, in the Duke's strong, resonant voice. I could not believe it and thought it must be a mistake. I was getting not only my diploma, but also the Fidelity Prize, awarded to that scholarship boy who, during his four years, had done the most for the school community, as exemplified by his spirit and growth.

I had goose bumps running up and down my back. My knees were weak as I left the pew to walk down the aisle amid the clapping from the sea of faces on either side. And there, down at the other end, stood the Duke, like some fortress of strength, waiting to catch me if I stumbled or fell.

"Congratulations," the Duke whispered, as he shook my hand. I felt him draw me closer, until nobody else was there, just he and I. "I have done all I can. This prize is as much for what you've done for the school as for what I still expect from you. Now, it's up to you. My best wishes are with you, always."

Forty years later, I can almost feel the Duke – that is, Mr. Van Santvoord – hovering over my shoulder as I write these words. Wouldn't he perhaps consider that repeating publicly this story about Dr. Renny and Mr. Hale amounted to a far more monumental case of rumor-mongering than my original mealtime gaffe? And what would he think of the literary license inherent in reconstructing dialogue after so many years – regardless of how brightly it remained emblazoned on one's mind?

Of course, this would not be the first time in all those years that I had felt the Duke's unmistakable presence when confronted with a moral dilemma – advising me, remonstrating, chastising, or encouraging in his inimitable way. I would like to think that in this case, after some inevitable and protracted examination of the principles involved, he would finally betray his approval with a few contented puffs on his pipe. Whether that might indeed be wishful thinking is for the reader to decide as the Hotchkiss story unfolds.

2   Minutes from the Past

Hotchkiss versus The Hill

How has the Hotchkiss School managed to accommodate a hundred years of unprecedented change – a century during which horse-and-buggy trails have become less familiar than the fiery trails of space-bound vehicles, and Victorian propriety has yielded to unabashed self-expression?

The short answer – carefully; certainly not without considerable tension and the constant need to mediate between the forces of tradition and innovation. Oh, yes, also by following the golden rule: do not disturb the cherished memories of alumni – and, more recently, of alumnae as well.

In the splendor of its bucolic isolation in the northwest corner of Connecticut, Hotchkiss has always been selective about innovation. Some advances, to be sure, have been eagerly adopted. In the school's first catalogue, published in 1892, parents of prospective students were given a reassuring picture of the up-to-date facilities for the fifty boys who would each be paying $600 as boarders: "The buildings have a frontage of 325 feet, and are connected by a corridor which runs their entire length," boasted the modest square pamphlet with pale blue covers – an obvious reference to the protection students would receive from colds and other boyhood diseases. Such ailments, according to the latest medical theory, were caused by venturing outside during the winter months into the microbe-laden air; hence classrooms, masters' rooms, offices, chapel, dining room, gymnasium, and other facilities would all be within this enclosed complex of buildings, where each boy would also have a separate room. "[The buildings] will be lighted by electricity, and will be abundantly supplied with pure water. . . . As the School site is on high ground, perfect drainage has been secured."

Before the first year of operation was over, a potentially intrusive innovation was causing excitement. On May 13, 1893, at a board of trustees meeting held at the Wononsco House in Lakeville, a short carriage ride downhill from the school, it was voted that "the executive committee be instructed to provide the School with a telephone."

Yet Hotchkiss was not about to succumb to every convenience dictated by the times. Even a casual glance through the minutes of those early board of trustees meetings reflects an abiding respect for tradition. The graying pages of the red leather-bound volume are filled with gracefully rounded letters inked by careful hands. Inserted in the front of the albumlike book are the Articles of Association. It is not too farfetched to note their formal resemblance to the Constitution of the United States. In subsequent pages, the painstaking penmanship creates the impression of a family journal or ledger and conveys the personal concern these original overseers had for the school.

The decision to record the trustees' minutes by hand, of course, may have been made partly because the typewriter was still at a rudimentary stage. If so, what started out as a temporary convenience acquired a momentum of its own. The quaint format continued through the retirement and death in 1904 of the personally impressive first headmaster, Edward G. Coy, who was responsible for transforming the newly erected buildings into a functioning school and who, with a do-it-or-I-shall-resign ultimatum to the trustees, expanded the faculty and facilities to accommodate some 150 boys. The handwritten format continued during the two decades when Hotchkiss doubled in size under the reign of Dr. Huber Gray Buehler, one of the original six faculty members of the school, whose honorary doctorate [D. Litt.] was supplemented by the more popular agnomen "the King." The same format continued during the brief interregnum of another seasoned master, Walter Hull Buell, inevitably nicknamed "the Bull" and immortalized by his ringing declaration in morning chapel after expelling a boy, "Hotchkiss will lower her standards for no one!" And it continued through the ascension in 1926 of George Van Santvoord, who had himself been graduated from Hotchkiss in 1908 and then, as headmaster, showed no hesitation in cracking down on hazing – a practice which other eastern prep schools would tolerate well beyond the twenties.

The Crash of '29 likewise failed to affect the traditional recording by hand of the trustees' minutes. But the Depression did impose drastic adjustments on many Hotchkiss families. Previously affluent parents suddenly were hard pressed to pay the all-inclusive $1,500 fee. "My grandfather gave the first regulation pool in honor of my father," observes William L. Bryan '39. "When I came to Hotchkiss after the Depression, I was a full scholarship boy. That tells you something about American life and history." Another Hotchkiss graduate of that era, James A. Linen III '30, who later became president of the Hotchkiss board and publisher of *Time*, accepted a personal loan from George Van Santvoord to complete his studies at Williams. As an afterthought, the Duke inquired, "Are you still seeing that young lady you were so attached to?" When the young man nodded, his benefactor concluded, "Well, I'm going to give you a few hundred dollars so you can get a car and maintain the relationship, because she's probably the best thing that's happened to you in your life." And indeed, that young lady, sister of William W. Scranton '35, would become James Linen's wife – and mother of another Hotchkiss generation.

At last, on May 6, 1939, the final pen and ink entry was made. War was about to engulf the world for the second time since the founding of the school, and again Hotchkiss boys would die in action. Among them: short-statured Eugene C. Brewer '39, nicknamed "the Admiral," who had his classmates stretch him by tying his feet and arms to his bedposts for the night to help him qualify for naval officer training. The Admiral was destined to make it – and lose his life when his navy fighter was shot down over Guadalcanal. Yet it was not the looming calamity of World War II that provided the symbolic marker for the switch to the typewriter, which by then had been in general use at Hotchkiss for several decades. The reason was that there were three hundred prenumbered pages in the first volume of the trustees' minutes, and when those pages were finally filled that was the signal to make the change. Rather than yielding to innovation, the trustees let a tradition simply exhaust itself.

Too bad there were not another hundred or so pages within the scuffed bindings of that daunting volume! From today's perspective, it certainly would have made sense. For the most prominent break in the school's history was not to come until the tenure of A. William Olsen, Jr. '39, who, as headmaster from 1960 to 1981, transformed Hotchkiss into a coeducational institution of more than five hundred students – and otherwise responded to the realities of the world beyond the boundaries of the school.

ii /   A closer examination of those handwritten minutes begins to betray details missed at first glance. The impression of the family journal or ledger is partly dispelled by the realization that most of the entries were not personally penned by the trustees whose signatures they appear to bear, but by no less committed, though anonymous, hands. Then, as one continues to scan for content, various inconsistencies gradually crop up which hardly make sense yet cannot be ignored. Perhaps most puzzling: Why were the minutes of a board meeting held in 1896 sandwiched between two meetings held three years earlier? Were the minutes being adjusted or amended ex post facto – in other words, doctored? If so, to what purpose?

For nearly a century, the flowing artistry in that unique first volume has inadvertently helped to obscure some of the most dramatic events of the early years of the school. The handwritten minutes are a chore to read – and discourage anything beyond a cursory examination whenever they are periodically dusted off. Moreover, the authors deliberately employed language which blunted any edges that could prove unnecessarily sharp. This often meant leaving out details of the most critical sort.

Yet the essential information is there; enough key pieces exist so that in juxtaposition with fragments from other sources a composite picture takes shape. It is a picture, alas, which may cause loyal alumni to wince the next time they sing "Fair Hotchkiss" in celebration of the school. Portraying the relationship between Maria Hotchkiss and the trustees, this composite shows hardly anything that can be construed as fair in the treatment of the benefactress of the school. That she also happened to be the only woman among the trustees adds a modern dimension which retrospectively puts to the test what it meant to be a gentleman in those days.

When Maria Hotchkiss signed the founding articles of association in 1891, her name headed a column of eleven trustees, among them two relatives from the Bissell side of the family and three prominent business leaders from the vicinity of the future school. Right beneath the endowing widow's name was that of Timothy Dwight, the president of Yale, followed by that of Frederick J. Kingsbury, a Connecticut banker from Waterbury. Though Kingsbury was elected to head the board, there was little doubt where the power lay. Five members of the board, besides Dwight, had graduated from Yale, including Kingsbury, who was a Yale trustee, and two professors who taught there. One of them, Andrew W. Phillips, an urbane, gentle mathematician with a flowing beard, would eventually succeed Kingsbury as president of the board; the other, Arthur Wheeler, a historian nicknamed "Waterloo" because of the rousing lecture he gave each year about Napoleon's decisive defeat, was the board's secretary. No college besides Yale was represented on the board, and most of the meetings during those early years were held neither in Lakeville nor at Kingsbury's Waterbury bank but in the office of the Yale president. Mrs. Hotchkiss at this time listed her residence as New York, and Timothy Dwight may have volunteered his New Haven office as a convenient place for her to reach by train. Whatever the pretext, the effect was the same. Surrounded by the trappings of his office and embodying an august family tradition, Timothy Dwight was in a unique position among the trustees to handle, in

whatever subtle ways, the reputedly difficult woman whose intran-
sigence vis-à-vis her late husband had recently been publicized in the
Herald's scandalous revelations about Berk Hotchkiss's life.

From the start, the relationship between Mrs. Hotchkiss and the
board was akin to another frustrating marriage, this one maintained
for the sake of a child. (The Hotchkiss School would often be called
"Son of a Gun," in jesting reference to the source of the founding
widow's wealth.) Some of the tensions in this union were a reflection
of the times: any woman in an influential position outside the home
was likely to be looked at with reproach for forgetting her proper place.
There seems to have also been an awareness of intellectual disparity on
the board between the farmer's daughter, whose credentials amounted
to one year at Amenia Academy, and the other trustees, all men of
learning or business accomplishment. And beyond such estranging pe-
ripherals was a conflict of aims. As Stephen Birmingham has suggested, Mrs. Hotchkiss would have instinctively preferred a modest
academy to prepare local youth for useful tasks in the surrounding
communities. What Timothy Dwight and his cohorts had in mind was
a substantial "feeder" school for Yale to prepare privileged young men
from the Northeast – and from throughout the United States – for
their inevitable leadership roles. If those concepts were to clash, Mrs.
Hotchkiss could not automatically count on any block of votes – not on
the three trustees from the vicinity of the school, not even on her own
Bissell relatives. One of them, a distant cousin, Dr. William Bissell,
had graduated from Yale and might have understandably preferred to
accommodate rather than oppose the president of his alma mater.*

iii /　　　I n the minutes of the board's first meeting, held in
　　　　　　Lakeville on August 11, 1891, a simple declarative
　　　　　　statement would turn out to be the smoking gun several years hence in the final rift between Maria Hotchkiss and her

---

*Dr. William Bissell would serve as the school's first physician for some twenty
years and his son, William Bascom Bissell, for another fifteen.

namesake school. "It was voted to accept the deed," reads that innocuous phrase on top of page 2 of the handwritten first volume, "presented to the board by Mrs. Hotchkiss, of a tract of land for the use of the School." What could be more routine than that? Far more attention was devoted to the next order of business, whereby the board voted to accept "the gift of seventy-five thousand dollars for buildings, but with the understanding that . . . [this] deed of gift . . . be modified and perfected." Apparently Mrs. Hotchkiss had encumbered her gift with a far broader provision for tuition scholarships to local youth than the board was prepared to accept. On being "perfected" by the trustees, the scholarship clause set a limit on the "deserving boys" not to "exceed three in number . . . at any one time" from the town of Salisbury and the same number from Sharon. The most likely reason Mrs. Hotchkiss consented to this numerical limitation (rather than a percentage of the total number of students) was that she had been led to believe there would be no rapid or dramatic expansion in the size of the school. She also seemed to share at this stage her Yale-educated cousin's desire to cooperate.

Cooperation – and more cooperation – is what it would take. The original $75,000 gift proved inadequate even before construction began. At the next board meeting, held again in Lakeville less than two months later, "it being evident . . . that the cost of the plan adopted would exceed by at least $50,000 the sum already appropriated for buildings, Mrs. Hotchkiss was appealed to to make up the necessary sum, and she very generously consented to do so." She was not told at this time that related construction costs would still leave a shortfall of more than $20,000. Maybe the gentlemen on the board knew the limits of their sponsor's generosity. The bills would not be due for some time, and the next order of business was "to receive $200,000 in bonds from Mrs. Hotchkiss as an endowment fund for the School." A committee headed by Kingsbury subsequently traveled to New York, where the endowment transfer from the machine gun heiress was made.

With the school's construction well under way in the spring of 1892, the board placed Waterloo Wheeler in full charge of ensuring that the facilities would be ready for students that fall. Professor Wheeler's profile as a trustee and board secretary was thus visibly raised – setting him up for an eventual Waterloo of his own. He was now also appointed, along with his Yale faculty colleague Phillips, to the committee for staffing the school, chaired by Timothy Dwight. Some of the personnel decisions about to be made – without a hint of discord at this stage – would play a pivotal role in the troubles ahead.

For headmaster, the committee proposed, "after a very careful and thorough search," just one candidate, Edward G. Coy. Head of the Greek department and second only to the principal at Phillips Academy in Andover, Massachusetts, Coy was well known at Yale. Not only was Andover Yale's top feeder school; Greek was an entrance requirement which Yale often cited as evidence of its preeminence over Harvard. A Yale graduate himself, Coy had married a New Haven woman, and his wife's home often served as their second domicile. It seems likely that the prospective headmaster had known Dwight for years. The two might even have discussed the desirability of a new feeder school before the subject had ever been broached with Mrs. Hotchkiss. In a letter Coy wrote shortly after his appointment to Huber Gray Buehler, whom he was trying to recruit to teach English, he referred to Dwight as "one of our most valued trustees and a personal friend of myself." In that era, one did not become "a personal friend" overnight.

Coy's official title at the school was then written as two words – *head master*. His salary was set at $3,500 per year, plus "the use of a suitable house" and "the privilege for himself and his family" to eat in the school dining room "during term-time." The candidate's one condition for accepting the position was that his colleague David Y. Comstock, head of the Latin department at Andover and the next most senior member of the faculty there after Coy, join him as associate master "in the conduct of the enterprise." Messrs. Coy and Comstock were both men of commanding presence, and together they had commitments from several Andover students to transfer with them to the new school. As associate master, Comstock would receive $2,500 and perks similar to Professor Coy's.

Also appointed by the Dwight committee at this time was the

school's first master, Joe Garner Estill, a tall, ebullient Southerner with a boyishly wispy walrus mustache who had graduated from Yale the previous year. As a student Estill had heard of the prospective school from Professor Wheeler and then had trudged more than fifty miles along muddy roads to inspect the site of what was known as Yale Junior. As teacher of mathematics and head of the department, he was to receive $1,500 with "board at the common table and the use of a furnished room free of charge."

The most routine appointment, or so it seemed, was that of the curator, who was essentially the school's bookkeeper. His name was W. W. Goss. He had previously managed a resort hotel in Vermont, where several Yale faculty members, including committee member Phillips, often spent the summer. Goss's salary was to start at $800, with annual raises to a maximum of $1,200, and he would be provided a "suitable house" and "free tuition" for his two boys when they became old enough – "the understanding being that the incumbent may hold the position so long as he gives satisfaction."

Those would prove to be loaded words.

iv /   "For a considerable time there is to be a rigid limitation of the number of pupils," the *New York Weekly Post* reported shortly after Coy's appointment, "who are not to exceed fifty boarders and a smaller number of 'day' scholars." According to the prospective headmaster, this limitation would make it possible to enforce "a high grade of scholarship" without being hampered by the bureaucracy and "old lines of instruction" which existed at larger institutions.

Despite such theorizing about limiting the school's size, the building expenses continued to mount. The first time Mrs. Hotchkiss balked at fully accommodating her colleagues on the board occurred as construction of the school was being completed, only days before students were due to arrive. "The cost of the school plant being considerably in excess of the sum already given by Mrs. Hotchkiss in 1892," reads the entry in the minutes of that early-October meeting, held in Timothy

Dwight's office at Yale, "this meeting was called mainly for the consideration of ways and means." In other words, how to pay the bills? Since providing the supplementary $50,000, Mrs. Hotchkiss had recently taken care of other outstanding bills, and the board had voted their thanks for this "very generous additional gift to the building fund." The bills still to be paid had been incurred partly by Professor Wheeler in his push to have the school finished as scheduled. (Even so, opening day had to be postponed by a week to October 19, 1892.) This time, Mrs. Hotchkiss declined to come across with more cash, as if to let her colleagues know that they had expanded the project beyond anything she had intended – or beyond what they had originally represented to her. But she evidently did not want to create an impasse at this stage. By consenting to modify the deed to her $200,000 endowment in securities, she provided the necessary collateral to borrow "such sums of money as are needed to complete and pay for the school plant as now contemplated, but not to exceed in the aggregate the sum of $60,000."

As her desire for accommodation wavered, was the wealthy widow becoming apprehensive, too? At the next board meeting some two months later, again held in President Dwight's office in New Haven, there was "some discussion of the rather loose financial management prevailing at the School," and the recently installed headmaster was directed to "make such arrangements as will keep the expenses within income." Minutes of future board meetings would provide ample evidence that the "discussion" could have been instigated only by Mrs. Hotchkiss.

As if heeding the signals of a distant storm, the gentlemen on the board took a precautionary step. The deed Mrs. Hotchkiss had presented to the board for the sixty-five-acre tract on which the school now stood either had been mislaid or perhaps had never been picked up from her. In any case, it had not been registered. So now, after more than a year of apparent unconcern, a committee was formed "to procure a deed" to this land and to "have the deed put on record."

Though the deed in the form of a quitclaim was obtained from Mrs.

Hotchkiss within less than two months, it was not registered by the recipients for another two months. More pressing matters may have understandably taken precedence during this first year of running the school. When the entry was finally made in the official land records of Salisbury, there was reason to do so without further delay, for virtually on the same day notices were being mailed out from the school for a crucial board meeting at which Mrs. Hotchkiss would find herself thrust into a most uncomfortable position. The trustees knew what was coming and, not surprisingly, did not want to be technically squatting on her land.

That meeting was held on April 15, 1893, once again in Timothy Dwight's office. The opening paragraph of the minutes indicates the magnitude of the problem: "The Head Master and Associate Master having presented to the President, sometime in February, a list of grievances, and having, early in April, sent to the Board letters of resignation. . . ."

What was going on? The promising team of Edward G. Coy and David Y. Comstock resigning even before giving the school a chance? And the problem was more extensive. According to the memoirs of J. G. Estill, written shortly after his retirement some forty years later, Coy and Comstock were supported by the entire faculty. "The *young fry*, of whom I was the oldest and ranking member," recalled Estill, or Uncle Joe, as he came to be known, "got together and voted to support our chiefs, informing them that if their resignations were accepted, ours *ipso facto*, should be too. Of course we did not consider ourselves of sufficient importance to submit our resignation to the Board."

Among the most vociferous of those "young fry" was Huber Gray Buehler, who had acceded to Coy's entreaties to join the faculty and now headed the English department. He had been promised "a cottage" in time for his forthcoming marriage in June, yet nothing had come of that promise. "For reasons which need not be mentioned here," Buehler wrote, in offering his resignation to Coy, "I find myself in spite of all my precautions and to my great mortification, in the position of a man about to assume the responsibility of a wife without knowing how he is to provide for her." Estill was also planning marriage and needed housing, and there had been grumblings throughout the school about such inadequacies as the much heralded supply of "pure water" and "lighting by electricity." But all that was secondary to a far more fundamental problem which touched on the basic presuppositions about the school. As Joe Estill explained, "Mr. Coy and Mr. Comstock could not get the trustees to make provision for more boys, and they said they had not come down from Andover to run a school of 50."

The headmaster was, in effect, issuing an ultimatum: expand the size of the school or else! It was a step he had thought about long and carefully. "I am resolved on the course . . . which will bring matters to a crisis," Coy had written to Buehler, in response to his complaint, "because I am satisfied that nothing short of this can arouse the Board – particularly madam."

The gravity of the situation could hardly have been lost on the trustees gathered in the office of the Yale president. According to the minutes, "There followed a general discussion of the situation, with special consideration of the probable additional cost of providing accommodation for, and maintaining, fifty more students." What was said by Timothy Dwight or anyone else on that occasion has not been recorded, but the scene can be readily imagined. It is unlikely that any of the gentlemen seated in the red leather upholstered chairs on either side of the massive table in the oak-paneled room offered much in the way of a solution. There were no alumni to appeal to, no devoted parents to solicit, no friends of the school to snag. As for the more prosperous of the trustees, they were pikers in comparison with Mrs. Hotchkiss. Besides, why should they or anyone else donate funds to a school bearing her name when she could very well do so herself? The entire board, including the petite "Madam" – sitting beneath a Trumbull landscape at the other end from the lanky, black-frocked Timothy Dwight – must have all along realized against whom the resignations were aimed. Again, in the words of the minutes, "After careful consideration of the situation, Mrs. Hotchkiss has expressed a willingness to consider the subject of a new dormitory and houses for the teachers, and of such changes . . . as the necessities of the case may demand." The trustees, in turn, expressed their confidence in the expected results of Mrs. Hotchkiss's "liberality," and the crisis was defused.

A logical question: To what extent did any of the gentlemen in that critical face-off, especially Timothy Dwight and Edward Coy, conspire to separate the reluctant Mrs. Hotchkiss from the necessary funds? The conspiracy need not have amounted to anything more than a tacit understanding between two colleagues of that era – a gentleman's agreement sealed with a nod and a wink. Perhaps Messrs. Dwight and Coy had felt all along that fifty students were too few for the kind of influential and prosperous institution they had in mind, and they had been merely waiting for the right opportunity to make their move, just as had been done on three previous occasions in obtaining additional funds.

A brother of Mrs. Hotchkiss who was on the board, Charles A. Bissell, was appointed to a three-member committee for "getting [her] approval" on this latest move to expand. Was he there to protect her interests or because he was the one most likely to be able to handle her or both? When the trustees subsequently voted to name the new dormitory Bissell Hall, perhaps they had more in mind than merely honoring the donor's maiden name.

v / In the give-and-take between Mrs. Hotchkiss and the trustees, it had thus far been a one-way affair. Now, in expressing a willingness to accommodate her colleagues on the board once more, the school's benefactress clearly set down a quid pro quo. She did not make any demands to increase the number of local scholarships to correspond to the growth of the school; nor did she seek to influence the curriculum or in similar ways further her original views of the school. Keeping an agreement was a virtue that may have been no less important to her than the Yankee thrift she had acquired as a child. What she now wanted in return was some degree of control over the additional money she felt she was repeatedly being compelled to spend. The minutes spelled it out: "Economy both in construction and administration, and that some arrangement be made for an efficient financial manager, to have general oversight under the trustees of all the business affairs of the school and to be its sole purchasing agent." What this meant was that Waterloo Wheeler, the Yale professor who had been in sole control of building operations, would have to resign. According to Estill, Mrs. Hotchkiss had become very much irritated with the professor, "and she was unwilling to give anything further to the school so long as he remained a member of the Board." Her implicit message in wanting "an efficient financial manager" was no less specific. That was the job now almost entirely performed by W. W. Goss in his expanded duties as curator.

"Goss suddenly blazed out as a star of the first magnitude in the way of target for the spite of . . . Mrs. Hotchkiss," wrote David Comstock several months later to the vacationing Buehler. "Since the term ended, Mrs. Hotchkiss, for some reason, has been in a most unpleasant frame of mind. She seemed to be all bristles and Bissells" – an obvious reference to Bissell Hall, for which ground was soon to be broken. "She was suddenly seized with an idea that there was to be an enormous outlay of money for all sorts of things; conceived a suspicion of the architect's propositions; made all kinds of halts, advances, and retreats."

No doubt with good reason, considering how she had been repeatedly maneuvered into a greater and greater outlay in financing the original school complex. Maria Hotchkiss had other charitable interests, including the Sharon library, which bears her name. If the estimate of her inheritance at $1 to $2 million is accurate, she may have felt her reserves were being unduly drained by the demands of the school. Yet relations between Mrs. Hotchkiss and the board were about to take a dramatic turn. What brought about the change of heart was a trustees' meeting held in Lakeville on July 25, 1893. By an act of the Connecticut state legislature, The Hotchkiss School Association had just been granted tax-exempt status, and in the process, become

The Maria H. Hotchkiss School Association.* Of more relevance than any such personal recognition to the modest widow, however, was that the board accepted the resignation of the influential Professor Wheeler. In his place, Mrs. Hotchkiss nominated her Lakeville lawyer, Frank E. Randall, and "Mr. Randall was duly elected," assuring her of a reliable ally on the board. But Mrs. Hotchkiss was also unrelenting in wanting to have her "efficient financial manager." Here she found the board much less willing to yield. The meeting at that point was adjourned until after dinner, when "a conference was held between Mrs. Hotchkiss, Pres. Kingsbury and Professor Phillips." The result was a resolution which accommodated Mrs. Hotchkiss's concern and pointed directly at her target. "There seems to be a good deal of dissatisfaction with the Curator, Mr. Goss, in regard to his management of the School property," the resolution read, calling for obtaining not only "a suitable man," but also a "general financial manager for the affairs of the Corporation."

Mrs. Hotchkiss had reason to believe she was at last being listened to. The resolution had spelled out what she wanted, and she seemed optimistic that she would soon have her way. "When we think how Mrs. H felt last July, and what she is now doing, the change in her is wonderful," observed Edward Coy in a letter apprising the vacationing and just-married Huber Gray Buehler of the cottage the board would build for him to share with the Estills. "Everybody congratulates us on the immediate outcome of the meeting . . . on the temper of Mrs. H's mind, on the general good feeling that seems to prevail, and on the prospects of the School from this day forth." Summarized David Comstock, "Mrs. Hotchkiss had been in a cloud as to many matters, and the outcome of the day's proceedings was a promising token of the future."

The headmaster had personal reasons to be optimistic. He had just been elected a trustee and board secretary, thereby establishing a precedent which would automatically place all future headmasters on the board. He was a recognized insider now and at last in a position to

*Her maiden middle name was Harrison.

take action on something that must have been gnawing at his self-respect for months. Turning back several pages in the minutes to the meeting which had referred to "the rather loose financial management at the School," the just-elected keeper of the record placed an asterisk by the word "loose" and at the bottom of the page noted in his stylish Spencerian hand, "The facts at no time warranted these words." Signed with his unmistakable flourish, the addendum seems to have been as much in defense of Curator Goss as of Mr. Coy's own pride.

The good feeling between Mrs. Hotchkiss and the board would not last. Almost a year after first agreeing to accede to Mrs. Hotchkiss on the matter of "an efficient financial manager" – and more than nine months since the accusing finger had been pointed at Mr. Goss – no action had been taken by the school or the board. Now, with Bissell Hall almost completed, a misunderstanding arose over the bill for $54,985; in the words of the minutes, "Mrs. Hotchkiss having been represented as ready to assume the entire cost of the building, whereas she had assumed responsibility for only $50,000." The difference between those figures was no trifle for a school whose total receipts from tuition in the first year were $29,106. With Mr. Buehler again growing restless about his promised cottage, the gentlemen on the board may well have commiserated with one another over Madam's intractability at this crucial stage.

Using the $5,000 misunderstanding over Bissell Hall as leverage, Mrs. Hotchkiss pressed for what she had every reason to feel was her proper due – now overdue. At a board meeting held in Timothy Dwight's New Haven office on April 28, 1894, she agreed to cover the unpaid balance in return for a motion to hire "Mr. Frank Ingersoll, or some other suitable person" for the financial position she wanted filled. Yet, despite some convincing words of intent from the board, Mrs. Hotchkiss did not succeed in bringing that motion to a vote. Wanting to replace the curator was hardly the same as having Professor Wheeler resign from the board, which had in no way affected his tenure at Yale and doing his annual Waterloo bit. Dismissing Curator Goss would have imposed an economic hardship on one of the original members of the Hotchkiss community – already then characterized by an exceptionally strong sense of family. Besides, as the loyal lieutenant to Head Master Coy, Goss had merely been carrying out the policies of his chief.

Reconvening in President Dwight's office a week later, the board seemed no more ready to act. In fact, after numerous conferences which included Mrs. Hotchkiss and Mr. Coy, the board took a distinct step back – dropping the specific mention of Mr. Ingersoll's name. But, as usual, there was no shortage of promises. The board resolved "that the Executive Committee, together with Mrs. Hotchkiss and Mr. Coy, be instructed to hire a bookkeeper for the Hotchkiss School, as soon as practicable, it being expected that he shall also fill the position of Treasurer and Curator, if in their judgment his experience and ability warrant it."

To think that the focus of this protracted and intensifying storm was "a bookkeeper" – and that men of the stature of Dwight and Coy were putting forth their considerable efforts on an issue such as this to thwart the woman whose generosity had financed the school! To Mrs. Hotchkiss, the verbiage of her colleagues must have sounded frustratingly familiar, and in fact, that is still all it was, for the minutes state that "no action was taken on this motion." How tenaciously she then persisted to get the board to stop waffling can only be surmised. To speak up to these men could not have been easy for a woman in those days, especially for one with the retiring disposition ascribed to Mrs. Hotchkiss. Nevertheless, "it was subsequently" voted that the preceding motion be implemented "as soon as practicable," and to "notify Mr. Goss that his services will not be needed after October 1, 1894." In a gesture that was surely kindly but also lent credibility to the board's stated intention to fire Goss, the trustees voted that his son be permitted to complete Hotchkiss free of charge.

If Mrs. Hotchkiss was temporarily mollified, it did not take her long to conclude that all those resolutions were still just so many words. A month later, on June 9, 1894, a showdown of a different sort came about at yet another special meeting in Timothy Dwight's office. What had happened in the interim was that Mrs. Hotchkiss had hired her own financial man – most likely, the aforementioned Frank Ingersoll – whose household goods had already been shipped to the school. The result was that for the second time in a little over a year, Coy was putting his job on the line. The minutes describe the board's response: "In view of the serious injury likely to result from the resignation of the Head Master at this time, and after consultation by some members of the board with each other, and with Mr. Coy, the following votes are proposed. . . ."

When the votes passed, the headmaster was in sole charge of running the school – with specific power "to employ a curator and other such servants as may be required." Though the votes also assigned financial prerogatives to the board, there was nary a word about Mrs. Hotchkiss. In fact, she may have been totally ignored. She certainly had ample reason to interpret the entire proceeding as a direct rebuff, if not a slap in the face. The financial man she had hired was promptly notified by Coy of the change of plans. His baggage was returned to him, accompanied by a generous check to cover the expenses and trouble he had incurred. As for Curator Goss, he would in due time receive a raise "to the maximum salary agreed upon" and continue serving the school until his retirement in 1904.

vi /   In this ongoing strife between the founder and her namesake school, the personality of Edward G. Coy may have tipped more than once the balance of the scales. "[He] was handsome, distingué, and of a carriage so erect and proud as to seem almost haughty," noted his junior colleague Joe Estill. "His resemblance to Kaiser William I was so striking as to make him rather decidedly the 'observed of all observers' when travelling in Germany, which was far from displeasing to him."

A kaiser look-alike who enjoyed that role would not be apt to look kindly on anyone crowding his terrain – especially a woman. But Mrs.

Hotchkiss was not the only one to transgress in that way. Stumbling into the headmaster's privileged path at this time was his own deputy, the associate master David Y. Comstock. A glance at pictures of these two men makes it understandable how this could have come about. Though radiating a far more approachable attitude than Coy, the associate master was no less magnificently bewhiskered and impressive in bearing. And he had attained an unusual popularity throughout the school and a reputation for excellence. "Mr. Comstock had one of the quickest minds, and was one of the best raconteurs, I ever knew," Estill wrote about him. "His old pupils, almost without exception, said, 'Commy never had an equal as a teacher of Latin.'"

If Messrs. Coy and Comstock had got along at Andover for years, it is well to remember that their relationship there had been one of independent department heads. Their coming to Hotchkiss to join in a common cause may have had an effect not unlike releasing two bulls into the same ring, especially on the headmaster in his dominant role. Yet that alone might not have been sufficient for them to lock horns, had it not been for Maria H. Hotchkiss. According to *A Portrait*, the history of the school published on its seventy-fifth anniversary, Comstock knew Mrs. Hotchkiss while he was still teaching at Andover, and she was the real reason he had been offered the new job. While none of that information can be confirmed, it appears that after coming to Hotchkiss, Comstock did gradually develop a unique relationship with the benefactress – one which diverged from the adversarial sort she had with the headmaster and the board. According to Estill, Mrs. Hotchkiss personally turned over to the associate master the sum of $4,000 to purchase books for the library – a task which Comstock carried out after consulting with other members of the faculty. Whether or not the headmaster felt slighted or bypassed can only be surmised. Far more revealing is that in submitting his resignation for the second time, Coy was not joined by Comstock, although once more the entire faculty stood by their chief. Why did the associate master's name not appear? Did he decide not to join in because he had become aware of the real facts of the situation and instead of assuming Mrs. Hotchkiss to be "in a cloud" now recognized the justice of her cause? Or was it perhaps the other way around? Did the headmaster feel secure enough and no longer wanted to share his status with David Comstock at the school – not even in a letter of resignation? Or was it altogether something else? Whatever the case, Head Master Coy made his displeasure with the associate master widely known and did not shrink from passing out misleading information to buttress his own primacy at the school. "[Comstock] was *Associate Master*, which was interpreted by all at first as associate *to*, or *with*, the Head," observed Estill in his memoirs. "Certainly the younger men never thought of it as meaning *their* associate. Misunderstanding about this or 'incompatibility,' in spite of nineteen years of life with Mr. Coy at Andover, led to his resignation in 1895 – a great blow to the school."

vii /   Whether or not Mrs. Hotchkiss felt further estranged from the school by Coy's treatment of her faculty friend remains a matter of conjecture. Even so, there is little doubt that she harbored deep-seated resentments against the board. She may have felt by now no less deceived in this relationship than she had been by her faithless husband in France. But she recognized the need to bide her time. Only two board meetings were held in the next two years, one of which Mrs. Hotchkiss attended, with no evident participation reflected in the minutes. But as soon as the next meeting convened on April 25, 1896, in Timothy Dwight's office, she launched her counteroffensive. Flanked by Frank E. Randall, her Lakeville lawyer, she made the attack through him. The strategy was as subtle as it was complex, involving a long written communication which "recited an outline of the history" of the board. This version of events from Mrs. Hotchkiss's point of view was marked by such phrases as "matters of vital importance . . . law applicable thereto . . . existence and usefulness of this association." It all sounded ominous, and the handwritten page in the minutes still looks that way today, bristling with a half-dozen underlined *whereas*es and several *resolved*s.

Mrs. Hotchkiss, it turns out, may have wanted nothing short of getting "her money back." * And she was doing it by challenging the legal basis for the board's actions over the past three years. Her case rested on a technicality going back to 1893, when the original Hotchkiss School Association received its tax-exempt status and became the Maria H. Hotchkiss School Association. Claiming that the transfer of assets and authority between those similar but separate entities had not been properly carried out, Mrs. Hotchkiss wanted to have the board's actions for that period declared invalid. She seemed intent on turning back the clock and starting anew.

The effect of the salvo fired by the embittered widow and her lawyers, despite some of the bombastic rhetoric, was more like buckshot – unpleasant but not particularly damaging. It sent the board scurrying for cover, though only under reams of paper. The administrative work needed to set the record straight was tedious and convoluted. One of the many steps in that process consisted of resurrecting for a single meeting the former Hotchkiss School Association – which explains why those minutes from 1896 ended up so startlingly sandwiched between two meetings in 1893. A rash of legal jargon also appeared at this time. For the previous five years, the minutes had begun with the phrase, "The meeting was called to order by President Kingsbury, there being present . . ." Now, just getting to this stage required a lengthy preamble containing language like, "According to the provisions of the 2nd By-Law . . . a notice of which the foregoing is a copy was deposited in the post office at Lakeville as required by By-law 3." Only upon Mrs. Hotchkiss's death would such legalese disappear from the minutes, just as noticeably as it had appeared. [†]

The gentlemen on the board thus were uncomfortably aware of having their every move legally scrutinized. That Mrs. Hotchkiss

---

*Thomas H. Chappell '24, headmaster from 1955 to 1960, wrote that he had heard from an old friend and business acquaintance of Mrs. Hotchkiss that that is what she wanted – "to get her money back."

[†]In 1927, by an act of the General Assembly of Connecticut, *The Maria H. Hotchkiss School Association* became *The Hotchkiss School.*

should resort to such harassment reflected the depth of frustration and animosity she felt – almost as if she had been violated and was bent on taking revenge. Yet even at this irreconcilable stage one of her fellow trustees on the board managed to handle her sufficiently so that she ended up "concurring with the President that her communication in writing to the Board [which had formed the basis for this involved action] need not be copied into the records, provided it is placed on file." A thorough search of all possible repositories has failed to bring such a document to light. How instructive it might have been to examine Mrs. Hotchkiss's version of events in her "outline of the history" of the board!

That was the last meeting Mrs. Hotchkiss attended – a decision which was interpreted by the trustees in their own peculiar way. According to Andrew Phillips, who was surely as kindly and understanding a man as any on the board, Mrs. Hotchkiss was upset at being only one of a number of trustees and, in her thwarted ambition to act as dictator, stayed away.

The most acrimonious exchange between Mrs. Hotchkiss and the board, however, was yet to come. The minutes of a meeting held on January 11, 1897, at the accustomed location, Timothy Dwight's office, provide an all-too-familiar prologue to the drama. "After Bissell Hall, erected by Mrs. Hotchkiss' order, had been turned over to the possession of the board, it was found that $10,000 were needed to settle unpaid bills incurred for its construction. The surprise and disappointment caused by this discovery were increased when it was learned that Mrs. Hotchkiss entertained decided objections against the sale of a piece of land, containing ten acres . . . from the proceeds of which – $6,000 – it was planned to pay for Mr. Buehler's cottage. As the result of this combination of circumstances, the Board finds itself obliged to make extraordinary provision for raising immediately the sum of $16,500."

Although the "extraordinary provision" meant taking out a mortgage in place of the aborted sale – "upon Bissell Hall, the adjoining cottages, and a specified portion of the surrounding land" – the situation provided the undeceived widow with a high-minded rationale to take an extraordinary step of her own. For it was only through her alacrity that she had staved off the sale of those ten acres, which represented an integral part of the school grounds (stretching from the boathouse on the lake to the Millerton Road). Now, she may well have considered the far more extensive mortgage – within the framework of her Yankee views – tantamount to pledging one's soul to the devil for temporary gain. Accordingly, on May 21, 1897, Maria Hotchkiss had a new deed drawn up for the sixty-five-acre tract of land she had originally given to the school. In this deed, she acknowledged the quitclaim she had provided in 1893 after it was "represented to me" that the original deed of trust "after its delivery to and acceptance" by the board, "but before it had been put upon record, had been mislaid." The purpose of the new deed was "to declare and put upon record the trusts and uses" which had been specified in that original deed "according to the true intent and meaning of the grantor." The bottom line? "That no lien shall be created upon said premises and said premises shall not be incumbered for any purpose, and shall not be conveyed or otherwise disposed of."

There, no more mortgages, no more attempted sales of land on which the Hotchkiss School was "forever to be maintained." Mrs. Hotchkiss had the new deed promptly registered in the land records of Salisbury and notified the board by letter of what she had done.

Perhaps because they knew what was coming, both of her Bissell relatives as well as her lawyer, Randall, chose not to attend the meeting that was immediately called. The consternation of the trustees on this occasion thus comes through in the minutes undisguised. Referring to the document sarcastically as the "so-called deed," those in attendance barely stopped short of labeling the school's benefactress a liar. They repeatedly and vehemently denied the existence of any deed prior to the quitclaim of 1893, asserting that no one on the board had "seen such a deed, or that it was ever delivered to the Corporation, excepting that Mrs. Hotchkiss maintains such a belief." They voted to lodge a formal protest with the Town of Salisbury for having recorded the latest deed, declaring "that the statements contained therein are untrue."

But were they?

"To impeach the integrity, high purpose, and honest judgment of such men," observed J. G. Estill, in assessing the credibility of the gentlemen on the board, "was out of the question." Yet should not the school's founder be accorded the same trust or at least the same benefit of doubt? If those overwrought gentlemen had paused to glance through the minutes, they would have found the evidence right there, in the official account of the first meeting on August 11, 1891, recorded at the very top of page 2 of the red leather-bound volume: "*It was moved and voted to accept the deed, presented to the Board by Mrs. Hotchkiss, of a tract of land for the use of the School.*" The 1891 date would have irrefutably confirmed Maria Hotchkiss's claim that there indeed had been a deed prior to the 1893 quitclaim. Today, that sort of evidence would fall into the category of the smoking gun.

viii / What a denouement between the benefactress and her namesake school! To have the Hotchkiss name bandied around town in such an unfavorable way by the public challenge of her deed! What exactly were her adversaries on the board whispering about this woman with her recently inherited wealth? Given every conceivable – and even inconceivable – benefit of the doubt, those trustees must have known perfectly well what the donor's intent concerning the land had been all along. How far would Timothy Dwight have got when he first approached Mrs. Hotchkiss with his idea for a school if he had insisted on reserving the right to sell or mortgage the land she might donate?

Still, the gentlemen on the board did not fully comprehend how Mrs. Hotchkiss felt. The evidence suggests that subsequent to this final encounter with the school's benefactress, they formed a committee to solicit her for more funds. Heading the deputation? Atholl McBean '00, then a mature, enthusiastic lower mid who went on to found the Stanford Research Institute and in 1968 received the Hotchkiss Man of the Year award. Fortunately, the school was on the verge of the sort of prosperity which would obviate the need for any further desperate measures to make ends meet.

As bequests and purchases started to expand the school's holdings to today's five-hundred-acre domain, the board periodically sought to establish an unrestricted title to the original sixty-five-acre tract. Among those involved in that endeavor was Morris W. Seymour, a lawyer and a trustee,* who also contributed his legal skills toward acquiring the land for Taylor Field and the forested area that would become the picturesque site of the ski jump. In 1906, Seymour reiterated the opinion of the former president of the board, Kingsbury: "He thinks the last deed was drawn by an attorney of Mrs. Hotchkiss at a time when she was particularly angry with all the trustees, and was a crafty effort on his part to import a trust into the matter, which never had existed nor would be allowed to exist." Ironically, at about the same time as such misconceptions about the founder of the school were being perpetuated, the board was unveiling a portrait in her memory.

The controversial deed not only survived Mr. Seymour's challenge, but in time came to articulate the school's own feeling about the inviolability of its site – vindicating, in this case, the judgment of the farmer's daughter over that of her formally more accomplished colleagues.

This is not to diminish the achievements of the gentlemen on the board. Timothy Dwight, Edward Coy, and other trustees selflessly pursued what they saw as the best interests of the school. For that, future generations would bestow on them due praise. It should also be remembered that during the same contentious meetings involving Mrs. Hotchkiss, myriad other matters were taken care of. These ranged from hiring new masters to protecting the ecology of Lake Wononscopomuc (yes, way back then) and even handling such mundane details as providing slate for blackboards and improving seats in the chapel. Moreover, Edward Coy and other board members who authored those

---

*In 1916, Seymour – by then a Litchfield judge – would succeed Phillips as president of the board of trustees.

handwritten minutes of the early years deserve applause. Their obliquely presented record is startlingly frank when compared with the rest of the volume covering the next forty years; and even more so alongside the three thick, typewritten volumes covering the rest of the school's first century. Now, at the end of that century, those early minutes provide a glimpse of what the sombre woman whose portrait hangs in the dining room went through on her way to that prominent niche. Her family's motto, *In Recto Decus*, carved into the oak panel-ing just above the portrait becomes invested with meaning beyond the translation, "Glory consists in fair dealing."

What would she think of her school now? Perhaps the best evidence is that even in her day, Maria Hotchkiss held an affection for what it then was. "She was present at our baccalaureate exercises, and enjoyed them exceedingly," noted David Comstock at the completion of the school's first year in 1893. "She was also present on Monday, the 26th of June, at the boys' closing exercises, and enjoyed *them* immensely. She 'received' with us on Monday evening and had a royal time. Then came a sort of relapse, and we began to be alarmed." According to Com-stock's account, this "relapse" had been brought on by the thought of still more financial demands about to be orchestrated by the trustees.

Mrs. Hotchkiss died in 1901 without leaving a will. It should by then have come as no surprise to anyone on the board that she had made no financial provisions for the school that bore her name.* The significance of the occasion was such that Timothy Dwight decided to handle Maria Hotchkiss personally this one final time. On the day of her burial, he inserted into the board of trustees' minutes a lengthy tribute to her and the school she had established "by her munificent gift . . . and generous endowment. It was evident that she had medi-tated long and seriously on the question as to the best means and man-ner of accomplishing her desire. The result . . . was dictated by wis-

---

*In 1923, the brother of Maria Hotchkiss, Charles Bissell, bequeathed to the school $10,000 and a 175-acre tract of land on the condition that an agricultural course be offered as part of the Hotchkiss curriculum. The gift was declined by the trustees.

Portrait of Maria Hotchkiss in the dining hall

dom as well as by generous sentiment." This was a grand tribute, since it revealed that he, for one, understood the thoughtful and logical nature of her acts. It cost him nothing to say so now and perhaps relieved his soul. Then, in what appeared to be a customary final refrain, the now-retired Yale president and erstwhile parson offered comfort to

*Timothy Dwight (right) circa 1915 at Yale with Walter Hull Buell, future
headmaster of Hotchkiss*

"those who are nearest to her in relationship and affections" and expressed the hope "that the thought of a happy reunion in the future life may be a delightful inspiration for their minds and hearts." Considering the relationship he and the trustees had experienced with Mrs. Hotchkiss in this life, it is understandable why Timothy Dwight pointedly failed to include himself in any such future reunion.

Timothy Dwight died in 1916. Besides having provided the influential trappings of his office for so many meetings, what was the full extent of his contribution to Hotchkiss? There is surely far more to it than his own files reveal. Being a thrifty Yankee himself, he disposed of most of the letters he received by scribbling his responses in the margins or somewhere on the page and sending them back by the next mail. The most telling indication of how vast a role he played comes from the minutes of a board meeting held on June 3, 1916: "*Resolved*: That amidst the universal grief that the Educational world feels at the death of Dr. Dwight, this Institution, which in a large sense was the child of his creation, feels an especial loss, appreciating as it does that it was his wisdom that largely dominated its inception, creation and upbuilding."

3   A Paradise for Boys

Head Master Coy flanked by entire faculty, circa 1894, including Joe Estill (far right), David Y. Comstock (third from left), and Huber Gray Buehler (third from right)

"I can't tell you how I happened to end up at Hotchkiss, but I can tell you why I didn't go to St. Paul's," recalls Robert S. Pirie '52, in his classically ornate New York office of Rothschild, Inc., where he is president and CEO. "I was dragged around on the usual tour of boarding schools. I remember we went to St. Paul's and they served us cold macaroni for lunch in the dining room. Mother said to me afterward, 'That's the end of that place. You're not going there!'"

To be fair, Hotchkiss has served its share of cold macaroni in its time – surely one of the less hallowed traditions held in common with other boarding schools throughout the Northeast. And if St. Paul's antedates Hotchkiss in such culinary offerings, it does so in some of the more enviable traditions as well.

Chronologically, Hotchkiss is about in the middle of the pack. Among the first to articulate the purpose of these schools was Samuel Phillips, who wrote that it was his "chief concern to see to the regulation of [the boys'] morals" by "early diligently painting in the purest simplicity the Deformity and odiousness of VICE, [and] the Comeliness and Amiableness of VIRTUE." With that in mind, he founded in 1778 Phillips Academy in Andover, Massachusetts. Three years later another member of the family established, in Exeter, New Hampshire, a second Phillips Academy. Andover and Exeter were followed by the founding of such schools as Lawrenceville in 1810, The Hill in 1851,

St. Paul's in 1855, St. Mark's in 1865, and Groton in 1884. Though differing in emphasis and approach, these schools shared the goal of instilling in their boys a pristine blend of Christian values, an aristocratic noblesse oblige, and a Darwinian self-reliance abounding in all sorts of manly virtues. "To develop what was good in boys," is how the founder of St. Paul's, George Shattuck, described his mission, "[and] to discourage and check what was evil; to train & educate all their powers; mental, physical and moral." And the best way to accomplish this was to have the boys placed together in country settings, away from the distractions and temptations of the cities and under the constant supervision of "masters." Through a combination of inspiration, persuasion, and an assortment of unforgettable personality quirks, these masters would seek to work their magic on their unruly charges in the classrooms, in the dormitories, and, increasingly, on the playing fields. The goal was to bring forth in the boys their most desirable characteristics while preparing them for leadership roles. Another way of saying that: *Moniti Meliora Sequamur*. Derived from Vergil's *Aeneid*, this motto was included in the bylaws approved by the Connecticut legislature in establishing the tax-exempt Maria H. Hotchkiss School Association. Even Mr. Coy's elegant translation, "Let growing wisdom guide us to better ways," falls short of conveying all that the motto implied.

Hotchkiss opened its doors in 1892 as part of a greatly accelerated trend which saw the establishment of such schools as Taft in 1890, Choate and St. George's in 1896, Salisbury in 1901, Kent in 1906, and Berkshire in 1907. Ironically, what contributed to this spurt in private schools was the unprecedented expansion in public education during the latter part of the nineteenth century. The increasing availability of "free" high schools in effect put out of business many of the small academies which had been the pride of towns and villages throughout the Northeast. As semiprivate day schools, these academies had produced some top-notch applicants for the leading colleges that would become known as the Ivy League. Many college presidents, among them Timothy Dwight, now feared that the public high schools, because of their massive scale and bureaucratic structure, would not be able to do the job that had been done by the displaced academies. "The Hotchkiss School is the outgrowth of the conviction that the interests of higher education call for more and better secondary schools," reads the preamble to the school's first handbook. At the same time, the demand for this "better" education greatly increased. New fortunes were being made in the industrialization of America; yet such schools as Groton and St. Paul's looked askance at first- or second-generation wealth, especially if its possessors resided beyond the Northeast. St. Paul's also insisted on sound Episcopal credentials. With the simultaneous appearance of even greater urban sprawls and the correspondingly conspicuous "unhealthy" aspects of life in big cities, it became more imperative than ever to whisk impressionable boys into the bucolic innocence of the countryside. "So long as people dwell in great cities, where the atmosphere, physical and moral, is in a large measure unwholesome," observed Endicott Peabody, many years after founding Groton, "so long the boarding school will continue to minister to the children of those who can afford to send them out of town." In Peabody's day, almost any aspect of that male sybaritic triad of wine, women, and song would have qualified as "unwholesome" for boys – especially the "women" part.

Endicott Peabody and other educators of that ilk may also have been responding to a subtler reality of the times, namely, that the sons of aristocratic, wealthy, or otherwise notable families were likely to inherit power regardless of their educational background. The implicit responsibility of institutions such as Groton and Harvard or Hotchkiss and Yale was to prepare these boys to wield that inherited power in the most constructive and enlightened way. As one current witticism put it, "The dimmer the boy, the more urgent the task." And the sooner this educational process was started, the better the chance of overcoming any of the natural tendencies in boys to resist such edification. Just as Yale and Harvard were looking to the likes of Hotchkiss and Groton to prepare and premold their candidates, so these prep schools were now looking to feeder schools of their own. One of the first on the prepreparatory level was Fay, founded in 1866 with grades one through eight. Similar schools followed, including Allen Stevenson in 1883,

Fessenden in 1903, St. Bernard's in 1904, Buckley in 1913, Harvey in 1916, and, beyond the Northeast, most notably St. Louis Country Day in 1917. A boy starting out in the first grade at one of these schools could virtually count on progressing through the system to a diploma from Yale, Harvard, Princeton, or some other elite college of his choice. Those falling by the wayside for disciplinary reasons would usually find another path open to them within that same system. Boys expelled from Hotchkiss, for instance, would often be granted sanctuary at Deerfield or Choate.

Yet it was not an entirely closed system. At various junctures, this special path to influence had openings for boys from beyond the small circle of privilege. Scholarship programs provided entry to a limited number of needy boys, whether the deserving sons of missionaries or teachers, or of single mothers impoverished through widowhood or divorce, or from other families of character but modest means – or just boys who happened to be qualified in some particular way. But the objective was far broader than to benefit merely the recipients. As Frank H. Hamlin '24 has observed, "A lot of the rich and famous sent their sons to Hotchkiss partly because they would be pretty sure of getting into Yale, Harvard, or Princeton, and partly because they would be closely associated with the bright sons of the non-rich who were there on scholarship." He might have added that many of these promising boys would eventually join the family enterprises of their privileged classmates and with astounding frequency marry their classmates' sisters – who, in turn, had been prepared for their roles at such colleges as Smith, Wellesley, and Vassar and their growing network of preparatory schools.

In starting out with fifty boys and a handful of day students, Hotchkiss was considered to be of respectable size. Taft at that time did not have even half that enrollment, and Groton, which had opened with twenty-four boys eight years earlier, was only then approaching the fifty mark. The notable exceptions in the 1890s were Andover, which already then had close to four hundred students, and Exeter, almost three hundred. Though an academy, Andover had always taken in boarders, lodging them with families in town. This had severely restricted the academy's growth during its early years. In 1810, after three decades of operation, Andover's total enrollment had been only twenty-three. The big change came in the second half of the nineteenth century, when Andover started to build its own accommodations and was converted to a boarding school. Other academies, determined to survive the new competition from public schools, did likewise. Deerfield, a small day academy since 1797, became a boarding school in 1902 under the leadership of Frank Boyden. He served as headmaster for the next sixty-six years and became one of the legendary members in that unique coterie of prep school overlords.

In one respect the Hotchkiss School had an enviable advantage. "It is incredible for a school to start off like that, with land, buildings and everything else," Horace Taft, brother of the future president of the United States, is reported to have said wistfully as he struggled to provide the necessary facilities for his own school, which had just relocated from New Jersey to Watertown, Connecticut. And the growth of the Hotchkiss School continued at an enviable pace. Within two decades of welcoming its first students, Hotchkiss reached a symbolic milestone. Just as the school had drawn on Andover faculty for administrative talent in 1892, Hotchkiss was able to pass on the favor to Loomis in 1912. Nathaniel F. Batchelder, head of the English department at Hotchkiss, moved with his family to Windsor, Connecticut, to become headmaster of the school which was just then preparing to welcome its own initial contingent of fifty students.

ii /   When the first Hotchkiss boys arrived at their gleaming new school of lemon-colored brick overlooking a circular lake with an unpronounceable name, they surely had not much of an inkling of what it had taken to make everything ready for them in time – or of the approaching conflict between the distant lady they occasionally spotted on the grounds and her ever-present escort, the imposing gray-bearded gentleman who was their headmaster. He, along with the associate master, was an especially reassuring sight for the dozen or so transfer students from Andover, who recognized many other aspects of their old school. As at Andover (and, of course, Exeter), Hotchkiss masters were respectfully addressed as *professor*. The other most obvious borrowing was the designation for grade levels, which was quite unlike those at other secondary schools or colleges, including Yale. The youngest of the new boys were called juniors or, more popularly, preps. They were followed in the hierarchy by lower middlers, upper middlers, and ultimately by the lofty and near-almighty seniors. It was considered as much a senior prerogative as a responsibility to remind the preps of their lowly status by having them wear black ties and always be touching a wall with an elbow while walking along the endless corridor in Main. "Sir" was the only permissible form of address by preps to seniors. But whether seniors or preps, there was a class equality of sorts in that all of the boys had their rooms cleaned and made up daily by maids. Another carry-over from Andover – this one shared with virtually all boarding schools of that era – was a daily chapel service of about ten minutes and, on Sundays, a longer service with a sermon and then brief vespers at the end of the day. The unspoken theory was that even if the boys happened to be half asleep, such passive exposures to godly wisdom would have the same cumulative effect as the rays of the sun, ennobling the attendants in due course with an inner spiritual glow. As for the curriculum, it was devised by Andover's two most exacting former academics. "I may assure you," wrote Coy, as the headmaster-designate, to his prospective English teacher, Huber Gray Buehler, "that the Hotchkiss School under the present administration will adopt no cheap substitutes for a liberal education. . . . To be sure, we shall recognize Scientific education as a branch of liberal education . . . but we shall make no provision whatever for boys who may wish to enter college, like Harvard, for instance, without Greek." Shortly thereafter, Coy declined to accept an applicant who did not want to study Greek but was otherwise fully qualified – a luxury the school could hardly afford. Fortunately, it was the boy's father who relented. "In that case," resolved the father, "I will have him study Greek!"

Thanks largely to the more mature of those transplanted Andover boys, an unusual record of that first year has been preserved. Overcoming the disorganization inherent in the starting of a new school, these older boys managed to muster their talents to put out a yearbook, called the *Hotchkiss Annual*. The significance of their accomplishment looms even larger because the school newspaper, the *Hotchkiss Record*, would not be inaugurated until the following year, and the next yearbook, in the guise of the present *Mischianza*, did not come out until 1896. Originally spelled *Meschianza*, the title derived from the Italian verbs *mescere*, to pour out, and *mischiare*, to mix, and essentially meant "a medley." The foreign-sounding nomenclature was in line with similar publications such as *Pot-Pourri* at Andover and *Olla Podrida* at Lawrenceville.

That unique *Hotchkiss Annual* of 1893 was a slim volume in rich lavender covers with the whimsical Gothic lettering of the title imprinted in gold. Among the Andover-transfer editors was Henry L. deForest. "I intend to leave large footprints in the sands of time," he predicted in one of the few attributed quotations. Indeed, young deForest would have a distinguished business and philanthropic career – and also become the first Hotchkiss graduate elected to the school's board of trustees. He would serve in that capacity from 1919 to 1939, nurturing a school which, he once confided to George Van Santvoord, he considered "a perfect paradise for boys."

In that original publication, unlike those of subsequent years, a considerable amount of space was devoted to descriptions of the embryonic Hotchkiss:

"One of the most pleasant features connected with The Hotchkiss School is the character of the surrounding country. Standing on top of a high hill, the buildings command a superb view in every direction. To the north looms up old Greylock, forty miles away, like a dim spectre; to the west can be seen the hazy outline of the Catskills; while to the east and south the view is broken by innumerable hills. The lakes on both sides of us also add greatly to the beauty of the locality. The village of Lakeville, about a mile distant, seems to lie far below us as we stand upon the summit of the hill. . . . Tradition relates that once, as John Trumbull, Connecticut's famous painter, was passing over this hill, he became so entranced with the marvelous beauty of the scene which lay spread out before him that he ordered the coachman to stop so that he might enjoy more thoroughly the prospect; even the imprecations of the driver and the entreaties of his fellow passengers to re-enter the coach, were unavailing, and it was not until a threat was made to drive on and leave him that he reluctantly consented to comply with their wishes. . . .

"When one takes into account all the influences which here favor high thinking and right living – the bracing air, the strength of the hills, the goodly fellowship – it seems as if he must be perverse indeed who falls out by the way."

To get away from the temptations and evils of the city – after all, that was the reason for locating the school in such a remote bucolic spot. The natural splendor remains as precious today as it was in John Trumbull's time. The countryside has been dotted with sparkling white houses (even the modest ones now going for more than it cost to build the school), and the pristine beauty of the fields and the woods remains largely unscathed. The view from the hill is as superb as ever.

The *Annual* was no less enthusiastic in depicting the functioning of the new school: "This school is the first in the country, to our knowledge, to adopt the self-governing plan. The students study together in one large room with absolutely no faculty supervision, but are bound by a stringent pledge neither to communicate nor to disturb the order of the room in any way. . . . It has been, indeed, an impressive sight to see sixty boys working there quietly at their desks from 9:30 to 11:30 A.M., from 2:30 to 3:30 and 7:30 to 9 P.M., without the supervision of any school officer, yet keeping, by their own voluntary self-control, better order than is usually secured in most study halls by the presence and authority of a master. . . . We should not recommend this plan for all schools, but for one situated as this is, where character building is the first end in view, we heartily recommend it. It strengthens a person's self-reliance and prepares him much better to go out into the world."

The idealistic observations about the boys' conduct in study hall reflect the school's initially lofty expectations. Over the next seventy-

five years, every boy would be inescapably exposed to a compelling reminder of this ideal in the rotunda in Main, the internal crossroads of
the school.* Emblazoned in large white lettering around the rotunda's
frieze was the quotation, "I sat obedient, in the fiery prime of youth,
self-govern'd, at the feet of Law." No matter that the nineteenth-
century English essayist and poet Matthew Arnold had meant those
words more as a lament than an inspiration; the boys also did not take
their exemplary intent to heart. By the time that first senior class had
been graduated, the school's governing ideals had to be modified by the
realities of life – especially by the behavior of adolescent males with
energy and ingenuity to spare. Study hall was placed under the constant and strict supervision of a faculty member; even so, it remained
one of the most inviting places for students to perpetrate pranks. These
probably did not change much over the years and represented a varia-
tion on the same theme as when I sat in study hall in the mid-twen-
tieth century – not in the original room but at some of the same desks,
embellished by layers of predecessors' initials, some artistically carved
out and others impetuously scratched in. The most common trick involved turning out the lights during the two-hour evening session. As
in the original room, all of the switches were on a control panel outside
the door, and the culprit was in little danger of being caught. He might
even abscond with the master circuit breaker and extend the students'
relief from books, while providing a rarely missed opportunity to create all sorts of bedlam in the dark.

Faculty-supervised study hall continues to this day for students with
academic and disciplinary problems. And the ideal of self-supervision
remains. "The student-faculty council recognizes the need for students
to take greater responsibility for the daily concerns of campus life,"
reads a memo of 1990 from the school's student body president, Amit
Basak. "As one step toward this end, we propose to the faculty that
seniors supervise Main Building study hall."

---

*As the school increased in size, the rotunda also became the site of individual
post office boxes for students and faculty.

iii /   "The Faculty have proceeded on the assumption that any boy who is worthy of a place here must be trustworthy," stated the *Annual*, "and that whenever, after a fair probation, a boy is unwilling or unable to respond to appeals to his self-respect and sense of honor, he must give up his connection with the School."

The propensity for less-than-ideal behavior meant that this ultimate punishment inevitably had to be invoked. In his memoirs, Uncle Joe Estill provided a faculty participant's account of how this was done:

"Going back to the first year . . . every effort was made to have boys feel that, as young gentlemen, they should do right without the compulsion of rules. So rules were not promulgated. *Announcements* were posted, printed on one side of a two-page buff-sheet. Mr. Buehler often quoted the boy who said, 'We don't have any rules, but if you break one, you get it in the neck.'

"The *announcement*, the non-observance of which has brought more trouble throughout the years than any other, was the one about leaving the grounds after 7:30 P.M. Another important one was that not more than three boys should ever be in a boat at the same time.

"Only a few weeks after the opening that first year some master reported to the faculty that he had seen four boys in a boat, but too far away to identify them. As this was the first serious case calling for discipline, there was prolonged discussion as to how it should be handled. I took the position that as we were trying to start a new school on a higher plane of manliness and cooperation than any of which we knew, and in which we expected boys to do right or to make manly admission when they did not, the Headmaster should call the school into the study, with all the faculty present, and after some such statement as above, call for the boys who had been out in a boat on a certain afternoon to rise. It was agreed by the faculty that they should be told to go to their rooms and pack their things in preparation for going home. It was some shock to the faculty when eight boys, without a moment's hesitation, arose, one-seventh of the whole school. No member of the faculty had the slightest suspicion that more than four boys were involved. Mr. Coy did not hesitate for an instant to dismiss the bunch in agreement with the decision of the faculty. There followed a long discussion in the faculty as to whether the dismissal should be temporary, permanent, or changed to a suspension. I pleaded with all the fervor of my being, even to the point of tears, for temporary suspension of boys who had previously been exemplary, insisting that suspension was punishing parents instead of boys. But colleges and schools in those days made very frequent use of the six-weeks suspension, rustification, as it was called. So all these boys were suspended, five of them for six weeks, the other three indefinitely, as they had previously shown themselves not up to the desired standard. . . .

"The fight over suspension continued till Mr. Buehler was brought into the faculty. A few years after he became headmaster, the sequestration program, one of the best constructive suggestions to my mind he ever made, was started. It had scarcely been adopted before it was brought into play, to mete out punishment to the greatest number ever of offenders on a single occasion, to my knowledge, except where a class or dormitory was in some mix-up."

In the presequestration era, the most extensive disciplinary action came in 1901, when fully a quarter of the senior class of forty-two was dismissed. The indirect cause of the trouble was the rapid expansion of the school – partly driven by the need to bring in additional revenues – and the consequent permission for seniors to live off campus. Rooms were readily available in Lakeville in private homes for $2.50 per week, and for a dollar more, at the inn, which was closer to the school. The precise nature of the boys' infraction has not been recorded, but they certainly were in a position to break the no smoking, no drinking, and other cardinal rules. Professor Coy attributed the trouble to "the social leadership of the class [which] by accident fell into incompetent hands." He assured the board that "the refractory spirit . . . not only did not affect seriously the spirit of the school, but did not even carry the senior class as a whole." Nevertheless, that was the end of the "experiment of going outside of the school grounds to accommodate excess of students." In future years, more and more students would be housed on the top floors of masters' cottages, which were beginning to mushroom on the school grounds.

iv /   The failure of off-campus housing only reenforced one of the basic premises on which Hotchkiss had been founded: the constant need for masters to exert their character-building influence. Beyond the interaction in classrooms and in the dormitories, where each corridor was supervised by an unmarried master residing there with the boys, what better opportunity to do so than on the playing fields?

Athletics were a relatively recent phenomenon for teenagers in boarding schools, going back only about half a century to such British private "public" schools as Rugby and Eton. (Eton at that time had already been around for some 350 years.) Athletics thus represented a truly novel opportunity for channeling some of the rowdiness and mischievous idleness of teenage boys into a structured outlet. In franker parlance, daily exertion on the playing fields was expected to drain away some of the pressure of adolescent sexuality – in that era of no other permissible or untabooed outlets – while instilling the qualities epitomized by the accolade, "He's a good sport." In the United States, organized sports were institutionalized only a couple of decades before the founding of Hotchkiss. Groton's headmaster, Endicott Peabody, was one of the major forces of this movement to build "manly Christians." The first interscholastic football game, Andover versus Exeter, was played in 1878.

"The Hotchkiss School boy believes it his duty to be first a gentleman, then a scholar, and then an athlete, if possible," declared the *Annual* of 1893. "To secure the fullest benefits from exercise and yet to avoid the dangers and evils of over-indulgence in matters purely physical is the policy of The Hotchkiss School towards athletics."

The *Annual* spelled out the school's specific goals for athletics: "First, the recreation of minds whose first business is genuine hard work in study and classroom. Second, the maintenance of health and the development of the body. Third, the acquisition of those qualities of nerve and character which are so well developed on diamond and football field. Lastly, the making of records and winning of games."

To achieve these goals in their "order of importance," the Hotchkiss School decided to foresake all outside competition and instead divided the student body into two intramural teams, the Pythians and the Olympians. "Every student is compelled to belong to one of these, thereby bringing fellows into a close relation with athletics, and stirring up an enthusiasm which otherwise would not be shown towards school teams," stated the *Annual*. "The principles of the School look towards making its reputation not by athletics, but by its collegiate record."

Such athletic modesty would not survive beyond the school's first year – with the impetus for change coming entirely from the students. They were the ones who turned the school's athletic priorities upside down. They yearned to represent Hotchkiss and bring glory to the school, and no doubt a smidgen of the same to themselves. Though the Olympian and Pythian societies continued to provide athletic opportunities for everyone, a school football team began training in earnest in the fall of 1893. Their only game that season was against the previous year's Hotchkiss class at Yale, which the older boys won 6–0. The baseball team that spring had more luck finding opponents, taking the field against several small nearby academies. And by the fall of 1894, the school's football team began to fill out its schedule, too. Among the rivals: Taft, whose new location in Watertown placed it about halfway between Hotchkiss and Yale. But this level of activity was still too low-key and provisional for some of the more competitive spirits in the school. "We all feel great pride in Hotchkiss of a quiet kind," editorialized the *Record* in 1895, "but great school enthusiasm can be aroused among students only by the exertion of schoolmates with other schools . . . when we can vie with other schools and show our superiority over them." Such aspirations could finally begin to be realized with the arrival at Hotchkiss in the fall of 1896 of a compact young man named Otto F. "Monnie" Monahan. For more than four decades, he would teach Hotchkiss boys not only the principles of good sportsmanship, but also how to win. His most intense rivalry during those years was with the Hill School in Pottstown, Pennsylvania, and many veterans of Monnie's training techniques, including the headmaster's son, the legendary Ted Coy '06, went on to achieve football fame at Yale and elsewhere. Ted's most vaunted moment at Hotchkiss came when he was taken out of a baseball game that was being won to save the track team from defeat. As a fullback at Yale, he was hailed for introducing "the new tactic of running down opposing tacklers instead of dodging them."

Athletic opportunities even in the school's second decade were in no way comparable to those of today. Except for Wednesdays and Saturdays, classes in those years continued into the afternoon and sporting endeavors had to wait until after 3:00 P.M. "The school was channelled very definitely into studies and a very limited range of athletic things," recalled George Van Santvoord '08, in a taped interview with Lael Wertenbaker for the 75th anniversary history. "The faculty were, by and large, people in their thirties, but we thought of them as people who were fifty or sixty and a very few of them took part in the athletic life of the school. There was Mr. Monahan, the physical education director, and only two or three others who were involved. The rest didn't do anything at all except come out and watch. Baker Field had been given to the school some years before, and there was a rather rough place by the crossroads where boys who were not on the school team could play football and baseball. There was no athletic sport at all in the fall except football. In the winter, there were the gymnastic teams, and hockey was a very uncertain sport. You might have a week when the lake was good skating, and then people just went out and skated, and there were some scratch hockey games. In the spring there was baseball and track and tennis, and then about the first of May, you could swim in the lake. The only out-of-town trips were once a year. A team in football or baseball in alternate years went to the Hill School. The other schools we played came to Hotchkiss, and they came by train. The automobile had been invented but the roads were dreadful."

Under these conditions, it was not easy for Monnie to maintain the appropriate athletic spirit from year to year. The following letter from him appears in the *Mischianza* of 1908:

"I desire to call the attention of the student body to one or two impressions which have been growing on me during the last two years.

"In the first place I have felt that the fellows do not appreciate and covet the letter as much as formerly. If this is in any way true, it is deplorable. The fact that there has been some reason for this impression should stimulate and arouse the energies of every fellow. It does not seem necessary to state the reasons which have caused the writer to question the appreciation of the H, it is sufficient to say that there has been cause."

Monnie's "cause," specifically, was that fewer than a dozen "fellows" earned the *H* in the preceding year, and far too many other fellows were content to make class teams. "What we want is more of the old Hotchkiss spirit," he wrote. "What I want to make strong is, that every fellow should be ambitious to make his class team, but when it is made he should use extraordinary effort to climb higher and win the H."

Monnie's exhortation may not have been directed at the students alone, many of whom were eager to carry on and expand the school's sporting tradition. The following editorial entitled "A Few Statistics" appeared in an issue of the *Hotchkiss Record* in 1912:

"It is an undeniable fact that scholarship at Hotchkiss is each year rising to a higher plane. We do not exaggerate when we say that the present Senior Class is doing the work on a par with the work of the Senior Class at Yale of forty or fifty years ago. Many of the older graduates who are in a position to know have assured us of this fact. . . .

"From the educational point of view this is doubtless a most satisfactory record, but to those who glory in the athletic prestige of Hotchkiss it is anything but welcome. The big men of years gone by, who barely kept up in their work, can no longer hold their positions in the School. But one member of last year's football team came back this year.

O. F. MONAHAN
DIRECTOR OF ATHLETICS
THE HOTCHKISS SCHOOL
LAKEVILLE, CONN.

My message to the Class of 1938 and to Hotchkiss boys, past, present and future, is, that to my mind, there is no better way to instil the right attitude towards life into the lives of the youth of the Country, than can be obtained through the training and participation in competitive athletic sports.

Long after the last scores have been posted, be they victories or defeats; long after the cheers and groans have died; long after cheer leaders and players have become dignified men; the sportsmanship, the fair play, the quick and straight thinking which leads to the making of right decisions and the carrying in ones soul of honorable methods of dealing with ones competitors, these qualities should linger in the lives of Hotchkiss boys as among their principle assets of good citizenship.

For the splendid way in which members of this and previous Hotchkiss classes have cooperated with me in trying to instil this Hotchkiss spirit, I am indeed grateful.

I would have you and others carry with you through the years, my recent, publicly expressed slogan:

"No boasting or gloating in victory
And no excuses or alibis in defeat."

O. F. M.

Monahan's letter

Again, as we look at the picture of the present Senior Class when they were preps, we find that nearly fifty percent have dropped by the way. This is not a protest against the high standard of the School, but a statement of figures that talk for themselves. We do suggest, however, that more regard be taken for the strong men. Let their strength be considered one of their qualifications, since we all admit that studies alone do not make boys into men, and it is by her men that the Hotchkiss of the future will be known."

A quarter of a century later, on the eve of his retirement, Otto Monahan penned a letter (opposite page) which articulates to this day the sporting philosophy for legions of Hotchkiss alumni — and a growing array of alumnae as well. Many of these men and women, in fact, would consider what they learned on the athletic field by far the most valuable aspect of their Hotchkiss experience. Playing by the rules, self-control under pressure, and a willingness to put out 100 percent are the same principles which brought them success in life. Yet these returns from the school's athletic program have not come without exacting a price. The lesser athletes in each class often have felt diminished by the big wheels of sports, by the jocks; and nonathletic accomplishments, including excellence in class, have rarely managed to evoke the same sort of approval or applause. Moreover, the effect of early fame has not always been positive on the great athletes. Tantamount to a cautionary tale was the well-publicized lot of Ted Coy, who, after a failed second marriage to the glamorous actress, Jeanne Eagels,* settled into a notably lackluster existence. Was that perhaps a reflection of "the dangers and evils of overindulgence in matters purely physical" against which the founders of Hotchkiss had sought to alert the school? What exactly was the ideal balance among the physical, intellectual, and moral aspects in character development? Where did the desire to win, to cultivate an intense adversarial relationship on the field fit in with the solitary competition against the selfishly pleasurable temptations within oneself?

With the recent revival of the Olympian-Pythian tradition at Hotchkiss, these questions are being asked again. The primacy of recreation and keeping fit originally assigned to the role of athletics by the founders of the school seems to be more timely now than a hundred years ago.

---

* Portrayed in a 1957 film *Jeanne Eagels* with Kim Novak. Sonny Tufts played the role of Ted Coy.

v /   **W**hen Otto Monahan came to Hotchkiss in 1896, he joined a faculty which had already doubled from its original six – and more would join to keep pace with the rapid growth of the school. From the very beginning, the quality of the faculty was considered as much a key to the success of the school as the personal trustworthiness of students. The first Hotchkiss catalogue promised "the most favorable conditions for instruction and study," which would come from "the intimate contact of students with masters in social as well as in other relations."

That promise soon brought reassuring dividends. "Professor H. P. Wright, who came up from New Haven to conduct the examinations," noted Head Master Coy after the completion of the first year, "was carried away with the spirit of the place, and with the boys themselves. Of the 12 Seniors, 7 were admitted to college without conditions, and the rest with very light conditions." (The word *college* as used by Coy was synonymous with Yale.) "We are overflowing with applicants for next year. The exact situation is this: 30 old boys return; 40 new ones have applied. Of the 40, some have been refused for various reasons, leaving about 35 from which we must now make our selection. Of this number 25 have already shown satisfactory evidence of being ready for classification in Sept." By 1896, thirty-five seniors were graduating. Twenty-five of them had been accepted by Yale, and the rest were heading for Harvard, Princeton, and other predominantly Ivy League colleges. "But one school in the country sends a larger delegation to the next Freshman class at Yale," Mr. Coy noted with pride, "and that is Andover Academy, and four years ago, the Andover contingent was not as large as that of Hotchkiss this year."

Some Hotchkiss masters were already beginning to earn recognition beyond the school grounds. "During the past year," reported Professor Coy to the trustees in 1897, "text books have appeared from the hands of Mr. Estill, Mr. Buehler, Mr. Pierce and Mr. Barss, which represent the results of their efforts to improve their capacity for service. . . . Some of these books have had very wide sale, all have been received with high commendation." The trustees in turn commended the head-master for his "ability to surround himself with strong and able teachers [and for] his influence and leadership in the important educational associations of New England and the eastern section of the country."

Yet, for whatever reason, the master who was perhaps even more influential with the boys than Professor Coy had been lost to the school. David Y. Comstock received barely a nod of recognition when he resigned in 1895 as associate master: the trustees thanked him rather curtly if enigmatically "for his services during the first three, and very eventful years, at the School." Precisely what happened or how the departure was related to the broader conflict between Mrs. Hotchkiss and Mr. Coy may never be known. But half a century later, one of Mr. Comstock's students would give us a measure of the sort of human being that he was. The following excerpt is from a longer piece sent to the Hotchkiss *Alumni News* by the late Judge Jesse Olney '93, shortly after returning home to California from his fiftieth reunion at the school in 1943:

"I wish to revive the memory of a great man, of a Professor whose brilliance as a teacher of Latin, I believe, outshone any other in the United States, and who made his classroom hour one for which no Hotchkiss boy would take a cut – a big, full-lived Human whose kindly sympathy and knowledge of human frailties made him beloved of all the boys under the affectionate nickname of 'Commy.'

"I feel the historical background of these first years at Hotchkiss is far, far indeed, from complete, and this overwhelming, dominating character of the School has been signally overlooked.

"Beyond the suffusing reputation which preceded him to Hotchkiss emanating from the Old Boys at Andover, my personal knowledge of Prof. Comstock dates from my entrance into the School in October 1892. I found at that time that Prof. Comstock was convinced that though the preparatory education for college at that period quickened youthful minds, it also often envenomed their hearts. His idea was to so dramatize it as to make it lovable. He felt that the Preparatory Schools instead of using their techniques as a broad thoroughfare up to Collegiate gates, instead had made it a blind alley.

"I want the later alumni to know the ground on which they stand – to realize the primal fostering of a great genius of a School free from barriers to opportunity and class distinctions. . . . He saw on the horizon on the hill between two lakes a school world in which there would flourish that science and art of gentle culture which is peculiarly Hotchkiss – a house built upon a hill, where boys lived peacefully and comfortably together in a society of honor and dignity as true gentlemen should.''

Comstock would never again hold a position at a school comparable to Hotchkiss or Andover. ''Professor Comstock does not at present know what he will do after leaving the School,'' concluded a tribute in the *Record* from the students. After a year of ''writing,'' he became the principal of a small academy in Vermont, and at the time of his death in 1920, he was teaching Latin at the Fall River High School in Massachusetts.

Was the departure of this humane man from Hotchkiss the beginning of the school's reputation as lacking in caring and warmth?

vi /   Though the boys surely had a pretty good idea about the Coy–Comstock strife, they probably had only the barest inkling of the fateful differences between Maria Hotchkiss and the board. Within a year of Professor Comstock's departure, the school's benefactress attended her last meeting, and virtually all avenues for any kind of cooperation were closed. Yet even on that contentious occasion she might have found herself nodding approval on hearing the following report from Professor Coy: ''Arrangements have been made whereby several boys of limited means are able to render some service to the School in return for tuition, etc. Four boys have thus been able to enjoy the privileges of the school whose chief compensation has been their priceless fidelity and industry. That boys do not suffer in their social standing from this arrangement is shown by the fact that one of these four boys was the Ivy Orator, by the election of his classmates for Class Day.''

The genesis of a thriving scholarship program may represent a contribution of Mrs. Hotchkiss's as valuable as any of her more tangible gifts. The stipulation she made to provide free tuition for a number of deserving local boys dovetailed with a similar Andover tradition of helping needy boys irrespective of geographical bounds. Scholarship boys thus became an integral part of Hotchkiss life even when the school was still severely strapped for funds. As the financial situation improved and the facilities expanded, the scholarship program kept pace. The original proportion of around 10 percent, which Mrs. Hotchkiss had acceded to in numerical terms – six students in total – continued to be honored in correspondingly larger numbers, though drawn from an area by no means limited to the vicinity of the school. By 1922, Headmaster Buehler could proudly report that in a student body of approximately three hundred, Hotchkiss had forty "free pupils," and he listed two dozen prominent boarding schools that still had none. While the number of local Foundation Scholarships among those forty free pupils cannot be readily ascertained, the *Hotchkiss Record* in 1928 stated that "for many years now [the school] has annually carried on its rolls ten or more local boys as recipients of scholarship aid."

Professor Coy's observation that these "boys do not suffer in their social standing" would be resoundingly confirmed in future years. Many jobs which had originally been performed by maids, such as cleaning classrooms and waiting on tables, were taken over by these "free students," or scholarship boys. (The maid service in individual rooms was continued until the start of World War II.) "Waiting on tables you got to know people by the way they responded to somebody who was serving them," explains the Pulitzer Prize winning author John Hersey '32. "You got to know the faculty very well, too, by the way they presided over their tables. I thought it was a privilege to be at a kind of nerve center." John Hersey and other scholarship boys made their work seem so desirable that some nonscholarship boys felt excluded. A two-week period was eventually set aside during the spring term when any senior in the school who wanted to give it a try could do so. Among the volunteers was a quiet, small-framed boy named Benson Ford '38. The first time he put on the white waiter's jacket and came out of the kitchen balancing a large soup tureen on a tray, he tripped and spilled the contents all over his Latin teacher, Richard Bacon '30. The scion of the founder of America's automobile industry cleaned up the mess and completed the two-week waiting stint he had requested, bringing closer the day when all students at the school would rotate at the task.

Other scholarship tasks, such as sweeping classrooms and washing the blackboards were not without allure. "I always regarded the pail and broom as sort of a badge of honor," says Swarthmore College professor Thompson Bradley '52, whose two brothers also went through Hotchkiss on scholarships. "I felt we were fortunate."

The presence of scholarship boys at a school nominally for the sons of the rich made for some memorable combinations. "I couldn't believe the first night in the dining room when we had supper as new kids," recalls Frank A. Sprole '38. "I sat with my father and mother next to Mr. and Mrs. Thomas Watson and their son Arthur. God knows, Watson was then in 1934 already one of the world's wealthy men and my own father was unemployed, and we were stony broke." Frank Sprole today is the retired vice-chairman of Bristol-Myers Squibb Pharmaceuticals, a former president of the Hotchkiss trustees, and one of the school's all-time great fund raisers. "Arthur thereafter became quite a good friend of mine, and he'd always remember himself that evening we had sat together with our parents."

The unbiased treatment of scholarship boys did not imply egalitarianism in every respect. "My exposure to the world of privilege was a shocking one at first," relates John Hersey. "I remember walking along the Main corridor where people left their papers and stuff on the windowsills and along the floor. I happened to see the bill that Walter P. Chrysler had run up at Ma Dufour's [a popular snackbar-with-taxi-service in Lakeville] – 'swilling in town' as we called it. It was more money than I saw in a year." But the future author of *Hiroshima* and some two dozen other notable works had his way of keeping up. "I only had one pair of trousers when I first got there, and I used to put it under my mattress every night to have it pressed in the morning."

Similar stories could be told by less conspicuous graduates of the

school, including some of the local boys who benefited via Maria Hotchkiss as recipients of Foundation Scholarships. Among them was the
grandson of the owner of Ma Dufour's, William "Doof" Dufour '52, a
good-natured classmate who stayed in the area to run and expand the
family transportation business before his untimely death. A year behind him was John J. Roche, who became a school trustee and a senior
partner in the Boston law firm of Hale & Dorr before starting his own
firm. Here is his story as a recipient of a Foundation Scholarship:

"We actually lived in New York City until 1937, when my father
suddenly died – leaving no assets – and my mother moved the family
to what had previously been our Connecticut summer home in the
Taconic section of Salisbury. There were some large barns in the back
part of the property which she used to start up a chicken farm. One of
my earliest memories is feeding about three hundred or four hundred
chickens with my older brother. The sale of eggs and chickens was
what kept the family together.

"In the second grade, I had an experience which bore on an event
years later at Hotchkiss. It was an exceptionally cold November day,
and the teacher, Mrs. Mathesson, took me aside to ascertain whether I
didn't have a coat for this weather. That night, when I appeared at
home with a slightly used but 'really neat' overcoat, my mother gave
me a stern lecture about how she got this far raising the family without
accepting charity or welfare, that we were not about to start now, et
cetera. Much to my regret, the coat went back the next day, and during
the balance of the winter, I wore two sweaters. Anyway, my mom was
a hardworking lady who at great personal sacrifice raised the family
alone. You cannot imagine how proud she was a few years later when,
at the urging of one of the teachers at the Salisbury Central School, a
Mrs. Hemmerly, I applied for and was granted a scholarship at the
Hotchkiss School.

"Prep year at Hotchkiss was a time of great anxiety for all of us, not
just the farm kid from Salisbury. The question was whether we were
going to survive in that academic environment. We were all in the

same boat. That being the case, I did not feel different from anyone else. Another reason for the commonalty, I believe, was the more or less standard uniform everybody wore – wash khaki pants, beat up sports jacket, and scuffed loafers or dirty white bucks. Furthermore, acceptance by one's peers at the school depended upon your accomplishments, especially in the area of athletic prowess. If you were an achiever academically or received recognition in some extracurricular activity, you would have no major difficulties fitting in. In that sense I didn't really feel I was treated any differently from anyone else. That would not have been the case if I had stayed at the Regional High School where I went for one year to prepare for Hotchkiss. Acceptance there depended upon the kind of car you drove, what your father did for work, how large a home your family lived in, and a lot of other things which had nothing to do with your own basic makeup.

"One incident at Hotchkiss which I will always remember occurred in the spring of my lower mid year. I was walking from the gym back to the Main Building when I found myself in stride with a senior who was a member of one of Hotchkiss's dynastic families. He questioned me at great length about what it was like to grow up on a little farm in Salisbury, Connecticut. He was genuinely curious. Because he was an upperclassman interested in me and my background, I was enthralled and opened up like a flower in the sun. We must have stood there in the middle of the campus for fifteen or twenty minutes before we finally walked back to Main. When we arrived there – and this I will never forget – he formally shook hands with me and said with great sincerity, 'I want you to know, John, that I really have enjoyed this conversation. This is the first time that I've had a talk like this with anyone who's underprivileged.' Well, that kind of knocked my socks off because I had never thought of myself in those terms. Actually, I was more embarrassed for him than I was for myself. Nevertheless, I knew well enough *not* to share the experience with my mother. She had always regarded a scholarship as something which is awarded, something which one wins, a prize given to people who are superior and that type of thing. If she had any notion that scholarships were granted to people who were characterized as underprivileged, I would have very quickly found myself back in the local high school. Just like with the overcoat, she would have made me give it back. She died in 1967 – and I never did have the heart to tell her."

John Roche's scholarship job in his senior year was supervising the dining room cleanup after lunch. "When I first became a trustee some thirty years later," recalls John, "the president of the board, Fay Vincent [Francis T. Vincent '56], reminded me that he had been one of the lowly preps wielding the broom on my dining hall crew. You could say it was an interesting change of roles."

A personal note: I was John Roche's cleanup crew predecessor, and he was my assistant for a year. After World War II, I was attending a boarding school in England when my father resigned as a Czech diplomat at the time of the Communist coup in Prague in 1948. Among his American colleagues was a friend of a Sharon resident, Admiral Thomas Hart. Admiral Hart conveyed to the Duke the story of our family's situation – with the result that only days after arriving in New York, my older brother and I found ourselves at Hotchkiss. The Duke enrolled us on the spot, neither asking for transcripts nor giving us any tests. "I don't want you worrying about the tuition fees," I remember the Duke telling Father. "I am instructing our bursar, Mr. Brooks, to consider as payment in full whatever you are able to pay. And I shall let *you* be the judge of that. If it turns out you can't afford anything right now – well, we have other boys here on full scholarships. It won't be anything unusual."

The Duke's voice was matter-of-fact, as if he were merely doing what anyone in his place would. Years later, when I tried to thank him during tea at his Vermont Shadowbrook Farm, his forehead became slightly tinged with pink and he puffed on his pipe several times. "But you really have nothing to thank us for," he finally said, in that same matter-of-fact tone. "We took you in because we simply wanted to see what we could learn from you."

vii /

W

hat kind of a man was the Duke's earliest predecessor? And how did he fulfill the role of a gentleman in his time? "Mr. Coy enjoyed the blessed distinction of not looking like a school-master," wrote J. Edmund Barss many years after he had joined the faculty in 1894. "A picture that I well remember is Mr. Coy seated in a light buggy, a soft, black, rather broad-brimmed hat on his gray hair, tooling his fine mare 'Daisy' delicately along the road. When he walked down the corridor he had a way of hitching his right shoulder as if settling his coat in place. . . . Like most men fit for leadership, Mr. Coy had a quick temper, which he habitually kept well controlled. An angry flush was sufficient warning to most people not to press him too far. I once saw a boy make the dangerous experiment of testing the limit of his patience: his insolence brought instantaneous dismissal. I think the dismissal was just, but it was rarely that such things happened without the safer, if less picturesque formality of faculty debate. Generally, Mr. Coy was long-suffering, so much so that on one occasion a lady who knew him well, and thought that he was unduly patient with some young scamp, implored him, 'Mr. Coy, *get mad!*'"

The school's first headmaster favored the appropriately measured response. "Never sacrifice a boy to a rule," was one of his maxims. He often put forth the theory that at adolescence a boy's nature "fermented" and would settle and clear if only given enough time and sympathy.

Professor Coy was also known for his humor. One day, when he repeatedly failed to elicit a response from a bright student who had just returned to class after an appendectomy, the headmaster remarked with slight exasperation, "Apparently, they removed not only your appendix, but also your table of contents."

This is how a member of the class of 1899, unfortunately unidentified, remembered his headmaster thirty years later in an article in the *Record*:

"It was a privilege to have been under Mr. Coy's influence. An imposing figure, very erect, with high color, making even more striking his snow-white whiskers, Mr. Coy was very human withal, much be-

loved, and had the distinction of causing even Greek to be very interesting. I can see him now, standing before a class, rolling out Greek in
his deep, melodious voice, and giving real meaning to every shade of
inflection. His handwriting was a flowing Spencerian type with curves
and flourishes, tempting to copy, so that often the blackboards were
filled with excellent imitations of his signature. A considerable number
of the boys at that time, sooner or later, had to call on him alone, at
least once. The rules then were not so strict on first offense smoking.
Mr. Coy, though very fond of smoking himself, never indulged during
the School term. Any student caught smoking was summoned to his
office, and together he and Mr. Coy would shake hands and solemnly
'swear off.' Second offense meant immediate dismissal as quickly as a
boy could be packed either by the boys or faculty. Going to Millerton
was also not subject to review. In those pre-Volstead days Millerton
was strictly 'out of bounds.'"

That solemn handshake was not merely symbolic. A boy committing a second offense would be immediately expelled *not* for the smoking itself, but for breaking his word. That was something a gentleman
simply should never do – and a tradition was thus born, which would
be enforced for most of the school's first century. A different sort of a
tradition initiated by Professor Coy was that, unlike Andover, Hotchkiss would tolerate no secret cabals, cliques, or societies. Open associations for whatever purpose were encouraged. The oldest of these was
St. Luke's. Named for the saint on whose day the school first opened,
this organization was devoted to furthering Christian qualities, especially through charitable deeds. But any organization with telltale secretive mumbo jumbo was considered destructive of what the first
handbook described as "the unity of school life."

The headmaster had more than one way of handling such hidden
societies, as is related by that anonymous graduate of 1899: "The
winter term was quite a problem to the faculty and students alike.
There were not all the facilities and activities of the present school, so
surplus energy was hard to work off during those weeks of slushy,
muddy weather. [An incident] . . . arising from this fact . . . was the
formation of a local chapter of a school fraternity. For a short time it

caused great thrills as well as heartburns. We were very select and even more secretive. A room was rented over one of the stores in the 'ville, in which regular meetings were surreptitiously held, unknown to the faculty, as we innocently imagined. We were soon disillusioned, however, as one weekend three or four impressive grads came up from New Haven, and in no uncertain terms told us collectively and individually exactly where we got off. The chapter disbanded, and the 'sacred' paraphernalia was rowed to the middle of the lake and sorrowfully dumped overboard."

Maintaining the harmonious balance within the school and doing his melodious bit in Greek daily in class would have been a taxing job in itself; but Edward G. Coy also personally carried on most of the school's correspondence – and that, by hand. A letter sent in those days prior to typewriter carbons was the only copy available and could not be readily retrieved. But the small packet preserved in Huber Gray Buehler's file gives an indication of what was involved. In just trying to recruit Buehler for the faculty, Professor Coy while still at Andover dispatched a half dozen detailed letters in a single month between June 7 and July 8, 1892. Since the telephone was not yet in general use, every minute contingency had to be worked out in this laborious way. "For the first year, at least, we can make no engagements with married men," Coy wrote, referring to the lack of housing. "Would you defer marriage for a year? And yet since writing this last sentence, I feel that it is an unkind suggestion." When the deal was eventually sealed, the headmaster's complimentary closing reveals the intensity of his feelings. "Anticipating our labors together with genuine pleasure, I am, Cordially yours . . ."

And that was correspondence with just one master on one specific subject. Professor Coy's dedication to the school was reflected in every line and in every turn of the phrase, and the natural artistry of his pen exemplified the elegance and grandeur of *his* style. The headmaster would eventually deal with a faculty of 15 and a student body of more than 150 in equally personal detail. This is revealed in the same batch of letters written by Mr. Coy in the summer months when either he or Mr. Buehler was away from the school. Here in its entirety is one of the shorter ones:

> Brevoort House
> Fifth Ave. and Washington Square
> New York, July 2d 1897

Dear Mr. Buehler:

As I sit here I am thinking how important and necessary a service to the School you rendered through your admirably conducted interviews with Sills, Kellogg, Shonninger, and McCall; and I cannot resist the inclination to send you special assurances of my full appreciation, not only of the service to the School, but also to myself. For it was a very great relief to me, under the circumstances, to have you so kindly take up those cases. I wish you again and again a most enjoyable and profitable summer.

Mr. Goss, of Waterbury [no relationship to Curator Goss] has just come in and has been talking about the son who wishes to enter our School in Sept. May I ask you to find the examination books or papers of C. P. Goss, Jr. in my office and send them on to Waterbury. From all that Mr. Goss tells me about the boy, I think that we ought to encourage him to prepare for entering the Upper Middle Class. We can scarcely do otherwise, under the circumstances. Yet I have also suggested to Mr. Goss that Chauncey may find more work involved than he anticipates; and difficulties which are insurmountable. I am satisfied, however, that the boy will be of great advantage to the *tone* of the School, should it be found best for him to enter when he naturally feels that he belongs. Very faithfully yours,

E. G. Coy

Surmounting whatever difficulties he may have encountered, Chauncey Porter Goss graduated in 1899, the first in one of the most prolific of all Hotchkiss families. Numbering nineteen graduates by the end of the school's first century, they include George A. Goss II '38, after whom the Goss Gymnasium was named; Richard W. Goss II '51, who served two terms as a trustee; and Chauncey Porter Goss II '84, the great grandson of that first Hotchkiss Goss. His father, Porter J. Goss '56, is a U.S. congressman from Florida.

viii /   Huber Gray Buehler knew his predecessor, E. G. Coy, as well as anyone beyond Coy's immediate family. When he was starting out as a teacher of Greek and Latin at a small Maryland school, the youthful Buehler undertook the journey of several hundred miles to Andover solely to meet Professor Coy and consult with him about some finer points of teaching Greek. Buehler made quite an impression on the future headmaster, who then continued to try to keep his prize recruit a contented member of the Hotchkiss faculty to the very end. Only weeks before his death at his wife's New Haven residence, the ailing headmaster assured Buehler, in the same exemplary script, that "in the twelfth year of your continuous service . . . I shall have little or no difficulty in persuading the Board to grant you a leave of absence of a year, for purposes of rest and recreation, at half pay."

A few months after Professor Coy died, his successor drew this portrait of him: "The things about Mr. Coy which always impressed me most from the first time I met him and which will linger in my memory longest were his magnificent presence and his unfailing courtesy of manner. Professor Warren of New Haven told me a few months ago that he received his first idea of a gentleman from Mr. Coy when he was his pupil at Andover, and I think that all the masters and boys who knew Mr. Coy here at The Hotchkiss School were impressed with this same thing. One of our masters said to me recently, 'When Mr. Coy introduced me to anyone as his colleague, I felt an inch taller.' In his ideals for his pupils he stood for manliness more than for scholarship, and we sometimes felt that he underrated scholarship as one aspect of character. He impressed his masters and pupils as a man much more than as a teacher, a scholar, or a speaker to boys. In these latter particulars he easily had superiors; but he was a significant specimen of the genus man. . . . He never appeared to better advantage than when, clad in evening clothes, he presided at the meetings of the University

Confidential

April 6th, 1904
New Haven, Conn.

My dear Mr. Buckler,—

I hasten to tell you of my interviews yesterday with Pres. Dwight and Professor Phillips. I spoke to Dr. Dwight first about a sabbatical year for you. While he was not ready to favor the introduction of the sabbatical year as the settled policy of the School, he fully sympathized with my wish to have you enjoy this advantage as an acknowledgment by the Board of the exceptional services which

With best wishes for the last term of the year, as ever

Faithfully Yours

Edward S. Coy

Part of a 5-page letter written a few weeks before Coy's death

Edward G. Coy

Club of Litchfield County, of which he was President, or at the meetings of the New England Association of Schools and Colleges.

" . . . Parents were always greatly impressed by him, though they did not always agree with him and sometimes 'hit back.' But the ordinary 'pestiferous parent' could completely subside here under his very presence. One look at his splendid appearance was frequently enough for a parent who had come to see him about some questionable acts.

"I used to admire greatly the apparent ease with which he carried heavy burdens. . . . He frequently stayed in his office from eight in the morning until ten at night, and he always declined to appoint office hours, saying that he wanted to be accessible to masters and boys at all times. . . . He never lost his poise or showed that he minded those burdens at all, but I now know that in spirit he sometimes staggered under them and that some of his trials ate into his heart. . . . He loved The Hotchkiss School with a love passing the love of women, and I think he would have lived longer if he had given his time and strength to his work more temperately."

The first tee

4 The King's Domain

J oe Garner Estill was bitten by the headmaster bug before he ever came to Hotchkiss. "Prof. Wheeler spoke to me in my Senior Year at Yale of a possible opening in a new school that was to be founded," Uncle Joe explained in his memoirs. "As plans grew and developed, it was seen that it would be folly to put such a large foundation into the hands of a fellow just out of college."

What Estill seemed to imply was that he had taken Waterloo Wheeler's words to mean the possibility of becoming headmaster – and then had to be eased back down to earth. Yet young Joe had not been as wildly presumptuous as it may seem. Born in Tennessee at the close of the Civil War, he grew up in the hard years of Reconstruction and went to work at nineteen. Before entering Yale, he had already had several years of teaching experience, including positions as principal and co-principal at two small academies below the Mason-Dixon line.

As the first faculty member hired at Hotchkiss, Estill was technically senior to Huber Gray Buehler by a matter of weeks. Though both had quickly become popular at the school, the more athletic and rather blustery Uncle Joe had a bit of an emotional edge over the narrow-shouldered, constrained English teacher. A case in point: Buehler had inaugurated, during the first year, Sunday night readings in the library, but they never quite caught on. When Estill took over the following year, the readings became so popular that they continued until his retirement almost forty years later. "How he could read Southern dialect," recalled one student who first sat in in 1895. "In some of Thomas Nelson Page's sadder stories he would get so into the spirit of it all that his voice would break and tears roll down his cheeks. He had nothing on us, though, for most of his listeners would be crying too." As Estill would explain years later, Buehler "read instructive things, whereas my chief aim was entertainment."

Estill may also have held another initial advantage. He had graduated from Yale, while Buehler was the only faculty member not to have come out of a New England college. The quiet, methodical Buehler had studied classics at Pennsylvania College in Gettysburg and then was trained as a minister at the Lutheran seminary there. Although he had never held a pastorate and had gone immediately into teaching, he did not altogether shed his clerical ways. Coy often baited him gently by engaging him in such seemingly serious arguments as to whether or not it was profanity to say "Damn!"

With the departure of David Comstock in 1895, Estill moved from the cottage he had been sharing with Buehler into the associate master's house. There was an element of irony to this; for when he had first been hired as a bachelor and told he would be heading the list for "a cottage," Estill scoffed that he had no more use for it "than a dog has for two tails." He changed his mind shortly after meeting "pretty, pink-cheeked Miss North in a lovely yellow waist" on a visit to New Haven, and the Estills were married at about the same time as the Buehlers. But Uncle Joe had never made an issue about the promised housing the way his colleague Buehler had. Now, a modicum of equity was retained by renaming the associate master's house Estill Cottage — perhaps with the additional intent of obscuring the lingering Comstock legacy and dampening any "associate" tendencies Estill might entertain. It should also be pointed out that both of the cottages belied their modest designation. The smaller one, occupied by the Buehlers, was a three-story white frame house of New England colonial design with a half dozen bedrooms and three bathrooms.

For the resident of Estill Cottage, the first indication that all was not well with Mr. Coy came shortly after the start of the school year in the fall of 1898. At that time, "in consequence of an unexpected illness," the headmaster gave up his professorial duties in class "with the approval of those familiar with the facts." What those facts were would never be fully revealed. That was not a proper subject for detailed discussion in those days. The *Hotchkiss Record* termed it a "malignant disease" which "preyed on him" with "attacks." J. G. Estill noted that he "advocated surgery for Mr. Coy's trouble all along, and it seems to me a great pity from all sorts of considerations that the doctors in charge of the case should have been so slow and so long in reaching this conclusion."

Whatever the diagnosis, Edward Coy was able to continue on his reduced schedule for another four years. But with the beginning of the term in 1902, at the age of fifty-nine and after a decade on the job, the white-haired, white-bearded headmaster who had the look of a distinguished elder statesman asked the trustees for a leave of absence. Voicing sympathy "with Mr. Coy," the board expressed "its entire satisfaction with the temporary arrangements he has made."

Thus in October 1902, without being specifically named in the minutes, Joe Garner Estill became acting headmaster of the school.

Estill was not a resounding success. Exactly what Uncle Joe did or did not do has been obscured by time and lack of documentary evidence. It seems that the very attributes which had made him such a flamboyant reader of stories on Sunday nights and a scintillating teacher in class worked against him when he tried to run the school. Perhaps partly because he had been brought up in the courtly romantic tradition of the Old South, he was governed as much by emotions of the heart as by logic of the mind. And in his case, the two were not always synchronized. He alternated bestowing benevolence on everyone at the school with threatening mass expulsions and other draconian measures. He also lacked both the talent and the temperament for the voluminous administrative work inherent in the position.

The school nevertheless made it through the year, as did J. G. Estill – though feeling somewhat nervous and harried from the experience. At a board meeting held in October 1903, the trustees "voted that Mr.

Estill be given $500 for his extraordinary services last year," along
with their "appropriate" thanks. That was far from a ringing endorsement either in terms of the money (only half of what his immediate
successor would get) or the thanks, which sounded like the faint gratitude accorded to Associate Master Comstock in bidding him adieu. Yet,
nothing was put down in writing about remedying this undistin-
guished leadership at the school. The most likely explanation is that
Estill was exceedingly sensitive to any challenge of his status and had
to be handled more carefully than nitroglycerin. If, in expressing their
"appropriate" thanks, the trustees had also suggested that Estill take an
"appropriate" rest, they presented it as a purely temporary measure
and hence of not enough consequence to be recorded in the minutes.

The drama that played itself out in the next few days can only be
inferred from another packet of letters preserved in the Buehler file. At
first glance, these letters reflect in an earthier way a similar devotion
and commitment to the school as the previous batch penned with such
elegance by Edward Coy. Written in a brash, almost overbearing hand
that conveys a sense of grand urgency, they were signed "J. G. Estill"
on a Winchester, Tennessee, letterhead. The first of these "My dear
Buehler" letters was dated November 17, 1903, exactly a month after
the last board meeting. What is immediately clear is that Uncle Joe
Estill had suffered some kind of a psychological breakdown at the
school and was recuperating at his hometown in Tennessee.

"They say 'open confession is good for the soul,'" Estill wrote to
Buehler, who now was his temporary stand-in back at the school, "but
had it not been for the extreme condition of my nerves, wrought upon
as they were by the (intended) sleeping powder and tablets given me
by Dr. Bissell, I very seriously doubt if I should have ever brought
myself to talk with quite the brutal frankness I did, not only with reference to others but myself as well."

The story that emerges from the half dozen letters of varying length
written over the next four months is one of an unintended "drug trip."
Pharmacology in those days was hardly a science, and it should not be
surprising that a powder mixed with the greatest care for a patient
seeking relief from insomnia and nervousness could have untoward or

Part of a letter from Uncle Joe Estill

unexpected effects. In Estill's case, his "vision became very unusually clarified," and he could "understand" and "see clearly" many of the things "I was not willing to allow my mind to dwell upon before." Exactly where Uncle Joe chose to apply this new vision and cause the incident which created widespread consternation at the school – and perhaps in itself sent him packing for a rest – cannot be ascertained. It may have taken place in the smoke-filled faculty room or perhaps in the rotunda in Main, where legions of boys could have also witnessed the scene. What is clear is that the acting headmaster shared in a thoroughly public way a revealing array of those "brutally frank" perceptions he had not allowed his "mind to dwell on before." (Did he perhaps yell at the exemplary Otto Monahan that he should watch his drinking, and at Buehler that he was a pompous fraud? And at somebody else that he was inappropriately fond of boys?) It must have been an arresting spectacle to see this hulking man, his ruddy face flushed a red even deeper than usual and his walrus mustache quivering, as he disencumbered himself of the innermost secrets he harbored about his faculty colleagues and, for good measure, interjected a few choice insights about himself. Obviously, Uncle Joe had failed to appreciate how perilous such a "gift" of clarity could be for the visionary involved.

Technically still the acting headmaster when he left for his Tennessee convalescence, Estill vacillated between "feeling tip-top" and wanting to return to the school by Christmas – and sheer panic at the thought of going back before "Sept. 1904." "I hope a few of my friends appreciate that it is one of the hardest trials of my life to desert them at this time and leave all the burden on them, but it is absolutely necessary. Anything else would be suicide." And he was apologetic to Buehler for having included him in his exposé. "I hope that any of my other friends who may have occasion to reproach me for 'giving them away' during the time when Dr. Bissell, with his sleeping powders, helped me get 'off my base,' will be as charitable towards me about it as you were." Estill's overriding goal was eventually to have his "honor, reputation and character" restored, even if it meant having "to force an open investigation."

Estill finally resigned as acting headmaster at the end of 1903, and the title went formally to Huber Gray Buehler, who had been performing the duties of the position de facto. At the next board meeting in March 1904, the trustees took the "opportunity to express their deep regret that the Institution has, during the greater part of the present school year, been deprived of the efficient services of Mr. J. G. Estill." After a touching tribute to "the unusual strength and force of his personality, his unselfish devotion and zeal," the trustees concluded with the hope that "he may so fully recover his health that he will find himself able to resume at the opening of the year in September, his work of teaching."

The titular headmaster, who at this time was still alive (and perhaps uncharacteristically cantankerous due to his illness), disagreed vehemently. He did not want Estill back, not even to teach. "He is so discredited with the public, as a consequence of the events of the year," wrote Edward Coy several days later from his sickbed in New Haven to Buehler, "that he cannot be permitted to return to service in the School; and Professor Phillips has already begun correspondence with him which will gently but decidedly lead him to abandon all thought of again being entrusted with the responsibilities of a master at *The Hotchkiss School*, should he still entertain the thought of doing so." The wavy underlining of *The Hotchkiss School* by the dying Coy visually emphasized how he felt. To be a *master at The Hotchkiss School* he clearly considered an honor second to none. "While I am exceedingly sorry for what I am sure is likely to prove a bitter disappointment to Estill, issuing perhaps in the most disastrous consequences, I cannot see how, as guardians of the School, the Board can take any other course."

In Coy's eyes, Estill had committed the unpardonable transgression of allowing himself to be seen in a bad light. That was something a gentleman should never do, and for the good of the school, Coy was ready to risk the possibility that Joe Estill might even take his own life. Considering such an attitude, it is understandable why Estill had earlier wanted "to force an open investigation" in connection with the "sleeping powder" prepared for him by the physician-trustee, Dr. Bissell.

Fortunately for Estill, Coy was not long for this world, and Uncle Joe then managed to fend off those gentle efforts by Professor Phillips and the board to get him to forsake his cherished ties to the school. He was found to be well enough and fit in time to return to Hotchkiss as a master in the fall of 1904 – though this did not mean that he had also been permanently cured of the headmaster bug.

ii /   Huber Gray Buehler had just turned thirty-nine when he officially became acting headmaster in January 1904. In appearance, he could perhaps best be characterized as seriously distinguished. He was a man six feet tall with a rounded build which was slightly wider and fuller at the hips and the waist than at his shoulders and chest. His thin hairline had receded to the very top of his head. He had a fleshy look from his chin down to the high stiff collar pinching his neck, a condition which revealed that he did not exercise beyond taking occasional walks. The sort of vigorous activities he advocated for the boys would not be considered dignified for someone at his stage in life. Always formally dressed in one of his dark, impeccable waistcoated suits, he offered the ultimate example of what it meant to carry oneself ramrod straight. Only the thrust of his presence kept him from looking noticeably stiff. And of course, his mustache, which had a life of its own. Unlike the drooping adornment of his ailing colleague Estill, Buehler's was a bristly dark outcropping covering a slanting area between his upper lip and the width of his nostrils. It was the sort of mustache that was increasingly favored by young European noblemen who had their feet firmly planted in modern times.

Buehler had not sought the provisional top position but accepted it as a responsibility to the school. He had recently turned down a number of interesting offers, including a full professorship at a western university, "a half-interest in a flourishing private school," and a position at Lawrenceville at twice his Hotchkiss pay. One of his more emotional

Huber Gray Buehler

decisions was his refusal to be considered for the presidency of Midland College, a Lutheran institution. "Both Mrs. Buehler and I are Lutherans through and through," he wrote the Midland trustees. "Lutheranism is bred in our bones, and we shall never forget our early training and never shall we cease to have a living and acting interest in our church and its institutions. . . . [But] if I should at this time accept an offer to go elsewhere for either personal advantage or for other reasons, it would look very much as if I were deserting the School in the time of its utmost need."

Besides sharing a Lutheran heritage, the Buehlers were a team in just about every conceivable respect. Of Germanic descent, their fathers had both been professors at the same seminary in Gettysburg, and Huber and Roberta (née Wolf) may have been childhood sweethearts. To what extent the small, energetic Roberta motivated her husband can only be deduced from those determined letters to secure an appropriate domicile.

Buehler had come a long way since stepping in to relieve the emergency created by Estill's breakdown. The English department head at first had harbored serious misgivings about his own qualifications for the task. As George Van Santvoord noted, in his partial history,* "Years later, he told me he tried to escape. His wife cried all night long, and he felt he could not do the job. 'No one knew then I had the gift of executive ability,' he told me. They soon learned he *did* have it in abundance." But what continued to disturb Buehler was the "acting" qualification. In a letter to Professor Phillips, president of the board since 1901, Buehler called it "a double burden;" for in addition to his stand-in responsibilities, he had to carry his regular teaching load "without proper compensation, and without the prestige, dignity and influence which always attended a permanent appointment. You know how Mr. Estill chafed under such a burden."

Then there was the uncertainty. Coy had been on a leave of absence for almost two years and continued to believe he might yet be able to return to the school. While the acting headmaster did not share Coy's optimism, he realized the situation could remain unresolved indefinitely. Buehler was determined not to suffer Uncle Joe's fate, powder or no powder. On April 8, 1904, he wrote Coy about the possibility of

* Several days before his death, George Van Santvoord filled some sixty pages of a spiral notebook with annotations to *A Portrait*, the 75th Anniversary version of the school's history by Lael Wertenbaker and Maude Basserman.

taking a year's sabbatical "not as a reward for service, but as a necessary rest." A scribbled line on the working draft which he later crossed
out indicates how strongly Buehler felt: "I desire my year of absence
before I break down rather than afterward." (And not at half pay, either, as Coy had proposed.)

Part of the uncertainty ended six weeks later, at a trustees' meeting
held on May 23, when the board accepted "the resignation of Profr.
E. G. Coy from the Head Mastership of the School." Now that he was
the leading candidate to become full-fledged headmaster of the school,
Buehler no longer seemed to feel the same pressing need to take a
leave. On the contrary; the evidence suggests he may have engaged in
a subtle campaign for the post. "We learn on good authority," reported the *Millerton Telegram* in a dispatch reprinted in the *Record* at
precisely this time, "that Mr. Buehler, Acting Head Master of The
Hotchkiss School, has declined during the current year four invitations
to other educational institutions." If that was designed to whet the appetite of the selection committee – headed again by Timothy Dwight –
Buehler nevertheless maintained he was not actively "seeking the
Headmastership, for I know too well its burdens and difficult duties."
He also wanted it known that if the trustees still considered "Mr. Estill
eligible . . . I should not wish to put myself in his way" by being a
candidate. Obviously, there was hardly a chance of that, and Buehler
could well afford to take this position with respect to his friend. "If the
Trustees should wish me to continue the duties of Headmastership, I
would of course expect the usual accompaniments of the position."
What this indicates is that Buehler was not entirely sure that he would
get the appointment without a lengthy search. If that were to be so, he
wanted it understood that he would be willing to continue on the provisional basis only if he were given all the perks. Buehler's notations
on his rough draft make it clear this meant moving into the headmaster's house and furnishing it to his taste.

He need not have hedged his bets. The board acted with unusual
speed, and within three weeks of Coy's resignation, Huber Gray
Buehler was unanimously elected as the second headmaster of the
Hotchkiss School – the title now formally written as one word. This

time, Buehler had no misgivings about being able to do the job, and the only tears his wife might have shed were those of happiness over a muted anticipation at last fulfilled. In applauding the selection on behalf of the senior class, the *Record* stated that "our respect and esteem for him have steadily increased. We have found him consistent in his aims and always ready to view our claims in a charitable and open-minded way."

iii /   The new headmaster from the start sought to establish for himself an elevated niche. According to George Van Santvoord, Buehler was a naturally shy man who "covered up his shyness by a formal, aloof manner. Many people were deceived by this." In fact, Buehler was made uneasy by familiarities of any sort. When he overheard a master address a visiting clergyman by his first name, he asked the clergyman afterward, "Even if you knew him before you were ordained, how can you retain respect for your position if you allow anyone to use your first name?"

It would be difficult to pinpoint when Buehler came to be heralded as "the King" throughout the school. This sobriquet probably followed rather than preceded the honorary doctorate of letters (D. Litt.) he received in the summer of 1909 from his alma mater, Pennsylvania College. With both Coy and Comstock now out of the picture, the Andover title of "Professor" was falling into disuse, and Buehler seems to have encouraged being addressed as "Doctor" for some time prior to his formal investiture.

Far better documented is how the new headmaster and Roberta Buehler achieved a pinnacle of another sort. Several brief entries sandwiched into the trustees' minutes over the next half dozen years tell the story. The first one was a seemingly insignificant privilege, already granted to Buehler by the board several weeks before he became headmaster, whereby he was "authorized to take such meals as he may desire with his family in his own house, making written requisition on the school stores for such ordinary supplies as he requires, these supplies to be cooked and served at his own expense." Then on October 6,

1906, it was "voted that in view of the large number of official guests which the headmaster and his wife must entertain for the school, one servant should be employed by the school for service at the Headmaster's House." On October 30, 1909, a special meeting was held "to take into consideration the general affairs of the School, and particularly to consider the alteration and improvement of the Headmaster's House." And on October 15, 1910, it was voted "that Mr. Buehler be authorized to employ a man servant at the expense of the School, and also that the wages of his cook be paid by the School."

What the Buehlers ended up with was an impressive domain, royal or otherwise. It was within this domain that the noted character actor and impersonator, the "candid satirist" John M. Hoysradt '22 (known professionally as John Hoyt), spent much of his youth. His mother was Mrs. Buehler's sister, and John Hoysradt to this day recalls watching in 1904 "my Aunt Roberta drink a glass of stout, as beneficial for her pregnancy with my cousin Barbara."* And he has a vivid recollection of "Uncle Huber's" residence: "The large addition was built around 1910. Counting the six-room third floor 'Alumni Dormitory,' there were eighteen bedrooms and seven baths. Quite a 'cottage' to keep in top shape. Mrs. Buehler was a superb housekeeper. She surrounded herself with quality servants of whom very few 'lived in.' Outstanding was the Mantas family. John Mantas was first-generation Greek, a super butler, often wearing livery. His younger brother, Tommy, was second in command, and his wife Ethel 'helped out,' for the most part, in the kitchen. The basement kitchen might have been a hotel in its expert operation. Over the years, Mrs. Buehler had two different cooks, both of them superb. Meals at the Buehlers' were like those in world-famed restaurants. The wondrous roasts, the perfectly prepared green vegetables, the succulent desserts, combined to assure memorable occasions. There were seldom fewer than twelve around the table, with more at frequent parties. Costs were borne by the school, and they were anything but minuscule."

* John Hoysradt died in 1991. The acknowledgments at the end of the book provide a listing of others who have died since being interviewed for this history.

Not exactly a tableau of a typical headmaster's residence, but the school had good reason for bearing the costs. The Buehlers through their entertaining had given Hotchkiss a name and an image no less important than the top ratings Hotchkiss students were earning year after year on College Entrance Examination Boards. The shy, rigid young man from Gettysburg had become a cosmopolite who duly impressed even the most powerful and worldly captains of industry about the desirability of sending their sons to the school – while admissions officers in Ivy League colleges besides Yale were vying for their share of Hotchkiss graduates.

"The Trustees of The Hotchkiss School take this opportunity to most heartily congratulate Dr. Buehler on the completion of ten years of service as Headmaster," wrote the board president, Andrew Phillips, in the minutes of a meeting on June 6, 1914. "In these ten years the School has grown in numbers from 160 to 250 students: the net earnings of the School have amounted to $200,000, and gifts in the amount of nearly $100,000 have come into the treasury, largely through the efforts of Dr. Buehler. . . . The Trustees appreciate still more highly how much the wisdom, the inspiration and the whole-souled devotion of the Headmaster has meant in the esprit de corps of the faculty; the great strides in scholarship, the high manly tone and ideal spirit of the student body, and the great name and fame of the School. Nor are they unmindful of the gracious and leavening influence of Mrs. Buehler through all these years."

Her nephew, John Hoysradt, has drawn for us a detailed portrait, as he remembers "Aunt Roberta" to this day:

"She was the Queen. My cousin, Barbara, was the Princess, and her brother, Reginald, was the Prince. But he was never around and didn't need to be called that. Aunt Roberta held a great many high teas for the various classes, and they were always called the Queen's teas. She had the royal sense of noblesse oblige. I remember her greeting the mother of my roommate upper middle year who was sick. The mother came in the front door, and Mrs. Buehler rushed up to her, took her hand, and said, 'You poor child, in this awful weather,' or whatever,

Roberta Buehler (third from left) in 1904, the year her husband became headmaster

'Let's see if we can get you to see your son right away.' She loved to take care of people in distress.

"She was also awfully social. Anybody with a title was fair game. There was a woman in Sharon named the Countess Zeckendorff. Aunt Roberta was very impressed at having the Countess at her elbow, so to speak. One day the Countess called, and my aunt said, 'Who is this?' 'Countess Zeckendorff,' was the reply. 'Who?' Again the reply, 'Countess Zeckendorff!' Aunt Roberta for the third time, 'Who?' The answer, this time, 'Julia!' My aunt: 'Oh, Julia, how are you my dear!' She wanted to make her come off her high horse by getting her to say, 'Julia.'

"Roberta dressed as the Queen all the time. She had a most impressive clothes closet, almost like Imelda Marcos. Fifty pairs of shoes and a most impressive array of clothes hanging up. It was almost more like a separate room than a closet, and it was lighted by a window from the bathroom. She always wore high heels. I never remember seeing her in sporting clothes.

"Aunt Roberta was by no means beautiful, but she was not plain. She was distinguished in a sharp fashion. She had a sharp face, not a bland, contented face at all. Her voice was always in ruins. She had a voice that always sounded as if she had a cold. People who didn't know her would say, 'Oh, you have a terrible cold.' She'd say, 'No, that's just the way I talk.'

"She was a character, but so was my Uncle Huber. I remember him at a mealtime once saying, 'I see the moon, and the moon sees me, and the moon sees somebody I'd like to see.' He loved little humorous rhymes like that. I never heard a stern word between my uncle and my aunt. I never heard my uncle shout or give a command. He was not at all that kind of a monarch.

"I remember once in the locker room discussing the King, and somebody said, 'The King is your best friend, and don't you forget that!' I remember being quite impressed by that. Of course, he might have been your best friend, but Dr. Buehler always remained aloof. He was not an arm-around-the-shoulder man at all. He realized that and wished he could have been more intimate with the boys. But he was the King, he was His Majesty."

iv /   Beyond the royal family domain, what was it like at Hotchkiss in those days? Under the benevolent influence of the King, the students were also allowed to feast – especially at the senior class annual banquet. It was held in New York at the end of the spring vacation, usually at the Hotel Manhattan. A typical menu included oysters, cream of asparagus soup, shad *à la Manhattan, filet de boeuf avec chervilles, sorbet au rhum* to provide a breather and perk up the appetite in order to continue with *poulet hongrois, salade panachée,* Neapolitan ice cream, *gateaux assortis,* and, of course, coffee. It was not clear whether school rules were in force, and brandy and cigars were most likely winked at by the faculty members who were present. "As most of the class intended to go to the theater later," reported the *Record*, "the banquet began exceptionally early so that there would be no hurry." It was an attestation to the power of manly youth that anyone could walk after this feast.

The fare at the school was less royal but no less plentiful. The *Record* on March 2, 1909, provided a summary of the consumption patterns of that year's 223 students and 21 faculty members: "Roughly speaking, the School consumes over 100,000 eggs a year; it requires 100 loaves of bread for a single day, from 500–600 rolls for breakfast, 50 pies for dinner and 1500 tea biscuits for supper. During the course of a single year we use 50,000 quarts of milk, and over 5½ tons of butter. Five bushels of potatoes have to be peeled every day. For a long time members of the School have been proud of their capacity for shredded wheat biscuits. The present record is, we think, in the neighborhood of six for one breakfast; hence we do not wonder that last year over 90,000 of these went the way of all good cereals. So each fellow eats approximately 450 a school year."

Then, of course, there was the traditional "swilling" in "the Ville" at various favored spots, whose proprietors had figured out that nothing could ever be too sweet, too creamy, or too much of, for the appetites of Hotchkiss boys. Among the favorites: a gigantic ice cream concoction called a Double Buffalo.

"Colds (125) and digestive ailments (85) constitute as usual most of the illnesses," the headmaster reported to the board of trustees at the end of the school year in 1909. "If some way could be found of keeping boys from imprudence in dress and eating, the need for an infirmary and a resident nurse would be only occasional." This was Buehler's way of saying how fortunate the school had been in having escaped any outbreaks of scarlet fever, polio, and influenza which, in the past, had forced the school to close or be quarantined—and would do so again in future years.

That report of 1909 to the trustees was also a revealing document about the composition of the school. "The 223 pupils have come from 29 different states," wrote Buehler, listing the states, with a high of forty-six for New York. "These figures indicate that the school is more national in its constituency than Yale and Harvard Universities. In those universities more than 50% of the students are drawn from within a radius of 100 miles. The same radius provided this year only 38% of Hotchkiss pupils." The headmaster also figured out, at the other end of the spectrum, that since the school's founding an average of eleven boys from Sharon and Salisbury had attended Hotchkiss each year.

Hotchkiss was branching out in another important way. Of the forty-six students in the graduating class of 1909, Buehler reported that thirty were bound for Yale, thirteen of them for the Sheffield Scientific School. Of the remaining seniors, five were going to Williams, three each to Harvard and Cornell, two to the Massachusetts Institute of Technology, and one each to Princeton, Colgate, and the University of Minnesota.

"Every place for next year has been filled since mid-winter, and already 108 applicants have been informed by printed circular that we shall have only chance vacancies at our disposal between now and September," continued the headmaster's report. "The large excess of applicants over available places makes it possible to select pupils carefully, according to the best information obtainable regarding their character and previous school record. Vacancies are given to those boys who seem most likely to adjust themselves satisfactorily to the standards of the school."

Among the more rigorous of those standards was that the boys rarely if ever could leave the school during term time. The few lucky ones who were on the football and baseball teams did get away on alternate years for the Hill game, but there were no "away" debates, glee club concerts, or activities of that sort. The only other temporary reprieve was through situations such as death in the family or a wedding. "The word 'weekend' had not yet come into use in the United States," recalled George Van Santvoord in the interview with Mrs. Wertenbaker. "It was imported from England around World War I. Travelling took so long that whenever people went somewhere, they

usually stayed at least a week or two. When I was at Yale, my roommate's family had a car. We left New Haven at noon one day, and we
got as far as Waterbury and spent the night. That was some twenty-
five miles. The next day, in a long trip, we drove up to Lakeville. That
was fifty or sixty miles. As I remember, we had one flat tire in the
morning, one in the afternoon. So the business of moving around all
the time was physically impossible. Life at Hotchkiss for the boys
wasn't very exciting, but I think this was what they expected."

Adjusting to Hotchkiss life, nevertheless, continued to have its trying aspects. The sentiments of "The School-boy's Lament," which
appeared in the *Mischianza* for 1913, were surely shared by many
contemporaries:

I

They have fed me on their Latin, and they've tried to teach me
   Greek,
And they've rammed their mathematics down my throat;
They have said I know no English, that I blunder when I speak,
And I know their lectures all by rote.

II

I must waken in the morning to the clanging of the bells,
And I'm hurried off to breakfast by their call;
Then I'm run into the chapel, and all day the ringing tells
Of appointments, study, recitation hall.

III

If, perchance, in recreation I am seeking for a lark,
In the way that only *real* boys do and can,
Then there always comes a master, who of fun has not a spark,
And he tells me how I ought to be a man.

IV

O I'm nothing but a school-boy, but I'm human just the same,
And I wish that I were better understood;

For sometimes I'm called 'rebellious,' but that's not the proper
  word,
I'm just full of boyish spirits, and they're good.

O it's joy, joy, joy just to be a lusty boy,
And I'm proud to have good red blood in my veins;
It's the very biggest grade of stuff that sturdy men are made of,
And may God preserve it there while life remains!

v /   Among the alumni from those early Buehler years who were still alive at the close of the first Hotchkiss century was Francis A. Cochrane, who had entered the school as an upper mid in the fall of 1908. "Dr. Buehler started out as a minister but got waylaid somewhere to head up the Hotchkiss School," reminisces the second oldest living graduate with a gleam, at his country home about twenty miles from Lakeville. "To a little fellow from Hudson, New York, he seemed impressive. Tall, narrow shoulders. Maybe that's the reason he was so erect in his carriage, to offset the narrow shoulders by being very erect. Yes, very nice man, very nice wife. They invited me over for dinner one night. It was quite a privilege eating dinner with the headmaster."

Cochrane's view of the Hotchkiss curriculum jibed with that of the author of "The School-boy's Lament." "I don't think there was any of that fancy stuff that they're teaching nowadays," avers the lively near-centenarian. "It was classes and learning – Latin, Greek, English, French or German. In mathematics, I had Joe Estill. He was quite a character. As a teacher up in front of class, he had a great way of expressing himself. He'd use one of those yardstick rulers, bang on the desk! Everybody would jump. He made a lasting impression on me."

It was a different world for which Francis Cochrane was being prepared. "When I got my first job with Bankers Trust in New York," continues the old alumnus, looking obviously satisfied with the course of his life, "I didn't get hired because I knew this or I knew that. It was because they said, 'Cochrane, he went to Hotchkiss, he went to Yale. Cochrane he's a nice fellow, he's a responsible fellow.''

Personal idiosyncracies rather than subject matter often made classes memorable. The faculty included an array of characters with such names as "Bull" Buell, "Peanut" Hall, "Puss" Grant, "Pop" Jefferson, "Doc Rob," "Doc" Brown, and plain Mr. George Creelman, who could endlessly fascinate students by writing sums on the blackboard simultaneously with both hands. And those were by no means all of the legendary masters of that era. In George Van Santvoord's retrospective estimation, the small, peppery Buell, who looked like an old world professor with his graying mustache that merged into a pointed goatee, was "probably the most distinguished recruit to the staff at Hotchkiss, including Mr. Coy." The closest this scholarly gentleman came to bullish comportment was when he exclaimed at a faculty meeting, "That boy ought to be kicked by a jackass, and I want to be the one to do it." A more deliberate source of wit was J. Edmund Barss. He had taught Latin at the school since 1894, had written several widely used textbooks, and wrote the school hymn, "Almighty, merciful and wise. . . ." At one faculty meeting when he rephrased in overly frank language an overly cautious statement the headmaster had just made, Dr. Buehler protested, "Not so bald as that!" Retorted Mr. Barss in a flash, "I'm afraid it lost all its hair in transmission." On another occasion, a great commotion issued forth from his classroom and distracted the attention of boys in an adjoining class. "The word *furore* came up in the lesson," explained Barss blithely to his disturbed colleague, "and I was trying to get the meaning across." Joe Estill often said he felt indebted to the large, outgoing Barss because he was the only one on the faculty "to fly off the handle faster than I."

Surely on the opposite end of this emotional spectrum was the spare, bespectacled Doc Rob – that is, Dr. J. J. Robinson, Princeton Phi Beta Kappa; Yale Ph.D.; advanced work at the University of Leipzig, Germany, in Greek and Latin literature, comparative philology, and Sanskrit; member of the Yale faculty for a half dozen years; author of a book on Roman law; head of the Latin department at Hamilton College for four years. (His was a résumé that sounded almost on a par with that of the present headmaster, Dr. Rob Oden!) But there was a problem back in 1904 about hiring Dr. Robinson for the Hotchkiss Latin department. The problem was that he could hardly be offered a subsidiary role; yet the school already had a senior faculty member in charge of teaching Latin, the witty, versatile Barss. His M.A. from Harvard was no match for Robinson's credentials, but Barss had the advantage of having proved himself over the past decade at the school. In being apprised of the situation, Barss did not fly off the handle. He said he would heartily welcome the new master and was "quite willing that Dr. Robinson should have that share in the counsels of the department and of the School which his experience entitles him to." His dark, curly hair began to quiver only when he added, "Provided Robinson's name is not listed above mine in the catalogue." By a decision of the board of trustees, who feared they might otherwise risk losing a rare talent for the school, the name of Dr. J. J. Robinson did, however, appear first. The implicit slight put a crimp into the otherwise jovial step of Edmund Barss from which he never quite recovered. In 1919, a year after his son had graduated, the gray-haired Barss accepted an offer from his former Hotchkiss colleague Batchelder, the headmaster at Loomis. Barss then taught there for another twenty-six years. As for Dr. J. J. Robinson, he may well have wished at the outset of his Hotchkiss career that he had never heard of the school. Whether because of his overly rigid style or some subtle spillover from the controversy with Barss, the lean, sandy-haired Latin teacher became the target of perhaps the most severe assault on a master in the history of Hotchkiss. It happened while he was tending evening study hall. The lights suddenly went out, but instead of the usual hoots, whistles, and catcalls until power was restored, a flowerpot came crashing onto his desk. Robinson was sprayed with dirt and geraniums, and then other flowerpots, rulers, inkwells, books, and similar objects rained down on him. He dove under his desk, where he weathered the rest of the storm. When he crawled out in the ensuing calm, the study hall was deserted. He turned on the lights and personally cleaned up the mess. He never reported the incident; and though everyone at the school knew about it, nobody talked about it openly. It would have, no doubt, struck too sensitive a chord all the way around. But it did have a cathartic effect, and from then on Robinson's position at the school steadily improved. His classes became known not only for drilling Latin, but also for dispensing all sorts of interesting information from the rich intellectual domain of Doc Rob, as he was soon dubbed; though still, if he happened to see a boy's attention wandering, he would suddenly whirl around and say, "Now, [so-and-so] translate this sentence!" A lover of music, Doc Rob often led his class in song and, by 1908, combined his musical and German talents to found Der Wagner Verein, which featured periodic trips to attend Wagner operas in New York. By providing a legitimate way to get off the school grounds and enjoy a sumptuous feast in New York before imbibing the cultural benefits, Der Wagner Verein became one of the most prestigious of all Hotchkiss clubs — with a waiting list for its dozen slots.

vi /   Of the letters Huber Gray Buehler dictated on August 11, 1908, the longest went to Professor Henry P. Wright. He was the Yale dean who kept an alert eye on all Hotchkiss graduates after they arrived in New Haven. A quick glance at the three typewritten pages makes it clear that the headmaster was giving the professor his personal evaluation of the boys who would be coming that fall. "[It] gives me pleasure to say that the two leaders in our Senior class during the year just closed have been Arthur Howe and W. Kirk Kaynor. . . . Howe is a fine all-round fellow of great personal force and sterling character, but only ordinary ability in studies. He is from Orange, N.J., and is a brother of Henry Howe of the Yale crew. He is perhaps the 'biggest man' as boy judgment goes among the Hotchkiss members of the next Academic Freshman Class. Kirk Kaynor came to us five years ago from Dakota, where he had been a cowboy. He worked his way through the School and was always dependable for support of any good cause or movement in the School. He was faithful and loyal to his duties as a beneficiary student and immensely popular with the boys, over whom he has always exerted strong influence for good. At times his enthusiasm for this or that good thing in student life has seriously interfered with his studies, in which he has never been conspicuously good. On the contrary, he is the only member of our graduating class who failed to be admitted to college [meaning Yale] in June. I hope he will try again in September with better success. Both Howe and Kaynor have been class presidents."

Interestingly, especially from the perspective of today, neither Kirk Kaynor nor Arthur Howe distinguished himself academically. Yet Howe would become a professor at Dartmouth, and then head the Hampton Institute, strengthening it as a major pioneering force in black education. As for Kaynor, the Dakota cowboy who went through the school as a free student, taking five years to do it instead of four, he did make it to Yale that fall. He subsequently became U.S. congressman from Massachusetts and an alumni trustee of the school. His promising career was cut short by a fatal airplane accident in 1929.

Another contemporary of Kaynor and Howe followed an even more startling career path. Howe's son, Arthur, Jr. '38, explains: "That was my father's twin brother, Harold. They had arrived at Hotchkiss at the same time, and Uncle Harold was just an extraordinarily fine human being as well as a superb athlete. My Dad became all-American in football and outstanding in hockey and baseball at Yale. Uncle Harold was better at all three – but never went to college. Year after year he was failing a course or two and had to drop back. After he had stayed at Hotchkiss a couple of extra years, helping the school win athletic victories and completing his diploma requirements, he began to coach, and then at some point, without formal appointment, melded into the faculty. By 1912, he was teaching a little and was great with the young people. Well, it so happened that overlapping with Uncle Harold was George Carrington, whose son George was a classmate of mine. George's Dad, who did eventually graduate and went on to Yale, always claimed that he competed with Uncle Harold for the longest undergraduate stay at Hotchkiss. Uncle Harold finally left after several years in this quasi-faculty position to join the flying corps in World War I, and later had a successful business career."

Hence no mention of Harold Howe in that letter of 1908 to the Yale dean. In the same letter Buehler offered a thumbnail sketch of a score of other New Haven-bound students, among them the following two, who were characterized one after the other only because of the inexorable order of the alphabet but were about to be joined in an unforeseen historical role:

"Selden Spencer, son of Judge Spencer of St. Louis. He has a good head, but admitted to college [again, of course, meaning Yale] on probation because of his careless attitude toward school appointments at Hotchkiss.

"Van Santvoord – a thoroughly nice boy and a good scholar, but shy and retired. Here only one year."

The significance of the latter characterization needs no elaboration; yet it was Selden Spencer with his "careless attitude" who would provide the primary motive for co-starting a tradition that would affect, in a most welcome way, every Hotchkiss student from that year on until today. Among the first to benefit was Carle Parsons, then a senior in his fourth year at the school, who has described the historic event in an *Alumni News* article of 1965: "Imagine the scene in the old Chapel on a usual October morning. The brief service was over, and Dr. Buehler stepped to the lectern to make what everyone supposed was a routine announcement. Instead, he announced that Selden Spencer '08 had won the Chamberlain Greek Prize (awarded to the person making the highest mark in the entrance examinations in Greek at Yale) and that George Van Santvoord had won honorable mention. There was still no sense of anything unusual. But then came the world-shaking moment when Dr. Buehler added that, to honor these scholars, the faculty had voted to give the school a holiday! At first the silence was almost palpable. Then the thunderous applause and cheering broke loose."

There were to be several more holidays announced that year – on crisp fall days with the foliage a perfect blend of yellows and reds; in midwinter when the hilly countryside, freshly blanketed in snow, sparkled in the brilliant sun; and on refreshing days in spring as the greenery was about to burst forth. During every season of every year since that historic event, occasional holidays have been declared. And there has never lacked some accomplishment by a Hotchkiss graduate to justify the occasion in the tradition of Selden Spencer and George Van Santvoord. A notable departure came when the King seized on the ending of World War I as an appropriate cause, explaining to the school that he had been told by many interested parties he would, like the kaiser, have to abdicate unless he proclaimed a holiday.

As for Carle Parsons, he was to become over the years a Hotchkiss tradition in his own right. A well-dressed, trim, fine-featured man of Victorian dignity and a hearty laugh, he had been tagged mischievously with the nickname "Pansy" while still a boy at the school. It stuck for the next half-century while the mild-mannered teacher of prep English became famous for some highly original classroom ploys – including one which brought his nickname into play. During the spring term, by which time he and the class had gotten to know each other well, he would have a student read out loud a passage involving a character named Parsons. As the boy struggled to resist the urge to substitute "Pansy" whenever the name came up – egged on by the muffled snickers of the class – Mr. Parsons would feign total amazement. "What in Sam Hill is going on?" That would only increase the commotion in the room, prompting Mr. Parsons to come out with one or more of his "Judas Priest!" expletives, and then exclaim, with seemingly mounting impatience, "Now, stop acting like a bunch of fuzz-bonnets!" And if the unfortunate reader did happen to slip up and come out with "Pansy," he would be promptly shown the door by the apparently outraged gentleman teaching the class. In later years, the graying, urbane Mr. Parsons became famous for the set of large metal bolts he kept at the ready in the top drawer of his desk. As he tried to activate the brain of some somnolent prep, the increasingly agitated Mr. Parsons would move unmistakably closer and closer to the repository of those bolts. If need be, he would escalate the pressure by opening the notorious drawer and even taking out and kneading the massive bolts impatiently in front of the apprehensive boy. Tradition had it that at least once each year, the seemingly exasperated Mr. Parsons would let fly those bolts with full force, though intentionally wide of the mark.

That was all a part of his act, enjoyed by almost everyone – just as the boys on his corridor enjoyed the periodic feeds of ice cream and cookies he institutionalized in his two-room quarters on the third floor of Alumni. What *was* intimidating about Carle Lawyer Parsons were the three little words he would append to an obviously foreshortened list of examination grades posted on the school's main bulletin board: *All others failed.*

vii /   Carle Parsons and George Van Santvoord were both from upstate New York. "I went down on the train from Albany, and curiously, the first person I met on the train was Mr. C. L. Parsons," the Duke recalled in his 75th anniversary interview. "I was entering as a senior, he as an upper mid. I got to know him then, and he was my friend from then on. Another curious thing is that he was one day younger than I. This was a great cause of superiority. I was a class above him and I was a day older, so if there was an argument, I could remind him of that, and that ended it."

Also arriving at Hotchkiss in the fall of 1907 with these future faculty colleagues was a shy, undersized boy called Archie MacLeish. Son of a prosperous midwestern businessman – his father was a founding director and manager of the Chicago department store Carson Pirie & Scott – Archie almost did not make it to Hotchkiss. "My husband has never been so enthusiastic over sending the boys East to school, as I, who am a Connecticut Yankee," Archie's mother, the former Martha Hillard, wrote to "Mr. Buehler" in explaining the delay in completing the school's application forms. "It was with difficulty that I secured [my husband's consent], and later when Archie became very much interested in a chicken business which he has been conducting for a year with real success, and wanted to stay home one more year to watch the development of his fancy stock, and reap the benefit of his spring labors, his father thought that might be the best course for him."

Archie's other hurdle had been that he miserably failed the school's entrance examinations in algebra and Latin. Fortunately, he had already completed his freshman year at his high school in Glencoe, Illinois, and this deficiency was routinely overcome by having the boy drop back a year and start out at Hotchkiss as a prep. "I greatly fear that if he takes up work so very easy as beginning Algebra and your first year of Latin," his mother protested in another letter to the school, "he will drop at once into slovenly habits of study, which is just what we want to avoid. . . . English is exceedingly easy for him, so that the first year's work alone will not furnish enough for him to do."

That would never again prove to be a concern for this woman, whose forthcoming correspondence with her son's headmaster would evoke in telling detail a tableau of the Hotchkiss School during this period. Some twenty years younger than her husband, whose third wife she was, Martha MacLeish probably was less representative of the mothers of that era than her son was of what it meant to be a Hotchkiss prep. "I had a few moments' visit with Archie last Saturday as I passed through Lakeville, en route for Chicago," Martha MacLeish wrote to "Dr. Buehler" on October 18, 1907, a month after her son had settled in and undoubtedly informed her of the preferred form of address. "I thought he was looking in very fine condition, and he seemed very happy. He is greatly pleased with his new room, and I want to thank you for making the change for him. . . . Please remember me to Mrs. Buehler and believe that Mr. MacLeish and I thoroughly appreciate what you are trying to do for all your boys, Archie among the rest."

That rooming change Mrs. MacLeish referred to helps to place the following undated letter, written with evident care on a sheet of the school's stationery:

Dear Dr. Buehler:

I have heard that there is a vacant room in the third story of Dr. Robinson's cottage. Would it inconvenience you a great deal to let me have that room? I know I could study a great deal better over there, because it would be so much quieter than the main building room which I now occupy. I am pretty sure I would get along better in every way. I would have a little time to myself and have a chance to read a little from my Bible in the morning. A thing which, without exaggeration, I hardly dare do over in Main unless I get up very early. I don't say this to try to have you pity me or anything like that. It is the honest truth. There are many other reasons also and I hope very much you will let me make this change. I know Mother would be only too glad to have me get the room, and I hope you will at least speak to me about it. I am

Yours very respectfully,
Archie MacLeish

The change of residence, however, failed to resolve the concerns of this new boy. Within a week after seeing Archie in Lakeville "looking in very fine condition," his mother was inundated with letters of such despair that she took the radical step of talking to "Dr. Buehler" on the phone. "In view of our conversation concerning the hazing at Hotchkiss," she wrote in following up with the headmaster, "I am sending you a part of a letter just received from Archie. He has been in a very homesick and low-spirited state for the past week, and this letter would seem to account for it. It will give you an inside view that I think you may be glad to get. Evidently some of the Seniors are somewhat overwhelmed by a sense of their individual importance, and forgetting the responsibilities of seniorhood."

The portion of Archie's letter which his mother copied began *in mediis rebus*: ". . . still naked, while the fellows snapped him with wet towels. He was pretty sick I can tell you. It does no good to tell the faculty. The fellows are afraid to tell the truth. Now what do you think of that for a nice state of affairs? I simply hate it here. I hope you will consider sending me to some other school next year. I don't believe I could live here for four years.

"I am getting along well in my work except when I am too homesick. This homesickness is usually brought on by fear of those bullying seniors. I hope you won't laugh at this. I am not talking for effect. It is the truth. One of them came up to me the other day and told me I was going to get it for not holding a door open for him. I just barely got off, but I can tell you I was most certainly homesick for a few days.

"Please don't laugh at this letter and say all this is for my good. It is very real to me. But I know you'll understand, won't you?

"Your very loving son.

"Archibold MacLeish"

Archie's mother drew two arrows pointing to the "bold" part of the name, which she underlined three times and noted, "His signature shows there's a gleam of humor left in him."

It was not until November 21, almost four weeks later, that the headmaster responded. Explaining the delay as necessary to properly observe and evaluate the situation, he wrote:

"The fact seems to be, as you hinted when you were here, that your son shrinks from the kind of contact with other boys that accompanies life in a large school, and since this contact is similar to what must be expected in life it seems to me that it is exactly what he needs. Mr. Estill, who is one of my trusted confidential advisors, thinks I made a mistake in removing your boy from the main dormitory, and that it would have been better to let him stay there and fight it out. However that may be, he told me this morning in a talk which I had with him that he felt much better now than he did and 'likes it better.' I asked him if he felt homesick now, and he said that he felt better about that, too, although he did not seem very cheerful."

The headmaster concluded by inviting Mrs. MacLeish to keep in touch, which is what she did with a grateful and detailed response. But the crisis was clearly abating. There were no more desperate letters from Archie, and his mother's goal at this point was to have Archie moved back from the cottage to be with the other boys in Main. "Of late the letters are more cheerful," she wrote. "I think he realizes that too much of melancholy is a bit hard on me, and is trying to write more cheerfully; also I think he feels better. The one thing I do not like about the letters is their self-centered character. His talk, and evidently his thoughts, are too much about himself. I am trying to urge him to take his full part in all the things that are open to him: St. Luke's, the literary society to which he belongs, and so forth. Also I have told him not to consider whether or not the boys like him, but to be just as cheerful and jolly and helpful a companion as possible to all the boys with whom he has to do. . . . I believe that Archie will make his adjustment all right in time, but it is going to be a longer process than I thought. I doubt if it will be complete before he goes back next fall in the satisfaction of being an 'old boy.'"

Martha MacLeish proved to be right. By the start of his lower middle year, Archie was back in Main with the rest of the boys, and he had matured enough physically to try out for varsity football. Archie was also a member of St. Luke's and heeling the *Record*. There had been no letters between his mother and the headmaster for more than nine months, until the winter term of Archie's lower middle year. "I write to congratulate you and Mr. MacLeish on Archie's success in winning the Helen Yale Ellsworth prize for the best essay on 'The lesson of Lincoln's Life,'" Buehler wrote in part. "The award will be announced to the school at our Lincoln exercises on Friday at 12 o'clock, when Archie will be presented with the prize and required to read his essay to the school."

This was not meant as an invitation to attend; even if it were not for the distance, parents did not participate in their sons' school life in those days. "It is certainly gratifying to know that he is developing the ability to write well," Archie's mother responded, "but I am even more pleased to know that he is gaining the power, perhaps I should say the capacity, for honest, earnest, steady work. His marks would indicate that this latter is true, and it is a capacity that he lacked when he went to Hotchkiss. Mr. MacLeish and I both feel that Archie has gained very much in every way from his year and a half with you, and we look forward with pleasure to the two and a half years more of the same influences. I do not believe there is a school in the world that does more to produce moral earnestness and manly self-reliance than Hotchkiss, and I am very glad that this particular boy has the good fortune to be there.

"You will perhaps remember what a struggle he had with home-sickness when he first went there. Now his loyalty and devotion to the School are in the same measure."

Again, silence for more than a year – perhaps confirming the adage that no news is good news; especially considering the nature of the next letter, sent during the spring term of Archie's upper middle year. It was addressed not to Mrs. MacLeish, but to Archie's father:

April 20, 1910
My dear Mr. MacLeish,

Last Sunday we were obliged to omit our chapel services because a strong east wind and the unfinished state of the new organ chamber together made it impossible to heat the chapel sufficiently. Without asking permission, your son and four other boys left school during the morning, engaged a local automobile and went to Pittsfield, Mass., forty miles away or thereabouts. This was perfect folly. If permission had been asked it would have been refused, and the boys admit that they knew it was against the rule. [Dr. Buehler explains the rule and the significance of its being starred.] By breaking this rule in the manner described, your son and his companions . . . made themselves liable to dismissal or suspension. We are not disposed to say that we want no further dealings with them; therefore, they have not been dismissed. Suspension, on the other hand, is a very clumsy instrument of discipline in a boarding school, which should if possible find some way of dealing with school boys' conduct on the spot without interrupting his school work and training unless things reach a pass which makes further dealing with the boy inexpedient or impossible.

Accordingly we have determined to apply as an experiment a substitute for suspension which we call sequestering. Sequestering is an attempt to punish a boy without trouble to his parents and injury to his own school work. It aims at cutting him off for a time from the pleasures of school life without interrupting his studies and the School's supervision of him. [Dr. Buehler details the restrictions imposed by sequestration.]

I myself have talked with the boys and tried to explain the folly and wrong of such conduct, especially in boys who are good at heart and usually stand for right things. Unfortunately boys are wise, thoughtful, etc. only in spots. As they grow older under good training, their wisdom, thoughtfulness, etc. become more pervasive and all embracing. They have a common and pernicious tendency to measure the importance of a school rule by the 'sin' or 'lack of sin' in the thing which is forbidden. They are slow to realize that our school rules are reasonable and necessary, and that their duty is always obedience. They must be made to see, and also *feel*, that it matters not what the forbidden thing is; the fact that it is forbidden by the school is enough.

I cannot tell you how distressed I have been over the folly of the boys, of whom in the main we think very well. I hope you will approve the action we have taken. I am sure you will co-operate with us in our effort to bring the boys to a right attitude toward these things.

With kindest regards,

Very sincerely yours,
H. G. Buehler

Archie had forewarned his parents by telegram of what to expect, and the response Mr. MacLeish sent to Dr. Buehler reflected his son's "realization of the folly and impropriety of his conduct. . . . The salutary feature of the affair is that Archie was thoroughly scared at the possibility of his being expelled from school, and expressed the deepest penitence to his parents for his disobedience and thoughtlessness, and his willingness to submit to any punishment that might follow. His expressions of love for Hotchkiss explained his fear lest his offense should prove unpardonable."

Archie's sequestration was over in a few weeks, just prior to the end of the school year. That summer before he was to return for his senior year – as a member of the football team, chairman of the *Record*, and one of the leaders of his class – Archie joined his parents on an extended visit to England. Yet, even on the other side of the Atlantic, Archie felt the aftereffects of his near-expulsion, which he communicated to his Hotchkiss liege: "My chief reason for writing this is to unburden my mind of certain things that have been weighing on it rather heavily since my automobile escapade. I have felt at other times that anything I might say on the subject would be taken as needless. By that I mean that, had I spoken of it before my term of sequestration was up, I might have been suspected of false motives.

"Of course that was a foolish fear but it hindered me. All this explanation simply leads up to the statement that I am and have been heartily ashamed of myself for my part in the trip. . . . I'm afraid I've made quite a bungle of the three years that I've had at school and I am thankful that I have a fourth left me. I feel so because of something Mr. Buell very kindly told me about the opinions held by the faculty about me. He said that I had a reputation for being very irresponsible and 'kiddish,' and even for not being straightforward. I was very much surprised, I'm afraid, and it made me feel kind of shaky for a while. I don't doubt but that I had been conceited before.

"Please believe that I say these things knowing myself that they must be true if you believe them so, and hoping that you will believe me when I say that I want to try to live them down. . . . I love the school as much, I believe, as my own people, and I am very thankful that I shall have one more chance. If ever you can use me, and you feel that you can trust me, please do."

Aug. 25, 1910
Mr. Archie MacLeish
32 Charlotte St., Manchester, England
My Dear Archie,

Returning to Lakeville I find your very good letter which has pleased me very much, and it gives me great pleasure to assure you that the joy ride has not permanently shaken my confidence in you. I am quite ready to forget all about it, and I feel sure you will fully redeem yourself during the coming year, and by the whole course of your future life make us proud of you as a Hotchkiss boy. I am grateful to you for your willingness to co-operate with me in anything that may be best for the school – that is, for the boys. I know you love it as much as I do, and I should be very much grieved if you were not coming back to us. . . .

This letter from the supposedly cool and emotionally detached King was signed, "Affectionately yours,"

Archie MacLeish would prove worthy of that special commitment almost to the end of his senior year. With only a few weeks left before graduation, he was censured for an unspecified dining hall misdemeanor, which clearly had not been his first. "Archie was glad to admit the utter folly of his table pranks," the headmaster wrote to Mrs. Mac-Leish, "and he assured me he was always ashamed of them as soon as they were committed. I have been more concerned about the mental and spiritual experience through which he is passing."

The incident provided impetus for a final exchange between the headmaster and the mother of one of his most esteemed seniors. She was not upset by the censure – "I can understand exactly how he did what he did. It doesn't mean much, but you were right in noticing it." Martha MacLeish was, however, eager to take up another aspect of that affair: "I was glad to note in your letter received yesterday that you have had a good talk with Archie. I was just on the point of writing to ask if you would try to do so, as his last letter to me indicates that he is having a difficult time in his religious experience. He is at sea in the matter of faith, and his spiritual life does not mean to him what it once did. . . . He intellectually wants to see to the very bottom, the last end of everything. He takes nothing for granted, and he doesn't realize that spiritual truth is not to be discerned by the same logical process as intellectual truth. Also I'm afraid he doesn't do the things that are necessary for the feeding of his spiritual life. He admitted to me last summer that he had not taken the place in St. Luke's and in the religious life of the School that he ought to have taken. . . .

"I cannot help fearing that Archie's success in his literary work has not been altogether good for him in point of character. He needs to realize that any ability he may have is a gift to him, and that he is responsible for the use he makes of it.

"Also he is selfish, with the selfishness of a strong nature. It means achievement and power, but it means limitation and emptiness of life unless he makes something far bigger than himself the object of his living. He hasn't had the big vision yet, or if he has he hasn't been obedient to it.

"Forgive me for troubling you with so long a letter, but I am sure you who know boys so well, and who have his respect, can help him. If you have not covered the ground already I hope an opportunity to talk further may occur."

March 16, 1911
My dear Mrs. MacLeish: –

Your fine letter of March 13 is just at hand, and I feel that Archie cannot get very far astray with you behind him. I agree with you in thinking that his success in his literary work has not been altogether good for him, and I notice that it has led him into an attempt at smarty writing, which is something very different from the literary quality which has aroused our admiration. I think he will get over this speedily when he moves on to college and becomes a freshman instead of a senior, especially if he goes to Yale. This present phase in his development makes me feel perfectly sure that he ought not to go to Harvard now. I think he needs the democracy of Yale.

With Archie and some other boys in mind, I requested Dr. Henry Wright to take 'Doubt' as the subject for one of his talks last Sunday. If Archie says anything about these talks I should be very much interested to know whether they impressed him at all. I am very much interested in the boy, and I shall have him constantly on my mind.

With sincere regard,

Very cordially yours,
H. G. Buehler

Whether Archie was in any way impressed by Dr. Wright's sermon that Sunday cannot be known; he did, however, heed the advice to go to Yale – where he was honored in his senior year by a Hotchkiss holiday declared "partly in recognition of the acceptance of your poem by the *Yale Review*," and a year later by another holiday partly for "win-

ning the Cook Prize in Poetry." Then this telegram to Archibald Mac-
Leish at the Harvard Law School in 1919 for yet another honor:

Gave boys holiday this morning because of Fay Diploma. Congratulations and thanks. Can you be with us Sunday morning?

H. G. Buehler

viii / As distinguished a niche as Archibald MacLeish would attain as a lawyer, professor, statesman, and America's poet laureate, another Chicago boy of approximately the same vintage would ultimately play a more pervasive role in the annals of the Hotchkiss School.

To his classmates he was known as Bert. When Bert entered as a
prep in 1909, he was already eighteen because of the circuitous route
by which he had come to the school. Only the previous year, he had
been a runner for a Chicago bank, and in his spare time emptied spit-
toons and otherwise helped out at a bar owned by his stepfather. (His
father had died some years before.) It was on one of his bank errands
to the commodity exchange that the hard-working youth chanced on a
Princeton graduate known as Captain Bradley, who had founded a
small farm school for orphans where Bert had spent some time a few
years earlier. Captain Bradley had just returned from a Princeton reunion at which one of his classmates had told him about the promising
New England boarding school where he was a master. Best of all, Captain Bradley said, the school offered scholarships, and he would help
Bert apply through that Princeton classmate – who turned out to be
Dr. J. J. "Doc" Robinson. Determined not to miss out on this chance
of a lifetime, Bert ironed his one suit so assiduously that during the
long journey East by train, he repeatedly checked if the seat of his
pants had not dropped out. He arrived in fine form, only to be told by
the splendidly clad headmaster that he would have to take examinations in English, history, Latin, and algebra. Whereupon the young
man said he would be glad to take the first two, but as for Latin and

algebra, he did not even know that such subjects existed. Whether or not he took any exams at all is unclear, but when Bert found out that he did not qualify, he asked the headmaster if there was any job he could fill around the school. He needed the money for train fare back to Chicago.

If some of the foregoing details have been distorted by time, the rest of Bert's saga is amply documented. Dr. Buehler let the boy stay, and Albert William "Bert" Olsen graduated with the class of 1913 and later married a sister of a classmate and future Nobel laureate, Dickinson Richards; the couple's son would become the school's fifth headmaster and lead Hotchkiss through the two most tumultuous decades of its history. "Dr. Buehler will always be something of a hero in my book," says A. William Olsen, Jr. '39. "I judge that underneath all the pomposity was a heart just about as big as he was."

Perhaps it was Dr. Buehler's big heart, combined with his affinity for the famous, which exposed the entire school to a lecture that was as disturbing as it was edifying. The speaker was Jacob Riis, a Danish-born former newspaperman who had spent a quarter of a century as a police reporter on the *New York Sun*. He was a friend of President Theodore Roosevelt and the author of such books as *How the Other Half Lives* and *New York Slums*. His subject on this particular evening was *The Battle with the Slums*. "Mr. Riis began his lecture by showing a picture of a typical tenement house block on which between six and seven thousand people live. The reason for this overcrowding is the greed of man," reported the *Record* on December 8, 1908. "Mr. Riis next showed some pictures of the interior of these tenements and described the filth and squalor in which these people live. . . . Often fifteen or twenty people sleep in a single small room. . . . Mr. Riis told of the playgrounds and gymnasiums which he has built in the slums and which now provide for the children healthy places in which to exercise."

Jacob Riis had come to the school as a part of the long-standing practice of inviting prominent speakers from the outside world to this privileged country haven, safely tucked away in the northwest corner of Connecticut. In one year alone Buehler had brought in Charles W. Eliot, Woodrow Wilson, and Arthur Twining Hadley – the presidents of Harvard, Princeton, and Yale – to talk on education. Other speakers included a professor from Amherst lecturing on German peasant life, an editor of *Scientific American* revealing the techniques of "the American amateur photographer," and a faculty member of the Hampton Institute speaking on "Negro education, preceded and followed by Negro singers."

Though startlingly graphic in its presentation, the message Jacob Riis brought to Hotchkiss was not an unusual one: the responsibility of the more fortunate members of society to lend a helping hand to those in need. This was one of the implicit premises on which Hotchkiss had been founded, and already back in 1894 the school's St. Luke's Society was raising funds and collecting clothes for a nearby retreat for destitute boys with "marked criminal tendencies." Such charitable acts were not only part of being a "good Christian," but represented the sometimes neglected noblesse oblige aspect of being a gentleman. In December 1895, the *Record* had put it in the form of a cautionary tract:

"The Hotchkiss School has always had the reputation of being a school of and for gentlemen. There is no fellow in school who would not resent any imputation to the contrary, and yet in certain instances at various times, the behavior of some members of the School has given rise to just censure. A fellow who stoutly maintains, despite any doubtful conduct of his own, that he is a gentleman from the top of his head to the sole of his foot because his ancestors have been so before him is likely to err. We are gentlemen of 1895, not of the Restoration. It is not customary now as then for gentlemen to treat all inferiors with an overwhelming insolence, to be entirely unmindful of the convenience of others and when not in one's own home or circle of society to deport one's self with a superior and patronizing air. We are living in an age when even a little unintentional politeness goes a great ways, in an age when it is inconsistent with no man's dignity to treat those beneath him with some consideration, and his less fortunate fellowman with charity and tolerance. . . . We have two models of gentlemanliness before us: the first is the man who wastes the heritage of good reputation which his ancestors have left him; second is the man who increases his inheritance by living up to the standard which is before him."

The standard which Jacob Riis implicitly put before the school in his lecture in 1908 was to do something about those city slums. By the following summer, a program was launched to do just that. Eighteen boys, variously referred to in the *Record* as "urchins" and "street boys," were brought to Hotchkiss from the Lower East Side tenements of New York for two weeks of "sunshine and happiness." That was the beginning of what came to be known as the Riis Camp. Fortified by hearty fare in the dining room, the campers engaged in day-long outdoor activities, supervised by Hotchkiss boys who had volunteered to postpone their vacations and stay behind at the school. Others contributed clothes, athletic goods, and money to make the camp self-supporting. Soon, the Riis Camp was running double sessions and averaging a total of about forty boys each summer. "The days are spent in outdoor work, tennis and baseball being the chief sports," reported the *Record* in 1911. "Twice a day the boys go down to the lake for a swim. Sometimes a few fish are caught. . . . We may easily see how much pleasure the little fellows find in their outing by the fact that two of them made their way back here just to see the fellows and the place where they had such a good time."

During the school year, Hotchkiss boys were engaged in similar endeavors closer to home. On the other side of Lake Wononscopomuc across from the school was Ore Hill, which had provided much of the raw material some years before for the Hotchkiss family's munitions business. Inhabited by miners' families, many of them now unemployed, Ore Hill represented the proverbial other side of the railroad tracks. A collection was regularly taken up in the school chapel to help the more destitute of these families. After hearing one such case dramatized by Mr. Estill before a Sunday offering, several Hotchkiss boys became interested. They investigated the conditions on Ore Hill and came up with a plan that would bring together boys from the two opposing hills. They secured permission to use an abandoned school-house and founded the Ore Hill Club. According to the *Record*, "1908 was the first year of this club, and in that year Hotchkiss boys went to the old school building and played games with the Ore Hill fellows or took musical instruments, making the evenings so jolly that every one had a good time. These gatherings proved such a success that every one at Ore Hill and Hotchkiss agreed that the one thing to do was to erect a permanent building for a club house. This was a rather expensive prop-osition, but Hotchkiss boys, Hotchkiss alumni, together with a few kind friends in Lakeville, made the plan possible."

The Ore Hill Club and the Riis Camp were to remain a part of the Hotchkiss scene for years to come. This did not mean that Hotchkiss was brimming with altruistic goodwill. It took a concerted effort to keep these relatively modest endeavors going. An editorial in the *Record* in 1914 found it necessary to chide those who had missed their Ore Hill commitments: "Fellows who do not care to go should not sign up and then refuse to go at the last minute. . . . This is not the kind of spirit that we care to tolerate." Important to note is that activities of this sort continued to be held out as an ennobling ideal toward which every Hotchkiss boy should strive. In Sunday chapel, one minister counseled that students should occasionally "withdraw from life for a short time in order to study one's self and life as a chess player looks down upon a chess board to see what to do." He pointed to life's dual aspect: "There is our ambition [and] selfishness in achieving success for ourselves. Then there is the idealistic side, the desire to be a good influence and to be unselfish. That's why we came to school; to learn the proper outlook on life."

When the Ore Hill Club was finally disbanded in 1918, it was actu-ally because most of the mining families had moved away. The Riis Camp was discontinued in 1925, after a contingent of campers housed in Main were left inadequately supervised on a weekend, and went on a rampage during which they damaged the building to the tune of $6,000. The Depression then turned the school's altruistic reserves in-

ward. The boys would chip in to help a classmate whose parents had
been wiped out in the crash or extend a helping hand within the surrounding community.

Despite its unfortunate denouement, the Riis Camp set a tone and a
precedent for similar activities in years to come. The most radical
would be the Greater Opportunity (GO) program inaugurated in 1965
by Headmaster William Olsen and directed by a social worker from
New York, Father David Kern. What the Riis Camp had tried to do for
underprivileged white boys, the GO program endeavored to do for a
much larger number of underprivileged young males who were mostly
blacks—with the extra dimension of providing remedial schooling.
And Hotchkiss students again volunteered to assist as proctors, this
time for six weeks—giving up almost their entire summer. Observed
the *Record* in evaluating their contribution to the first GO program:
"The proctors worked ten hours a day, from noon till ten, every day,
always on the go, and the warm feeling which they generated and displayed to the boys was a vital factor in aiding the students in becoming
oriented to the Hotchkiss campus and way of life, which after all is as
markedly different from their environment as if they were in another
world." Symbolic of the charges' appreciation was the "entertainment
night" the proctors organized toward the end of the summer: "The
boys really sang, read, and acted their hearts out, and by this proctors
could see just how proud and grateful the boys were to be in the
program."

Among those who participated in the GO program was Jonathan
Garrett. Today a photojournalist for the Reuters News Agency, he as-
sesses the meaning of his experience:

"I came from the north end of Hartford, which was one of the more
depressed areas of the city. The toughest thing was confronting an environment that I wasn't accustomed to. You look around the school,
and there's money. Money is a big factor here. My family was working class. There were no luxuries afforded to us. Here we had everything. You couldn't ask for a more beautiful place, a more beautiful

countryside. But to benefit, I first had to overcome the environment I came from.

"The GO program for the three summers I was at Hotchkiss represented the turning point in my life. It gave me an opportunity to prove to myself that I could deal with a situation like this. It placed me around some very positive people in a positive environment, and it was impressed upon our minds to succeed. We discovered that whatever we did, failure or success was going to be the result of our own doing.

"I had always felt a spark within to keep going. One of the most overwhelming experiences when I first arrived here was in the dining hall. The names that are engraved on the wall there—to look up and see some of the alumni, endless names of famous people—that to me was like, 'My God, I'm here in the same place!'"

One of the proctors for the Hartford GO recruits was Donald G. Block '71, whose grandfather had donated the money to build the school's chapel in 1932:

"As an upper mid, I stayed at Hotchkiss for the summer, and I was a proctor on a dormitory floor for some GO program kids. They had to appear tough, and the façade which they carried in the inner city didn't break down very much. There was one kid who used to like to tackle me in the hall and tried to wrestle me. He was upset when I just sat there like a brick. I remember him very well, a streetwise kid from Hartford.

"A small group of us continued to go to Hartford once a week throughout the school year to tutor. I think I was going through so much learning being with these kids, I probably wasn't thinking much about what they were getting out of it. Father Kern, who ran the program, was a great influence on me, and unlike most students of my day, I found the chapel an important experience. The School gave me a chance to explore moral values, which was important to me. I got interested in education, particularly education for the disadvantaged. After graduating from college in 1975, I joined the Peace Corps and went to West Africa."

Don Block then put on hold any plans to go into the family publishing business. (His father, William Block '32, headed the *Pittsburgh Post-Gazette* and several other newspapers.) Since 1984, the former GO proctor at the Hotchkiss School has been executive director of the Greater Pittsburgh Literacy Council. "What I want for schools such as Hotchkiss," sums up Don Block, "is not simply to be a preserve for the elite, but to continue the tradition of exposing that group to responsibility for service."

The GO program was eventually phased out, primarily because of the withdrawal of outside financial support, but also because of a concurrently waning interest at the school. Again, this did not mean the end of social work at Hotchkiss; on the contrary, the new awareness drawn from the late 1960s and early 1970s provided impetus to broaden this work on many fronts. Not to be overlooked was the continuation of the kind of sharing – and leveling of inequalities – within the school, which had characterized Hotchkiss since its earliest days. "My dad was a very sharing guy," says Stuart H. Watson '76, whose father had entered the school with Frank Sprole in the class of '38. "I remember we had at home an IBM typewriter I wanted to take to school. It was an old '50s model, which typed cursive, and I loved the way it made the words look on a page. But Dad said to me, 'The only way I'm going to let you have this typewriter is if you promise to share it with your classmates. It's not just for you. If anybody needs it, you have to let them use it.' Well, I had no problem with that. Unfortunately, it turned out that a lot of the teachers didn't like the script type, and after a while, that beautiful typewriter was hardly used at all. But that's the way my dad was. He didn't want to spoil us. I used to have a forty-dollars-a-month allowance at the school, and I had to send him a complete tally of every dollar I spent."

Besides following in his father's footsteps in being generous to the school, Stuart Watson is currently called "Dad" by some eighty-eight orphans he sponsors in the Philippines.

Spearheading the school's social work today is the oldest student organization, St. Luke's Society. "As goes St. Luke's, so goes Hotchkiss" has been one of the oldest bywords of the school. In the past, St.

Luke's was at times religiously oriented; at other times, it was exclusionary and manifested traits of social snobbery; and for a time in the early seventies, St. Luke's even served as a front for the Dubious Film Society, which specialized in adult fare. But spanning the century of St. Luke's existence has been the desire to render social service, and this has now become its primary and virtually only goal.

Louis H. Pressman, faculty adviser to St. Luke's at the close of the school's first century, offers a contemporary perspective: "All told in a year, we probably have 175 kids involved in one activity or another – candy striping, visiting with retirees, acting as big brother, big sister at the grammar school, tutoring on the kindergarten level, helping to run a soup kitchen on Saturdays in Torrington, hosting the Connecticut Special Winter Olympics. When I consider the course load our kids carry, and that sense of relentless demand on one's time in boarding school life, I think the fact that we've got as many kids involved is remarkable.

"I've heard some of the youngsters who aren't involved say, 'Oh, she or he is just doing that for college suck.' In other words, that it'll help them in the college admissions contest. Well, they may do it once, they may do it twice for that – but that's about it. Those who do keep coming back frankly know it isn't going to make a big difference on their college record, but that's not why they're doing it. They're doing it because for so many of them it really is the time of their greatest satisfaction at the school. Practically everything else at Hotchkiss is subject to graded appraisal. Even in athletics you get an imaginary grade in what the coaches say or whether they start you or bench you. Here the kids have the chance to discover the satisfaction of giving. In the Torrington soup kitchen, our kids learn to see those people neither as statistics nor as sort of idealized victims, but as real human beings who can be funny, who can be obnoxious, who can be touchy; in other words, just like anybody else. In working with the elderly, they learn what it means to be infirm and disabled – something which in our society is usually kept pretty much in the dark. The lot of the very elderly is sometimes like the old Tarzan movies, in which the elephants went to the graveyard in the jungle, leaving only their ivory behind as the remains. Helping an elderly person who maybe can't make it to the bathroom lets our students learn about human dignity in a way they just couldn't have imagined before.

"We now allow special projects, including social service, in lieu of athletics. Melissa Brown, who was one of the recent winners of the Frank Sprole Social Service Prize, had done a special project at the Town Hill School during the winter, and then continued coming during the spring, just on her own at odd times, while doing varsity softball. She was also doing the soup kitchen, as well as being probably the single most important leader in the Special Olympics. And she wasn't even an officer of St. Luke's. She was just this wonderful, extraordinary person who wasn't interested in claiming credit for herself."

The opportunities for service within practical reach of the school continue to expand; so do the numbers of Hotchkiss students wishing to serve, giving a contemporary meaning to that traditional concept of noblesse oblige. With girls better than holding their own in this respect, the old adage, "Be a gentleman!" hardly says it all.

ix /   Ah, yes, girls. Back in the old Hotchkiss days, they were the stuff dreams were made of – and that was as far as things went. Virtually without exception, Hotchkiss boys in those days did not feel they were missing out on anything akin to ultimate carnality by being cooped up at the school. Their contemporaries who had remained at home certainly did not engage in anything of that sort. Such base activities might well go on on the wrong side of the railroad tracks but were hardly worthy of gentlemen. Altogether imponderable was that the co-participant might be your sweetheart or a classmate's sister. Nothing could lead to a quicker punch in the teeth than an improper reference or a smirk within that hallowed context. The subject of sex was riddled with multitiered standards and overall uncertainty, in itself reason enough for Hotchkiss boys to appreciate the benefits of being in an all-male enclave. They seemed to prefer relegating the fairer sex to their fantasies rather than having them around to complicate life. "See thyself, a lover, as others see thee," soliloquized the president of a mythical Bachelors' Club in the *Mischianza* of 1912. "Woman hast bereft thee of thy reason, thou art insensate, fatuous, feeble, and flighty, as woman is herself." No wonder Maria Hotchkiss did not stand a chance with those gentlemen on the board!

Yet there remained a yearning among boys to be occasionally rendered bereft of reason, insensate, fatuous – and whatever else the presence of the opposite sex might do to them. The socially acceptable vehicle for bringing that about was The Dance. The first one reported on by the *Record* was held in 1894, and social decorum was the paramount theme:

"On Saturday evening, the twentieth of October, Mrs. Coy and Miss Coy gave a dance in the gymnasium in honor of the Senior and Upper Middle Classes. Nearly all the members of these classes were present and enjoyed a most delightful evening. The gymnasium was furnished with extra rows of electric lights, and was therefore brilliantly illuminated. The floor was made smoother and more slippery than ever by the lavish use of wax, so that it was almost perfect for dancing purposes.

"Although the gentlemen were greatly in the majority, the pleasure of the evening was in no way lessened for them; the ladies used so much tact and kindness in distributing their dances that every one had a fair share. The music, furnished by a violin and a piano, added greatly to the charm of the dancing.

"An interesting feature was the various grades of formality displayed by the gentlemen in the different styles of apparel which they wore. One would glory in full dress, while his neighbor contented his spirit in a sack coat. Cutaways and tuxedos, long tails and short, were all mingled in the common enjoyment of the dance; and all seemed to be equally proper for the occasion.

"The program of dances contained sixteen numbers, which, according to the prevailing custom, were distributed evenly between the waltz and the two-step."

From the list of the young ladies present, it appears that there were nine of them, including Miss Coy, to be apportioned among approximately forty seniors and upper mids. Presumably, Mrs. Comstock, Mrs. Estill, and Mrs. Buehler, who were listed as assisting "the hostess in entertaining," were also twirled around on that highly polished floor. The "lavish use of wax," incidentally, was characteristic of the school; not only prior to a dance, but weekly, on all of the parquet floors, especially on the long corridor in Main. It might be safe to say that anyone graduating from Hotchkiss before old Main was torn down would still remember the fresh smell of that aromatic wax and the drone of the old aluminum rotary buffer that was inched along the length of the corridor every Friday afternoon.

The first dance to become institutionalized on a year-to-year basis was the Mid. So-called because it was held in the middle of the winter term, its purpose was to offer the senior class a marked respite from the season's gloominess, which often gripped the school. One non-negotiable prerequisite for holding a successful Mid emerged over the years: a plentiful supply of female guests. And this often meant resorting to all kinds of appeals. Editorialized the *Record* shortly before one Mid: "Do not hesitate to offer your invitation because of a false sense of modesty or an inferiority complex. Let us remind you of the ancient and time-proved adage, 'Faint heart never won fair lady.' We scarcely need to mention, so manifest are they, the incomparable advantages that would of necessity follow upon your inviting the girl of your choice. Increased prestige, influence, and 'savoir faire' alone would be your ample reward. And when we peer into the future, and reckon your chances of increased chances for connubial bliss and matrimonial fecundity, it is with difficulty that we find justification for your reticence.

"As a matter of class pride, if not of personal interest, we are morally bound to have present at least a goodly number of girls. . . . No man is justified in throwing his towel into the ring until Thursday night [before the dance]. The problem of success or failure, of a good time or a bad time, finds its solution in the girls who come. That puts it squarely up to you."

Another *Record* editorial sought to redefine what it meant to act like a gentleman: "Every year around Mid time we are disappointed by the conduct of a few people we have heretofore admired greatly – and another ideal is shattered. There is an unwritten law that no dance-cards shall be made out until a specified day in order that all may have an equal chance to arrange a good program for themselves and their guests. And yet each year there are those who, regardless of public opinion and the example of others, fill out their cards ahead of time. They may call it a desire to give their guest a good time or frankly acknowledge it to be selfishness, but it isn't fair and an occasional strain like that certainly does no one's code of honor any good. We also find the dance hog (no other term is strong enough) who keeps from eight to twelve dances for himself. It may give him great pleasure to monopolize his guest, but good taste should tell him his partner may not appreciate this monopoly of her dances, and his friends may feel that this gentleman does not consider them good enough to associate with her."

With the young lady invited and the dance card filled out, nervous anticipation took over the senior class. Perhaps the best-informed perspective on what happened next comes from one who observed the Mid from his student days in 1908 until the mid-fifties, when he retired after more than a quarter of a century as headmaster – George Van Santvoord. Written in a shaky, barely legible hand only a few weeks before the Duke died, the following account is a part of his last-moment attempt to set down for the record the history of the school:

"For the Mid careful and elaborate preparations were needed. Sometimes the last ten days of February were snowy and cold. Sometimes there was sunshine, temperatures in the sixties, and deep mud.

"The would-be host invited his guest and requested Mr. and Mrs. Blank as a special favor to accommodate her for three nights, and arranged with Peabody's livery for a carriage or sleigh to provide transportation. The bill for this was formidable, as he found later.

"On Friday afternoon he was driven to meet the train at Millerton or Lime Rock, lucky if he shared his vehicle with a classmate or two. They greeted their girls, drove with them to their host and hostess, and after introductions, parted to don evening clothes. (The girls were never called dates until long after World War I, and the dance was never called a prom.)

"Then came dinner, with lower classmen all agog to view and appraise the guests. In my time, 'a queen' was the standard term of enthusiastic approval.

"After dinner the whole company gathered in the auditorium where Glee Club, Banjo Club, and Mandolin Club performed, and unhappy judges had to decide which of the three deserved the award of a championship club. . . .

"After the Concert, the boys took their guests to the Gym across the corridor and proceeded to introduce them to all the faculty ladies, especially those entertaining girls as houseguests. Then came the dancing until 1 A.M. Music was supplied by a professional orchestra. (For afternoon dancing in later years, the music came from the 'Society Syncopators,' a lively group of boy-performers.) For refreshments guests walked to the Lower Mid room, normally a classroom, fitted up grandly as a 'Turkish Corner,' for lemonade and cookies.

"Saturday morning brought the 'Gym Meet' with feats of strength and agility on flying rings, parallel bars and sidehorse. Pythians wore red, Olympians blue. They performed in spectacular fashion, trained by Monnie, later assisted by Howard Taber. In the early 1930s, this exacting form of physical training evaporated and disappeared."

Saturday afternoon, according to the Duke's account, was taken up by attending a play – a custom dating back to the first production by the Hotchkiss Dramatic Association in 1908. Then on Saturday evening "came the climax with a formal dance at 8 P.M." Though GVS did not elaborate, an obviously more involved observer provided this glimpse in the *Record* of the highlight of the Mid of 1914:

"The President of the Senior Class and Miss Heywood led the grand march into a scene of such colour and gaiety as scarcely to be recognized as the prosaic gymnasium of ordinary days. The myriad banners flaunting on the walls, the dim lights, and the witching, tantalizing strains of ragtime from the marvelous negro orchestra in the corner, all blended with the spirit of the occasion and lured even the most staid onto the floor and into the swing of the dance.

"Down the corridor, the Lower Mid room enticed the weary with its cozy corners and cooling refreshments. It afforded a most charming retreat.

"But the relentless clock still pursued his round, and all too soon his hands stood at the fateful hour of a quarter to one. The spirits of the company sank with the 'dip' of the lights, for the Mid was over."

Well, not completely over, as the Duke made clear in a continuation of his account:

"Sunday was a long day. After breakfast there was Chapel at 11, lunch at 1 P.M., a long void in the afternoon, a brief vesper service, and Mr. Estill's reading after supper. On Monday morning everyone was glad to say good bye to the girls.

"Not until the 1930s did there appear the enlivening custom of taking the girls for an informal Sunday lunch at a log cabin in the school woods, and with the coming of the motor car, the 2-day house-party was brought to a close by midafternoon Sunday – a great relief to all participants!"

It was not the girls, but the social protocol that would finally wear thin. The most enjoyable part for the boys and their guests may well have been that "long void in the afternoon." Weather permitting, the couples could walk around on the school grounds or otherwise negotiate a moment or two of relative privacy. Not that they would have been in a position to let their emotions run amok. Even if through ingenuity or stealth they could have found an isolated spot, there were other obstacles to surmount. A *Mischianza* editor in 1917 offered this thinly disguised parable:

"A youth of literary longings in this school had a girl, for whom he had a well-diagnosed case of puppy love. He had gotten as far as holding her hand several times, but for some unaccountable feeling of temerity, perhaps because he felt that he and she ought to be engaged first, had never progressed any farther. The summit of his ambition was a kiss. And he so conceived the clever idea of working his trouble up in the form of a story and handing it in. Being written under the stress of real inspiration, the story was a winner and when the magazine came out he promptly sent a copy to the girl. Two days later, he received a letter with this quotation: 'A faint heart never won a fair lady.' It is understood that there was a question mark after the word 'fair,' but of course that was only maiden modesty."

Such quasi-Victorian attitudes remained virtually unchanged over the first half of the twentieth century. When I arrived at Hotchkiss in 1948 as a prep, some of my classmates were still smarting over having been told the facts of life, which implied that their parents must have indulged at least once in that causative, unwholesome deed. Then there was the classmate who was overly worried prior to our upper middle dance that he might become inappropriately aroused while doing the foxtrot on that highly polished floor. How mortifying it would be to "give himself away" in so obvious a way! He resolved his dilemma by wearing two athletic supporters beneath his tuxedo pants.

Of course, the upper middle dance and the graduation dance, which supplemented the traditional Mid, were not the only opportunities at the school for getting together with the opposite sex. There were lesser dances organized with such schools as Emma Willard and Ethel Walker, and various collaborations, such as the French Play put on annually with the Masters School in Dobbs Ferry, New York. In extracurricular activities of a different sort, a few of the boys were occasionally enticed by semiprofessionals who plied their trade just beyond the limits of the school grounds – sometimes resulting in subsequent visits to the infirmary. But that was not at all typical of what went on at the Hotchkiss School. Far more reflective of the drive and ingenuity to relieve this pressure of adolescence – beyond the rumored saltpeter added to the meals – was this letter submitted in 1939:

To the Editor of the *Record*:

Lately I have been involved in an interesting and curious affair. I write it down on paper and send it to the *Record* only as proof of the old adage, 'What fools men are,' and as a warning to my fellow males.

Not long ago I observed on a certain desk in a certain classroom the following illuminating inscription: 'Want a good kiss? See Dot xxxxxxxx, 612 xxxxxxxx Avenue, xxxxxxxxxx, Conn.' Because I have some interest in such affairs, I decided to fire a shot in the dark. With my best English 4 style, I drew up the following epistle:

'Dear Dot,

'More from the desire of satisfying my curiosity than from another desire which might, I admit, immediately crop up in your mind, I am writing you. For yesterday, I ran into an advertisement which praised you in the highest terms. It said: 'Want a good kiss? See Dot xxxxxxxx, 612 xxxxxxxx Avenue, xxxxxxxxxx, Conn.' My curiosity aroused! I have no way of knowing when this inscription was engraved on the desk, so I would like you to notify me if it were at any date previous to the [first] World War. Also if you are married, let me know, and we will drop the whole thing. For I can then go back to the 'Hearts and Hearths' magazine through which agency I have already made several conquests. But this letter, understand, offers no grounds for a lawsuit of any kind. I cannot tell you to whom you owe your recommendation, but I can think of no better one, nor of any better place, to inscribe it. Perhaps you will be glad to know that I have removed it to insure no competition.

Respectfully yours,

Sam Mills, IV'

I posted this letter to the given address. Impatiently I waited for the reply. Today I received a letter from the same address. It had the heading Mrs. George Wickham Styles, Jr. As I tore open the envelope, my hand lacked its usual steadiness. The letter read, and there I quote:

'Dear Sam,

'I was delighted to receive your letter, although I am afraid you are going to be disappointed in whatever you were hoping to get out of this.

'You see I married him. Naturally he denies putting that ad on the desk, and of course I believe him. Better luck next time.

'Dorothy Louise Styles (Dot), H'30

'P.S. If you ever are passing through stop in to see our daughter.'

Gentlemen, my advice to all of you is to fire a minimum number of shots in the dark. The casual mention of 'our daughter' was, of course, the crowning blow.

What fools men are!!

S. M. IV

Only the coming of coeducation would finally begin to change this state of affairs at the Hotchkiss School.

x /   "One break was not having the women up there," recalls Robert E. Blum '17, as he glances through the sliding glass doors of his Ore Hill home across the Lake toward the distant silhouette of today's Hotchkiss on the opposing hill. "But I liked it when they came up for the proms."

The silver-haired, spritely Robert Blum had devoted his life to the family department store business, Abraham & Straus, and a seemingly endless list of civic and charitable organizations. He has remained active in many of those even after retiring in 1964 and building a home in the same area where, during his Hotchkiss days, lived impoverished miners.

"We had a strange class because it was the middle of the First World War," explains the ninety-one-year-old gentleman, after bringing out a large battered scrapbook filled with mementos of his prep school and college years. "They had us marching around with wooden guns on the athletic fields. Those of us who had a decent average at the end of my senior year stayed at the school and did victory gardening that summer. I got a certificate from Governor Holcombe of Connecticut saying that we had farmed for sixty days, and Yale accepted that instead of entrance examinations. So we literally farmed our way in."

Robert Blum had been on the staff of the *Mischianza* and a member of the mandolin and gun clubs. But his favorite activity by far had been the *Record*, where he worked closely with Briton Hadden, whom he had known in Brooklyn, and Henry Luce, a scholarship boy whose parents were missionaries in China. "They were the editor and managing

TIME

NEW YORK

October 8, 1923.

Dear Dr. Buehler:-

It gives us great pleasure
to send you under separate cover, a
bound copy of Volume 1 of TIME. We
hope you will accept it together with
our renewed thanks for your early encouragement of our efforts.

Editors.

Dr. H. G. Buehler,
Hotchkiss School,
Lakeville, Conn.

BH/HG

Announcing the first issue of Time

editor of the *Record*, and I was business manager," continues Mr. Blum. "The same trio then ran the *Yale Daily News*. After I graduated from Yale, Briton Hadden came and visited Brooklyn one night, and spent the night with us. The next morning he came down to breakfast. My father was there, and Brit said to him, 'Luce and I are thinking of starting a news magazine. What would you think of it?' Father said, 'Why do we need another news magazine? I don't think the idea is worth a damn.' That didn't discourage Hadden. I put in a hundred bucks at the time and sold out just recently when *Time* merged for quite a tidy sum. I would have gone into *Time* with them, but I had a family business that I was headed for."

Among those receiving a complimentary copy of the first issue put out by Hadden and Luce was their onetime headmaster. Surely an appropriate historical footnote is his response:

October 18th, 1923
Messrs. Hadden and Luce,
236 East 39th Street,
New York City.
My dear Boys:

I thank you very much for your courtesy in sending me a bound copy of Volume 1 of TIME.

You are certainly going after this business with your usual ability and energy. I wish you all possible success.

> With kindest regards,
> Sincerely yours,
> H. G. Buehler

Five years later, with *Time* a renowned national and international publication, one of those boys was inevitably asked by his successors on the Hotchkiss *Record* for what was expected to be an endorsement. The following response from Briton Hadden undoubtedly caused consternation, both on the *Record* and among the faculty:

"I have been asked . . . to state what, in my opinion, are the advantages of being on a preparatory school newspaper. Personally I don't see any advantages. It's a lot of drudgery and, unless you have a competent Faculty adviser *who has been an active newspaperman himself* – not just an English instructor – it is not journalism. . . .

"Dr. Robinson, who had a study next to our old *Record* office in North Bissell Hall, aptly characterized the 1916 *Record* board by telling a fellow faculty member that 'they spend hours in there asking one another how to spell 'cat' – and look at what they turn out!' On hearing this, we were sorely vexed. 'Let's put rats under his door.' With the years (twelve of them now) came realization that 'Doc Rob' had been 100% correct.

"The trouble with us was that we did not know what constituted news or how news should be written. All might have been well had we had a competent newspaperman to instruct us. Because we were Editor-in-Chief or Managing Editor or Sporting Editor we considered ourselves to be authorities on school journalism. Later certain members of our Board moved to New Haven and 'edited' the Yale *News* under similar hallucination.

"Perhaps I am too critical. Certainly there was good in the *Record* work – no question but that it sobered us with a sense of responsibility. The point that I had better make is: The work would be more valuable if you had a coach who could make you stop printing the same old stories that have been printed every year since the School and the *Record* were founded. Stories like: 'Dr. Flubdub will speak at Vespers,' and 'Hadden 1916 says that journalism is a good career.'

"An excellent test to apply to each story on any newspaper is: 'Is there anybody in this entire community who really wishes to read this story?' If there is not, throw the story OUT.

"Also for the *Record*, an excellent rule to follow would be never to permit your heelers or editors to read the bound volumes of past years. One set of heelers and editors imitates another. Are all the original thinkers on the *Lit*? Your *Record* men are using (just as we did) formulas and 'ideas' for stories today that actually were evolved in the nineties. Suppose Mr. Monnie should do that in football?

"I guess I've been far too 'indiscreet' by now. So I'll ring off. To summarize: School journalism is of some use to a potential newspaperman, but it is only about ten percent as effective as it might be because it is not *coached*. Of what value would the Greek course be if you had only the grammar book and the *Anabasis* and the *Iliad* and no 'Doc' Brown? About one half of one per cent.

"I, for one, should like to see the *Record* and the Yale *News* abolished as social organizations and courses in journalism established in their places, with these periodicals properties of the courses.

"If this be treason, go ahead and sue."

A word of consolation for those *Record* editors of 1928, for their predecessors and their successors: Mr. Hadden could not have possibly foreseen that those myriad stories that failed to qualify as timely news would prove to be such a treasure trove when the time came to prepare this centennial history.

xi /   "When my brother Os and I came to Hotchkiss, he was fifteen and I was fourteen – and the school was only twenty-six," says Arthur "Squidge" Lord '22. "Yet I don't think it ever occurred to any of us that Hotchkiss was really very young compared to other New England prep schools. One reason for that probably was that Hotchkiss had been founded back in the preceding century. Of course, when we came to Yale some of our friends who had gone to St. Paul's, Andover, Exeter, and so on, acted as if Hotchkiss was something they'd never heard of. Who were these guys from Hotchkiss? Even though out of our class of around seventy who graduated, fifty of us went to Yale."

Squidge and his slightly older brother Os (Oswald B. Lord '22), along with brothers William G. Lord '18 and John C. Lord '23 and three of their sisters would combine to attain a unique distinction in the annals of the school: producing more Hotchkiss graduates than even the Goss family. As classmates, Squidge and Os shared a wealth of schoolboy experiences of that era, including almost drowning in Lake Wononscopomuc – Squidge, when he foolishly skated out on ice that was too thin; Os, when he went out with comparable abandon in a canoe on a lake still filled with ice floes and tipped over. "Os was fished out in the nick of time by the head groundskeeper, Fred Ellis, who happened to be passing by. I was numb and going under when a classmate, Dan Lindley, spotted me and managed to pull me out. We always laughed about it because the following fall, playing class football, my brother Os tackled Dan Lindley and broke his leg. Dan said, 'This is the family's way of showing its gratitude.'"

Though Os died several years ago, Squidge is a fount of memories: "I loved Hotchkiss from the start. It puzzles me that anybody could possibly go there and not have a good time. I angered each of my successive wives by saying that the best four years of my life were spent at Hotchkiss.

"Typical of the kind of fun we had was going to the village. We'd usually walk down, take in a movie and go swilling – just stuff ourselves – then coming back, we'd take a taxi. There was an Armenian fellow, Black Harry Ablahadian, who had an old Model-T, no heat in it. He'd get six or eight kids in there, sitting in each other's laps. Going up the hill to the school grounds, we'd be barely chugging along. The temptation was to jump off the running boards and run for it. Black Harry didn't look at that with any favor at all. My nickname, Squidge, was too much for his English, and he always called me Squash. So as we'd start up the hill, he'd say, 'I'm looking at you, Squash, don't you jump now!' Of course, I used to pay him the next time around. But we loved to run and hear him holler.

"My study habits were good, and I had done well at the local country day school. My first term at Hotchkiss I was on the first honor roll. During the second term I slipped to the third honor roll, and then I disappeared from the honor roll category altogether. The marks were passing but nothing to startle anybody – though my senior year I shared the prize for American history because we had a wonderful teacher, Mr. Hall, Peanut Hall.

"I think I held the record for sequestration – five times. The punishment wasn't as fearsome as it sounds. There were always three, four, or five people sequestered, and we made a good time of it together. In my day, probably twenty-five percent of every class was sequestered at least once – including my brother Os."

Squidge Lord would have been in even more frequent trouble had he not taken preemptive action: "In those days, the headmaster's office was in the old Main Building. It had three windows, and one of them opened onto the porch as you came up to the building. That window was never locked. If you missed Sunday chapel you automatically got a censure. My friend Al Luke and I would occasionally find that one or both of us had missed Sunday chapel, and already had two censures. One more would mean going back on sequestration for six weeks. So we would wait until after dark, after lights, and we'd go out the window from the second floor of Main onto the top of the corridor. There was a drainpipe which would bring us down into some bushes on the lefthand side of the entrance to the building. Then we'd wait. There was a night watchman, known as Cascarettes. He got the name from liver pills advertised in those days. Their slogan was, 'Cascarettes, they work while you sleep.' Naturally, we attached the name to the night watchman who worked while we slept. We pretty well knew his timing, and we'd wait in the bushes for Cascarettes to go by. Then I would go up on the porch, while Al acted as a lookout. I would raise the window to Dr. Buehler's office and climb in. I would have on one of those heavy blue Hotchkiss sweaters and carry a flashlight. If you missed Sunday chapel, the absentee slips were put through a slot in his door. They would be picked up the first thing the next morning and handed to the disciplinary people. So I'd grab all the slips out of the box, maybe ten or twelve on a given Sunday, and take them over to Dr. Buehler's desk. Shining the flashlight through my sweater, I'd quickly flip through the batch to find Al Luke's, or mine, or both, whichever we were after. I'd stick them in my pocket, shove the others back in the box, pop out the window, pull it down, climb back up the pipe and go back to bed for a good night's sleep. If Dr. Buehler ever knew that anybody was in his office at eleven o'clock Sunday night – well, that was probably as risky a thing as we ever did."

For Squidge Lord, the most valuable aspect of Hotchkiss was "the association with a very fine group of fellows and a very fine faculty, a devoted faculty. Men living on tiny salaries because they wanted to teach. Real teachers at heart. Uncle Joe Estill was going to teach us mathematics if it killed him. He used sort of a green stone chalk, and he'd always fill the board with big equations. If you didn't know the answer, he'd bang the blackboard and shout. I'll always remember him banging out equations on the blackboard. He'd practically go through the wall, but he managed to drive the material into some awful dumb heads, too. He adored Hotchkiss, and he couldn't stop teaching.

"The whole atmosphere at the school was so tremendously stimulating – healthy, outgoing, companionable. There were practically no weekends, no Thanksgiving holiday, and we didn't have the distraction of coeducation. We were interested in boys' activities, and I guess we were a naive bunch of boys. The fundamental aim of Hotchkiss, however, was no different from what it is today – to produce in this country a continuity of culture. What little culture we have in the United States is nurtured in the prep schools. They are the last holdout, more so than the colleges which are jammed with tens of thousands of people. It's these little oases – Andover, Exeter, St. Paul's, Hotchkiss, Taft, and the rest of them – they are the last bastion of young people in a position to get the preparation necessary for leadership in our public and private life."

xii /　　Two years behind Squidge Lord – and following in the Hadden-Luce footsteps on the *Record* and the *News* at Yale – was Frank H. Hamlin II '24. He was offered a job at *Time*, but like Robert Blum he went instead into the family business; in Frank Hamlin's case, manufacturing farm machinery in upstate New York. Writing, however, remained a lifelong avocation. After retiring as CEO of Papec and with the compulsion of having a story to share, Frank Hamlin put his *Record*-honed talents to work and completed an autobiography titled *My Time*. Though intended primarily for his grandchildren, the story has sections that are of no less immediate relevance to this Hotchkiss School chronicle.

Fourteen-year-old Frank arrived at the school after changing trains three times and being humiliated by a dining car steward: "Needless to say, this journey took all day and then some. The school, when finally reached, was alive with men and boys, all of whom seemed to be on the most intimate terms and to know exactly where they were going. I was told where my room was in an outlying cottage, how to find it in the dark, and that the dining room was closed.

"I was pretty tired, hungry, and confused when I got to my room, which was already occupied by my roommate: He said his name was Dick Goss and that he came from Waterbury, Connecticut, which he claimed to be, without question, the toughest town in all the Northeast.

"I got into my cot with the least possible delay. The tough guy from Waterbury said, 'Hamlin, in this room we say our prayers *every* night and we say them on our knees *before* we get into bed.' I said, 'I say my prayers *after* I get in bed.' With no more discussion, Dick yanked me out of bed, beat me up, and gained full compliance from then on, and I *mean* from then on. I *still* say my prayers on bended knee before bed. Incidentally, Dick and I corresponded for sixty-one years until his death five years ago.

"Next day in somewhat battered condition, I found and reported to my classes, including Mr. McChesney's English I. He immediately noticed that, when called on, I blushed fiery red. His antidote was invariably to call on me by announcing, 'And now we shall hear from Little Sweetness.'

"Mr. Mac was the best teacher I ever had. At our forty-fifth class reunion, John McChesney was there and greeted me with, 'As I live and breathe, it's Little Sweetness.'

"After English, algebra, Latin, and history I was told to report to the gym. There, I stripped down, and Mr. Monahan examined me thoroughly and with obvious interest. He weighed me in at seventy-five pounds. 'Hamlin,' he said, 'you are without a single exception the smallest, skinniest boy I have ever checked in, in all my years at Hotchkiss. Go and pick out the smallest football gear you can find, put it on, and report to the practice field for scrimmage.' I ended up ingloriously on the third prep team.

"Strict discipline and athletics were held to be essential parts of the learning process at Hotchkiss, and many a renowned athlete came to and from the school. Ducky Pond was a senior when I was a prep. He captained both the football and the baseball teams, which no one else has done before or since. At Yale he again distinguished himself in both sports and subsequently became head football coach. Gene Tunney, when he was light-heavyweight champ, used to be on hand to referee school boxing matches and give us suggestions on the manly art of self-defense. Bill Tilden came to show us how to hit a tennis ball. He even played doubles with some of us. I had that never-to-be-forgotten experience. I can still hear him call out, 'Peach, Chape!' as his professional partner, Chapin, smashed one out of reach.

"Hotchkiss also attached considerable importance to religious training. Famous divines of the day came to preach at school, including Fosdick, Dean Brown of Yale Divinity School, and 'wet-the-ropes' Goddard [trustee and board secretary for some thirty years] – so called because of the same old punch line of the same old sermon he dished out every year. Step by step he would unfold a tale about the huge obelisk being erected in St. Peter's Square in Rome. A series of blocks and tackles were in place. All available horses, mules, and men exerted every ounce of pulling power. The obelisk refused to budge. The discouraged crew secured the tackle under full tension and agreed that their best efforts were hopeless. But just then a young student appeared, took in the situation at a glance and called out in a loud voice, 'Men, wet the ropes!' They did. The ropes began to shrink and presently the great obelisk settled into place. At Hotchkiss whenever anyone was faced with a task beyond him, some wiseacre was bound to sing out, 'Wet the ropes, you dope!'

"At chapel, stiff, starched white collars were required. These were conveniently stored in mailboxes just outside the chapel doors. After breakfast one fished out his collar and fastened it with his tie over his regular button-down soft shirt collar. After chapel the collar was restored to its post box.

"I grew to love the place, and, after four years of it so many years ago, I still do. My son, who is of tougher stripe than I, seemed to have no trouble settling into the life of the school when it came his turn. In fact, when his mother and I drove three hundred miles from Canandaigua to reassure ourselves that he was not pining away for home and family, I found him in his room concentrating on the work spread out before him on his desk. I knocked on the open door to call his attention to the arrival of his concerned parents. He looked up briefly and said, 'Hi, Pop! Have a chair, I'll be with you as soon as I finish this.' "

xiii /   Frank Hamlin's class of 1924 produced an impressive roster of lawyers, financiers, and similar corporate types – as well as the Reverend Thomas H. Chappell, whose unenviable task it turned out to be to follow George Van Santvoord as headmaster when the Duke retired in 1955. The class also produced an unusual array of graduates who made their mark in public life, including Roswell L. Gilpatric, who was deputy secretary of defense for President John F. Kennedy, and Charles Yost, who served President Nixon as ambassador to the United Nations. Then there was, in Frank Hamlin's words, "Paul Nitze, with whom I still correspond as Class Agent. [He] went to Harvard, and on a bet, paddled a canoe from Boston to New York, where he subsequently made a fortune on Wall Street. He has now served seven U.S. Presidents and knows more about dealing with Russians than anybody else."

As a student at Hotchkiss, Nitze had at first appeared lackadaisical. His father, a professor at the University of Chicago, had sent the lean, precocious youth East for a couple of years after he had passed at age fifteen his college entrance exams for the University of Chicago. "I certainly had no interest in the subjects I was studying," reminisces the still-lean, dark-suited elder statesman in his Washington office; "so I developed all the bad habits which stuck with me later in life. I didn't pay attention to the assignments I was supposed to do, and I spent my time reading things which I wasn't supposed to read. I can remember going to study hall and reading Dante's *Purgatory*. It had nothing to do with any course I was taking. I tried to hide what I was reading so that I wouldn't get caught."

Paul Nitze did not exactly fit the mold of what the "administration of the school thought a boy should be." He acquired several censures, one of them for perpetrating an outrageous disturbance in the middle of the night by rolling down the corridor in newly built Memorial Hall a sealed barrel of construction material that had been left behind. He was then sequestered for hiring the town taxi to take him "to Meadowbrook School where there was a girl I was interested in." Like Archibald MacLeish before him, Paul Nitze had traveled beyond permissible bounds; on top of that, he had returned late. "There were three of us sequestered at the same time, and among other punishments, we had to run the triangle daily, and we had to walk with our elbows against the wall during normal hours, just like preps," Nitze explains. Edging his clasped hands forward on his desk, the veteran disarmament negotiator looks intently over his half-glasses as if about to reveal a strategy of global consequence. "I proposed to the other two sequestrees that it would be great to send off to New York and have a medal struck to form a club, the Sequestered Club. So we had a triangular medal struck with this little triangle etched in and the figure of a man running in the center. Around the edges was the lettering, 'The Sequestered Club.' We put it on our watch chains, and as the three of us walked with our arms against the wall, we exhibited this medal. When it was discovered that I was the one who had architected this thing, I was asked to come in and see the Reverend Dr. Buehler. Dr. Buehler began by pointing out that this was not just making fun of discipline, but an intolerable offense. I thought he was going to fire me, but then at some point as I was defending myself, he began to smile. Frankly, I developed a great respect for the Reverend Dr. Buehler."

Paul Nitze developed respect for other aspects of the school – even for Latin. "The change came because of Vergil. I'd loathed the other Latin authors that I read. Caesar, I thought, was just an ambitious, dictatorial politician, not an admirable man. Cicero, I thought, a hypocrite and one of the most unattractive men I had ever read the works of. I was all with Catiline! Cicero should be totally condemned. But I did then read Vergil, and I became persuaded that Vergil did really have a sense of beauty. That converted me from being totally bored with Latin to being interested in Latin. So I did pick up something in those two years by bits and pieces; I did learn something, and I changed my mind on my original discouragement with the school. And then amongst the people there, I made a lot of very close friends. At first I couldn't play football, because I had water on the knee. When it turned out I could play, the world changed. Those people have remained friends for life."

Paul Nitze was also on the *Lit*, which gave him an untrammeled opportunity to articulate his thoughts – as he did so presciently in the following editorial in April 1923:

"How often have you gone out on some clear night and looked up at the myriads of bright stars in the heavens? Those stars, bright points of light forever twinkling and casting their bluish light on our small earth, never seem to move or grow dim, but keep on shedding their beauty on us every night throughout the ages. As Emerson says, 'If the stars should appear one night in a thousand years, how would men believe and adore; and preserve for many generations the remembrance of the city of God which has been shown!'

"If one looks at the stars for any length of time, they invariably fill one with a sense of awe and wonder. They seem so far distant, so unchangeable, and so vast that in comparison, we seem puny. Think of the vast multitude of stars, of their tremendous size, of their inconceivable age, and of the possibility of life on some of their planets. All these thoughts have but one effect, to make one feel quite insignificant. One thinks, in a universe of such immensity, what difference can the actions of a single human being make in the period of a lifetime?

"If, however, we keep in mind the fact that for us the world is everything and that each one of us is the center of his small universe, we realize that we are not such an unimportant thing after all. . . . Each one of us has been entrusted with one life to do with as he thinks best. If he makes the most of his life, he may accomplish things which will not only bring him his reward but which will give an infinite amount of happiness and comfort to the rest of the world. At present each of us is developing and directing the course which his life must later follow. Let us see to it that we do our job well and make the most of our opportunities."

Sixty-five years later in his Washington office, Paul Nitze was shown the piece he had written on the threshold of adult life. The commanding, white-haired nuclear strategist seemed momentarily transported back in time as he read it. Then he said, with a hint of a smile, "It's better than I thought, better than I remember writing it. I still think it's amazing what you can do over a long period of time, over five or ten years. Yes, I remain an optimist."

xiv /   In the spring term of Paul Nitze's senior year, Huber Gray Buehler was taking it easy. Perhaps the most taxing project of all – raising funds and then overseeing the construction of Memorial Hall in honor of the twenty-two Hotchkiss graduates who had lost their lives in the war – had been completed the previous year. (Among the memorialized was Archibald MacLeish's younger brother, Kenneth '14, who was killed in Belgium.) For the King, this had been an emotion-filled task. Despite his reputed aloofness, he had personally known each one of those former boys; some of them, he may have regarded as if they had indeed been his princely sons. He had spent many hours sitting quietly on a green bench by the old tennis courts, gazing at the embodiment of his memories taking form from red Georgian brick.

As Buehler's twentieth full year of headmastering drew to a close, the school was academically strong. A 1922 compilation of CEEB scores over the preceding eight years showed Hotchkiss leading "in the total numbers of highest ratings" over Andover, Exeter, St. Paul's, and a dozen other top schools, including Boston Latin. The headmaster had earned an influential niche in regional and national educational groups, where he cut an impressive figure with his royal bearing and impeccable tailoring. An entry in the records of the Headmasters' Association noted, "This was the year when Boyden [the headmaster of Deerfield] put a fur collar on his coat, and thought himself as good as Buehler." Within his own domain, the King could well take comfort over some of the additions to the faculty he had made. The likes of Doc Rob, Pop Jefferson, Peanut Hall, and Doc Brown were supplemented by a new cast of memorable characters, including "Spud" Murphy, "Monk" Taber, "Howdy" Edgar, and the choirmaster, Denison Fish, who was enough of a character without an embellishing nickname. Two neophytes who would cut perhaps the broadest swath in the memories of Hotchkiss alumni were both English teachers who looked so young they could be mistaken for new boys. One was John Mc-Chesney, the same one who had dubbed Frank Hamlin "Little Sweetness" for life. Mr. Mac's bag of tricks for turning boys' minds to literary pursuits was startlingly physical. A boy with a wandering mind might suddenly find the pixyish English teacher sitting in his lap and twisting a piece of chalk into his hair. John McChesney married Molly Scoville, the sister of Robert Scoville, a trustee and treasurer of the board in whose memory the Georgian entrance to the school was built in 1935. The union made Mr. Mac independent of his teacher's modest salary and helped him earn renown as a formidable host. Like many of the greatest masters at Hotchkiss, he was to remain controversial beyond his thirty-year teaching career at the school. Legions of students to this day speak of Mr. Mac in affectionate, almost worshipful tones. "He opened my eyes to what was really happening in literature," says John Hersey. "He got me out of Galsworthy and into Faulkner at a time when Faulkner had published only three novels and was far from famous. His teaching was mixed up with so much slapstick and comedy. Everybody spent half his time laughing and half his time taking in what could really awaken his mind." Far less numerous, but no less vociferous, have been the debunkers of Mr. Mac, including Paul Nitze. "I did not take to McChesney. I think his was kind of a fake, fancy admiration for the superficialities of literature, books, and collection of books," recalls the classmate of Little Sweetness. "But he didn't have his mind on the content."

The other faculty appointment with boyish looks was Carle Parsons. Suffice it to add that this former Hotchkiss boy of gentle manners, faultless gray herringbone jackets from J. Press, and ever-polished elegant shoes (except when wearing white bucks on sunny spring days) immediately became the headmaster's confidant. With him the King shared his hopes and his fears and even talked about his ever-growing dependence on his wife. "You know, Carle," he reportedly confided, "when some hovering case is haunting my mind, I'll ask Roberta, and just like that, she'll come up with the answer."

Roberta Buehler's contribution to the school would be difficult to overstate. Beyond whatever emotional and practical support she provided for the King, the Queen had a reputation for remembering the name of every alumnus, what he was doing, and his children's names. She also tried to interact with every boy at the school – if not always with unqualified success. "She'd have each class over one day a week for cocoa and cookies," recalls Robert V. Massey, Jr., another classmate of Paul Nitze. "Those were rather forbidding affairs. Mrs. Buehler wasn't a warm, friendly type; certainly not in the atmosphere of a class tea. But she was feisty; she had a lot of spunk." She also had her conquests. Says Thomas P. Blagden, Jr. '29, "I remember when my mother first brought my older brother Gus up here, she felt Dr. Buehler was the coldest thing and the school the grimmest. It almost destroyed her to put her little son there. But Gus ended up rooming for a while on the third floor of the headmaster's house. Roberta Buehler befriended this homesick little guy, and that's what turned him around."

The other woman in the King's life was his young secretary, pretty, apple-cheeked Mary Meehan. Brought up in Lakeville, she had been working in New York for Appleton, Century, Croft Publishers, when a friend employed at Hotchkiss told her about the opening. "My friend set up an appointment, and I met Dr. Buehler at Wake Robin Inn," recalls the ninety-four-year-old secretary to four headmasters. "I'll never forget my impression. He was a handsome big man wearing a white suit with a light-colored vest and a big watch fob. You rarely saw those anymore. And white shoes. White suede shoes. Again, that was new for this area."

Mary Meehan would forget no less her five years of working with the King. "He would dictate in his big study in the headmaster's house. There was a huge fireplace, and he would stalk around and look out of the beautiful window overlooking the flower garden. He hated to dismiss a boy. He would dictate a long letter, and he'd say, 'Miss Mary, type it out, and I'll sleep on it.'

One aspect of office work, however, remained within the exclusive purview of the King's wife. "Mrs. Buehler opened all the mail, which was a good policy," explains the former Miss Mary. "It helped her keep up with what was going on at the school. I think maybe she also had a lot of bills and didn't want him to see them. That could have been serious for his condition."

The King's health was the main reason he was taking it easy during that spring term of 1924. He had suffered a mild heart attack a few months earlier and was under the care of a local specialist and another one in New York. The King's appearance by this time could best be termed as roundly dignified. As with authentic monarchs, whether Henry VIII or the Roi Soleil, the fifty-nine-year-old Buehler showed the side effects of privileged life. Though still holding himself ramrod straight, he had acquired a comfortable paunch. Anyone suggesting a link in those days between diet or a sedentary life and physical health would have been dismissed by the medical profession as a quack. (In fact, one respected physician visited Hotchkiss to conduct tests on volunteers from the football team to garner support for his theory that strenuous exercise dangerously enlarged the hearts of young people.) From today's vantage point the King would have been quickly diagnosed as a cardiac disaster waiting to happen. That he had survived so many years of royal fare and minimal physical exertion was a tribute to his constitution. "Some of the food was so rich," says John Hoysradt about the dinners at his Uncle Huber's "palace," "I often felt almost ill afterward."

The King's medical Rx dovetailed with what would be convenient for him as well as for the school. After taking care to finish up the year with a minimum of stress, he was to depart in the fall on a year's sabbatical of relaxed traveling in Europe. The change and rest would practically guarantee recovery, the doctors predicted, and enable him to resume his reign at Hotchkiss in the fall of 1925.

The most immediate result was a recurrence of Joe Estill's headmaster bug. Twice before in the past dozen years, Dr. Buehler had left the school for several months abroad with his family. On both occasions with the approval of the trustees, he had appointed his longtime colleague as acting headmaster – though not without misgivings. The day he was to depart for Europe in 1912, the King was so distracted by the prospect of leaving Estill in charge that he rose in chapel for prayers and said, "Let us provoke God!"

Uncle Joe had managed to make it through that time, and once again for several months in 1916. But there had been signs of the same kind of administrative chaos and emotional disruption that had typified his tenure when he stood in for the ailing Coy. "Uncle Joe, in control of the ship during the skipper's absence, makes things lively for us," noted the class historian in the *Mischianza* chronology for 1916. "During his first day as captain, in his calm Southern manner, he declares the school quarantined; sequesters one boy; expels one boy; calls two special faculty meetings; keeps us in chapel an extra twenty minutes, trying to dope out how many have not had the mumps; and gets seniors and faculty together at 9 P.M. Nice, quiet day!"

This sort of memorable performance left many lingering doubts. To put Uncle Joe in charge for the entire year of Dr. Buehler's sabbatical would have inflicted on the King the kind of stress he could not escape, no matter how far he traveled. Moreover, the headmaster in his royal palace and the school's perennially most popular master had drawn further and further apart over the years. They differed vastly on what was considered good form, which so often took precedence over substance at the Hotchkiss School. Whereas Estill as a Yale graduate had started out with a slight edge in the appropriate savoir faire over his Pennsylvania College colleague, the King had long since drawn far ahead as a paragon of urbanity. Two parallel glimpses symbolize the gulf between these two men and perhaps help explain why one was respected and the other loved. John Hoysradt '22 on his Uncle Huber: "He came into the library one time and there were several boys doing some writing, with vests on, but not with a coat. Dr. Buehler said, 'Here we either just have the shirt sleeves or the full vest and coat –

but never just the vest." Paul Nitze on Uncle Joe at about the same time: "I remember Estill coming down to breakfast one day. He used to wear a stiff collar, but he had forgotten to put on the collar and he just had this gold collar button sticking out. It didn't seem to bother him at all – and it didn't bother me." Estill was the only person in the school who neither addressed nor referred to the headmaster as "Dr." Buehler, but as "Mr." Buehler or just "Buehler."

With the approval of the trustees, Buehler's choice for his stand-in fell on the wiry, professorial gentleman with a goatee, Walter Hull Buell. He had been headmaster at a boys school in western Pennsylvania before coming to Hotchkiss in 1899. Now, after a quarter of a century of exemplary and versatile service – he could teach with equal skill Greek, Latin, French, German, English, history, and mathematics – he was ready to retire. Standing in for the King during the year-long sabbatical would be the Bull's final service to the school.

Yet, how to tell Uncle Joe, who might take it as a slap in the face, a public repudiation of his performance as acting headmaster in the past? The easiest way would have been for the board of trustees to notify Estill, along with everyone else at the school. But the King favored a more straightforward, personal approach, if only for old times' sake; after all, he and Estill had joined the faculty together three decades earlier as the original young fry. Pacing up and down his study in the latter part of April 1924, Buehler dictated a "Dear Mr. Estill" letter, on which he may well have slept before telling Miss Mary to drop it in the school mail. "The retirement of Mr. Buell offers an opportunity to entrust the work of the headmaster to an experienced man," read the key paragraph, "without raising any question of precedence or disturbing in any way the distribution in teaching. Everyone would know that the arrangement grew out of the fact of Mr. Buell's retirement." Elaborating on this face-saving explanation, the headmaster detailed the need for Mr. Estill's cooperation and help and concluded with a friendly, "How does the thing strike you?"

The King should have known; maybe he did, but had tried anyway. Uncle Joe was standing by the school post office in the rotunda (beneath Matthew Arnold's misleadingly exemplary lines emblazoned on the frieze) as he finished reading the letter, oblivious of the groups of students walking by to check through the glass portion of the individual boxes to see if they had any mail. Just then out of the corner of his eye, Estill caught sight of the ailing portly headmaster making his way from the end of the long corridor in Main toward his residence. Interrupting the King's measured, upright gait in the middle of the rotunda, Estill could barely control his rage. There was no misformulated sleeping powder to blame this time, only the agony of wounded pride. His graying hair and mustache quivering, Estill hissed, "You can't spit on me like this!"

The headmaster's first concern was to avoid a scene in front of the boys. Except for flushing a deep red to the roots of the remaining hairs on top of his head, the King managed to maintain his outward composure while he excused himself as expeditiously as he could. It was not until several days later that he revealed in his typically understated way the grave consequences of the encounter. "Mr. Estill stopped me in the corridor," Buehler wrote to Dean Jones of Yale College, who was then the president of the board. "Our short talk was pleasant enough, and I invited him to come over and talk about it more if he desired. . . . Fifteen minutes later, however, I had a severe recurrence of angina, followed by three other attacks the same day. Our good friend's insistency and persistence, of which you know something, make it difficult sometimes to avoid the unconscious 'stress and strain' which doctors have cautioned me against!"

Estill's "insistency" did not stop with the King. "In an interview which Mr. Estill sought," wrote Buell in a memorandum to Buehler, "he regarded the proposed action as implying a vote of lack of confidence in him, and that he was not inclined to be tramped upon or spit upon. About his last words [to me] were: 'The situation is full of dynamite.'"

And it was. Through his persistent campaigning, Estill had secured the support of several of his old-time colleagues, creating a rift within the faculty which threatened to extend into the student body. Under the circumstances, Buell made it clear he had no desire to get caught up in the fray and would go ahead with his original retirement plans.

The King, in the meantime, had been restricted by doctors to his residence, with specific orders to avoid Estill, no matter what.

The president of the board at this point came to Lakeville to take matters personally in hand. Frederick Scheetz Jones, dean of Yale College, had a personality that seemed specifically designed to handle the likes of Uncle Joe. A practical man with frosty hair, a red face, and the gusty manners of a hunting squire, he had a reputation for being able to spit farther and talk straighter than anyone on the faculty of either Hotchkiss or Yale. What exactly transpired between the board president and the perennial headmaster-aspirant will probably never be known. The King had counseled resolving the matter simply by sending Estill away on a year's sabbatical at the same time that he, Buehler, would be gone. But another version has it that the earthy, nononsense Jones issued an ultimatum to Uncle Joe: apologize and get in line or resign.

Whatever the case, the visitor from New Haven made his point. For someone who loved Hotchkiss and teaching as much as Estill, it was preferable to swallow any amount of pride than risk losing everything, and he promptly fell in line. It was not the first time, nor would it by any means be the last, when the interests of the school unequivocally took precedence over individual aspirations and needs. Yet it was in no way a personal repudiation of Uncle Joe. The disparate talents of Estill and Buehler were no less integral to the Hotchkiss School than two sides are to a coin.

By the time Paul Nitze and the rest of the Class of 1924 were ready to graduate, peace had been restored on the hill. The King was feeling well enough to hand out the diplomas and personally wish each of the seniors farewell. As the school began to empty of faculty and staff, one of the last to leave was Carle Parsons. He had a long, warm chat with the King, and the headmaster asked the former student to do all that he could to help Buell in his task. He then took the young man's hand in both of his and wished him a happy vacation at his cottage in Nan-

Portrait of Huber Gray Buehler presented by class of 1924

tucket. Toward the end of the third week in June, Hotchkiss was virtually deserted. Even the Queen was away. Roberta Buehler was in New London for the boat races, staying with the family of Tom Chappell, who had just graduated. The Queen felt secure in having entrusted her spouse to John Mantas, the family butler for almost twenty years.

The weather on the morning of June 19 was glorious, and the freshly cut lawns smelled of the lazy summer ahead. Dressed in a light, three-piece suit and a high stiff collar, the King sat in a large rattan wing chair on the expansive verandah on the lake side of the headmaster's residence. Next to him on a smaller wicker chair was Mary Meehan, dictation pad in hand. Whether he was feeling some of his former energy – or because he wanted to complete a vital task – the Europe-bound Buehler passed the entire morning dictating letters of acceptance for the new boys who would be coming that fall. Mary Meehan then spent the afternoon typing in her office in Main, determined to have the letters ready for the King's signature the first thing the following day. But when she arrived at the school that morning, John Mantas had just called. He had gone upstairs with the King's coffee – and the King was dead.

5   The Duke's Garden

(Above) *The old Main;* (below) *the corridor in Main*

H e spanned the Hotchkiss century in a unique way. George Van Santvoord was born in 1891, the same year the Articles of Association of the Hotchkiss School were signed. He graduated seventeen years later and returned to preside as headmaster over much of the middle third of the school's first century. He died in 1975, a few months after coeducation began and just seventeen years short of the start of the school's second century.

To the end, Hotchkiss was uppermost in the Duke's mind. Surely the most unusual document passed on to me for possible use in this centennial history was a limp, yellow spiral notebook, its lined pages filled with a shaky, at times almost illegible rendition of George Van Santvoord's unmistakable hand. An accompanying letter written by the Duke's stepson, the late Thaddeus "Ted" Beal '35, reads in part, "I discovered the enclosed in rearranging papers in desk drawers here. . . . It was written in the last months, I believe, when he was in pain from ill health and short-tempered and unduly critical."

What had provoked the Duke's ire was the previous version of the school's history – *The Hotchkiss School, A Portrait* by Lael Tucker Wertenbaker and Maude Basserman – published in 1966 in anticipation of the school's seventy-fifth anniversary. The Duke had at that time expressed his displeasure in no uncertain terms. "[The] work seems to me very shallow, unnecessarily caustic and unkind," he wrote in one of several letters to William Olsen, the headmaster then in charge. "It makes me half-inclined to wish I had never accepted the trustees' invitation to go to Hotchkiss as headmaster." George Van Santvoord subsequently sent several annotated copies of the book to the school, each with penciled marginalia and corrections similar to the markings of a teacher on a student's essay or a test. Yet that was not the end of the matter for G V S. For more than eight years he apparently continued to contemplate Mrs. Wertenbaker's version of the school's past; and when he finally put down his thoughts on paper, it may have been because he sensed his end was near. The yellow spiral notebook reflects, in both form and content, the urgency felt by a man intent on unburdening himself before it was too late. "What shall we say of [Mrs. Wertenbaker's] account of Maria Hotchkiss?" demanded the Duke in one of his first tirades. "Where did our historian find evidence to justify her remarks about a divorce, a broken marriage and court decrees? All these are highly suspect unless supported by precise evidence. Even if there were any truth in such malicious tales, why would they be apropos?" A few lines later, G V S endeavors to debunk Mrs. Wertenbaker's description of how Timothy Dwight had reasoned with Mrs. Hotchkiss "over a marble-topped table" while they sipped tea. "Was the 'Widow Hotchkiss' so gauche and ill-bred as to serve tea on a marble table *with no cloth?*" queried the Duke. "Gossip, rumor, imagination and fiction replace fact."

The Duke's sixty-five pages of final jottings had a practical intent beyond venting his wrath. "When someone – preferably an alumnus – comes to write a book about the school," the retired headmaster had previously informed Bill Olsen, "those notes may be worth looking over." What made this suggestion so hauntingly personal was the familiarity of the criticisms in the Duke's assorted notes. They bore the unmistakable stamp of the headmaster who had chastised this Hotchkiss boy forty years before for thoughtlessly fomenting strife between the school's two senior math teachers, Dr. Renny and Mr. Hale. To be sure, I was not the only former student still responding to G V S years after graduating from beneath his direct tutelage. When I interviewed baseball commissioner Fay Vincent '56, he had a framed photograph of the Duke on his desk and allowed that he often glanced at it for advice – whether preparing a speech or grappling with some sensitive issue. And Fay Vincent surely was not the only *other* Hotchkiss graduate who to this day involved the Duke in his life.

The standards implicit in the Duke's critical notations turned out to be particularly relevant for presenting a balanced account of *his* life. Not only was George Van Santvoord an intractably multifaceted and, frequently, an unfathomably self-contradictory subject; his personality tended to arouse a full range of conflicting and vehement emotions. "I loved him dearly and admired him enormously, but could have shot him on a few occasions," says Arthur Howe, Jr. '38, whose father had been the Duke's classmate and who had known GVS as headmaster from the perspective of a student, faculty member, dean of admissions at Yale, and lifelong fishing companion. "I felt very close to the man, but had friends who felt only dislike, even anger. All they could see were his flaws, which stuck out all over the place." Stories about the Duke could not be dismissed simply because they seemed to be too farfetched. The most farfetched of stories were among the most characteristic of him, though the Duke ultimately was a thoroughly straightforward man governed by a few basic principles. "Think what the world would be like if everybody did it," he chided many a boy in whom he detected leanings toward some seemingly harmless form of selfish behavior. "How would you like to live in such a world?"

Perhaps the most outrageous "Duke story" that, I regret to say, I believed was related by a Hotchkiss classmate. It concerned this classmate's recently deceased cousin, who throughout his life rarely missed an opportunity to publicize how the Duke had spitefully prevented his going to Yale. As a student at Hotchkiss in the early thirties, this boy had family connections going back to the first years of the school. His connections at Yale were no less impressive. Yet when he sought to apply to Yale, the Duke had told him that he was too immature to go there – or so the boy later claimed, attributing the headmaster's stance purely to a personality clash. In those days, the Duke's recommendation was the single most important factor in helping a student gain admission to college, especially to Yale. Drawing on his New Haven connections, the boy's father then arranged the requisite interviews and entrance examinations for Yale, entirely independently of Hotchkiss and the Duke. In preparation, the boy spent several vacation days being crammed by a tutor with answers to the exact questions likely to appear on the test. The crux of the story was that the boy was accepted; however, when G V S found this out, he drove to New Haven in a fury and informed the Yale admissions people that he would not bother writing any further recommendations. Needless to say, or so the story went, the boy's acceptance was summarily withdrawn by Yale.

What made the story credible was that G V S in certain matters was adamant – allowing himself to be neither persuaded nor dissuaded – and that impulsive drive to New Haven would have been especially characteristic. But a glance at the records revealed an altogether different situation. The cynical adage, "The thicker the file the thicker the boy" seemed to hold true in this case. The boy in question had previously attended several other schools, and his multiplicity of academic and other problems were detailed in a half dozen letters exchanged between the boy's mother and G V S. From this correspondence emerged a headmaster who was acting as an extraordinarily patient and sympathetic counselor. Then this letter from the Duke to the dean of admissions at Yale:

Mr. Alan Valentine
Yale University
New Haven, Connecticut
Dear Valentine:
[The boy's father] informs me by telegraph that his son, [xxxxxxxxx], has passed all his College Board examinations and will be a candidate for admission to Yale in September.

Our previous correspondence will give you the story of this boy's schooling up to the time he came to Hotchkiss. We took him in last fall largely because of [his grandfather's and father's relationship to Hotchkiss]. His grades for the year are as follows:

Senior English 52
U.S. History 49
Chemistry 48
Senior English 52
French 50

We recommended to the family that the boy should spend next year at some school where he could receive individual attention, suggesting particularly the school run by Mr. Lloyd H. Hatch at Dexter, Maine.

[The boy's father] arranged for his son to take College Board examinations in New York after the close of the term here. They were taken without our recommendation. I suppose we might have given our consent had it been asked.

I hope you will feel free to deal with this boy's application in any way you see fit without feeling it will cause us any embarrassment.

Sincerely yours,
George Van Santvoord

The boy did end up at the special school in Maine. Subsequent correspondence, which now included Mr. Lloyd H. Hatch of Maine, reveals that GVS continued to provide advice in the same magnanimous spirit. Yet, for the next half century this thwarted boy would use the Duke to explain away his failure to get into Yale.

"I'm fairly observant of people, always thinking about what really makes them tick," says Art Howe. "There was a lot I didn't understand about the Duke, but in literally hundreds of relationships over many decades, I never saw him do anything deliberately mean or vengeful. I question the motivations and the real source of the problem of people who quote such stories."

This is not to attribute to the Duke some sort of perfection or saintliness. Zeph Stewart '39, a trustee emeritus and lifelong admirer of the Duke, recalls an unfortunate incident: "One of our outstanding classmates, who was an excellent athlete and scholar, had diabetes. He was horribly embarrassed about it and tried to hide his defect, as he saw it, from everyone. At some point this boy was sitting at the headmaster's table, and the Duke asked him loudly something like, 'Do you have a lot of trouble in life dealing with your diabetes?' To GVS, it was an interesting intellectual problem. My classmate, of course, never forgave him.''

In matters large or small, the Duke was all too prone to human fallibility. Even in criticizing Mrs. Wertenbaker over a plethora of details such as misspelled or wrong names, GVS made some similar blunders himself. Perhaps his most revealing error was in identifying the first head of the Hotchkiss board of trustees as Timothy Dwight (instead of Kingsbury). As an undergraduate at Yale, George Van Santvoord had seen the lanky Dwight striding across the campus and, no doubt, assumed that such an august personage played a secondary role to no one – clearly the same conclusion to be drawn from the trustees' final tribute to Dwight.

The Duke, in fact, was not totally immune from lapsing into what he so vehemently condemned. "Rumor had it," he wrote at one point in his critique, "that [Barss] and J. J. ["Doc"] Robinson were very uncongenial." GVS must have had a fair hunch that this was so, since he had been a student at the school when both men were on the faculty. What the Duke did not know was the reason for the strife. He lacked the evidence showing how adamant the seasoned faculty member Barss had been about not having the newcomer Robinson's name listed first in the Latin department section of the school's catalogue. The same sort of elaboration could now be made on the Duke's mystification over the departure of the associate headmaster, Professor Comstock. "Whether he and Coy disliked each other at Andover or drew apart at Hotchkiss, who knows?" GVS wondered at another point. "Mr. Harry L. deForest, who came from Andover, liked and admired both. He once told me their hostility began and developed at Hotchkiss."

Ultimately that was the Duke's purpose in filling up the yellow spiral notebook – to provide information about the Hotchkiss School from his unique vantage point. Other documents which he left behind abound; yet in writing with the ebbing remnants of his strength, whether about the Mid or subjects yet to be excerpted, GVS imbued these final notes* with a circumstantial dimension that in itself is compelling.

"Here he is, trying to the end to set the record straight," wrote Ted Beal in that letter accompanying the notebook. "Perhaps the most interesting passage begins [with] the setting down of what *he* thought he did during his time as headmaster. . . . What he says he did is markedly limited compared to what I think he did – even apart from spirit and leadership. I can't believe he didn't know what he had really done; perhaps he couldn't permit himself to acknowledge it."

ii /   George Van Santvoord much preferred acknowledging the accomplishments of others. And in his view, no one's accomplishments were worthier than those of his interim predecessor, Walter Hull Buell. "He was a splendid teacher, orderly, generous and patient, and very much respected and admired by his pupils," GVS wrote in his unsteady hand. "[He] had been Headmaster of a school in Scranton, Pennsylvania, thus beginning a long and important connection with that town, bringing to Hotchkiss boys from families like Brooks, Connell, Linen, Warren, and Scranton. . . . At Hotchkiss he taught French and German. But he was an expert in classics and my classmates in 1907–1908 read under his guidance the Book of Acts in Greek. In the summer he tutored boys in all the current curriculum except science."

The one idiosyncrasy for which Buell would be remembered by a generation of mercilessly surveillant teenage boys was his laugh. When annoyed, this dignified professorial man with a pointed white goatee, a handsome bald head, and a rimless pince-nez had a habit of emitting what started out as a mirthful sound but came out as more of a bark, which he followed by a snort and a poke at his nose. That mannerism may have been partly responsible for the "Bull" nickname. The boys inevitably imitated him behind his back, and some of the more daring ones vied with each other as to how far they could mimic

---

*Hereafter referred to as such whenever excerpted or used as source material.

him to his face without giving away their game. Professor Buell's wife, whose name was Louise – and who, in the Duke's words, "brought back into the social life of the headmaster's house some persons long alienated" – came to be referred to by the boys as Vesta Buell.

The appointment of Buell as acting headmaster for the King's anticipated sabbatical proved to be providential. "The trustees wish to announce that the sudden death of our headmaster, Dr. Huber G. Buehler, has in no wise altered the plans for the immediate conduct of the school," read the notice "to our patrons and alumni" issued on the day of the King's funeral. Instead of filling in until the King returned, Buell would fill in until a new headmaster had been selected. And there would be no Uncle Joe to contend with at the helm.

Although Buell had no intention of transforming the stand-in position into a career, he did not particularly miss retirement. "We expected, until last spring, to repeat this year some of [our experiences with you] in Europe," he wrote in December of 1924 to Paul Belin, one of those Scranton, Pennsylvania, acquaintances who would send generations of offspring to Hotchkiss. "Fate willed it otherwise, and we are trying to do our best in guiding the fortunes of a school that has grown dearer and dearer to us."

"Doing our best" for Buell meant keeping the status quo. "The masters and the boys have all tried to work in harmony and to make the year as effective as possible," the acting headmaster wrote to Professor Robert D. French, who had briefly taught English at the school before leaving to join the Yale faculty and eventually become master of Jonathan Edwards College. "It is naturally a trying year for the school, and we have not endeavored to do much except to hold to the best of our traditions and steer a straight course on an even keel." Somewhat cryptically, Buell added, "There are, however, things to be done here, and many of the men are aware of the opportunity."

The trustees, in the meantime, were not making much headway in finding a successor. When Coy and Buehler had been selected, no other candidates had come up for serious consideration by the board. But the selection committee appointed shortly after Buehler's death – and headed by the prominent Yale administrator and board president, the earthy Dean Jones – could come to no such agreement. Among the contenders for the post was the history teacher A. B. "Peanut" Hall. As the efficient head of the school's ongoing $1.5 million capital fund drive, he enjoyed a particularly high visibility among the trustees. But he was approaching fifty, and having spent half of his life teaching at the school, he may have been considered too set in his ways. Moreover, as a would-be successor to the King and the Bull, Hall was burdened with a nickname which could hardly project the appropriate image of the school. After several meetings of the selection committee and considerable wrangling over many months, no decision could be reached.

The search for a new head, at that point, was temporarily given up. At a meeting held on March 20, 1925, the acting headmaster, Walter Hull Buell, was appointed as full-fledged headmaster, his salary was almost doubled to $7,500, and he was made a member of the trustees and of the governing board. "Yes, we are settled in the headmaster's house at Hotchkiss for another year at least," Buell wrote enthusiastically to a friend in Minneapolis. "It was certainly kind of the trustees and I am hoping that we shall be able to make good and do something for the school." And Buell personally felt up to the task. Though approaching seventy, he could still outdo most of the boys on the frequent treks he led over the hilly terrain well beyond the boundaries of the school.

Whether deliberately or through lack of sensitivity, the president of the board, Dean Jones, reminded Buell of the facts of life. After congratulating him by letter on June 25, 1925, "on the success of the year at Hotchkiss," Jones wrote, "I can appreciate from my own feeling how much you desire to be freed from the burdensome duties of office and how much it means to you to give up your European trip in order to continue service to the school." Jones attributed a similar appreciation of Buell's desires to other trustees as well, concluding, "We all realize this, and we shall make every effort to relieve you in the near future, although at the present time I must confess we are quite at sea as to the man to pick as successor."

Buell hardly felt put upon by the board's predicament of remaining "quite at sea." It was with renewed confidence if not gusto that the Bull declared in chapel, after firing a boy, "Hotchkiss will lower her standards for no one!" And he was no longer loath to consider long-range moves. Following the rioting by the Riis Camp contingent during that summer of 1925, Buell not only abolished the camp but set up a summer program for boys from Hotchkiss and similar schools, putting his colleague Lawrence "Spud" Murphy in charge. Over the next thirty-eight years, this summer school would save countless Hotchkiss boys from needlessly flunking out and help countless others to meet the school's entrance requirements.

With no apparent candidate on the horizon by the following April, it must have looked to Buell as if his tenure would be extended still another year "at least." Buell's one reservation concerned timing. Having already canceled two European trips and about to cancel a third, he asked for more advance notice in the future. Thus, at a board meeting on April 14, 1926, the future policy of the school established February 15 as the deadline by which any notice must be given to terminate "the headmaster's and masters' employment" for that school year.

It did not work out that way. With the sudden, unanimous election less than two months later of George Van Santvoord as the school's fourth headmaster — effective July 1, 1926 — the Bull found himself retired at least a year earlier than he had anticipated and with less than four weeks' notice. In a lengthy tribute to their colleague, the trustees betrayed their embarrassment, concluding, "We extend to him and to Mrs. Buell assurances of our profound gratitude and affection." (In tributes to other notables of the school, "expressions" rather than "assurances" had always sufficed.) As if to prove further they meant it, the trustees bestowed on Buell an honorarium of $5,000 and gave him the title of headmaster emeritus.

Buell responded in the best Hotchkiss tradition. Whatever pique he might have felt was offset by his respect and affection for George Van Santvoord, whom he had already befriended when the future headmaster was a student at the school. In fact, when Buell had first taken over the reins after Buehler's death, he had asked the trustees to bring in the then-assistant professor at Yale to help him run the school. But GVS had already made a commitment to head the English department at the University of Buffalo. As GVS recalled on that tape with Mrs. Wertenbaker, his eventual appointment came about in a somewhat haphazard way: "I was to go down from Buffalo and speak at a Yale News dinner, and I had a letter or a telegram from Dean Jones, saying, 'Come and see me in New Haven.' I didn't know what it was all about. But I had to go there anyway, and so I did see him. Then he said, 'Would you take it?' I said, 'Well, it had never occurred to me they were thinking about me, but yes, if you want me to, I think I would.' And that was all there was to that."

Buell's departure for Europe began a new chapter in his relationship with the school. "Old Hotchkiss boys have greeted us on the streets of various cities and one is expected here next week," Buell wrote in another open letter, this one to the *Record* from Florence. "The world is small and the Hotchkiss fellowship unlimited. . . . Nothing which the boy does in school will be lost to the man in the future. The languages which he studies, the history and literature which he absorbs, the bits of information which he picks up about art, archaeology, etc., will some day prove useful. The past year has established contact for us with the names and works of many men who have enriched their native cities and the world by the breadth of their interests and the loftiness of their aims. May there be not one but many sons of Hotchkiss who will make her name famous for sound scholarship, broad culture, and high spiritual endeavor!"

The Bull continued to stay in close touch with Hotchkiss from his home in Bronxville, New York. Even after the death of his wife in 1935, the headmaster emeritus continued to take private pupils, and at age eighty was still helping to prepare boys for the school. When he died in 1944, he left the bulk of his estate to Hotchkiss, which made him one of the school's more generous benefactors up to that time.

In writing this relatively placid finish to the life of Walter Hull Buell and his wife, it would be a significant omission not to follow up on

Roberta Buehler, the Queen, who had played such an integral role in the affairs of the school. "Dr. Buehler and his wife were one," Buell had declared at his predecessor's memorial service. The trustees had voted to continue her husband's salary for a year and thereafter provided the Queen with the same pension the King would have received if he had served until his retirement at age sixty-five. The monthly amount was to be $188.70, about what a senior faculty member was paid.

As was the custom at that time for grieving individuals of her former means, Mrs. Buehler departed promptly with her daughter, Barbara, for Europe. One of the boys who had graduated in that last class of 1924, John D. Leggett, Jr., ran into the pair in Paris that summer. "I got the impression Mrs. Buehler wasn't too well off," he recalls. This may have been partly because the former queen had depleted her reserves through her regal spending ways and partly because she and her daughter had been robbed. "I still remember seeing the bare footprint they showed me on the ledge outside of their hotel window," says John Hoysradt, who met up with his aunt and cousin in the French capital. "They had an awful time trying to get new passports and papers at the American embassy."

After her return from Europe, Roberta Buehler settled near the school where she had been the queen for so many years. It was not a fortunate choice, if only because the reminders of another era were all around. And while no one in the community was challenging the Buehlers' role in building up the school, a certain amount of revisionism had set in. "The school had become fashionable, thanks to Mrs. Buehler's throwing house parties on weekends for the socially prominent," observes Archibald C. Coolidge, who had been hired as an English teacher not long after the Buehler era ended. "But she had been spending an awful lot of money. I understand that Rob Scoville, who was treasurer, said that if Dr. Buehler hadn't died when he did, this business of spending money simply would have had to stop. The Buehlers' household was costing something like forty thousand dollars a year – at a time when starting faculty salaries were still fifteen hundred, with an occasional raise of a few hundred dollars." Also well known throughout the Hotchkiss community was the tidbit that after the trustees had authorized Mrs. Buehler to take with her from the headmaster's house those pieces of furniture with special sentimental value, she interpreted the gesture more liberally than anyone had anticipated.

John Hoysradt takes up the story of his Aunt Roberta: "For several years, she lived down the hill from the school where Mr. White, a Latin teacher, lived later on. She was never happy there because instead of being the headmaster's wife, she lived in a small house away from the center of it all. Later on, she had to move even further down the hill. She told Denison Fish, who taught music in my day and had been a close friend of the Buehlers, that she thought about doing away with herself. He earnestly tried to talk her out of it and went over the situation with her. But it didn't work. One day she took a train to Philadelphia and checked into the Bellevue Stratford, which was then the ritziest hotel in town. She asked for a room high up to be away from the noise – and then threw herself out of the window. She was decapitated on striking the glass marquee down below. I don't think her suicide was related to her husband's death as much as to not being Mrs. Buehler, the Queen of Hotchkiss, anymore."

At the time of Roberta Buehler's death in 1930, the trustees entered into the minutes a tribute which read, in part, "She gave herself unsparingly to the task that fell to her during the years of Dr. Buehler's life, and faced with rare courage the suffering and sorrow that came to her at his death."

iii / "I graduated from Hotchkiss in 1908. Six years later my world burst into flames, and much that was of most value and importance to me was destroyed," the new headmaster would note later in life. "There seemed to be everywhere a perverse insistence on taking the wrong turn, and on following courses that were disastrous, obviously leading to misfortune and catastrophe. From the end of the War in 1918 until 1928 this continued. Many were unnerved, depressed, and even desperate. Some concluded that they at least must see to it that they should build their own lives into structures that might have some strength, validity, and constructive purpose. . . . If a man cannot solve all the resulting problems and dangers, he can at least set himself to work doing something with his own life which will embody and symbolize his own ideals and aspirations. He may not transform the world, but he can cultivate his own garden and make some good things grow.''

Those words serve as an eloquent summary of George Van Santvoord's purpose at Hotchkiss. He had witnessed the senseless atrocities of World War I, the trench warfare which snuffed out promising youthful lives (the Hotchkiss machine gun was one of the foremost weapons) and left others permanently crippled. Of the forty-four freshmen in 1913 at Oriel College, Oxford, where he studied as a Rhodes Scholar after graduating from Yale, by 1918 half had been killed by enemy fire. "I knew personally many who are become as though they had never been born," he wrote. The same was true of his students at Winchester College, a traditional English public school where he taught briefly just prior to the United States' entry into the war.

"He never talked about the war, and then suddenly one day, we were in his study when something triggered it," recalls his stepdaughter, Allelu Kurten. "He turned and started to tell me about it, and he made it live – the trenches, the mud, the dirt, the stupidity of it. It was so horrendous that I remember it to this day. The sheer horror of it came to me, the death of all these young people, the senseless death. He had been a volunteer in the ambulance corps prior to U.S. entry into the war.* I think the memory of taking bodies of the wounded and the dying off the battlefields of that war never left him. Later, he was a lieutenant at the front and was decorated for an action in which his arm was nearly blown off. He spent close to a year in a French hospital. I did see his arm once, when he was fishing in a

---

* This ambulance corps eventually became the American Field Service, an international youth exchange program headed for many years by the Duke's friend Arthur Howe, Jr. '38.

T-shirt, and he had to support it when casting." It also left him without strength in his grip for shaking hands, which most people attributed to a typically incongruous personality quirk. Never did the Duke publicly mention his disabling wound.

As headmaster of the Hotchkiss School, George Van Santvoord had his own garden to tend "and make things grow." Perhaps symbolically, the tall, rugged thirty-five-year-old with an inherently aristocratic demeanor was talented at the real thing, too. Gardening was one of his countless avocations, and to this day the school grounds are graced with bushes and shrubs which GVS personally planted with the Hotchkiss virtuoso gardener, John Cardoza. ("Mr. Cardoza could make grass grow on a bald man's head," GVS once remarked with admiration.) Possessed of an encyclopedic knowledge of flowers and ferns, the Duke also showed his mastery in coaxing vegetables out of the ground during World War II. He often said he learned a great deal about his faculty members by the way they tended their victory garden plots. "No two people did it the same. It was like the touch of different people on the piano; some of them much better at it than others, and it wasn't the amount of time they spent on it, either. The plants know the difference."

When he first took charge of the school, GVS had yet to perfect some of his cultivating skills. He did not appear to be the assured headmaster that he would become – perhaps reverting to his days as a student at Hotchkiss, when he was voted "the meekest" by his classmates. In reckoning Dr. Buehler's aloofness as a means of compensating for a basic shyness, GVS perhaps revealed the cause of his own often abrupt manner. Among those who remember the new headmaster's first days is Lewis A. Lapham '27, who had come to Hotchkiss from San Francisco in the fall of 1923:

"My prep year we had Dr. Buehler, who died at the end of that year. Then we had a holdover, Dr. Buell, for two years, and then Van Santvoord arrived for our senior year. By that time we thought we knew all about the care and house training of headmasters. We filed into the first chapel the first day he was there. As seniors we all sat down in the front, and we expected him to say he was a new boy and that he was going to like us and that we'd like him, et cetera. Nothing. Right straight into the service.

"He was to teach a class in senior English, which I happened to be in. I remember our first assignment was on the bulletin board. Mostly you didn't bother much the first couple of days about assignments, but I cheated a bit and looked at the material, which turned out to be my luck.

"We went into the classroom and Van Santvoord read the roll. He called us all 'mister,' and that upset us a little bit. In writing he had a kind of a Greek script, and he had put on the board, 'God.' Just God, underlined. And when he got finished calling the roll, he ran his hand down the list and said, 'Mr. Lapham, please address yourself to that topic.'

"I arrived at the blackboard with a piece of chalk. It was me and God and that piece of chalk. I had a lot of Sunday school training as a child; so I just made up my mind. While he turned to address the class, I put down everything I had ever heard or thought about God, and what I had read in *Paradise Lost*. I covered half the blackboard, and to this day I'd give forty dollars to see what it was I wrote. I got back to my seat, the bell rang, and Van Santvoord said, 'The next time, the next two hundred lines in *Paradise Lost*. I hope the class will be better prepared than it was today.' When we got out in the corridor we wondered, 'What the hell kind of a guy was this?' I don't know if he ever read what I wrote on the board. He never talked to me about it, but that was our introduction to Van Santvoord."

Lewis Lapham soon got to know G V S better: "I was president of the class, and we had a couple of robberies, out of bureau drawers or something, and I saw quite a lot of the Duke for a couple of weeks. He was advising me as to what the class ought to do and how we ought to do it. I don't remember what came out of it, but I realized he was extraordinarily kind. He used to take me aside and ask me how I was getting along. Then when I was at Yale, he came down a couple of times a year, and he'd take me and Roberto Heurtematte [Lapham's Hotchkiss and Yale roommate] out to dinner. Once he spent the night on the sofa in our room. I was very high on the Duke. I subsequently became, I think, a great pal. I corresponded with him long after college. I thought he was fine, but he sure had problems with a lot of the parents because he was quite off-handed about things. My wife gets irritated still today when she thinks about his attitude during the time our sons were there.

"But the incident I remember best has nothing to do with that. We had off-loaded Lewis, our older son, in Main where he had to check in after the weekend. Van Santvoord was there in the corridor talking to a prep. He saw us come in, and he just beckoned me over, and he said to the prep, 'This is Mr. Lewis Lapham, a distinguished graduate of the school.' Then he said, 'Now, Lewis, if you had committed a murder in Saigon, and you had only a motorcycle on which to escape, into which countries could you escape?' This was back in 1949, long before anybody had ever heard of Saigon. I said, 'Mr. Van Santvoord, if I went north I'd be in China. If I went northwest I'd be in Laos. If I went south I'd be in Thailand.' The Duke then said to the prep, 'Now you see the advantages of a Hotchkiss education.' And he turned and left. This prep had his mouth wide open, and I said to him, 'You want to know why I know that? Because I'm in the shipping business, and I run ships to the South Pacific. I look at a map of the area every day. If I was running ships to South Africa, I wouldn't have had a clue.'"

It had not been merely by chance that the Duke had queried the then-president of Grace Lines about Southeast Asia rather than Africa. As headmaster, GVS took the same sort of interest in each boy, knowing his special strengths and interests. And when the Duke remarked to the prep, "Now you see the advantages of a Hotchkiss education," he was summarizing, beyond the obvious flippancy, his lifelong educational goal. Among the qualities GVS included in defining a gentleman was the Renaissance concept of taking for one's province all human endeavors. He wanted Hotchkiss boys to understand the world around them – its beauties and its challenges – in terms significant to their own lives. "One of the most valuable things [a student has to learn] is how to spend time when he is not working at routine tasks," GVS said in his speech to the *Yale Daily News* in 1926, on the same visit to New Haven that he was offered the headmastership. "Our aim is not to teach a man how to earn his living, but rather how to be a finer human being." The Duke deplored the idea of studying anything merely to pass a test. In fact, his own parting from Yale had come partly from academia's insistence on testing professors by its "publish or perish" requirements, which he believed often served to promote the author rather than knowledge. "What shall we do about poor Socrates who was so foolish as to publish nothing?" GVS asked his *Daily News* audience. "Fortunately, for his fame with posterity, his disciple Plato wrote for him, so that we know perhaps more about Socrates than any other man who ever lived. But he did not advertise himself."

The Duke's paramount interest was in teaching boys, in imparting to them wisdom and making them think. "What is it that a poor man leaves in the dirt and a rich man puts in his pocket?" the Duke would query a senior Bible class. After an appropriate pause of stumped silence, he would put his finger to one nostril and make as if he were about to blow his nose, explaining, "That's the poor man's way." On another occasion, he would seek to put a nervous student at ease: "If what you have to say isn't more important than your standing up and saying it, then you might as well sit down." The Duke's ways of making the materials unforgettable were likely to shock his colleagues. "How would you like to live in a town called Shittim?" he would ask deadpan in that Bible class. "Do you suppose it was anything like living in Greenwich, Connecticut? And what kind of a sewage system do you imagine they had in Shittim in those days?" He also taught a class in Latin for boys who had hopelessly failed Latin 1b, the most elementary course offered. It was variously called Latin 1c or 1z or 1x. Much to the encouragement of one boy who could never quite figure out the difference between declensions and conjugations, the Duke awarded him almost full credit for the wrong endings which the boy had in desperation devised. "I think some of them showed a great deal of inventiveness," GVS said magnanimously, puffing on his pipe. "Besides, there are no set endings in life. We all have to be constantly devising our own." I happened to be that boy, and it was the single most valuable lesson I learned at Hotchkiss and at Yale.

iv /   GVS often likened the academic standards of the Hotchkiss School at the time he became headmaster to Procrustes' bed. Procrustes was a mythical highwayman who stretched or amputated the limbs of vic-tim-travelers to make them fit to the length of his bed. "Our boys were all promoted, the bright ones and the stupid ones, the industrious ones and the other ones. Hardly anybody got held back. The good ones were told to go slowly, so as not to leave the other ones too far behind. The stupid ones would have to study all summer."

Endemic to virtually all college preparatory schools of that era, the situation was largely created by the demands of the college entrance examinations. As the Duke explained, "They tended to freeze the cur-riculum. Everybody read the same works. The English examination, for instance, depended on a very close reading of Macbeth, Milton's minor poems, Burke's 'Speech on Conciliation,' and some essays of Macaulay and Samuel Johnson. You went through those with a fine tooth comb. It didn't mean that anyone had to read widely. The library at Hotchkiss was negligible when I came there. It was in charge of a boy who was going through on a scholarship, and it was open – if he remembered – for about an hour after lunch each day, and all books were behind glass doors, and he had the key. None of the schools had very good libraries then.

"By the time World War I ended, a whole lot of new and younger people were beginning to come into the schools and say, 'This is ter-ribly dull to teach Burke's 'Speech on Conciliation,' which somebody had decided in the 1890's – the Carnegie Foundation or somebody – that this is something the boys should read. And Macaulay's essays were going out of style as a literary fashion anyway, so that the mate-rial itself they had put in was under attack, and they just said, 'These are stupid things to take. We would rather have more freedom.' Of course, some of the older people were perfectly content to stay in the old harness. One school where I was invited to meet with some of the trustees [before coming to Hotchkiss] with the idea that maybe I'd be their headmaster, I said, 'We can go way ahead of what you're doing now.' I told them some of the things that I thought ought to be done, and they were very much shocked. This seemed to them almost destroying the whole academic structure they knew."

The faculty which George Van Santvoord inherited in 1926 was predominantly of the old school. To be sure, there were exceptions, including a few of the old-timers such as Dr. J. J. Robinson, who led his Latin classes in singing "Gaudeamus Igitur" and digressed so often to fascinating but seemingly unrelated topics that some of his students worried about how well prepared they would be for their college boards. Most of Doc Rob's contemporaries, however, prided themselves on being able to drill material into their students' heads and have them retain it long enough to excel on their college boards. Some of the old-timers, like Dr. Brown, could even predict with astounding certainty many of the questions that would be asked on the Greek section of the test. "Lester Dorman Brown, Doc Brown, was famous for getting all his people the highest marks on the Greek college boards," says Zeph Stewart, who is director of the Center for Hellenic Studies in Washington, D.C. "He was a marvellous teacher and showed me the power of old-fashioned discipline." Yet, so absorbed sometimes was Doc Brown in exercising this old-fashioned discipline that he failed to convey the greater meaning beyond. "I remember the Duke saying to me that he didn't think that it ever occurred to Dr. Brown that Homer was a poet," recalls Archibald Coolidge, one of the first group of teachers hired by the Duke. "But to some extent, that was part of the age and that generation. Alfred Hall, whom I liked very much and who was a very good man in a great many ways, taught memorizing facts of American history for the college boards. That's the way you got through." Richard Bacon '30, who returned, at the invitation of the Duke, to teach Latin and Greek at Hotchkiss for the next thirty years, elaborates: "A. B. Hall, otherwise known as Peanut Hall, taught American history four periods a week, and each period he had a ten-minute quiz. You read so many pages for the next assignment and you assimilated the facts. Okay, 'How many men went down with the sinking of the Maine in the harbor at Havana?' I think I wrote two hundred and seventy-five. Whatever the figure was, I had the right number. But the paper came back the next day all scratched out in red ink. 'Two hundred and seventy-two men, three officers.' I thought, 'Why you so-and-so!' Fortunately, I had a chance also to see a different side. I had taken my college board in English at the end of upper middle year, and there were about ten or twelve of us who had done well enough on that exam to be put in a select, if you will, a select section of senior English. In that case McChesney was free to do what he wanted. That course really meant something because this was literature and not, 'Who was Silas Marner, and when did he live and what did he do?'"

If Mr. Mac was fast becoming the most popular teacher at the school, Estill, nevertheless, remained the sentimental favorite, a living embodiment of Hotchkiss as an institution. "In those days, he seemed to be older than God," says Lewis Lapham. "White hair, ruddy face, mustache, deep voice – quite a character." As Uncle Joe shuffled along the long corridor in Main toward his excuse office domain, he was likely to be besieged by a veritable flock of boys, vying for his attention with their heartrending reasons for lateness or missed appointments. Uncle Joe enjoyed playing the never-ending game of try to fool me. He had a well-known routine of coming to class and, weather permitting, opening the window so that he could spit out unimpeded throughout the period. More than once the students distracted his attention long enough to close the window. They then tried to stifle their snickers as Uncle Joe continued spitting during the rest of the class as if the window had not been closed.

Estill, of course, had his difficult, opinionated side. "He always reminded me of a sort of a Colonel Blimp," says Lapham. He was famous for his tenacious bridge and golf playing, and the *Mischianza* in 1926 voted a special honorable mention for "the bold preacher who dared to denounce golf and bridge while the chapel service was being conducted by Uncle Joe." Estill was also the man who mobilized the forces of reaction on the faculty – including such stalwarts as Peanut

Hall, Doc Brown and Pop Jefferson – against the former meek student who had now come back to tell them how *their* school should be run.

A staunch ally of GVS from the beginning was Carle Parsons, whom the headmaster had first met as a fellow student on that Albany train. In a taped interview with Mrs. Wertenbaker shortly before he died in 1965, Carle Parsons recalled one of the first faculty meetings presided over by GVS: "It was sort of an inquisition, and I got madder and madder but fortunately, kept my mouth shut. When we left the meeting, I followed Mr. Jefferson down the hall. In those days, the masters' smoking room was right beside the reception room just inside the front door. When we got there, I lit into Pop, and I said, 'I know I'm one of the younger men here, but I'm sick and tired of this idea that a certain handful on the faculty think that they have the welfare of the school in the palm of their hand.' I said, 'I think it's absolutely insufferable for them to question the headmaster the way they did tonight.' Well Pop backed up against the radiator and said, 'Why Carle, you're practically accusing me of disloyalty!' I said, 'I don't give a hoot what you call it. I'm just furious that you and those others would carry on this way.' And I said, 'If anybody comes along the hall, we'll call this off, and tomorrow, when I've calmed down, I'll come up to your room, and I'll say this over again because I believe it from the bottom of my soul.' Well, someone did come along, and we quit. But I knew this would get around. The others involved were Mr. Hall, who had a very orderly mind and politic manner, and Uncle Joe, who could make me madder than any man I've known. I don't recall how many days passed. I was on the morning train going to New York, and Mr. Hall was on the train, and I thought, 'Now, this is going to be fun to watch. I know that he knows that I lit into Pop. I know that Pop's told him, and I know he's going to pour oil on the waters, and just how he's going to begin to use the squirt gun, I don't know.' But he finally got up from his seat and came and joined me, and it was just fascinating to watch him sort of ease up to the subject in his suave, logical manner."

GVS took a philosophical stance in faculty confrontations of this sort. Never raising his voice, he showed his irritation only by addressing Doc Brown or whoever was taking him on with a frosty "Sir" – the same as in his student days. Recalls Archibald Coolidge, "I remember the Duke saying to me of some of the older masters who were a trial to him, 'Well, if I can keep my temper longer than they can, they'll die or resign first.'

This would indeed take patience. "My guess is from '26, oh, for the next ten years, the Duke must have had a very difficult time with his faculty," says Dick Bacon, who entered Hotchkiss as a lower mid at the beginning of the Duke's second year. "When the Duke tried to introduce things and bring the school up to date, in one way or another, there was invariably this, 'No, no, no, at Hotchkiss it's never done this way, and we see no reason why it ever should be.' And of course, these people were entrenched because they'd been around here for years. But eventually, they began to retire, and the Duke was bringing in his own faculty, much younger in age, and in general began to mold them in the way he thought that things should be done. Along towards the last few years before the war, the Duke had pretty much his own faculty, and we would argue and dispute in meetings. The Duke would be sitting there at his desk, chain smoking, just calmly listening. Finally, when he figured everybody had shot his mouth too much, he would say, 'Well, gentlemen, any further comment? I hear no comment? Therefore we will now do it this way.'"

v / To free the school from the academic version of Procrustes' bed, one of G V S's first innovations was to create advanced levels in all the major courses of study. If Uncle Joe Estill, as head of the mathematics department, had protested the creation of advanced math (or Math V, as it eventually came to be designated), it was at least partly because he did not know any calculus – just as some of the other long-time stalwarts would have been at a loss to teach anything beyond the very limited material they mastered so rigidly well. But it was not only these faculty fossils who sought to put a brake on the Duke's pedagogic ideas. "In making any curriculum for Hotchkiss we are limited somewhat by the exacting requirements for admission to college," an unidentified master was quoted in 1927 in the *Record*. "No very sweeping changes could be made at present, even if we should wish to make them." Although the college boards began to loosen up considerably in the thirties, the questions continued to be more a test of short-term memory than of genuine understanding. Ironically, that would be a dilemma still unresolved at the end of the Hotchkiss first century – and debated with ever more insistence. To what extent should Hotchkiss be "covering material" for the sake of tests at the expense of useful, lifelong command of the subject matter? Students thus continued to agonize on tests, "My God, is that the third provision of Jay's Treaty or the fourth?" Or, "Am I getting my political and economic causes of World War I mixed up?"

Unable to entirely unshackle the school, GVS sought to expand the boys' horizons with a variety of liberating steps. Perhaps his most revolutionary move was to bring in a full-time teacher of art. This was a subject which no comparable prep school offered as a part of the regular curriculum. Singing and musical instruction had, of course, always been included for the practical reason that each of these religiously concerned schools needed somebody to play the organ in chapel and train the choir to dispatch heavenward praise. But instruction in art? What did that have to do with passing college boards or anything else besides being a frivolous distraction?

The Duke's choice was a recent Yale graduate, Robert Osborn, from Oshkosh, Wisconsin, who was in Paris trying to become a great American artist before he ran out of funds. When Osborn realized he would not meet that deadline, he wrote the Duke to take him up on his invitation to come and teach art. "There was no reply and no reply," recalls the debonair eighty-eight-year-old artist, who still resides only a few miles from the school. "The money was getting short indeed. Finally, I was down to about a hundred and fifty dollars when the cable came. I picked it up at Morgan and Company. I opened it, and it said, 'Yes, do come. We'd love to have you.' I still have chills when I tell you this." What Osborn did not know on receiving that telegram was that the Duke had apparently decided to reach into his own pocket for Osborn's first year's pay.

Robert Osborn: "I was in heaven; imagine having a job, *and* encountering that marvellous landscape. It was 1929 and the Depression was taking place. People were losing jobs all over, and here you had a room which was on the third floor of the headmaster's house looking out over the lake, and you had food and heat and were paid twelve hundred dollars for the year. That was mightily solid and comfortable in those times, I assure you. Too, there was the excitement of starting something new like that, particularly when you began to see it working. The thing started out down in the basement of the headmaster's house. The ceiling, I'd say, was about seven and a half feet. It was very low, just a basement. But we whitewashed all the stones and the walls, so it became a very pleasant room. You could look out at the lake and your eyes were right on ground level beneath the big back porch. We put a small stove down there so we would be warm.

"I had a still life or something set up, and we had every prep come down for an hour just to check them out and see if there were any students we ought to be encouraging. We ended up with a group which varied year by year; maybe eight, maybe ten, maybe twelve. I had a two-seater, open Ford, which I had bought for about twenty dollars, secondhand. It also had a back seat. So, on any of those wonderful, explosive holidays the boys who wanted to go out and paint or draw all day, would pick up picnic lunches and we'd set off. I can tell you it was very pleasant. At the Duke's behest, I also went down to the public school in Lakeville to teach there once a week."

Bob Osborn sought to accent the artistic sensitivities in every way: "That long corridor as you go down toward the dining hall from the headmaster's house was an ideal place to show things. We put up beaver board that you could put thumbtacks into. I began making exhibits so that the lads going by could see them. I had beautiful prints from France and put those up. But everyone was walking right by, not even looking at them. I sensed that I was going to have to do something to capture their attention. I began using cartoons either to kid them or say, 'Look at this or that!' Pretty soon they did begin to notice. I developed a whole set of exhibits on what design is, what pattern is, what texture is, what form is. I was turning those out once a week, which was quite a task, but it was keeping the whole thing fresh. In the process, quite a technique for teaching art evolved. And pretty soon people of the Art Association began to ask me to explain this method and how one did it.

"Among the young men in my classes, Bill Kienbusch ['32] became an outstanding American artist. His father being German – a collector of armor which he gave to the Met – was really tough on the boy. Kienbusch told me later how much difference the art work made by just having somebody there encouraging him instead of saying, 'Do this, do that!' the authoritarian style. So you felt that.

"There was one boy who came along, Richard Rossbach ['32]. He was a very lean, handsome Jewish boy, and he really had it. If you were sitting here and you gave him that amount of clay, the perception of your head was so good, so prompt, that he could make an impressive likeness in no time at all. I'd never seen anything like it. Rodin came to mind later. It used to take my breath away. However, when he got out, and I guess he went to Yale, he was forced into Wall Street by his family, swept into the making of money. His older brother, who was also here, became a well-known judge in New York. But the artistic Rossbach, you never heard of him again, and he probably became richer."

In his fifth year at the school, Bob Osborn had a perforated ulcer, and the school's physician, Dr. Harry Wieler, rushed him to a hospital in Pittsfield: "Dr. Wieler rode all the way in, sitting beside me in the back of the ambulance. They didn't have antibiotics in those days, and three days after the operation they called my mother to come out from Oshkosh. It was apparently nip and tuck. George Van Santvoord also came to see me. I was at that time teaching a class in religion and Greek philosophy with him, which was quite trying, I can tell you. Now he wanted to know what the assignment should be for next week, and there I was barely holding on!"

Getting that assignment was obviously not among the reasons the Duke had made the eighty-mile round trip drive. "Robert Osborn . . . brought gaiety and good cheer to the school," George Van Santvoord wrote in his final notes. "A very serious illness and operation ended his stay at the school. It was commemorated by his sketch of Drs. [Harry] Wieler and Reynolds examining what looked like a long garden hose. The title read, 'Harry, we're looking for a slow leak.'"

vi / **B**ob Osborn recovered to go on to cartooning fame, and Tom Blagden '29 took over the teaching of art, joining a faculty on which the Duke had already begun putting a notable imprint. As was the case with Tom Blagden, some of the Duke's new teachers were former Hotchkiss boys, although that was nowhere near the top of the qualifications he was looking for. "In the first place, you try to get people who are interested in boys," GVS told Mrs. Wertenbaker. "Some of the old-timers weren't interested in that, really. A faculty member shouldn't be like the bank officer who only cares about the status of the customer's loan, and once that is paid off, loses all interest and most likely wouldn't know that customer if he came back in a few years." Second, GVS wanted faculty members who would teach not only the subject, such as Greek, but also the architecture, the drama, the government, the law, the philosophy, and every other aspect of life connected with that subject. "That way, even if the boy drops the subject after his exams, he's still got something for life," noted GVS. "Of course, our aim was not to teach the boy in a way that made him feel he knew enough about a particular subject to last him for the rest of his life, but to inspire him with a lifelong interest to learn more." The third criterion for GVS was the variety of the teacher's previous experience, which was not quite so readily defined. Although many of the newcomers had spent at least a year in Europe, one science teacher found himself on the faculty because he had mentioned to the Duke the successful Caesarean section he had performed on a goat. More typically atypical, however, is the story of Archibald Coolidge:

"My freshman year at Harvard I was very much impressed by a classmate who had everything I did not. I hate the word, but he was sophisticated. He was very good looking. He was beautifully dressed. He was extremely intelligent, and he came from a very wealthy family. I said something about this man to my roommate, who had gone to Andover, and he said, 'Oh, he went to Hotchkiss!' I was so impressed by this fellow that I thought the school that turned out somebody like that really must be quite a school.*

"When I decided to write to various schools saying that I would be interested in getting a teaching job, I wrote to Hotchkiss and didn't get an answer. I got answers from other schools but not from Hotchkiss. So, I sent a copy of my original letter and wrote a nasty little note saying I was very much surprised that a school with its reputation hadn't bothered to answer my first letter. I was at Oxford at that time, and I promptly got a nice letter from George Van Santvoord saying that his answer must have gone astray in the mails. He said I sounded like the sort of person they'd be interested in, but he was afraid there would be nothing for the next year.

"I came back to this country at the end of July, and I made a date to go up and see him. He met me in the little railroad station at Millerton, and he had a lot of timetables on his lap. He said he was going to take a trip someplace or other. He spread the timetables out in front of us and he covered the name, but not the initials, of the railroad with his hand. Then he asked me what railroad it was. I almost guessed Louisville and Nashville for 'L & N', but was too rattled to risk it. He said, 'You're not very good.' But we continued to talk, and eventually he asked me what I had written my B.Litt. thesis on. Well, I'd written it on the reaction against the French heroic romance, and the reaction to an extent took the form of some rather scandalous novelettes. He said, 'What kind of an impression do you think it would make on a head-

---

* And who was that Hotchkiss sophisticate at Harvard? In preparing this centennial history, a request for reminiscences in the *Hotchkiss Magazine* brought forth this response from John A. Carter '33 of Fairhope, Alabama, shortly before his death: "Did you know that Arch Coolidge came to Hotchkiss because at Harvard he admired Fred V. Field '22 so much? Fred went to jail in the '50s for contempt of McCarthyites. He wouldn't squeal on his friends. His book *From Right to Left* is fascinating – especially the chapter about his showing Mexico City to Marilyn Monroe."

master when you're looking for a job to say that you chose a subject about really indecent literature?' I was sufficiently annoyed by then to say, 'Well, anybody who took that attitude I shouldn't care to work for anyway.' He said, 'You've answered these questions a great deal better than I think I would. I hope very much you come to work for us.'"

Archibald Coolidge would spend two decades teaching English at Hotchkiss – and acquire the nickname "Starchie Archie" – before leaving in the early fifties to become headmaster of Manlius Military Academy. During its first century, Hotchkiss would serve as the training ground for more than a half dozen future headmasters of other schools. Another career goal for promising members of the faculty was to depart after a much shorter stay to pursue their interests at a higher level, usually Yale. This inevitably deprived the school of some of its most talented young teachers, whether the brilliant "fair-haired boy" of the 1950s, Charles Garside, who could light a lifelong intellectual flame even within the most fireproof brains;* or his contemporary, the dashing Lothario with a generous heart and understanding mind, Louis Connick '41, whom legions of boys hoped to emulate – some rendering to him the ultimate tribute of offering their older sisters as potential dates. Alas, both Charlie and Louis left to do graduate work and teach at Yale. A generation earlier, Robert D. French moved on to Yale to become, eventually, master of Jonathan Edwards College, and Harry R. Rudin, to head the history department there. Gordon S. Haight, who taught English at Hotchkiss from 1925 to 1930, was another of these transient faculty luminaries – and one of whom John Hersey has a lifelong memory:

"Gordon Haight put me in a seminar of four students on nineteenth-century English novels – his lifetime field of scholarship. He eventually wrote a superb biography of George Eliot and edited her letters, and when the British could finally face placing someone who had lived

---

*When Charlie Garside left after only two years at Hotchkiss, the senior class dedicated the *Mischianza* to him – an honor normally bestowed only after decades of teaching.

in sin with a man in the sacrosanct Poet's Corner in Westminster Abbey, Gordon Haight was the man invited to make the address – remarkable that an American was invited to speak on such an occasion. Anyway, he brought to life those nineteenth-century novelists for us students in a way I've never forgotten.

"More than thirty years passed, and I was invited to become Master of Pierson College at Yale. One of the main reasons I wanted to accept was because Haight had held that post, and the idea of following in his footsteps thrilled me. Shortly after my wife and I moved to New Haven, he invited us to dinner at his house. After we ate, he disappeared into his study, and he came out and put into my wife's hands papers I'd written as an upper mid at Hotchkiss! You can imagine what that meant to me. But then he said, in his typical caustic way, in case I might have a swelled head coming on, 'Hersey, don't get the idea that yours are the only Hotchkiss papers I have in my office. I have lots.'"

As much as he undoubtedly regretted losing the likes of Gordon Haight, the Duke had the ability to set aside parochial interests and counsel the departing masters to do what was genuinely best for them. Most of these teachers were single, living in a room or two on a corridor with the boys, often sharing their facilities, which made the logistics of any replacement a simple affair. And there were many young men who were eager to fill the teaching ranks under the leadership of the Duke. "One of the things that impressed me the year I was teaching," says Edmund K. Trent '32, John Hersey's roommate at the school, who briefly joined the Hotchkiss faculty before taking up law, "was the devotion of the masters to teaching the boys. That was their whole interest, to do a good job teaching. At faculty meetings, it was always, 'What about so-and-so, what can we do to help him?' There was one boy, a senior, who came to see me and said, 'You once told me if I ever needed any help, to call on you. I think I do now.' This was in the spring, and he was trying to get into Yale. He asked me what he should do. I said, 'Mr. Taber mentioned in faculty meetings you hadn't turned in any homework in physics for six weeks.' The boy said, 'Oh, you know how it is.' I said, 'All right, instead of going out and playing before dinner and on Sundays, you go into the library. No one will bother you there, and you do all that back homework and hand it in.' Well, I didn't say anything to anyone about it, and the next week at faculty meeting Taber said, 'Just look what so-and-so has done! He started handing in his homework. We've got to get behind him and see that he gets into Yale.' So, as soon as this boy showed some interest, they were all behind him. That to me is the mark of a good teacher. The boy, incidentally, did get into Yale but flunked out two years later. He was a poor student who just couldn't make it without the sort of faculty nurturing he'd had at Hotchkiss."

vii /   Building a new faculty was but one aspect of the Duke's total absorption with the school. He was no less interested in a far more literal building up, and from his own student days he was fascinated with the physical plant. "The whole design was simple, unpretentious and completely effective and convenient," he wrote in his final notes. "The long corridor was like a village street promoting daily and even hourly social contacts. In time its south window sills (called 'the Ledge') were brightened by geraniums in bloom or daffodils or tulips, and on the north wall were hung all sorts of ornamental, artistic or historical materials – plaster casts of figures from the Frieze of the Parthenon, photographs of European cathedrals, and in later years Medici prints in color, or lively kaleidoscopic exhibits by Robert Osborn and Thomas Blagden and their pupils. Some of these exhibits were very amusing and some of quite remarkable excellence. They made the Main Corridor come alive."

The original architect of the school was Bruce Price, whose other distinction was that he happened to be the father of a young woman who came to be known as Emily Post. Thirty years later, when Dr. Buehler was casting around for an architect to build Memorial Hall, he picked the prominent New York firm of Cass Gilbert. It was Cass Gilbert and his elaborate plans for the school which Van Santvoord had inherited.

There was conflict from the start, which GVS details in his final notes: "In 1926 our Building Committee and Cass Gilbert began a

Architect Cass Gilbert's plan for the Hotchkiss School drawn in 1925

furious argument over Alumni Hall [in 1980 renamed Tinker Hall], then about to become our second new building. Cass Gilbert was at the height of his fame and activity. He had designed two state capitols and was now at work on the George Washington Bridge. His son, Cass, Jr., was helping his father. . . . Mr. Gilbert suddenly realized that [the] main floor of [Alumni] would not be on a level with Memorial Hall, about a hundred yards to the East, but nine feet lower.

"Raising the level of Alumni would now mean bringing in thousands of yards of topsoil and accentuating an already difficult problem in surface drainage.

"The very next year, 1927–1928, an even more contentious problem arose with the new infirmary.

"Mr. Gilbert had never yet designed a hospital. Now he wanted *two*; one for contagious diseases – smallpox, measles, mumps, diphtheria, flu, etc. – the other for fractures, sprains, and other nonnoxious ailments.

"Harry J. Wieler, M.D., had [just] joined our staff. His advice was accepted, and Gilbert was again overruled.

"The third battle with Cass Gilbert now drew near. Mr. Paul Block, proprietor of the *Pittsburgh Post-Gazette* and the *Toledo Blade* offered the headmaster $100,000 toward a new chapel. Our trustees reported that Cass Gilbert said the building he had in mind would require $300,000. So we must raise more money.

"Mr. Gilbert would have placed his new chapel about on the site of the Scoville Memorial Gate (not yet built). Its entrance, at the north end, would have been surmounted by a tall and graceful tower, one hundred feet or more in height, a memorial to Hotchkiss alumni lost in World War I. I believe there had been no great objection to Mr. Gilbert's tentative design except perhaps that (1) the building would probably be too large, and (2) it was too far from other buildings, with no approach under cover. Mr. Gilbert is said to have replied that he didn't approve of daily chapel. One service Sunday morning would be better. This looked ominous. Should architects decide policy?

"The trustees failed to resolve the problem and directed the headmaster to confer with Mr. Gilbert. There was difficulty in finding a free hour in [Mr. Gilbert's] busy schedule. But at last I was given an appointment for 9:00 A.M. on a Monday in June, the day after our school graduation.

"I left school at 5:30 A.M., drove to Brewster, New York, and caught a commuters' train; so I was at Mr. Gilbert's office before 9:00 A.M. He and his son were said to be conferring with Federal authorities at the New York Customs House. So I waited, looking through the *New York Times*, reading Thornton Wilder's reviews in the *World*, and enjoying the *Conning Tower* in the *Tribune*.

"At noon the Gilberts were reported to be still detained. So I went out for a cup of coffee and a breath of fresh air. At 12:30 P.M. they were said to have not yet returned. I waited until 3:00 P.M. Then some unwary clerk opened the door into Mr. Gilbert's office. There at a long table sat the Messrs. Gilbert, Junior and Senior, with several other gentlemen, evidently discussing details about the George Washington Bridge.

"'The Lord has delivered them into my hand,' I thought. A hasty note left with the ranking secretary stated that I had been waiting from 9 : 00 A.M. to 3 : 00 P.M. for our appointment, and must now start back to school for an evening meeting.

"The following day, Mr. Gilbert called up Mr. H. L. deForest, told him he found it impossible to work with me, and resigned as the school architect.

"So Messrs. Delano and Aldrich took up our long-range planning. . . . They soon produced plans for the new chapel and for Coy Hall, enthusiastically approved by all at Hotchkiss. The contracts were let; and in the fall of [1931] the chapel was dedicated by H. K. Sherrill '07, Episcopal Bishop of Massachusetts; and Claude Fuess, Principal of Phillips Academy, Andover, [came] to do honor to Edward G. Coy."

Over the next quarter of a century, GVS worked closely with Henry S. Waterbury and other principals from Delano and Aldrich, whom he had met when they were designing the Divinity School and Pierson, Davenport, and Timothy Dwight colleges at Yale. At Hotchkiss, they were to expand vastly the facilities under the headmastership of the Duke. To the four major buildings completed after 1926 were added Buehler Hall, Monahan Gym, Edsel Ford Library, and the new Dining Hall as well as tennis courts, Hoyt Field memorial stands, the Scoville Gate, and many other additions and alterations which began to give Hotchkiss the look it has today.

viii / P lanning new buildings, hiring new masters, and making such innocuous changes as renaming the curator business manager and otherwise devoting himself to detail made the Duke more and more pervasive in Hotchkiss life. When the class of 1930 was graduated, it was the first one he had nurtured through its entire four years, and they made him an honorary member. Forty-five years later, the names of some of the students were still burnished on his mind: "Harold Zeamer, Ramsey Minor, Graham Reeves, George Ranney, James Linen, Fred Kammer, Norton Miner, Richard Bacon, Charles Reynolds, Bruce McPherson, William McKnight, Churchill Carey, Bruce Hill, Lewis Clarke, and many more

– what a splendid group of boys, loyal, courageous, and generous, bound together by experiences of joy, hardship, and even tragedy!''

The Duke continued in his final notes, ''Fortunately for me a U.S. Army Life Insurance Policy which I had taken out while in service came due about this time. The 'Great Depression' was upon us, and I was able to use my insurance money as a sort of Emergency Relief Fund for Hotchkiss 1930. There were many calls for help in the next few years. The money came back to me as time went on, and went out again to others.''

Whether there had indeed been an insurance windfall or that it fully covered the Duke's largesse cannot be ascertained. While he was rumored to have far more family wealth than he probably did, the Duke might have been hard pressed to expend even his $10,000 annual salary for personal needs. He did not consider his influence as headmaster to be dependent on any expensive external trappings or habits. He was sufficiently impressive in his wash khakis, raking leaves or hoisting a shovelful of mud out of one of the school's several ponds. ''He didn't care what he wore; he didn't care what he ate,'' says Archibald Coolidge. ''I think life for him was a good deal easier than for many people who did care what they ate. He was altogether unaware of money in his own life, and if anything, he believed it could have a negative influence. He once said to me, 'I don't think it would be a good thing if our salaries were such that people came here to teach just because of the money.''

The special relationship with the class of 1930 prompted the Duke to take a highly controversial step: the abolition of hazing. Technically speaking, it was the class that abolished it, since the seniors were the ones who imposed the euphemistically called ''new boy rules'' – both written and unwritten. Yet, without the Duke's unmistakable influence, this revolutionary break with tradition would not have taken place for years to come.

What exactly constituted hazing at Hotchkiss? Squidge Lord '22 details its practice and function toward the end of the Buehler era: ''Dr. Buehler headed only one aspect of the school's disciplinary system.

There was another level imposed by the seniors. All prep year you had to walk with your elbow touching the wall. Anywhere down the main corridor, you always walked with your elbow theoretically touching the wall. It didn't actually have to touch, but you had to be right up against the wall. If you wanted to go over to the other side, you made the crossing at right angles. The idea was to keep you properly humbled and not too big for your britches.

"The next step in this student enforcement was calling you into the senior room. Adjoining the old library was a room about the size of an ordinary classroom which was known as the senior room. You'd be brought in there, and a strong light was shone in your face, and then these mighty seniors would haul you over the coals and tell you what a fresh brat you were and so on. Some of these kids had been big shots at small schools at home, and they'd come in fresh as paint. So the seniors would try to scare the daylights out of them. They'd give them one or two shots in the senior room. If that didn't do it, you were really in for it. If you were a fresh kid and you just wouldn't respond, word would be whispered around school, 'He's going to get a bath!' They'd take you up to the top floor of old Bissell Hall, which for some reason had a much wider, more open corridor. They'd take off all your clothes, put a jock strap on you, and throw you in a hot shower until your skin was nice and soft and tender. Then they'd make you run the gauntlet of kids standing on both sides with bath towels, the ends dipped a little bit in water. There were some experts who could just take a piece of hide off you. The offending prep would have to run past maybe thirty seniors on each side, and he'd get maybe half a dozen pretty good cracks before he got through. And then he'd go back to his room. I don't think any kid ever went back for a second bath. I haven't any idea why the faculty tolerated it, except that it didn't happen often – maybe once or twice a year – and the kid pretty generally straightened up after that."

As Dr. Buehler had written to Mrs. MacLeish, "This contact is similar to what must be expected in life." The basic reason why the faculty tolerated hazing, however, was that it represented an integral aspect of senior rule. Throughout the Hotchkiss community, it was generally believed that the school would not be, and could not be, what it was without this senior rule. The following communication appeared in the *Record* shortly before Dr. Buehler died:

"The senior class must take all the responsibility for the good name and reputation of the school. By the quality of the senior class the name of the school is valued. If certain boys do something to stain the good name of Hotchkiss, the seniors get the blame thrown on them. . . .

"Many of us, when we were preps, thought that senior rule was unjust. We complained bitterly when we were forced to shovel off the hockey pond, we cried out against senior rule when we were forced to walk with our arm against the wall day after day. But when we became old fellows, we began to view the matter from a broader perspective. We realized that something had to be done to us to prevent us from becoming unbearably fresh. Something had to be done to us to make us realize that we were but a small portion of a big pudding, and that we must make a name for ourselves before we could be Hotchkiss boys in anything but name."

The senior rule system had not been without its critics all along, and from the beginning of George Van Santvoord's tenure they were being listened to by a widening segment of the school. The following letter appeared in the *Record* on November 29, 1927:

"Even though we admit that new fellows need 'training' – do they need it, or do seniors like to do the training? It is doubtful that every senior in the school ought to have the power to administer the rules and contribute to the training. One of the older boys of the school said in my room the other day that in his prep year the new boys were unnecessarily and unreasonably hounded, bullied and persecuted by two of the weakest seniors in the school. These two 'trainers' amounted to nothing in their class; they were frankly 'puds,' but into their hands, as well as into the hands of the president of the class, is given the power to whip new boys into line. One 'glaring defect' of the present system is the creation of the bully who exists every year and who exasperates the better element of the entire school."

To the Duke, the repressive aspects of senior rule were not merely flawed, but wholly unjustifiable. The exercise of genuine leadership, the Duke pointed out, should not require resorting to such reprehensible means. *Moniti Meliora Sequamur* should quite suffice. So, forty years of "senior prerogatives" and "new boy rules" came officially to an end, the sole remnant being the symbolic requirement for preps to wear black ties until Christmas vacation. "Think how much time you'll save by not having to decide what tie to put on every morning," the Duke rationalized to the preps in subsequent years.

ix /   The official abolition of hazing did not suddenly bring total harmony to the school. Such expectations would have been no more realistic than thinking that all abuse could ever be eliminated from a Marine Corps boot camp or a Roman Catholic seminary. Hotchkiss inevitably combined some of the characteristics of both – perhaps exacerbated by the involvement of young males at an even more volatile age. The *Record* back in 1906 eloquently warned of the "conditions both good and evil that exist within the student body."

The most prominent and pervasive aspect of this evil was called baiting, and it was by no means directed only at preps. Some of the boys continued to be picked on throughout their entire four years. Whether or not a boy was popular with his classmates depended on a complex of intangibles rather than any single factor. Being athletic, good-looking, dressing casually in the right clothes, and embodying the appropriate attitude and school spirit certainly helped – while an absence of those qualities did not augur well for the boy. Whatever the elusive reasons for a boy's unpopularity, the baiting would tend to be focused on his most obvious idiosyncrasies: "weird" colored hair, "funny" regional accent, different wardrobe, or stereotypically ethnic characteristics. On the other hand, if the boy for whatever assorted reasons happened to be popular, any idiosyncrasy was likely to be overlooked. One of the most popular students of his time was a stunted boy with a partially malformed face and a hunchback. He was a veritable dynamo and an arbiter of taste against whom no one would think of making a slur.

Another boy of that era who happened only to be congenitally short was cruelly baited for his stature throughout his four years at the school. He became the victim of one of the most insidious pranks when his classmates elected him vice president for one term as a lark.

Some of the abuse originated with the faculty in the normal course of teaching and "dishing it out." Bob Massey '24 recalls one such incident in Dr. Robinson's class: "There was a fellow in our class named Charlie Yost, who later capped a distinguished diplomatic career by becoming ambassador to the United Nations. He was very much of an underdeveloped guy; thin, no beard, light-colored hair, with mild and inoffensive nature. I think he was younger than the rest of us. Anyway, in one of our Vergil classes he translated something that 'somebody had caused the spear to be hurled at somebody else.' Robinson was one who loathed literal translations. He thought they should be translated into English to sound like poetry. He landed on this slim boy very hard and said, 'Yost, how in the world can somebody cause something to be hurled at somebody else?' He said, 'Yost, have you ever killed a man? Well, go out and kill a man and you'll see what I'm talking about!' That sort of thing can wound you pretty badly or it can be a source of hilarious entertainment."

Doc Rob's approach would be memorable precisely because of incidents of this sort, which alumni would recall fondly for decades to come – just as they would Pansy Parsons's unique variety of threatening ploys. But being tough and vituperative in class was considered essential by many faculty members just to be able to teach anything to resistant, unruly boys. "You have to have sweat on the walls," says Archibald Coolidge. "When you go in the classroom, there's going to be sweat on the walls – and it isn't going to be the teacher's."

The practice of baiting among students went considerably beyond this type of purposeful intimidation in class. While the abolition of hazing put a stop to organized physical abuse, the individual knotted towel did not disappear. Other means of intimidation ranged from repeatedly dumping a boy's bed to throwing him into a shower fully clothed. The clothes, however, would be quickly stripped off if his tormentors had previously detected a hesitancy to expose himself in the communal showers, which were standard at the school. As an under-endowed lower mid, I once deflected the interest of my potential assail-ants to my best friend, who felt similarly insecure about his attributes. While being showered, he was also shorn of his lengthy locks. The whole affair could have turned into a tragedy, as my desperate friend bobbed and weaved in trying to avoid two sets of scissors lunging at his hair. Though he graciously disclaims any memory of the fate which be-fell him on my account, it was an event I still shudder to contemplate.

The imagination applied to the baiting endeavor – if not its incidence – remained at a fairly constant plateau from year to year. "We could certainly be quite cruel," says Zeph Stewart '39. "I didn't really enter into it because I was too close to being a victim. But I would guess that sort of thing goes on in any school."

What bothered Zeph Stewart more was the primacy accorded to ath-letes. Otto Monahan's tenure as the director of physical education was drawing to a close, but he was to be succeeded by another formidable figure: William C. Fowle, a man of movie-star looks and one of the greatest all-round athletes ever to come out of Williams. Definitely a nonathlete, the slight, cerebral Stewart felt his only status came from the respect openly accorded him by the Duke. (Zeph Stewart would win that same Chamberlain Greek Prize at Yale for which Van Sant-voord's honorable mention thirty years earlier had contributed to the school's first holiday.) "Athletes were definitely top dogs at the school as the people who did things and ran things and had the most fun," says Zeph. "One memory I have is of a weekend when I was in the infirmary. Everybody else was going off to play a sport somewhere. I thought about my life at the school, and I realized again that if you were on one of the athletic teams you could get away more easily, and there I was, confined. Of course, I was sick, but the other people who had to stay at the school were the non-athletes."

This feeling of alienation, of not belonging, of not being one of the "wheels" has served as an intriguing dynamic throughout the school's first century. Though reluctant to talk about it because he was thinking of sending his daughter to Hotchkiss, Lewis H. Lapham '52, son of

Lapham '27 and also my classmate, consented to do so "for old times' sake":

"My misalliance with the Hotchkiss School, is, I'm sure, as much my fault as the school's. I was a year younger than the other boys in my class, and I hadn't reached my mature weight, strength, or height. Most of the other students were from the north shore of Long Island, from Connecticut, from New Jersey and Massachusetts – very much the Eastern establishment. I was from California, which in 1948 was considered a foreign country. I knew none of the proper dress codes, none of the *in* words. I didn't know any of the girls who came to the dances. I thought of myself as a stranger.

"I was also deeply interested in reading, especially history and poetry. Most of my classmates were interested in sports. In the first month of my prep year, October 1948, I remember there was some kind of a reading in our common room in Buehler Hall. Either a master, or visiting professor, or somebody's wife was giving an hour's talk on Browning, a poet whom I deeply admired. At the time I knew nobody at the school, and I showed up for the reading, enthusiast that I was, intensely excited because this person was talking about poems I had read and memorized. I still can remember coming out of the common room and being seized by a number of the boys who lived on the first corridor. They took me to task for showing what they deemed to be an effeminate interest in poetry and hung me by my tie on a doorknob – to the point where I felt I was being choked to death. They made it clear that they thought anybody interested in poetry was probably a flit or a queer and certainly not one of the favored few deserving the preferred sobriquet, a big wheel.

"During my first three months at school I worked very hard at my homework assignments. I had been a highly disciplined student in grammar school, and throughout that first fall term at Hotchkiss I did all my assignments at least three weeks in advance, the papers lined up in neat rows on my desk.

"By the winter term, I discovered that neither the school nor the other students were interested in the intellectual virtues. I was lonely, an adolescent desperately wishing to be accepted by the other guys at the school. By then I had figured out that one had to affect an air of bored indifference. It was a matter of attitude, one of seeming languor and implied sarcasm summed up in the word *casual*. Something of the same style made itself manifest in the figures of Humphrey Bogart and later in the early 1960s, in the persona of John F. Kennedy. I am by nature an extremely uncasual sort of person – far from indifferent. I still write four or five drafts of every manuscript. That temperament ran against the Hotchkiss grain, and so it occurred to me that if I were going to succeed at the school – not as a scholar, but as one of the guys – then it behooved me to become more casual than anybody else, to carry the pose to its extreme statement. I stopped doing any serious reading. I never prepared work for class. I cultivated an image of care-less insouciance. To my eventual sorrow, I mastered the act. If I re-member correctly, the senior yearbook voted me the title of 'The Most Casual' boy in the class."

Toward the close of the interview in my classmate's book-lined office, I handed him a token of gratitude which I thought would be particularly appropriate. It was a framed copy of a letter written in 1952 by Arthur Howe, Jr., then the assistant dean of freshmen at Yale, to the Hotchkiss assistant headmaster, George P. Milmine. Howe, who had been Lew Lapham's corridor master during his prep year in Buehler Hall, was reporting on several Hotchkiss seniors he had just interviewed for possible admission to Yale:

"[3] *Lapham*. Lapham made a very poor impression on Mr. Noyes and myself, the poorest of any of the fifty-odd boys we interviewed. He appeared with his shirt unbuttoned, ragged tie, torn trousers, sloppy shoes, coat halfway up to the elbows and tousled hair. His man-ner was casual to the point of being rude at times. His indifference leads me to believe that he is liable to be a very poor candidate for Yale. For his own good I felt this should be brought to his attention."

The urbane host of the weekly PBS series "Bookmark" and editor of *Harper's Magazine* put down the framed letter. "It took me four years of conscious effort at Hotchkiss to develop that impression. At the time I considered it a triumph." He paused and momentarily cupped his face in his hands and then shook his head. "What a waste of energy and time – what Wordsworth would have called a waste of spirit. At the same age of sixteen, my great-great-grandfather was a captain of a sailing ship trading tea and silk in the South China Sea."

A different though no less typical response to the same set of circumstances prevailing at the school was fashioned by Lapham's classmate Richard W. Adams. Though younger than the rest of the class, Dick Adams was already over six feet tall, and his height only called attention to his predicament:

"My mother sent me to Indian Mountain* to get me into the country amongst men and boys. I used to see Hotchkiss in the distance up there on the hill, and I'd hear about it. It was sort of like when you're at Hotchkiss hearing about Yale.

"I was the youngest member of our Hotchkiss class, and I was maybe a little bit shy by nature. I came with probably better-than-average preparation, which also may be the only reason why I started out at the head of the class. It's terrible to remember something so petty as marks, but I remember getting a 97 in Latin. There was something about those grades. Every number between one and one hundred had its own special aura. An 88 was different from an 87.

"To be the first and the youngest in the class and not to be an athlete – that was a bad combination. I remember being sort of embarrassed. I remember feeling a certain shame. There was a stigma attached to doing well in school and also to not being much of an athlete. Not being an athlete was particularly upsetting. I had to face the fact that I was a weenie and I wasn't a big wheel. And I began to feel fear. I began to feel fear of the superior physical strength that I imagined was all around. I can remember walking down the corridor and there were guys loitering along the walls, and I remember it was like running a gauntlet. It was scary to be stared at by these guys.

"I suppose I should have been proud of possibly being a little ahead of myself because I had already reached puberty at Indian Mountain. But my social experience was very, very limited. My classmates were

---

*The Indian Mountain School, less than two miles away, was one of the traditional "feeders" for Hotchkiss.

talking in three-letter, four-letter, and five-letter words about what they were doing to girls, and that was a little intimidating.

"By my third year at Hotchkiss, because I had a very beautiful stepsister who was an actress, I put her picture on my bureau because I didn't have anything else to put on that bureau to compete. She was much more sensational looking than the girlfriends that other people had on their bureaus, but it was slightly embarrassing to secretly realize that I hadn't *done* anything with my stepsister."

Dick Adams continued to fear his older, tougher classmates: "One morning during the third year, I set out from Alumni Hall to go to the infirmary – I had a cold or something – just when most students were going to chapel. As I stepped out of the building, I heard some voices calling me, and I looked up. Looking down at me from the third floor were at least three jocks, big wheels. These weren't the more aristocratic wheels like Charlie Lord. These were the jock-type big wheels, the most intimidating of them all. So I was outnumbered, and I was having to look up to them on the third floor, which doubled my intimidation. They said, 'Hey, Adams, you going to the infirmary? Would you sign our names on the list?' [Being on the list authorized a boy to miss morning chapel.]

"The voice of my conscience was totally overwhelmed by this incredible opportunity to win at least a smidgen of approval from these big wheels. I went to the infirmary, and it's hard to believe, but I guess I signed those names. I don't consciously remember trying to fake the handwriting or change the style for each signature. Yet I can't believe I was stupid enough to write each name in my own handwriting. I guess I was in a bit of a daze. It turned out I had a pretty high temperature, and I was put in the infirmary.

"I don't remember if I heard anything more about it that day, but the next day George Van Santvoord came into my room. He told me with great gentleness, warmth, and understanding that the other boys had been punished. I think they may have been sequestered. I hadn't explained anything to the Duke, but he had somehow realized that I had been intimidated. He said, 'We're not going to punish you, but you should really learn to stick up for what you know is right.' That was pretty impressive on his part. I don't know that I can swear that that was a turning point in my life and that I became a courageous defender of the right and the truth as a result of that. But it certainly was something I shall never forget."

Dick Adams for the past thirty years has been making documentary films, many of them on starvation budgets. They include *Men of Bronze*, which chronicles a black infantry regiment from Harlem in World War I, and *Citizens*, a portrayal of Poland's first "Solidarity Period" of 1980–81.

x /   Any generalization about big wheels at Hotchkiss has to be judged in terms of the unique circumstances and personalities involved. It is with good reason that the differences between the various classes over the past one hundred years have often been compared to the different vintages produced from the same vineyard. Some have been smooth and concordant, some have been distinctive and bold, and still others, a bit rough and unbalanced. Moreover, among the biggest wheels to have been wrought at Hotchkiss, some have rolled up records no less impressive in academic work than in athletics: John Hersey was the president of his class, of the student council, and of St. Luke's; he was chairman of the *Mischianza*, Ivy Orator, and winner of the Treadway Prize; and he was on the school's football, hockey, and baseball teams.

Yet even if virtually every class could point to individuals who embodied both physical and intellectual prowess, many more athletes had no easier time of it academically than the majority of the students at the school. Just to survive, they often had to expend far more effort on their studies than did Dick Adams – and the reproach he may have felt was for raising the class average unattainably high.

Among the most notable athletes in the same class as Adams and Lapham was Donal C. O'Brien. Holder of the school's javelin record and a member for three years of the swimming team, he shared the distinction of being on the only back-to-back undefeated football teams (1950 and 1951) and the following year was the team's captain.

Don O'Brien: "I think athletics were extremely important to all of our classmates who had the ability to participate – as well as to the faculty and to Hotchkiss as an institution. Some of the most respected and influential faculty members were the most qualified and respected coaches. Years later, I remember Dick Gurney [football coach and legendary English teacher 1935–1971] telling me that Nels Corey taught the best course at Hotchkiss. I duly bit, and I said, 'What's that?' And he said, 'Football. Nobody does a better job teaching anything than Nels Corey does of teaching football.' He was also a great lacrosse teacher. Corey happened to have taught my son in both of those 'courses.' So I knew firsthand what Gurney meant.

"One of my most vivid recollections of Hotchkiss sports is the incredible leadership Blair Torrey ['50] demonstrated when he stepped in for Don Ross as substitute captain of the football team during my lower middle year. Ross had broken his leg, and I replaced him as fullback on that team. Blair certainly led by example. He was never a fellow who gave off-handed speeches. But he was such a fierce competitor, such a fierce team player. I can remember him at each huddle, going around the huddle and talking to almost each member of that team, urging that person to carry out his share, his assignment so that the team would be successful. To this day I will not forget being so astonished that somebody so young could be so effective."

Don O'Brien's own unforgettable moment came when he was injured in one of the early games during his upper mid year: "I took myself out, and I remember coming to the sidelines. All these coaches whom I had the highest regard for – Gurney, Kiphuth, Stearns, Best – they said, 'Just shrug it off and jog up and down the sidelines, and then go back in the game.' So I jogged up and down the sidelines, and it hurt like stink. I mean it really hurt. After I did that for a while, they said, 'Okay, now get back in.' So I went in. I played, I guess, two or three more plays. By this time I could barely stand on my leg, let alone push off and play on it. So I came back out. I had no idea what was wrong, and I did not want to admit defeat, did not want to admit that an injury would take me out of the game. When I got to the sidelines, they had Joe Black there, the trainer, and they told Joe to get some Red Hot and rub some Red Hot on it, which Joe proceeded to do. It hurt even more. I was pretty much in agony at that point. I finally said, 'Look, Coach, I just can't possibly play on this damn thing. I don't know what's wrong with it, but I can't play on it.' They weren't happy with that decision on my part, but they said, 'All right, if that's the way you feel, go to the infirmary and have Doc Wieler take a look at it.' So I climbed the hill, mostly hopping on one foot, from the field to the infirmary. Doc Wieler was there, and he took an X ray and said, 'You goddam fool, you've got a broken leg!' Well, I don't think he said 'goddam fool,' but words to that effect. That evening, I had four very embarrassed coaches coming to visit me in the infirmary.

"Without doubt, the major pressures – and the major rewards – I received while at Hotchkiss came from the playing field. I worked like a dog in class, but not with the same results. I guess the faculty had written me off early on as a jock, which I didn't particularly like but could do little to change. In retrospect, I think one reason for my difficulties was that I was dyslexic and had enormous problems with foreign languages and math. I wouldn't come into my own academically until sophomore year in college.

"The people who did best with their athletic success at Hotchkiss were the ones who turned it into becoming strong campus leaders. It was certainly true of Blair Torrey. Going back to our prep year, there were seniors like Bob Bryan, Baird Brittingham, Tommy Dorsey, Sandy Muir. These were athletes and leaders and they were hardly the ones who were baiting or intimidating people. Some of the most notorious baiters in our class were nonathletic. Some weren't even big or strong. It is unfortunate but youngsters can be cruel. They were cruel when we were around, they were cruel a thousand years before us, and they are cruel today. But I do think that some of the people who did the baiting didn't mean anything by it. It was the sort of thing to do at that time, and it wasn't meant to be mean.

"Among many of the athletes, and I would include myself as one of those, we developed strong friendships with people who were not athletic at all. George d'Almeida, for example, I was very close to. I was overwhelmed by his artistic ability – not just with sculpture, painting, and drawing, but in the way he was so original about everything. I was also close to Dick Adams. Many years after we graduated, I contacted him and asked him to do a film for one of my clients."

Don O'Brien's own most lasting interest had little to do with athletics: "Boker Doyle, who was a senior when I was a prep, introduced me to the great sport of robbing nests of baby crows. We'd climb up the trees with a laundry bag with a string on it, put the baby crow in the laundry bag, and then lower it down to the person who was below. I kept the crows in my room as pets. It was against the rules; but the Duke knew of this interest, and nobody ever said anything. As a matter of fact, lower mid year he left a baby woodchuck in my wastepaper basket and set it on my desk. His dog had killed the mother, and the Duke probably figured I was the most appropriate recipient. I carried that woodchuck around in my breast pocket and initially fed it milk with an eye dropper out of an iodine bottle. Eventually, I put it into my side pocket. It was an incredible pet. By upper middle year, I had a whole menagerie in my room. I had squirrels and crows and other things, but my favorite was a great horned owl which George d'Almeida found in the woods. Like with that woodchuck, I raised that owl from when it was tiny, and I kept it in a cage in the Duke's garden behind the headmaster's house. My main problem was finding the right food. I had no problem getting a good supply of frogs, but my owl didn't particularly like frogs. It finally dawned on me that one of the great sources of food for this fellow would be the pigeons which the Duke kept behind Mr. Beaumont's house. So I would go down there at night with a shoelace and sneak up on a dozing squab. I always picked the very young birds because I didn't want to kill one of the Duke's championship racers or anything like that. I figured nobody would miss these very young birds. I made a little noose and I'd slip the noose around the little thing's head and pull quickly and that was that. Then I would take it back and give it to the owl, and that was his menu. I don't know if the Duke knew about that phase of my interest – but then maybe he did."

Since graduating from Williams and the University of Virginia Law

School, Don O'Brien has spent most of his career as the family lawyer for the Rockefellers. And his Hotchkiss interest in wildlife has continued to this day. He was for a dozen years on the board of the National Audubon Society – five of them as chairman. "One of the reasons Audubon is interested in working with young people is to instill in them some of the awe and wonder about our environment, so that when they are in positions to make decisions, they'll make them based on that kind of awareness. If the Duke were around today, I'm convinced he'd be in the forefront of the ecology movement. My God, he was articulating the fundamentals of today's conservationist agenda forty years ago!"

xi / With the abolition in 1930 of their traditional privileges, some of the seniors felt as if they had been deprived of their birthright. The Duke followed up with an edict which evoked far more widespread groans: no more jitney rides, which had been the time-honored conveyance for getting down to the Ville and nearby spots. The jitney operators had far too often in the past made illegal runs with boys to New York or other beckoning destinations that were strictly out of bounds. Archie MacLeish and Paul Nitze had not been the only ones to have been sequestered for the illegal use of jitneys. Others had been kicked out, and legions more had never been caught. GVS also had another concern, which had been dramatized for him by an incident involving the car of a young master, George P. Milmine. With his ever-present bow tie, George Milmine was a meticulous man for whom no detail was too small, and when the quarterback on the football team started to borrow his car for joyrides after dark, it was not long before the Duke's recent faculty recruit noticed the extra mileage on the odometer. For several nights, he lay in wait with a policeman, and sure enough, the unwary boy returned. He was about to jump-start the car when Milmine and the officer, gun drawn, emerged out of the dark. The boy was sent packing home the following day. What disturbed the Duke no less than the "borrowing" was that there could have been an accident. That is what happened on the night before graduation in 1930, when a senior was killed driving his car. The rule the Duke finally crafted was that under no circumstances could a boy take the wheel while within the jurisdiction of the school; moreover, riding in cars was forbidden except with adult members of one's family or with a master or his wife.

The headmaster did not limit his faculty prerogative to just stopping for boys walking down to the Ville. With astounding frequency, the Duke would drive Hotchkiss boys to catch trains or buses in emergencies as well as embark with them on a variety of special trips. Trying to encourage young John Hersey to choose Harvard over Yale, the Duke personally drove the promising scholarship boy to Cambridge, a round-trip of more than three hundred miles. ("I think the Duke was always disappointed that I did not go to Harvard," remarks Hersey in retrospect.) On one occasion, when he had to dismiss two boys whom he particularly liked for breaking the no-smoking rule, the Duke drove them and their belongings to another school some fifty miles away, where he had arranged with the headmaster for the expellees' admission. Both were readmitted to Hotchkiss the following year and returned with a colorful account of the Duke driving his new Buick in second gear all the way while engaged in an uninterruptable conversation.

The Duke was gradually developing his own inimitable style. He had tempered the "mister" or last name format in class and increasingly employed first names. In certain cases, he just spoke in a boy's direction in a wholly unmistakable way. He had also developed his characteristic approach, whenever he had something of vital importance to impart, of taking the boy by the elbow so as to better guide him down the corridor during the obligatory tête-à-tête. Because of the war wound which left him without a grip in his right hand, the riveting contact was maintained by a forward thrust rather than any viselike attachment. That is why the walking part became an inseparable adjunct to this approach. And when the Duke had completed the interaction with a particular boy or spotted a student to whom he had something of even more vital importance to impart, he would release his quarry with a flick of his lame hand on the rear – as a football coach might do in sending a player back into the game – a sort of symbolic slap for being a boy with potential for mischief that was being successfully kept in check by the civilizing forces of the school. The elbow action and the occasional pat were a radical departure from the distant demeanor of the King, who once confided to Carle Parsons that he would give anything if he could bring himself to put his arm around a student's shoulder.

The boys by now had a distinct yet kaleidoscopic picture of what their headmaster was all about. "The Duke unwound to entangle us in intricate discussions of the use of the bassoon in Tasmania or what is Al Katz going to name the expected kitten," wrote the class historian in the *Mischianza* for 1931. He concluded, "The Duke has called us perfect boobs. At least we are perfect in something!" In the next year's *Mischianza*, Corwith Hamill referred to the headmaster as "George the Duke" and indirectly appraised his influence: "For the benefit of any future candidate for the four-year demolition process known as prep school, the translation of the school motto, 'Moniti, Meliora Sequamur,' . . . means, 'Having been warned, may we know better the next time.'"

Among Hamill's classmates in 1932 was William Block, who today heads the family newspaper interests. His brother, the late Paul Block, Jr., preceded Bill at Hotchkiss by two years, and it was their father, Paul Block, Sr., who gave the money to build the present school chapel.

Bill Block: "I don't know when my father pledged the money, but I think it was before the Crash – and then he had to make good on it. He was heavily in the stock market, and he really took an awful beating. Frankly, it must have been very difficult for him to come through with the money, but he did, and our class graduated in that chapel.

"I entered Hotchkiss in the fall of '28. The Duke had come in '26, and as far as I was concerned, he was scary. He would ask you these way-out questions. 'Do you think Sanskrit is what we ought to adopt for our writing system?' I probably had never heard of Sanskrit to start with. I was cowed rather than stimulated. But others responded very well. The Duke liked intellectual challenge, and he sought response.

"I think my best experience lower middle year was studying under Dr. Bickford. He was a witty and stimulating teacher. He used to tell us the story of the man who wanted very much to be a minister. He took the required theological exams several times but never seemed able to pass. Finally, the accreditation team gave him one last chance. They said, 'We're going to ask you only one question. Who was the first king of the Hebrews?' And this man smiled and said, 'Saul!' They said, 'Very good!' Then as the man went out toward the door, he turned around and said, 'Later called Paul.' So, on our exams, whenever we had put something down and then erased it and had written in something else that was wrong, he would mark L C P – Later Called Paul.

"I was not the greatest athlete. I was the smallest boy in my class, but I took boxing as my winter sport because George Salling, the boxing coach, talked me into it. I was so small that he had a hard time finding opponents for me. But after I had taken boxing for two or three years, he was anxious for me to be in the Bryan Belt bouts. He found a prep named Charlie Wright as my opponent. Charlie outweighed me I think by ten pounds, but he and I were considered to be of about equal skill. We were to be in the first bout because they went from the lightest to the heaviest. Gene Tunney, who had retired a few years earlier as the world's heavyweight champion, came up to Hotchkiss to be the referee. It so happens Gene Tunney also liked to lecture on Shakespeare. So, there we were in the gym, very cold in the middle of winter, and Charlie in one corner and I in the other waiting to start the bout. And Tunney decided to make a speech about Shakespeare to the student body. We were getting colder and colder. I was absolutely frozen by the time we started the bout, so frozen that when I saw this punch coming almost from the floor, I couldn't get out of the way, and Charlie hit me within the first thirty seconds of the bout and knocked me down. Whereupon Gene Tunney gave me the longest count that anyone has ever had. I took a pretty good pounding that night, and by the third round my thoughts were not on the Bryan Belt, but how to hang on to the end."

Continues Bill Block, "In those days you couldn't get away for weekends, and we used to look forward eagerly to Saturday night movies at the school. My father knew a lot of the people at Twentieth Century Fox and MGM, and he was devoted to doing anything that he thought would help his children. So he was in a position to get movies and he would arrange to send them to Hotchkiss, and we therefore saw some very good current movies."

Among the Saturday night movies sent to the school through the courtesy of Bill Block's father was *The Love Parade*, which promptly resulted in the following communication from the Duke to Mr. Block: "The real trouble with a picture like 'The Love Parade' is that its primary interest is sex, and it treats the whole question at rather an objectionable angle. Even if it were handled carefully, it would still not be a desirable subject for boys at this age. Naturally they are interested in a picture which is new and which they read about in the picture magazines, but I think that other considerations should lead us to withhold these from them and supply something of a different quality. There should be plenty of films available which will be interesting, yet wholesome. If not, we would do better to heed the wishes of some other friends of the school who are anxious to have us increase still further the number of concerts and other entertainments. . . . Apparently, Mr. Jones [the school's business manager] had seen this film elsewhere and realizing it was unsuitable, telephoned your office requesting that it should not be sent. Even so, on Saturday the film arrived. Perhaps it would have been best for us to announce that we would not have any performance, rather than show a picture which is so objectionable. . . . It is rather wrong to go to such lengths to provide good conditions for our boys to live in here and then allow such influences to come to bear upon them through a Saturday night entertainment. It is a mistake which I hope will not happen again."

This letter to one of the school's major benefactors reflects the primacy which the Duke accorded to matters of principle. He could be relied upon to express himself with forthrightness in matters of this sort — and on virtually every other subject as well. It is not necessary to look far and wide in the Hotchkiss files to come across letters such as the one written in 1933 to Warren F. Kaynor, who, like his brother Kirk, had graduated in 1908 in the Duke's class:

"Many thanks for your note. Your story of the college president and the athletic director is of course an indictment of many bureaucratic organizations. . . . A friend of mine at Oxford tells me a story which seems to me the prize one to illustrate this mass of red tape. Some acquaintances of his visited the Isle of Sark. While inspecting an ancient manor house, they were shocked when someone within fired a shotgun at them out of the window. Very indignant, they complained to the police when they returned to the village, and were informed that the house belonged to the seigneur, the Supreme Magistrate of the Island. They were very angry and decided to take up the matter in London. On arriving there they first went to the Home Secretary, who told them Sark was not part of the United Kingdom. He directed them to the Colonial Office, where they found Sark was not a colony. They then went to the foreign office, but were told Sark belonged to the British Empire; so there was no ambassador maintained there. Some bureaucrat with imagination suggested they go to the War Office, from which they were solemnly sent to the Admiralty, since it would be impossible to make a land attack on Sark. At the Admiralty they were told that war with Sark would probably mean a loss of several battleships, since the coast was very rocky. A kind clerk who happened to come from the Channel Islands informed them that Sark was one of the possessions of the old Duchy of Normandy, and they could get redress only through the King, who reigns in the islands as Duke of Normandy. However, they did not want to bother the King and through the friendship with the Sheriff of Alderny, the clerk finally got an apology from the Seigneur of Sark, on condition that the offenders would promise not to trespass on his property again!"

No less notable than the content is how such letters were composed. After helping for two years to guide Walter Hull Buell through the paperwork maze of the headmaster's office, the young secretary hired by Dr. Buehler in his last years became secretary to George Van Santvoord. She had married a Lakeville railroad man, and instead of Mary Meehan, she was now Mary Finney:

"I'd open the mail and leave it there on the headmaster's desk. At a certain time every morning he'd dictate and get the mail out. Sometimes he'd hold a letter up before he'd answer it. He was very well organized, and he dictated beautifully. He could compose a letter, and there were no changes. He stuck to it. Now, Dr. Buehler would sleep on the letters dismissing boys. Mr. Van Santvoord never did. He made up his mind. That was it. For a man as brilliant as he was with the vocabulary he was capable of using, he wrote very simple letters to parents. I think there again his modesty is showing through. He never claimed anything for himself, but he was brilliant. I think he could size up a person without any trouble. And he was so kind. I thought it was one of the nicest things when he invited so many of the local boys to stay as boarders.

"Mr. Van Santvoord was always the same, very even. You'd know it, though, if something was wrong. He wouldn't run and tell you, but you sensed it from his manner. He never got angry with me, never said a cross word to me, but for a long time I didn't know whether I pleased him or not. You know, you like a little praise or appreciation. Then when he was about to retire, I also wanted to retire, but he told Tom Chappell, 'Don't let Mrs. Finney go. There's too much in that office that I don't know anything about.'

"I think I was very lucky to have worked for Mr. Van Santvoord. I wrote him that after he became ill. I said, 'I never told you but I want to tell you now that I enjoyed working for you. It was a challenge and an education.' He never wrote back, but he sent my letter on to somebody to read."

xii / T he Duke was not quite as even in his comportment as he appeared to Mrs. Finney, before whom he undoubtedly felt that it was just as important to maintain the appropriate good form as it was before the boys. The most outlandish example of his self-control occurred when G V S was clearing trails in the woods with a group of boys. One of his mightier swings with an axe missed and went right through his boot. He acted as if nothing out of the ordinary had happened, gradually dismissed the boys, and then walked more than a mile to the infirmary. Even the perennially imperturbable Dr. Wieler was disturbed when he removed the bloody boot and saw the severity of the wound.

The Duke was likely to show more emotion in front of some of his close faculty colleagues. "The thing about the Duke was that something perfectly trivial would drive him into a towering rage, and the hairs in his nose would stand erect," says Arch Coolidge. "If you had committed a murder, he's the first guy you'd want to talk to, and he would have understood and done everything for you. But when somebody dropped a firecracker down the dust shoot, which is a natural place for a firecracker — made a fine noise and what not — he'd just almost tremble with rage at something like that."

What was likely to make the Duke tremble — and what he might simply ignore — is elaborated upon by Woods McCahill '33, retired counsel for General Electric and president of the Hotchkiss board of trustees from 1970 through 1975.

By way of background — when Woods was an upper mid, a group of seniors asked Pop Jefferson to lead them in prayer for the recovery of the kidnapped Lindbergh baby. Pop Jeff was a devout and somber man who spent considerable time each day on his knees, and the students' motivation in inspiring the Lindbergh prayers was partly to bait Pop Jeff. Woods McCahill picks up the thread the following year:

"During our senior year, a few of us were one day going down to the village, and Potter Stewart, who was in our class, conceived the idea of tapping into the radio and announcing that President Hoover had been assassinated. The only radio we had was in the senior common room, which assured us of a captive audience. So we got the necessary equipment and hooked the thing into the radio. We sat in the bushes outside, and a number of us spoke, primarily Potter, who had the role of today's anchor man. We swore in Curtis and described the scene along Constitution Avenue and provided a lot of other convincing detail. Then it was suggested in the broadcast that a responsible person in the area, someone among the listeners around each radio, lead the group in prayer for the deceased president. So they got the corridor master, who happened to be Pop Jefferson, to lead them in prayer. He took it in hook, line, and sinker. His voice trembled, and he was very solemn. Of course, we knew it was only a matter of time before he'd find out. So that evening, the class president, Jack Wiltshire, was designated to tell Mr. Jefferson that this was a hoax. Coincidentally, not too long thereafter, President-elect Roosevelt was in Miami, and someone took a shot at him and killed the mayor of Chicago, who was riding in the car with him. When the paper came out with the big headline – in those days, the paper was often put out on the window sill in the long corridor by the old dining room – when Pop Jefferson saw this headline, he thought it was a hoax, too. He made it clear he wasn't about to bite again.

"Everybody in the school knew about that broadcast, but the Duke never said anything about it. The really serious incident happened after our graduation. An orderly from the infirmary who was gravely ill confessed to Dr. Wieler that he had been getting liquor for a group of people in our class, and Doc Wieler reported it to the Duke. I happened to be having lunch with one of the classmates involved when a telegram arrived saying that he should immediately return to the school because there was reason to believe that his diploma should be withdrawn. I think there were six or eight of them. They all came back, and they had their honorable dismissals withdrawn, which meant that none of them could get into Harvard, Yale, or Princeton. I always thought that was a lousy deal after they had graduated."

Dismissing those boys was far from the end of it for the headmaster. Among the follow-up letters dispatched by the Duke was one to Potter Stewart, which began:

"As onetime President of the class of 1933, you will be interested to learn that seven of your classmates have been definitely proved to be guilty of serious offenses against the regulations of the school – so serious as to lead the faculty to conclude that we could not give them Honorable Dismissals."

Though the Duke's letter went no further than to name the boys, the future justice of the Supreme Court crafted the following response: "The first news which came to me of the seven members of our class having been dishonorably dismissed was when I received a letter from [one of those boys]. This letter was more of an apology to the class than anything else, and it expressed intense humiliation. I feel very badly about the whole thing; I am sorry that our class at the end caused so much trouble for the school, and I cannot help but feel sorry for some of the boys and their families.

"It is true that the Student Council never took any action on this matter, nor did they in fact ever even discuss it. At the same time I am sure that almost all of us knew, or heard rumors, that there was drinking and smoking going on in our class. I talked to two of the boys, trying to dissuade them from their actions, but I did this purely as a friend, and I failed miserably in my purpose.

"It is natural that Student Council members, as members of their class, hear of various misdeeds in the class. These misdeeds often concern friends of the members of the Council; often they are backed up by no real evidence; often a member of the Council hears of these things in confidence. It is thus not hard to see why a member of the Council hesitates as to what course to take. We certainly took the wrong course this year when we weakly shut our eyes to the things that were going on in our class.

"It would seem wise to me for the council next year to formulate a definite course of action that a member of the Council should follow when he hears of any misdeeds in his class. . . . [I believe] that there were only two boys who were essentially bad in this group, and that the other five were only very weak and very foolish. Thus if these two boys had been weeded out by the Student Council and the faculty earlier, five boys would have been saved.

"As fall approaches and I look forward to entering a new environment, I cannot help but appreciate even more fully the happiness and benefits that I enjoyed while I was at Hotchkiss. Some day I hope to express my appreciation in something more lasting and definite than words [and] live up to the trust you have put in me."

On being shown his classmate's letter for the first time some fifty-five years after the fact, Woods McCahill chuckled. "When we passed the applejack around," observed the gentlemanly lawyer who continues to serve the school as trustee emeritus, "I don't remember seeing Potter turn it down."

Potter Stewart died in 1985. At a memorial service at the Washington Cathedral, his younger brother, Zeph, also a trustee emeritus today, made these remarks: "What a show he provided for his younger brother and for his not altogether admiring family in his youth! Those who have known [Potter] only in the more serious and careful character of his later career could hardly imagine the fun and tricks and mimicry that made every day with him a comic drama when we were boys. What I was seeing, I now realize, were the sources of that energy and wit that were later tamed to the service of his profession and country and that fueled his capacity for work and showed through in his marvelous aphorisms. . . .

"Potter never lost his sense of the comic and the dramatic, but he was never blinded by them either. I remember that years ago he was amused by the imagery of a poem by Robert Louis Stevenson, some simple stanzas from "A Child's Garden of Verses", and he read them to me with a flourish. But then he copied down these verses and carried them in his wallet for the rest of his life. In their simplicity and whimsy they reflected the unpretentious courage of his own attitude at the end of life:

> "Must we to bed indeed? Well then
>   Let us arise and go like men,
>   And face with an undaunted tread
>   The long black passage up to bed.
>
> "Farewell, O brother, sister, sire!
>   O pleasant party round the fire!
>   The songs you sing, the tales you tell,
>   Till far tomorrow, fare ye well!"

xiii / "When Potter was at Hotchkiss, Henry Ford's grandson was there," relates Zeph Stewart, who had entered Hotchkiss as a lower mid in the fall of 1936, only three months after the graduation of Henry Ford. "Because of the Lindbergh kidnapping, Potter told me that they had groundsmen who were, in fact, detectives, watching him, guarding him. Everyone at the school was conscious that Henry Ford the Second was around."

In depicting Henry Ford's sojourn at the school, Mrs. Wertenbaker made a similar assertion, which greatly aroused the ire of George Van Santvoord. "We catch Mrs. Wertenbaker in a complete and deliberate lie," GVS wrote in his final notes, "[when she] tells of the arrival at Hotchkiss of Henry Ford, II, attended by a bodyguard, disguised as an assistant to Monnie. Why not get the facts? They are pretty simple. After several uneventful terms, the presence of Henry Ford, II, was given undue publicity by *Time* magazine. Three runaways from Hotchkiss were interviewed by a reporter who quoted one of them as 'almost successful in persuading Henry Ford to come with them.' Henry's comment was, 'Nonsense!'

"Soon after this came a letter to his father, threatening kidnapping. It was turned over to the F.B.I., who sent to Hotchkiss a vigorous young law student to investigate. Monnie was absent on leave. The visitor helped compile an alumni addresses list and gave his afternoons to helping our swimming coach. After two or three weeks he reported that it would be incredibly difficult to kidnap Henry at the school and went back to Washington. All was quiet and unexciting. But Hotchkiss boys who read *Time* magazine were horrified at the absurd errors they found in the detailed story of the runaways. It began with the school dining room 'with Homer looking down from the mantelpiece.'

"The figure there is *not* Homer but *Olympian Zeus*. And doesn't the fool know *Homer* was blind? A dozen more howlers followed."

In fairness to the writer of that article in *Time*, it should be mentioned that the Duke at one point did convey his displeasure to Henry's parents over their son's choice of friends at the school. Ironically, a dozen years later, when GVS visited his former entrustee in his Dearborn office, the new chairman of the Ford Motor Company said that "Hotchkiss was the last time in my life I could tell who my friends really were."

In 1953, Henry Ford II, at thirty-six, became the youngest winner of the Hotchkiss Man of the Year award. He served as a trustee from 1960 to 1967. The generosity of the Ford family to the school over the years is symbolized by the Edsel Ford Memorial Library and the William Clay Ford indoor tennis courts.

xiv /   "**W**hen we were at Hotchkiss, we knew that we were having a wonderful experience," says Thomas S. Quinn, Jr. '35, now retired from his family-owned steel business in Lebanon, Pennsylvania. "It isn't something that dawned on us many years later. We knew it at the time. I think that fully 80 percent of our class were of the same mind. We not only knew we were having fun; we knew that we were in a historic setting in an educational institution that was second to none. And, of course, the God-figure there was George Van Santvoord. If there was one thing he instilled in that whole faculty and student body, it was an incentive to be curious about what's going on around you. I learned to become deeply interested in current events, and he re-inforced my interest in public service. The Duke was personally inter-ested in every boy in the school."

Tom Quinn's class of 1935 was also the class of James Humphrey Hoyt, after whom Hoyt Field was named. "He was a wonderful guy, the number-one guy in our class," says Newton I. Steers, Jr., former congressman from Maryland. "Jim's close friend Bud Humphrey* was also in our class. Jim was a good athlete though he wasn't quite as good as Bud, who was the captain of the football team. But Jim was ex-tremely handsome and extremely hard-working. He was always near the top academically. He won all the prizes at Hotchkiss. I can't re-

---

*Gilbert W. Humphrey '35 became a trustee and a Hotchkiss parent and grandparent.

member the names of them now, but this guy who stood for the best at Hotchkiss then snuffed out his own life while he was a freshman at Yale. It was a terrible thing to hear, a terrible shock to all of us."

Beneath the veneer of good form and cheerful attitude, life entailed inescapable sorrow at the school. Tragedies seemed to strike with all the greater intensity because the Hotchkiss community was so tightly knit. In the final years before reaching mandatory retirement age, the venerable Uncle Joe Estill tried not to betray the grief he felt over his younger son, in whose memory the Estill Prize is awarded to this day. At thirty-two, incurably ill, Wallace Estill withdrew into the Arizona wilderness, where he killed himself with a shot to the head. And the brilliant Dr. John Bickford, who defected from the Exeter faculty to Hotchkiss after reading the Duke's speech of 1926 sponsored by the *Yale Daily News*, succumbed to gastric ulcers in 1937 – bringing Potter Stewart back to the school to deliver a eulogy.

Uncertainties that in our time have been largely eliminated still plagued everyday life. "I became friendly during my prep year with a guy named Bob Kaufman," relates Newton Steers. "He was known as Rip. One day he had a sore back and asked me to rub it with liniment. My God, it turned out he had infantile paralysis! His was a very light case, but they had to close the school." Another classmate, G. d'Andelot "Don" Belin, elaborates: "Six boys contracted polio, including two sets of brothers, and we were sent home in mid-November, given various assignments to do, and brought back the twenty-sixth of December. It was a rather unusual prep year calendar."

Don Belin had come to Hotchkiss as part of a contingent of thirteen boys including Tom Quinn, who had prepared together at Fessenden. Also among them was Don Belin's neighbor from Pennsylvania, William W. Scranton, whose parents had registered him at Hotchkiss when he was eight years old. This would seem not at all premature by the reputed standards of such schools as Groton, where the parents of a newly born son with the proper bloodlines supposedly dispatched two telegrams, one to the paternal grandparents and the other to Groton's headmaster, Endicott Peabody. Under Dr. Buehler, Hotchkiss too had devised an advanced registration form; no doubt partly for the snob value, but also for the practical reason that in the pre-Depression era the school was indeed heavily oversubscribed.

"You can apply for Billy's admission in the fall of 1930 as you suggest," Mr. Buell, then the acting headmaster, had written in 1925 to the prospective student's father in a friendly "My dear Worthington:" letter. "The application can later be postponed for a year without loss of priority."

"Billy," who became governor of Pennsylvania and U.S. ambassador to the United Nations, explains why it was postponed: "I'm deeply indebted to Hotchkiss because I was a problem child in one sense of the word. Physically I was very immature. To give you one idea, in 1934, the last part of my upper mid and the first part of my senior year, I grew seven inches. So you can imagine what size I was when I first came. Dr. Wieler and all the teachers were very considerate of my physical condition. The Duke used to do just little things to give me encouragement and make me realize I had support."

One of the governor's first and most lasting memories goes back to being at the Duke's table as a prep: "We sat down, and he said, 'Scranton, there's a minister in Salisbury who weighs one hundred and twenty pounds, and he's married to a woman who weighs two hundred and sixty pounds. What kind of a buggy would you design for them?'"

Young Billy's relationship with the Duke quickly evolved beyond respect: "I was very fond of him, and not many people were. They all admired him, but I was fond of him. He was a very loving man. It was all very indirect. He didn't kiss you or hug you, not him. Just a little touch. He would come up to you in that long corridor and just quietly put his hand on your elbow and quietly speak to you about something or other. Of course, if he didn't like a person, which was really rather rare, that person knew it. There was not much diplomacy in the Duke."

There also was not much diplomacy involved if the Duke was intent on correcting a boy's misconduct – as Newton Steers soon found out: "I came to Hotchkiss from the public school system in White Plains, where we lived. In a bourgeois way, I felt I had been a little above the people in that area. Then I got to Hotchkiss and it was exactly the opposite. Here was Bill Scranton of Scranton, Harry Whitin of Whitinsville, Henry Ford of Ford, Bill Atterbury, whose father headed the Pennsylvania Railroad, then the nation's largest. I was not over-whelmed, but I was impressed, dazzled. I was also horrified at first to hear so many of my classmates swear. I wasn't very popular, and I was quite introverted, and being at the same time very talkative, it shouldn't be surprising that instead of ignoring what I'd heard, I be-came the biggest user of these words;* so much so, that the Duke called me in. He said in his majestic way, scaring me to death, 'New-ton, your language makes you sound like a sewer running down the main corridor of Hotchkiss.' Those were strong words and I've remem-bered them for sixty years.''

Newton Steers's classmate Don Belin was taken by another aspect of the Duke: ''He was interested in some of the less conventional, less successful boys. I remember being impressed one day when people at his table were making sneering remarks about a shy boy in our class who obviously was having a tough time. He said, 'Now listen, you fellows, just don't get on your high horse about so-and-so. I'll bet there isn't a boy in the school who knows as much about eagles as he does.' The Duke happened to know that, and he impressed us with that.'

Belin, the former general counsel for the U.S. Treasury and now law partner at Boston's Choate, Hall & Stewart, recalls another experience he will never forget, if only because of its somewhat nightmarish qual-ity: ''At our commencement, I had been made the valedictory speaker. I cranked up a little speech that I had to give, with enormous apprehen-sion. The main outside speaker was the president of the University of Pennsylvania. He was interminable and absolutely boring, but we got through that, got through the prizes and everything else. The Duke

---

* Years later, Newton Steers felt challenged to ''keep up'' in a somewhat different way after he married Nina Auchincloss, stepsister of Jackie Kennedy: ''I think I was affected by the fact that women were throwing themselves at Jack. That was before he became president. God knows, after he became president, it was really ludicrous. Anyway, I saw all these women who were anxious to become groupies to poli-ticians, and it went back to my unpopularity at Hotchkiss. So I took up politics, thinking of it as a way of overcoming my lifelong tendency to introversion.''

got up with this distinguished guest and started to walk off the chapel steps. He actually was walking down the aisle, when he stopped and looked at the program and said, 'Oh, my goodness, we've forgotten something. We've forgotten the valedictorian.' So he went back up and sat there for my speech. I got out of there in about ninety seconds. That was a real scare.''

Newton Steers has his own particular recollection of the event: "It was an extremely hot day, and if Don Belin had been less smart, he would have talked us all into prostration. But he got up there and in effect said, 'It's too hot so my speech is going to be short. It's now over.' At Yale, Don would be Bones, chairman of the *News* – really, one of the biggest men in our class, which also produced Cy Vance, Bill Bundy, Stan Resor, and, of course, Bill Scranton.''

Another member of the Fessenden contingent in Don Belin's Hotchkiss class was Thaddeus R. Beal. During the summer prior to coming to Hotchkiss, Ted had broken his neck; and when he arrived as a prep, he was in a rigid metal brace. GVS took special note of the youngster imprisoned in this contraption, and before long Ted and the Duke developed the same sort of outgoing relationship already characterized by Bill Scranton – who happened to be Ted's Hotchkiss roommate. Ted's parents came up several times during his prep year to thank the extraordinary headmaster for whom their son could not say enough.

During Ted's lower middle year his father died, and the bond between the boy and the headmaster became even more that of father and son. His widowed mother now also placed her younger son, John, in the Duke's hands. Her interest in Hotchkiss took a new turn. "Mother used to come to Hotchkiss to see me," recalls John W. Beal '37, "but she didn't really come to see me."

Alice Dresel Beal was not the only mother of a Hotchkiss boy to take a personal interest in the Duke. "People would ask him, 'How come you aren't married?'" recalls Archibald Coolidge. "He once said to me, 'I suppose the right answer is, 'None of your business.'" According to Coolidge, the mother of a student in the class of '30 presented GVS with a superb Great Dane named Rugnir, who reputedly understood only German. Alas, the Duke's ready affection for the dog failed to extend to the donor, and one day when GVS was away, the mother drove to the school and absconded with the dog. "The Duke was much upset by the dognapping," recalls Coolidge. Determined to avoid any disruption in the school's routine which would undoubtedly result if the disappearance of the headmaster's conspicuous companion were to be noted, the Duke immediately took himself to the nearest Great Dane kennel and returned with a virtual look-alike whom he also named Rugnir. Although the new Rugnir responded wholly to English, this was a difference which was picked up by almost no one at the school.

Why Alice Beal succeeded where so many mothers failed perhaps could only be elaborated upon by the principals; suffice it to say that the Hotchkiss community as a whole, and the trustees in particular, welcomed the prospect of a union which promised a more sympathetic presence for visiting parents at the school. "Parents had trouble with the Duke because he wasn't the kind to engage in idle chatter, particularly with mothers," says Bill Scranton. "There's an interesting story about my mother and the Duke. She and my father came up for a visit in the fall, and there was some kind of entertainment on Saturday night. At the end of the entertainment, the Duke came up to Mother and said, 'Mrs. Scranton, would you and Mr. Scranton meet me in my office tomorrow after lunch?' They went, and when they got there the first thing he said was, 'Well, now, what do you want to hear about Bill?' Mother looked at him and said, 'I don't want to hear anything about Bill. I think I know more about him than you do.' From then on the Duke loved my mother."

Mrs. Worthington Scranton was a formidable character in her own right; a Republican national committeewoman referred to in her part of the world as "the Duchess." When her son graduated, she sent George Van Santvoord perhaps the only letter he ever received with a "My dear 'Duke'" salutation. "Under your guidance, Hotchkiss has not only developed [Bill] physically, mentally, and spiritually," she wrote in part, "but it has made him so deeply happy, that I think no headmaster could possibly have done more for his boys than you have done for yours."

More than half a century later, after a distinguished career in public life which included making a presidential bid, William Scranton has returned to pursuing that love of knowledge which he first acquired from the Duke – this time, studying the Italian Renaissance. Surrounded by mementos of his life in his Scranton, Pennsylvania, office, which he frequents between terms at the University of California in Santa Barbara, the trim, shirt-sleeved gentleman with a rep tie stands up to bid his Hotchkiss interviewer goodbye. "If you happen to talk to John Hersey," he says with an impish grin, "tell him I hold him responsible for all the trouble I've gotten myself into since Hotchkiss. After all, he was my senior advisor when I was a prep."

xv / Three years after graduating from Hotchkiss, Bill Scranton along with his Yale roommates, Don Belin and Ted Beal, served as ushers at the wedding of George Van Santvoord and Alice Dresel Beal, Ted's sensuously elegant mother. The slim, immaculately clad Carle Parsons was best man at the simple ceremony, and at the outdoor reception Hotchkiss faculty members and students mingled with the relatives of both families. Among those helping to launch the Duke on this new, unpredictable voyage was Frederick Delano. An uncle of FDR and a friend of both of the principals involved, he considered the Duke to be such a confirmed bachelor that he had promised to come with bells on if the wedding indeed took place. True to his word, this jovial elderly gentleman came with a harness of sleigh bells strapped over his suit.

One of the youngest members of the wedding was Ted and John Beal's little sister, Allelu – in my time a decade later, an unattainable blond Vassar heartthrob for us boys at the school – now Allelu Kurten, mother of three adult children and general secretary of UNIMA-USA, the international association of puppeteers. Allelu's portrait of her brothers' headmaster takes on a special dimension now that Hotchkiss is coeducational:

"When I moved to Hotchkiss at the age of eight, it was a pretty scary thing suddenly to have that man as my father. I never called him my stepfather, because I'd never known my own father. I was from the outset allowed to sit in Father's study provided I was seen and not heard. He had this wonderful Great Dane, and Rugnir and I would curl up by the fire and I would do my homework. Rugnir was my father's dog and no one else's. If anyone shook hands with my father for a longer time than usual, Rugnir would take his hand and pull it away. But I loved animals and animals loved me. I remember thinking to myself, 'Anybody who has a dog like this must be all right.' He, I think, felt that anybody whom that dog loved as much as Rugnir obviously loved Allelu must be all right. So, over the dog we got to be friends.

"My father prefaced a lot of remarks by saying, 'I'm packing your bags for the future. You won't hear me now, but one day you will.' And he made me his companion. He loved the woods and all the natural things. We used to canoe in the Adirondacks, and he'd read me books out of his memory. He read me *Tom Sawyer*, and *Huckleberry Finn* from memory. I could almost see him turning the pages in his mind. He had complete recall of these wonderful things. When I'd ask him questions, he'd always amaze me with his answers.

"I remember saying to him, 'Father, how much money is enough?' He'd say, 'Enough to put food in your mouth, keep a roof over your head, pay the doctor's bills and keep you out of hands of unscrupulous people.' Then he looked at me and said, 'Any more than that and you'll get into mischief.' He really thought that women were the ones who got into mischief. That's the reason why I have a puppet show now where God is a woman and Adam picked the apple. I was tired of being blamed for that apple, and I was tired of being blamed as the eternal Eve. Father said, 'One thing about women in the old days – they had too much to do to get into mischief.'"

When Allelu was twelve, her own potential "to get into mischief" began to appear: "I was developing as a girl, and I had a boyfriend in the school. My parents thought, 'This is extremely dangerous. We must have her go someplace else.' My father was a trustee at Emma Willard, and that's where I ended up. The problem was that I had been around only boys, and I didn't know how to act as a girl. In my eighth grade at Emma Willard, there were five of us girls. So it was four against one, and I cried myself to sleep every night. When I came home for vacation, I said, 'Father, I want to quit.' He asked me, 'Allelu, are you ahead or behind?' and when I told him I was behind, he continued, 'Get ahead, and I'll let you quit.' So I went back, and the tiger in me came out, and I said to myself, 'All right, how do I get ahead?' And I started to figure out how girls think. I was watching and listening, and by the next year there were a few more girls who were a little more like me. I kept saying, 'I'm going to get ahead, I'm going to get ahead!' Of course, what father knew that I didn't was that as soon as you get ahead, you don't want to quit. I was at Emma Willard for five years, and by the end I was a class leader and having a marvellous time. Father gave the graduation address, and when he gave me my diploma and two of the top prizes and kissed me, it was a moment for both of us. To this day in many situations I hear him asking, 'Are you ahead or behind?'"

Allelu, not surprisingly, grew up with an idealized picture of Hotchkiss life: "Later on, Mother would say, 'Allelu, that's because you didn't know.' There were two divorces, and she named some other things. I said, 'Mother, you're kidding.' She said, 'No, I'm not, but this was not worthy to be mentioned.' They never gossiped. Father always inveighed against talking mischievously. Whenever I remarked, 'Well, they say . . . ,' Father would bellow, 'Who are they?'.

"At the school, Father didn't allow himself to have a private life. He said to me once, 'When you're in a position of responsibility, you must be above reproach. You cannot let down for a minute.' It took about fifty miles to get the school out of his system. When I was eighteen, Father took me on a trip to Quebec with him. As soon as we were off on our own, he was a different person. He'd sing and teach me silly songs and quote limericks. He took me to dinner and ordered a bottle of wine, and then we walked along the boardwalk, arm in arm. He was a father showing his daughter how to be grown up."

Allelu often found herself serving as a bridge between her parents. "For my mother, coming to Hotchkiss must have been difficult. Her

The Duke and the Duchess with Rugnir in front of the headmaster's house

first husband had been twenty-four years older than she, and I think he pampered her very much. What Father was to her romantically, I don't know. He was a Victorian man, and he was not easy to live with. Hotchkiss was his domain, and he put his stamp on everything. But Mother was also extremely strong. Father was always respectful of women who were strong-minded and weren't ditherers. He didn't put up with dithering for a single minute, and as headmaster, he was besieged by a lot of dithering mothers worrying about their sons. Yet I don't think Father realized how strong-minded my mother really was. This inevitably led to a great many arguments. Of course, in those days people stayed together and they worked together. In a way, Mother was perfect for the school because she was strong enough to create her own role. She was wonderful as the headmaster's wife. I remember her arranging flowers in the chapel, welcoming visitors. Mother really made people feel at home. The faculty wives came, and she would talk to them and be supportive. I remember the dinners she gave for the new boys; the after-game gatherings with wonderful glazed doughnuts and cocoa for parents and alumni; the endless coffees and receptions; the Christmas parties with the huge tree in the big room. Mother added a very necessary note to the Hotchkiss community, and I think she truly enjoyed it.

"My father never felt that happiness was a worthwhile goal. He used to say, 'There's fun in life!' But one did not pursue happiness. One really tried to live a useful life, one really tried to serve others with whatever special talents one had, and if you did these things, then you were going to enjoy life. And you never dwelt on yourself. He had a couple of suits, an odd jacket or two, but nothing in abundance, nothing in excess. In our house if you were a girl or a woman, you didn't look in a mirror except to see if your hair was combed, or your lipstick was on straight.

"My father was an intensely simple man. He lived a very clear life, and you knew who he was and what he was. 'Do your best, Allelu,' he always said to me. 'If you do your best and fail, that's the best you can do. The important thing is, you tried.' His own best was considerable because he was a considerable person. He was made for the job. He was made to be the Duke. The school was lucky to have him, as it was lucky to have the people who came before him and after him, each putting his mark on the school.

"To me, of course, he was unique. He was my father, and he was my friend – a friend I could rely on without fail. As one of The Lost Boys said of Peter Pan, to me he was the sun and the moon and the stars."

xvi /   Others beyond his immediate family and the Hotchkiss community were able to benefit from the Duke's ubiquity. As one of the founders and president of the Connecticut Headmasters Association, it was

George Van Santvoord's task to assist some of the less prominent private schools. "We had to inspect, advise and often give temporary accreditation to schools of exotic or unusual character," the Duke noted. "For example: a group of Lithuanian monks, fleeing from Soviet annexation, came for refuge to [Thompson, Connecticut] with a handful of refugee pupils and no knowledge of English; or perhaps it was a very orthodox rabbi in Bridgeport, teaching a tiny group of boys exclusively in Hebrew." The Duke was also vice president of the New England Association of Colleges and Secondary Schools, a position he filled until his election as a member of the Yale Corporation.

Despite such affiliations, the Duke did not place undue stock in academic credentials. "Think of all the wonderful boys we would have missed who went to Hotchkiss if we had accepted only those from the ninety-eighth percentile," he once told Allelu. "I put my trust in the middle-of-the-roaders. The dumb ones get into mischief because they don't really know any better. The bright ones have so many possibilities that quite often they can't settle on anything. They're good at everything, and they often come up with nothing. The middle-of-the-roaders who really care often find one thing that fascinates them. They pursue that for the rest of their lives."

Among these middle-of-the-roaders was a boy from Colorado, Raymond "Doc" Freeman '39. The most formidable obstacle he encountered at Hotchkiss materialized in the person of Archibald Coolidge in senior English. As Doc Freeman recalls, he reached a point when he doubted whether he would make it: "Arch Coolidge was stiff. He was very requiring, very meticulous. He insisted that you have your papers in on time. When I handed in my term paper ten minutes late, I got a zero. This made me pretty distraught, because I knew if you didn't pass senior English, you were wiped out, you wouldn't graduate. But here is where the Duke came in. I was walking along the long corridor near the post office, and he came up from behind. I didn't see him, but I felt him take me by the arm and direct me a little bit off to the side. We walked along slowly, and he said, 'Freeman, Mr. Coolidge likes you. He says you're going to make it. He says don't worry.' Of course, it meant everything to me to hear that. I thought, well, this is the final word! The Duke then said, 'Just keep working!' Which I did, and I felt, yes, I will make it. I think it was the psychological boost that turned the corner. I wonder how many other boys the Duke did that for."

Doc Freeman returned to Colorado, where he went to college and entered medicine, which he has been practicing with devotion ever since. In fact, it was at Hotchkiss that he acquired his nickname. Doc's class president, William L. Bryan, had bestowed it on him, as Bill had done likewise on so many other of his classmates at the school. Bill Bryan's own nickname was "Boner," which he cherishes to this day.

Boner Bill came from a fiercely loyal Hotchkiss family. His father, "Whispering Jim" Bryan, had been in the class of 1911, and it was he who subsequently introduced Gene Tunney to the school. Explains Bill, "You know, before my parents married, my grandmother took aside my mother-to-be for a word of advice. 'Hazel,' she said, 'there are two things in life never cross Jim on. One is Hotchkiss and the other is Yale.' A half dozen other family members attended Hotchkiss – or would attend – and Bill had a unique status at the school:

"My contribution was that I held up the class from below. I was the world's worst concentrator – and still am. I'd go to the library early in the morning, and everyone thought, 'There goes the most conscientious person that ever lived.' Word even filtered back to my family. But I'd be sitting there in the spring, thinking of baseball and fishing, and in the winter, saying, 'Oh boy, can't wait for the ice and skating to begin.'

"Lower mid year, Dick Gurney was my corridor master and English teacher. He and I immediately had one bond. I was a Boston Braves fan; he was a Boston Red Sox fan. Dick knew I got the old *Boston Post* to keep up with the team. It arrived a day or two late, and I would quickly read it, and then sneak it under his door every night. I'll never know how I did it without a classmate seeing me and thinking, 'Oh, boy, that Bryan, he'll stoop to anything to pass English!' But Dick Gurney never mentioned it, never gave it away. He was my favorite teacher, and he could see through everything. He used green ink to correct our papers. I got a theme back from him once, with just one comment: 'This is so awful it doesn't make nonsense!'

"The one person my father never stopped talking about was Monnie, Mr. Monahan. He was a figure of strength and encouragement, but also discipline. I remember the time my brother Jim came up from Yale to see us in the Taft game, which was always a big ball game in my upper mid year. I was playing center field, and in the second or third inning, my brother came by the dugout and put his head around the corner to tell me something. He just spoke to me one word or two. The next inning, someone else was in center field for the rest of the game. Monnie was unbending. You didn't talk to another person. Your concentration was on the game, not on the girl that's sitting up in the third row of the stands. He was a great sportsman, stood for the best. In the last game he ever coached, I'll never forget him coming around to each person and mentioning something we had done well and shaking hands. That was the biggest moment; that was something. He had never done that before. After three years, to see this side of him!

"My dad had been head of St. Luke's, and I was too. In those days, we used to work with the Boys Club in New Haven. Gave them old baseball uniforms, and then in the summer, we'd spend two or three weeks with them in summer camp. That feeling of service at Hotchkiss, of helping others was a strong part of the school spirit. Another part was the chapel program. I think there were forty-two Sunday services, or forty in the year, or thirty-six. Whatever it was, you could be asleep in thirty-five out of the thirty-six, and then one day you heard something, or were inspired to do something, or had your mind opened up to do something. It could change your whole life.

"The Duke, of course, had great standards. The most valuable thing I got from him and took away with me from the school was a shoring up of my own conduct of living. I was lucky to have gone to a school which pushed the same kind of ideals as my family. My grandfather used to say, 'You're either honest or you're not honest. There's no such thing as being ninety-five percent honest.' I think that was so clear at Hotchkiss, that honor. They used the word 'gentlemen.' What it meant was honesty, integrity, decency."

After World War II service on a Coast Guard cutter, Bill Bryan completed his education at Colby College. Forsaking his family roots on suburban Long Island to settle in rural Maine, he returned as an administrator to Colby, where he met a thin, jug-eared student named Art White, whose future he helped to change – and in the process, the school's as well:

"I knew Art because his wife-to-be, Cynthia, was working in the dean of women's office at Colby, and I was working with the dean of men. Art was then a senior, and I asked him what he was going to do next. He said, 'I want to go into teaching – private school, a boarding school.' I said, 'Great! What do you have in mind?' He told me about Vermont Academy, where he knew the headmaster. I had to do some fast talking to convince him that he should also look at Hotchkiss.

"Art didn't have a car, and neither did I. But I borrowed one, and off we went. The whole six-hour trip I was hepped on the subject of how Hotchkiss was so democratic. I had visited Art's home and seen a large, devoted family trying to help one another. His parents had to work hard to make ends meet. Now here's Art driving with me to Hotchkiss. So the whole time, I'm telling him about scholarship boys. I had them nearly coming down in sack cloth, trying to convince him it wasn't a rich man's school.

"We finally drove through the gate and pulled up in front of the school. Right ahead of us in a big car – a Lincoln or a Buick – this kid is in the back seat. The kid jumps out, never even turns around. The chauffeur gets out a couple of big suitcases and golf clubs, and follows the kid. Art turns to me, and with a perfectly straight face, he says, 'Very democratic school, eh Bill?'"

Arthur W. White eventually got the job – and after thirty years as a teacher of mathematics, varsity baseball coach, and dean of students, he became the most popular headmaster ever at the Hotchkiss School.

Bill Bryan himself briefly joined the Hotchkiss faculty when his classmate, Bill Olsen, became headmaster and appointed Boner Bill to the post once held by Otto Monahan. "My most vivid memory as athletic director is of the day Bob Kiphuth visited in the fall of '63," recalls the white-haired, sun-blushed Bryan. "Bob Kiphuth was the Yale swimming coach and many times Olympic coach. He was also on the board of trustees, and he said, 'I want to see the pool.' So over we went. He looked down and growled, 'It isn't filled!' And he hollered at me again, 'It isn't filled!' I'm standing there and I look in, and of course, the pool is as filled as it's ever going to be. He said, 'Let me show you something.' And he took a golf tee out of his pocket. There was no one in the pool and the water was perfectly smooth. He dropped in the tee, and he said, 'That pool should be filled so completely that when we drop in the tee there's a little overflow. How can you set world records here?' I'll never forget that as long as I live."

Bill Bryan left Hotchkiss to become director of admissions at the University of Maine. Now retired, Bill has metamorphosed into something of an institution in northern Maine, appearing as a lay preacher, working with local boys clubs, and coaching Little League. A director of the Labrador-Quebec Foundation (founded by his brother, Archdeacon Robert A. Bryan '49), Bill also happens to be a part-time scout for the Pittsburgh Pirates.

Bill lives in a tidy red farmhouse built more than a century ago; a hand-lettered sign by the RFD mailbox reads, "Fresh Eggs." "The challenge for Hotchkiss and the whole educational system is to have a little extra vision," says Bill, who likes to think of his homestead as the biggest in the world, because anybody is welcome from anywhere at anytime. "Yes, keep the academics high, but do not overlook the intangibles of a person. I think we want to keep turning out people who have gone through the fire and have their values straight."

xvii / By the time Bill Bryan was graduating in 1939, World War II was beginning to engulf the world. In Europe, Hitler had violated the Munich Accords by marching into Czechoslovakia, and then launched his blitzkrieg against Poland. The following year France fell to the Fuehrer without resistance.

There was now serious concern on the other side of the channel that Britain would be next. Among the defensive measures under consideration in bomb-beleaguered London was sending large numbers of children to safety in the United States. One of those involved in this project was Arthur L. Goodhart '08, a noted teacher of jurisprudence and the first American to be named as master of an Oxford college. The following handwritten letter to the Duke from his former classmate needs no elaboration:

Aug. 26, '40
Dear George,

Thank you so much for your letter of July 13th. I am glad that Hotchkiss is taking some of the English boys. I doubt whether many more will be coming over, especially those of school age. There is a growing feeling here that too much emphasis can be placed on safety, and that everyone ought to be in the same boat. There is also the danger of submarines which, although not large, seems to be as real as that from aeroplanes. The astonishing success of the R. A. F. during the past two weeks has been most encouraging, although at no time was there ever a feeling of depression here. . . . It would take a tremendous number of aeroplanes to do serious damage to London, especially if they have to come over at night.

Cecily and I are having a busy and cheerful time. I am enclosing a letter which I wrote in the *Times* two weeks ago, and the *Times Leader*. . . . As a result, I had a most interesting few days as I was called to London for various meetings. It seems to have annoyed the Germans who have attacked me in three broadcasts – I never expected such an honor.

I am now a full member of the Home Guard with a uniform which looks rather like a pair of rompers. The tin helmet, however, gives me a rather fierce and military appearance. . . . My fellow guard is a distinguished professor of philosophy who has hated Hegel all his life: he is anxiously waiting his chance to shoot a German parachutist in revenge. I have explained to him that this is an unphilosophic point of view, but he answered that he has never allowed philosophy to interfere with his pleasures.

Please give your wife our kindest regards. It is disappointing that we were not able to visit you at Hotchkiss this year, but perhaps we shall have better luck in 1941.

Ever yours,
Arthur Goodhart

Instead of better luck, 1941 brought Pearl Harbor. "World War II began while I was sitting in the common room at Coy as a lower mid," recalls John A. Luke, Sr. '44. "Among us students when we first heard of Pearl Harbor, we didn't quite know where it was, and the early reports either weren't completely descriptive nor could we appreciate the magnitude of what happened. But we knew that it was terribly dramatic. It changed the outlook and activities at the school. Pretty soon, travel to sports events, to away games, became restricted. Some masters were acting as air raid wardens and watching for planes at night. Other masters put on uniforms and began to leave. The school progressively moved to a wartime footing."

"Everybody wanted to be patriotic and go off to enlist," says G. Guthrie Conyngham '42, who was a senior at that time. "I remember the Duke addressed our class. He had a terrible time trying to keep everybody in place."

"There was no football schedule," says John N. Conyngham '44, Guthrie's younger brother. "Instead of athletics we'd go pick apples and dig potatoes. All we talked about was what we were going to do in the war. It was a very abnormal boarding school life. I guess what it did was to remove the tendency to play at the kinds of things upper mids and seniors usually play at."

There was little question as to what lay ahead for the graduating seniors. "I gave one of my favorite teachers, Bob Jerosch who taught French, my raccoon coat when I graduated," says the older Conyngham. "I told him I was going into the service and wouldn't be needing it." And indeed, a few months later as a freshman at Yale, Guthrie Conyngham enlisted in the Marine Corps. Beyond whatever patriotic fervor he felt, there was a practical reason for doing so. Once you reached eighteen, the draft would get you no matter what.

This prompted GVS to make a unique move. "At the end of our upper middle year, with the war going on very actively," explains John Luke, "it appeared to the Duke that those of us who would turn eighteen in the middle of our senior year would be drafted right then and there. So the Duke said he would be happy to have those of us who would be affected go to summer school at the end of our upper middle year, take courses from McChesney, Spud Murphy, and Taber, and he would let us graduate in September if we passed those courses."

"Out of our class of around eighty or ninety, there were eighteen of us who came back that summer," says the younger Conyngham. "We didn't have a graduation or anything, but we eventually got a diploma in the mail. And that's how we finished. I never spent my senior year at Hotchkiss."

Today, John Conyngham runs a prosperous supply business in Pennsylvania, along with his brother Guthrie (and another brother, William L. Conyngham '38). An easygoing, gregarious man, the younger Conyngham smiles as he recalls how quickly he learned the value of his Hotchkiss education: "About three weeks separated being a student in that pristine surrounding and being on Parris Island with fifteen thousand recruits and not having a hair on your head. They did their damndest to break you down. That's the bootcamp philosophy. But those people at Hotchkiss had made you realize you could do things that you didn't think you could. That was the kind of attitude you began to acquire from the time you were a cowering little prep. And it helped me make the quantum leap from Hotchkiss to being a marine recruit."

Yet John Conyngham and the handful of his classmates in that special summer school program felt they had forfeited something irreplaceable. "We were all enthusiastic and gung ho about the military effort and didn't mind so much at that time," explains John Luke at his Westvaco Corporation office, where he is president and CEO, and his brother, David L. Luke III '41, is chairman. "But to this day I feel quite a gap in my total fulfillment by not having had a Hotchkiss senior year and experienced the dimensions of Hotchkiss as a senior. The friendships, the perspectives, the accomplishments that come by virtue of the fact that you were an older boy – whether on the football team or the *Record* or whatever – one looked forward to his senior year and being able to fulfill or try to fulfill his boyhood dreams. Also intellectually, a more mature relationship with the Duke and his faculty would have been very meaningful to my own development. I feel as if there's a gap, and I am genuinely sorry it happened that way. But I would make the same decision again, and I was very excited about joining the Army Air Corps. It was the right thing to do under the circumstances of the war."

Some fifteen hundred alumni served in the armed forces during World War II. The school's Roll of Honor lists forty-nine names, including that of a member of the class of 1944 who did finish his senior year, Thornton A. "Gus" Lyttle. One of the most promising artists ever to have graduated from Hotchkiss, he died in the battle for Iwo Jima.

xviii / Among the preps at Hotchkiss during the final year of the war was John L. Loeb, Jr., who would have a controversial career at the school. In rating him "very high" four years later as a candidate for Harvard, the Duke summed up as follows: "John is chairman of the editorial board of the School newspaper. He is not a popular boy, and his election as Chairman is evidence of the respect he has won for integrity of character, honesty and intelligence. He has largely overcome the traits of sensitiveness and quick temper which brought him many difficulties during his early years here. He now handles himself very well, and with a start in a new environment should win popularity as well as respect."

"I was thinking what I could do for this history," says the towering, uncommonly handsome man as he welcomes his Hotchkiss visitor more than four decades later to his Park Avenue office in New York. John Loeb's dark hair is only slightly flecked by gray, and his English-tailored blue pin-striped suit accentuates a powerful, trim physique. "One of the things that has interested me most over the years – and which really developed out of my time at Hotchkiss – has been the whole Jewish question."

The principal events John Loeb wants to relate go as follows: "When I arrived at Hotchkiss in the fall of 1944, I met an extreme amount of anti-Jewish feeling. I remember that in the fall of 1944 they showed the first pictures of the holocaust. This was just towards the end of the war, and these pictures were a part of the regular newsreel before the feature film on a Saturday night in the old auditorium. It's hard to believe, but when they showed those terrible pictures, the entire school cheered.

"Looking back now I realize that anti-Semitism was at its peak in those years. Hitler had a tremendous influence around the world. People said, 'We don't like Hitler but at least he's killed the Jews.' At Hotchkiss I met a great deal of hostility because I was Jewish. There were only a very few Jewish boys there at the time. Some of them pretended they were not Jewish, and several of those who were Jewish left the school, including one who was later a classmate of mine at Harvard. He asked me how I could have taken it. But I understand that anti-Semitism was prevalent at all the top boarding schools in New England at this time.

"My mother and father had felt comfortable about sending me to Hotchkiss. A few members of my family had gone there before. I had a cousin, Robert Lehman, who had gone there, and another cousin, Arthur Goodhart, who became a great professor in England and was knighted by the Queen. So I don't think my parents had any awareness of the situation until I came home and told them how terribly upsetting this was.

"Somehow this got to the attention of my grandmother. She was from an old southern family, a hundred percent Jewish family, but she was also a member of the DAR, and her father, my great grandfather, had been a captain in the Confederate Army. She told me, in her own inimitable way, 'When your great-grandfather went off to the Civil War as a captain in the Confederacy, he met someone who called him a dirty Jew, and he knocked him down; afterward they became best friends. What you must do, the next time anybody insults you, just sock him!' Of course, coming from my grandmother, I thought that gave me total permission. I really didn't know exactly how to go about it, but my father at that time was a senior partner at Loeb, Rhoades, and there was a marvelous man who was a runner there who'd been a lightweight boxer, called Eddie Galorie. So, during the summer between my prep year and lower middle year, I trained with Eddie.

"When I got back to school my lower mid year, I was primed. My chief tormentor was a fellow from Butte, Montana; he was sort of the ringleader. We had quite a number of fights, and this came to the attention of the teachers. I don't think Hotchkiss had any Jewish masters then. There was nobody on the board who was Jewish. As I said, this went on for some time, and finally the teachers – who, may I say, were totally indifferent to my situation – finally said, 'We've had enough of all these scraps. If you guys really are angry with each other, put on the gloves and fight in the ring.'

"Of course, this was great because I felt prepared. We went into the gymnasium one afternoon and put on the gloves with several teachers looking on. We had three rounds of one minute each, and at the end we were pretty even. But by some miracle my Montana adversary got a black eye. Pretty soon the story was around the whole school that I had won. And from that moment on, the baiting gradually declined. Of course, what also helped was that the war was now over, and anti-Semitism was on the wane. Then when Israel became a state in 1948, anti-Semitism stopped pretty much altogether. Israel looked like a winner, and one thing you can say about people at Hotchkiss, they love to go with a winner."

As one researches the school's history, a curious parallel to the holocaust cheering comes to light: cheering during the announcement of FDR's death. Without in any way implying a moral equivalence, it seems that in both cases the reaction was at least partly a reflection of attitudes the students brought with them from home, perhaps concentrated by the close contact of like-minded individuals in an isolated milieu. Moreover, it was a well-entrenched tradition for Hotchkiss boys to cheer any grizzly, violent, or tragic movie scene in the auditorium, as if to rambunctiously deny – or scoff at – human mortality.

This is not to detract from John Loeb's overall charge. Indeed, when Hotchkiss was first established, it was to serve almost exclusively a Protestant clientele. This was implicit in the school's compulsory attendance at daily and Sunday chapel, which alone was probably enough to discourage some potential applicants. The application form inquired about both a religious preference and membership in a church.

There is no documentary evidence as to what role being a Roman Catholic or a member of any other non-Protestant but Christian sect played in the admission process. The school's policy toward Jewish applicants, however, is clearly reflected in a confidential letter dated August 30, 1906:

My dear Mr. Van Duesen,

Replying to your letter of Aug. the 20th, there is, of course, some prejudice against admitting boys of Hebrew families, and it is not the policy of the school to admit many such boys. This year there will be three with gilt-edge credentials, and one of them the brother of an old boy.

In reply to your question about the likelihood of a vacancy, I do not think there is much chance for young Cullman, and it will be wiser for his parents to make application elsewhere.

With kindest regards,

H. G. Buehler

In Buehler's time, one such boy with "gilt-edge credentials" was Robert Blum '17. "I was confirmed as a Jew in 1911, but my parents saw more of Christians; so I was always conscious about being a Jew, whether it was at Hotchkiss or not," Robert Blum explains. At Hotchkiss, young Robert's problem was that he had been assigned a roommate (perhaps as much because he was his relative) who also happened to be Jewish. "I didn't like the idea of segregating the two of us. I fought against it, and my family went to bat for me. I finally succeeded in being separated. You see, I was afraid that I'd not be liked by my fellow classmates because of my association with this roommate, who wasn't at all popular."

Robert Blum implicitly articulated what seems to have repeatedly manifested itself as a fact of student life at Hotchkiss. Whether or not the students liked somebody was based on a complex of intangibles rather than on any single factor such as whether or not he was Jewish. Of course, if the boy happened to be unpopular, his Jewishness could become the target of subtle and not so subtle barbs – as might, no less, a student's Roman Catholicism, national origin, or almost any distinguishing characteristic. To be sure, in a group of people as large as that at Hotchkiss, there were bound to be also some out-and-out bigots.

Buehler's policy on admitting Jewish students was not widely known. When the question was raised rather insistently at a faculty meeting during the interim headmastership of Walter Hull Buell, he is said to have calmly replied, "Oh, I always thought we would take about as many as we wanted."

The drama picks up again in the summer of 1926, with a relative of the Cullman who had been discouraged from applying in 1906 – a peppy fourteen-year-old, Joe Cullman:

"I was very happy at a school called Ethical Culture in New York. I was the oldest of four boys, and I remember very well one day my father came home and said, 'Son, you're going to Hotchkiss.' I said, 'Why is that?' He said, 'It's a very good way to get into Yale. Besides, my friend Harold Pumpelly ['11] went to Hotchkiss. He's the guy that drop-kicked the winning field goal in the last minute of the Yale-Princeton game, and that's a good reason to go to Hotchkiss.'

"About a month before the entrance exams for Hotchkiss, my father said to me, 'How's your Latin? You have to take an exam in Latin.' I said, 'You know that I've never taken Latin.' 'Oh,' he said, 'we'll have to correct that.' So he got me a tutor, and this tutor was a woman, and she used to come in around four-thirty when I came home from school. We lived in a brownstone just off Central Park West, and that was the time when I usually played stoop baseball. So I always had a conflict between my stoop baseball game and my Latin. You can imagine which got my priority. Besides, it was ridiculous. Even if I was a genius, which I'm not, in thirty days I couldn't have possibly learned enough Latin.

"When the expected results came back from Hotchkiss, my father said, 'We're going right up to the school, see the headmaster, see what happened.' So we journeyed up to Hotchkiss, took probably two and a half hours in the family car. We went straight to the headmaster's office. There was George Van Santvoord, towering over my dad, who was only five foot six. Mr. Van Santvoord was having one of his good days. I mean he was rather patient because my father kept saying, 'My son's a great young man, a great young man. I can't understand how he could not have been admitted to Hotchkiss.' You can imagine how I felt standing there, but my father persisted. "It's very important to me that he go to Hotchkiss. Isn't it, Joe?' I said, 'Yes, yes, it is, Dad, sure.'

"George Van Santvoord said, 'Let's go take a look at the records.' Out came the blue books, and I could see the red crayon marks all over. I got fifty in English, fifty in math. The Duke said, 'Let's see what he did in Latin.' It turned out I got fifteen on that. He finally said, 'Apparently your son is not scholastically prepared to go to Hotchkiss. I would recommend that he go to a place called Fessenden School for a year.'

"Driving back to New York, my father was pretty upset. He kept saying, 'They can't do that to us!' He took it as a personal insult. He then said, 'O.K., you're going to Fessenden.' I asked where it was, and he said, 'I'll look it up.' So I went to Fessenden, and I got into Hotchkiss with flying colors."

He also graduated with flying colors. "I met some of my best friends in my whole life at Hotchkiss," says the chairman emeritus of Phillip Morris, Inc., Joseph F. Cullman 3rd '31, who, in 1961, became a Hotchkiss trustee and, in 1973, Man of the Year. Of his three brothers who also went to Hotchkiss, one withdrew lower mid year for health reasons; another was sequestered three times for such offenses as causing a commotion in the dining room by wearing a morning coat that the family had sent him to try on for his sister's wedding. The other brother who went to Hotchkiss was Edgar M. Cullman '36; he, in 1987, became president of the Hotchkiss board.*

For much of the first half of this century, discrimination at Yale, unlike that at Hotchkiss, was institutionalized; not only with respect to joining campus fraternities or being tapped for the far more prestigious secret societies, but even in being accepted by one of the more "desirable" of the residential colleges. Thus we find George Van Santvoord sending an appeal to the master of one of these colleges on behalf of a recent Hotchkiss graduate: "Of the various freshmen I have talked to, he seemed to be the most intellectual and sensible of the group who had chosen your college and it will be a great disappointment for him not to get in. . . . The family are Jewish. The boy is a singularly attractive and agreeable youngster. He is very intellectual and was a distinctive and popular boy in his class here. . . . If any vacancies occur later on in your enrollment, I hope you will give this boy a chance of getting in."

The Duke was not wholly successful in transforming his own school into an enlightened enclave. The multifaceted tradition of baiting continued, and as John Loeb has pointed out, Jewish students found themselves disproportionately the targets in the 1940s. Although his own situation improved markedly after he bestowed that black eye on his chief adversary, Loeb was again victimized when a number of his clay sculptures on exhibit in the main corridor were defaced in patently anti-Semitic ways, such as deforming the noses into exaggerated stereotypes. "There definitely was anti-Semitism at Hotchkiss during those years," says a friend of the perpetrator. "John Loeb probably was the target of it because he was the smartest guy in the class at that time, and he was a hard worker. There probably was a certain amount of jealousy among the students." Another friend of the perpetrator

---

*In 1970, Woods McCahill had become the first Catholic to head the board.

phrases it somewhat differently: "John Loeb was terribly conceited. I won't deny there was anti-Semitism, but John also offered a perfect target."

Although the perpetrator escaped official detection (and was subsequently kicked out for another offense), any discord brought about by religious causes was particularly odious to the Duke. "It is sad to think what most religions started out to be and what they became," the Duke noted. "The Christian fold is too narrow and not lacking in men I shudder to have as colleagues." No less revealing was George Van Santvoord's own religious stance: "Religions worthy the name are attempts to find and follow a pathway to the Divine Power & Grace, 'merciful compassionate Owner of the Day of Judgment.' Religious differences are not of our own making, [and] quarrels and recriminations among the followers of these different ways are unseemly and unreasonable. Perhaps Buddhism has been most free of such unseemliness; I believe that Islam has been less stained by it than Christianity."

The Duke was thus not only nondenominational, but, unlike Dr. Buehler and most of the ministers with whom he shared the pulpit in chapel, did not subscribe to the absolute primacy of the Christian faith. While he devoted himself to such "Christian" tasks as revising the school hymnal in conjunction with three other schools, the Bible course he taught did not have the customary agenda of demonstrating the unique virtues of Christianity but recognized the similarities and good points of all religions. "It actually was the five great philosophies of life," says Bill Scranton. "I have the book still that he used in that Bible class he gave the seniors, in the headmaster's house. I learned more about philosophy in that course than I did in all the official philosophy courses I had at Yale."

Above all, the Duke was able to apply his commonsense perspective to this traditionally divisive aspect of life. "I once had a curious inquiry from the Northern Baptist convention as to how many Baptists we had at Hotchkiss," GVS recalled on that Wertenbaker tape. "So I got a religious census of the school, because religious preference was one of the questions asked on the application. Guess how many Baptists there were – two! We had 27 Jews that year, we had eight Quakers, and we had three Mormons.* It looks as if we were very anti-Baptist. But we were never bothered by any of that really at all. The only question was, 'Are these people going to be people who will gain from the experience, and who are worth our bothering with, and who are not going to be too intractable?' And occasionally, there would be all kinds of reasons for taking a boy. I remember one man who came and said, 'I never expected to send my boys away to school, but my grandmother has just given the oldest boy a motorcycle. I think it's time for him to go to boarding school.' So he came."

As for what GVS meant by intractable, he harbored a stereotype to which he occasionally succumbed. "Go easy on South Americans," he cautioned, in spelling out his admissions policies. "They're scamps, terribly sophisticated." According to the Duke, these applicants were often too rich, too spoiled, and lacking in a sense of social responsibility. But from interviews with some of the people who knew GVS, it seems that the headmaster's underlying concern about such boys may have been that their level of experience with the opposite sex could exert an unwholesome influence on other boys at the school.

xix /   George Van Santvoord was thought of as a god-like figure most often in the context of his capacity for righteous wrath. Those who had experienced it, for whatever cause, were likely to have a far more vivid understanding of Jehovah's ways. Yet a subtler analogy has often been overlooked – the Duke's unfathomable reasons for bestowing or withholding his grace.

---

*The Duke neglected to mention that an even larger contingent than the Jewish students undoubtedly consisted of Roman Catholics. Required by their faith unfailingly to attend Sunday Mass – which they were able to do at 9:00 A.M. at St. Mary's in Lakeville – the Catholics' main complaint of discrimination was that they also had to attend just as unfailingly the nondenominational service at 11:00 A.M. in the school chapel.

"I try to think of the basis for his affection – I don't think I'm over-stating it – for me," says Art Howe, whose father had been GVS's classmate. "I was certainly one of his middling students, and a guy who had to be disciplined to get anywhere because I didn't have the smarts to do it easily. But I think I always had enthusiasm, and the Duke loved anyone who dug in and did it enthusiastically. I grew close to him, particularly after I came back there on the faculty. We had not only the formal relationship of the school year, but we went off in the summers on fishing trips, repeatedly. I'll never forget the day back in the woods somewhere, after about two summers of this, he turned to me and said, 'You know, I think it's time you started calling me George.' Well, I couldn't handle it. I kept trying, for the next two weeks, quietly, out of the side of my mouth. After about six months, it finally became easy, and then it just strengthened the tie."

Not too many people, regardless of age, called GVS "George." Don O'Brien '52, a student when Howe was a young faculty member, draws a more inclusive picture: "I don't think the Duke had any favor-ite type of boy. His counterpart at Deerfield, Boyden, I think liked the athlete, straight-arrow type. The Duke was sort of a maverick. Because of him, there was a tolerance at Hotchkiss for boys who didn't really fit in."

What has not been often publicized, however, has been the Duke's seeming lack of generosity toward certain boys at the school. "You hear the stories that this man was so understanding of boys, such a great humanitarian," says Jay H. Lehr '53, whose letter detailing his unfortunate relationship with GVS appeared in the *Alumni Magazine* in 1985. "Afterward, I had calls from several people. Most were in their seventies, and for the first time, somebody had verbalized the thoughts they had carried with them all these years. They said it was just a wonderful feeling to realize they were not alone."

Jay Lehr at the time of this interview was training to become the world's fittest man of his age. A recreational parachutist, Iron Man Triathlon competitor, author of a half dozen books on water pollution, and executive director of the National Water Well Association, he liked to bill himself as "the happiest person on the planet."

Jay Lehr was anything but happy at Hotchkiss: "My parents were very old when I was born. My father had retired, and they decided they wanted to travel a lot. So they felt the best place for me would be in prep school. They couldn't have cared less that I liked the high school I was in. Basically, my parents bound me and gagged me, and dropped me off at the front step of Hotchkiss.

"From the beginning, the Duke called me Lear. I've always pronounced my name Lair. I used to hear that the Duke was one of the ten smartest men in America. Years later, when I got my Ph.D. and studied German, I found out that Lehr is a very common affix. I wondered if the Duke mispronounced it on purpose, or if he wasn't as intelligent as people thought. Whatever the case, the way he said 'Lear' was always kind of biting, like he was sticking it in me.

"I got excellent grades at Hotchkiss from the very beginning. My run-in with the Duke started over chewing tobacco. I didn't like chewing tobacco, but it helped me be accepted by my peers. The vogue in those days was to carry a beer can that had been cut open at the top. You kept it in your pocket as a spittoon. It wasn't against the no-smoking rule, but the Duke was extremely stern and called me a social dinosaur.

"I have no warm, fuzzy memories of the Duke. I was an unhappy, undersized person who was two years younger than many of the kids in my class. Looking at myself as an individual who was having difficulty adjusting because I really didn't want to be there, I can say that the Duke never made any contribution to making life easier. In my three years at Hotchkiss, he either wasn't perceptive enough to see that I needed help, or there were just too many students and I didn't stand out, or he couldn't have cared less. And he not only failed to reach out to me, but he was harsh, stark, and reprimanding. He typified the attitude of the old English type of prep school, trial by fire. Maybe that was his philosophy. He did me good indirectly, but it was in such a negative way.

"I do have one positive memory. All new students at the school were invited once to have dinner with the Duke. I remember that night clearly, my lower mid year, going over to his house. There were six of us, and he treated us as bona fide guests. I remember Mrs. Duke being extremely nice. She reminded me of the queen of England, and she carried herself that way. This was the only occasion I can recall when there wasn't any effort by the Duke to put on an austere façade.

"I guess I've placed a great deal of the blame on the Duke because he was the head of an institution that was not making me happy. Yet the situation was not altogether strange to me. My father, too, had been incredibly strict, and I lived in eternal fear of him. He also never said anything nice to me; so the Duke was just one more of his type. Of course, in retrospect, I realize I would have never gotten into Princeton without Hotchkiss. I've devoted a lot of time over the last twelve years to raising funds for the school."

It would serve little purpose to offer armchair psychoanalysis as to what might have gone wrong between George Van Santvoord and Jay Lehr. Any generalization would be too simplistic and in no way account for the lifelong anger felt by so many others besides Lehr, some of whom can cite a single incident which forever turned them against the Duke. Jodie Stone, whose husband, George, joined the Hotchkiss faculty as a mathematics teacher in 1949, witnessed two incidents of this sort: "Do you remember Thanksgiving dinners, and how they put white tablecloths on the tables, and we all came in and all the boys were in gray flannel suits, charcoal gray Sunday suits? Anyway, we were all standing waiting for Mr. Van Santvoord to ring that big bell and say grace, when some boy at our table reached over and took a mint from a little basket. Mr. Van Santvoord saw it, and he came across that dining hall, and that kid died. He never did eat any Thanksgiving dinner. Mr. Van Santvoord laid him out six ways to Sunday about being a boor, having no table manners, being rude to everybody else. He was a frightening man when he got going. Another time, there was a boy who had graduated and gone to West Point. He came back his sophomore year to visit, proud as a peacock of his uniform. He got out of the car and walked up to the porch of Main. Mr. Van Santvoord was standing there, and he just said, 'Well!' and turned his back and walked away. You never knew why he acted this way, when something seemed to be bugging him. The rest of the time he couldn't have been kinder or more considerate. I loved him. He was one of the great influences in my young life."

The Duke's wrath, however, was not always what it appeared to be. "I remember once he had just chewed out someone in my presence," recalls Robert Hawkins, then a young English teacher whom GVS had brought in from South Dakota because he wanted to have a faculty member from "one of those big square states." "I don't recall exactly what the boy had done, but he certainly deserved it. What I do remember is that when the Duke got through, he winked at me. Somehow it made me feel pretty good about him. He could wink in a very charming manner."

Under certain circumstances, the Duke was known to change his attitude toward a boy. One of the more dramatic turnabouts involved a student who was being expelled primarily at the Duke's behest. When GVS phoned the parents to come and pick up their son, he found out that the boy's mother was not living at home, and the father was too busy to do anything other than send a chauffeur. The Duke reversed himself and kept the boy.

xx / "The Duke was a snob, but there was an intensely democratic basis for his snobbery," says Marcellus "Gus" Winston '55, a member of the last class over which the Duke would preside. "I don't think he cared where anybody came from, how they looked, so long as they were interesting. If somebody came in who was selling brooms or greeting cards, and if the Duke had the time and got interested in how brooms or greeting cards were made, and that person evidenced knowledge about those subjects, he would talk to him for as long as it took to pull out all that knowledge. And he would respect him precisely for knowing about it."

Gus Winston's insight comes from the perspective of having been the first black student at the school. All other qualities aside, that alone made him interesting to GVS. "Tolerance is desirable, but it is a rather neutral stance," the Duke noted. "Isn't it better to prize the admirable qualities of those unlike oneself?" One of his favorite cartoons, drawn by Hotchkiss alumnus Peter Arno (C. Arnoux Peters '22)* for the *New Yorker*, showed two matronly ladies considering schools for their boys. One of them limited her choice to Groton and St. Paul's, but the other said that since the boys would go out into the world and have to deal with all sorts of people, perhaps they should go to Hotchkiss. The Duke's admiration for President Roosevelt was largely based on FDR's ability "to be sympathetic and friendly to all sorts of people." As Zeph Stewart recalls, "The Duke was considered a terrible radical. My brother told me that some parents were having their children report on what GVS said because they considered him a dangerous New Dealer."

As headmaster for a quarter century, the Duke consistently sought to bring some of the variety of the world to the school enclave, whether through visiting speakers such as Sergeant York depicting life in the Tennessee mountains or faculty members such as Chingis Guirey '40, a practicing Moslem and a superb equestrian who, according to the Duke, was a direct descendant of Chingis (better known as Genghis) Khan. Above all, GVS sought to intermingle interesting boys into the student body as the most effective antidote to the Greenwich, Connecticut, mindset. He recruited several Chinese-American students; he established exchange programs which placed a student from England and from Scandinavia in the senior class each year; and he was ever on the lookout to bestow scholarships on students with unusual backgrounds.

By 1950 George Van Santvoord was actively looking for a qualified black applicant, with the approval of the trustees. Andover and Exeter had been admitting black students for more than a hundred years, but most other prep schools had no plans to do so, and for the conservative Hotchkiss community, the Duke's intent evoked strong emotions. His staunchest ally at the school was John McChesney. Though his spouse's wealth enabled him to maintain a chauffeured Lincoln and hire faculty wives to grade his more routine tests, the ever-popular

---

*Arnoux Peters changed his name to Peter Arno to avoid embarrassing his family by cartoons satirizing America's social elite.

Mr. Mac considered himself philosophically a socialist. Taking the affirmative in a major article in the *Record* on the question "Should Negroes be admitted to Hotchkiss?" the white-haired, pixyish English teacher who was soon to retire wrote, "No educational institution can afford to be left behind the Major Baseball Leagues, the National Bowling Congress, and the United States Contract Bridge Association. . . . The man who even murmurs 'Untouchable' is guilty of great disservice to education, to democracy and to humanity." The rebuttal was authored by a group of unidentified seniors. "There is quite a difference between competing with a Negro and living with him," they asserted in the *Record*. "Wouldn't he be just an oddity, pointed out to passersby and kept as a monument to the racial tolerance of the Hotchkiss students? Is it fair to completely disregard the Negro's own personal emotions?"

There were other considerations. "We realized we had dynamite on our hands," noted Carle Parsons in his interview with Mrs. Wertenbaker. "If just for the sake of taking a Negro, we took him and then judged him by the same standards we did our ordinary students and kicked him out, people would say, 'Oh yes, this is just window dressing.' I was at that time marking all the entrance papers for the prep class. I remember recognizing that some papers were from Negroes because they were just abysmally poor. But finally, in the spring of 1951, I marked a perfectly phenomenal paper. I think probably no more than a dozen times in all the years I was there did I put a 95 on an entrance English paper. I noticed the name was Marcellus Winston, which was unusual, and when all of the marks in his other subjects came in, they were all above 85. The admissions people realized that here was our chance."

For Gus Winston, the chance was not altogether an unexpected one: "I was attending Banneker Junior High in Washington, D.C. It was a kind of a feeder to Dunbar High School, which was considered to be the best and most prestigious segregated high school in the country. Ralph Bunche's parents, who lived in Los Angeles, devised a way for him to attend Dunbar. Being at Banneker meant you already were on the right track. As a matter of fact, out of the thirteen boys in my class, five of us eventually reunited at Harvard."

It was hardly the normal school policy for the assistant headmaster to visit prospective students at their homes. George P. Milmine '17 was well suited for the task. A discreet, tweedy gentleman known for his bow ties and early use of audiovisual presentations in medieval history, he had been GVS's student at Yale. The Duke's invitation to Milmine in 1927 to join the Hotchkiss faculty was meant at least partly to help his former student recover from a severe emotional breakdown. For many years now the headmaster had trusted his deputy's judgment as if it were his own.

Gus Winston picks up the story: "My old man worked as a postal clerk, but both of my parents were college educated. We lived in a short block of distinctly middleclass housing, and the neighbors were schoolteachers and so forth in the black world of middleclass status. So George Milmine came to our house, sat down in the living room, and there we were. He was there to poke around, to look around, to see what was what, and we knew it. I was wearing a coat and tie, and I'm sure my old man was, too. My mother wore an attractive dress, and we were doubtless less boisterous than we normally were. But there was no strain. Mr. Milmine struck me as a nice and decent man. Shortly thereafter, we were notified that I was accepted at Hotchkiss."

As Carle Parsons explained in his interview with Mrs. Wertenbaker, "George laid the cards right on the table. He told Gus, as he was known, 'You're a pioneer, since you'll be the only one. It's going to be a very real challenge.'"

Gus Winston: "When the word got around at Banneker, there was some apprehension as to what I might experience and confront, how I might react and perform, and whether any black student could live through what the stress might be. My science teacher at Banneker, who was really a superb man, had been appointed to the Naval Academy in the late 1930s, but because of the nastiness and hazing he underwent, he hadn't lasted more than a year or so. Then there was the daughter of a neighbor, about ten years older than I. She had gone off to Wellesley, but the strain had been too much. She wound up transferring to a black college."

The logistic problem of getting Gus from Washington to the school was solved when a friend drove him and his parents there: "On the front porch of Main we met the Duke and Milmine and maybe somebody else. I frankly experienced no unusual apprehension as I watched my parents drive off that first afternoon. I wandered outside behind Buehler Hall, and just kind of walked around the fields. There was a touch football game going on, and I got into it, and I never looked back. I had played games all of my life, and this was just another game. I remember I met the guy who was to become my closest friend at Hotchkiss, Leigh Ardrey. He was a Texan, from Dallas, and he had the same sense of the kind of moves to make in those games. We were both basically southerners. We walked away together, sort of buddies, commenting on the styles of running and what not, and life started at that particular point.

"I never felt any personal or communal or political pressure to perform as such. Like other new boys, I looked around and got a sense of how people acted and talked and how they dressed. By the time I went home at Christmas of prep year, I knew enough to put together some money and went shopping at the right kind of a shop. I got some new jackets, trousers, and the right kind of loafers and that kind of thing. But it's not as if that sort of thing doesn't go on in every environment. I also came to the conclusion that it was not too good to be at the top academically, to appear to be a grind. It was all right to be near the top, and to excel in some area of your choosing, such as sports. Or I should say, especially sports."

Gus Winston did not succeed in holding himself back. At the end of his second year, he received the prize for being outstanding in scholarship *and* athletics. "He was in every way a superior boy," observed Carle Parsons with obvious pride in talking to Mrs. Wertenbaker.

By his upper middle year, Gus Winston felt he thoroughly understood the system: "I came to the realization that it was all right to be dispositionally a little bad, to run up against the rules a bit. There was a group of us, including Leigh Ardrey, who took to wearing gray suits to class at the same time as we began playing poker. We were all tacitly pretending to be professional gamblers. Sometimes we'd carry a deck of cards in a coat pocket, so that it would bulge a bit, but you probably wouldn't notice. That was all part of the mystique. The game rotated from one person's room to another, and we had a way of locking the door with a nail. We didn't exactly exchange money, but we kept a kind of a ledger on a hand-by-hand basis. One night we were playing in my room when Carle Parsons knocked on the door. We got busy moving the ledgers out of sight and stuffing the cards and every-thing under the mattress. Mr. Parsons was soon hollering and banging away; so I opened up. There may have still been a card or two in evi-dence. I don't remember what we told him, and I don't think anybody got charged with anything, but I do recall being invited to see the Duke in his office. He recounted to me the report he'd gotten from Carle Parsons and wanted to know what it was all about. I fudged a bit and told him that we had been playing bridge. The Duke gave me one of his sharp looks, and said, 'Well, that's a fine game if you don't spend too much time at it. My wife and I often get together with friends and play it on Saturday evenings. You probably would find it pleasant to come over some time and make a fourth.' Well, I had never played a hand of bridge in my life, and the Duke knew it. Over the next two or three months, he'd stop me occasionally in the corridor and say, 'Mr. Winston, we may well be playing bridge this Saturday evening. Do you suppose you might be free to sit in on a couple of hands?'

"I think it was about December of my senior year, the Duke called me into his office and said, 'It's time to think about colleges.' He said, 'This is my last year, and I'm terribly busy with any number of obliga-tions. People are going to be putting in these multiple applications, and it would save me a great deal of paperwork if we could just settle where you want to go.' He said, 'That way, I shall have to write only one recommendation.' I said, 'I was thinking either Amherst, Yale, or Har-vard.' He smiled and said, 'Well, Amherst is a wonderful place, but if you want to continue what you started, I suppose it would be better to be a big fish in a big pond than a big fish in a little pond.' Then he said, 'As you know, I have many ties with Yale, and they're very old and very deep. But I think if I were genuinely interested in learning, I'd go to Harvard.' I said, 'Sounds good to me.' Anyway, that's what I felt. I think I actually said, 'Harvard is what I'm interested in.' Shortly thereafter, the Duke took me up to some sort of Hotchkiss alumni meeting on the Harvard campus. Zeph Stewart was there and a few other people, and the Duke asked me to talk about the basketball team.

"Hotchkiss for me was an adventure, and the adventure was to experience it and to be good in the place on its terms, and if possible, to conquer. I can't think of a single instance during my four years that caused me to feel discriminated against or biased against on any sort of a level. Maybe when guys went off to a dance at Emma Willard or wherever, I knew I was expected not to sign up. But if the truth be told, I may have been a little privileged. I had become immensely good friends with a number of my classmates and faculty members, especially George and Jodie Stone, when I was on George's floor in Coy Hall. Other students had privileged relationships with the Stones, but that did not detract from what I felt I had with them. It also happened that our senior play was *Othello*, and naturally it might appear there was only one person who could play Othello. And Desdemona was the Duke's stepdaughter, Allelu. We became very good friends. I remember the final dance or prom, or whatever it was called. I didn't have a date, but she just sort of turned up and we strolled down to the dining room, and my friend Ardrey came out with his date. The next day he said, 'So you had a date, after all.'

It was, nevertheless, a different story beyond the boundaries of the school. As Jodie Stone relates, in at least one instance the Duke had tried to pull some behind-the-scenes wires to surmount the barriers of the outside world: "In those days, it was extremely hard to get a weekend. I know for a fact that Mr. Van Santvoord approached a very good friend of Gus's who was flunking a subject, and he said to this boy, 'If you will invite Gus home for a weekend, I will give you the weekend.' The boy said that he'd love to but his mother wouldn't let Gus into the house.' Gus was a very fine, charming, bright, good-looking person. If that wasn't enough to overcome the prejudice of the early fifties, no wonder the Duke's inducement didn't work."

Gus Winston: "I remember the Duke telling me that the world after Hotchkiss would probably always be a little less democratic, which it has been. At Harvard there certainly was no question of my being asked to join Porcellian, though there were lesser clubs whose members kind of apologized for not inviting me to join; not that I necessarily wanted to. I was aware while at Hotchkiss that it was an idyllic world, and looking back thirty-five years later, I can still say that it was as idyllic a world as I've ever known."

Carle Parsons provides a postscript on that world: "The year before Gus graduated, Barry Loncke and Bob Martin came. Barry, again, was beautifully prepared and went straight into lower middle English. Barry came from New Haven, where one of our alumni [Eugene Van Voorhis '51], who was at Yale, started an evening school for Negroes interested in going away to prep school. That's how we got Barry, and he, at the end of his lower middle year, was awarded the same prize as Gus for being outstanding in scholarship and athletics. Bob Martin was not an athlete and the only one I taught. I remember in his themes, no matter what the subject was, he'd drag in the race problem. Finally, I called him in and said, 'Now, Bob, don't let this thing just sit on your mind.' I said, 'So far as I know, everything is going very well. You have an opportunity here, so don't drag it in just to get it out of your system. I don't want to see this in any other theme you hand in.'"

Commented GVS, "We had several very good Negro students, and no newspaper said anything about it. When Groton took the first one, it was in the headline of the *New York Times*."

Robert M. Martin today is an official of Adoption & Foster Care for New York City; Barry R. Loncke is a municipal judge in Sacramento, California; and Gus Winston, after a career in international finance with Chase Manhattan Bank, is a private investor and writer.

The real drama in changing the face of the Hotchkiss School was yet to come.

xxi /   The graduation of the class of 1955 was to be George Van Santvoord's last. He had another year before reaching mandatory retirement age; however, the Duke felt that after twenty-nine years at the helm, it was time for him to go. "He told me he was finding it difficult to remember boys' names," recalls Bob Hawkins. "Mr. Van Santvoord felt he could no longer be effective if he didn't know every boy in the school."

It was also a different world. "By the early 1950s, the atmosphere in which independent secondary boarding schools functioned was beginning to change," explains William Olsen '39, who had returned to Hotchkiss in 1945 as the Duke's junior assistant, and then – after graduate study at Columbia and a few years on the faculty at Deerfield – had come back to Hotchkiss yet again in 1953 to teach English. "Parents wanted quality education, but they also wanted to remain a part of their sons' upbringing. Their power was enhanced by another fact of life – relative scarcity of teenage boys. The Great Depression had come of age. Hotchkiss in the early fifties had some difficulty filling its dormitories. No longer was it possible to balance budgets and replenish physical resources without reliance on an alumni appeal. My sense is that the Duke knew all this, [but] had little stomach for the kinds of responses required."

Yet, GVS was not quite through; for in his ever-startling repertoire was one more original piece to be performed. He had been mulling over how best to symbolize the great contribution made to the school by a number of special families – those who since the earliest days of Hotchkiss had sent their children there, generation after generation. At any one time, a quarter of the student body might consist of the offspring, relatives, or friends of Hotchkiss graduates.

The Duke's overture came in unexpected form. After handing out diplomas at the graduation exercises in 1955, GVS picked up a letter-sized document and read, "This certificate is awarded to Mrs. Charles E. Lord in commemoration of her presence for the eleventh time at the graduation of her sons and grandsons from the Hotchkiss School, and in appreciation of the honor and distinction which she and the boys of her family have brought to Hotchkiss." The Duke then walked down from the chapel lectern and handed the certificate to a grandmotherly lady seated in one of the front pews.

The most immediate result was that one of her younger descendants in St. Louis vastly augmented his pocket money by betting his friends fifty cents that his great-grandmother had a diploma from Hotchkiss.

In the longer term, Grandmother Lord's Hotchkiss descendants have continued to proliferate. The grand total at the end of the Hotchkiss century stands at twenty-two, including several under the name of Galey, Keene, and Dale – and the family's first bona fide female graduate, Deirdre R. Lord '85. Her father, Charles P. Lord '52, headmaster of the Holton Arms School in Bethesda, remembers his grandmother's partner in launching this Hotchkiss line: "My grandfather died when I was only sixteen, and my favorite story about him was told to me by my father. The family textile business had been in New York, and my grandfather commuted from Tarrytown, where he lived. The day my father and all the kids looked forward to most each week was when their Dad had stopped at Brentano's and came home with a new collection of books. The whole idea that one sat down and read, and that families read together and that books were important in life, grew out of my grandfather. He knew the value of education, knew the value of literature, loved literature. He was a very bright person. He used to love to invent games to play with the kids."

Among those kids: Squidge and Os from the class of 1922. "My father [Oswald B.] believed to his dying day that Hotchkiss was the most important experience of his life," continues Charlie. "He gave money for a Lord Scholarship with some sort of wording that this is the place that made him the man he was."

For Oswald Lord, his mother's symbolic investiture was a doubly special occasion: he was also at the ceremony to see his younger son, Winston, graduate. "Winston Lord is one of the ablest and most promising seniors," wrote GVS in recommending him to Yale, "with promise of development into a man of great power and usefulness."

If the Hotchkiss of Winston Lord was different from the carefree, joyous place depicted by his Uncle Squidge, this had as much to do with Winston as with any changes in the school. More than thirty years after the days of Squidge and Os, Winston acutely felt the family's lengthening Hotchkiss tradition and was determined to honor it by doing his best. Anything on the order of breaking into the headmaster's office, as Squidge had done to retrieve his chapel absentee slips, would have been as inconceivable to Winston as robbing a bank. Even if Winston had been inclined toward some lesser escapade, it would have been too far down on his list ever to be put into effect. "I hate to complain, but this is too much," he wrote home in the fall of 1954, shortly after starting his senior year. Winston listed the work to be done that week: "A 600-word editorial for the *Record* – helped by the Managing Editor; all of the normal work of the *Record*, except that it is the most difficult issue yet, and involved more work than any other issue . . . because of the Duke's retiring; make-up of last week's paper; 350 pages to read in *Tom Jones*, and a full period test on it; 50 pages of *Paradise Lost*, and a 1,000-word theme on it; a French theme of 300 words; a 200-page book to read, and a theme on the book for Greek; a full period review test in Greek; a debate in Public Speaking; write-up of longest student council meeting minutes yet; plus all the regular homework; and the longest, five toughest football practices yet." No wonder that the only splotch on Winston's record was a censure for "repeated lateness to bed."

Years later, when Winston Lord returned to Hotchkiss to accept the Alumni Award for 1989, Henry Kissinger introduced him as "an American statesman who has made great contributions to American foreign policy." Lord had been ambassador to China, member of the National Security Council Staff, president of the Council on Foreign Relations and had held numerous other consequential posts. Here is in part what Winston Lord said on that occasion at the school:

"One winter evening in my senior year, I sat in the basement of Old Main, congratulating myself on the editorial I had just published as editor in chief of the Hotchkiss *Record*. I luxuriated in reading each scathing syllable of our attack against Senator Joseph McCarthy for his wild branding of innocent people as communists. Then, the Duke, as our headmaster George Van Santvoord was known, stomped into my office in high dudgeon. While he remains one of the most brilliant people I've ever met, his humor is not to be confused with that of Robin Williams. Surely the Duke, a Democrat and a scholar, had no equal in his disdain for the senator from Wisconsin. The sole object of our terrifying conversation, however, was the editorial's inclusion of the allegation, widespread but unproven, that the senator had been a draft dodger. The Duke lectured me mercilessly on the imperative of fairness. In effect, he asked me, is this the best you can do? It was not, and I have never forgotten it."

Winston Lord's association with Henry Kissinger began more than a decade after the Duke's retirement and spanned the critical Vietnam years, when the country was agonizingly split as to what might be best. Was it the concept of "best" which Winston Lord brought with him from Hotchkiss that prompted Henry Kissinger to often characterize Winston as the conscience of our foreign policy?

The chronicling of successive members of the Lord family offers a revealing flash-forward into the rest of the Hotchkiss first century. While Kissinger's protégé was grappling with Vietnam in Washington, the school's headmaster, William Olsen, was entering the most tumultuous period of his career, and Winston's cousin, John C. Lord '68, was on the other side of the world, a combat medic crawling through the jungles and rice paddies of Southeast Asia. Jack Lord, the son of Arthur Squidge Lord and his first wife, explains: "I took it as a part of my heritage that Hotchkiss was the place I would go, but I also came to realize Hotchkiss was an isolating experience. Beyond the school boundaries, civil rights marches, the war in Vietnam, drugs and the youth culture were changing America. The decision to enlist right after Hotchkiss and go to Vietnam was my own self-prescribed shock therapy."

Continuing the Lord family tradition – eleven years after Jack Lord had graduated and toward the end of Bill Olsen's twenty-one years at the helm – were the twin sons of Charlie and his wife Gay, a Hotchkiss trustee and a teacher at the Sidwell Friends School in Washington, D.C. "I think that Tim and I went to Hotchkiss despite the fact that our family had gone there," says Charles P. Lord '83, now a student at

University of Virginia Law School. "Even before we were born, my grandfather's story of how he had almost drowned in the icy lake had become a code word in the family for something that's been told too often. And I think we were only eight when he said to me, 'I know you boys will love Hotchkiss and Yale.' At that point my brother and I swore we would never go to either place. When my grandfather finally did take us up there – with the understanding we were only looking and were free to decide on our own – we just had a great time. We chose Hotchkiss because we really did like it the best of all the boarding schools we looked at."

Tim and Charlie's achievements at Hotchkiss in the early 1980s turned out to be no less impressive than those of their Uncle Winston – as scholars and athletes and in extracurricular activities. Yet they also had fun in the tradition of their family forbears in Dr. Buehler's time. One of young Charlie's pranks was to paint all the speed bumps pink and green, the classic preppy colors. He also was nabbed in a more contemporary transgression: puffing away on a joint. The school at that point happened to have the same two-chance policy instituted by Head Master Coy toward tobacco. "It was good that I got caught, and it was good to have a second chance," recalls Charlie. "My grandfather called, and I knew he wasn't too pleased. But he said, 'You know, your Uncle Squidge and I were sequestered so many times we lost count. So take it as a lesson, but don't worry about it.'"

Charlie in his senior year was awarded (for the third time) the history prize that his Uncle Squidge had won, and he also became one of the first students to co-teach a history class. Among the lower mids taking it was his sister Deirdre:

"I started out with a different perspective from my brothers. I had grown up hearing my grandfather say to them, 'You'll love Hotchkiss and Yale, and thank goodness for that!' I was never included in that, and I didn't care. But by the time I was ready to leave my day school and go to boarding school, Hotchkiss had become coed. So my parents gave me the same option as they had given my brothers, and I looked at a whole range of schools. But from the start I went into it saying, 'I'll never go to Hotchkiss' – especially since my brothers were there at the time.

Then I went to visit, and I saw my brothers in plays and athletics and just being in that environment, and the decision became apparent on its own."

Not until her senior year did Deirdre Lord become aware of a highly disturbing aspect of coeducation – at least to her – at the Hotchkiss School.

xxii / George Van Santvoord was still alive when the school made the move which eventually enabled Deirdre Lord to attend. "Hotchkiss takes in its coeds in September and begins its expansion to 500," he noted in the spring of 1974. "I have wished them *bon voyage* and waved goodbye.

"Neither of our mares is to foal in 1974; so they go again to be bred."

The juxtaposition was hardly coincidental. Since his retirement as headmaster almost two decades earlier, GVS felt progressively estranged from his former domain. His first disappointment was the tenure of his immediate successor, the Reverend Thomas Huntington Chappell '24. Besides recommending Tom Chappell to the board, GVS had been his teacher at Yale and brought him to Hotchkiss as a member of the faculty briefly back in the 1930s, before Tom went into the ministry. In retrospect, it was surely unrealistic to expect that anyone could return after more than two decades on the outside and fill the vacuum left by the Duke, who had embodied so much of the administrative structure of the school. Within five years, Tom Chappell resigned to return to the ministry.

The Duke had good reason to be relieved when his former protégé, Bill Olsen, took over as the sixth headmaster in 1960. The son of the impoverished boy from the class of '13 thoroughly understood the school's traditions and its inner workings and had already proved himself as associate headmaster during Tom Chappell's final year. But then as the boyish-looking, forty-year-old Olsen began to put into effect changes he thought long overdue, the strains between him and his former mentor became more and more palpable. Beyond the obvious generational gap lay a veritable chasm of style, which was conspicuously dramatized by the dust jacket of Mrs. Wertenbaker's 75th anniversary history, *A Portrait*. Filling almost the entire back cover, normally reserved for publicity blurbs or the author's picture, was a commanding photo of the executive-like Olsen, who by then had been headmaster for a half dozen years. Whatever he may have felt in his innermost self, the Duke had always insisted that Hotchkiss was far vaster than any individual or single group.*

In the spate of letters GVS sent to his former student and aide shortly after receiving an advance copy of the Wertenbaker book, the Duke left no doubt how he felt. "It [the book] will reflect, I fear, on the School, and upon you too for failing to provide adequate safeguards against error and bad taste. . . . It is now too late to censor (or to sequester!) But I would suggest very earnestly that you consult your father for his advice. . . . Perhaps he will say DO NOTHING. If so, I would say O.K. – do what he advises."

The Duke was also otherwise engaged. Besides operating a thriving farm adjoining the family home in Bennington, he had been repeatedly elected to represent the area in the Vermont state senate. "Ne tirer pas le grand bouton du parti," he advised his French-speaking constituents in a fourteen-line handwritten playlet in the Bennington newspaper while campaigning as a Democrat in the solidly Republican area, "mais choisir chacun des candidats que tu veux, soit en haut, soit en bas, et

---

*At his farewell dinner in New York back in 1955, GVS had enthralled the packed ballroom of the Waldorf-Astoria with an almost hour-long extemporaneous speech, reminiscing about those who had made Hotchkiss great – everyone from Mr. Cardoza, the groundskeeper, to an array of staff, faculty, students, alumni, trustees, parents, and friends of the school – without any direct mention or claims concerning the role he had played. And when Whitney Griswold '25, then the president of Yale, predicted a touch too effusively on that festive occasion that GVS would one day be joined in heaven with the likes of Aristotle, Plato, and Erasmus, the Duke responded that he didn't care very much personally about those people, but would like to meet the country schoolteacher Ichabod Crane.

ATTENTION ! AU SECOURS!

Lui : Tu es troublée, ma cherie — pourquoi ?

Elle : J'ai peur de la machine-a-voter.

Lui : Écoutes-toi ! D'abord etudier la liste des candidats. Quelques noms te fâcheront tant que tu vas oublier ton peur.

Elle: Tu as raison — alors?

Lui: Ne tirer pas le grand bouton du parti, mais choisir chacun des candidats que tu veux, soit en haut soit en bas, et tirer son bouton.

Elle. Merci. Ainsi je pourrai voter pour le candidat démocratique, pour le sénat GEORGE VAN SANTVOORD et encore des autres!

Lui: Pas de quoi ! Bonne chance.

GVS's political campaign ad

tirer son bouton." This man of universal interests also served on the board of the Bennington Free Library, the Bennington Museum, and the Bennington Farm Bureau. He liked to quote an old-timer who had once advised him, "On retirement you'll be as busy as before, but you'll not be paid for your work." During one especially busy moment, GVS indirectly revealed a startling aspect of his past. "If things go on this way," he noted, "I must get a secretary and begin dictating again – a labor I solemnly foreswore after twenty-nine years of such serfdom at Hotchkiss." So it had not been all as effortless as he had made it seem.

George Van Santvoord continued to give priority to maintaining ties with his many friends from the school. One such occasion was when the late William V. Brokaw '48 flew his former headmaster to the wilds of Canada for a family fishing trip, along with teachers L. Blair Torrey '50 and Richard Crocker Gurney. "Where the Duke really shone was in the tent," recalls Blair, who eventually succeeded Dick Gurney both as the school football coach and head of the English department. "A couple of days it rained hard and the fishing was no good, and he kind of took charge. We had a lot of little kids, the Brokaw children, and I remember the Duke reciting from memory Gray's 'Elegy in a Country Churchyard.' That's a mighty long poem, and he hadn't boned up on it or anything, but there it was. The Duke kept a journal, and at the end of each day, he would sit at the table and open the journal and gather us around and ask, 'What did you see today? What did you do?'"

The Van Santvoords' stately colonial house in Bennington remained a destination for countless Hotchkiss boys, many of whom regarded the trip to Vermont as not unlike a pilgrimage. During the head-master-and-boy tête-à-tête, Mrs. Van Santvoord would bring out tea in an old silver service, along with an assortment of homemade cookies, while the conversation somehow drifted back to where it had left off years ago at the school. To this visitor, GVS kept stressing how much harder it was to be a "good man, a good person" – and how incomparably easy to be a "good guy." He left not the slightest doubt as to what he meant by his terms, or that attaining the good man, good person qualities was his ultimate criterion for evaluating success.

Then there was his vast correspondence. Former students were always writing letters, and it would be difficult to overestimate with how many alumni he kept in lifelong touch. At Christmastime, the walls of his expansive parlor were almost entirely covered with a kaleidoscopic array of greeting cards. Each would be acknowledged, in due course, with a handwritten note that was likely to include some detail which revealed how well the Duke remembered the boy.

"My last chance for a good conversation with George occurred in October 1973, about six months after he had a pacemaker installed in his heart," remembers his disciple and friend Art Howe. "I was uneasy over having pressed him to attend a reunion dinner in New York City of American Field Service ambulance drivers. Not only was he there, but this eighty-two-year-old told me with some glee how he had taken three different buses to reach New York, and clearly had engaged in intensive conversations with a number of startled passengers along the way. At the end of the dinner, he enthralled the assembly with perhaps the most witty, learned, and moving talk I ever heard him give."

That seems to have been the Duke's last public hurrah. "As life goes on," reads an entry in his journal three months later, "I find it more and more desirable to pass by on the other side of things that don't have to do with the vital quality of the surrounding world: perhaps time is getting short and the inconsequential and trivial are less deserving of attention? Or is it that we haven't the attention to give?"

The handwriting was controlled and firm, not too different from the way it had always been. A year later, in response to one of those countless season's greetings, the Duke dispatched a card with an old-time painting of a New England winter scene. "I am told the man in the sleigh is my grandfather," he wrote in a labored, shaky hand. "I have no way of knowing if that is so, but maybe I shall before too long."

Judging by the barely legible script in the yellow spiral notebook, GVS's final legacy was most likely written about the same time. One can only imagine the sort of determination which the ailing former headmaster brought to the task. He and Mrs. Van Santvoord had closed their Bennington house for the winter and were staying at the Williamstown Inn across the state line in Massachusetts. GVS had made arrangements to be moved to a nearby nursing home at the appropriate time. He did not want to be the cause of any problems for the inn either by becoming incapacitated or dying there.

It was a coincidence that Allelu happened to be visiting him on February 19, 1975, when her father indicated that the critical time had come. At that point Mrs. Van Santvoord became distraught and left the room.

Allelu: "I sat down, and we started to talk. I asked, 'What's it like being old and unable to sleep and being in pain?' He said, 'I'm glad I learned all the poetry I did when I was young. Sometimes, the endings still surprise me.' Then he said, 'Now, Allelu, here are some envelopes. Here are the people I want to have things from the house.' He gave me the papers, and then asked me to help him get dressed. I thought, 'That's impossible.' He had never before asked for help of this kind. He said, 'Well, bring me the pants.' He knew what was happening, and by the time we finished and I had all the papers, he said, 'You'll take care of it?' I said, 'Yes.' He said, 'Now help me to the car.' He leaned on me. It was a power of will that got him to that car. By the time we arrived at the nursing home, he had to be put in a wheelchair because he had no feeling in his legs. They put him in bed, and I held his hand. He quoted several lines from *Alice in Wonderland*, and suddenly I realized he wasn't there anymore. It was just the way I prayed he'd go – in control, because he always was in control. He had arranged it to the last minute."

xxiii / A memorial service was held for George Van Santvoord on May 17, 1975, in the school chapel. John Hersey '32 delivered the final tribute:

"What looms first in memory is the forehead. Up and up and up it went, incised crosswise with swooping wrinkles which seemed to be the tracks of endless thought. What a castle that long head was! In its keep there must have been brains enough for three normal men. When I first read 'Kubla Khan' I could not help picturing Coleridge's 'stately pleasure-dome' as George Van Santvoord's forehead.

"Second in memory: his eyes. They were as deep as the Atlantic rift. The range of temperature in those eyes was universal – from the heat of the sun to the unimaginable cold of the gaps in the galaxies.

Their look could penetrate every fiction and falsehood; they could make a transparency out of a lower mid. But behind every powerful look in them, no matter how accusatory, there lurked a glint of mischief, an ember of something still boyish in the marvelous intellect, and with that glint every student, even in terror, could ally himself.

"And a third memory: his right hand. It was broad, spatulate, and extraordinarily dry – as dry as papyrus. His handshake was limp, flaccid; our student awe of him was sharply heightened when we learned that the weakness in the hand had been caused by a grievous injury in the First World War, in which he had won the Croix de Guerre. And yet what voltage there was in those flattish long fingers! When one was idling, a bit too loudly perhaps, in the Main Corridor, and suddenly from the rear one felt the big limp shape of that hand slip into the crook of one's arm, it was as if one were being electrocuted.

"The first time that happened to me was no more than a week after I had arrived at the school. The hand slithered under my elbow, and I looked up and saw the great forehead, the grim features, and Jupiter's eyes. A voice that seemed to come from a stone statue asked me a question: 'What was Stradivarius's first name?' There I stood, brainless, in the dim light of the varnished wainscoting, faint with the smell of floor wax, dizzy with homesickness, and all I could force from my lips was, 'Uh, sir, I don't know.' It was not much comfort to discover very soon that this was the standard student answer to the Duke's questions.

"Within a few days, I was shocked again by the flexible hand, and this time the question was, 'Is it true that eeny, meeny, miney, mo is counting in Chinese?'

"This time I knew the answer. 'No, sir.'

"'Then how *do* you count in Chinese?'

"I heard my cracking voice, just recently changed, intoning, '*Yi, erh, san, sz, wu, lyou, chi, ba, jyou, shr.*

"'I think you are wrong,' Mr. Van Santvoord gravely said. 'I believe the correct way to count in Chinese' – this time he mimicked the singsong tones I had used – 'is eeny, meeny, miney, mo.'

"My heart leaped then with fear and joy – and it still does today, remembering – because I knew that I was right and the man with the three-story forehead was wrong.

"Only later did I realize that this austere personage, who had to cope with the total energies of three hundred and fifty mostly miscreant students, and with endless problems of bricks and mortar, and with ever-furious parents, and with towering eccentrics on the faculty like Doc Rob and Pop Jeff and Uncle Joe Estill and Howdy Edgar and John McChesney, had nevertheless been able, within the very first days of my arrival in his amazing ambit, to breathe an identity into the shapeless clod of a homesick fifteen-year-old that I was, for not only had he known my name, he had known that I had been born in China, he had known that I played the violin. And I became convinced then, and I hold the conviction today, that he knew much, much more, right down to the innermost secrets of my groping adolescent mind.

"And much later still I realized that by putting me in the right and putting himself in the wrong, in the matter of Chinese numbers, he had given me my first small sand grain of self-confidence.

"In this way, and in many other ways, he taught. For he was, above all, a teacher. In the First World War, as an enlisted sergeant, a former Rhodes Scholar, he was designated to lecture the officers of his battalion on military campaigns. At Hotchkiss he could step into any class in place of an indisposed teacher, whether of Greek or trigonometry or modern history or physics, and could teach there at least as well as the incumbent expert. After his retirement, he even made a kind of school of the Vermont Legislature, where, according to the *Bennington Banner*, 'his colleagues listened when he spoke.'

"Any boy who was fortunate enough to attend the Sunday-evening open house at Mr. Van Santvoord's would be treated to one of his astonishing monologues. The first week, it would be on beekeeping; the next on Zoroastrianism; the next on the methods of construction used in building the Pyramids. We were not old enough to know how truly dazzling those performances were, products of total recall and of a gift for shaping an essay, and yet even our crude perceptions could be jogged into a kind of grudging juvenile uneasiness, the first stage perhaps of wanting to learn, by the spectacle of that beautiful mind at play in the fields of knowledge.

"He was born, it may have been, two centuries too late. His mind was as large and wide-ranging and noble as those of the men who wrote *The Federalist Papers*, who designed octagonal Monticello, who tempted the charges of a thunderhead with a wired kite. 'As a member of the Yale Corporation,' Dick Gurney wrote in the *Lakeville Journal*, 'he sat between Senator Robert Taft and Secretary of State Dean Acheson without awe or embarrassment, for the excellent reason that he probably knew more about most things than they did.'

"Yes, he was a man of the Enlightenment. He was a poet. He painted watercolors of wildflowers. He was an aviarist and an apiarist; a topographer and a cartographer. He was an angler who in his seventies scorned the use of rubber boots or waders in frigid Northern streams. He was a moderator of town meetings, a legislator. He was a dairy farmer, whose fine bulls gave their seed for breeding throughout the Northeast. He was a Puritan, an equestrian, a philosopher who sweetened his thought with pipe smoke.

"Like a true eighteenth-century man, he was completely in tune with nature, as many a student can testify who learned woodcraft from him. He revered all creatures of the meadow and woodlot – horses, woodchucks, badgers, bears. He was a botanist. His heart was torn between the beautiful rare ducklings he raised on the hockey pond in the warm seasons and the equally beautiful owls that snatched them away for prey. He was a trainer of homing pigeons who, scorning Western Union, released the birds in Pottstown, Pennsylvania, to wing home to Hotchkiss carrying in their message capsules the scores of just completed football and baseball games against the archrival, The Hill.

"Some years after I had graduated, Mr. Van Santvoord invited me to give the Hotchkiss Commencement address. The day before graduation, he was sitting on the veranda of the Headmaster's House with half a dozen pairs of parents – not his most beloved category of humankind. He said, 'Well, John, you have an audience here. Why don't you rehearse your speech for tomorrow?' I thanked him and said I

George Van Santvoord

thought one performance would be more than enough. 'All right, then,' he said, '*I have a commencement speech for them.*' He went into the house and fetched a volume of short stories by the colloquial satirist George Ade, and he read out loud the whole of 'The Fable of the Last Day at School and the Tough Trustee's Farewell to the Young

Voyagers,' a story of a small-town businessman's exceedingly practical advice to a graduating class. Mr. Van Santvoord read in the tone of a kind father reading his little children to sleep. I will never forget his mock solemnity as he read the last sentences of the story: 'I will now ask you – the Trustee said – to come up and get your Sheepskins. Take this precious Certificate home and put it in a Dark, Cool Place. A few Years hence when you are less Experienced, it will give you a Melancholy Pleasure to look at it and Hark back to the Time When you knew it all. Just one word in Parting. Always count your Change, and if you can't be Good, be Careful.' He looked up. There was a stunned silence. He broke it, that little fire of mischief burning bright in the deeps of his somber eyes, by saying, 'Since you enjoyed that story so much, I'll read another.' And he read 'The Horse Maniac and What Caused the Filing of the Suit.' *Then* he read 'The Two Wives Who Talked About Their Husbands.' And THEN he read 'The Old-time Pedagogue Who Came Down from the Shelf.' And after that the parents fell over each other heading for the nearest exit. Mr. Van Santvoord looked very surprised at their sudden departure.

"Was his notorious treatment of parents mere rudeness for its own sake? I am certain it was not. I think it was a combination of a deep, deep shyness he had, along with a shrewd sense of alliance with the secret souls of the boys in his school, who were condemned by nature in their formative years to a helpless war with the very idea of parenthood. They could see that on this painful battlefield, as elsewhere, the Duke was on their side.

"And so again and again we come back and back to that quality of mischief in him. It could be heard in his Socratic questions. His massive severity had a bubbling laughter close beneath the surface. He was a whole man, and he wanted his charges to open their eyes to the many shades of light in life. Character in a boy was more important to him than high marks. His smoking pledge had sharp teeth – students were kicked out not for their smoking but for breaking their word. But grim rectitude was not his aim for us; to be whole and healthy, a person had to see the force in human affairs of irony, of absurdity, of folly, and of fun. And so he always teased as he used his luminous mind to teach – his mind that was like a display of aurora borealis on a north-wind night. He wanted a man not just to be learned, but rather to be wise, decent, humane, generous, forgiving, and light of heart in heavy days. As to all these traits, he gave us the great gift of his example."

Part Two

Hotchkiss circa 1960

6   In Transition

Scoville Gate

Surely the most interesting legacy of the Reverend Thomas Huntington Chappell '24 – at least for the preparation of this 100th anniversary version of the Hotchkiss history – is an elegantly handwritten letter offering advice on how best to put together the 75th anniversary book. "A school history is most difficult to write," the former headmaster cautioned four years after the end of his brief tenure. "For instance, Claude Fuess [the principal] of Andover, prepared an address to deliver at the dedication of Coy Hall [in 1936], giving a fair and objective view of Mr. Coy. He told me three or four years ago that when he found that Maida Coy [daughter of the school's first headmaster] was to be in the audience, he simply had to throw away his whole speech. . . . When Coy left Andover for Hotchkiss (really, having been fired from Andover), it was said that both Andover and Hotchkiss were greatly benefited.

"I myself am responsible for destroying many historical documents. When I arrived at Hotchkiss [in 1955], I found my desk full of papers going back to 1893. Many were complaints against the Buehlers by the faculty (utterly unfounded, arising from that curious envy that so many faculty have towards anyone who has one more dollar). Why Dr. Buehler kept them, I cannot imagine. At any rate, I destroyed them. I see Barbara Buehler [the Buehlers' daughter, who died in 1978] quite often, and I cannot dream of letting her know of such things.

"I knew the Buehlers particularly well; in fact, Mrs. Buehler was down here in New London with us when Dr. Buehler died. . . . Henry Sherrill '07, Presiding Bishop of the Episcopal Church, loathed [the Buehlers]. I loved them. I could write a novel about Mrs. Buehler, and make the readers love her; but if the facts were seen in cold light, without understanding, Bishop Sherrill's viewpoint emerges.

"The solution, of course, is simply to say what people *did*. Both Coy and Buehler contributed enormously to Hotchkiss. One can write about that, without mentioning all the disastrous qualities which some people imagined, with reason, Coy and Buehler to have had."

Tom Chappell's advice seemed especially apropos in writing about headmasters who were still alive. Bill Olsen, who dominated the post-Van Santvoord era, resided with his wife, Jean, a seven-minute drive from the school. In any unabridged account, what was to be said about Jean Olsen's reluctance to this day to visit any of her close faculty friends on the school grounds? And what was to be said of Bill Olsen's successors, one of whom left after only two years, and the other one – although clearly the most popular occupant ever of the headmaster's house – retired under circumstances which caused turmoil throughout the school? Perhaps most sensitive of all: what approach to take toward the present headmaster, Dr. Robert A. Oden, Jr., the bespectacled, boyish pundit endowed with the magnetic attributes of a cult personality, whose full humanity traditionally should be portrayed in a quasi-perfect light for the good of the school?

Indeed, schools such as Hotchkiss enjoyed a virtually unbroken tradition of presenting to the outside world an image thoroughly bleached out and ironed flat, with just about the only true-to-life wrinkle left being the occasional account of some humorous student escapade or clever faculty ploy. Legions of graduates as well as a goodly number of trustees, administrators, and faculty members preferred this sparkling one-dimensional rendition of their school's past. Anyone tampering with it risked being charged with violating good form, as Uncle Joe Estill was back in 1903, when he "gave away" a number of his colleagues under the influence of "Dr. Bissell's sleeping powders." Revelations from the school's recent past might well be considered disloyal on top of that.

There was also a purely practical argument for focusing on deeds à-la-Tom Chappell during the post-GVS years and overlooking everything else. This was an era which coincided with waves of turbulence and social change surging through the United States. The central point of what the Hotchkiss School was all about during these years could thus be obscured by a series of highly visible crests – rebellion, drugs, sex, race, even violent death. "What is important to remember," points out Peter A. Thorne '73, who was at Hotchkiss in the vortex of this storm, "is that except for some dramatic incidents, life went off pretty normally and the school continued to graduate about a hundred seniors each year, who were in many ways a step ahead of their contemporaries when they got to college."

The president of the board, Edgar M. Cullman '36, made the strongest argument against abbreviations of any sort. "Hotchkiss today is a different place from what it was when the Duke left," the affable, seventyish industrialist told the centennial history committee, as he savored a cigar made from leaf grown on his Culbro Corporation's tobacco fields. "I want to make sure we explain fully how the school got to be that way. I'm proud of what we have accomplished. I don't know of anything that cannot be said, provided it isn't said with malice."

Though the committee reached overwhelming consensus in mandating this open approach, Edgar Cullman's endorsement carried special weight. Since succeeding his older brother, Joe [Joseph F. Cullman 3rd '31], on the board in 1971, Edgar had increasingly taken time from his numerous business and philanthropic activities to devote himself unstintingly to the school. As head of the student life committee for many years, he kept in firsthand touch by inviting groups of students and faculty members for Sunday luncheons at his country home in Stamford. Rather than sitting quietly and minding their p's and q's, the guests were encouraged by this perennial Hotchkiss benefactor and patron (jointly with his wife Louise) of the school's art center to engage in a lively give-and-take on even the most sensitive issues. (This was not surprising, considering that while a student at Hotchkiss, Edgar had delivered as his senior speech a spirited critique of movie censorship by the Catholic church.) Now, he was heading the campaign – and personally passing around the hat – to raise $100 million for the centennial development fund.

There was one seeming anomaly not to be overlooked within the scope of the mandate to tell all: wasn't there a conflict between Edgar Cullman's role as one of the leading tobacco industrialists and heading the board of a school which had sought to expel from day one those of its students caught lighting up? "You can't embarrass me or make me feel uncomfortable," the gentlemanly third-generation tobacco mogul responded after dinner, as he relaxed in the drawing room of his Fifth Avenue apartment, appointed with understated classical good taste. "Some of the trustees look at me askance when I light up a cigar in the boardroom. I look back at them. I'm comfortable with the way the school has handled the no-smoking rule. I don't think young people should smoke until they've had more of a chance to make their own decision. Some people can smoke and enjoy it; some people may have problems. I resent the way smoking is attacked in this country. There's a lot of lore and romanticism that goes with tobacco and the making of cigars. I'm smoking a cigar now, and I'm enjoying it. I'm sorry for those who can't enjoy a good cigar."

Thank heavens for Edgar Cullman's lifelong belief in an unfettered press! It was his guest who was left embarrassed for having raised the question in such a hospitable milieu.

ii / There is little cause for embarrassment in examining the five-year tenure of Tom Chappell as headmaster in personal terms – not because he is no longer living, but because to this day he and his wife, Jean, are remembered by the Hotchkiss community with unusual affection.

Jean Chappell, who now resides not far from their old New London home, provides a uniquely personal glimpse of what led up to the nomination of her spouse to head the school: "My husband and Mr.

Van Santvoord had known each other since Yale, where Mr. Van Santvoord taught him English. I was abducted to Hotchkiss on my wedding day. We had been married in New Jersey and were heading for Cape Cod, when I suddenly realized we were going in the wrong direction. I asked my brand-new husband, 'Where are we going?' 'Oh, it's opening day at Hotchkiss, and I've made it a habit for fourteen years to be there.' This was 1935, and he had entered the school in 1921. We stopped in Lime Rock, and he took off the flower and swept the rice out of the car. When we got to the school, he went to see Mr. Van Santvoord at the headmaster's house, and told me to stay in the car. He obviously didn't quite know what to do with me at that juncture.

"My husband used to go up to Hotchkiss for many years after that to preach, and he saw a lot of Mr. Van Santvoord. One Sunday Mr. Van Santvoord said, 'I've put you down to be the next headmaster, and if you're not going to do it, say so now, and it will save a lot of trouble.' And Tom thought, 'This is going to be great. I know Hotchkiss inside and out.' Our girls were now getting older, and we needed more money for their education than the ministry could provide. He also knew it was time to get out of Harrisburg. We had been there for twelve years. Tom felt that if by then you haven't accomplished what you had set out to do, you're never going to."

"Tom Chappell was indeed handpicked by the Duke," confirms Robert B. "Dud" Parker '29, a trustee emeritus and a member of the board at that time (May 1955). What remains unclear is whether or not he was the sole candidate. "I don't remember specifically any alternatives," says Thomas Fisher, Jr. '33, another trustee of that era, "but I'm sure it wasn't a complete railroad job." In any case, Tom Chappell was speedily approved, supposedly when he gained the support of one of the most powerful members of that board, Charles Edison '09, son of the inventor, and governor of New Jersey. This was the era of Senator Joe McCarthy's hunt for Communists, and, though a Democrat, Charles Edison was said to be deeply concerned about possible infiltration of Communist thinking into the country's institutions. In interviewing Tom Chappell, one of the questions Governor Edison reputedly asked was how he would describe a typical Hotchkiss boy.

"There's no such thing as a typical Hotchkiss boy," the candidate is said to have promptly rejoined. The governor was decisively impressed. To him, the answer was unmistakable evidence (or so the story went) that Tom Chappell believed in individualism and was obviously untainted by any collectivist heresy.

Jean Chappell defines her late husband's overall approach to running the school: "I believe Tom felt his job at Hotchkiss was to make it a warmer, more welcoming place for parents. I heard several times that Mr. Van Santvoord had said if the parents would just stay away, he could do a fine job on the boys. So Tom was determined to change that. There was one mother who had come to see him about her son; when she returned a few weeks later, Tom met her and said how nice it was to see her again. They had a pleasant chat walking down the main corridor. When Tom said he had to turn off here, and reiterated how glad he was to see her, she said, 'It's been so nice seeing you, too. Now, who exactly are you?'"

It is doubtful whether anyone could have taken over readily from the Duke, who had personally fulfilled so many of the school's administrative tasks. There were no deans, no department heads, no student counselors, and the one assistant headmaster, George P. Milmine '17, carried an almost full teaching load. Moreover, the trustees expected the new headmaster to become more involved in such peripheral activities as meeting with alumni and raising funds, which his predecessor had not sufficiently emphasized.

"I think everybody would admit that Tom had an almost impossible job," says Bill Olsen, then a member of the English department. "That job was made virtually impossible primarily because Tom was unprepared for what he was asked to do. There seemed to be a perception on the part of the trustees that running a school like Hotchkiss required a certain set of attributes, and that a certain kind of experience would be adequate for that role. If somebody looked like a headmaster, then he could probably handle the role. Those of us who were here when Tom came almost had the feeling that the board was trying to clone the Duke – bright guy, big guy, big voice. The fact that he was also a clergyman was seen as a plus for bringing about the sort of warming up the school needed after the Duke."

Tom Chappell did not at first realize what he had bargained for. "I met him in the corridor after he'd been here three or four months," recalls Tom Blagden, who was about to retire as head of the art department, "and I asked him, 'Well, how's it going, Tom?' He said, 'Oh, it's just marvelous, Tom, it's just marvelous. You know, when I had my parish I was on call twenty-four hours a day. Here, well, I'm in the office in the morning and then my day is free.' I thought, 'Tom, you've got a lot to learn.'"

Tom Chappell in some respects antedated the Duke. "I always thought that Tom saw himself as a character out of a Trollope novel," recalls retired faculty member Bob Hawkins. "He was a fine-looking person, but he was a bit of a dandy and loved to be noticed. Whenever he went somewhere, he'd put on a homburg and carry kid gloves and occasionally would drape himself in a black cape. He assumed Victorian attitudes and held himself in a very erect manner." Yet Tom Chappell's was not an aloof pose; he also liked to dispense communion in Wellington boots, and he was perhaps the only headmaster in the history of the school to stand up when a faculty member entered his office. His sartorial preference was a genuine reflection of a period man in a period costume. He mistrusted the modern age, whether travel by air or inventions with a dehumanizing effect. He acknowledged every gift to the school with a handwritten note, and at his first alumni dinner at the Ruppert Brewery in New York, he pushed aside the proffered microphone with the remark, "If you use machines to do what you're supposed to do, it leads finally to artificial insemination."

He was no less of a traditionalist with respect to his family. "My role in life was to do what my husband wanted me to do," says his widow, Jean, who is most often remembered at Hotchkiss as being singularly attractive and adoring of her spouse. "In the parish I had done exactly what he wanted, and at Hotchkiss, I did, too. The one thing I was not allowed was any close friends. 'You've got to be friendly with the whole place,' he told me. 'You can't have any favorites. You can see more of Molly Milmine because I knew them before they were married.'"

"Jean Chappell was absolutely charming and great fun," observes Anne H. Bowen, who was then a young faculty wife, "but she was also a very shy woman for having been a clergyman's wife all her life and having always to deal with people. Instead of having lots of hired help around for the after-dinner coffee on Sunday when one was expected to go over to the headmaster's house and drink a demitasse, she'd bring it out and you'd help yourself. She was always in the kitchen or the butler's pantry because she didn't want to be out front dealing with the people."

Explains Jean Chappell, "We continued what Mrs. Van Santvoord had done on a more modest scale. The difference was she had money, and we did not. Our two older girls enjoyed themselves thoroughly. They were the same age as the seniors, and they just had a whirl. The next year they felt Father ought to move on to Yale."

Traditionally, it was the seniors who provided the faculty with vital support in running the school. Tom Chappell strengthened their role in a way which has functioned to this day. By approving and implementing a proctorial system, the headmaster extended the seniors' influence to the lower class residential halls, where each of the designated proctor-seniors was assigned a corridor to supervise. Tom Chappell also gained renown for his handling of what was perhaps the most elaborate prank in the school's history. When Van Santvoord Hall was being built, a restless group of seniors helped themselves one night to enough cinder block and brick to erect a six-foot-high mortarless barrier, wall to wall, in that long corridor in Main. "When Tom Chappell came out of his house the next morning to walk down to breakfast, he was blocked by this wall," says Bill Fowle, the former physical education director, who had been appointed early in Tom Chappell's tenure as a second assistant headmaster. "Tom didn't say anything, but walked outside to get around it. When the dining room doors had closed and everyone was seated, he banged the plunger on the bell [normally used for saying grace before lunch and dinner, though not before breakfast, which the boys could begin devouring right away], and announced in his booming voice that no one was to be excused until he said so. He ate a leisurely meal while everyone was wondering what action the headmaster was going to take. When he was good and ready, he banged that bell again and said, 'Okay, you've had your fun. Now I want every one of you to go back there, grab a brick, and return it to where it came from. Off you go, hup, two, three, four.' That's all there was to it. He didn't get excited, and I think the kids had fun doing exactly what he told them to."

"My husband often remarked that it was a beautifully built wall," says Jean Chappell. "He was exceptionally good-natured, and the boys called him the Saint."

Among former students remembering this saintliness is David W. Bentley '56. As a senior, David had been nabbed turning on the master switch after lights out in Memorial Hall to enable him and most of his classmates to continue working on the year's most important essay, due the following day. "About a week later, Mr. Chappell called me into what had been the old library, and at that time was the old alumni room," recalls David Bentley, who became a trustee in 1985. "It was a dark room, and he was sitting in one of the wing chairs with one lamp on. He had on his black turtleneck that he used to wear after hours, and with great trepidation I went over to see him. He sat me down and said, 'David, I've got to inform you that we've had a meeting of the faculty, and we have decided to supersequester you.' That meant I had to do double the time, and I was distraught. As I stood up to leave, he put his hand on my shoulder and looked at me and said, 'I would have done the same thing' – which made it all worthwhile. I felt totally wonderful."

Comments Jean Chappell, "My husband had been a chaplain at Norfolk and Charlestown prisons as well as at the state mental hospital in Harrisburg. He was used to dealing with people with serious problems and serious crimes. How could he be upset about boys turning the lights on after 10 P.M.?"

The headmaster's saintly sobriquet seems to have been sufficiently in vogue so that it might have eventually become as institutionalized as *the King* and *the Duke*. But saintliness was not a particularly desirable attribute for those in authority at the Hotchkiss School. "He was a very compassionate person," says George D. Kellogg, Jr. '35, a faculty member since 1942, whom Chappell had taught Bible and French as a prep. "If the people who chose him to replace the Duke thought it was time to ease up on things – he sure did. I remember crossing swords with him once on a discipline matter when, in my opinion, he was being far more compassionate than he should have been. It's not a popularity contest. You have to keep things in order."

"He didn't have it in him to make the tough decisions when boys got into trouble," says Mary Finney, whom the Duke had asked not to retire with him, but to stay and help orient his successor. "I knew Tom as a boy and as a master, and when he came back as headmaster, I tried to make suggestions. He had a wonderful disposition, but he wouldn't listen. He also lacked the ability to finish a job. He had a place on the water near New London, and he'd take college applications down there with him and never mail them. Things like that were important to me."

Tom Chappell was not entirely to blame. "The Duke's system for college placements was essentially to do the whole job himself," says George Kellogg. "The trouble was, when Tom Chappell tried to do the same thing, it was already a much bigger job. The number of students was about the same, but the number of colleges was getting to be more and more numerous. Just filling out the wretched blanks was more than Tom could handle. I don't think he had any help until he got Jack Bodel [science master since 1929] to do it."

Explains Jean Chappell, "My husband was trying to move parents away from their expectations that their sons must be accepted at Yale or Princeton or they were failures."

The expectations that parents had of the school's headmaster were changing, too. "We had a kid there at the time Tom was headmaster," says Woods McCahill '33, whose fond memories of Chappell also go back to when Tom was his teacher, "so my wife and I were eagerly awaiting the headmaster's comments on our son's reports. On one of them Tom wrote that it was nice to see us. On another, he wished us a Merry Christmas. That was all."

Bill Olsen, who by then was acting as an admissions assistant, provides the necessary perspective: "The Duke often added nothing more than his GVS on the reports home, and there was nothing written by masters. The big joke was that you heard from a school if you succeeded monumentally or if you failed. That's why no news was considered to be good news. Now parents were expecting to be kept better informed. They wanted to remain a part of their sons' upbringing."

Tom Chappell's leadership style eventually led to dissatisfaction among faculty members accustomed to the Duke's seemingly infallible ways. "I can remember wandering down to Dick Bacon's house one night," says Blair Torrey, the youngest member of that coterie. "Dick had a group of teachers there airing their grievances and talking about getting together and kind of unionizing. I always felt vaguely uneasy about all that because Tom hired me. I loved him as a person, as a human being, and I really wasn't aware that he was not competent as an administrator."

Tom Chappell was feeling disappointments of his own. "He thought he was going to have a chance to talk to the boys and do things the way Mr. Van Santvoord had done when Tom was a teacher there," explains Jean Chappell. "It turned out to be not quite the way we thought it was going to be. There was so much paper work. That's not what he was cut out to do. He was a personal approach type. It was also mostly about raising money, always more money. He went out with Bill Olsen's father, Bert, to several cities to visit alumni. They traveled by Pullman, and Tom enjoyed that. But he was at heart a minister, and he missed the larger parish problems. One of Tom's great frustrations was that there was little chance in those days for the boys to get out into the community and do work in the hospitals and so forth."

The administrative structure being put in place in lieu of the Duke was further expanded in 1959, when Bill Olsen became associate headmaster. "The role was essentially a combination of dean of faculty and

Thomas Huntington Chappell and his wife, Jean

dean of students, which put me in close touch with the day-to-day workings of the school," says Bill Olsen. "Tom was spending more and more time on the outside, on more ceremonial things. It was a big pyramid at that time, a headmaster, an associate, and two assistants. It was a delicate situation, but Tom couldn't have been nicer. I never felt at any point that he saw me as intruding on his turf. I don't know totally what the trustees' theory was, but I hope what they were saying was that they wanted to give Tom every chance in the world to succeed by appointing me to help. Why it never could have worked, it seems to me, was because the impetus came not from Tom, but from the trustees."

"I think the job was not right for Tom," observes John G. "Jerry" Bowen '42, a nephew of G V S and an English teacher at Hotchkiss for thirty-six years before he retired in 1989. "He was a warm and delightful guy, and when he was eased out by the trustees, I thought he handled it very well."

The official reason given for Tom Chappell's resignation in the spring of 1960 was his desire to return to the active ministry. Like GVS before him, he was voted one year's salary, and the trustees expressed their gratitude to him and his wife, emphasizing Tom's "great affection for Hotchkiss and profound understanding of its spirit." "I had no idea it was going to happen," recalls Blair Torrey. "I remember being shocked by his announcement to the faculty in the old library the day he resigned, with tears and so forth. I even wrote about it later in a Middlebury graduate school composition paper. I described that moment. It made a big impression on me."

It was perhaps a measure of the man that his experience as headmaster did not affect Tom Chappell's loyalty to the school, and he remained for many years an enthusiastic class agent. "Until he died, he always came to see me when he visited the school," says the ninety-four-year-old Mary Finney, "and I still hear from Mrs. Chappell. She was a lovely woman."

iii / After the Saint came the O.
Although this sobriquet also failed to gain the currency of its two chief precursors, it was perhaps no less appropriate in that it revealed characteristically little about the man.

"I remember he always wore very shiny shoes and tweed jackets, and he was always well turned out," says David Bentley about the O before he was elevated from the teaching ranks. "He seemed to be a nice, easy-going guy, a guy you just naturally looked up to."

That was the image Bill Olsen would continue to perfect during his twenty-one years at the helm. "To sit opposite Bill in the front of the chapel at the start of the service," observes Lou Pressman, whom Olsen appointed as chaplain in 1980, "was rather like sitting opposite Yahweh on Mt. Sinai. You think, 'My God, if I look in his face. . . .'"

After the O stepped down as the sixth headmaster of the Hotchkiss School in 1981, his portrait was commissioned by Forrest E. Mars, Jr. '49, a trustee and generous donor to the school from the family's candy bar fortune. Selected to do the painting was Everett R. Kinstler, whose subjects were more likely to be statesmen, CEO's, and movie stars than a headmaster of a small New England prep school. It should therefore not be surprising that the life-sized image of the distinguished-looking man with a full head of slightly graying hair and symmetrical features emphasized by an ambient thrust of the jaw could well be that of a statesman, CEO, or movie star. Yet those who know A. William Olsen, Jr., will attest that the portrait is indeed a remarkable likeness of the man. No less remarkable is the artist's success in conveying some of the enigmatic quality of the O. The subject has a powerfully mirthful look which radiates outward and overwhelms; yet there is no way to tell whether it conveys friendliness for his former youthful clientele or self-satisfaction over having won at a difficult game. Or is there a measure of both? That thrusting-outward smile serves as a screen against anyone's trying to peer within.

Except for a few well-noted occasions, a generation of Hotchkiss students encountered that screen. "Everything Bill Olsen said seemed so edited," observes Lawson R. Wulsin, M.D. '70, who headed the *Record* and now is in charge of psychiatric residency training at the University of Cincinnati. "I assumed at first it was all because that's the way students had to see a headmaster. But the more I heard Bill Olsen give speeches to alumni and talk to faculty or friends, the more he remained the same. It seems that nobody I know gets the unedited version. He was a shy person in a 'public' position."

Bill Olsen to this day holds out that screen, which some of his closest associates reenforce. "I think that Bill made an absolutely superb contribution to the school," says David Luke '41, the Westvaco chairman who headed the Hotchkiss board during the latter part of Bill Olsen's tenure. "At the time of social turmoil in the country – and great turmoil in the university system – Bill steered a very good course for Hotchkiss." When pressed to provide specific incidents reflecting on the character or modus operandi of Bill Olsen, David Luke demurs. "Excellence speaks for itself," he explains.

Not to be overlooked is the unprecedented role of the headmaster's wife. The former Jean Stryker Rohrbach had her own long-standing ties to the school. Her brother, John, had graduated with the class of 1942, and Jean had often attended the school's dances while a student at Emma Willard. After one such dance, when she had stayed in the headmaster's house, she wrote in her diary, "Can you imagine anywhere a better job than being the wife of the headmaster of a school like Hotchkiss?" Some of the most trying episodes at Hotchkiss during the Olsen headmastership would be the result of Jean's determination to break out of precisely that tradition-bound role she had once so idealized.

Bill Olsen's appointment to the top post in 1960 was the culmination of a spectacular rise from within the teaching ranks. Only the previous year, with Tom Chappell's headship visibly faltering, Bill Fowle appeared to many of his faculty colleagues to be the logical successor. As assistant headmaster, Fowle was second in seniority only to George Milmine, who was nearing retirement age. "Fair is foul, and foul is fair, but Fowle is not fair," went a good-natured ditty among the students, which nevertheless reflected why this well-seasoned, pipe-smoking family man and former athletic hero was favored by many at the school who yearned for a strong hand.

Bill Olsen at that time – to use his own words – was still "a fairly run-of-the-mill New England boarding school master." In seniority, he stood exactly in the middle of the forty-four-member faculty."

"A total bolt out of the blue," says Bill Olsen about his appointment in the summer of 1959 as associate headmaster. "I was at home, cutting grass, when Tom Wagner ['28, secretary of the board] came up and plopped the idea at me. My first question was, 'How about Bill Fowle or George Milmine? Why me?' To this day I haven't the faintest idea why I was picked. If I had plans to become head, it was to succeed Tom Chappell after he'd been there fifteen years. Now, I had to assume this was more than just picking me to be associate head."

Curiously, Bill Olsen's question, "Why me?" – why not Bill Fowle? – is still asked sometimes at the school today. Was it because Bill Fowle had been on the Hotchkiss faculty for more than twenty years, and, as in 1926 when Peanut Hall was bypassed for a younger man, the trustees were looking for somebody who would be not quite so cemented in his ways? Was it because Bill Olsen had graduated from Hotchkiss, as had also his father, who at that time was working closely in fund raising with the trustees? Was it because one of the trustees was Olsen's relative, the Nobelist Dr. Dickinson Richards, who resigned from the board as soon as his nephew's pivotal appointment was confirmed? Was it because Olsen's three years on the faculty at Deerfield had exposed him to an alternate way of doing things – especially to the legendary Frank Boyden and his unique style? Or was it simply that Bill Olsen was the best-qualified person for the job, and the foregoing circumstances combined to put him in that position?

"I remember the Duke telling me once," Bill Olsen points out, "that becoming head was largely a matter of being in the right place at the right time."

Bill Olsen's implicit designation as heir apparent did not escape the Hotchkiss community for long. "In college I had never been sure whether it was better to be an assistant professor or an associate professor," noted George Stone, Bill Olsen's Yale classmate and faculty member since 1949. "Bill made it absolutely clear that an associate headmaster ranked higher in the system of things than an assistant headmaster."

Bill Fowle also knew what it meant. "That signaled what was going to happen," he says, "and Bill Olsen worked very hard as soon as he got to be associate head."

"There was a job to be done," explains Olsen. "The problem, I know, is that if you get in there and you start working hard, it looks as if you're bucking for the job."

In an effort to master some of the subtler details of his task, Bill Olsen called on Mary Finney at her home, an unusual step in that era when the lines between faculty and staff were rigidly drawn. Mary Finney had just retired, and as secretary to four headmasters knew more about the inner workings of the school than anyone else. Jean Olsen often accompanied Bill on these visits to tie up loose ends. "She even came down with a gift for Christmas," recalls Mary Finney. "That was unheard of."

With Bill Fowle out of the picture, the board met at the school on Friday evening, May 6, 1960. Surprising though it may seem, by the time the meeting adjourned for the night – and Tom Chappell's lot had been cast – it was not yet a foregone conclusion that Bill Olsen would get the nod. As associate headmaster, he was obviously the leading candidate. But would the board perhaps want to interview others, too?

Dud Parker, who participated as a trustee, explains what happened when the board convened the following day: "I was at the meeting, and I just happened to glance out of the window, and there was Bill Olsen in his car. I turned to those in the room and said, 'Why do we have to look any further? Here he is.' He offered everything we wanted."

A few weeks later, Bill Fowle accepted an invitation to become head-master of Mercersburg Academy. "I felt I'd be better off going some-where else, and I think Bill wanted it that way," says the still athletic-looking seventy-five-year-old Fowle, who has returned with his wife, Toni, to spend retirement in nearby Salisbury. "And that's all right. That's the way life is."

iv /   "The first day I got here in the fall of sixty, after dropping my bags off at Buehler, I walked over to Main," recalls John H. Perry, III '64, who today is an investment banker in Santa Barbara, California. "The moment I set foot inside the doors of the old Main, two seniors grabbed me, one by each elbow, and said, 'Hey, prep, what are the words of the Hotchkiss school song?' I told them I didn't know. They said, 'Okay, you're going in the showers.' They dragged me across the corridor and opened the two doors that went up to the second floor. And as they were pull-ing me up on the tops of my toes, Mr. Olsen came by and said to my abductors, in a very calm voice, 'What are you doing?' The seniors looked at him, and you could see they respected the authority he had in the school. They said, 'Well, sir, we're taking this prep on a tour of Main.' Bill Olsen said, still in that calm voice, 'I think you could let him take his own tour.' I had been shaken by this, and it was nice to know there was authority around so that you didn't have to be subjected to this kind of hazing."

The incident and the way the newly appointed headmaster handled it could just as easily have come from the Duke's era. Hotchkiss was indeed still very much the same school it had always been. While such revered figures as Mr. Mac and Carle Parsons had retired and lived nearby, the faculty with a few exceptions were holdovers from the Duke. In taking over the reins, however, Bill Olsen had one enormous advantage over G V S in 1926. There were no Uncle Joe Estills or Pop Jeffersons or Doc Browns ready to challenge him in whatever he tried to do. "Bill came in with considerable faculty support, including from those who had been partial to Bill Fowle," explains one of the senior holdovers, Dick Bacon, who would continue to teach until 1977. "For the past five years, the school had been very poorly run; everything was at sixes and sevens. Here was somebody who would at last take the school in hand, and though we disagreed with Bill about some of the ways he went about doing things, the school was being much better run."

Bill Olsen, moreover, was not coming in with a new academic program that would disrupt the status quo and threaten its old-time practitioners. Many of the Van Santvoord holdovers were pedagogically still well ahead of their times, as the new headmaster astutely recognized. There was the great Dick Gurney, a former Rhodes scholar who taught senior English, coached school football, owned an Aeolian harp, and reputedly operated an efficient still in the back of his house. There was Dr. Alan S. Hoey, a vibrant, twinkling little man who taught Latin and Greek with the sort of communicable enthusiasm that brought the subject matter buoyantly to life, not only for the moment, but in many of his students, for the rest of their lives. Then there was R. R. "the Hun" Miller, who taught senior French and was reputed to have a genius I.Q. Having been granted a patent for an automatic radar anticollision device at sea, he had just closed a sale with the Italian government and was returning on the *Andrea Doria* when it collided with the *Stockholm* some fifty miles off Nantucket and sank. Miller's cabin was not in the impact area, where all the casualties were, and he made it back to Hotchkiss only somewhat bedraggled and sans luggage. Another French teacher was Peter Beaumont, a transplanted British ex-pugilist and Oxford graduate whose instructional technique of musical chairs made his classes only slightly less animated than Grand Central Station at rush hour. A correct answer enabled you to move up one or more seats over those who had not answered correctly. At least once a week at the end of the period, this dynamic, chunky man with flashing eyes would enter your final seat number as a portion of your grade. Nobody ever dozed off in that class! The Duke's final innovation, an extracurricular course in Russian, was to be carried on formally by the immensely popular Clinton N. Ely '45, a man whose Neanderthal-like physique harbored a tender heart, and his capacious head sheltered a poetic brain.

A young Van Santvoord holdover destined to gain a unique niche in Hotchkiss history over the next quarter century was George Norton Stone. "We were just getting into new math, and we were using a book being written on an almost day-to-day basis by George Stone," says William R. Boyer, Jr., who entered as a prep in 1960. "I can still see George Stone striding back and forth in front of the class, window open, with a little butt of a cigarette between his thumb and forefinger. He would take a drag off the cigarette and stare up at the ceiling and with a kind of an upside-down smile say, 'Boys, you're learning things that freshmen at Yale don't know.' I think everybody felt they were participating in some special magic, something unique and extraordinary. To this day I can count to thirty-two on one hand by using his binary digital numbering system.

"Yet what I learned at Hotchkiss was not so much particular skills as things about myself," continues Bill Boyer, now a civilian in the Pentagon. "I learned the pragmatic cause-and-effect relationship of doing your work and not doing your work. I learned about succeeding and failing from that moment of truth when your grades were posted on the bulletin board in the hall for all to see. Above all, I learned how to discriminate. At that time discrimination was a kind of a socially bad word to use, and Mr. Hawkins said to us in class, 'You must learn to discriminate.' I thought, what is this? Then I came to understand he meant not to enter a situation without a willingness to look at both sides and try to evaluate the relative pros and cons – yes, to discriminate and make a choice. I learned that life is indeed a series of choices all along the way."

The faculty's continued pursuit of traditional values in traditional ways by no means received uniform applause. "I think Hawkins was perhaps one of the most sadistic people I've known in my life," says still another member of that class of 1964, Washburn S. "Burn" Oberwager. "He certainly showed his discrimination against those of us in class who didn't do well. His approach was to beat us further down rather than raise us up. But that wasn't unusual. Hotchkiss was in a time warp. It was a school that had lived since the previous century under almost a puritanical mentality, and we were probably one of the last classes that went through under that kind of mentality. Olsen still had that mentality, too. It's hard to believe that he could have been so out of touch with our generation."

Burn Oberwager, who today runs his own leveraged buy-out company in Philadelphia, elaborates: "In my senior year, I was expelled from Hotchkiss along with two other people just four weeks from graduation. My parents had dropped me off on a Sunday evening at about five o'clock. Figuring I was still on the weekend, which technically ended at midnight, I took it upon myself to leave the campus. I went down to Millerton with my friends and drank and had a good time. We were caught, and nothing has been as indelible in my memory as getting kicked out. It was a traumatic experience. In my class, I'd say that about twenty people were expelled during the four years. Most of them had characteristics that were nonconforming. I think Bill Olsen was a man lacking in compassion. I don't think he really understood kids. He left us unprepared for what was beginning to happen in the outside world in the early sixties."

Oberwager's classmate, Strobe Talbott, gives an altogether different picture. "Olsen had the right combination of compassion, sternness, and good humor that I thought the job required," says the editor-at-large of *Time*, author and noted Sovietologist, whose father had been in Olsen's class of '39. "He defined for me what a good headmaster should be." Talbott credits Olsen's handling of the Cuban missile crisis in October of 1962 "for contributing to my decision to devote my professional life to understanding the Soviet Union. At the low point of the confrontation, Bill Olsen assembled the entire student body and had us literally pray for deliverance. We were down on our knees basically saying, 'Please, God, may these two jerks not get us into a nuclear war.' Bill Olsen made us appreciate the magnitude of what was happening while giving us a sense that reason could still prevail. I thought the way he used the chapel and the spiritual underpinnings of the school on that occasion represented great leadership."

That brings us back to the persona of the O. "We were good friends," says English teacher Blair Torrey, who has himself attained legendary status with an unusually small array of detractors, "but I always wanted him to be a little less combed and polished, more down to earth."

Lawrence W. Becker, now headmaster of the Brooks School, who joined the faculty in 1964: "Bill had the ability to communicate with kids in a language they could understand and relate to. I can remember his auditorium speeches about popcorn on the stairwells. 'If there is any more popcorn on the stairwells, the snack bar will be closed.' Miraculously, there was no more popcorn on stairwells."

F. George Anastasio, today head of the drama department, who joined the faculty in 1963: "Bill was a shy man, but he had a flair. He proved in faculty productions that he could act well and sing well and exert a powerful presence. He capitalized on these abilities to become a strong PR headmaster."

James L. Marks III, now headmaster of Lake Forest Country Day School, who joined the faculty in 1964 and stayed through Olsen's entire career: "Bill was a mentor to me as I moved through the ranks, and I came to understand how difficult and complex running a school could be. There was so much more to the man than his formal exterior."

The go-around about the O, like that about the Duke and the King, could go on and on. What is different is that Bill Olsen is here in person to impart to this verbal carousel a turn of his own.

v /   "**W**hen I was first asked to be head," recalls Bill Olsen, "probably my initial reaction might well have been, 'Wow, isn't it fun! Imagine being headmaster of Hotchkiss. Now what do I do?'

"I didn't have to have any learning period there. I knew the place in personal terms; I knew the kids; I knew the faculty. No matter how you slice it, your relationship as the head with your former peers changes. You become a whole new authority, with the power to hire and fire and do all those kinds of things. The relationship with the kids changes also. Before, you were down there with them. They saw you horsing around in class. Now, you're up front, the authority figure. A headmaster can lose the game by perfectly silly little things. It may be something as small as whether you speak from your clipboard or from cards or stand in front in the auditorium or on the podium. It can be the first comment you make; if that's wrong, it will stick with you forever. The kids are your most critical constituency.

"There was probably a lot going on under the surface in 1960, but outwardly there weren't major issues that any school of our kind had to face. There wasn't an awful lot of initiative you could take except to keep the school moving forward on an even keel. More than ninety percent of what a headmaster does day by day is react; react to what the kids do, react to what the faculty does, react to what's happening in the immediate community. What you've got to do, however, is to keep alert for any changes beyond the horizon which you're eventually going to encounter. What the Duke had not recognized – and, of course, the Duke had been brought into the modern world kicking and screaming – was that the school could no longer remain an isolated entity on a hill where youngsters came in September and from which they went in December, and anything important that happened in that period happened here and nowhere else. That isolation was beginning to break down, and it was breaking down because people on the outside, particularly former graduates of the school whose children were students here, or would soon be coming here, began to make it happen.

"One of the first things I did was to suggest that we have a Thanksgiving vacation. This was in part responding to reality. What was happening was that seniors who had weekends that they had stored up took the Thanksgiving weekend. So the old idea of having everyone here at the school together for the holiday was falling apart. The seniors would go off and have a wonderful time in New York, or wherever, and come back on that old Millerton train. I'm glad I wasn't the conductor on that.

"Another early suggestion that was in its own way revolutionary was to give in on the radio issue – to allow students to have radios in their rooms. To keep people so isolated from the world that they couldn't even hear what was happening out there was insane. I can remember going home from school when I was a kid here and my mother asking me about such and such and my saying, 'I never heard of it.' This could be something as important as Czechoslovakia being taken over by the Nazis. If we got caught with a radio, we were slapped on sequestration. It was one of those God-awful things. Now, you couldn't have enforced it, even if you tried, because of transistors.

"Then somewhere in there – I don't remember if at first it was by fiat or by persuasion – I said, 'This school is far too discipline-oriented. The faculty is worrying about kids doing perfectly ridiculous things that kids are going to do, and we're spending well over fifty percent of our time in faculty meetings and discipline committee meetings – what were then called dormitory committee meetings – talking about kids doing what kids have always done.'

"My suggestion was that we eliminate the old system. My major objection to sequestration was that it removed from participation in the school program the very people who ought to be in there contributing. To me it made no sense to say to them at the very point you run out of string, 'Okay, we're going to have you here, but we're not going to let you be a part of this society.' So sequestration was eliminated, and nobody knows what the word means anymore. Censure was eliminated, and that eliminated one of the Duke's favorite arguing points: do you know the difference between *censor* and *censure*? I told the faculty, 'We're still going to keep the same general principles of what we want kids to do, but as far as how they're going to be persuaded to do it, we're going to do what was not very different during the early years of the school.' The words *moral suasion* were used by Dr. Buehler before he brought in sequestration. We felt the offenses that had previously been automatic dismissal now could be handled more constructively if the kids were given a severe warning, put on probation, and in many cases, suspended for a period of time to get the families involved. Then, if subsequent to that the youngster indicated by doing the thing again that he didn't belong here, he was sent home for good. So that was the two-chance system. I'm still comfortable with that. Kids are kids.''

How George Van Santvoord felt about these first changes instituted by his onetime protégé can only be surmised. No doubt, Bill Olsen's appointment to be headmaster was as much a relief to the Duke as it was to the senior faculty holdovers, and the new relationship started off on a festive note. ''When we took over from Tom Chappell, the first thing we did was to have Mr. and Mrs. Van Santvoord down, instantly,'' recalls Jean Olsen. ''We also had him stay with us and gave him a dinner party with the friends he knew in the community, so he could see some of his old buddies – Carle Parsons and some of the people he knew. He really appreciated being asked back.''

Recalls Bill Olsen, ''One of the funniest scenes I witnessed after I became head was George Van Santvoord and Harry Luce confronting each other in the headmaster's house. 'What are *you* doing here, Harry?' 'Well, I've been invited to give the graduation address.' 'Oh. . . .' 'And what are *you* doing here, George?' 'I guess I've come to hear you, though I didn't know you were the one.''''

According to Bill Olsen, his admiration for the Duke never changed. ''I think the guy was just terrific. He was one of the two headmaster models I could draw from. The other was Boyden, for whom I worked at Deerfield. What really motivated me as headmaster from the beginning was the feeling that if we were able to merge some of what Deerfield was trying to do with some of what Hotchkiss was trying to do, we'd have a wonderful setup. Hotchkiss was clearly a better school academically. Deerfield was seen to be less severe than Hotchkiss. We labored under that characterization for generations. I thought if you could meld those perceptions, you'd have the ideal kind of a school.''

Bill Olsen's abolition of sequestration was, in fact, partly an attempt at changing perceptions rather than substance. For the new headmaster, it was a way of putting his imprint on the life of the school. "As always, for violation of any major school rules such as smoking," reported the *Record* on October 1, 1963, "the boy is placed on special discipline: on bounds, no visiting, study hall, no social commitments, and no athletics for a period of six weeks." There, little had changed except the word sequestration. Moreover, the new two-chance policy failed to save Burn Oberwager and his two classmates from that traumatic expulsion the following spring. The reality was that traditional ways at Hotchkiss could rarely be eliminated overnight. Some offenses by their very nature continued to demand an instant casting out, including, apparently, sneaking off to Millerton to guzzle beer.

Bill Olsen's other innovations represented a more tangible break with the past – and GVS. The Duke's case against radios had been that students used them only to tune in to such programs as *Mr. Keene, Tracer of Lost Persons*. "Read the *New York Times*, read the *Herald Tribune*, and not just the sports pages," GVS had often admonished the school. "You might be surprised at some of the things you will learn." And his rationale for keeping everyone at the school for Thanksgiving had been based not only in trying to be fair to those who lived too far or could not afford to go home, but also in wanting to avoid needless exposure of Hotchkiss boys to the undesirable influences of the outside world – though GVS sought to make the holiday at least partly a family affair. "On Wednesday evening . . . the Fall Play is presented in the auditorium [and] seats are available for guests," he had notified parents. Parents whose sons were in the production, the Duke invited "to supper in the School dining room at 6:30 P.M."

As a trustee emeritus, the former headmaster was not a docile member of the board. "He used to come to the meetings, and he'd ramble on about something that didn't have anything to do with the subject at all," says Woods McCahill, who became a trustee in 1960. "But Jim Linen [James A. Linen '30, then president of the board] didn't hesitate to tell him to get back to the point. Jim knew the Duke very well, and they had a wonderful relationship. Jim never forgot what the Duke had

A. William Olsen, Jr.

done for him back in the Depression. When Jim got married, I think the Duke was his best man."

The Duke's comments did not remain quite so muffled. "When I became a trustee," says Zeph Stewart, who joined the board in the fall of 1964, "the greatest problem was the fact that GVS came back to the meetings and criticized everything that was going on. I was terribly embarrassed because he would sit next to me and whisper about all the things that were being done wrong."

One issue seemed especially to rankle GVS. "He was desperately against the GO [Greater Opportunity] program, which would bring black ghetto kids to the school for the summer," explains Zeph. "He said, 'If you're going to help people, why don't you help the farmers in New Hampshire or Connecticut or Vermont? They're much more in need of help than these black people from the cities.' He didn't use the word *black*, of course. It came into use later."

The Duke's lifelong liberality, apparently, was suspended when it came to keeping out what he considered to be undesirable influences of city life. In this connection, the Duke recalled the costly incident leading to the termination of the Riis summer camp, whose inner city sojourners had been virtually all white. "History repeats itself," he said about the proposed new campers, and cautioned, "You can throw plates in the dining room right through Mrs. Hotchkiss's portrait. One [is all it takes]." Whether over this issue or because of other differences with Bill Olsen, such as the 75th anniversary history, GVS would attend no board meetings throughout most of the final decade of his life.

vi / 	The trustees liked what they saw of Bill Olsen's substance and style. His report of May 4, 1963, outlining his proposed disciplinary system, "was enthusiastically received and accepted." He was voted a salary raise from $14,000 to $16,500 as of July 1, 1963, and given an "unlimited allowance for school-connected travel and entertainment," with an exhortation "to exercise this privilege generously."

During that same summer a casual meeting gave impetus to the GO program that so distressed the Duke. "We were vacationing down at the shore, and we bumped into John Morton Blum in the Yale Co-op," recalls Jean Olsen. "John was known throughout New England as an outstanding educator. [Though a graduate of Andover, he became a Hotchkiss trustee the following year.] We had dinner with him, and he very gently prodded Bill. He said, 'What do you do with your campus in the summer? Do you just let it sit there? This is a great chance to play a role in what's going on in the United States.' This was the height of the Kennedy era, and of course, he meant the civil rights movement. Then as Bill and I drove home, we agreed we weren't doing enough with our lives beyond running the school and helping to build up the endowment fund. Billy is a completely unprejudiced man, and not a fearful man. He saw there was a chance, and he was going to take it. He wrote up a proposal, which the Rockefeller Foundation agreed to fund for three years. That was the origin of the GO program."

Bill Olsen prefers to emphasize the historical perspective; he sees the GO program as his response to a subtle educational and social revolution gaining momentum over the previous twenty years. "It goes back to Truman's integration of the armed forces during World War II; to the G.I. Bill of Rights, which opened up a first-rate college education to large numbers of people who couldn't previously afford it; and to the civil rights movement, which was then gaining momentum. As the composition of Yale, Harvard, Princeton, and other colleges began to change, the composition of schools like Hotchkiss began to change. In the past, Hotchkiss helped disadvantaged individuals by admitting them on full scholarship. My dad would have qualified on that score. But that was a very narrow definition of disadvantaged. It was financial and to a lesser extent educational. The Greater Opportunity program was directed at young people from inner cities who had been deprived culturally, educationally, and in virtually every other way except, of course, in terms of what's known as street smarts. We asked, 'Is there something we can do to help?' Hotchkiss already was a founding member of ABC, A Better Chance, which operated out of Dartmouth College and sought to increase the enrollment of minority students in independent schools. ABC was primarily trying to identify, place, and provide scholarships for the top black students. There was no need to duplicate that. What we came up with was a team approach with inner-city schools that was designed so we wouldn't be taking their best kids out and giving them a Hotchkiss education and having them lose touch with where they came from; instead, we would have them come here for the summer and supplement their own program and then have them go back. The hope was to enrich these youngsters intellectually and emotionally, and they would in turn make a positive difference in their schools."

To direct the program, Bill Olsen chose an outsider, Father David Kern, who was experienced in educational work with inner city youth. The Hotchkiss School was to provide the facilities and make up any financial deficits in excess of the $165,000, three-year Rockefeller grant. While there was no dearth of Hotchkiss boys willing to give up a large part of their summer to act as GO program proctors, faculty enthusiasm was not quite so uniform. Bill Olsen explains: "There were certainly people who resisted strongly the move into the GO program because this brought to the Hotchkiss campus the kind of youngster the school never dealt with. These were all boys still, but the majority of them were black, and those that weren't black were Puerto Rican. There were a few white faces in there, but damned few.

"Yet it was not a difficult problem to handle. There was a strong idealistic strain, particularly in the younger-to-middle-range faculty who were attuned to what was going on out there and wanted to be part of it themselves. Enough of the older-timers were either eager to do this or certainly willing to do this; so where there was a segment that resisted it, they didn't have to participate. Much of the faculty that we wanted were people teaching in the inner city schools, and David Kern brought them in."

Among those inner-city teachers was Walter J. Crain, recruited from Wadleigh Junior High at 114th Street between Seventh and Eighth avenues in New York City: "One of my colleagues had written to Hotchkiss in early 1964 asking if some of our kids could get involved in the GO program. When David Kern came down to interview them, it turned out I knew him from the days that he had been an Episcopal minister in the Bronx, and he hired me to be part of the public school faculty at Hotchkiss.

"About 120 kids were enrolled in the first GO program – fourteen of them on my corridor in Memorial. The summer was set up as a microcosm of the regular Hotchkiss year; study in the morning, athletics in the afternoon, study hall in the evening. On weekends, we tried to take the kids to some enrichment event that they wouldn't have had a chance to be exposed to on their own; it could be Riverside Park, the Long Wharf Theater, and so forth. The kids liked the fun parts of the program, but to have school and study for seven weeks during the summer was foreign to them. They didn't take to the regimentation easily. For a lot of them, it was compounded by the fact that they were away from home for the first time. So it took a lot of coaxing, coercing, and tugging along to get the kids involved.

"The advantage of the GO program over other programs developing around the nation was that it was an ongoing three-year program. The same kids would be coming back for three successive summers. During the winter, Father Kern would visit them at their schools, get their report cards, and talk to their parents. Then in their senior year we helped them with their college plans, their applications and so forth. I remember Bill Olsen telling the kids on graduation that they were always going to be Hotchkiss men, and that they were as much a part of the Hotchkiss tradition as anyone coming for the four years. I think the kids really did feel it. Almost twenty-five years later, I still occasionally get calls from some of them."

Walter Crain, who joined the regular Hotchkiss faculty in 1970, is today dean of students and head of the school's discipline committee.

For Bill Olsen, who had taught alongside Walter Crain on the GO faculty, one incident typified the program: "It happened at the end of the first summer, and the buses had just loaded up. The proctors were standing out on the front porch, and left behind was one guy. I went up to him, and I suddenly realized he was crying. He looked at me, and

I looked at him, and I knew why he was crying and he knew I knew why he was crying. That was the kind of emotion that was involved.

"George Stone characterized it a bit differently. He said, 'You know, I learned through the GO program that very often just touching somebody is the most important thing you can do.' It seems to me a lot of people fought the GO program because it disrupted all the old patterns. But it also seems to me that if it can have the kind of impact it had on this youngster and on a lot of the faculty, then it was worth doing. And that was what the program was designed to do – to get people to understand each other a lot better."

Even those who did not directly participate in the GO program were touched. "I think we became aware," says John A. Luke, Jr. '67 (whose father had been deprived of his senior year because of World War II), "that there was another world out there that we didn't just see when we rode the train through 125th Street, but one that we had to be more sensitive to."

vii /   "For me, 'Mr. Olsen' represented Hotchkiss," says Stephen D. Greenberg '66, former trustee and today deputy commissioner of major league baseball. "I'm sure people who lived in the Van Santvoord era would find it startling that anyone other than George Van Santvoord could represent Hotchkiss. To this day when I think of the school, I have the image of Bill Olsen come to mind."

Yet Hotchkiss still was not a fundamentally different school from the days of GVS. "Drugs were not on campus, to my knowledge," says Steve Greenberg's classmate William H. Conyngham II of the Pennsylvania Conyngham clan. "The biggest transgression in my time was that a guy would run out in the woods and smoke a cigarette or maybe have a rum and coke. Or he might have his hair a little longer than they chose us to have. One thing I distinctly remember is walking down the hall and all of a sudden feeling this very strong grip on my shoulder, and Bill Olsen telling me in a firm voice to sign up for the barber shop." No less characteristic of the times was the written comment at the end of Will Conyngham's upper mid year from his corridor master: "He has kept a neat room, has had careful regard for bed hours, and has been so judicious in his use of his illegal hot plate that I never managed to catch him at it."

Will Conyngham, however, would not finish his senior year. Bill Olsen's two-chance policy had yet to be fully implemented, and it was the rum and coke that proved terminal for Will: "I had to leave school during the fall term, along with four other guys, because of drinking at a dance weekend picnic in the woods. All told, seven of us had been reported, but when they questioned us, five of us took the tack that we were going to be totally forthright, hoping that some value would be placed on that approach. We were commended for that forthrightness – and were expelled. The others were not. Coincidentally, three of us who got kicked out had fathers in the class of '38, one of whom was a trustee. I felt I was in good company, although that made it no less painful."

Will Conyngham's predicament would be debated to this day. Should you tell the truth when doing so meant being expelled? Or should you try to save your skin and silently be branded a liar in the Hotchkiss community? Some of those who took the seemingly easier course would feel no less pain than Will Conyngham for years to come. As one student analyzed it, "Damned if you do, damned if you don't."

Despite his role in accentuating this paradox, Bill Olsen was held in high esteem by Will Conyngham's class. "The Headmaster's constant effort and interest in all facets of Hotchkiss life," commented the *Record* on the dedication of the *Mischianza* of 1966 to Olsen, "is the force that makes the school tick, and the Alumni showed their recognition of this fact when they elected him Hotchkiss Man of the Year in 1964. . . . Indicative of the Headmaster's participation in school life is the fact that he managed to find time away from the demanding duties of the school's administration to coach the Varsity swimming team to a highly successful season. . . . He will be remembered for his good humor, for his patience, and for his great inspiration."

"The world rolled over about 1967," says Bill Olsen. "That was the first time two or three kids were caught smoking marijuana and reported. That was when we recognized that as far away as we were from the horrors of the world, the world had gotten to us. I can still hear Steve Bolmer [Stephen T. Bolmer, then director of admissions and mathematics teacher since 1947] in the back of the faculty meeting when he heard the report, saying, 'We're ruined!' Little did he or anybody know that what we were facing was what everybody else was facing; that was, that the world was changing radically, drugs were coming, the generation gap was upon us, the civil rights movement had burgeoned.

"What accelerated everything was the nastiness of the Vietnam war. We got the ripple effect from what was going on at college and university campuses. The one advantage we had was having about a four-year lead time. If something happened on a college campus, we could expect some kind of a reverberation three or four years later. So in a way we could prepare ourselves. The downside was that we had no idea what our seniors would be getting into in college. The class of 1965 was in college during the worst of the counterculture and protest period. The class of 1966 had it even worse. They were in college when the climax was hit in 1970. Yet we had no idea when they left here what they were going to hit – or what was going to hit us."

Hotchkiss was beginning to experience the pangs of finding out. A new mood was increasingly pervading the school – a mounting disillusionment and disaffection dating back perhaps to the shattering end of JFK's Camelot. When a group of boys rushed into the coffee room after lunch on November 22, 1963, to tell Mrs. Olsen that the president had been shot, she had good reason to think they were trying to pull a typically Hotchkiss prank. Those who had experienced this wrenching event shortly after entering the school as preps could hardly be expected to harbor much boyish levity by the time they became the graduates of the class of 1967. The intervening years had deeply affected many of them with a cynical distrust of society and authority; often they questioned the meaning of their own existence. If some of them wanted to tune out with marijuana and heavier drugs, it was perhaps symptomatic of a broader desire to escape who they were. The class of 1968 felt it even more acutely as the chant "Hey, hey, LBJ, how many kids did you kill today?" went up, followed by the assassinations of Martin Luther King and a second Kennedy.

Jack Lord '68 chronicles his alienation from everything he once loved – and the drastic step he took: "One of my most vivid memories of Hotchkiss is that of Dick Gurney and his massive, awesome character. He used to watch the Saturday afternoon football games, and while everyone would be running up and down following the plays, he'd usually stand in one place. He'd have on his kind of floppy hat, and he'd move his head slightly to follow the action, smoking his pipe. One game it started to rain, and it just rained more and more heavily. Everybody else was scattering around, dealing with it in different ways. If they had an umbrella, they'd use it or they'd pull their coat over their head or they'd run for shelter. The only thing Gurney did, he reached up and turned his pipe upside down.

"I was fascinated to be [at Hotchkiss] with kids who had traveled all over the world and lived in fantastic homes. My best friend was Orin McCluskey, and his parents had an apartment on Park Avenue and Sixty-Second Street. Several friends and I would visit him in New York or go out to their house on Long Island. Boy, I embraced it all. Yet, I also came to realize Hotchkiss was an isolating experience. In 1968, my classmates weren't nearly as aware socially and politically as the classes after ours would become. For all the unique characters at Hotchkiss like Gurney, they were still part of the same world I grew up with. And it was a small world.

"What brought this home to me, literally overnight, was an incident during spring vacation of my senior year. It wasn't so much something that happened, but kind of like a light went on. I had gone down to Jamaica with my friend Orin, where his family had a house on Montego Bay. It was the epitome of privileged lifestyle, and I loved it. Then I went to Florida, where my mother lived in more modest circumstances. She is someone who admires people of wealth and power and wouldn't be much impressed with the virtues of a Dick Gurney. Suddenly, I guess, the contrast struck me, and that the values she embraced were kind of like a caricature of what I was embracing. I said, 'Wait a minute, I've got to get away from all of this. There's other stuff going on in the world besides getting into the right college, landing a job that would bring me a lot of bucks, and get me a B M W, and the nice things in life.' That was a one-dimensional reflection of reality, and I needed to walk through the mirror and see things from the other side. Going into service right after Hotchkiss, going to Vietnam, specifically as a corpsman, was my way to gaining that reverse perspective.'' *

Even if unique in his response, Jack Lord had not been too far out of the mainstream at Hotchkiss in recognizing his misgivings about the direction he was headed in. The prevailing mood at the school in the late sixties is reflected in MacDonnell Gordon's article in the *Mischianza* for 1969, which appeared just as America's youth were about to gather in the historic protest-celebration at Woodstock, New York:

''All that is Hotchkiss came to me in May with one very isolated experience. On a very beautiful and deceptively calm evening I went to a party given for a former class at the boathouse. One of the couples there were friends of mine, and their son is a student here. It all seemed very innocent to me. Fireworks were being shot over the lake, and even the officious appearance of a Mr. Royce [the school's business

---

* ''My biggest surprise in Vietnam,'' says Jack Lord, ''was when my Hotchkiss friend Orin McCluskey showed up. He was a freshman at Yale, and he got press credentials, I believe, through another classmate, Kit Luce [Henry C. Luce '68] and his *Time-Life* connections. One day I was out in the field with our platoon when a resupply helicopter swooped down, and Orin walked off. He carried a little Brownie Instamatic, and he really wasn't going to be a journalist for anything other than the *Yale News* and some local papers like that. But he just wanted to be there. He had the courtesy rank of a major, and he could hop a helicopter and say, 'Are you going to Saigon? I'm riding with you.' This gave him the option, after a few days in the boondocks – going out on patrol with us and taking real chances – to go back and stay at the press club, take a shower, eat lobster and drink Jack Daniels.''

manager until 1991] questioning permits could not shatter the beauty of the night. But things changed very quickly. Mr. Carlisle [a young English teacher] had volunteered to answer questions the alumni might have. Soon he looked like a Christian in a field of Romans. From the start there was an incredible wave of archconservatism and imperceptive feelings that bordered on the sickening. The questions centered on the idea that Hotchkiss was not doing enough to teach 'our children' the true and beautiful benefits of the free enterprise system; that Socialist works were taught without presenting the other view, and so forth. The beauties of free enterprise aside, what amazed and saddened me was that they were not asking, 'Why aren't you making our son a man?' They were asking, 'Why aren't you making our son a capitalist?'

"I grew uneasy just watching. Mr. Carlisle was trying very hard to answer the questions, but he was either ignored or laughed at. After all, he is young. A voice in the back of the room yelled out, 'Let's hear what Gus [Dick] Gurney has to say about all this!' A chorus rose in agreement. Mr. Gurney had been standing with his back to them. He turned and very quickly said something to the effect that worrying about the profit motive, systems of economics, and the like, are not what is taught at Hotchkiss, because it believes in something else larger and more important. He said that he and others tried to teach what it meant to be a man, and all else was crap. He was obviously angry. He walked out. The room was silent for a few moments as if an ally had suddenly turned traitor. A few nervous laughs were heard, and soon all was happy again. I left; and as I walked by the front, I saw Mr. Gurney sitting on a pile of logs smoking his pipe. For some reason I went to him and thanked him for what he said. But I don't think he really heard me. The whole thing fell on me in the one question, 'What's the use?' I started to cry. I cried for all the people Gurney had tried to teach a little humanism to and had failed. I cried for my own damned idealism. I felt like giving up any contact with humanity or any attempt to help make the world any better. I felt like committing a symbolic suicide and moving to Billings, Montana, and never looking back. . . ."

G. MacDonnell Gordon today is an attorney in Santa Fe, New Mexico. John C. Lord is a physician's assistant working in emergency situations and teaching. "I have a wonderful relationship with a wife who is philosophically in tune with me," says Jack Lord. "My life has clicked in a way I had never imagined possible at Hotchkiss."

viii /   For Bill Olsen 1967 was a watershed year – and not just because of that first marijuana incident at the school. This was also the year that the original Main Building was torn down. As the wrecking ball swung inexorably to demolish the old structure of lemon-colored brick, a movie camera recorded the scene for the generations of old Hotchkiss boys who would have wanted to be there to bid farewell to this treasured landmark. Bill Olsen was not about to disregard their feelings in building anew: "There's a very strong strain of traditionalism in schools like this, and you tamper with it at your peril. If you've got any brains at all, you take advantage of it. What you try to do is to tie today to yesterday. The thing people relished about the old Main Building was the long corridor, and the fact that the buildings were connected. They were connected for ridiculous reasons when you think about it – to keep people indoors because they'd be healthier. The theory was that they wouldn't be susceptible to all those germs that were outside during the winter, which contradicted the whole idea of moving to the country in the first place. Nevertheless, we certainly made a clear effort to tie the new design into that nostalgia. When I showed the trustees the first plans for the Y-shaped building with long corridors, there was actually a suggestion to use blue brick because that symbolized Yale."*

* Planning the new Main had been in fact a long and arduous process for the trustees. As Zeph Stewart explains, "At one point, after final plans had been inspected and approved, Bob Flint ['23] sent to his fellow trustees an incisive, eleventh-hour criticism of that somewhat ostentatious version. As a result, the plans were

The year 1967 also happened to be the school's 75th anniversary. Bill Olsen's portrait on the back cover of the Wertenbaker book not only dramatized his stature at the school, but was symbolic of the way he chose to play his role. The recognition he received among alumni was perhaps most convincingly reflected in the success of the anniversary's fund-raising drive, which surpassed its goal with a total of more than $11 million. The trustees, in turn, expressed their appreciation by upping Bill Olsen's salary to $22,000. And at the suggestion of the board's new president, IBM's World Trade president Arthur K. "Dick" Watson '38, "It was voted to grant the headmaster a leave of absence for whatever date in 1968 he chooses and extending through the summer, with full salary and travel expenses paid."

Perhaps the trustees also felt Bill Olsen needed the rest. Nineteen sixty-seven had seen long-simmering tensions among the faculty begin to bubble up. Part of the problem was the perennial one of the generation gap between the older, more traditional masters and the youthful headmaster with his relatively liberal views. The good will Olsen had started with in 1960 had been increasingly eroded by a nostalgia for GVS and his ways. "The greatest criticism of Bill came from the stalwarts of the Van Santvoord era; people like Jack Bodel, Bob Hawkins, Dick Bacon, Charlie Berry, Stearns and Gurney," says Larry Becker. "I do remember an unfortunate quote attributed to Jean Olsen which made the rounds of the school: 'Well, a few more years and those people will all be gone, and every appointment will be Billy's.'"

Yet it was the young newcomers who at this point felt the strongest pressure to let off steam. "One of the most devastating things about teaching is you spend so much time educating other people's children that sometimes your own suffer in the bargain," says John R. "Rusty" Chandler, Jr. '53, who joined the faculty in 1964 and today is assistant

---

dropped and the whole concept rethought, giving us the present structure. It was Woods McCahill who guided the project throughout, working with Bill Olsen and the architects. Several years later the rather forbidding main entrance was lightened and softened by alterations donated by another trustee, Fred Godley ['38]."

headmaster. Coming from a family replete with Hotchkiss relatives and steeped in the school's traditions, Rusty was the one to broach the subject to the man he admired and worked with closely: "I remember in 1967 we were flying to California for a Hotchkiss dinner. I was sitting with Ted Cooke who was then the alumni secretary. I had a Bloody Mary on the plane, and Ted and I were talking. Then I decided I'd go back and talk to Bill Olsen, who was sitting four or five seats behind us, working on some speech. I sat down next to him and said I thought he had some problems with his faculty. He looked up from his papers, and in that low-key way of his said, 'What's that?' I told him I thought he had a morale problem. 'Oh?' he said. He seemed more curious than surprised. I told him there was a bunch of us fairly young – twenty-eight, thirty-year-olds – and we were under tremendous stress: 'We have kids growing up, and we never see them. We're expected to be at three meals a day, go to chapel six days a week, and twice on Sunday. There are athletics to coach in the afternoon and corridors to supervise in the evenings. It just is a life that is beginning to frustrate us and our spouses, and to some extent, our kids.' Well, Bill was very good. He said I had made some interesting points, and we talked about them. When we got back to school, he came to my office and said, 'I'm going to appoint a faculty morale committee. Do you want to chair it?' I accepted. He left it to me to select the members. Blair Torrey was on it, and Dick Bacon, who just recently had lost his wife to cancer. He and I were close, and I'd had a high regard for him since I'd been a student. So the first meeting was at Dick's house, and it was terrible. Nobody opened up. Everybody kept sidestepping the issue with the same pleasantries and platitudes. I was discouraged. For the next meeting, I brought along a bottle of bourbon and that unlocked everything. All the pent-up feelings just came right out on the table. We sat there and shared one another's frustrations. We had two or more meetings. I had a notebook of goodies, and Chris Carlisle took the notes and reduced them to a dozen or so recommendations which the committee presented to Bill Olsen. Within four years every one of the recommendations had been acted upon. Whatever Bill did, he did only with due deliberation."

Comments Bill, "In a school where whatever is done for younger faculty impinges on the hoary privileges of an older generation, making haste slowly is often the only way to make haste at all."

Whether in matters large or small, Bill Olsen was increasingly becoming the center of controversy. A case in point was his around-the-world trip. When he departed in January 1968 with his family, the school was entrusted to George Kellogg '35, a faculty member for more than a quarter of a century and Bill Olsen's assistant headmaster for a half-dozen years. A tall, methodical man with an open approach and an unassuming style, George Kellogg had a calming effect all around. "People were great, and it was fun," says George, who retired in 1982 and lives with his wife, Kit, near the school. "I don't remember a lot of hang-ups. I remember being plenty busy doing three jobs at the same time. I do remember thinking, 'Will Bill be back for graduation or not?' He did come back just in time to address the class. I remember that. And that it was a pretty good class."

Of the headmaster's decision to abbreviate his family's travels, Larry Becker says, "I can well understand why Bill would want to come back, but it was a mistake. Even some of the kids wanted George Kellogg to preside over their graduation, and they went out of their way to make a special presentation to George."

Explains Bill Olsen, "Our daughter, Lisa, was beginning to get homesick, and I had three and a half years personally invested in that graduating class."

A perennial, more proprietary emotional issue concerned faculty salaries. As associate headmaster, Bill Olsen had served on a committee "to study and report on what would constitute an ideal Faculty salary schedule . . . The Trustees would like to have Hotchkiss take an advanced position on this subject, so that we can hope to lead rather than compare rank." This represented a sharp policy break from the Duke. Although he tried to be solicitous about individual faculty needs, G V S did not want to attract teaching talent through monetary rewards. "The Duke personally didn't care about money and felt the faculty shouldn't either," says Steve Bolmer, whose starting salary in 1947 had been $1,750, "and Tom Chappell wasn't around long enough to do it. But Bill did get interested in that, and that was a very positive thing he did." Though in office less than ten years, Bill Olsen had doubled the starting minimum to $6,000, and raised the top compensation of $8,000 for nonadministrators to $15,000.*

The generous salary increases, however, became a source of controversy. "Part of the problem was that we didn't have a formal salary scale, and there was no requirement of an annual meeting between the headmaster and each faculty member," says Jim Marks, one of the young teachers brought in by Bill Olsen in 1964. "That would have provided a forum to answer questions and straighten out any misunderstandings."

Salary review was among the issues about to be taken up by an altogether different morale committee than Rusty Chandler's. Heading it by virtue of his official position as the Senior Faculty Member was John Knox "Jack" Bodel, who had little respect for the young headmaster. Since his graduation from Wesleyan in 1929, Bodel had taught biology at Hotchkiss and for many years had headed the science department and college placements. This small, lean, humorless man who parted his silvery hair in the middle and still wore long, white flannels on the tennis courts year-round had at one time enjoyed a formidable reputation at the school. ("Jack's understanding and compassion meant a great deal to me," recalls Nelson S. "Bud" Talbott, a member of Bill Olsen's class of '39.) The intervening years, however, had taken their toll. "Jack Bodel was an interesting man and obviously had mastered his subject matter, biology," says Larry Becker, "but he wasn't a popular teacher when I came. Kids called him 'Bugsy,' and he couldn't have felt good about coming to work every day for reasons other than Bill Olsen."

As a counterbalance to Bodel and other old-time stalwarts on the committee, Bill Olsen appointed several younger faculty members, in-

---

* How much administrators were earning was no longer a matter of open record. Having raised the headmaster's salary after he returned from his sabbatical to $25,000, the trustees thereafter ceased the traditional practice of listing all – or any salaries – in the minutes.

cluding Jim Marks. "I was struck by the venom of Jack Bodel's first draft," says Marks, whose great-grandfather had founded Pittsburgh's Kiski School, where his grandfather had followed as headmaster, and his father was then passed over for the top post because of academic intrigue. "I knew Hotchkiss wasn't perfect, but I thought we had a terrific school. Suddenly I realized there was a lot of very strong negative feeling about Bill Olsen and the way he ran the school. A couple of us spoke up and said, 'This doesn't really reflect the full faculty, especially not some of our younger people.' We said we weren't going to sign until some of the language was toned down."

Faculty strife of this kind was invariably kept under wraps. "I had no idea anything of this sort was going on," says Michael A. Davis '70, an editor on the *Record*, "and I don't know if anyone else in our class did." What Davis acutely sensed, however, was a continuing decline in the headmaster's popularity among students. "I had been a GO proctor for a couple of summers," says Davis, "and Bill Olsen's unqualified support for that program really made him come alive for me. I thought he was a man of broad perspective, with an eye for where Hotchkiss ought to stand in the world."

About the time Jack Bodel was readying the final version of his committee's report, Davis and several of his *Record* colleagues decided to put their feelings to work. The result was surely the most arresting issue of the *Record* published in the school's first century. Dated November 8, 1969, the front page was filled with a commanding photograph of the school's headmaster bestriding the auditorium stage in a studiedly casual pose, his houndstooth jacket hanging just a tad loose off his shoulders, and his cordovans visibly glistening. Surrounding Bill Olsen's image in discreet black type was a listing of twenty-five accomplishments under the heading "Evolution 1960 – 1969." Superimposed in the top righthand corner of the page in prominent white lettering was a quotation from Ralph Waldo Emerson: "An Institution is the lengthened shadow of one man."

Within a month – on December 2, 1969 – Jack Bodel presented his report to the faculty. "An important premise in every discussion," the report began, "was the belief that the school, as frequently stated by the Headmaster, was not an institution run by one man, but rather a faculty-run school." Now politely worded within the scope of Hotchkiss good form, the document criticized the administration for interference "without prior consultation" and "bureaucratic incivility" and even questioned whether "real excellence in carrying out the academic program of the school is genuinely prized." Although the lack of formal salary procedures was one of the issues addressed, heading the list of "specific proposals for immediate consideration" was the "institution of a permanent faculty association . . . to represent the interests and needs of the faculty as a whole and individually." The zinger implicit in the committee report was that this faculty association would be empowered to communicate directly with the trustees.

Mulling it over during Christmas recess, the headmaster made his response on January 19, 1970. "We gathered in the Alumni Room, and Bill had a podium," recalls Larry Becker. "He never had a podium in faculty meetings. The message was very clear that there was not going to be a discussion. He said, 'There's going to be no faculty association. You know how I feel about it.' And that was the end of the meeting."

Jerry Bowen elaborates: "It was the only time in my thirty-odd years that I had ever seen a headmaster at a faculty meeting at Hotchkiss bring out a rostrum and stand behind it. The Duke, everybody knows, from his name down, was a martinet. But he never did anything of that sort, ever. He never addressed the faculty like a Dutch Uncle, though he was a Dutch Uncle. Bill said something like, 'I'm not George Van Santvoord and I don't intend to try.' Well, nobody thought he was."

Recalls Jim Marks, "When Bill said he wasn't George Van Santvoord, my feeling was, 'Thank goodness! Why would you want to try to emulate somebody who was just different?'"

According to the unverifiable folklore surrounding that event, Bill Olsen pointed to the painting of GVS, which then hung just to the right of the fireplace and dominated the Alumni Room. Shortly thereafter, the GVS portrait was moved to a more discreet position on the opposite wall, next to portraits of Buehler and Coy. While some faculty members cite this as evidence of Olsen's extreme sensitivity to any comparisons with GVS, others marvel at Olsen's forbearance in allowing the GVS painting its undue prominence for so long.

And what happened to Jack Bodel's association? "I think clearly the majority of people felt they didn't want to work for a school that had a union," says Larry Becker. "Let's face it, the faculty could have certainly rebelled if it wanted to. I can still remember thinking, 'Bill is absolutely right. This should not happen at the Hotchkiss School.'"

Jerry Bowen: "The real purpose of Jack Bodel's faculty association was to provide direct access to the board. Bill wasn't letting anyone on the faculty other than a few handpicked people near the trustees because we might say to them something that Bill didn't like. Bill wasn't going to let that happen."

Larry Becker: "I'm still not sure I know completely what Jack's gripe was about Bill. The thing came to a head when Jack was retiring in 1972, and Bill made a presentation to him on the back porch of the headmaster's house at an evening party. Jack responded with a very biting speech about being 'a weed in Olsen's garden.' I don't think there was a person there who didn't think it was inappropriate. Bill certainly carried it off beautifully, but it must have hurt."

Jack Bodel died in 1986, and perhaps no one will fully know what his gripe was about Olsen. But then perhaps Jack Bodel answered the question in a feature article which appeared in the *Record* during his last year of teaching. It was a paean to the Hotchkiss School of the past, its graciousness, civility, and unity of purpose: "Tuesday morning assemblies are remembered by many as occasions for hearing informed and often humorous comment about national and international affairs, about coming visitors to the school in the fields of art, music, drama, education, religion, and public affairs. They were by no means confined to admonition or exegesis of school requirements." Bodel clearly identified GVS as the source of that Tuesday morning wisdom and wit and detailed the wealth of far-ranging activities and contacts in those days, concluding, "In a curious way it almost seemed that the school was in better communication with the world around it then than it is today and, perhaps, that it made less noise about it."

ix /   "**I**n my first year there were two events," says Peter A. Thorne '73, who came as a prep in the fall of 1969. "One guy had a bad acid trip and went out of control in Dana. Then there were two prep friends of mine and a couple of invited girls at a dance who got caught smoking marijuana. One of the girls thought she was having a bad time and turned herself in, and the others then did likewise. That forced the recognition that drugs now involved the young preps. The school took immediate and dramatic action. They brought in a bunch of heroin addicts who were in a treatment program and had them lead small education and counseling groups with all students. That turned out to be a pretty positive step."

Peter Thorne arrived at Hotchkiss when the national psyche was still filled with images of liberating abandon at Woodstock, which were increasingly penetrating the school's protective bounds: "I remember waiting in my room in Buehler for my brother and his wife, who were coming to take me to dinner. I was looking forward to it and watching out for their Country Squire station wagon. Suddenly I heard this roar down the road. It's my brother on his Honda, just back from Morocco, in full leathers, long hair flowing, doing a turn around the main gate and driving up the walk and parking this huge bike at the door of Buehler Hall. Then he sort of clunked up the stairs. People wondered if maybe Hell's Angels had not arrived. After lunch, they rode off, doing another turn around the loop. It was a striking contrast between the life at the school and the life outside."

Peter Thorne's arrival at the school coincided with the entry of the first sizable contingent of the wholly "underprivileged" as year-round students. "Bringing in kids from the inner city was a bold gesture. I remember Leif Thorne-Thomsen [a young classics teacher] had a major effect in trying to give them grounding within the Hotchkiss world. Some of the ways of Hotchkiss must have seemed absurd to these kids, like tardies if they were late for class. On the other hand, it seemed like these city kids got more chances to screw up, and there was a more lax academic standard for them. Some of my friends felt these kids were taking advantage of the system – and that the liberal white teachers and administration were being duped by them. There was a time one of these guys literally drove a station wagon up to the dorm when everybody was at a hockey game and just loaded up with stereos and other stuff from the kids' rooms. It came to be a personal test for me, too. I remember being in my room in Coy as a lower mid. A friend of mine was being hassled on the corridor by a couple of these kids, apparently because he had something they wanted. I had once told him, 'If they give you any more trouble, tell them that whatever they want is in my room.' This was a Saturday afternoon with nobody around. All of a sudden, knock, knock, knock at the door. My friend had taken me up on my word and brought these guys around. I remember being in fear of serious abuse. They threatened me and tore my room apart. We got out of the situation without anybody getting hurt, but it shook me to the core in terms of the liberal values I held dearly. I thought, 'There's got to be some way to reconcile these huge gaps between people who have things and people who don't.''

Peter Thorne's years at Hotchkiss also coincided with the peak of the Vietnam protests. "As I recall, it really wasn't a major issue at the school. Some of us had family in the military, and some of the older kids were concerned about the draft. But most people were ignoring it, hoping it would go away before we came of draft age. That was one of the shortcomings of Hotchkiss in being so isolated. I remember during the Panther trial in New Haven, some of us going down to where the indoor tennis courts are now, and building a peace memorial out of rocks. There we were, making this pathetically small gesture, crying in the wilderness in a sense. I had a brother in New Haven, and consequently heard about a very different awareness at Yale.

"But that isolation at Hotchkiss had its advantages, by focusing your mind on schoolwork. Bill Olsen was flexible and was ready to draw lessons for all of us from some of the events going on on the outside. During the first Earth Day celebration, he suspended classes for three days and put on a special program focused on the environment. I still remember a couple of BBC movies on nerve gas testing and firebombing, radiation and toxic waste. It had a dramatic, lasting impression on me. I thought that was a very bold thing for the school to do.

"Bill Olsen's approach was interesting in a comparative way. Looking back, you get a sense that the 1950s was a much more stable time, and Van Santvoord was a mythical, dynamic personality. During a stable time, you want a dynamic personality there, to work people up and get them inspired. Conversely, in a dynamic time you want a more calming influence, like Olsen. He had a way of defusing situations. What comes to mind is one of his unscheduled all-school meetings, this time around the issue of smoking – specifically dismissing one of the really popular kids. He happened to be a black kid, but that didn't matter. The kid was smoking. It felt as if dismissal for smoking no longer was an appropriate response at this time in the country. At the meeting he called in lieu of classes to approach this problem, I could clearly see the conflict that Bill was feeling. I remember seeing his face. He was struggling with how to balance the different constituencies he was working with. Personally he didn't believe you should be thrown out for smoking, but he had to put on a professional role. It was a revolt, and the students felt a whole new sense of empowerment. Bill was sensitive and intelligent enough to let that grow rather than trying to sit on it."

This sense of empowerment, it should be noted, was doled out in carefully measured doses. Like Charles de Gaulle with his plebiscites, Bill Olsen was astute in knowing which of these all-school meetings to call to obtain the desired results. Moreover, by their very nature some issues the headmaster regarded as not subject to debate – such as, during Peter Thorne's time, the suicide of a popular young French teacher. "I expected we'd all have a chance to talk about it, perhaps have an all-school meeting in the auditorium," says Peter D. Adams '63, who returned fresh out of college in 1967 in an administrative capacity. "Well, there was a eulogy by Bill in chapel, and he suggested that we all send comforting letters to the deceased's mother. But there was no encouragement to really express our feelings. I had an advisee on this teacher's floor, and it took the kid several months to deal with it. The whole community went through the rest of the year all bottled up. It was as if we hadn't been given permission to mourn. Bill seemed generally afraid to delve publicly into the psyches and emotions of people."

In this respect, Olsen was at least partly acting in the tradition of GVS. After a similar tragic event, the Duke limited himself to a terse chapel announcement, concluding, "I suppose one way to think of this is that there are interesting novels, and interesting short stories. Mr. [xxxxx] chose to make a short story of his life."

Another young master, Christopher Carlisle, who also would eventually take his life, was just coming into his own at this time. He is remembered by Lawson Wulsin '70: "When I took Chris Carlisle's lower mid English, I considered him to be a good teacher. Then as a senior, I was in his advanced placement class, which was held at his house. It was an arrangement which was just starting then, and within this environment, it now seemed natural to set him up as a mentor. He was a young man who sort of looked the way I looked, had gone to the same kind of schools, had the same kind of background. He had drive, he had intensity, he had creativity, and he really loved thinking about how you expressed yourself; really loved thinking about what the second and third messages were in a paragraph. He could thumb his nose at some of the school's more rigid requirements but still demand a lot from you. He gave us a chance to work out of devotion rather than to meet some standard. Going to his house, eating his wife's cookies, playing with his kids, talking for two-and-a-half hours – it was close. He was a shy person by nature but he would let us get close to an extent. It's not as though he would tell you a lot, but he would throw out these little carrots. Just watching him play the banjo in his study there, with his two kids nearby, those brownies, and *A Portrait of the Artist as a Young Man* in our laps about to be talked about – that was sort of the essence of what we did down there. He *was* the artist as a young man, and had even studied art at Yale for a while. He really had a feeling for what people who had written these novels had messed around with, and he got us to feel it, even though his own exterior was fairly conventional. I mean he was a golf coach, and he played paddle tennis, and he dressed like everybody else."

Back to Peter Thorne, who graduated as an upper mid, planning to take a year off before college: "I remember sitting in the admissions office at Yale and telling the dean that my goal was to work for IBM or Union Carbide or Citibank, and I wanted to get an internship and learn what business is all about. The dean is a guy sitting there behind this huge oak desk, with his feet kicked up, saying, 'Uh huh, uh huh, real interesting, yawn.' Then he said, 'That's what your father wants you to do. Now what do you *really* want to do?' He said, 'It makes no difference to us what you do next year. It's your free year, and you should do with it whatever you really want. You should explore your dreams.' So I did just that. I went to Massachusetts and worked for the head of Vietnam Veterans Against the War who was running for Congress. Then I went to New York and worked for the Museum of Natural History. I had wanted to follow up on the environment situation, being stimulated by that earth week we had at Hotchkiss a couple of years earlier. The museum didn't offer enough of that. After *Roe versus Wade* was decided by the Supreme Court, I continued my interest by working for Zero Population Growth. Lastly, I worked as a carpenter building a school in Colorado."

Today, co-owner of *New Age* magazine and a Hotchkiss trustee, Peter Thorne heads a real estate company which buys, designs, and renovates buildings in "economically transitional neighborhoods in Boston, New York, and Chicago." A graduate of Harvard Business School, he is a board member of the Boston Food Bank and is active in Amnesty International.

x / "It wasn't business as usual to be able to sit on that horse in those days," says Rusty Chandler about Bill Olsen's task. "The horse wasn't just trotting, but galloping and bucking."

Whether drugs, Vietnam, environmental concerns, or the presence of a sizable contingent of unacculturated students – those were but symbols of a vast array of changes impinging on the school's traditional ways. In the previous ten years or so, Bill Olsen had taken some far-reaching steps, among them introducing dormitories of mixed classes after prep year, allowing student participation on discipline and other faculty committees, and appointing a dean of students. But what would have been considered forward-looking at another time was hardly sufficient now. There was constant agitation for more and more. Peter Adams, by then Rusty Chandler's assistant in admissions, provides an insight into the era circa 1970: "I remember sitting in a dorm meeting, and we were discussing changing some rules. George Stone had been running a corridor something like twenty years at that point, and one statement he made was just classic Stone frustration. Everything he had grown accustomed to doing, which was by the book, was changing. And we were changing it at the request of the kids, giving them some voice in managing things. He said, 'God damn it, I'm sick and tired of you young Turks and your ideas!'

"The way of doing things was coming unraveled. I remember another great faculty meeting, involving Dick Gurney. He had been in an accident and had to whisper, and for a while he had to carry around an amplifier with a speaker attached. So he set it up in the faculty meeting, and we were talking about hair length. When Dick wanted to speak, he'd blow in the microphone. He went, 'Ahh, Mr. Olsen, I've been listening to this discussion for the past three hours, and I just have one comment to make. My concern is that when these boys go in to take a leak, they won't know whether to stand up or sit down.' At that point, the whole faculty just burst out laughing. Mr. Olsen said, 'Faculty dismissed.' He was disgusted, and we hadn't resolved it. So we just never had a rule about hair length, and the kids grew it. We could only agree that it had to be clean and neat.

"The next year they wanted to grow hair on their face. Why not? We had people on the faculty then with beards. Arthur Eddy had always had one, and now Dick Hughes, Peter Wade, and I grew beards over the summer. I remember standing in the new Main Building with Dick Hughes and Peter Wade during the GO program summer session, when this kid Jamie came up. He looked at Dick Hughes and said, 'Mr. Eddy, I'm real sorry I didn't get my math homework in. I'll get it done as soon as I can.' Dick looked at him and said, 'Jamie, I'm not Mr. Eddy.' The kid turned to me and said, 'Mr. Eddy, I just couldn't get my homework in.' I said, 'Wait a minute, Jamie, I'm not Mr. Eddy.' Peter Wade said, 'Don't look at me.' Here's this black kid confronted with four white faculty members with beards, and he can't tell us apart. I looked at my colleagues and said, 'Hey, let's keep these beards into the school year and see how they go over.' We walked into the first faculty meeting after the opening of the school, and no doubt about it, we got some dirty looks. I don't think Bill Olsen was at all pleased that I had a beard, and I was in the admissions office. It was a symbol of the times, and it actually went over very well with some of the kids who were applying. Gradually our colleagues realized our beards weren't so bad."

Not only such symbols of the times, but even seemingly mundane matters could acquire the momentum of bitter controversy. "I was replacing a faculty wife," says Walter E. DeMelle, Jr., hired by Bill Olsen as the school's librarian in 1970. "The fact that I was a member of the faculty without being a classroom teacher raised a lot of hackles. Then there was the controversy which came from having changed the lock on the library because no one could tell me who had keys. This put an end to the clubbiness of those who did previously have keys, and they found it offensive."

Tensions of this sort again ended up being reflected at the Monday night faculty meetings. "I've never been at a faculty meeting where comments were made that were as objectionable as those often made at Hotchkiss," observes Larry Becker from his perspective today as headmaster of Brooks School. "Outspoken comments from Steve Bolmer; when some poor faculty member who taught two sections of something or other would try to say something, Steve would say, 'Now that we've heard from the part-time people . . . .' Bob Hawkins would sit back in his corner and mumble, 'Well, are we going to hear from the librarian again?' Everyone heard these things. We were not terribly civil to one another."

The influences from beyond the school's portals during those tumultuous years had some memorable results. "I am not a religious
man particularly," says Leif Thorne-Thomsen, who eventually headed
the classics department, "but I strongly believed in the traditional
chapel program. Now there were some pretty nontraditional goings-
on. I remember Chris Getman – one of the young Turks – once led the
service. We bowed our heads and prayed to some six-armed Hindu
god. On another occasion, the chapel service was presided over by a
student, and he read from Nathanael West's story 'The Dream Life of
Balso Snell.' He read *The Hymn to St. Puce*, which is the single most
blasphemous piece of writing I have ever heard.

"Then there was the whole series of events surrounding the hiring,
tenure, and departure of the school's chaplain. I was in charge of the
dorm, and he was on the second floor. He was handsome and athletic;
iron-gray hair, crewcut, really all-American looking. His wife was
beautiful, and they came highly recommended by Blair Torrey, who
had met them at a summer writing program in Vermont."

Blair Torrey: "He was fashionably avant-garde, and everybody
loved him. At one point he gave a sermon in chapel that blew the kids'
minds. It was called "The Gospel according to Simon and Garfunkel."
He had a record player up there with the "Sounds of Silence" on it,
and so forth. You can imagine what it did to the old guard.

"During that year [1969–70], his wife had an affair with one of the
boys in the senior class, and the reverend was having an affair with a
woman up in Pittsfield or Williamstown. By the end of the school
year, they were both gone. She left to follow that student to Harvard –
and the reverend just vanished. I still get blamed for the whole fiasco."

That fall, at the first board meeting of the new school year, one of
the items highlighting the headmaster's report accepted by the trustees
read, "Chapel is no longer required on Sunday, though it is available,
and morning chapel is held on two mornings a week."

The unconventional minister and his like-minded wife may have
hastened but did not cause this radical departure from one of the
school's most fundamental traditions. The increasing multiculturalism

of the student body combined with the rediscovered pride in one's own heritage outside of the White Anglo-Saxon Protestant fold had produced a powerful tide which no prep school headmaster – no matter how absolute a potentate – could either ignore or hold back.

Bill Olsen's response to that inundating force was not universally acclaimed. "I think the reader of this piece can call it an obituary," wrote Bob Hawkins in the *Record*. "In any case, it's about an institution that recently died a lingering death at Hotchkiss – Sunday chapel. Even its sister observance, daily chapel, gives every indication of moribundity; five weekly meetings reduced to two hardly suggest health. And I am sad, sad the way anyone is when an old friend dies."

Other problems associated with those times were beginning to converge on the headmaster; among them, whether to allow cigarettes. Bill Olsen provides his perspective on how that historic change in the school's no-smoking rule came about: "By the early seventies, the college world almost got blown apart. We had the May Day thing down in New Haven. We had Kent State. We had the bombing of the physics lab in Wisconsin. This was getting serious; yet, the principal issue on the Hotchkiss campus was smoking. I felt I had other things to take care of than to sit around and worry whether someone's enough of a jackass to want to smoke. Marijuana and other drugs, that was another matter. But this was cigarettes!

"What brought the matter to a crisis was the case of one of the black students, Ronnie Kelly, who had been caught for the second time and was on general probation. Theoretically, he should have been kicked out. The faculty was considering the matter, when suddenly the door opened and the president of the senior class said, 'Mr. Olsen, I think you'd better come. There's a protest meeting taking place in the Alumni Room.'

"I left the faculty meeting and walked over there and said, 'What's the problem?' They said they were annoyed because the faculty was meeting to kick Ronnie Kelly out of school. I said, 'Okay, what do you want?' They said, 'We don't think he should be.' I said, 'I have an idea. We'll meet in the auditorium tomorrow morning at eight o'clock, and we'll stay there until we've talked this issue out.' I said, 'I'm assuming one of the issues is Ronnie Kelly, and the other issue is smoking.' They said, 'Yes.' I said, 'Okay, I'll expect everybody. Not just the people in this room. I want the entire student body. I'll have the faculty there.'

"So I went back to the faculty meeting and said, 'Sorry, fellows, I hate to disrupt your classes, but I've committed you to a school meeting tomorrow.' I then arranged with George Anastasio from the drama department to have ready a mike with a long cord.

"'There are two conditions to this meeting,' I told them at the outset the next day. 'When you get up, you're going to identify yourself by name and class, and if there is one hint of inflammatory language, the meeting is over. Second, what is happening here is most likely not going to have any effect on what the faculty decided in Ronnie's case. He was operating on preexisting rules, and that's the way we're going to handle this thing.'

"For the next four hours we talked about smoking. Some were for it; some were against it. Most felt there were more important things in life than that. In the process, Ronnie Kelly seemed to have been entirely forgotten. It interested me that the real issue obviously was smoking. We adjourned for lunch, and came back for another hour. When the meeting broke up, someone said, 'Sir, what do you plan to do about all this?' That was on a Tuesday, and I said, 'I'll have something in writing by Friday morning.'

"That's when the rule was changed. For one thing, the surgeon general's report had come out, and there was ample evidence that smoking is bad for your health. Anyone with any intelligence should have enough sense not to smoke. My concern was to protect the large majority of people who didn't smoke. I said, 'Smoking will be a personal decision from now on, made with your parents' consent. But I'm going to have policy here different from what you find in most places, and it's going to be tilted towards the nonsmoker. If you want to mess up your own room, that's your problem. But there will be no smoking in any public place. In fact, we'll start with the elimination of smoking in public places by the faculty, and there will also be no smoking outside.' This was back in 1971 and not at all a popular restriction on the faculty. But they approved it. The only recommendation I didn't get through was that the school would repaint the room of each smoker at the end of the year at his own expense."

The changing of such a fundamental rule was not without its anticipated outrage. "Bill Olsen allowed smoking at the time the surgeon general came out with the first study saying how bad it was for you," says Steve Bolmer, the perennial conservative on the faculty. "I was sitting on the discipline committee when that came to a vote. I said, 'I will not be a part of a discipline system that says it's okay to do this. If you're the headmaster and the kids pressure you to do this, you're abdicating your responsibilities.' I couldn't believe that Bill was actually going to give in."

There was to be another fundamental concession soon. With the war in Vietnam drafting eighteen-year-olds, the cry went up, "If you're old enough to fight, you're old enough to drink." Accordingly, the Connecticut state legislature in 1972 lowered the legal drinking age to eighteen. Hotchkiss adapted by allowing drinking off-campus in the company of a teacher or family member.

"Dropping the drinking age to eighteen was one of the great disservices legislatures visited on growing kids," says Olsen. "Their argument now was, 'If I can drink legally when I'm home, why aren't there circumstances when I can drink off campus?' The parents were squawking about it, too, and most of the sanctioned drinking was done with parents. You cannot segregate a school from the society that it's a part of."

Despite such protests, the new regulation undoubtedly afforded some relief. Downing a beer off campus hardly compared to the drug problem and other challenges to authority which the headmaster had to face.

And what happened to Ronnie Kelly, the hapless catalyst for the most fundamental change in the school's policy since its founding? True to Hotchkiss good form, he was not kicked out but allowed to withdraw voluntarily. "Ronnie is a good person," wrote Arthur White, the dean of students, to Kelly's mother, "and his smoking is certainly not a moral issue, but we feel the school must uphold the rules that it has established."

xi /

Among the students entering the school with Peter Thorne in the fall of 1969 was Dennis Watlington, who had the looks and demeanor more of a world-class heavyweight boxer than of a lower mid. Enrolling with him was his Harlem friend Noel Velasquez, who was a head shorter and chunky rather than muscular. Over the next three years, Dennis would become the leader of the black student faction at the school as well as of his entire class, while Noel was destined for an end unprecedented in Hotchkiss history.

Dennis Watlington came to Hotchkiss as part of Bill Olsen's determination to reflect the social realities of the outside world by setting a 10 percent target for blacks and Hispanics in the Hotchkiss student body. This was far easier said than done. The snide joke of the 1950s was becoming a reality of the late sixties: "What are you going to do when you run out of Ralph Bunche's sons?" The kind of care that had been devoted to selecting Gus Winston and other black students who followed him was no longer possible. Hotchkiss was not alone in trying to tap the talent pool through ABC [A Better Chance], which Bill Olsen helped to found. The slogan *Black is Beautiful* reflected the political temper of the times, and independent schools were literally lining up for qualified candidates.

"When I joined the faculty in 1964," says Leif Thorne-Thomsen, "there was one black student, Ellis Bagley, and a lot of effort was being made to find, recruit, and keep other qualified black students. We didn't have any black alumni to help or faculty who knew what was going on. I had been educated at Princeton, which was even more rigidly white than Hotchkiss."

The one advantage Hotchkiss did have was the GO program. Contrary to its founding philosophy, the GO program became the leading source of full-year candidates. "The school received a steady infusion of the best sort of candidates," says Thorne-Thomsen. "David Burrus, Jim McBee, Edgar Inigo were the first three. The next year we had people like Elliott Fennell and Robert Woodbine. Then I lose track. These were the best sort of students we could possibly have. Robert Woodbine was the finest leader I think I have seen operating. He *was* the GO program. Elliott Fennell was my proctor. David Burrus became a classics major at the University of Pennsylvania. Fennell and Woodbine went to Harvard." Dennis Greene was also from that era. He went on to television's "Sha Na Na" fame and kept a summer home not too far from the school.

This is not to imply that all of those students went through Hotchkiss without difficulties. "Ellis Bagley came from a solid home, his family visited him on weekends, he was enthusiastic, and we were all very good friends," says John Luke, Jr. "My impression on the surface was that he and other blacks who came during my time managed just fine. However, over the years I've often thought about how little we understood about the difficult transition that they were each undergoing."

"I don't think that any of us had any idea what a kick in the fanny it was to these kids to be brought to Lakeville, Connecticut," says Bill Olsen. "I guess our assumption was, 'If you can come to God's country, you're lucky.' In reality, we were pulling kids out from one home without being able to provide another. Our greatest asset was goodwill and a conviction that we really could be helpful to these kids. But we were jumping into uncharted waters in many ways, then learned by doing."

Toward the end of the sixties this learning process was to be vastly accelerated. With public funding replacing Rockefeller funding, the GO Program after its first three years became more dependent on bureaucratic criteria – and no longer produced the same kind of qualified full-year candidates. At the same time, there was the commitment to strive for that 10 percent goal of minority students within Hotchkiss ranks. The obvious dilemma – where to find these boys?

Enter the late William V. Brokaw '48, a big, hearty businessman around whose life swirls a drama reminiscent of Saul's transformation on the Road to Damascus. While at Hotchkiss, he had engaged in his share of that schoolboy diversion known as baiting. What was different about Bill Brokaw was that in subsequent years he experienced a violent reaction against the callowness of his youth. Although his classmate John Loeb does not remember him as one of his tormentors, Bill

Brokaw sought out John to tender his apologies. "Bill Brokaw went to his grave regretting what he had done back then," says Bill Olsen, "and he devoted most of his life to doing good. He was one of the most generous-spirited people that I've run into, and he was among those during the late sixties who saw a need for the country to take corrective action. He was the guiding light behind the program called Broad Jump, which helped disadvantaged kids in New York, hooking them into independent schools there and boarding schools outside of New York. That has grown into a program that is still running today, called Prep for Prep."

Bill Brokaw also happened to be simultaneously a trustee of the Hotchkiss School and of the New York Boys Club Federation. It was through membership in the club's East Harlem community center that Dennis Watlington encountered the man who changed his life: "You could say I was a chip off Harlem's heroin bloc. I was just coming to the end of a three-and-a-half-year addiction. I had gotten hepatitis, which almost killed me, and in the hospital I made my own choice that I'd had enough of the drug. One of my closest friends, who was also a recovering heroin addict, was Noel Velasquez. When I got out of the hospital and Noel got out of rehab, the community center we belonged to sent us on a tour of various colleges and family groups. That was in the very early beginnings of white people getting hip to drugs as a threat to their children. We comported ourselves very well, and they just fell in love with us.

"This was what I call from the old Spanky and Our Gang song the 'give a damn' period. Martin Luther King had just been killed, and Bill Cosby was the first regular black cat on television with 'I Spy.' A torrent of attention, money, genuine concern, et cetera, came flooding into the ghettos. It was the liberal chic thing to do.

"At my community center was a singing group that was becoming popular. A man named Bill Brokaw was having some huge stock-brokers' ball at his home in Greenwich, Connecticut, and this group was invited as a portion of the entertainment. Noel and I both had girlfriends in the group, and we just traveled along on the bus.

"So we met Brokaw that night. He came up to us, and he'd obvi-

ously had a few drinks, and he said, 'D'you guys want to go to Hotchkiss?' Neither of us knew what the hell Hotchkiss was, but we knew
better than to say no to a guy who owned all of this, especially given
the sentiments and feelings of the time. We said, 'Sure,' and probably
within a couple of minutes forgot all about it.

"Next thing we know, we get a call about two weeks later from Brokaw's secretary, or someone like that, telling us we have to take some
tests. Brokaw was a trustee then, and I guess powerful enough where
he could stack the deck. Instead of SAT's and other exams, which I
subsequently learned are the really tough things you normally have to
go through to get into that school, we were to be examined by a psychologist. I'm not exaggerating, but the psychologist would put an ink
blot in front of us and ask, 'What does that look like?' I said, 'A don-
key.' A bunch of questions like that, and Noel and I were in.

"Now that I was faced with it, I didn't want to go. Four years earlier,
the community center had sent me away on this program where I'd be
trained to go to prep school. But I screwed up and got thrown out. As a
matter of fact, the shame that I had experienced in coming back to the
ghetto after getting thrown out at thirteen is what drove me into
heroin. I wanted to destroy any visions anybody may have had of me
of being a good kid. I did it by becoming the worst, which was a street-
shooting junkie. Besides, I was enjoying the magic carpet I was on,
being the boy who came back from drugs, talking it up and playing
football on the community team, and everybody kissing my behind.
What did I need prep school for?

"The head of the community center was named Chuck Griffin, a
powerful-looking guy who was also the football coach. He threatened
me with physical violence. He said if I didn't go to Hotchkiss, he'd
make sure I'd get an ass-whipping every day and I couldn't show my
face on the block.

"Two weeks later Noel and I were on our way up there to report for
early football. The campus was empty except for players, and that was
kind of nice. We could enjoy the beauty and the luxury, and the reality
of being at school hadn't crept in yet.

"I remember the first day the rest of the kids came. Noel and I were seated alongside of the road, not far from the brick entrance. We were watching these really fine cars coming in with little white kids and huge amounts of stereos. And here we were, robbing-and-doing-any-thing-for-a-fix junkies seven months earlier. I thought what a tremendous sense of humor God has, to take us from where we were to where we were seated then."

Dennis and Noel were not alone. A dozen or so other minority students from similar circumstances were enrolled at the school that fall of 1969, most of them selected in a comparably haphazard way. It was Leif Thorne-Thomsen, a strong partisan of Bill Olsen's efforts, who asked to be the advisor for several of them, including Dennis and Noel: "There was practically no documentation on either of them, and just about all that I knew was they were self-cured drug addicts who had been stars in the street academies, stars on the football field. They were both running backs, impressive locomotives. Bill Brokaw and Chuck Griffin – who would become Dennis's father-in-law briefly – apparently convinced the two boys to drop everything and come up to Hotchkiss, telling them, I think, 'If you stick it out at Hotchkiss, that's your ticket of admission to the establishment.' But the period between playing football for the Federation Chargers and graduation from Hotchkiss was left a sort of merciful gray blank. So when they got here, they didn't have any idea of what they were going to face. Mercifully, neither did Hotchkiss."

Dennis Watlington: "They had a sort of a storybook tale in their heads. They bring us up here, we learn, we change. We become what they call good men. We go off to college, and they have reconstructed us. What they didn't bargain for was that they were going to get hustlers as a way of life. We may have looked cute and cuddly, but we were cunning and manipulative. We never considered being changed. We were there to be a part of it, to take advantage of it. I remember telling some white cats the second week I was there, 'Look, the way this deal is going to work is, I don't want to be like you, and you shouldn't want to be like me.' I said, 'If we can stay ourselves and jam, then we have something happening.'

"The first months, even the whole first year, it was like being fussed over by a bunch of doting rich uncles. Hotchkiss wanted so much to extend themselves to us. They made us stars, and they spoiled us to death. And we were stars. White folks have always been fascinated by black stars. Noel and I called it our dance period. We were dancing our asses off, but the pay was good. Why did Bo Jangles dance? Because they paid him, and he got to do it with Shirley Temple.

"We abused the system, because they came to us with a sign painted on them that said, 'Abuse me, please abuse me.' When I was a lower mid and Noel a prep, we were supposed to get one maybe two weekends a year. He and I would go to Bill Olsen and tell him someone at home got shot, someone got stabbed. Olsen would reach into his pocket and peel off some money and let us go. They didn't even start to pull the plug until the twelfth or fifteenth time. Another time Noel wangled two hundred bucks out of one of the real conservative stalwarts on the faculty, Bob Hawkins. Noel told him his sister needed an abortion, and he then went into the city to buy dope and brought it back to sell to the kids. I think Hawkins had a sort of a love-hate thing for Noel, based on the challenge of trying to teach him *David Copperfield*.

"That was the only area of resentment, I think, that existed between the students and us. They couldn't get away with half as much. We had those guys saying, 'Yeah, I bet if I were black I could do such and such.' And there we were, in their school that their fathers built, and we flaunted it.

"The big challenge for us and for them was to be honest and get real and develop relationships. What I discovered early on was that bringing me into that environment, as closely knit and sewn as it was, eliminated my fear of white people. Coming in you have all sorts of feelings and thoughts; spend the winter term in Dana Hall with fifty other guys, you emerge in the springtime liking or disliking each other on merit.

"An Italian [American] kid who lived down the corridor from me became my best friend – John Terenzio, the guy who would be the godfather of my daughter twenty years later. I first got to know him when I hustled him for some cigarettes. He thought I was going to rob him. I saw the fear in his face, and I knew I had a chance to break that barrier by exposing my intentions, which were to go out and have one together. This was at a time when you could still get kicked out for smoking, and I think going off into the woods and puffing away built this initial bond between us. Gradually we became very close. I remember the weekend I spent at his home, and we drove to the Yale Bowl for a game. The woman who would become my first wife was my girlfriend then, and she left me for another man. I cried and wailed as we were driving, and he was like my pillar of strength. I think it affected him in a positive way, to see that the image of a big tough man from the ghetto was only an image, and that I could come apart at the seams."

John J. Terenzio '72, executive producer for many years of NBC television news programs – and more recently of *A Current Affair* – elaborates: "The stereotypes many whites still have today were the prevalent stereotypes then – that blacks were related to crime, that you had to be afraid of black people, that blacks could not achieve any kind of an intellectual or educational level. You not only didn't think of blacks as going to prep school, but of graduating from college as doctors, lawyers, businessmen, and things like that.

"Dennis and I realized very quickly that despite the enormous cultural differences we had, the fact is we lived about a mile apart from each other in New York City. We both lived on the East Side – culturally worlds apart, but geographically close. So it was easy for us to maintain our friendship outside of Hotchkiss during vacations. I came from a liberal family, and he was a welcome guest in my home. My parents loved him and took him in. Obviously, the other dynamic was me going to visit him. I don't think I had ever been north of 96th Street before. So that was fascinating, as a young man, to go to Harlem. I'll never forget a hot summer day watching New York City policemen literally drive through the pedestrian walkways of the housing projects in early afternoon and knocking over tricycles. I said, 'What in the world is going on?' He said, 'Oh, they just do that once a day to kind of let everybody know they're there.' That's the first time in my life that

I had ever viewed police as hostile. In the society I grew up in, police were your protectors. Now, I'm standing on the corner watching this scene, and I realize that the police are not the protectors. They're the antagonists. I had never understood that before."

It was owing to the presence of Dennis Watlington and Noel Velas-quez that the most cinematographic event perhaps in the entire century of Hotchkiss came about. Dennis Watlington: "Anybody from that time period who was at Hotchkiss always talks about *the* game. About three busloads of black people came up from Harlem. The sand-lot team we had played for the previous year in Harlem was playing Hotchkiss JV's. In the warm-ups, the black kids were dressed in gold satin with black stripes up the pants, and they ran like the wind. They were running and making these great catches, and they had a whole set of hot black cheerleaders. Just watching them, the white boys were scared to death. They were younger, they were smaller and not half so slick. But this was Noel's greatest moment. He and I had discussed this the day before. It was our job to get the white boys to believe that they could do it. It was our job to convince them that race wasn't such a big deal. So it was Noel who now rallied the guys in warm up. He said, 'Don't be afraid of the blackness; don't be afraid of the streetness. You're worth something; you're somebody!'

"There was a hang-up even before the game started. The coach, Chris Getman, wasn't going to start me at quarterback. I'm the type who plays by instinct rather than memory, and Chris wanted to try out some of the plays that he had rehearsed. The black team was coached by Chuck Griffin, the guy who had pushed me to go to Hotchkiss. When Chuck discovered I wasn't playing quarterback – that some guy who was half the quarterback I was, was playing – he came up and started a tirade on the sidelines about what kind of racists they were. 'Four hundred years,' he was shouting, 'and nothing has changed.' A great big, flam-boyant black man who wore this tentlike dashiki – imagine this at Hotchkiss, on Taylor Field – and he's going bananas. Anyway, I did wind up playing quarterback.

"The game was pretty even, and our JV's were holding their own. I don't know who was ahead, but there was a dispute when Chuck accused the refs and everybody of cheating. Next thing you know, this big guy in the dashiki is pulling his team off the field. So the players in gold, their hot cheerleaders, and everybody is grumbling and heading for the buses. It was like Martin Luther King marching on Selma, Alabama. Our coach was all caught up in the fury. I don't know what possessed him, but he rushed up to Chuck, who was striding away from the field, and yelled, 'What's the matter, Chuck, you chicken?' If a hundred people can turn silent, that's what happened. This powerful black man spun around and said, 'Chicken? I'll show you!' And with one sweep of the hand he waved all the seventy-some blacks back onto the field, and they came running back onto the field like it was Africa or someplace. The students told me later they were never more afraid in their lives, seeing all these blacks running toward them. For the rest of the game, I don't think anyone on the sidelines sat down. The black team and their cheerleaders were yelling in unison, 'Oh, go! Oh, go! Oh, go!' So with the blacks cheering on that side, the whites cheering on this side, the game going on in the middle, it was so hotly contested that Chuck's wife was screaming to kill us at the top of her lungs as we were winning in the fourth quarter. Here was my future mother-in-law, and she was telling the black team to kill Noel and me. 'Kill them! Kill them! Kill them if they play for the white man! Kill them!' The white kids took some pretty strong mouthing from the black cats, but they pulled together and played a hell of a game. I ended up scoring one of the touchdowns, and Noel scored the other. They missed the extra point, and we won fourteen to thirteen. But it was really Noel's game because of the way he had psyched up everybody on our side.''

Perhaps the most fundamental difference between the black and the white students at the school was not one of color. ''Hotchkiss was basically a school for kids,'' explains Dennis. ''They had to take Noel out of the prep dorm because the kids were in there playing cops and robbers with their fingers. They'd go around the corner on the corridor, 'Bang, bang!' Noel had shot people. This was too much. So Leif talked to the administration about getting him out of there and putting him in the regular dorm.

"Leif Thorne-Thomsen became the most influential man for me at the school. I think he understood that I was a person, not a project. He was and has remained my brother. He again showed me that white boys could be cool. I idolized Leif. He was wearing his hat on one side, hanging out, the whole thing. He was a strong supporter of the civil rights and peace movements, and his life was deeply influenced by the death of a brother in Vietnam. He cared passionately about people, and I can't count the number of times he saved my ass. I remember the time the worst of me got the better of me, and I ripped off a stereo amplifier from one of the kids' rooms. This kid had already left for Christmas vacation, and I was going to take the stuff home with me the next morning on the bus. It was the middle of the night; suddenly I felt terribly confused and found myself running through the snow across the campus to wake up Leif. I explained the situation and said, 'I probably could have gotten away with it.' He said, 'So why didn't you?' I said, 'Because of people like you around here.' When I asked if he was going to turn me in, he shook his head. 'You did something a hell of a lot tougher. You turned yourself in.'

"I was so successful the first year, they took my brother in the next year, and I was elected class president, I think more by virtue of my capabilities as opposed to being black and playing off all that. I became the leader in my class because I was vocal and strong – and about a decade older than anyone in my class, coming from the background I did. They used to love it when prospective parents would be taken around the school, and they'd see me and introduce me. 'Here's Dennis Watlington, the first black president of a class.' And I played it to the most. I guess I loved the school so much because I understood the game."

Leif Thorne-Thomsen: "Dennis is one of the finest minds that has come through the school in the years I've been here. He was capable of dealing with almost anything. He was a powerful speaker, quick on his feet. And he was intimidating – a big, tall, strong, heavily muscled, fierce-looking man with a great heavy face and an impressive regal nose. Dennis was skirting around the rules in all sorts of ways, but he was not tainted the way Noel was with drug dealing. Many of us were working with tremendous commitment to keep Dennis and Noel straight. Noel lasted a year and a half, during which time he got into a lot of trouble with drugs. He got into a lot of trouble with little girl babysitters. He got into a lot of trouble because as far as he was concerned, he considered anything fair game. He got mixed up in a couple of bad three-way male triangles, which included a predatory proctor on one of the corridors. This provoked a turmoil which would be felt at the school for many years after Noel left."

Dennis Watlington: "Noel was too ghetto, too much into the instant gratification syndrome that prevails in the ghetto. You want to grow up and do it before it does it to you. Hotchkiss was about white boys entering in the ninth grade and having the next four years mapped out for them. So what was a grind to them was unbearable to Noel, day in and day out. Studies killed Noel.

"The national mood was now beginning to change, as we got further and further into the Nixon administration. The chic of Lyndon Johnson's Great Society was fading. This was the time of the Kent State shootings – though I think Noel and I were the main reason why attitudes changed at Hotchkiss. We had abused them, and they weren't going to take it anymore. They said, 'Okay, we're not going to let you use your poor little black boy angle anymore. We're going to make you play by the rules.' The patronizing stopped, and they respected us insofar that they demanded our best. Equality was sinking in by virtue of necessity."

This new equality progressively depleted the ranks of the Hotchkiss blacks. Leif Thorne-Thomsen: "Dennis followed Noel out of the school gates shortly before the end of his upper mid year. It was sort of by mutual consent. I think he wanted to take a break from it all, and the faculty couldn't have been happier. He was also woefully behind in his French. But Dennis and I wanted to keep the door open. We exacted a promise from Bill Olsen that if Dennis successfully got his French under control, he could come back again in the fall.

"Noel by now had become president of a Harlem street gang called the Slum Lords. He had good organizational instincts and managed to get some federal renewal money with a proposal to open street academies and to keep the peace among the various rival gangs. During the summer, Noel put Dennis on the payroll as his minister of war. Their main task seems to have been to visit the different gangs and be entertained by the ladies' auxiliaries. At one point Dennis visited me in Connecticut for a couple of weeks and insisted on a diet of nothing but liver. For whatever reason, I think he felt revived by the time he left.

"The outcome for Noel took a different turn. He had the misfortune to sample the hospitality of the girlfriend of the president of a gang called Satan's Spades. The gang leader didn't go after Noel. That wouldn't be appropriate. He just beat up the girlfriend. But Noel, though he had his own regular girlfriend and a daughter, felt obliged to go out and defend the honor of this girl he'd been fooling around with. So he put on his ruffled shirt and his gold chain, and put his derringer in his pocket. He went out as if he were a character in a movie to do battle with this leader of Satan's Spades. Although Noel was playing by the rules, the other guy was not. He had two bodyguards stationed on fire escapes, and when Noel drew his derringer, they shot out his lungs from behind."

"He was the first Hotchkiss kid who was murdered, to my knowledge," says Bill Olsen. "Thank God it was back home and not here. Noel was an awfully bright kid who was trying to get what he could out of us, in more ways than one, and yet never pulled himself out of where he lived." *

During that fateful summer of 1971 as Noel's minister of war, Dennis was also leading another, altogether different life: "Leif had set it up for me to go to a tutoring school in New York. I hated French, and I

---

* Noel was not to be the only fatality from among the black students at the school. One dropped out promptly and went to California, where he killed himself. Another strong leader from the Hotchkiss black contingent had his throat slashed in Harlem in a drug deal gone awry.

knew there was no way I was going to be able to make it up. But the teacher and I became good buddies. He introduced me to the world of French restaurants, French plays, and French things going on around New York. I introduced him to night life in my part of town. When Hotchkiss sent the test down to the tutoring service he worked for, he sat in the room with me, and we discussed every answer. We designed it so I would get a B-, not too low, not too high, but convincing enough.

"When the word got around the school that I did well, the faculty was up in arms. They weren't about to let me back in, no matter what. Leif continued to present my side of the deal so fiercely that it came down to the trustees' dinner, the first week of the school year. Leif pushed Brokaw to get on Bill, and Brokaw said, 'Aw, come on, Bill, you've got to let him back in.'"

Leif Thorne-Thomsen: "The matter came up in a turbulent meeting at which faculty speakers made it clear there was going to be big trouble if Dennis came back without a vote. So Bill Olsen put it to the vote of the faculty. He said, 'Leave Leif out of it. Any beef you have is with me. Leif is doing only what we're all expected to do as advisors.' When the vote came, I don't know what the against score was, but the pro score was either one or two. I can account for one. I don't know who the other was. As a headmaster, especially at Hotchkiss, you have power only until you use it. There the matter lay until the following week, when Bill came in and said, 'I've decided to admit Dennis Watlington. I gave him my word, and that's the way it's going to be.' It took courage to take that stand."

Dennis Watlington: "Leif had a great influence with Olsen because Leif represented everything Olsen would love to have been – especially a rebel. Olsen had to be stuffy and look like a politician, which I guess the headmaster really is. Freedom is what Leif represented to Olsen, and freedom is what Noel and I represented to the kids. Those kids were dominated by their parents at home, and by the teachers at the school. It was the fear of having their power and authority challenged that probably played an underlying role in the faculty's determination to keep me out."

Dennis Watlington's readmission as a senior proved dramatically fortuitous for the school. Leif Thorne-Thomsen: "That fall, about a pound or so of marijuana found its way into the hands of some white kids at the school. It had been a while since any dope had been around; so this was precious stuff. The situation developed when a group of black kids came up to one of these white kids in Memorial to buy some of the stuff – and were refused on the grounds that their credit was bad. Apparently, they had welched on paying the previous time. So the black kids went out and got reenforcements and staged a sit-in, demanding the dope. As the thing went on, it got progressively nastier and nastier, and a knife or two were shown. I remember one of the white kids came running out of Memorial, looking wild-eyed, saying, 'Where's Dennis? My God, where's Dennis? Only Dennis can save us now!'"

Dennis was not around; he was living off-campus at that time. Although Leif and a phalanx of faculty members managed to keep the situation under control, it was up to Dennis to ease the resulting tensions that were barely being kept in check. Dennis Watlington: "A lot of the black cats weren't righteous, meaning they wouldn't play fair. I may have played tough at times, but I always played fair. Now the black guys came to me, 'What're we going to do 'cause they won't sell to us?' They wanted to beat the white kids up. I told the black guys, 'You ain't going to do shit! Did you pay the man? No! Well, then? You know damn well if you was on the streets and didn't pay for your drugs, they'd kill you.'"

That helped the situation but didn't end it. Leif Thorne-Thomsen: "There were a lot of people involved, and almost all of the black kids. A series of meetings took place in which the school tried to assess the importance and damage of this and get some feeling about what to do. Dennis was nothing short of heroic during all this, serving as a bridge between the black and white students at the school and a conduit with the faculty on behalf of both groups. The faculty was nothing short of frenzied. I remember at one point they voted to expel all of the black kids for violating property, and put all of the white kids on probation for importing drugs. Bill Olsen thwarted the expulsions by instituting a two-thirds majority requirement. Feelings were running high, and that was a courageous move. The final solution was to put everyone involved on probation. But the faculty lay in wait for a few of the blacks. The following year, they threw out Dennis's brother for being off his corridor and watching 'Monday Night Football.'"

Dennis Watlington also did not receive a Hotchkiss diploma. Instead of taking courses to complete his credit requirements, he opted for courses which he felt he needed the most. Then a few weeks before graduation he left the school, again more or less by mutual consent. "Whatever else Hotchkiss may have done to me, the point is they took me in," says Dennis. "They did not exclude me at a time when the rest of America was doing just that. Hotchkiss showed me what America was all about. I didn't live in America before, I lived in Harlem. I ended up with the best of both worlds – Harlem boy street smarts and Hotchkiss boy know-how."

The benefits were not one-sided. "Dennis Watlington touched more people – kids and faculty – and challenged more aspects about the school than anyone before him," says Peter Adams. "He represented the one kid that the school really struggled with, and when the end finally came, many of us who worked closely with Dennis felt defeated – yet satisfied that we had given it everything we had. Still, it was not enough."

David Luke, who was then a trustee, provides an administrative perspective: "With the best of intentions, we had moved too fast and reached beyond our capabilities. So we made a conscious decision to narrow our focus a little bit, maintain the same objective, but try to deal with individuals who were a little more easy to read and for Hotchkiss to assimilate."

Dennis Watlington puts it more bluntly: "Me and Noel fixed it so that the only blacks they would take in the future were ones who were really qualified in their definition of what the school meant."

Dennis today is a successful author. One of his recent pieces for *Vanity Fair* was "Between the Cracks," a depiction of his bout a few years ago with crack cocaine. "Pilgrim among the Privileged" was his feature article on Hotchkiss for *American Way*, the in-flight magazine. "Dennis sometimes embellishes on the truth," cautions Leif Thorne-Thomsen, his former mentor and still close friend. "He is a follower of Gail Sheehy, who has one of the most warped pens as far as I'm concerned. She did a whole chapter on Dennis in *Passages*; so I know."

Dennis Watlington's latest project is a screenplay on Eugene Lang, the New York businessman who has devoted millions to helping inner-city boys and girls go to college. "Me and Lang are very tight right now because to me he is Bill Brokaw. Exact type of figure with the exact type of purpose. He's doing en masse what Bill Brokaw did for me and Noel for the same reasons. He believes that it's an investment in society. This is in effect me paying off in part on Bill Brokaw's investment."

xii /   "**M**r. Olsen says he is a chameleon," read the minutes of a trustees' meeting held in the spring of 1970, at which the subject of co-education received its most comprehensive airing, "being almost at the same time for and against. The time is not now [according to the headmaster]. . . . Hotchkiss should not take one girl on campus until it could give her the kind of experience she ought to have. He feels no pressure [and recommends] a friendly attitude toward coeducation, facing that it is coming and awaiting the [right time]."

Comments Bill Olsen, "Actually I did not say I was a *chameleon* on the subject of coeducation. I said I was *split down the middle*."

The most significant achievement of Bill Olsen's tenure is widely held to be that he brought coeducation to Hotchkiss. A more accurate statement would be that he successfully, even masterfully, implemented the introduction of coeducation at the school. The single most influential person at Hotchkiss in promoting the idea of coeducation may well have been Bill Olsen's wife, Jean. Her involvement in this cause – and in other affairs of the school – helped precipitate the most acute crisis in her husband's career.

"They fired him!" exclaims the woman of modest stature yet prepossessing presence, at her Lakeville home not far from the headmaster's house where she had reigned for more than two decades. "This, after Bill had raised the school until it was nose to nose with Andover, Exeter, St. Paul's, and Groton!"

As a thirty-three-year-old wife with a young child in 1960, Jean Olsen understood the traditional responsibilities of the school's first lady. "She cared tremendously about the faculty," says Jane C. Hughes, who came to Hotchkiss in 1959 as the wife of English teacher Richard D. Hughes '52. "She made it a point to go and visit every new wife who came on campus, to make certain they knew that her door was always open to them should they need any guidance or any kind of friendship from her. She was a terrific hostess, and she and Bill made certain that they had small dinner parties including all the faculty over the course of the years. And she was a very caring person. If anybody was in trouble or had a problem, she would be there to help."

Being the wife of a Hotchkiss headmaster was not what Jean Olsen had once so idealistically imagined. "The person who receives the paycheck is the headmaster," says Rusty Chandler. "The person who has to put up with a hell of a lot is the headmaster's wife. It's tougher than being the wife of a CEO of IBM, or P&G, or Pepsi Cola. Those wives don't live at the corporate headquarters. They aren't under a microscope all the time. They don't have their husbands' employees or directors dropping in on them all the time – which is what literally happens to a headmaster's wife."

This was something Jean Olsen at first was only too happy to handle: "It was evident the trustees were anxious to have the house opened up, more people coming in and out. I was young and enthusiastic, and I was a people person. I refurbished and redecorated the place, and we entertained the trustees for the first time for more than a day. They stayed with us, and we entertained them for dinner, breakfast, lunch, dinner, breakfast. I included the women, the trustees' wives, and I got to know most of them very well. We also traveled for the school a great deal because for the first time it was possible to go by jet all over the country. We had a wonderful time visiting with alumni.

"In the early years, the faculty were very close, and the school was like a big family. I went to New York and bought a lot of games for the boys. When you're thirteen, fourteen, or fifteen, you're uneasy. You can't get into a room easily, and once you get in, you don't know how to get out again. If you have something to do with your hands other than eat, you're much happier. So I had about fifteen games spotted around the room, skill games, that the kids would play when they came over for cocoa. Nowadays, the kids are so close to the adult world that they don't need any props. But back then, there was a real barrier – so everything helped.

"The revolution started in the latter part of the 1960s. Suddenly, people seemed to have lost their sense of humor – completely. Everybody hated everybody over thirty. Nobody smiled. Nobody joked. The faculty was testy. At the same time, I saw a new world opening up. I read everything about the female revolution and was thrilled because I had been unable to do those things. I would have loved to have gone to law school or get an advanced degree, but it had never occurred to me that that was an option open to me. Also, with the use of the pill, it became possible for women to readjust and be themselves."

"We were on the brink of the women's movement," explains Cynthia White, who would eventually succeed Jean Olsen in the headmaster's house. "Jean had gone to Smith, was very bright, and had very definite abilities. I think she tried to find expression for those, to find a position for herself in the school. She really got to resent the social aspects. She referred to herself in the end as 'I'm just a cookie cutter,' or a 'cookie passer.' She felt she had more to contribute, and she was right. But at that time the school was completely male-dominated. It was difficult and painful for her to find a position in which she could offer the best of herself in this very Victorian society. While Bill would support Jean, his thinking was very male-oriented. All our husbands were."

Far from being a cookie passer, according to a number of faculty

Jean Olsen

members from that era, Jean Olsen exerted an unprecedented influence on her husband in running the school. Recalls Peter Adams, "She would come into somebody's office and say, 'I think things ought to be done this way. I have a very strong sense that this is the way it ought to be done.' And we'd say, 'No, we don't do it that way, Jean. We do it this way.' A couple of weeks would go by, and Bill Olsen would kind of step in, and in some way let you know by what he wanted to do that Jean had gone to him. I felt Bill was caught in the middle."

Jean Olsen's approach at times was not quite so subtle, as others in the Hotchkiss community have pointed out. She would not hesitate to take on people one-on-one if she thought they were somehow thwarting her husband's goals. Unpredictably, these confrontations were sometimes intense, sometimes calm. And there were few activities around the school that she considered irrelevant to her concerns.

"She liked to be a part of important things that were going on," explains Dick Hughes, who was one of Olsen's faculty loyalists. "You can say that's being a busybody, or you can say that's a woman in the world trying to make her mark. I think in one way they were a great team. She complemented Bill and was very ambitious for him. But like any team, they didn't invariably see eye to eye. I know they had their differences about, 'Why don't you do this, Billy?' or, 'You should do this and that.' I think he would try to temper her extremes, but I think at times she had a major influence on him."

Specifically, what prompted Jean Olsen to put herself behind co-education was the disintegration of traditional morality: "Bill and I would travel around to other schools, and they'd say to me, 'How many of your faculty are sleeping around or divorced?' I'd say, 'Oh, none, none, none. Not at Hotchkiss, not at our school.' Well, that's absolutely asinine, asinine! Because the whole thing began to fall apart. Marriage wasn't sacrosanct anymore. And that's very difficult when you think of adolescents and you want that as an ideal, and you know and they know that that's not the way it's being played.

"I came to feel very strongly that our Hotchkiss youngsters should be prepared to move into that real world they were going to have to live in. Even though they had girls over for dances, that was pretty much an artificial relationship. And by that time Andover and Exeter and St. Paul's and Taft and Kent and Choate had all either become co-educational or had amalgamated with another school. So, Billy had talked round about it, round about it, round about it, and finally, he agreed, 'Yeah, the school has to change.'

"That wasn't going to be easy. I suspect that Hotchkiss was by far the most male-oriented, chauvinistic school in the country. Dick Gurney hated the idea of admitting girls. George Van Santvoord, still alive, was schizzy about women – 'If Hotchkiss goes coed, get rid of Olsen.' Bob Hawkins, terrified of taking in girls. Always, 'No! No! No!' And, of course, the students: 'Don't rock our boat. We like it this way.' They had no idea what the other way was, but 'not at our school.' The students at other all-male schools and colleges were often in the forefront of those for coeducation. Billy was astute enough not to ask them their preference here."

The kind of opposition Jean Olsen was talking about was perhaps best articulated by Dick Gurney. "If Hotchkiss ever became a coeducational school," he warned in a feature article in the *Record* in early 1972, "Hotchkiss would be dead. What the word *Hotchkiss* means to thousands of people would have no significance except as a symbol of the past. It would be a misrepresentation, a fraud, if the school continued to use the same name." Relegating coeducation to a "recurring fad," Gurney asked, "Are seventy-five years of established freedom, excellence, and independence trivial when compared to a change or following the lead of some of our neighbors? Why shouldn't Switzerland join the Communists?"

In the same issue of the *Record*, Bill Olsen informed the school of his decision: "In November of 1971 I fell off the fence," the headmaster wrote. "It was a noisier fall than I had expected! I recommended to the Trustees that Hotchkiss become coeducational as soon as possible. . . . We are moving into a new world; there can be no return to the old, no matter how much we may wish to go back. . . . One of my charges as headmaster is to protect the best of the past . . . but my biggest responsibility is to prepare students for the future."

Bill Olsen's falling off the fence was a prerequisite but not empowerment for the most critical move in the school's history. "The trustees had been discussing the issue vigorously and consulting widely for more than two years under the leadership of Woods McCahill and later Rhett Austell ['43]," says Zeph Stewart. "The decision to go coed remained to be hammered out by the whole board in concert with Bill."

As the board's discussions continued, among the possibilities explored was associating Hotchkiss with one of "the several girls' schools that had indicated interest." This proved impractical, and at a meeting on December 7, 1972, after a "long discussion of Mr. Olsen's *Revised Summary of Timetables and Targets for Coeducation*," the trustees reached "a consensus that we would take in girls in the fall of 1974."

Jean Olsen's efforts did not stop with this implicit victory. As a member of a faculty committee approved by the board, Jean took the lead in exploring how other schools handled coeducation: "I was very fearful that Hotchkiss would be too chauvinistic to do it right. I spent weekends at St. Paul's, and Exeter, and Andover, and I talked to them at Kent and Taft. At some of the places they were doing it very well, and at some of them not at all well. The worst was where they had brought twenty girls on campus in the middle of the year. That was absolutely ridiculous. It was horrible for some of the women faculty. It seems they weren't allowed to have an hour off to themselves. They had to be around to prove to everybody that there were women on campus."

To see her efforts about to be implemented should have been especially satisfying for Jean Olsen. Yet this was also the time that her husband's delicate balancing act was beginning to come undone. Inappropriate as Jack Bodel's farewell speech may have seemed a few months earlier, many of the faculty members at that party felt their own disenchantment with the way Bill Olsen was running the school in matters of both substance and style – not the least of which was the perceived intrusion of his wife. Now, entering the final school year before going coed, these misgivings seemed to gain a new intensity and thrust.

Whether by osmosis or more direct means, the faculty attitudes spread to the student body to an unprecedented degree. "In our senior year we had a classmate who went on a rampage against the Olsens," says Charles A. Denault '74. "He was on the *Record*, and every week there were articles about Mr. Olsen not being an active headmaster, not being available to the students and spending too much time out fund raising. This pounding away at the Olsens just went on and on, and I remember one Sunday after dinner a group of us going to the headmaster's for coffee. We were just standing there, when all of a sudden, Mrs. Olsen out of the blue says, 'Do you believe the things in the *Record?* Do you think this is right?' I was not a rebellious child, and I surprised myself when I heard myself say, 'Well, yes, I do.' Mrs. Olsen wasn't angry or anything, but she was obviously looking for support for her husband."

For Charlie Denault, it was a positive experience. "I realized that we were allowed to think freely, to have our ideas and express them — which is probably the strongest thing I've taken away with me from Hotchkiss."

Bill Olsen took an unusual step in confronting this personal onslaught. "I'll never forget the talk he gave in chapel, clearly in response to criticism that he wasn't terribly approachable, not a warm and cozy guy," recalls Larry Becker. "He almost apologized for being a private person. He said that didn't mean he didn't care, didn't have feelings for what was happening. He was a proud man, and for him to say that couldn't have been easy."

The students found some original and daring ways to express how they felt. Recalls Thomas V. Cholnoky '74, "Bill Olsen was giving a Wednesday morning talk in the auditorium when all of a sudden the curtain behind the stage opened up, and somebody came flying out on a rope like Tarzan and dropped a paper bag filled with something on Olsen, and then went flying back in and the curtain closed again. The perpetrator was wearing a mask, and both he and whoever was working the curtain managed to run out and were never caught. Olsen was shocked."

The lambasting in the *Record* was not limited to Bill Olsen. "Whatever the issue was — drugs, minority students, trust — it was sort of a life-and-death issue, and the administration became the whipping boy," says Peter Adams, Bill Olsen's onetime acolyte and faculty adviser for the *Record.* "I found it really difficult to play the role of adviser. As a faculty member, I wasn't supposed to agree with the things the kids were advocating, but I really did agree. The situation became so heated that the O decided not to mail out several issues of the *Record* because of how their content might reflect on the school. The *Record* was a PR piece for the school, and I remember Bill Olsen saying, 'I am the publisher of everything that's printed here.' The kids got the sense that if it didn't set well with him, it wasn't going to wash. So they started the *Whipping Post* as an alternative, as an outlet, and Bill Olsen was astute enough to provide financial support. The *Whipping Post* was strictly internal, not to be sent out."

Bill Olsen has a different recollection. "The kids were expressing themselves freely in the *Record*, and it was not taken out of circulation. The *Whipping Post* was started by a group of students who got sick and tired of the negativism."

Whatever its original raison d'être, the *Whipping Post* did not mince its words. "He's an absolutist," one of its issues in early 1974 charged, quoting anonymous student opinion. "He twists everything around. . . . He's tyrannical." An accompanying cartoon on the editorial page showed a closed door with the sign, "*major major major major HEADMASTER*," and underneath it a note, "I will be out until 3 P.M. Before then, I will gladly see anyone in my office."

What Bill Olsen had so forcefully sought to prevent in squashing Jack Bodel's proposed faculty association was now happening in an informal way. Rumblings were beginning to reach the board through several faculty members who were in contact with individual trustees whom they knew personally. These contacts continued until one day during that spring term of 1974, the executive committee found itself reaching unanimous consensus to ask Bill Olsen to resign. "We felt he had done a fine job, especially with the alumni," says Woods McCahill, president of the board and chairman of that committee, "but it was time for a change." The committee's feeling was that Bill Olsen could resign with honor; he had lasted fourteen years during a tumultuous period that saw the ousting of headmasters and university presidents on an average of every six years. Why not start with a new headmaster before final preparations for the transition to the new coeducational Hotchkiss began?

"I got a call from Woods McCahill who wanted to know what would be the effect on the parents of prospective students if Bill were let go," says Rusty Chandler, who was on sabbatical leave in the Western Connecticut public school system. "I told him I thought it would be just terrible. Here they had selected a school which was very much symbolized by Bill Olsen as the headmaster, and now he wouldn't be there. Yeah, I told him I thought it would be awful. What happened next was that other trustees who had learned what was going on confronted the faculty members who had been bellyaching. To a man they said, 'I really didn't mean it that way. I didn't intend for Bill to get fired.' It's a clear case where things really just got out of hand. What they didn't say was, 'We're not used to being told something by a woman.' That's the crux of the whole situation. It was a male club that was about to admit females, and there was a woman telling them directly or indirectly how they were going to do it."

"George Van Santvoord was leading the pack," asserts Jean Olsen. "He was old and evidently becoming senile, and he was terrified that something awful was going to happen to his beloved school. It wasn't anybody else's, it was *his* school – and he was going to save it. If it meant firing Bill Olsen, then fire Bill Olsen. And he got together a group of people who were his henchmen to do their darndest. Bill, I think, was absolutely stunned. He could see why George Van Santvoord was unhappy, and he didn't take it personally, which is extraordinary, because I did! He decided not to say anything to anybody, nothing at all, to anybody. I finally called a friend of mine on the faculty, Ellen Torrey, whom I adore. She and Blair are two of the finest people that Hotchkiss has ever had in the history of the school because of their devotion to the kids, particularly Blair. She came up and listened to me, and then she told Blair. The word gradually seeped out. Dick Hughes and others began to hear about it. The faculty went to bat for Bill. They began to call the trustees and said, 'What in the hell are you doing?'"

There was also heartfelt personal support. "Susan and I both hurt for you and Jean, as human beings," wrote Walter DeMelle, the school's librarian, to the beleaguered headmaster. "We wish there existed some sort of magic that could erase the frustration and sadness."

This is not to say that the community suddenly united in a common cause. "When we heard the trustees were ready to give Bill the heave-ho," says Anne Bowen, who had by then experienced almost fourteen years of the Olsen regime as a faculty wife, "there were a lot of us who felt it was time for him to move on."

Based on extensive interviews, it appears that the executive committee's action would never have come about solely because of Jean Olsen's role. How much of this crisis in the headmaster's career was attributable to his modus operandi and how much to his reversal of hallowed traditions is anybody's guess, though both form and substance undoubtedly were involved. Ironically, Olsen's operating style and his willingness to make changes were probably the very qualities needed in those days for successfully running the school – and the reason why gentlemen of a different stripe in similar positions at other institutions had failed.

"Bill among other things was a skilled politician," points out Robert J. Barker, a faculty admirer with a historical perspective. "He knew how to maneuver people, he knew how to maneuver situations."

To this day Bill Olsen is not sure what caused the crisis: "My interpretation is that when you're faced with major change, with major surgery, anxieties get intensified. Coeducation was the biggest change the school had ever faced, and quite frankly, probably ever will. This was partly a backlash of those who didn't want it. I know there were faculty who were trying to stop it, and they were using the Duke. We were moving into uncharted waters, and I understood their apprehension. Yet I'm sure I was also criticized two or three years earlier for not pushing coeducation fast enough. Sometimes you're damned if you do, damned if you don't."

Jean Olsen: "I had fought so hard for coeducation, and I felt maybe I was involved, having pushed him into this position. It's difficult because it's your responsibility, and it isn't. The school didn't pay me a cent. If I wanted a new covering for a chair, I bought it out of my father's money. If I wanted something particularly nice to eat for the trustees, I bought it out of my father's money. I bought special arrangements of flowers. I had made a plea at one point to the trustees that I thought I should be paid. They said no. I think I became just plain weary."

Whatever their individual reasons, the full board reversed the executive committee's decision on Bill Olsen.

"I would assume that Woods McCahill felt that he was crossed," observes Larry Becker. "He had done what he should do in his position, listening to various complaints and bringing them all together. When it came to the actual board meeting, some people clearly weren't saying the same thing they had said before."

An entry in the minutes for May 4, 1974, reflects the official end to the crisis: "The Board of Trustees affirms its confidence in William Olsen as Headmaster and in his leadership of The Hotchkiss School as it enters into coeducation."

"I remember Bill Olsen afterward coming into the faculty meeting room," recalls Geoffrey B. Marchant, who had been hired two years earlier as instructor in English, "and saying he would be back the next year. He had a sort of a quaver in his voice, which was the only real emotion that I saw or heard from him at that time."

To what extent Bill Olsen's close call transformed him into a more sympathetic figure can only be theorized. But there was one immediate practical change. "I had the sense that the trustees virtually gave Bill a directive to appoint a dean of faculty and give him significant responsibilities," says Larry Becker. "Jim Marks was named, and he clearly became number two. George Kellogg was still assistant headmaster, and he accepted the situation with true grace."

The ordeal left Jean Olsen emotionally drained, and she took a complete break from the school and everything associated with it: "When I came back, I realized Hotchkiss wasn't the be-all and the end-all of my life. I realized I'd be better served if I put my energies elsewhere. I accepted an appointment to the Connecticut Board of Education, and I was in Hartford a great deal of time. I was taking courses at Northwest Community College, and I was doing a lot of other things. I just felt there was no place at Hotchkiss for someone like me. I know very few classes after seventy-five."

Comments Bill Olsen, "To this day, Jean understandably feels strongly about the school for which she worked so hard. In my view, she has paid her price for feeling passionately about something that history has already proven among the most beneficial decisions ever made by the school."

Concludes Peter Adams, "Jean Olsen was stuck here in a time warp, and in getting unstuck herself, loosened up the whole place. She was the person I had the most difficulty with, yet also the one for whom I felt the most compassion. She deserves a monument for moving the school into the twentieth century."

xiii / The idea of a coeducational Hotchkiss had been entertained since the earliest days of the school – but as a fantasy no more realizable than Jules Verne's voyage to the moon. The *Mischianza* of 1914 published the following account of a mythical faculty meeting:

SCENE: Headmaster's study, Hotchkiss School. The Faculty lounging about the room, smoking Hotchkiss Perfectos (Headmaster's expense account).

DR. BUEHLER. The hour having arrived and a quorum being present, if . . . the faculty will throw away their cigar-butts and give me their undivided attention, I shall announce the subject for discussion this evening. Resolved: that *The* Hotchkiss School should be made co-educational. Before expressing my views on this momentous subject, I shall call upon you individually for your opinions. Will you favor us first, Mr. Estill.

MR. ESTILL. (Walking to the open window) E – h! My boy Wallie and my boy Joe never had any use for women. I think a lot of girls around here would be an unwholesome influence on my boys, and they'd cause too much trouble in my excuse department. *Cut it out*, I say! Nothin' doin'! *Absolutely* nothin' doin'! (again strolls toward window).

DR. BUEHLER. Well, Mr. Estill, you seem very decided in your views. What is your theory, Mr. Buell?

MR. BUELL. (Swaying as though in a heavy wind) Hm! Great Scott! I'll wager not half a dozen girls in the country appreciate Lessing's "Minna von Barnhelm." That's not the kind we want here at Hotchkiss! A little knowledge is a dangerous thing, and a few girls might turn the heads of our b'ys. Let the b'ys get their German every day, but keep away the girls! (Sits down, snorting violently.)

DR. BUEHLER. We are not concerned with the German department. Your views are too narrow. Will you cite some historical precedents, Mr. Hall?

MR. HALL. [History teacher Peanut Hall] I shall give the requested information. Now, the classic authors tell us that, in ancient Persia, each student had a harem of twenty wives. *Of course*, I would not go so far as to recommend this for Hotchkiss students. However, when we perceive to what heights of civilization Persia attained, we must admit the wisdom of their educational system. Although Alexander conquered the Persian empire, he retained this system. Now, Alexander was a scholar himself; therefore, we should respect his decision. And so, I would say that: though my family might not approve, I would *welcome* young ladies to *my* classroom!

DR. BUEHLER. This system is not intended for your especial benefit, Mr. Hall! . . .

The mythical debate continued, with a half-dozen other faculty members called on for their views. "There is much to be said on both sides of the question," Dr. Buehler concluded. "I think it is best to postpone any further discussion until a more suitable time."

Before taking up that postponed discussion – and at last being in a position to transcend theory with reality about the prospective male-female relationships – another reality needs to be examined. During the school's first eighty years as an all-male bastion, what were the corresponding relationships between the masters and the teenage boys under their tutelage – and among the boys themselves?

This has to be partly an educated guess. Though there have been hints of occasional activities fit for the scandal sheets, the chances are that the norm at Hotchkiss did not diverge markedly from what was current in the society as a whole. In the early years of the school, sexuality of any sort was repressed and deemphasized and hardly played the openly pervasive role it often does today. Boys did not even mature as fast and retained well into their teens an attitude unencumbered by such concerns. As Squidge Lord '22 remarked, "I matured late, I was interested in boys' activities, and we were a naive bunch of boys." This does not mean that nothing went on, as his classmate John Hoysradt makes clear: "We had a distressing incident with a faculty member during the early months of my prep year. He had to be dismissed by Uncle Huber because of improper behavior with a boy. I remember the boy's name and the boy very well. He was a very attractive boy. I also remember Dr. Brown's wife saying that she thought that Dr. Buehler had been too kind in his manner of dismissal. I don't know if she would have had him shoot the teacher, or dragged away in chains or whatever."

Such isolated incidents occurred from time to time. The most blatant story to be recounted during the interviews for this book came from a retired CEO of a major corporation: "Lower middle year I was living in Bissell, which was sort of dilapidated. The rooms were the size of cubicles. Between my cubicle and the one next to me I had drilled a hole so I could talk to the guy in there. It was a small hole, about an inch in diameter, and I'd cover it up for inspection during the day. One night, it was ten o'clock, lights out, and I'm lying there in bed, and next thing I know, my French prof is in bed with me, and he doesn't have any clothes on. I unplugged the hole as quickly as I could and hollered to the guy on the other side, 'Jesus Christ, the French prof is in bed with me, and he doesn't have any clothes on.' The prof panicked, and got the hell out of there. I clammed up, and he never did say anything. So there was no reason for him to get fired, or anything to happen."

The unanswered question: did this incident from the thirties represent a crude first attempt on the part of the prof or a time-tested approach?

"I don't think it's surprising that at schools such as Hotchkiss there should be some faculty members with homosexual tendencies," says Archibald Coolidge, the English teacher from George Van Santvoord's era. "I don't personally know of any homosexual instances among the students themselves, though I wouldn't say that such instances didn't exist. But I doubt very much if there was more of that sort of thing than could be reasonably expected at the better-known schools in this country. I know for a fact that it was more common in the great English public schools. It wasn't something that would have been tolerated at Hotchkiss if it came to light, whether between students or students and faculty."

Archibald Coolidge, nevertheless, did have occasion to turn in a faculty colleague: "It happened during the summer. It was brought to my attention by a friend in the town where the incident took place who knew that this fellow was teaching at Hotchkiss. I got a written statement from my friend and took it over to the Duke. I remember he was just coming back from his honeymoon, and I asked if anybody had resigned during the summer. The Duke said, 'No, not that I know of.' I said, 'Well, there's somebody who ought to.' I produced the evidence, and he called in Dr. Wieler. Dr. Wieler said, 'We are too busy around here without having to fuss with somebody like that,' and this master was let go."

Incomparably more characteristic than such unfortunate cases were those that might have taken place but did not. "There were probably quite a few men who gravitated to teaching boys because of their love for boys and the masculine sex," says Lael Wertenbaker, author of the 75th anniversary version of the school's history (which had been so maligned by the Duke), "but there was absolutely no question in my mind that they would ever do anything." Now in her eighties and living in New Hampshire, Lael Wertenbaker spent a considerable amount of time at the school in the course of her research a quarter of a century ago. Despite various inaccuracies, she wrote a book that certainly captured the spirit of the school with admirably lively prose. Formerly an international correspondent for *Time* and author in 1957 of "Death of a Man," a highly controversial account of her role in aiding her incurably ill husband to commit suicide, she nevertheless felt constrained in her commissioned work on the Hotchkiss School not to bring up such an unspeakable point. But it was uppermost on her mind in being interviewed for this centennial version of the school's past: "I think there were several of these teachers of the old kind at Hotchkiss. One or two were even married, but most were bachelors. Their love of young boys would probably be considered homosexual today. It may have been totally unconscious, and if not, it was totally disciplined. Their enormous love for boys made them great teachers because this love was converted to purity. I remember one marvelous old professor. He had a nickname which seemed most appropriate, but slips my mind. Devoted, absolutely devoted to teaching the boys, and to the school."

It was indeed Carle "Pansy" Parsons whom Mrs. Wertenbaker had in mind, the legendary English teacher who remains in the top rank of affection among generations of Hotchkiss boys, many of whom spent weekends with him in New York or vacationed with him in Nantucket or accompanied him on grand sightseeing treks through Europe. As helpful, considerate, and impartial as he was toward every student, it was no secret that Carle Parsons had a special relationship with three or four boys at a time, which he would carry on throughout their four years at the school. Handsome, athletic, and possessed of the appropriate social grace, they were known as Pansy's boys. Their most obvious (and enviable) privilege was that on weekends and holidays they would be seen riding with him in his mint-shiny Buick convertible, which was his one indispensable luxury on his modest salary. The most prominent member of this group in my class was Daniel C. Rebhun, Jr., whose father Carle Parsons had also taught. "He was a very prim and proper guy," says Dan, "a pure gentleman in every respect. He took me down to New York for a weekend to see *Carmen*, and he's responsible for my lifelong love of opera. Carle used to have Harry Wey and me into his apartment in Alumni on Sunday mornings, and we'd have tea and toast and chit chat. Another time he drove me down to Westover to try and see this girl from Cincinnati that I was just head over heels in love with. There was a wall around the damn place, and I called her to let her know I'd be driving by the wall. When we got there, I stood up on the back seat of Carle's convertible so I could see over the wall. He drove me around four times, while I was waving my heart out from the back seat. It was hardly the sort of behavior a Hotchkiss master would sanction for a Hotchkiss boy, but what the hell! I also have to tell you that Carle used to let me drive his car all the time. We'd get away from school, and he'd say, 'Do you want to drive?' So I'd be driving that Buick all over the countryside. I don't know why we were never caught. He was really taking a risk. What if we'd had an accident?"

Or what if the Duke had found out? The Duke was adamant about any student taking the wheel while under the jurisdiction of the school. And he was equally adamant about loyalty. What that would have done to the Duke's relationship with his closest faculty colleague is too uncomfortable to contemplate.

"I stayed in touch with Carle after I graduated," says Dan Rebhun, now head of a real estate concern in Cincinnati, and father of Daniel C. Rebhun III '76. "The last time I saw him was about six months or so before he died in the late sixties. He was a wonderful guy."

By that time, the sort of Victorianism which Carle Parsons symbolized had loosened its grip on masters whose dedication to the boys was in the same tradition. Yet there is no compelling evidence that faculty transgression of that thin line between the selflessness of *agape* and the self-interest of *eros* occurred with any greater frequency than before. As in the past, there were inevitably individuals on the faculty who would make some inappropriate move – perhaps to the boy's lasting distress – which was not reported or otherwise exposed. But as before, when an overt example did occur, Bill Olsen eased out the offender with the same consideration one would have for a member of the family.

To the very end prior to coeducation, Hotchkiss remained male-oriented – and, as some would charge, does so to this day. But it would be incorrect to view the coming of coeducation as the breaking down of the old ramparts by a phalanx of impatient females. One of the surprises in the ongoing debate came when the women on a mixed committee appointed by Bill Olsen to study the question reported that the time had not yet come. "We thought that probably the women would say, 'It's overdue and we should do it right now,' recalls David Luke, who was then one of the trustees most directly concerned with the issue, "but Mrs. Bodel [wife of Jack Bodel] made the point that Hotchkiss has been a boys' school for so long that you have to be certain that when you make the move, you don't envision that you're going to be just a boys' school which very warmly welcomed in a few girls. You really have to be prepared to be more than a single-sex school in attitude, readiness, and facilities in the broadest sort of way."

The faculty arguments delved into such questions as controlling the ardors of youthful romance and the distraction inherent in putting girls together with boys in the classroom. The alumni had more pragmatic concerns. Says Woods McCahill, then the board chairman, "Some alumni were afraid that in taking in girls, you would cut down the number of boys, which would have an adverse effect on the athletic teams." Others were concerned that taking in girls would reduce the number of chances to carry on in the family Hotchkiss tradition. Many, however, were quick to recognize the other side of the coin: now their daughters could also carry on that tradition.

"I was pushing for it like crazy because I had two daughters coming along," says faculty member and Hotchkiss graduate Dick Hughes. "I think another big factor was when Rusty Chandler stood up at one of the key meetings and said, 'In admissions, we're losing some top candidates to schools that have coeducation.'"

To meet all of these desires and concerns in going coed, it was also decided to increase the size of the school. "The size of an institution determines its economics," explains David Luke. "The decision to go from a school of roughly 350 to about 500 students would make an enormous difference in the unit cost of education. Coeducation was the means whereby we could enlarge the student body without in any way compromising quality, because we would be doubling our applicant pool.* This made an enormous difference at a time when we were trying to keep our costs in line with other schools and raise our revenues so that our average cost per student – and therefore our tuition – could be brought in line."

Yet with all this elaborate back-and-forth on the subject, one fundamental issue never seemed to have been fully resolved. "I was sitting in a discussion group that was trying to deal with some of the faculty anxieties about coeducation," recalls Peter Adams. "I said, 'I want to know what we're going to do as a school when the first girl gets pregnant?' One of the women who had just joined the faculty pretty much put an end to that. She glowered and said, 'Just who do you think we are?'"

xiv /   "**I**nstitutions like Hotchkiss are very conservative in accepting anything," Bill Olsen points out. "Yet it's always a surprise to people that the most conservative element in the school is the kids."

As his wife had observed about the boys' attitude toward coeducation, "Bill was astute enough not to ask them their preference."

There were, of course, those who could not wait. "I did not like being away from women for long, and I found that aspect of being at Hotchkiss depressing," says John N. "Jock" Conyngham IV '75, son of Jack Conyngham '44. Jock's other interest was hunting, which the school had also failed to fulfill: "The first time I came up and toured the school, the sky was dark with ducks and geese. Rusty Chandler, who was escorting me and my parents around, made it sound like I would be taking short breaks from my hunting and fishing to attend classes. I did get a lot of fishing in, but I hunted like three or four times that first year. So I was embittered and pissed off at Rusty Chandler.

---

*In the opinion of some people, among them Larry Becker, this increase in size, not coeducation, was the real fundamental change. "It meant losing forever the sort of intimacy that was possible only in a smaller school," says Larry.

No hunting, no women. I'd come back from vacation and see that blinking red light at the top of the hill, Route 112 crossing 41, and the blood would clot in my veins. I still have a visceral reaction when I see it today."

Jock Conyngham's first three years at the school exemplified the kind of behavior that movies are made of – and that many administrators of all-male educational institutions devoutly hoped would cease with the coming of coeducation. "In our frustration, we used to do wild stunts," says Jock Conyngham. "On a Saturday night and into early Sunday morning the place looked like between classes, with kids walking around everywhere. There was always some alcohol around, and sometimes drugs. We thought nothing of hot-wiring a golf cart and seeing how many people we could get in, and cruising all over the golf course, turning it over. It would fall on top of us, twelve or fourteen kids, and we'd flip it back over. We'd also build little jumps, though we'd try to be careful not to do much damage.

"Another time I was walking to class, and there was a sporty Italian car parked in the circle. I could see in checking it out that the guy left the keys inside. I had fifteen or twenty minutes before class, so I jumped in and took it down to Lime Rock. Unfortunately the gate was closed. I couldn't take it around the track. I started back and parked it and walked to class. I hear stories at reunions about things I did that I don't even remember anymore."

To think that only a few years earlier Jock's cousin, Will, had been permanently separated from the school for having a few drinks at a dance weekend picnic in the woods! And Jock was hardly alone in flouting the rules. "I did my share of illegal things, though I was never caught," says Stuart H. Watson '76, today a trustee, whose father had preceded Woods McCahill as president of the board. "One of our trustees' stepchildren was expelled for having a bad LSD trip. The state police came up to the school, and they arrested this kid. It was an embarrassing situation for everybody."

Jock Conyngham was intractable in other ways: "One day in English class, this new teacher was standing by the window, with his arms behind his back. He said, 'Master Conyngham should retire to his room to don a pair of socks.' I said, 'All of Master Conyngham's socks are in the dryer.' The class cracked up. He turned around and said, 'If you can't attire yourself properly, just leave.' Another time we got into a brutal argument in class about his teaching. He said, 'Anyone I've ever taught will know his Shakespeare.' I said, 'But if none of us ever wants to look at it again, what good is it?' It wasn't until he once saw me tying flies at Gus Gurney's, who was retired, that he changed his tune, and I could do no wrong in his book.

"Gurney was one of the people I respected the most. I used to fish with him, yet I had an argument with him already when I was a prep. I told him, 'I don't see how you can think it's a good idea to be isolated from women for four years.' I had grown up with three sisters and always found it easy to get along with women – unlike many guys in my class who sweated blood at mixers. I think what helped to keep me going at the school was knowing that Hotchkiss would go coed my senior year."

While Jock was an expectant upper mid, R. "Penn" Hulburd was a senior. Though coeducation would come too late for Penn, he had no regrets and confirms Bill Olsen's assessment of the boys' attitude: "I think the majority of my classmates were against coeducation, probably for all the wrong reasons. I think they said, 'I put up with it. Why should others have it any easier?' But I think it was also a matter of pride. The school was tougher then, no doubt about it, and there were more requirements. We had to go to breakfast. We got a cut if we missed. We had the waiter system. They never had a white coat big enough to fit me, and I could barely move my arms to pick up the tray. You remember that. The master sat there at the head of the table, and he served everybody. Even at the table he would start asking questions about courses. There was no free time. There was a lot of stress, a lot of pressure. Now looking back, I'm personally happy that I was in an all-male class. The world on the outside is tough. I work long hours with the Japanese, and the Hotchkiss of my time helped to give me the competitive edge.

"One of the people who had a great influence on me was Nels Corey [football coach and athletic director, 1966 to 1980]. Here was this legend who instilled cold fear in you if you didn't give him two hundred percent. I remember one game where we needed a couple of inches to make a first down, and we didn't make it. I had been playing the whole game and was totally delirious and exhausted. I came off the field thinking we had really given it our all. Nels Corey came over to me, and in his very eloquent language let me know I hadn't given it my best, that I had given up. I then realized he may have been right, that I had perhaps felt too much weight on my shoulders and was giving in to self-pity. It was shortly thereafter that I found a note in my mailbox from Nels – actually a four-page handwritten letter. He talked about the season, and he talked about the heartaches, and he said, 'Penn, I know you took a lot of this to heart, and I think you did a heck of a job.' That's the kind of a relationship we didn't want to lose.

"Once the decision to go coed was made, Bill Olsen lost little time in bringing sex education to Hotchkiss. He hired this gentleman by the name of Dr. [John] Money, who was supposedly a leader in the sex education field. It was in the middle of the winter, at that point when kids are probably in the lowest state of mind. I remember Blair Torrey stopped our hockey practice early and yelled, 'Everybody get up to the auditorium for this important lecture.' So the whole school is in the auditorium, all of the faculty, many of the wives. This guy gets up in front of everybody, real intellectual looking, and he starts talking in a monotone about sex education. It was just the blandest, boringest speech for about an hour. Everybody was on the verge of falling asleep, at which point he says, 'Now for the slide show.' And this screen comes down, and the first slide comes on, and there's a woman sprawled out on a bed, with a guy doing something to her, I don't know what it was. The kids went wild. There were more slides, one right after another for about twenty minutes. The one I remember is of this Marine with his privates hanging out and he's shooting down the enemy, and Blair Torrey in the back is howling that this is the best thing he had ever seen in his life. And way in the back I could hear Mrs. Olsen going, 'Oh, my God!' The place just erupted, and people were standing on their chairs. Imagine the scene in the dreary winter, late afternoon, four hundred males! The slides stopped, and on goes the movie. It was about this guy in a girl's room, chasing her and again doing all kinds of acts, all totally undisguised. That was a legend, absolute legend – and in a mandatory meeting of the school. It went on for more than two hours. We later learned that Dr. Money had a theory that if he showed this sort of material long enough, the viewers would get tired of it and lose their interest in pornography. It didn't work at Hotchkiss. Even as he left, the kids were yelling, 'More, more, more!' Next morning in chapel, Bill Olsen stood up, and sort of red-faced, announced, 'Dr. Money will not be coming back to the school. Thank you for attending.'

"I don't know if that sex lecture had anything to do with it, but the following year we had the Dubious Film Society. The president of the school and the guy who was the captain of the football team the year ahead of me used to order these films from New York. We would hold our weekly St. Luke's Society meetings in a room underneath the library, and we would show these films. The St. Luke's meetings got bigger and bigger every week, and the faculty couldn't figure out what was going on. And we'd be howling, just howling in there with these films. There was the evening we were in the St. Luke's room seeing one of the films, and we decided to streak. At that time streaking was very big. So, everyone took off his clothes, and we came charging out of the side door of the library and ran around the circle – a whole string of naked bodies. Peter Adams, who was in the admissions office, was just at that moment coming out of the front door to greet one of the first female candidates and her father who had driven up. Their car was coming into the circle when this vast herd of naked men ran right by them. There's a picture of that in our yearbook."

xv /   For Jock Conyngham, who today is putting his Yale Forestry School degree to work in Tanzania, the long wait was worth it: "The change of mood that Hotchkiss went through with coeducation was incredible. All of a sudden you'd look around the room and people were smiling. It was like a collective sigh of relief. The school had been kidding itself to have held off that long."

There were also some subtler shifts. "It was terrific to see girls on a daily basis and be able to be attracted to women my own age as opposed to masters' wives who happened to be pretty," says Stuart Watson, who had the looks which probably could have overcome a few years of age difference, and other barriers, too.

Nationwide, the tumultuous period which had begun in the late sixties was just about over by the fall of 1974. With the winding-down of the war in Vietnam and the abolition of the draft, the confrontational attitudes on campuses suddenly faded away. Not coincidentally, the phasing out of the GO program the previous summer was as much due to a lack of student and faculty interest as to the unavailability of funds. The issue which now aroused perhaps the greatest passion at the Hotchkiss School concerned parietal regulations. Although the administration made it amply clear that no interdorm visiting – also referred to as *visitation* – would be allowed, the theoretical arguments continued. Would such visiting encourage wholesome conversation or create an obligation to have sex? There were endless attempts to refine the definition of what constituted an open door. How many inches? What was the difference between a crack and ajar?

To implement the no visiting rule, the initial contingent of eighty-eight girls was to be housed in Buehler Hall, which was completely refurbished, including the installation of bathtubs (but initially lacking in provisions for the greater privacy favored by girls, such as doors on toilets and individual shower stalls). To feed the expanded student body, the traditional assigned seating in the dining hall was to be abolished in favor of cafeteria-style self-service. Because of limited seating capacity in chapel, only half of the school would be accommodated at a time, in effect reducing required attendance at morning chapel for each student from twice a week to once. (Sunday services were not compulsory, and the additional influx of attendees was not expected to exceed capacity.) To be sure, provisions were also made for girls' athletics, with part of the admissions process taking into account the athletic abilities of each applicant. And there were other considerations as well. "The admissions department was at that time run by Peter Adams," notes Stuart Watson, "and he certainly had good taste in women. But these women weren't just good-looking – and I don't mean that in any sexist way – they were bright as hell. I thought they really found the most qualified young ladies in every respect to come to Hotchkiss to start off coeducation."

On the human relations side, a professional team of outside consultants, members of the Harvard Counseling Institute, hovered on the scene to instruct the Hotchkiss community on the proper way to respond to the incoming females. "You would have thought we had never seen a woman or had a mother or a sister," grumbles Bob Hawkins.

Among the purely cosmetic changes instituted: the opening line of the school song, "Fair Hotchkiss, we thy loyal sons . . ." became, "Fair Hotchkiss! Hear our song of praise."

Over the previous couple of years or so, several faculty wives had taken up teaching; now, to accommodate the additional classroom load of the enlarged school, a group of faculty newcomers was also brought on board. "Bill told me, 'I'm hiring you as though you were a senior member of the faculty,'" says Blanche B. Hoar, who came with twenty-seven years of experience teaching art at Ethel Walker and four years at Smith. "He said, 'You're to be the symbolic woman for all the new female teachers that are to be hired. You're to be the mother, the senior woman for the girls.' When I told him that that was a heavy load, Bill said, 'Your shoulders are broad, and they're going to have to be broad and strong because you're going to carry much of a burden of jealousy and even hatred. Believe me, I know.'"

Despite a deliberate decision to start coeducation with students spread as evenly as possible in the four grades, the first group entering in the fall of 1974 included only four preps. Among them was Sarah Conyngham, for whom special provisions had been made by her brother Jock: "Sarah had not been altogether happy in her grade school in

Pennsylvania; so I asked all my friends to keep an eye out for her, check in with her, say hello to her. They all liked her, and they'd all sit and eat meals with her, invite her over to the table. Our group all had long hair, all the good athletes, the troublemakers. The teachers called us 'the Blond Bombers.' So Sarah was sitting around with the Blond Bombers all the time, which was a fast way to a bad reputation. She loved all the male attention. Finally, a month or six weeks into the school year, I saw her at a party where there was drinking. I dragged her aside and asked her what she was doing there. She said, 'What are *you* doing here?' I said, 'Not a bad point. But,' I said, 'you've only been here six weeks. You have a worse reputation than I've developed in four years. If you get kicked out, it'll really hurt our parents, and I'm going to be furious.' That toned her down for about a month. I wound up having to be the enforcer a lot."

Sarah Conyngham's roommate, also one of the original four preps, was Carolyn C. Wilcox: "That first year Hotchkiss brought in an unbelievable number of really good-looking girls. They formed sort of a clique and were called 'niblets.' I was a naive prep, and coming from an all-girls school in England, I didn't have any of the right clothes and I didn't do my hair right. I remember one of these girls trying to dress me to make me look a little better. The big thing in those days – besides wearing clogs in the ice and snow in the middle of the winter, which was crazy because you could kill yourself – was that you had on your shirt and your sweater, and you turned the cuffs back and folded them up to your elbow. She was doing this all to me, and I said to her, 'Oh, but it's freezing out.' She said, 'Sometimes you have to suffer to be beautiful.' She trained me so well that before long I said to one of my friends, 'You know, you really could be cute if you just tried.'

"I never had any problems with classes. Bob Hawkins was one of those most strongly opposed to having the girls come, and I was the first girl he taught. There were sixteen of us in his prep English class, and I was the only girl. In one respect, he didn't discriminate. For the first half of the year, he failed all of us on every paper. We all felt intimidated. This helped to build a strong bond between me and the boys in that class which would last throughout my four years. So prep English was a part of my foundation, not only academically, but in terms of friendship. I think Bob Hawkins called me 'Miss Wilcox' the whole year. He didn't seem to be able to bring himself to say 'Carolyn.' But I eventually won him over. I did quite well in that class, and he himself would make an example of me to the boys, saying, 'Well, she could do it. Why couldn't you get this right?' I learned early on to try not to be too smart around the boys I liked."

Carolyn Wilcox, today Carolyn Wilcox Galiette, details the long-awaited getting together: "Evening study hall ended at nine-thirty, at which time practically the whole school would rush behind Buehler. Everyone would run around and have pizza and kiss their boyfriends for half an hour. That was the big hangout. Then on Saturday, there were movies. Unless you were going with a boy, you always sort of hung around in the back, standing there looking as if you just came in. Then if the guy you had your eye on came in, you could pretend you just arrived and hope he would ask you to sit with him. If he didn't, you could pretend you were just leaving anyway. There were all these little stratagems.

"Sarah Conyngham and I were on Mr. Coughlin's corridor in Buehler. It was a corner room on the first floor, as far from his apartment as we could be. We used to have boys come in through the window and use our room as a transit point. The way I discovered it was one time in the middle of the winter we woke up in the morning and saw these huge hiking boot tracks across our floor and out the door. Someone had come in the window at night, walked through our room to go visit his girlfriend. Neither Sarah nor I woke up and heard him.

"The next time was quite different. Someone had been visiting his girlfriend, and we were startled by this guy rushing in. We had bunk beds and I was in the lower bunk. The guy flew under my bunk, and he was lying there panting real loud. I said, 'What's going on?' He said, 'Mr. Coughlin's in the hall!' Sarah and I are thinking, 'We're going to get thrown out of school. Our careers are over.' The guy was breathing really hard, and we heard these footsteps going up and down the hall. We were scared to death. Finally, everything quieted down, and we had this guy get out as fast as we could."

"The strictest rule was being caught in Buehler," explains Jock Conyngham. "It meant instant kick-out. I was the first to step into the girls' dorm that fall. A guy named Chip Halle and I. It was purely an exploratory foray. I remember I had a soccer injury. I was part-hobbling; my heart was throbbing. At seventeen or eighteen you have a certain thirst for danger, no matter what happens. The corridor master on the first floor of Buehler was Dave Coughlin, and he had the looks and attitude of a state trooper. So we opened the door to the first floor, and nothing's going on. We didn't want to chance anything there and went up to the second floor. There we started by knocking on the nearest door. Almost right away the door opened, and there were two girls. One of them I knew from the English course we both took. The other was a remarkably unattractive woman. That's interesting only insofar as she was the one who threw her head back and screamed at the top of her lungs. It's a horribly sexist thing to say, but she had no reason to scream.

"Of course, we turned around and bolted. Halle, who was captain of the track team, sprinted down the hallway and out of the building. I went clumping after him and somehow made it out of the dorm. Halle still does his imitation of sitting outside in the bushes, waiting for this hobbling figure. I had that torn muscle. The pain was so bad I fell down every once in a while. But I was going as fast as I could.

"On our next foray my leg was fine. This time Halle was going up to see his girlfriend on the third floor. I went in to visit my friend Lindy on the first floor. I was there only a little while when there was a hard, sharp knock on the door. It could only be Coughlin, the dorm master. Lindy was a small woman, but she slammed me against the wall in her haste to get me under her bed. I lay there for the next fifteen or twenty minutes, heart pounding. Then Lindy kicked me out, and I went back to my room – wondering how my friend Halle was making out. When I walked in, there was Halle sitting in my room, and he laughed and laughed. He hadn't been able to find his girlfriend on the third floor. She was off in somebody else's room; so he left, and on his way out, knocked on Lindy's door, pretending he was the dorm master.

"Coeducation wasn't exactly as I had expected it to be," concludes Jock. "Kids didn't throw themselves into each other's arms like hamsters. There wasn't much in the way of experimental sex or anything like that. It just didn't happen. By the end of that fall, there were maybe eight, ten, at the most a dozen relationships."

Jock Conyngham's classmate Katha Diddel, who had transferred from the Dalton School in New York as a senior partly because her brother had gone to Hotchkiss, experienced her share of novelty: "For one thing, it was the first time I started doing all-nighters. I was taking AP [Advance Placement] English with Uncle Roy Smith. Most of the guys had worked their way up through the various levels and knew what to expect. It was the toughest course I ever took, and I ended up studying for it two times a day, six days a week. I remember I wrote seventeen drafts of my first paper before Uncle Roy would accept it. A lot of evenings I'd go over to his apartment with other people, and we'd work with him through the various points. We'd get back to the dorms around midnight, and I'd continue working in my room. When you live at home, you don't do all-nighters. Uncle Roy had a real concern for the integrity of your work, but you felt he also had tremendous concern for you personally. He had a way of teasing people without being intimidating, and I think of him with fondness to this day."

Katha, now Katha Diddel Warren, also became the first girl to be suspended from Hotchkiss: "There was a lot of drinking on campus, and I was known to be very straight. Then one night at a big dance, I was invited to indulge in the evil alcohol. I had never had a drink at Hotchkiss before. I'm known for being a bad drinker, and that was the time I had been doing all-nighters. I happened to walk out of the dance and ran right into Mr. Kellogg, sort of a looming figure coming towards me.

"The school then had a two-chance system, and I was suspended for a week. It was a gentle punishment, but it was traumatic for me and a shocker for my parents. When I called them up, they sort of said, 'Excuse me?' as if they hadn't heard right."

For Katha Diddel that first year was, otherwise, very much a honeymoon with a lot of expectations and realizations: "I remember early on Mr. Stone cautioning me about starting out with too high a profile. He had been my brother's math teacher, one of the old guard and not at all keen on the idea of women coming to the school. But once we arrived, he was wonderful, very warm. He saw a lot of us start out as proctors, with all the younger girls looking up to us, and we hadn't gone through the usual three years of having to earn that position. 'If you start with too high a profile,' Mr. Stone said, 'it doesn't give you anywhere to go.' Another time he told me how the English tailored their suits. I didn't know anything about tailoring at the time. [Katha now imports specialty linens from China through her own company, Twin Panda, Inc.] He said, 'When they make a suit, to make it perfect they always put one button a little bit over to the side.' I had to think about that for a while, but obviously the lesson was that things don't have to be perfect to be perfect.

"I came to understand in other ways what George Stone meant about a low profile. Being a proctor, a lot of issues came up. Girls being away from home came to me with problems that I hadn't really dealt with before. Had I been at Hotchkiss for four years, I would have had a better sense for their questions, whether about drinking, sex, or what have you. One of the touchiest issues was what to do when several girls accused one girl on the corridor of stealing their clothes. Fortunately, that stopped after the word got around.

"A lot of people at Hotchkiss felt the pressure of money – having it or not having it. The father of one of my best friends was a pilot for American Airlines, and she had a picture of him on the dresser in his uniform. She said somebody walked into her room and asked her if he owned the airline. It was very matter of fact, as if that would have been the normal thing. She still remembers that. It stuck in her mind as sort of the attitude that prevailed at Hotchkiss.

"The attitude which I will remember is of the close friendships and warmth from everyone. Mr. Olsen was teaching, and one of the girls had a birthday, and he actually came in with a birthday cake. No one could believe it. It was something he probably had never done before. He was always congenial and kind. He was always interested in talking to us, and he knew all our names. He was great, and I think he was excited about the changes in the school."

Katha Diddel Warren in 1987 became a trustee, the second alumna to be elected to the board. Sarah Thornton, who entered in the fall of '74 as an upper mid, was the first. She was elected in 1984.

That pioneering class of '75 was a memorable one in other respects. For one thing, it was Katha Diddel's classmate Raymond J. McGuire who, in 1985, became the first black graduate to be elected to the Hotchkiss board. Recognized already in the fifth grade of the Dayton, Ohio, public school system as a promising student, he had transferred to a private day school, Miami Valley, and was eventually accepted by Andover, Deerfield, Choate, and several other eastern schools before settling on Hotchkiss.

Ray McGuire: "I couldn't have been at a better place at a better time to benefit from coeducation. The transition that occurred during that year from an all-male school to the coed school I know and love was as smooth as I think it could have been anywhere. From the administrative standpoint Hotchkiss for me will always be the school of the O, and the O was a fantastic leader. He had the uncanny ability to remember each student's name and to know something about that student. There was a terrific sense of rapport, which you could feel at events such as the first annual Brother Olsen bump contest. The bump was a dance, and the O was a part of it. To see someone who had been through the times that the school had been through and had weathered it with such dignity, to see him mingle and dance with the students was quite phenomenal. I can say that was a great year in Hotchkiss history."

Ray McGuire had a heretofore undisclosed role in an unforgettable event of that year: "This is the first time I'm going on record as being in any way connected with the midnight scream. Not to name names, but the other perpetrators were my classmate Mike Carroll and Ron Carlson, who was a teacher. Basically, we decided to wake up the town of Lakeville by having all the students at the school open up their windows at midnight and scream at the top of their lungs. It took a great deal of organizing and the timing was perfect. At exactly midnight every window flew open and out came a prolonged, sort of upwelling scream. I remember sitting in Dana Dorm, in my room on the second floor, and looking at the lights in Lakeville as they all began to come on. What we hadn't figured on was that at exactly this moment, the O would happen to be driving through the main gates. There was quite a commotion then around the school. The assistant athletic director, Rick DelPrete, who lived in Dana, hopped into a station wagon in his bathrobe and drove to the middle of the circle, trying to figure out what had happened. He never checked his own dorm. Perhaps he and everyone else thought that Buehler, the girls' dorm, was being attacked.

"The O handled it with style. He called an all-school meeting and vowed to get to the bottom of it, but he didn't look at all stern about it. I can remember at one point Art White, the dean of students, asking me if I had anything to do with the midnight scream. It was in the spirit of, 'Now you didn't have anything to do with *that*, did you, Raymond?' It was as if he was expecting me to deny it, which I of course did. George Stone, my guardian angel during and after Hotchkiss, also questioned me, but more in the tone of trying to find out something for which he should commend me. So the midnight scream was allowed to fade into history – but not before the O singled it out in his graduation address as an example of school spirit."

A graduate of Harvard College, Harvard Business School, and Harvard Law School, Ray McGuire is a corporate takeover specialist with Wasserstein, Perella & Co. in New York. An impeccable dresser with a towering, athletic figure and movie star looks, Flamin' Raymond, as he was known at Hotchkiss, treasures one other memory of the school: "I remember as an assignment in English class searching for a scarlet-crested cladonia, which is a rare growth that Blair Torrey said existed around the campus. I spent weeks searching for this scarlet-crested cladonia. Whether or not I'd find it was not important to Blair Torrey. What was important to him was that the city kid from Dayton go out and interact with the natural environment of Hotchkiss – the woods, the lakes, the countryside. Every free moment I would go out and search the woods looking for the scarlet-crested cladonia. It was an effort no less relentless than the search for Jean Valjean. I can remember spending the entire spring semester roaming around outdoors until I finally found that scarlet-crested cladonia."

xvi /   After several months of living within easy access of each other, the inevitable between liberated teenage boys and no-less-liberated teenage girls happened, that unwanted eventuality which Peter Adams had wished to talk through fully ahead of time. "When the girl found out she was pregnant," says Sarah Conyngham, "I thought, 'I fear for this girl's mental health.' Everybody knew about it."

"The school didn't know about it," says Sarah's brother Jock. "The girl took a regular weekend to go to New York and have the abortion she wanted. The problem was that her boyfriend was already on general probation, and he knew there was no way the school was going to let him take a weekend. So, as soon as he was through with classes and athletics that day, he borrowed a car from a kitchen crew member he was friends with and drove to New York. Of course, the word got around, and he was discovered to be off the school grounds, and the whole story came out. When he returned, the faculty met to decide his fate. The official charge against him made no mention of the pregnancy for which he was responsible, but merely that he had violated general probation. I found out that everyone on the faculty except two voted to expel him, which really embittered him. He thought most of the guys on the faculty would go to bat for him. Of his two votes, one came from Leif Thorne-Thomsen. He always championed the underdogs. The other vote came from Bob Hawkins, and when he voted, apparently the entire faculty swung around to stare at one of their most conservative, traditional members. For a moment, the Hawk sat there, absorbing his colleagues' outrage with a self-righteous smile and then gave a hint of a shrug: 'After all, the boy was only doing what a gentleman should.'"

The girl fared better; she was allowed to return that fall and graduated the following year.

"It was a big scandal because both of the people involved were respected," comments Stuart Watson. "The male individual had been sort of a role model to me, and I felt bad for him – especially for having to leave so near the end of his four years."

Blanche Hoar offers her rationale: "I think the fact that the boy was so charming *and* several years older than the girl swayed several of us. He had also taken the sex education course, which the girl hadn't; so he should have known better."

The entire incident was a reflection of the school's confusion in attempting to find its way under the new circumstances. Another difficult and not entirely expected challenge involved the faculty wives. "When we first came, wives poured tea after games and were expected to do a whole range of volunteer tasks, including informal counseling on their husband's corridor," says Jim Marks, then the newly appointed dean of faculty. "I had been brought up in that tradition, and my wife pitched right in. Then suddenly there were women on campus as students, there were women on campus as faculty. They were being paid for things, and yet you had this tremendous cadre of wonderful teachers' wives who had done this voluntarily all these years. It was a whole new ball game. Were they still to do the volunteer work? There were some very awkward times when some of the new faculty wives said, 'The hell with you. I'm here as a wife, not as a volunteer worker for the school.'"

For some of the traditional faculty wives who now took up teaching, the transition was also not easy. "I remember Steve Bolmer telling me I shouldn't expect to get paid because my husband already was on the school's payroll," says Marilyn "Sam" Coughlin, wife of the much-feared (by the boys trying to sneak in) Buehler Hall Cerberus, Dave

Coughlin, who first came to Hotchkiss as a chemistry teacher in 1961. "I don't think Steve was trying to put me down. He was merely stating what he honestly believed, though that made it no less upsetting."

Turning more than eighty years of the school's most fundamental tradition on its head also had unexpected positive results. For one thing, a number of the male faculty members now began to experience some of the same magic that their boy-oriented colleagues had previously been privy to: how thoroughly they could give themselves to these girls because of the affinity they felt for their sex as translated or sublimated into a pure, all-giving love.

This was no more blatantly obvious of anyone than that veteran teacher George Stone. Adamantly, passionately, almost violently opposed to coeducation, he was converted within practically the first eyeblink at his new charges. In periodic rhapsodies in the *Alumni Magazine* he unabashedly shared his feelings:

"All rumors to the contrary, I consider that I had been looking forward to a coeducational Hotchkiss. I had heard all manner of good things on all sides. But this good! Not even the wildest advocate of coeducation had prepared me in any measure for what is happening here. The gentling. The warming. The smiles. I never knew there'd be all these uncounted extra benefits, flung about the place casually like so many peanuts. Oh, lots of people had pointed out with leers that there might be some girl who would develop a crush on me. At my age and with my figure that seemed a) unlikely, and b) vaguely ridiculous. But why didn't somebody warn me that I'd have my crushes too? . . .

"The Taft-Hotchkiss football game. In Watertown. I'm on the sideline, drinking a can of ginger ale that I had just paid twenty-five hard-earned cents for. A girl on the Hotchkiss field hockey team, still aglow following a hard game, turns to me and says, 'Do you think I could have one sip, sir?' Is there a more ridiculous sentence in the English language? She calls me *sir*, and yet she's proposing to share my ginger ale. I pass the can over, aware that she doesn't realize the priceless thing she had told me. . . .

"These days I wake up with a recurring nightmare in which the Board of Trustees decides to go back to the all-boy days gone by. At odd moments, I find myself casting about for some word a little better than coeducation for the lovely thing we are undergoing. I think I may have stumbled on it the other day while poring over an old book by a very wise man.

"I think the word I've been looking for may be *education*."

No one was more amused by George Stone's transmutation than Bill Olsen: "George Stone was one of those stirring around on the edges trying to kill coeducation. Five minutes after the girls came, he was acting as if he had invented coeducation. Finally, we had to tell him, 'There are still boys here, George. What about them?'"

"The unhappiest memory I have of the transition to coeducation," recalls English teacher Dick Hughes, "is that some of the male students who were leaders in their upper middle and senior classes were over-shadowed. Everyone at the school was focused on how the girls were doing, and at the alumni reunions the girls were the ones in the spot-light. Some of those girls were really dynamite pioneers, and they relished the attention. They also became politically active and ended up running many aspects of the school – without putting in the usual years of 'heeling' time."

This did not lead to an outright declaration of war between the boys and girls, but rather to a subtle standoff, or at least a withdrawal of the previous special privileges. "The guys treated us more or less as one of the guys when we first came," says Carolyn Wilcox. "My prep year I played stickball with them, and they were very accepting and included us in things. I never was asked to play stickball after my prep year. As lower mids, we were no longer a closely knit, homogeneous group. I found myself spending more time with other girls."

Sarah Conyngham, who had the added advantage as a prep of having a brother among the Blond Bombers, details what she encountered over the next three years: "The senior class had graduated, and there were a whole lot of new people whom I didn't know. I'd had a fantastic summer working on a ranch in Montana, which was a great contrast to my little room on the third floor of Buehler, which was cold and had one dormer window. I began to spend a lot of time at my desk and grew more and more depressed. I must have lost fifty pounds in the next few weeks, and I clammed right up. When my parents came for a visit, they didn't recognize me and walked right by me. I'd sit on the side of the road and hope somebody would kidnap me, just take me away from there. Hotchkiss was no longer fun and new and different. It was the same and would be the same forever.

"I thought it was peculiar that nobody took me aside and said, 'You need help.' I didn't feel much like talking anyway. My advisor was a person I couldn't relate to – though I did have some great teachers. My art teacher, Mrs. Hoar, will stand out in my mind forever. She demanded peak performance; and if she didn't think you were trying your hardest, she was furious and showed it. She'd do things like kick a wastecan across the room, a tin wastecan. That makes a big sound in a quiet room. Or she'd say, 'Why do you continue to waste your time?' And her eyes would blaze, and her hair was swept back. She was suddenly behind you, and if you weren't trying, not concentrating, not on top of your game, you could expect to hear an explosion. It often happened. Or you'd hear her do it to another student, but that was enough to motivate you. She had a temper which she used to produce results. Or she'd come into class raging about some political situation. I never read a paper when I was there; so I wasn't aware of those things. But it was actually her positive side that I most appreciated. She could be very supportive if you were having trouble. It was my own choice that I didn't at that time want to open up to anybody. One of my first paintings was called 'Fear,' and she really encouraged me. She didn't tell you how to do something. She would talk about the concept, the goal. She would say, 'Now, what are you trying to do here? What is this area?' She left the decisions to the student.

"I got through this period of growing up which was not easy for me. After Hotchkiss, it took another five years or so. I went to Brown, and along the way I got interested in ecology and continued to paint. Today, my time is filled with a one-year-old and a three-year-old. [She is now Sarah C. Raithel.] I've been drawing but have trouble painting because the kids eat paint. I look forward to when they'll be old enough and I can go back to painting."

Blanche Hoar, who resurrected the art department from its gradual decline since the retirement of Tom Blagden in the late 1950s, adds her perspective: "Right from the beginning, Steve Bolmer was calling us, 'Cut and Paste.' I was serious about teaching 'art' per se, but I never thought of it primarily as that. I was teaching people to release their creativity, to release their narrowed eyes, to take off their blinders, to understand themselves. I saw teaching art as a gateway to the maturing process, where it often is so very, very lonely – yet it can be so joyous that you can hardly stand it. I don't know if Steve ever caught on."

Not surprisingly, Blanche Hoar became a confidante of the headmaster's wife: "Jean Olsen once said to me, 'I don't understand my husband. He's away all day, and when he comes home for dinner and to sleep, he doesn't release himself from that hold the school has on him.' Another time she visited me when I was in my garden pulling down wild grapevine that was climbing all the way up this huge tree. The tree actually had dents from the turning of the vine. I had managed to get quite a lot of it down, and when Jean arrived, here's this mountain of vine that I'd pulled down. She said, 'Why're you doing this?' I said, 'Because it's killing that tree.' Jean said, 'No one around here would care whether it was killing the tree or not.' And she got on the other end of the vine and started pulling along with me."

Despite her resolve to maintain a distance from the school, Jean Olsen welcomed Blair Torrey's invitation to take over an English class. "I taught the changing role of women in literature," says Jean. "I didn't want to teach the angry polemicists like Germaine Greer. In the first place, the students wouldn't have understood it, and in the second place it was irrelevant. But when you look back and try to think what was happening long ago to women like Edith Wharton, Anna James, Charlotte Brontë, or whomever, it was very interesting. And I'd say, 'Well, what do you think your wife should be like?' The boys in the class would say, 'She's going to be home, taking care of the children.' The girls would say, 'Like hell she is!' And then you'd start to discuss these things, and it was fascinating."

"For the girls, Mrs. Olsen definitely was there if you needed her," says Elisabeth D. "Lisa" Cholnoky, who graduated a year after Sarah

Conyngham. It was partly because of her older brother, Tom Cholnoky '74 – one of the *Whipping Post* founders and today vice president
in investment research at Goldman, Sachs in New York – that Lisa decided on Hotchkiss rather than Miss Porter's: "When I came to visit
my brother one weekend, I became enamored of the place. Hotchkiss
was in one respect almost genderless. There was none of that attitude,
'I'm going to go out and burn my bra and make an issue of it.' We
were comfortable wearing our brothers' Levi corduroys, and there was
a sense of family spirit. It wasn't a question of boys versus girls, but of
community. We were allowed to visit each other in the common
rooms at certain times. I think St. Paul's was at that time the first
school that was testing more extensive interdorm visiting. Many of us
frankly didn't care for it. It's a difficult time in your life, and at that age
you should still have a sense of privacy.

"Of my teachers, Geoff Marchant had the greatest impact," says
Lisa, now a trustee and member of the Strategic Planning Committee.
"The beauty of Geoff is that everything is different about him, and
he's not at all predictable. In my upper mid year, we were doing the
romantics. We had to memorize a lot of poems, and we used to have
poetry challenges between Geoff Marchant's and Blair Torrey's class.
A few years ago I was visiting here and walking down the halls. Geoff
was teaching a class, and when he saw me, he said, 'Come on in, sit
down.' He was doing *King Lear*, and he got to the mad storm scene,
and he said, 'Lisa, what do you remember about Lear?' I said, 'Well, I
can't quote anything from *Lear*, but I can quote you *The Daffodils*.' I
proceeded to recite this poem, and the kids in the class are looking at
me like, 'Where's she coming from?' This was more than eight years
after I had graduated."

An inevitable footnote to coeducation – and no easier to deal with
than that first pregnancy – was the first serious complaint of impropriety involving a male faculty member and a female student. It was
lodged in 1979 by an irate father who discovered that his daughter had
been sharing a room with her biking coach on an extended trip. The

accused was the school's perennial liberal, now known for reaching out to coeds no less than he had to blacks. Although Leif Thorne-Thomsen was exonerated, the incident raised the question of where to draw the parameters in faculty-student relationships with the *opposite* sex?

Another question unrelated to the foregoing case but receiving increasing attention in our national life: what constitutes sexual harassment and how to deal with it?

"Inappropriate personal conduct by any member of the faculty toward a student is a betrayal of a fundamental trust," states the school's present headmaster, Dr. Robert A. Oden, Jr. "Such conduct can never be excused and will not be tolerated – no matter how agonizing the necessary action may be."*

xvii / I mplementing coeducation and opening the doors to more than a token number of minority students were but two of Bill Olsen's triad of main accomplishments; the third and perhaps most notable was the relationship he established with the alumni and alumnae – and what that meant for the development of the school.

"A head has to take his entire institution as his responsibility," Olsen says, in an allusion to the absenteeism charge which had caused such a flap with students. "That often requires going out to where your constituents are rather than their coming to you."

Explains David Luke, who headed the capital fund drive at that time, "I told Bill very clearly, 'To get this job done, we're going to have to pull you out of the school, and the main burden of traveling is going to be on you.' We also told Bill, 'Once you pull someone out of an in-

---

*Shortly before we went to press, new questions arose about Leif Thorne-Thomsen's conduct, and after a thorough investigation, it was deemed necessary to separate him from the school. As in Greek tragedy, it would seem that the very qualities which had made Leif Thorne-Thomsen such a heroic figure for some students also harbored elements which produced an altogether different effect.

stitution, it's very hard to go back and reenter. You have to recognize it may prove to be a one-way process. So the cost may be more than a temporary one.'"

Certainly Bill Olsen had at one point found those words to be uncomfortably true. His efforts also earned him the temporary epithet "Dollar Bill."

"Bill was a master of reading the signposts of a situation and then acting," observes history teacher Robert Barker. "I think he read that the school needed a sound financial base, it needed an endowment, it needed buildings to bring it into the realm of a strong school. And that's what he set out to provide."

When Olsen assumed his duties as the school's sixth headmaster, the total endowment hovered around the $2 million mark. By the late 1970s, that figure stood around $25 million, all but a small fraction of it made up from alumni gifts. In the same period, an impressive array of major new buildings sprouted up: the new Main complex, Walker Auditorium, A. Whitney Griswold Science Building, and Dana and Watson dormitories. The biggest single gift led to the refurbishing of the old Alumni dormitory and to its renaming as Tinker Hall. There also was what Bill Olsen likes to call the dream wish-list category: the Tom Schmidt Hockey Rink, Ford Indoor Tennis Courts, Cullman Paddle Tennis and Squash Courts, and Fulton Field House. "Never have so many come so far to raise so much from so few," quipped a wealthy Dayton alumnus in welcoming an Olsen-headed fund-raising team.

"It is true that during the time that I was headmaster, far more money was raised than ever before," explains Bill. "But I believe strongly that institutions raise the money and individuals by and large don't. You have to have the mechanics through which people are informed about what the institution is doing. You also have to make sure that in the heart of the institution you've got the strongest possible argument for giving money to it."

Rusty Chandler offers a more graphic perspective on what fund raising is all about: "I like to tell people that when I was director of admissions, everybody wanted to take me out to dinner. Now, as director of development, nobody wants to see me. Bill Olsen was never perceived in the latter capacity, as a fund raiser, and he would feel cheapened if I used that term. He didn't like asking for money. Bill didn't come from money, and he didn't feel comfortable ever asking for money. I'm shameless, but Olsen was not. I was with him on a couple of occasions when he did ask for money and was shot down both times. Those are the only two occasions I heard him make a pitch for funds. But a lot of people came forth and were generous to Hotchkiss during this period. They respected Bill because they recognized what he was able to do during that period of monumental turbulence. From 1967 to 1973, some schools absolutely capsized or turned topsy-turvy and went in a totally different direction. Hotchkiss never did, and it was because of Olsen's guidance. Then came coeducation, potentially dynamite for the school and a dynamite issue with alumni. I think Olsen was able to be very much the conservative, yet a liberal in certain respects as well. It was a good combination for the school and a terrific combination for fund raising."

There was one other critical ingredient, according to Bill Olsen: "I think one reason we were successful with the alumni on coeducation was that nobody could say Bill Olsen doesn't know Hotchkiss. All these people knew me as my father's son, as a Hotchkiss graduate, the whole business. Those roots go all the way back to 1909."

Hotchkiss had always taken a special pride in the relation with its alumni. "I asked one of the masters what, in his opinion, distinguished the school life of the boys this far from that of its predecessors," noted in 1897 the school's first headmaster, Edward Coy. "He immediately replied the unprecedented strength of school loyalty among both the boys in the school and the graduates. He reminded me of the enduring loyalty of the alumni after entering college, in comparison with other schools . . . and called to my mind the frequent visits of the old boys, who always came as guests of the masters, and who seem always ready to come, and whose presence is always helpful to the life and order of the school."

Along with this loyalty came the first contributions. In 1898, as a purely spontaneous gesture, the grateful parents of several former Hotchkiss boys added $900 to the scholarship fund.

The first to actively solicit funds was Joe Estill, when he launched the Edward G. Coy Scholarship drive in 1902. As the most popular teacher and one who knew every graduate of the school, Uncle Joe was the ideal person to make the appeal – in those days by a handwritten letter personalized in every detail. According to Estill, he raised or had pledges by 1903 for approximately $43,000, including the first thousand-dollar-plus gift. (It was from George Baker '95, who also donated Baker Field.) In subsequent years, Estill proudly referred to his efforts of "raising a sum of $100,000"; however, the total officially attributed to him by the trustees was $25,000.

As the school expanded in prestige and size under Dr. Buehler, so did the financial recognition from alumni, their families, and friends. The generosity and grand style of entertaining by the Buehlers was often reciprocated by gifts to the school. On the King's tenth anniversary as headmaster in 1914, the trustees congratulated Buehler for inspiring gifts amounting to nearly $150,000, while "the net earnings of the school have amounted to nearly $200,000."

Yet only several years later, the situation had drastically changed. Owing to a sharp increase in expenses following World War I, the school in the spring of 1920, for the first time in its history, faced an operating deficit. The trustees appealed to parents for contributions to cover the red ink for that year and launched the first major building and endowment drive. They appointed a master, C. H. Banks '02, to activate the alumni files and publish the *Hotchkiss Bulletin*.

Raising the tuition in the next two years, from $1,000 to $1,400, did not stem the red tide. "As a result of [the school's] growth and because the annual operation frequently showed a deficit, due to the quality of service and the large number of free scholars," noted a statement from the trustees shortly after Dr. Buehler died in 1924, "the school is today burdened with mortgage loans and outstanding notes totaling $98,500." To what extent the King's personally royal ways may have contributed to this state of affairs remained unsaid.

Spearheaded by the school's first alumnus trustee, Henry L. de-Forest, the building and endowment drive of 1920 was revitalized into a modern fund-raising campaign, complete with an outside consulting firm. All told, about $1.5 million was raised in the two phases of the drive, which financed the construction of Memorial and Alumni halls. The balance of that sum was set aside almost in its entirety to fund a retirement plan for masters.

Among the more notable steps taken by the interim headmaster, Walter Hull Buell, to put the school back in the black was to expand the enrollment from about 300 students to 325 without enlarging the facilities. "Mr. Buell instituted a regime of austerity and more or less stopped the outflow," GVS told Mrs. Wertenbaker. "When I came, with Harry Jones [the business manager] there watching over expenses like a cat over a mouse hole, we could balance the budget. But there was no money to spare, particularly. You had to be fairly careful. A school that was well run could pay its own way very well, but it was not a great money-making concern. You didn't make money enough to build buildings; so if you wanted to build, you had to get the extra money to do it."

The Duke had his own fund-raising philosophy, appropriate to that era: to rely almost exclusively on the generosity of those who "liked to give," rather than coaxing donations from large numbers of alumni. The school chapel, financed by Paul Block, and the library, donated by the Ford family, were only the most notable of such gifts. Other sizable donations, combined with the regular operating surpluses, paid for several more of the Duke's building ventures.* And GVS was keenly aware of who the people were that liked to give. He did not hesitate to notify them of any opportunity to be of help, even if it were a request for no more than a few hundred dollars to cover specialized therapy for a scholarship boy who had come down with infantile paralysis. (Mr. Paul Block, the addressee in this case, promptly responded.)

---

* The infirmary, for example, was entirely financed by pooling some twenty-five donors, headed by the Chrysler family; financing the Monahan Gymnasium, on the other hand, came primarily from those school surpluses.

The headmaster, however, was hardly indifferent to the school's alumni-at-large, whom he called a "vital connection" which "demanded much time, thought, and energy," as he details in his final notes: "A week or ten days immediately after Christmas was spent on a special trip westward, to meet and interview applicants for admission, and to talk informally with groups of alumni. By train I went to Buffalo (or Pittsburgh), then on to (2) Cleveland, (3) Toledo, (4) Detroit, and (5) Chicago. Sometimes the journey went on to Milwaukee, Minneapolis, and even to Duluth (where I remember seeing Mr. Coy's elder son). Occasionally Carle Parsons joined me on these trips. Mostly it was not possible for masters to get off from home during this particular week. (For me it was a sacrifice to miss a traditional week with my father in our log camp at Beaver Lake.)"

It was under GVS in 1931 that the Alumni Award was instituted. Popularly known as the Hotchkiss Man of the Year award, it was presented each spring at the great annual dinner in New York "to an alumnus who through personal achievement has brought honor and distinction to himself and to the school." The first recipient: the Rt. Rev. Henry Knox Sherrill '07, then on his way to becoming presiding bishop of the Episcopal Church.

As World War II was drawing to a close, there were trustees on the board who felt that more aggressive fund raising was needed. Having approved long-range construction plans, including the complete rebuilding of old Main, they called for "raising $1,500,000.00 for buildings and $500,000.00 for maintenance fund." Archibald Coolidge relates the melodrama that ensued: "Right after the war the Duke asked me to go on a money-raising campaign with him. He didn't want to do it, but Harry Luce and various people put pressure on him to do it. He once said to me, 'If I have to do it, I'll do it; and then I'll resign. Let somebody else do it.' When he asked me to go along, he said, 'If you don't go with me, they'll just make me take someone else whom I don't like and can't work with.' So I didn't have much choice. I certainly didn't want to see him resign. But we were completely inexperienced. He'd say, 'Now we'll go see Mrs. So-and-So.' We'd go and see

Plans drawn up in 1945 for rebuilding Main

her, and he'd chat about this, that and the other, and he'd never come down to the point that we'd like some money. We stayed with the Swifts, the meatpacking people in Chicago [and generous donors over the years]. They had this enormous house, with a great swimming pool in the middle of it. We had to go out after dinner, and the Swifts went to bed, and there wasn't anybody around when we got back. In the meantime, the butler had unpacked us, and he had the top of my pajamas with the bottom of his, and I had one of his socks with one of mine. Our rooms were about a quarter of a mile apart, the lights were off, and we couldn't find either room. The only thing we could find was the swimming pool. We roamed around about a half hour trying to get sorted out. The whole thing sort of went that way."

To be sure, G V S and Coolidge did not constitute the entire fund raising effort, and although the drive fell considerably short of its goal, it provided the wherewithal for the most ambitious construction project since the founding of the school – the new dining hall.

But a confluence of factors in the postwar years pointed to the need for a vastly different effort. Because tuition could not be raised enough to keep up with post-World War II inflation, there was no longer a small operating profit each year; on the contrary, the school was again beginning to show persistent and mounting deficits. This was particularly troublesome because Hotchkiss was financially one of the less endowed of the New England prep schools.*

At the same time a deficit in applicants meant that the school could no longer do the usual picking and choosing if the beds were to be filled. Typically, the proposed solution was for George Van Santvoord to step up his schedule for visiting the usual Hotchkiss enclaves. Enlisted to help out was Art Howe, the Duke's young faculty friend. After Howe's departure for Yale in 1951, George Kellogg took up the part-time task, which was perhaps aptly defined by the $500 added by the trustees to Kellogg's $3,400 salary for his efforts.

When G V S retired in 1955, the alumni office consisted principally of the very competent Vassar graduate Martha Shouse. She kept track of every alumnus, helped put together an alumni publication (the former *Bulletin* under G V S had become *Alumni News*), and typed the individual letters the Duke dictated in acknowledging every gift. He referred to her rather devotedly as "My Miss Shouse," perhaps because her memory was in many ways as remarkable as his. The situation remained virtually unchanged under Tom Chappell, who took more frequent and extensive alumni trips than G V S, often in the company of Bert Olsen.†

One of the first steps the younger Olsen took on becoming headmaster was to hire Edward S. Cooke '37 to direct alumni relations. "I had a rather inauspicious beginning when I arrived in 1960," Cooke recalls. "The Duke used to come in those days and give the first Sunday sermon. I remember meeting him outside the dining room, and he said, 'Oh, Ted, what are *you* doing here?' When I told him I had come to assist Bill Olsen in alumni affairs, the Duke said, 'What do we need

---

* In 1960, St. Paul's and Exeter had a per-student endowment of approximately $40,000; Hotchkiss had less than $6,000.

† Sufficient funds were raised during Tom Chappell's era to construct Van Santvoord Hall and the Bierwirth Hockey Rink (John E. Bierwirth '13 was president of the board of trustees 1946–1962) as well as to cover much of the projected cost of a new science building (the future A. Whitney Griswold Science Building).

to do that for? Not that I have anything against you, Ted, but what we really need is just for the headmaster to approach a few of the alumni who like to give.'"

It was a sensitive situation for Ted Cooke: "I inherited Martha Shouse, and we eventually worked out a modus vivendi. It had been her bailiwick for years, and she was a quiet sort who had no family and put everything into her work. Thinking back on it, I'm sure she must have felt slighted for not having been offered my job. But in those days, I suppose that just wasn't considered."

Bill Olsen became directly involved in the first major fund drive even before becoming headmaster: "One of my earlier exposures to trustees was sitting in on the planning of the 75th anniversary campaign. I remember it with some amusement because Tom Chappell and I were supposed to talk at this thing. We got together earlier and decided that I'd talk about faculty needs, and he'd talk about something else. He got on first. The next thing I knew, I heard him talking about faculty needs. He had my speech."

As headmaster, Bill Olsen inherited the 75th anniversary campaign: "It was my task to go out on the road and talk about the school. I couldn't have done that without the background and experience that I had. I could talk about the place in personal terms, which is what it was all about. We also hired Marts & Lundy, the fund-raising firm, which brought Russ Browning into the picture."

Frank Sprole '38, one of the principal movers behind that campaign, and later president of the board, elaborates: "Russ was the outside consultant whose survey confirmed what we all knew – the vast, underlying good feeling about the school which had never been really tapped. I don't think Russ ever got along terribly well with Bill Olsen, but Bill knew where all the bodies were buried in the alumni group and also knew what we had to do. They got the annual fund really organized, and we became the outstanding school of our size in annual giving.

"I guess we got close to ten million in that first capital drive. Dick Watson, Jim Linen, Bill McKnight [William G. McKnight, Jr. '30] – it couldn't have been done without them. The problem was that we had to use much of what we raised for capital expenditures rather than endowment. The new Main Building alone cost over three million. What used to drive me crazy were the fellows I knew who had a lot of money, and some of them, boy – Dick Watson was very generous. Hotchkiss was tops on his list. He left a lot to the school. His widow, Nancy Symington, is still active in the sense of being interested, and his sons are. But I had a lot of other friends who could have bought and sold the school in a lot of ways with what they made. And they didn't begin to think about giving. That always bothered me. As a scholarship guy I could never really pay back the school. I'm sure I've done it many times over in the amount of dollars, but it was really because of what the school did for me and my life that I've been prepared to do all I can."

The next capital drive came in the mid-1970s. It was initiated by Woods McCahill and headed by David Luke, who succeeded McCahill as president of the Hotchkiss board. "Finances, females, and facilities – those were my priorities," says the Westvaco chairman. "The endowment had shrunk to around six million dollars, and the school was in the red. At the same time, Hotchkiss tuition was about a thousand dollars a year higher than our traditional competitors. Because of this difference, we were losing some of our best applicants.

"We set out to raise something like twenty-five to thirty million. I felt we had a very good story to tell, and I think we told it to a group of people who had reason to be interested in the school. Bill Elfers [William Elfers '37] played an enormous role, as did Frank Sprole, and there were many others, too. By the time I stepped down in 1980, the school's budget was comfortably in the black. One thing we recognized in particular was that as we expanded the school to accommodate coeducation, we obviously needed to do some building. But we didn't need to continue building bigger and better Georgian structures. It was clear that many of the students had never lived in such opulence, either before or after their Hotchkiss experience, and spending money on gold-plated facilities would create an inaccurate impression of the standards and purpose of the school. The most valuable money we could raise was money for endowment, where it could be used permanently to support scholarships and faculty salaries."

To be sure, Dave Luke, Bill Olsen, Frank Sprole, Woods McCahill, Bill Elfers, and the like were the generals, and they in turn relied on numerous lieutenants for the campaign to succeed. "We never forgot what all those wonderful class agents were doing on their own time, at their own expense, because of their loyalty to and love of the school," says Marie B. Trager, who retired in 1988 after more than two decades as alumni secretary. "Our job at the office was to assist them doing their job, and we made a constant effort to learn about the persons out there. We remembered to say small things like, 'Oh, how is your new job?' Or, 'You've just moved? How do you like Milwaukee?' Or, 'You're getting married in November? That's wonderful!' Of course, eventually the greatly increased volume changed things both in terms of the donors and the dollars. The solicitation system became very sophisticated, very refined, and the personal touch was not always there."

"Bill Olsen's was a good show, professionally done," says Edward B. "Ted" Leisenring, Jr. '44, who was cohost at several alumni dinners in the Philadelphia area over the years for the headmaster and his retinue. "He spoke with purpose and conviction; he spoke in grammatical sentences; he threw in the right amount of humor and generated the kind of admiration you want to have for a headmaster."

Did Bill Olsen prefer this sort of a milieu, in which he was surrounded by wealth and social glitter, over the more mundane task of running the school? The retired headmaster shrugs: "The real fun of alumni relations, parent relations, trustee relations, and all of those external relations is that they are basically just another form of teaching. The subject was always the school, which was easy to discuss because it was the subject I knew best and believed in totally."

He also believed that this form of teaching would come to be recognized as his primary contribution to the school. "In what was probably one of the last conversations I had with Bill when he was headmaster," recalls Robert Barker, who eventually became head of the history department, "he told me that he certainly felt that over the years he had guarded the academic program and tried to protect it. But he said he was under no illusion that his legacy was in that area. His legacy was in bricks and mortar, and the amount of money that had been raised over the years."

xviii / "I want to thank you for my most recent increase in salary," George Stone wrote to the trustees in 1980. "I was confident that I had reached the highest salary Hotchkiss could offer several years ago. After all, in the life I lead I am spared almost all of the expenses that make inflation painful for people who have to pay for their rent, their food, their medical services, their heat, their utilities, their pension. I want to thank you for my latest raise, and at the same time, assure you that I expect no others while I am at Hotchkiss. Years ago my wife and I made our wills leaving whatever we own at our death to the Hotchkiss School. To increase my salary further is simply advancing money to me that will come back to you eventually."

By 1980, the salary scale for nonadministrative faculty members ranged from $7,500 to a maximum of $20,700, though these figures at that time were not in the public domain, as George Stone's letter implies. Other procedures concerning the salary process had yet to be fully institutionalized, which eventually led to a bitter misunderstanding. "We didn't know each other's salary, but by mistake I got a slip of paper from the business office listing ten different salaries," says Steve Bolmer, the unreconstructed old-timer who prides himself on speaking up in faculty meetings on occasions when his colleagues considered silence to be the better part of valor. "I almost quit when I found out what some of my colleagues were getting.* They were friends of Bill Olsen."

Among those topping the nonadministrative category was indeed George Stone, who had been Bill Olsen's classmate and fraternity

---

* Bolmer's discovery came after Olsen had already retired.

brother at Yale. George Stone, however, also happened to be one of the most influential faculty members with students during his more than thirty years. Despite having a face-reddening temper which would sometimes get the better of him – he once inverted a full wastepaper basket over the head of a boy mimicking his lisp in class – George Stone would surely be remembered as one of the school's all-time greats. "One man's favoritism is another man's merit pay," comments Bill Olsen.

This is not to imply that there was nothing to Steve Bolmer's charge. "I think Bill very clearly rewarded those who he thought were doing a great job in the school and held back those he thought weren't," says Larry Becker. "Some of those who were held back were some of the more senior faculty."

Though his role was undoubtedly a pivotal one, Bill Olsen was not alone in setting salaries. The trustees, through the board's compensation committee, set the policy, determined the total amount available to be apportioned each year, and exercised general oversight. "The problem of the seventies was that we had inflation, voluntary wage-price restraints, and there wasn't that much money to parcel out," says Frederick A. Godley, Jr. '38, who headed the compensation committee at that time. "We were trying to keep our lower groups competitive so that we could attract good younger people. Yet we didn't want to antagonize the older group, whom we couldn't compensate quite the way we would have liked."

Most immediately involved in interviewing faculty members and making the individual salary recommendations was the dean of faculty, Jim Marks. "Bill would make some adjustments, but I was pretty much in charge," explains Marks. "Bill frankly recognized that younger faculty members with kids going through college deserved consideration over older faculty members who didn't have these expenses. Bill was the one who signed the salary letters and took a lot of the heat off me. I'm not sure the faculty really knew how much of a role I had in the salaries."

Comments Steve Bolmer, "Jim Marks certainly never interviewed me, nor did anyone else. I had three kids going through college in the seventies, so the policy of favoring that category of teachers obviously didn't apply to me. If they had any criteria for evaluating faculty, we weren't told what they were."

"Nobody ever interviewed me," adds Bob Hawkins, who also felt he had been discriminated against by Bill Olsen's salary system.

It may seem surprising to someone outside of the immediate Hotchkiss community how small these "merit" or "favoritism" salary differences were. In private industry, the stellar young executive with ten years on the job might be pulling down several times what the average executive with twice that seniority earns. The kind of differences Steve Bolmer was objecting to amounted to about a 15 percent salary edge accrued over twenty years of service versus thirty years. "It wasn't primarily the money, because I loved teaching," explains Steve. "It was the implicit judgment that my efforts were somehow falling short."

To debate the merits of individual faculty members would be an endless and inconclusive task. Suffice it to say that during what would turn out to be the longest teaching tenure at the Hotchkiss School, Steve Bolmer may have been misunderstood by an appreciable number of his faculty colleagues. What he thought was a forthright, outspoken manner was at times taken as a tactless and unnecessarily biting critique. If Steve Bolmer no longer recalls – or denies – making some of his barbed comments, not so his colleagues who were on the receiving end, though even they are often not unsympathetic to his point of view. "I don't think he ever meant to be personally unkind," says Marilyn Coughlin, who more than once found herself the target of those barbs. "I really think Steve played an important role in helping us see what one of the boundaries of the discussion was, and he helped to advance us in coming to some sort of a conclusion. But I must say I never wanted to be in the headmaster's shoes in faculty meetings when Steve's hand went up."

Money, of course, was not always the ultimate criterion for those who taught. "I was able to judge how much closer Bill Olsen felt to me by the way he signed my salary letters," says Robert Barker, whom Olsen hired in 1975. "The first one he signed A. William Olsen. Then it went to A. W. O. Then the last letter I had from him he signed just

Bill. The letter was a standard form, but he almost always used to write a personal note at the bottom. My eyes would invariably look for this note before traveling up to the salary figure."

Observes Jim Marks, "Far more difficult than salaries was the distribution of housing. Every time you made a teacher happy by giving him a nicer apartment or a nicer house, you disappointed two or three others who might have also deserved it in terms of tenure or for other reasons."

For the trustees, the salary issue went beyond the active Hotchkiss faculty. "I got a letter from Mrs. Gil Smith, whose husband taught French for some twenty-five years," says Dave Luke. "She wrote, 'Dave, you and I knew each other at school, you knew my husband's brother, Leverett. I'm writing to you not knowing whether you're the right one, but I was just overwhelmed with gratitude when I received the notice of the retroactive increase in our retirement pay. We've lived so close to the line, we've given up so much, that when I learned about this, I went over and turned up the thermostat.'"

On this emotional point, Bill Elfers, the trustee emeritus who as much as any single person over the past thirty years has helped put the Hotchkiss School on a sound financial footing, reflects the sentiment of the board. "Those great Hotchkiss teachers who retired when the economics were so different and are living on very marginal pensions is a problem every Hotchkiss person reacts to with feeling," says the courtly venture capitalist, who embodies the noblesse oblige of a more civil era. "Those great men of Hotchkiss like Dr. Hoey, who taught my son classics so well, are still not having the income they should have. It takes twenty dollars of endowment to yield a dollar in income. A real priority of our capital fund drive is to be able to meet more fully this very special human need."

xix /   "I remember my first year being in faculty meetings," says Julia Wu Trethaway, who was hired by Bill Olsen in 1980 and married her colleague Tom Trethaway '75. "There were about seventy people, and they seemed to be quite informally lounging around on the various couches and chairs in the Alumni Room. But Grace Becker [French teacher and wife of Larry Becker] had warned me, 'Be careful where you sit because everybody has an assigned seat.' What I found out later was that by tradition each faculty member sat in the same seat he or she had found available when first coming on board – and woe to the neophyte who didn't know any better. The other thing I remember from those meetings was the headmaster. Mr. Olsen was very, very commanding. He would allow discussion to go on, and then he would make his last comment, and everybody would end up voting the way he wanted."

Julia Wu Trethaway's first year at Hotchkiss was to be Bill Olsen's last. His retirement after twenty-one years at the helm typically did not come neatly bundled and tied up. As malleable and flexible as Bill Olsen had proved to be in introducing coeducation and responding to the turbulence of the times, there was one sensitive issue on which he did not want to budge because of a long-held personal belief. And that was the issue of scholarship students helping to earn their keep by cleaning classrooms and other areas around the school.

"I felt the work program for the scholarship students was a real plus," explains the headmaster who had been a scholarship student himself. "I felt it had been a privilege in my time, and I just did not buy the argument that it now was discriminatory."

Be that as it may, the accoutrements which had once been borne with such pride – the pail and the broom – were now perceived as symbols of an unwholesome caste system. "When the minority student hit campus, the whole notion of scholarship students working hit the fan," says Peter Adams. "They said, 'Hey, this is slavery. Is this what we came to Hotchkiss for? This is what we've been up against all our lives.'" Nonminority students performing scholarship tasks, moreover, were now being visibly stereotyped into this same servile category. With coeducation only accentuating such disparities, the question of scholarship jobs became a major issue at the school, discussed with as much passion as could be mustered in this more placid era of the late seventies.

"There was also a practical argument," says Rusty Chandler. "In the old days, nonscholarship students paid their way in full – and then some. But by the seventies, it really cost several thousand dollars more to educate the students who were paying full fare. So everybody was, in effect, on scholarship. What some of us on the faculty were saying was that there should be a universal work program at Hotchkiss, and that the artificial discrimination between those who are scholarship kids and those who aren't be eradicated. But Bill wouldn't hear of it. That was one of his blind spots."

Bill Olsen was encountering also some difficulties in town-gown relations, which were partly cumulative. The GO program inevitably had raised a few local eyebrows over the introduction of such an alien social element into the community – though many residents welcomed these youngsters and invited them to their homes. At about the same time, the wording in the catalogue concerning the "six Foundation Scholarships . . . for deserving day pupils" was amended to read, "deserving day pupils *who need financial assistance.*" Explains Bill Olsen, "We redefined the qualifications because local real estate agents began to use the availability of the scholarships as a come-on." After 1970, the listing of these scholarships was eliminated from the catalogue altogether. "We had by then joined other independent schools as members of the scholarship service out of Princeton, which bases all awards strictly on need," comments Rusty Chandler. Although this removed any theoretical limits on the number of scholarships for students from the area, the deletion in the catalogue was not always perceived that way within the neighboring communities.

Ironically, what brought things to a crisis was the discontinuation of the GO program after the summer of 1973. In casting around for the best way to utilize the school's facilities during the vacation months, the decision was made to rent out part of the premises to a private concern for use as a tennis camp. A Lakeville resident who operated a tennis court protested against what he considered unfair competition, and his action brought to the fore the lingering issue of the school's local tax exemption. It was an uncomfortable issue not only because of the school's apparent wealth, but because Hotchkiss was benefiting from a variety of the town's services – such as enrolling in the local grade schools a number of faculty children living on the Hotchkiss property. While the school had almost doubled its voluntary contributions in lieu of taxes to the Town of Salisbury in the second half of the seventies, some sentiment remained that the increased payments were still not commensurate with the means of the school.

But these were more annoyances than serious problems for Bill Olsen toward the end of his second decade as headmaster. Having Jim Marks as dean of faculty since 1974 undoubtedly had eased the headmaster's life. Dealing with individual teachers on a day-to-day basis had never been Olsen's forte; Marks, who came from three generations of schoolkeepers, relished it. Now, not only was there relative peace on the faculty front, but the sort of pervasive bitterness which had characterized the headmaster's relationship with students in the early seventies was no longer detectable, and even the absentee charge was muted. "If you looked at the schedule, the chances are that I was away just as much towards the end as in that earlier period," observes Olsen. "I contend that the difference was that I was now back in class. At any one time, there were probably forty kids who saw me doing what everybody else at the school does, rather than as just a guy up in front in chapel or the auditorium."

The most consequential change for Bill Olsen's career, however, was that since 1975, David Luke happened to be president of the board. A member of the executive committee which had unanimously decided in 1974 to ask Bill Olsen to resign, David Luke quickly established a unique working relationship with the reconstituted headmaster. "They were both strong leaders and they happened to see things pretty much eye-to-eye," says Frank Sprole, who was then vice president of the board.

"I openly admired and appreciated Bill Olsen's ability to handle the task," explains Luke. "He was the right man to do the extraordinarily difficult job which Hotchkiss was trying to accomplish in the aftermath of our coeducational decision. By the end of the decade, we were fully competitive with Andover, Exeter, St. Paul's, and Groton in our ability to attract students, as well as with such traditional rivals as Taft, Kent, and Choate. Much of the credit for that goes to Bill Olsen."

Not needing to worry about a renewed challenge from above, Bill Olsen was able to lower his guard throughout the school. This was especially notable among the coeds, with whom he seemed to have established a warmer relationship than he ever did with the boys. "I thought he was the epitome of what a headmaster should be," recalls Carolyn Wilcox Galiette, who graduated in 1978 and is now an investment banker with her own firm in Hartford. "He was very dignified, yet he was also warm to the students."

This did not mean that the O failed to exercise the same dispassionate impartiality with female students in matters of discipline. "My daughter got herself into a little jam the year I was to get the Alumni Award," says Frank Sprole, "and Bill Olsen wouldn't allow her to come down to the dinner in New York. I thought you didn't need that kind of a discipline, which was really punishing me. He could have taken away all her vacations or something instead. She was our youngest, our baby, and I would have loved to have her there. But there was nothing I could do."

Despite continuing to be involved in a multitude of ways in students' lives, Bill Olsen as headmaster played a vastly different role from that of his counterparts of earlier years. Whether it was because of the dramatically changing times or the individuals concerned, Olsen and his headmaster peers by and large no longer wielded the sort of personal, lifelong influence that the likes of Van Santvoord and Boyden had: "I didn't have many Epiphanies in his presence," notes Bill Olsen's admirer Mike Carroll '75, who had helped to orchestrate the midnight scream with Ray McGuire. "He was not a voice on the road to Damascus."

Bill Olsen, however, had become an indisputable model for other headmasters of his time. "He was a superb mentor for me," says Larry Becker, "and there are things I learned from him that are indelibly engraved on my mind and continue to influence my headmastership. I think it is a tribute to Bill Olsen that several of his faculty members are now running schools of their own."

Adds Jim Marks, "Bill Olsen bridged the transition from the Van Santvoord-Boyden era into modern headmastering."

In the spring of 1979 the school experienced a tragedy of unprecedented magnitude. A comparable event in 1930 on the eve of graduation did not have the same impact, since most of the students had left
for home.

Blair Torrey was especially close to the situation because his daughter was a classmate of the seniors involved: "The kids had a party
across the lake at the home of one of the day students. They had too
much to drink, and they were late getting back. It was a Saturday
night, and they had done all this illegally, sneaking off campus. Now
they were rushing to make it in time for the check-in. One boy had a
car, and he was driving too fast down Belgo Road, then onto Route 44.
One of the kids in the car actually said, 'Slow down, you're going to
kill us.' At about that time, the boy lost control, and the car skidded
sideways. A flatbed trailer was parked on the side of the road, and that
flatbed went right through the back side of the car and instantly killed
the couple in the back seat. The girl was a lovely, lovely person from
Detroit. My wife was very close to the family because she'd been an
adviser to her older sister. The boy who was driving was a nice kid. I
was close to his sister, who was the manager of my hockey team. This
kid got out and ran across the countryside, panicky. The whole thing
was a horrible time. One family sued the school. There was a lot of – oh,
it was an awful, awful period. The effects of that we've never quite
gotten over. There's a little garden out beyond Buehler by Dick Hughes'
house in memory of that lovely girl."

Recalls Jane Hughes, "Perhaps the worst moment of the whole thing
was when Bill Olsen and Arthur White went out into the street with
flashlights looking for bodies. That's a pretty hard thing to do."

Arthur White: "After Bill and I identified the two students at the
hospital – it was around 2 A. M. – we went back to his office. Bill said,
'I've got to call the parents,' and I said, 'Can I help you with that in any
way?' He said, 'No, I've got to do it. It's my job to do it.' He then
proceded to make the calls. It was very traumatic, very emotional, as
you can well imagine. We then sat around in Bill's outer office probably until four or four-thirty; George Kellogg was there as well. Fi-

nally we decided there was nothing more we could do and went to get whatever sleep we could."

Blanche Hoar: "I saw Bill the next morning. He said the impact had been so bad he couldn't even tell which one was the boy and which one the girl. His eyes welled up with tears."

Bob Hawkins: "Sunday services had been given up by then, but Bill had the whole school assemble in chapel at nine-thirty. This was the one time he really pulled all stops in venting the school's grief."

Jane Hughes: "It was a terrible time for Bill and Jean, the death of those children. I think that took the stuffing right out of Bill. To be then treated in the way he was by the lawsuits and so forth, the accusations that simply weren't so. That was a terrible thing for both of them."

Dick Hughes: "I think the trial was largely meant to test whether the school was following the procedures which were established for check-in and check-out. The lawyers claimed that this would never have happened if we'd been more on top of the situation. Their argument basically was that Hotchkiss is a small school, and the relationship between kids and faculty in the dorms is pretty close; and if we didn't know this was going on, we must have pretended to be an ostrich or something."*

The courts eventually threw out the case, clearing the school and everyone concerned. But it was not the same Bill Olsen after the accident. The distinguished gray around the temples seemed to spread out almost overnight and cover his head with a mantle of age. "If you ask me what was the worst thing that happened to me as headmaster, that was obviously it. Loss of life, the whole business, was terrible for everybody."

---

*"Kids think you know more about what's going on than you in fact do," says Bill Olsen. "Just because they know they're doing it, they think everybody else knows they're doing it." The argument nevertheless persists that the policy of the Hotchkiss faculty from the earliest days was to close its eyes to certain typical forms of teenage behavior. What *was* without precedent was that a transgression of Hotchkiss rules would lead to a tragedy of this sort.

Within less than a year, the headmaster was facing a situation of an altogether different sort: Dave Luke, the president of the board, with whom Bill Olsen had worked hand-in-glove for the past five years, was due to step down. At the next-to-the-last meeting presided over by David Luke, held on March 6, 1980, the following entry appears in the minutes: "Mr. Luke reported that, based on Mr. Olsen's fine record of leadership and achievement, the Executive Committee had warmly concurred for planning purposes in his continuing as Headmaster through June 1985, when he will have served twenty-five years in that position."

At the next board meeting, held two months later, on May 3, 1980, Frank Sprole was elected as the new president. The first meeting presided over by Frank Sprole was held that fall, and the trustees' minutes carry the following entry: "Mr. Olsen thanked the trustees for their support of him in his decision to retire at the end of this school year."

What accounted for the dramatic turnaround in the intervening months?

"Certainly the move from Dave Luke was not a factor in any way, shape, or form," explains Bill Olsen. "Frank Sprole was picked with very heavy input from me and certainly with my approval and encouragement. Frank and I had worked closely together over a number of years; specifically, when he was chairman of the development committee, and after that, there were his kids at the school. I had known Frank really since we were students here, and through Yale and beyond. If anything, a deterrent to the decision to retire was the fact that I was throwing a curve to Frank."

Frank Sprole offers his recollection: "Within a few weeks after I took over as president of the board, Bill called me and we had dinner. He said he would like to consider retiring at the end of the following year, and he wanted to know if the understanding still stood on continuing his salary until retirement age. That had at one point been proposed to him by Woods McCahill when he had been president. While Bill was a fine headmaster in the main respects, I felt we needed some new ideas, and he was giving us a year or so for a search committee and all the rest. So I said, 'Sure, Bill, you've got the deal. You'll continue to receive your salary until sixty-five.'"

Comments Bill Olsen, "Frank Sprole does not accurately recall the sequence of conversations I had with him about retirement. During the summer of 1980, I blind-sided him by suggesting that the time had come for a new headmaster. During the ensuing weeks, I talked with a number of individual trustees about a number of matters related to the future. One of those conversations took place with Edgar Cullman, a person who had consistently provided a friendly ear. It was Edgar who proposed the arrangement eventually adopted by the full board providing ongoing salary to age sixty-five. That suggestion had nothing to do with Woods McCahill, who by that time was no longer a full member of the board."

Regardless of whose memory is correct about reaching the retirement provisions, how does Bill Olsen explain his own change of mind? "If you look at the history of heads during that period, and even now, the average tenure was something like six years or less. There were very few people who stayed on beyond ten. The only thing that encouraged me to stay on was that the school was basically three different schools during the twenty-one years that I was there. The early part was the school I had gone to, the middle part was turmoil, and the third part was pure gravy. That was more fun than anyone could possibly have. The heat went out of the counterculture, the coeducation experiment worked like a charm. It was the seven years of the best fun I had, with one big exception – that automobile accident. Steve Kurtz, who was then head of Exeter, said, 'I hope your reason for leaving is not related to that accident.' Was that in there? I suppose there was no way to avoid it. My main reason, however, was strictly institutional. What changed my mind since David Luke had stepped down was a retrospective piece I was asked to write for the *Alumni Magazine*. In thinking about it, it became clear that there were significant new opportunities opening up for the school which I couldn't fulfill before I reached retirement age. This was principally the matter of internationalism and expanding and consolidating the curriculum to refocus on some of the things that were being taught and the way they were being taught. I felt that if somebody was going to do that – and do it right – he ought to have a chance to be here long enough not only to start it, but implement it. So, for me the reason was strictly institutional in feeling that this is where the school ought to go.

"Time and time again, retiring heads say, 'I've done what I feel I can do for this school. It's time for somebody else.' Or they say, 'I've done what I came to do,' which is a little pretentious because I don't believe most people have that kind of a plan. But really what they're saying is, 'Okay, guys, I've done it. It's time to do something else. It's time for somebody else.' You get worn down. It's partly being a public figure, it's partly being a court of last resort, it's all those combinations. You just figure you've had it. You say, 'Now is the time.'"

Sums up Rusty Chandler, "When he retired, I really think Bill Olsen was the senior statesman of the independent school headmasters."

More than comparisons with his contemporary peers, there was one standard Bill Olsen never forgot. How did he measure up against GVS? Here, let me offer a personal glimpse. At a cocktail party during a class reunion held at the school some years after the Duke's death, Bill and I became engaged in precisely this discussion. I hardly knew Bill then. My most vivid memory of him went back to the time I had visited the school in 1953 as a sophomore at Yale, and the Duke made a point of steering me to an old cubbyhole of an office, where he introduced me with obvious pride to "Mr. Olsen." During the early sixties, I came to think of the young, businesslike headmaster as one of the speakers at the New York alumni dinners at the Pierre, at which a speech by the Duke invariably highlighted the evening. In the second half of the sixties, when the Duke's annual appearances ceased, I was not alone in assuming that Bill Olsen was somehow the cause. Whether I had written to Hotchkiss to register my disappointment or whether it was because I did write a letter suggesting that GVS be interviewed on camera before it was too late (which was turned down), my impression is that it was Bill Olsen who had sought out this stranger in that reunion cocktail party crowd and brought up his relationship with the Duke.

Jean and Bill Olsen

He did it in a low-key, outreaching way, as if he had been aware not only of who I was but also how I had felt all these years. Expressing warm admiration for GVS, he said something to the effect that it was unfortunate that he had felt the need to compete with the Duke for so long. It seemed almost as if this unofficial dean of prep school head-masters was regretting a needless conflict between father and son, re-gretting the needless effort to get out from beneath a shadow that was never really obscuring what he was accomplishing in his own right. "We were different people in different times," Bill summed up in some such words. "I could have never done many of the things the Duke did so well, and he wouldn't have been interested in doing many of the things I cared about. Ours were two distinct and separate worlds which shouldn't have been compared."

It was a moment to remember.

xx /   "I thought it was absolutely brilliant on Bill's part to get out when he did," observes Larry Becker. "Jean was again becoming interested in being more in-volved with the school. Frank Sprole, I understand, was thinking of keeping Bill only two or three more years, rather than the full five. Bill was sixty, and still young enough to get involved in something else. At this point, he was immensely popular, especially with the girls. He was kind of like Ronald Reagan. I think in many ways his last year was his best."

Larry Becker and Jim Marks were the two candidates from within the school with a chance to succeed Olsen: "Jimmy and I both had in-terviews in New York, but we were very quickly eliminated. It was clear the trustees were going to go outside. They wanted someone with a fresh, new image who was in no way associated with the Olsen era."

Jim Marks: "I remember they asked me my vision of the school. Obviously, I thought the kind of person they should have was not un-like me. I was aware of the healing that needed to be done internally. My concern was not that I wasn't chosen, but that the board didn't seem to understand what was needed at that point."

Having several offers to head other schools, Jim Marks left shortly thereafter to become headmaster of Lake Forest Country Day.

Larry Becker: "It finally came down to Mike Stewart [Michael M. Stewart '53, former Rhodes scholar, noted humanitarian, and medical researcher with the Rockefeller Foundation] and Tim Callard. Mike was clearly the front runner, but Edgar Cullman asked him if he could give assurances that he wouldn't be lured away if a prestigious medical offer came by. Mike said he could not, and Tim Callard got the nod."

In an ironic twist of fate, Mike Stewart – surely one of the most versatile and popular Hotchkiss graduates of all time – died suddenly two years later of cancer.

Timothy C. Callard thus became the first headmaster since Edward G. Coy to be brought in from the outside, with no previous Hotchkiss experience either as a student or faculty member.

"When he first came, he seemed to be the all-American boy," says George Kellogg, then in his last year as assistant headmaster." He had gone to Gilman, gone to Princeton, where he was quite a football player. He had taught at Andover, been the head of admissions at Princeton. What more could you want?"

The account of Tim Callard's tenure in the trustees' minutes is also impressive. During his inaugural year, the school's seventh headmaster defused the intensifying crisis in town-gown relations by replacing the professional tennis camp with a bona fide academic summer program* and extending the school's involvement in community affairs; he eliminated the scholarship student work distinction by introducing a work program for all students in the school; and he recognized the contribution of faculty spouses, including his own, by obtaining nominal payments for the counseling and supervision of students that they did in connection with their spouses' roles. At the trustees' meeting on May 8, 1982, Tim Callard was given a raise, and the

---

*Headed by English teacher Dick Hughes, the six-week summer session in 1991 attracted 284 students from 33 states and 22 countries.

board's president, Frank Sprole, "congratulated him on his first year as Headmaster."

Yet a year later, still with nary an ambivalent word in the minutes, Tim Callard was asked to resign. To this day, some trustees and faculty members question whether he had been given a sufficient opportunity to orient himself to the ways of the school. One of Tim Callard's most startling miscues was his attempt to keep the championship girls' soccer team out of a postseason tournament because it would over-emphasize sports – a matter on which the faculty dealt him a unanimous rebuff. "To be shot down this way in the middle of a faculty meeting has got to be embarrassing," says Geoff Marchant, who was the coach of that girls' team. "Tim smiled and understood and re-thought it. He had an open mind, and I don't feel it was right to give him the hook so soon." But the consensus in the Hotchkiss community seems to be that he was given as much of a chance as the best interests of the school would permit. The litany of reasons why Tim Callard was not right for the job range from his tendency to retreat to his office or the headmaster's house rather than circulate among students, to his inability to get anything done and his unwillingness to listen to well-meant advice. Also invariably mentioned is that his wife, Pam, breastfed her newborn in chapel, and that the Callards made untoward alterations to the headmaster's house. "They built these little stairs coming down from the dining room to the main study," says Blair Torrey, "and when they decided to put chrome handles on the railing in that magnificently wooded room, it drove the old-timers out of their squash."

"The way they did it was in terrible taste," explains one of those old-timers, Bob Hawkins, "though the idea behind it was commend-able. The Callards wanted to open up this very dark room and devise a kind of area where students could come at any time, pick up food in the kitchen on trays, and then return them without having any servants around."

Yet perhaps the most damaging charge against the new headmaster was that he failed to establish bonds precisely with this constituency to which he had so imaginatively sought to open the headmaster's house: the students themselves.

"On a one-on-one with the kids, Tim was wonderful," says Larry Becker. "Any kid who went to see him with a problem invariably would come out feeling, 'This is a great man. He's heard me and dealt with my problem.' Unfortunately, what the kids mostly saw of him in the school was his standing in front of them in the auditorium. He would start many of his remarks with, 'I'm going to be brief.' You could after a while almost hear an audible chuckle from the kids. He would go on, and on, and on. What the kids wanted to know was what would happen if they didn't pick up the popcorn in the stairwell. They didn't need a lecture on where popcorn came from, who had to sweep it up if they didn't pick it up, and what finally became of the dropped popcorn. I would never believe that could kill a headmastership, but that undoubtedly was a large part of it."

Arthur White, dean of students and assistant headmaster after George Kellogg's retirement, offers another dimension to the same problem: "A lot of the personal qualities Tim had were terrific; his great shortcoming was that he didn't spend enough time with anybody on that campus – especially the students. It was not that he didn't work hard; on the contrary, he spent so much time in trying to learn about Hotchkiss and reading all of the things he could lay his hands on that he was constantly in his office. Hours on hours he wouldn't come out of his office. Then when he went home, he was closeted upstairs in his office, reading or whatever. There were people in school who were trying to convince him that he ought to spend more time in the dormitories, that he ought to be walking around, that he ought to be visiting classes. But he never did quite get to that."

"He just didn't get in touch with the kids," laments Frank Sprole. "When I finally had to tell Tim Callard it was the end, that was tougher than anything I ever had to do in my business career."

As a person, Tim Callard presents something of a paradox. "I couldn't believe that a guy who majored in religion could also be the president of the Ivy Club at Princeton," says Ted Leisenring, a Philadelphia friend of many Ivy members, and a trustee at the time Callard was headmaster. "You get a lot of heavy partying and swinging characters at the Ivy Club."

A sandy-haired, athletic man in a brown tweed jacket and gray flannels, Tim Callard projects far more the image of the quiet, introspective soul grappling with the downside of human life than of a carefree, hearty partygoer. He neither stands out nor tries to dominate – nor even to impress. He inspires the thought that if the meek indeed were to inherit the earth, he would be a leader in their midst.

With the benefit of hindsight, Tim offers his view of why events may have evolved the way they did: "When I was approached by the search committee, the message that I was given was that they were looking for a young, energetic headmaster who would bring a sense of family to the school, who would be sensitive to the quality-of-life sort of issues. I didn't feel I had a mandate to make major changes, to re-arrange the curriculum, but on the edges try to do a few things like getting the school service program going, reactivating the human relations and sexuality program that had come to a halt some years earlier, establish peer counseling, and so forth.

"I now understand there were from the beginning some serious questions in the minds of a number of the trustees about the quality of the search process – whether it had been done properly. I can remember that even in the first year there began to be almost immediately executive sessions of the board, which I later on learned were discussing my performance.

"Fundamentally, I was not aware of how important it is for a head of Hotchkiss to be attuned in a very particular way. All of the previous headmasters had some prior connection with the school and maybe understood more clearly how important certain things were for developing the support of the faculty and the board. They were steeped in how this organic institution operates. They could avoid some things that might be off-putting to some people, or realize how important certain relationships and traditions were.

"When we were still in the search process, my wife discovered we would have our fifth child. Some of the trustees were saying, 'Isn't that wonderful! A baby on the campus – adds some humanity to the place and focus on families of faculty. So my wife came in feeling that the search committee was delighted that a young family was coming into the school. She had breastfed all of our other children, and she was discreet about doing it now. I remember she would sometimes nurse in the dining hall, but I don't recall that she did it ever in the chapel. She assumed it was perfectly okay to do it. Well, it did get back to us that some faculty wives were upset and thought it inappropriate. It certainly wasn't meant to shock anybody. We had merely wanted to be together as a family in the dining hall.

"What I was finding out on the job was that many expectations of the headmaster conflicted with being a family-oriented man. Hotchkiss wanted somebody who was going to be on hand, visible throughout the school twenty-four hours a day, and at the same time be very attentive to development-office kinds of concerns, sending out notes of thanks to alumni and parents for this or that. I had a misunderstanding with the development office which led to an embarrassing incident. The library had just been renovated, and a lot of people had given money for it and their gifts had never been fully acknowledged. The principal donors were Frank Sprole and his wife, Sally, and one other family.* Frank wasn't pushing to have anything done for him. That certainly wasn't his style. But I thought we ought to, and I spoke to Bill Appleyard [director of alumni relations] and Rusty Chandler about it, and it was agreed that we'd do it. The development people were used to Bill Olsen, who would draft up his own thank yous because he knew more about the donors than anyone else. So Rusty didn't brief me, and I went ahead on my own and dug up folders on Frank and the other family and put together quite an elaborate presentation. I then discovered, after I had given this warm speech to Frank, that it was his wife as

---

* The late Ann Haebler-Frantz and her sons, William T. Frantz '76 and L. Scott Frantz '78.

well who had been one of the principals – that Sally's funds had gone into this. When I finished, Frank whispered to me that Sally had also given, and I ad-libbed briefly about that, but it was a bad moment.

"There were some things about Hotchkiss I found difficult to understand. David Luke was being honored as Alumnus of the Year, and he had come up to give a speech. He talked about the time he and some other seniors had painted a big blue *H* on a rock at the Kent School, which caused a great commotion. They were called in by Mr. Van Santvoord, who caught them literally blue-handed. Though Mr. Van Santvoord seemed upset, his frosty manner betrayed an admiration for what they had done. David Luke spoke of this as being in the great tradition of Hotchkiss pranks. Sure as shooting, within a week we began to have a series of pranks as if the students felt an obligation to live up to this tradition. One of the things they did was to lock all the doors to the classrooms and move the furniture around. While I could appreciate the human value of occasional, imaginative pranks, I didn't think this was a particularly good one. Some of the furniture had been damaged in the process, and it also bothered me that the students who were responsible didn't immediately own up. Our maintenance staff had to do all the work of putting things back in order so that classes could resume.

"Another old Hotchkiss tradition apparently was the spring raid on the preps. The senior proctors would rouse the preps out of their dorms at dawn and lead them out onto the grounds in their underwear, and in some cases tie them to trees and spray things on them. These sorts of things that happened bordered on sexual abuse. In my first year, I didn't learn about the prep raid until after it had taken place. It just didn't seem right for older kids to be doing this to younger kids, and I felt uncomfortable with it. Yet the prep raid had clearly been condoned by the faculty and had broad student support. The older kids claimed it was great for school spirit and that the preps would be disappointed if they weren't routed out. I decided to raise the issue the next year with the student council, trying to get the kids thinking, 'How can we do something that's in the same tradition without the blatant negatives? What's the moral equivalent?' They hemmed and hawed over this; finally I was able to persuade the proctors, and eventually the whole senior class got involved. 'Okay, let's get them up,' we said, 'but let them put their clothes on. They can then run down to the lake, dip in, then run back up.' They'd be cold, and we were going to have hot chocolate and Danish waiting for them at the headmaster's house to warm them up. So that's what we did. But in some minds it was a bit like kissing your sister. It didn't have the original spirit.

"That particular spring we had a lot of rain, and the people involved in spring sports were getting exasperated. Certainly, the morale was low, which may have had something to do with a big panty raid that took place during a Monday night faculty meeting. I remember clearly there were some faculty members who wanted us to call a meeting of the school right away, that same evening. The attitude was, 'Let's really stomp down on this thing, catch as many as we can, and chew out the rest.' My instinct at that time was to find out more about what had happened, talk to people, and draw out of it some sort of an understanding and awareness."

What was about to happen would prove to be one of those defining moments of history for Hotchkiss and, above all, for Tim Callard. Larry Becker provides an eyewitness account: "The first mistake was the way the panty raid was announced to the faculty by the teacher who got the word, as if it were a big crisis. Well, the school wasn't about to go down, but the faculty meeting went out of control, with people saying, 'This is it, this is it. The kids have taken over the school.' So the faculty meeting was adjourned, and there was going to be an all-school meeting at 8 : 00 P.M. in the chapel. I remember telling Tim, 'It doesn't matter what you say, just let them know you're mad, and this will not be tolerated, and they're all to go back to their dorms and lights are out for everybody at ten, and walk out.'

"Everybody crowded into the chapel. Traditionally, when the headmaster appears, things quiet down just like that. Well, Tim didn't appear. It was 8 : 01, and he wasn't there. It was 8 : 02, no Tim. I don't want to exaggerate that it was 8 : 10, but every minute after eight o'clock, the commotion got worse and worse. Maybe it was only five or six minutes, but it was a disastrous delay. Tim walked into a circus and he had a very difficult time quieting things down. He then went on at great length about what was wrong with what they had done. It was a most reasoned statement as to why this was the way it shouldn't be, and you had to be sensitive to the feelings of others. As far as the kids were concerned, it was just another Callard talk. It was a horrible mistake which was compounded by the fact that he didn't finish and then just walk out. He stopped for a moment. A hand went up. I can still see the girl today, and he called on her. You just don't do that in that kind of a meeting. Whether he thought she was going to support his point of view, I don't know. But he called on her. She said she didn't see what all the fuss was about. That did it. She was roundly applauded. Finally George Stone – and I'm sure he questioned to his dying day* whether he should have done it – interrupted and said, 'I'll tell you what's wrong with it.' He gave a ninety-second statement. No one remembers what he said, except that he said it with force and conviction, and it quieted everybody down. That's when it became clear to everyone that Tim didn't have control. Any faculty members who still had doubts about his headmastership would have said it was over."

Tim Callard did not attach any fateful significance to the faculty-perceived débacle: "This was in the spring of eighty-three. A couple of months earlier, I had a much larger increase in salary than I had the previous year, and my own feeling was that we were still sorting out some issues, but that things were going along fine. I knew there was some faculty unhappiness about this panty raid incident, and whether it had been handled properly. I told the faculty, 'If you have some concerns about the job I'm doing, I hope you'll come in and talk about it.' Some of them did and had constructive suggestions.

"In late May, Art White came to see me. He said he was concerned because he was picking up negative signals in talking with Frank Sprole and other board people as well. I immediately called Frank and said I wanted to talk to him. He said, 'Let's just wait until school is over, and

---

*George Norton Stone retired in 1986; he died of a heart attack in 1987. His widow, Jodie, continues to reside near the school.

Pam and Tim Callard

we'll address these matters then.' I followed up with a letter saying I believed that the concerns I had heard about were things we could deal with, and that I felt I was in a position to address them.

"After our last faculty meetings in mid-June, I went to New York to meet with Frank, Edgar Cullman, and David Luke. What I learned from them was that the day before the board had met and voted to ask for my resignation. They were going to pay me my next year's salary plus a housing allowance for one year. I wasn't told much about the specifics as to why this was taking place, and I was stunned. But I didn't see at that moment any sense in trying to resist, since I was serving at the pleasure of the board. They even had lined up consultations with one of those out-placement groups that work with executives who lost their positions.

"I now realize that in coming to a school with which I'd had no previous connection, I should have spent considerably more time with members of the board, keeping them more fully informed about what I was doing. In that sense, I wasn't probably as politically astute as I needed to be. Whether I would have been the right person to lead

Hotchkiss at that point in its institutional evolution is open to question. But with stronger political skills the whole thing would not have come to such an abrupt end."

xxi /   "Arthur White genuinely didn't want to be headmaster," says Larry Becker. "It wasn't one of those, 'I don't want it, but read my lips, of course I do!' Late that summer after Tim Callard left, Arthur was asked to do it on an interim basis. When he stood up on the podium in the opening chapel that fall, the kids leapt to their feet. That was the beginning of a love relationship that Arthur could not say 'no' to."

With Arthur White temporarily running the school, Fay Vincent – then head of Columbia Pictures – took charge of the search committee. "The reason I got to be chairman of all successive search committees was because I opposed the hiring of Callard," explains Vincent. "The fact that I turned out to be right sort of got everybody to say, 'Okay, wise guy, if you think you can do a better job, you do it!'"

Fay Vincent lost little time in taking up the task. At a trustees' meeting held shortly after the school opened in the fall of 1983, he reported that after two days of interviewing members of the faculty, they "to a person are extraordinarily supportive of Mr. White," and "the faculty is split on the most desirable qualifications for a headmaster – two thirds desiring a leader and a strong academic regardless of secondary school experience and the other one third desiring secondary school experience and achievement, with the academic credentials less necessary."

The trustees were not about to defer fully to Fay Vincent and his committee – despite his apparent prescience in the past. "The immediate strategy [according to the minutes] is to compile as long a list as may be of names . . . from all possible sources, and then to begin the culling and narrowing process. The full Board will be involved in the interviewing of the last three or four candidates and the final selection process."

As interim headmaster, Arthur White chose not to move into the headmaster's house and continued to teach mathematics and coach baseball. One of the reasons Arthur had consented to the appointment was that interim headmasters usually were automatically eliminated from consideration for the permanent job. "When I went to New York for a meeting with Frank Sprole shortly before the end of that fall term," recalls Arthur, "he said to me, 'Well, the search committee has found their man.' I said, 'Great, bring him on!' Frank said, 'Well, no, you're it.'"

The president of the trustees then came to Hotchkiss and gathered the school in the auditorium to make what was probably the most enthusiastically received announcement in the history of the school, holidays included. There was not a dissenting voice within the Hotchkiss community, not even in the innermost depths of thwarted faculty ambitions. The young man of modest means who had been brought by Bill Bryan from Maine more than a quarter-century before to teach at this "wealthy" school thus became the full-fledged ruler of the Hotchkiss realm.

Observes Larry Becker, "I think Arthur's original reservation had been, 'I don't want it,' because he thought, 'I can't do it.' He had by now found out that he could, and he began to feel, 'Hey, this isn't so bad.' And people loved him. It was clear the school would have had no part in the trustees picking anyone else. In a way, I think the kids fired Tim Callard and they appointed Arthur White."

"As soon as Arthur took over," says Blair Torrey, "the first thing that went was the chrome on those new stairs in the headmaster's house."

Virtually everything else from Tim Callard's days, however, the new headmaster continued. What was becoming implicitly clear was that Tim Callard had been lacking not substance or ideas but the appropriate Hotchkiss style. "One of the things that started under Tim Callard was bringing the larger Hotchkiss community together again," says Blair Torrey. "People had respected Bill Olsen, but he often lacked the human touch. When people retired from the faculty after twenty or thirty years and lived in the area, like the Bacons and the Beaumonts, they felt cut off from the school. Starting with Tim, these people were invited back whenever we had faculty parties – at the beginning of the year, at Christmas time, and so forth. In fact, I think it was Arthur and I who had originally suggested it to Tim."

That policy was now taken a symbolic step further. "The first tea Cynthia White had for the faculty wives, she called and asked me to come," says Mary Finney. "I told her I felt very flattered, but I had never been included when I was employed at the school, and I doubted I'd come. I didn't know anybody there anymore, and I didn't think I would mingle well, especially with the younger people. Still, it was nice to be remembered after all these years."

Above all, Arthur White created an atmosphere of good feeling among the students. "My first priority as headmaster was to make myself visible in the classrooms, in the dormitories, on the athletic fields, and around the school in general," says White, a wiry, balding man who could hardly fit the popular image of any duke or king. After thirty years as teacher of mathematics, varsity baseball coach, and dean of students, he had not even acquired a nickname. He was who he was – Mr. White to the students, Arthur to his colleagues, and he easily rated as the school's most prominent cheerleader. Anyone watching the relaxed, friendly headmaster conduct the traditional midweek assembly might readily sense the cohesive enthusiasm and goodwill between him and the terraced mountain of youth facing him eagerly from row upon row in the auditorium. There was no distance there, no feeling of separation. The students seemed to know that Arthur White was someone they could trust and rely on; that if a personal emergency arose and they had to get somewhere in the middle of the night, their headmaster would be the person most likely to drive them there.

Arthur White's routine involvement on the personal level often had startling effects. When Sean Nash left Chicago (where he had excelled in an inner city gifted program) to drive to Hotchkiss and enroll as a prep in the fall of 1985, he was anything but enthusiastic. "I didn't know what to expect," recalls Sean, now a senior at Stanford. "It was early morning, and there was so much fog that my parents and I had trouble finding the place. I remember my dad asking me why I wanted to go to Hotchkiss of all places. I could have gone anywhere in the

Arthur White – teacher, coach, dean of students, headmaster

world, and I couldn't answer him. What was weird was that when we finally got there, the first person I met was the headmaster. He showed us around the school, and took us to breakfast. I was pretty impressed after that, and so was my dad. It was a complete turnaround for me."

Most revealing of Arthur White was the perspective he had acquired in the course of his Hotchkiss years: "The reason I got into this business is because I love to teach, and one of my disappointments as headmaster was that I had to give up all but one class. Hotchkiss was an exciting place, with bright, highly motivated kids. When you went into a classroom, there was an electricity. We had a classicist from Harvard, where he had done graduate work, and he arrived to teach Latin and Greek. He took Greek 550, the most advanced course of all. First day in class, he outlined for the students a week's work. But he wasn't specific about that, and when he came to class the next day, they had the week's work done, beautifully done. He told me later, 'I suddenly realized I better be careful. These kids will do whatever I tell them to.'

"When I used to talk to prospective parents and they'd ask, 'What makes Hotchkiss special?' I think the first thing that usually came out of my mouth was, 'The wonderful relationship that exists between faculty and students.' These relationships aren't always formed quickly or easily. Sometimes they bristle; sometimes they're adversarial. Some of the strongest relationships are formed in the three or four years the students spend here when they're really banging heads. But I honestly believe that there is a member of the faculty for every member of the school. I believe that every youngster here eventually finds someone he or she can go to. And to that youngster, that's the most important faculty member that ever was, is, or will be – and rightly so.

"I often quote from Robert Louis Stevenson's *Apology for Idlers*, in which he states that perpetual devotion to a man's business can only succeed by perpetual neglect of many other things, and it's by no means certain that a man's business is the most important thing he can do. Not that there are a lot of people who are very idle at Hotchkiss, but we try to strike a balance to provide a well-rounded life of human interaction beyond the classroom. For whatever reason, the relationships that are started here become both long-lasting and meaningful. If you're here on any weekend in the fall or spring, you'll see the numbers of graduates who come back to reaffirm those ties. They literally come back by the hundreds, and it's wonderful to see."

Besides discovering a rather happy school, those alumni/ae returning during Arthur White's tenure did not escape being exposed to one of his vintage jokes. "Did you know that everyone in the Bible was terribly, terribly poor? Even the richest of the rich were always renting their cloaks." Or: "The student wasn't up on his current affairs. He thought Roe versus Wade was the choice George Washington faced when he came to the banks of the Delaware." Arthur was also known for his repartee. When an irate teacher came to Arthur to complain during the midwinter doldrums that a certain student's behavior was "jejune," Arthur shot back, "Good grief, and it isn't even mamarch!"

Some of Arthur White's homespun remarks served as advice for life. "The stupidest thing you can ever do," he often cautioned his players while coaching baseball, "is to get picked off first base."

Being perceived as a friendly sort with a ready quip did not mean that the new headmaster had eased up on school rules. On the contrary, he brought about a radical change. "It started with a case of a boy caught smoking marijuana," explains Arthur. "In talking with the youngster after the discipline committee had placed him on general probation, I said, 'You're one person I would have bet all my money on to be loyal to the school and uphold its rules.' He said, 'Oh, Mr. White, you don't have to worry about me ever again. I've had my one chance, I've taken it, and I'll never break a major rule again.' I said, 'You mean to tell me students feel they might as well use up their free chance as long as they have another?' He said, 'Absolutely.' So we put a pretty quick stop to that and went to the no-chance policy. The first time you get caught breaking one of the capital rules, that's it. We told the students, 'You've got to decide whether you want to be a part of the school or whether you want to be involved with drugs.' Of course, by far the toughest thing I've had to do periodically as headmaster has been to separate a student from the school. It is one of the distinctive – and treasured – aspects of Hotchkiss that it does demand this sort of behavioral excellence."

Arthur White's reversion to the first-chance system was aimed primarily at alcohol and drugs. Although not as prominent a scourge as it had been in the 1970s, substance abuse in the 1980s remained a Hotchkiss fact of life. Arthur welcomed the return to an unconditional ban on alcohol when Connecticut reinstated the twenty-one minimum drinking age in 1985. He also placed added restrictions on the smoking of cigarettes and set forth a firm timetable to return the school to a wholly nonsmoking status by 1990. "I had opposed the original decision to allow smoking, and the sentiment now among students and faculty was to reverse that." To encourage this pendulum swing back in a nonpunitive way, he established counseling staffs and support groups to help students with their resolve as well as to fulfill a broad range of other emotional needs. "The most common problems when I was head were drugs on campus and divorce and death at home," Arthur White explains. "But we were also dealing with issues that twenty years earlier were almost taboo to speak about except behind closed doors in the lightest of whispers. One of the outlets we established was the human relations and sexuality course – groups of ten seniors and two faculty leaders, male and female in each case, meeting for two hours a week for eight weeks, almost always in a faculty home. Each session was directed to a specific topic, whether homophobia, birth control, AIDS, and so forth. The message we tried to get across was the concept of tolerance and information over rumor and emotion. I think we had come a long way from the tough, macho image of the all-male school."

As a faculty wife for a quarter-century, Cynthia White felt during those years many of the all-male pressures herself. "Hotchkiss was a wonderful place to raise children, but from a woman's point of view, it was otherwise a difficult life," says Cynthia, whose first inkling about traditional prep school ways had come from her father, an Andover graduate. "Our entire lives as faculty wives were supposed to be bound up in the school but the school had been in no way bound up in us. We were *expected* to participate in such activities as pouring tea, cheering at games, chaperoning dances, but the school had no use for our minds – or even cared if we had them. So, we bit our tongues, and we bit our lips, and we did our good things – all the time repressing our abilities. Too many good women have given their lives there, for me to perpetuate the myth that it was all rosy." A sensitive, widely read, dynamic woman, Cynthia White eventually responded by devoting most of her energies to her own professional interests in Lakeville rather than investing herself primarily in the school.

On becoming a headmaster's wife, she found herself in a different role. "Cynthia, who had previously been almost invisible in Hotchkiss life, was a new person," says Larry Becker. "She was just wonderful, entertained beautifully, and clearly loved it." Besides the full whirl of teas, dinners, parties, and other social and cultural events proffered by the Whites, any student was welcome to walk into the headmaster's house at any time. "We both felt that the house and its occupants should be accessible easily and informally," says Cynthia. "Of course, with coeducation, the headmaster's wife became a much more visible presence. The women on the faculty might have liked me to be more verbal in their cause, but I didn't want to be heavy-handed about it. I saw what Jean Olsen went through. It had been an uncomfortable time for her – and the school. I envisaged my own role as rather an old-fashioned one, and I sort of went back to Mrs. Van Santvoord's era to spearhead the social life in small ways. Whenever I could, I would be supportive behind the scenes."

The most tangible result? The Cynthia White Day Care Center for children of faculty and staff members. Not as tangible, but far more pervasive, was the influence she had on the man who was her husband and created all that goodwill at the school. They had been sweethearts at Colby College in Maine, and during their occupancy of the headmaster's house, they radiated the sort of trusting closeness of a couple continuing to share life in the fullest sense.

Recalls Geoff Marchant, a faculty friend of the Whites: "Art would

Arthur and Cynthia White with Deco

say, 'Cynthia has an uncanny way of being right. I don't always agree with her, but whether it's her opinion on an Oriental rug or a policy matter, it invariably turns out she's right.'"

That is almost verbatim what the school's second headmaster, Dr. Buehler, had said about his wife.

xxii /   In the meantime, what was happening to coeducation? Charlie Lord '83 – scholar, athlete, and thespian who graduated with his twin brother, Tim, just as Arthur White was about to take over the reins – provides a dispassionate guide to the school of the 1980s which would surely make many of his Hotchkiss forebears take note: "You would meet somebody, and if you'd end up deciding that you were going to be involved, what you'd have to do in the warm weather is to go to the golf course. People would have more or less staked out different territories, and you knew who had the fifth hole and who had the fairway. You went to your own spot so you wouldn't overlap with anybody. But in the winter, it was sort of a scramble for certain couches in the Alumni Room. The pews in the chapel were also popular, offering both a certain amount of comfort and privacy. I know there were some people who used to go to the dorms at night, which was really taking a risk. The preps and the lower mids, of course, would mill around behind Buehler after evening study hall, but it was less serious."

Charlie's sister, Deirdre Lord '85, offers a perspective on a somewhat different aspect of coeducation at this time: "It wasn't until my senior year that I realized this was historically a school for boys that was now coed. Ironically, the incident which really awakened me came while we were celebrating ten years of coeducation at Hotchkiss. We created a committee of students and a few faculty members – all of whom happened to be women. There were about twelve of us, and we made up these T-shirts. On the front they had the male symbol with the logo, 'Hotchkiss 1893–1974 GOOD.' On the back were both the male and the female symbols with the logo, 'Hotchkiss 1975–1985 BETTER.' We sold the T-shirts to raise money for the celebration we planned for the spring. This happened in October, and everything went off normally. Well, springtime came around, and it was the first weekend after spring break. We were having one of those record hops, the big social event on Saturday night at the school. All of the boys suddenly started to take off their jackets and strip off their sweaters and shirts. Underneath they were wearing T-shirts which had a pair of man's feet and a pair of woman's feet positioned in a very obvious way, and the logo, 'Hotchkiss 1975–1985 THE BOYS ARE STILL ON TOP.' The boys in our senior class had orchestrated this whole thing without anyone's catching on until that very night. They sold the T-shirts to every boy in the school, except for a few who happened to be out of money at the time they were sold. Even our school president was in on it, though he was a real politician about it. He wore the T-shirt under his sweater, and he never unveiled it; but you could see it was under that sweater. Well, we were all terribly upset, those of us who had organized the celebration of coeducation. It may have been just a prank, an incredibly successful one, but we felt it had totally undermined the spirit we had been trying to create. What made it worse was that this had been perpetrated by our friends, people we had spent three or four years with, and they had done it as a big secret behind our backs. The boys, of course, just couldn't understand. They said, 'Hey, what's the big stink about? It was only a prank. Can't you take a little joke?' They also said that if we had really wanted them to be involved in the celebration, we would have had some of them on the committee. So there was some resentment that it had been a committee of women who had planned the celebration. We had not done that intentionally, and in that respect, it was a lesson for us, too."

Deirdre's disappointment after the incident had died down was that the student body as a whole had never gotten together to analyze the incident: "I think we could all have learned a lot. It wasn't only the boys who hadn't been able to understand why we were so upset; the underclasswomen at the school couldn't understand either. And that went back to my brothers' senior year when I was a lower mid. There had been a panty raid, and the whole school had been called together to discuss it. I remember sitting there, thinking, 'What's the big problem? Why are we gathered here?' I couldn't see that there was any big issue involved in invading the girls' dorm and stringing their panties up on trees. I still laugh about it today, yet there were a couple of girls whose clothes got dumped out of the window. It was an assault, and I didn't understand it at that age. Then I came to see it in a different form in my senior year, at which point I was upset because there were lower mids who didn't understand. So I had a chance to go through the whole process, to come full circle, so to speak."

Perhaps no one is in a better position to offer a faculty perspective on the "process" Deirdre Lord depicts than Marilyn Coughlin, who had started to teach in 1972 in anticipation of the school's becoming co-educational: "I think that what we did here for the first ten years of co-education is what most all-boy schools going coed did, which was to bring girls aboard and expect them all to be boys. We didn't make any substantial modification in the curriculum, in the sports programs, or in the facilities. Yes, we took out the urinals and put in bathtubs and things like that. But there remained a very male-oriented model of what the ideal person was. Girls succeeded to the extent to which they fit that model. Female faculty as well. Women here at the school had the feeling that there wasn't a place for them unless they were male-women; unless they bought into and participated in the old-boy kind of thinking."

To be sure, Marilyn Coughlin's was just one point of view, which did not lack an opposing view. "If I didn't know any better," commented Bob Hawkins after viewing the school's new video, completed in the mid-1980s, "I would say it was about a girls' school which had recently taken in boys."

Among Marilyn Coughlin's students was Jennifer I. "Jenna" McKee '84: "Mrs. Coughlin started opening my eyes to some of the women's issues in the world today," says Jenna, whose brother and sister had preceded her at Hotchkiss. "She really made you dig down deep inside yourself for what you felt. We had one or two guys in the class, and I think they really enjoyed it, too, because it opened their eyes a little bit as well."

But there was still another dimension to coeducation for Jenna McKee – perhaps the most important of all. "When I got to college, I found out there was a tremendous difference between those students who had gone to coeducational boarding schools, and those who hadn't," says Jenna, who recently completed her certification as a registered nurse. "The boys and girls who had gone to schools such as Hotchkiss knew how to have a friendship with someone of the opposite sex. The others just did not understand that kind of a relationship. To them, you either dated a girl or you didn't have anything to do with her. Some of my really dear friends are male, and if you didn't go to a co-educational boarding school, you often have no idea what that means. The main thing I took with me from Hotchkiss was to really know people for who they are. You see them twenty-four hours a day. You see them when they're down, when they're up. You see them for what they are. That's how you become friends."

xxiii / Her dismay over the T-shirt imbroglio notwithstanding, Deirdre Lord's overall experience at Hotchkiss was no less fulfilling than that of her older brothers. If anything, Deirdre felt she had the added advantage of having Arthur White as headmaster for her last two years: "There was an incredible energy and excitement when he was named interim headmaster. Hearing him talking to students and laughing and relating to everybody brought a noticeable change of spirit to the whole place. The class ahead of me at their graduation ceremony each gave him a marble, and he had a whole jar of them on his desk after that year. And then our year, we each gave him a piece of a puzzle with our name written on that piece."

It was during Arthur White's tenure that a curious fact of life came to light. "If a top-notch boy and a top-notch girl were accepted at Hotchkiss as well as at Andover and St. Paul's," says Dr. Parnell "Parny" Hagerman, whom Arthur White brought in as director of admissions in 1984, "the chances were greater that the girl would choose to come here than the boy."

This did not mean that such a choice invariably proved to be right. "I had a daughter go there, and she hated the place," says Fay Vincent, who succeeded Frank Sprole in 1985 as president of the Hotchkiss board. "Now, why was that? Obviously, she never hooked up with anybody who made her life there meaningful. She was not socially downtrodden, nor was she academically bad. She had a nonexperience. She passed through there like a bullet through water. There was nothing that attached. She bears responsibility, surely, but so, of course, does Hotchkiss. She had unexciting teachers in some of the main courses. There was very little counseling. Nobody noticed. I waited to see if anybody would pick up on the fact that this kid was floundering, and they didn't. They just missed it completely."

It was not for lack of trying. Arthur White increased the number of faculty from 82 to 97, some of them hired specifically for counseling. And he raised teachers' salaries to range from $17,000 to $55,000. (Correspondingly, the endowment during the eighties more than doubled to around $70 million partly through the appreciation of the school's investments.) His major disappointment was his inability to recruit minorities to teach at the school. Several were hired, only to resign after a year or two. Walter Crain was still the only black on the faculty. "Finding black teachers willing to come to this remote corner of Connecticut was even tougher than finding women," says Arthur White. "When Walter and Tessie Crain came, I think the most difficult thing for them was to be in a community where there are so very few black people. I remember them saying to me in their first years that they occasionally had to go down to New York to mingle."

This remote corner of Connecticut, however, did not remain altogether untouched by the latest trends. The 1980s were the years of the Reagan administration, whose gospel of success seems to have provided an added impetus to the already success-oriented school. "Many Hotchkiss students consider their school as the first important business venture, the first accomplishment for one's résumé," observed Susannah Bartholomew, who entered as a lower mid in 1987. "It is such a grave mistake to view Hotchkiss that way; it closes the door to so much learning, self-discovery, and growth because 'success' becomes all-important. A student so eager for success sacrifices the true value of the Hotchkiss experience – self-discovery through the 'experience' is the ultimate preparation for life."

The eighties witnessed other subtle shifts. This was the decade when the school began to realize that parents of students dismissed for smoking marijuana or for other capital infractions were likely to slap Hotchkiss with legal suits. "In the old days," says Arthur White with a touch of nostalgia, "the parents were the ones who backed you up." Comments Zeph Stewart, "In the yuppie Hotchkiss setting, a better translation of the school motto might be, 'On advice of counsel let's look for a better deal.'" The somewhat good news, duly noted in the trustees' minutes toward the end of the decade: "There are very little drugs and alcohol on campus as compared to home environments."

There was other good news. With glasnost just barely under way in the USSR, Hotchkiss was one of the first schools to have a full-year student and a visiting teacher from the Soviet Union. "I was most interested to follow up on Bill Olsen's efforts to make our community up in the northwest corner of Connecticut a little more interested and oriented in global issues," says Arthur White. "I didn't want our students to forget that there is a world out there that they should be aware of, that they should understand and care about. If there are solutions to be found to the world's overcrowding, hunger, pollution, or whatever, I do believe those solutions will come from students who are now at the Hotchkiss School or schools like Hotchkiss."

It was precisely in furthering scholarly objectives and giving due emphasis to the life of the mind that Arthur White was perceived as not being ideally suited for the task, especially by Fay Vincent. His reservations about the headmaster predated his daughter's unfortunate experience at the school. In chairing the search committee that elevated the former mathematics teacher to the top spot, Fay had openly sacrificed his preference to tap someone from the university world. At that juncture, he had felt the school's most immediate need after Tim Callard was for a familiar figure who would bring everyone together.

From the beginning, the new headmaster and the president of the board had been at odds. "Arthur was new as chief executive," explains Fay. "He didn't understand that you couldn't go out and appoint a dean of the faculty without checking with the board, because we wanted to know who that person was. So I had to reverse him on that, and it got to be public, and the board supported me. I had been a trustee of Williams for eleven years, and I understood completely what the board's role was. But Arthur would go wandering over the line and do things that we couldn't let him do, and when I pulled him back, the faculty thought, 'Fay is really the headmaster.'"

Though he resigned in 1987 as president of the board to join Yale's former president A. Bartlett Giamatti in overseeing organized baseball, Fay Vincent remained a Hotchkiss trustee with an unstinting interest in the school. His continuing criticism of Arthur White, by then, was not going entirely against the prevailing tide. Within the torrent of goodwill that still inundated Hotchkiss in the late eighties ran a current of palpable malaise. Not so easily characterized, this was the feeling that Arthur's administrative approach was much too amorphous; that there were too many power centers with no overall control. Moreover, Hotchkiss traditionally thrived on the appearance of being on the move in new and exciting directions, inspired by the vigorous leadership of the headmaster. Now, there was a perception that the school was not going anywhere. It was also beginning to run in the red again.

"My sense is that the fun Arthur had the first couple of years diminished rapidly, and the job began to weigh on him," says Larry Becker, who was White's assistant headmaster for three years before leaving in 1986 to become headmaster of Brooks School. "I think his first thoughts came back to him: 'What have I got myself into?'"

Though Cynthia White's zest for her duties as the headmaster's wife remained undiminished, both she and her husband were sensitive to the overall situation. "Schools need headmasters with different strengths at different times," Arthur had often observed since stepping in to pull the school together at its moment of need. "The time will come when the school will need someone with a different expertise." And so, after thirty-seven years at Hotchkiss, years during which he had enjoyed the kind of career that others in his profession only dream about, Arthur asked to retire at the end of the academic year in 1989. He pointed out in his letter to the Hotchkiss community that this was an ideal time for the school to start afresh as it approached the beginning of its second century and its greatest fund-raising campaign yet.

Fay Vincent again chaired the search committee. Determined to leave no academic domain unexplored, he recruited as a consultant his old-time friend Bart Giamatti, then the baseball czar, as well as the search firm of Ingram, Inc., headed by Thomas G. Aydelotte '58. "There are a number of qualified applicants," it was noted in the minutes of October 1, 1988. "The plan is to winnow the list this fall to a very few finalists for broad interviewing by the Board and at the School, with a decision to follow as early this winter as feasible. Mr. Vincent has himself talked with forty-five members of the faculty as to their views on the School's needs and desired qualifications for the position."

An unforeseen development interrupted this orderly process. According to the minutes of the trustees' meeting held the following January, the search committee "had planned to present to the Board at this meeting a stellar young college professor [from Dartmouth] who had visited the School, met with members of the faculty, and particularly impressed the committee. However, the candidate had unexpectedly withdrawn earlier this week. . . . There followed a general discussion of the process to date and the next steps to be taken. . . . Most important, as the president announced to the acclaim of all, Arthur White has agreed to continue as Headmaster for another year, thereby assuring the school of continuity of leadership during the continuing search." The subsequent announcement to the school of Arthur White's extension at the helm was met with comparable acclaim.

Agreeing to accommodate the school for another year had not been an altogether simple matter for Arthur White. In a similar situation almost sixty years earlier, Walter Buell merely postponed some travel plans. But Arthur had already made a firm business commitment, which he would have to break. Says Geoff Marchant, "I was very close to Art, and he said, 'Geoff, I've got to stay.' I said, 'But Art, you've already got everything planned.' He shook his head. 'I can't leave. I can't let the school down.' And so he stayed."

Within two months, another unexpected announcement was made to the school and the Hotchkiss community at large: the trustees had found their superlative leader after all – coincidentally another member of the Dartmouth College faculty – and Arthur White would be stepping down as originally planned. "The entire Hotchkiss community should know the great loyalty and flexibility that Arthur and Cynthia White have shown during the headmaster search," wrote Edgar Cullman, who had taken over from Fay Vincent as president of the board, in a postscript to the announcement. For his part, the new headmaster, Robert A. Oden, Jr., stated in his acceptance, "The wisdom and the loving care of the Board were of decisive importance to me in making my decision, especially because I have come to see that those same qualities characterize the larger Hotchkiss community."

Arthur White proved to be as good a team player as Walter Buell, when he had been summarily re-retired after being given the go-ahead to stay in office at least another year. The reason for the board's seemingly precipitous action was that if they had not acted immediately, they might have lost their highly promising headmaster-elect. The converse, Why mark time for another year with the status quo? was left unsaid. "I think it's great they got Rob Oden," says Geoff Marchant, "but why couldn't he have come in for a year just to observe? It wasn't the money, because they paid Art a year's sabbatical anyway." What was perhaps most distressing to the faculty was that while Arthur White's original retirement had been of his own volition, now it appeared as though he was being publicly hustled out. "How often has Arthur said, 'The school is family'?" wrote one irate faculty member in an unsolicited discourse on the situation for the centennial history. "God preserve me from the family that treats its loyal members in this way."

"It was an agonizing thing for the board to have to do," acknowledges Edgar Cullman in recalling the event. "We all loved Arthur and were grateful for all that he and Cynthia had done. One of my first and most difficult tasks as board president was to meet with the entire faculty and explain the situation to them."

That was not to be the end of the school's turmoil. As Arthur White

Arthur White (right) with incoming headmaster Dr. Robert A. Oden, Jr. in 1989

was completing his tenure on a high note, being feted with Cynthia in New York and at a number of celebrations at the school, an event took place that to Arthur was probably more agonizing than any apparent personal slight. On the night of the senior dance, the school's president and two other class leaders were nabbed in a state of inebriation that could hardly be overlooked. Hostage to his own no-chance policy, Arthur White had no choice but to enforce the disciplinary committee's verdict and send the students home. Though he did temper the punishment by letting the offenders receive their diplomas through the mail, this did not lessen the upheaval felt throughout the school. Dispensing this form of justice was an aspect of his duties in which Arthur White could not avoid sharing the concomitant pain.

"The great strength of Art White, the thing that has made him an unlikely giant at Hotchkiss," wrote Ron Carlson, who taught English at the school during the seventies before becoming a novelist, "is his fundamental empathy. . . . He can see past class, color, age, and sex and see the kid in everyone, and it's terrific to be seen that way. Whether we're getting an award or a probation, he treats us fairly, like the children we in some ways still are: 'There,' he seems to say, 'you'll be all right. Just like me, you're not finished growing yet.'"

Concludes Larry Becker, "Hotchkiss will forever be indebted to Arthur White. He pulled the school together quickly when it was in the depth of despair, and turned it around into a joyous place. If Arthur hadn't taken on that task, he could still be doing what he loved the most — teaching and coaching and being the dean of students. I don't think there's any school anywhere that had a dean of students who was as successful as Art was for such a long period of time."

7 Privileged to be There

The new Main

As the Latin department might put it, *tempus fugit.* And as time flies, how it changes the constituency of the Hotchkiss world! At the turn of the century, Dr. Buehler suggested that a member of the Cullman family would be well advised to apply elsewhere. Toward the end of the same century, not only has a member of that family become president of the Hotchkiss board, but his son, Edgar M. Cullman, Jr. '64, has come full circle by choosing *not* to send his children to Hotchkiss – or to *any* boarding school. "It's a disappointment that we haven't tried to hide," says the younger Cullman, in his New York Culbro Corporation office, where he is the executive president and his father is chairman. "My older son is in tenth grade at Trinity School in New York. My father naturally wanted him to go to Hotchkiss, and my son certainly was qualified. But it's hard for us to let our kids go. We want to be a part of their lives. My second son is in the eighth grade, and my father is now anxious for him to consider Hotchkiss. If he does go away, does my first son feel as if he's been denied an opportunity? Or does my second son feel as if he's been sent out of the house?"

"It's not easy for me to understand," says Edgar, Sr., about Edgar Jr.'s attitude. "He was president of his class, captain of the baseball team, quarterback on the football team, member of the hockey team – all the things I wasn't. He did everything better than I did, yet he found the school a cold place and never developed the good feelings I did. Fortunately, my daughter, who didn't go to Hotchkiss, encouraged her son to go, which he did, to his grandfather's delight."

Among the lessons of Hotchkiss history is to be wary of drawing simple or hasty generalizations. Another member of Edgar, Jr.'s, class of 1964 happened to be Burn Oberwager, who was forced to leave toward the end of his senior year for downing a few beers in Millerton; yet, he has brought his son to look at Hotchkiss and has encouraged him to attend. "The school has changed, much for the better; much, much for the better," says Burn Oberwager. "The curriculum is exciting, and the support groups are exciting. I think Hotchkiss today gives a tremendous education and a tremendous preparation for life."

Although Oberwager's son, and other Hotchkiss sons and daughters of today, are likely to be intimately involved in the critical process of choosing their school, that decision used to be made almost entirely by parents until well into the 1960s. One reason Hotchkiss had failed to compete fully with Andover and Exeter before the 1970s was that the applicant pool of those schools to a large extent consisted of the sons of their own graduates or of their friends' sons. During the seventies, these familial determinants were on the wane. The competitive parity with respect to St. Paul's, Groton, and such other schools as St. George's began at about the same time, though an additional consideration was involved. "Hotchkiss historically didn't have the same clientele as the schools which had attracted the old money and the landed gentry from Boston, and to some extent, from Philadelphia," explains Christopher "Kip" Armstrong '63, author of several sociological studies of New England schools. "The old upper crust historically went to Groton and St. Paul's and on to Harvard. That's not to say there wasn't any old money at Hotchkiss. But from the beginning the school catered more to industrialists, Wall Street executives, and a variety of newly rich gogetters. It appealed especially to people from Greenwich and New York who were out to make their millions, and it prepared these people to go predominantly to Yale. This same appeal spread westward, and more gradually, southward."

Toward the end of the school's first century, the total applicant pool has become approximately six times as large as there are places for new students; indeed, a dramatic departure from the days when the school could hardly fill its beds. Only during the latter years of the Buehler era was the winnowing process greater, with as many as eight applicants vying for each available place. Yet even in those days of pre-registering years in advance, instant admission in some cases might be arranged. "I had been accepted at St. Paul's, and my mother brought me East from San Francisco," recalls the senior Lewis Lapham about his situation in the fall of 1923. "When we got to New York, she called St. Paul's. There was a long silence, and then they said, 'Mrs. Lapham, there's a terrible mistake. He's entered for next year.' So there she was with a fourteen-year-old in New York and needing to get back to California in a hurry. I had a cousin, Ray Lapham, at the Hotchkiss School. My mother called his father, and he said, 'I'll call you back in twenty minutes.' He called back and said, 'Get him up to Hotchkiss tomorrow morning!'"

Hotchkiss family connections continue to play a unique role in the admissions policies of the school. "We had approximately one hundred legacy applicants last year and accepted seventy-five," says Parny Hagerman, the psychology Ed.D. in charge of admissions,* who still projects the youthful chic of a postdebutante she chose not to become. "I can't imagine a school that doesn't acknowledge the strength of its alumni. The reality of life in a boarding school which is independently funded by tuition and an annual fund is that alumni and alumnae support is crucial. I don't think you can discount the kind of attention you should pay to their children's application. That doesn't mean accepting one hundred percent of them. It means realizing that their contributions to the school have been significant, and maybe we could take a risk, if need be, with one of their offspring."

The abundance of Hotchkiss applicants today did not materialize spontaneously. Over the past several years, Parny Hagerman and her half-dozen assistants have been scouring the United States and the world, traveling well over a hundred thousand miles each year. This

---

* Officially referred to in the school's brochures in the singular, "admission."

talent search has been undertaken in the belief that as vital as the school's magnificent facilities are, as indispensable as the faculty's role is, the sine qua non for bringing this together in a meaningful whole is the recruiting of an appropriate student body. "All other considerations aside, the ideal student is one who has a sense of purpose," says Parny. "This is not to say we're looking only for somebody who's motivated to achieve great things. At fourteen, a child is seldom motivated to that kind of a goal. But there has to be some kind of spark about that individual which will enable him or her to benefit from being here – and to contribute to the life of the school. The interview gives us a chance to get an idea of that. Then there are the more tangible criteria: current classroom performance, standardized testing, teacher comments, and the way the child completes the application. There are a couple of questions that make the kids think about what they've done for others. We're more inclined toward those who are concerned with others before they're concerned with themselves. We also listen to constituents like David Sermersheim of our music department, who says, 'I need this kind of cellist, I need this kind of oboe player.' We go out and find that person. We check to see what the sports program needs, what the arts and drama programs need. Above all, we seek a balance for the school. If we take only the brightest kids so we get a high acceptance at Yale, Harvard, and Princeton, then I think you lose sight of the purpose of the school. Yes, we want the brightest, but we also want those so-called middle-range kids who we know will work hard and are motivated to do well despite their tested ability. Though we take only one out of six from the general applicant pool, five out of six probably can do the work."

Where is this pool drawn from? With the stream of applicants from the traditional feeder schools reduced because of demographics (these schools are the most expensive in the entire educational system and provide the smallest amount of financial aid), Hotchkiss has nurtured a new source – the burgeoning array of gifted programs that have grown up in the public school systems over the past twenty years. According to Parny Hagerman, this source was not easy to tap: "At first, these programs saw us as a threat and a potential drain of their participants. They didn't want to have anything to do with us and practically slammed the door in our face. They simply had no idea what Hotchkiss was and more likely had unfavorable stereotypes of boarding schools. It took persistence and patience to keep going back to these gifted programs, whether it was outside of Raleigh-Durham, where the Duke program grew up, or outside of Chicago, where the Northwestern talent search grew up, or outside of Denver at the Rocky Mountain talent search. We got there early and we did it with perseverance. The people we contacted were not the administrators but the guidance counselors. They are the ones with the commitment to helping the child find the best educational alternatives. These counselors eventually let us in to talk to the kids and present the Hotchkiss story. Gradually we came up with another approach. We'd say to a counselor of a gifted program, 'If you've got a couple of personal days coming, Mr. or Ms. Counselor, why don't we fly you to Hotchkiss and you can see the school firsthand?' Not only was it less expensive to do it this way, but our guests had a chance to experience Hotchkiss firsthand, the way no one could ever present it. The usual reaction was disbelief that these kinds of places exist. When you think we used to cater to less than a half percent of the population – because those were the people who could afford it – this approach has opened our doors to 99½ percent of the rest of the population."

Without coeducation that theoretical 99½ percent figure could not have been approached. "Right now we have about 60 percent boys and 40 percent girls, which is based on the respective numbers of those applying," explains Parny. "Culturally, we have more boys applying because families feel it's okay to send boys away, and not quite as okay to send girls away. That's been consistent throughout the first fifteen years of coeducation. If the trustees ever said, 'Let's make Hotchkiss the best institution based solely on academics,' then I would say, 'Perhaps we should consider accepting more females,' because at this age level, they're smarter. It's in the upper grades they start believing maybe they shouldn't be as smart as the boys and begin to hesitate a bit in the classroom."

Having worked for several years in the admissions office at Deerfield, Parny Hagerman offers a broader perspective: "I truly believe Hotchkiss does deliver a wonderful product to children, but I don't think any one of us should believe that only Hotchkiss does that. Applicants who choose St. Paul's over Hotchkiss will have a different experience because of the nature of the school, but trying to discern the difference between schools sometimes is like splitting hairs. I think when we start to believe in other schools in addition to our own, we will come closer to being the sort of individuals on which Hotchkiss prides itself."

At the end of the school's first century, every fourth student entering Hotchkiss was receiving scholarship aid. The average grant per scholarship student: $11,578. Moreover, with boarding tuition in 1991 at $17,000, *every* student at the school was being subsidized about $9,000 from annual giving and the endowment fund. The other accomplishment related to admissions: over 20 percent of the enrollment today consists of students of color. To be sure, this figure includes individuals such as a relative of the late shah of Iran and a daughter of a Latin American president, who hardly fit the usual minority image. But Hotchkiss is finally approaching the 10 percent target of African-American and Hispanic students set by Bill Olsen in the 1960s.

"I went back to Hotchkiss for the first time a year ago, and I took my wife and son up there," says John Terenzio '72, the close friend of Dennis Watlington and experienced television news producer. "I walked around the campus, and I liked the kids I saw. The girls seemed to be well represented, and I saw a lot of minorities. There was an ease and comfort among the student body. I'm a reporter; so maybe it's my reporter's instinct, but all of what Dennis and I went through together there, they would now shrug off as 'No big deal.' I got no sense of the kind of tumultuous rebellion that was manifest when I was there. We live in Greenwich, where the public school is practically all-white, which is not what I want for my kid. I liked the way the students were at Hotchkiss. It seemed exactly like the kind of place where I'd want my son to go."

ii /

As a result of the school's recruitment efforts, the response which reputedly clinched for Tom Chappell his appointment as headmaster back in 1955 is incomparably more apropos today: indeed, there is no such thing as a typical Hotchkiss student. Presented herewith are statements from several members of the student body at the close of the school's first century. Any generalizations beyond what they specifically say are left for the reader to draw.

Daniel Lammot "Dan" Belin '91, of Waverly, Pennsylvania, co-editor in chief of the *Record* and a member of the varsity soccer and lacrosse teams: "I applied to four other schools and was accepted at all of them. When I was younger, I remember my grandfather talking about his Hotchkiss experience and going to the Ville to get a double buffalo. He said it was something like two pints of ice cream with marshmallow, so I always associated going to Hotchkiss with getting a double buffalo. But he wasn't the first Belin. Looking through one of the 'View' books from the admission office, I saw a picture of the class of 1895 with a Belin there. My mom told me he was grandfather's something-or-other. But neither my grandfather nor anyone else in the family put pressure on me. I think I chose Hotchkiss because both of my older brothers had gone there, and I had visited them on a few Parents' Days, and in the spring, for a few lacrosse games. The campus just completely overwhelmed me, it was so beautiful, and my brothers told me how much they loved it.

"Still, I had little idea what boarding school was all about. I had previously been at a public high school in the ninth grade, which I repeated here. The first test I had was in biology, and with my public school mentality I thought, 'I won't have to study at all for this.' Well, I got a 53, and it really opened my mind quickly as to what was expected of me.

"I also learned about dorm life pretty fast. A friend of mine, Shep Wainwright, always left his door open. One Saturday night everyone was at a dance, and a few of my friends and I went into Shep's room and took everything out and put it in the bathroom – his computer, stereos, posters, clothes, absolutely everything. The idea was to see the expression on his face when he came back from the dance. I lost track of Shep at the dance, but my friends assured me they'd keep him from his room until I got back. When I did get back, Shep met me outside and said, 'Let's go up to my room and listen to music.' So we all went up there, and when I walked into his room, absolutely everything was back in place. Then I remembered that I had left my door unlocked, and thought, 'Oh, my God!' I sprinted down to my room, and it was absolutely empty.

"Things like that help to lighten the situation when it gets to be stressful here. I personally don't feel that much pressure, which bothers a lot of my friends. They're always stressed out, and it's common for people to say how much work they have and everything else. That's sort of the norm in discussions. But if you step back and look at it in the larger perspective, you see it's overstated or overblown. The pressure really is whatever you make it, or sometimes your parents put on you.

"Right now, English is one of my favorite subjects. I'd always been stronger in math and science, but then lower mid year I had Mr. Torrey and he just blew me away. Here's a man who's been teaching for thirty-five years; yet you bring up an idea which he must have heard at least five thousand times and he still reacts as if he's never heard it before, and it's the most brilliant thing that he's ever heard. It really puts a lot of confidence in you.

"What continues to amaze me about Hotchkiss is its diversity. I knew it was coed, but I had no idea there would be so many minorities and foreign students. It's a whole learning experience outside of the classroom, with the various organizations giving speeches and performances which inform you what they're all about. I may be naive, but I don't think money plays a role here in terms of status. There are a few kids that you know, or have heard, have obnoxious amounts of money. But generally it's not visible. You don't say, 'There's a kid whose father has ten million dollars; there's a kid who only pays a thousand to come here.' Unless they choose to tell you, you usually don't know who the scholarship students are. And even if you did, you take people for what they are at Hotchkiss. Actually, it's the really rich kids who sometimes have a tougher time. People say, 'You little mama's boy, your dad's got all this money, so why don't you take your plane and get out of here?' Just joking around, of course.

"The big athletes are the people everyone sort of looks up to and cheers for. They're singled out more than the artists or the scholars or the actors. I think everything else falls short of athletics in the students' minds, and it's a great way to build school morale. Last year we had a fiasco during the fall when all our teams played Taft. They brought two or three busloads of fans and had about three hundred people cheering them on. We had a few parents, and that was about it. They beat us in every sport except in girls' field hockey. They just crushed and humiliated us. It demolished the school spirit for the rest of the fall.

"So, that winter we organized a hockey game against Taft, which was to be played at night. That way we could still get the kids who were playing sports in the afternoon to come. We got a huge turnout, and the hockey team won 5–0. It was just a great experience.

"Now, if I could only find a place around here where they knew how to fix a double buffalo."

Dan Belin was interviewed as a senior. At that time, Keva V. Hobbs '92, of New York City, was an upper mid: "I was in the Prep for Prep Program for minority students in New York. When I reached the sixth grade, I found out about Hotchkiss. During that summer I was able to come up here for four days to get a feel for what the place was like. After I entered as a student, I think it was a lot easier for me to make friends than for a white person. A lot of people in my class were not accustomed to seeing black people regularly, and they wanted to get to know me.

"I'm looking at Stanford right now. As for my chances, I know I'm a black female coming from prep school, and being realistic, I know I get a little bit of leeway there. Not much, but a little bit. I've been about an average student since prep year, and right now I'm pulling in a B minus. I have participated in sports, and I'm in extracurrics, and the faculty likes me a lot – not to toot my own horn, but they seem to like me. I might even apply to Yale, though not Harvard. I think I have a good chance to go where I want.

"My philosophy is to relax, and I tell people to relax. I think a lot of students are under pressure from their parents. They're alumni kids, and their parents went from Hotchkiss to Yale, or from Hotchkiss to wherever, and they want their kids to do the same. If they aren't working for their parents, they're trying to get a grade to beat someone else. A lot of my friends are taking economics. I ask them, 'Why're you taking that?' And they say, 'For college.' I would never take economics because it bores me to death.

"I'm not going to say I came here because it was a good opportunity. I came here because I was applying to day schools, but my parents at one point were driving me crazy, so I decided boarding school was something to try. I'm grateful my parents drove me crazy so I could come here. I was reading Ann Landers, and she had a quote that said, 'The only people who go back to high school reunions are the rich and the skinny.' Basically, since most of the people here are rich anyway, or skinny anyway, they don't come back for that reason. They come back because of the Hotchkiss magnet. It draws you back. I'll always come back to Hotchkiss."

Keva Hobbs's classmate Emmett T. Berg '92 is from Kalispell, Montana: "The admissions office sent a recruiter, Caroline Kenny Burchfield, through the Rocky Mountain States. She would call ahead and ask schools to round up students who might be candidates for a private school. So Mrs. Burchfield, who's now my advisor, came to my hometown in Montana. I knew I was basically in a rut. I could see that my friends and I would go to high school and go to work in a factory for five dollars an hour. Mrs. Burchfield arranged for me and some other students to go to the house of an alumnus. We sat down and talked about the school. She showed a video and answered questions. Basically, from then on I was hooked.

"My mother brought me up for the first year. The school I went to before was just one building. Here, when you come in the main gate, the buildings just seem to envelop you. You wonder how you're ever going to make it around. There is such a variety of people. I'd never seen a black person before I came to Hotchkiss. There aren't any in Montana. There aren't any Jews in Montana. There're no minorities at all. People in Montana are all white. And they're laid back. I get here and people are always moving. They're sitting on the edge of their seat. They want to keep going. They talk fast. They think fast.

"I got my first bit of recognition prep year when I played JV football. In one game I played really well. I made an interception, and they wrote it up in the school paper. People who read the article finally connected the name with the face. For the first time I walked down the hall and people knew who I was. I wasn't a face in the crowd anymore. I guess it's easier to make achievements in sports than in something like music. In music you can say, 'He sure played well.' But you can't name the spots where he played well. In sports you can say, 'Wow, I made this shot here, just blew the guy away.' Athletes are also more outspoken than people involved in other things.

"The real difference between Montana and Hotchkiss is in the teaching. They have the tenure system at home, which means you get someone who teaches for five years or so, and they're assured a job. At that point there's no incentive for them. They kind of lose interest in what they're teaching. At Hotchkiss the teachers are living right next to you, and they really seem to be into the work. Prep year in math I had Mrs. Monserrat, whose name is now Miss Stone. She gave me the study habits I needed to get interested in math. I liked her because she was on fire. Always moving around the classroom and yelling. It kept me awake and in tune with what was going on. She made me a pretty good math student. I went from 110 to 380 math. And then I had Uncle Roy Smith for English last year. I've never seen a teacher more attached to his work than Uncle Roy. He loves his students, and he loves his work. He makes you think like he does. I loved him for that, and for noticing when a person's attitude was different or unusual. He'd take you aside and ask what's wrong.

"You get used to the ups and downs. Just about my happiest day came early in the fall of my upper mid year. For the first time in my life, everything that I planned a certain way actually happened that way. I had a good day at football. I got a good grade on a test. I asked a girl out and she said yes. It was terrific. I had this terrific grin on my face. I couldn't believe it was finally happening to me. Then shortly after that, I got another test back with a terrible grade. I had a terrible day in football. And the girl I'd met said goodbye. That's Hotchkiss."

Another member of that final class of the school's first century is D. Brooke Harlow '92, of Litchfield, Connecticut: "I came from a school where many of my friends in the eighth grade were going to a prep school. I can remember coming here for a play when I was in the sixth grade and thinking to myself, 'If only I could get in!' All my old babysitters went here, and I looked up to them. I applied to several schools, and it came down to a decision between Exeter and Hotchkiss.

"I came from a very sheltered atmosphere. Here, there are kids from Saudi Arabia, Hong Kong, and wherever. I try to be friendly with everyone. Beyond my group of close friends, I do know the majority of students. We integrate well in class, and I don't see any clear evidence of minority or racial tension. But there are cliques, and they're visible. At meals, if you look around the dining hall, you'll see who sits with whom. Teachers can basically tell what section of the dining hall the student they're looking for is going to be sitting in. But I'm sure that's true at every school.

"I would never have come to Hotchkiss if it hadn't been coeducational. I think it's an important factor in how students interact with one another. I'd say probably seventy percent of the students get involved romantically at some point throughout the year. The faculty knows basically where not to go in the evenings. But it's very difficult to carry on a romance. If you go out with someone for two months, it seems like you've been going out with them forever because of the stresses and pressures of the school. People make a big deal about interdorm visitation, but I don't know what they think they can do considering all the stipulations – door open, light on, and as the expression goes, at least three feet on the floor. It's really not that important for me to see somebody else's room.

"There are quite a few support groups at Hotchkiss. People don't just sit around and lament their problems. I remember on my floor for the past two years, they had a week when some of the girls carried an egg around, pretending it's their baby. They'd name it, and care for it, and trade off every other day with a boy. I know one girl who broke seven in that week.

"I'm very much involved with sports. One of the high points for me was when we won the state championship in swimming. It was like one of those things you read about the Hoosiers, except it wasn't in Indiana and didn't have corn and basketball. This was swimming at the Hotchkiss School, and we won. Having all the people in the stands cheering for you and being poolside with our coach, Mr. Trethaway, and getting thrown in with everyone else on the team was just terrific. Then to go to the auditorium the next Wednesday and present this huge trophy to Mr. White was really phenomenal. But that was prep year, and I think sports are becoming more and more a part of the routine here. The emphasis is more on academics.

"Every time I come back from vacation, I realize I've got less and less time left. It seems like only hours ago I had four years, and now it's only a year and a half. I tell people, 'Don't let your years here pass you by. Take advantage of all the opportunities. Go for it!'"

Subsequent to the interview, Brooke Harlow was elected editor in chief for the *Record* for 1991–92.

iii /   As an assignment in the spring of 1990 for one section of his lower mid English, Blair Torrey asked his class of mainly fifteen-year-olds to try their hand at writing something for the centennial history. Of the dozen or so pieces submitted, there was not one that did not have at least an image, an idea, a phrase, or a paragraph to commend it. "I have been here approximately a month, that has passed as quickly as mist disappears from glass," wrote Douglas De Couto; two pages later, he concluded: "My experience here has been like a ship on the seas. Sometimes in the doldrums, sometimes calm and pleasing, with swells of emotion, and sometimes with the angriness of the howling wind and whipping spray battering the ship."

The first piece is by Sanjeet Singh "Sammy" Lamba, who was originally from India. True to his Sikh culture, he wears – even in class – a black cloth covering his hair, which is braided into a bun on top of his head. Though still one of the smallest of the lower mids, Sammy has a mischievous look and is considered to be a unique and admirable character by almost everyone at the school. The title of his barely legible effort on a sheet of three-ring notebook paper that may well have been a first draft is *School Nights:*

"Freeze dried, beef-flavored Ichilan brand noodles in hand and red plaid night slippers on feet, I begin my journey. One step, two steps – and I remember my door. Turning on my heels, I dive back, seconds before my door slams, rudely awakening the rest of the sleeping lower mids on my floor. They are terribly quiet at midnight, and one becomes very cautious of his actions.

"Once again, I begin my quest to reach Harm Lucas's room. One step, two steps, even three – and I remember that I need a bowl for the noodle soup. Backtracking, I re-enter my room and pick up the filthy glass bowl with Aphrodite (or Athena?) on it, stopping to read the Latin words written about the goddess's head. 'Meliora, sequamur, man . . . who cares?' I whisper to myself as I effortlessly slip back out of my room, stopping the door with my heel.

"One step, two steps, three steps . . . eleven steps, twelve steps, bathroom! Phase one completed, I crumble the noodles into the 'Athena bowl,' and drown them in the 150° water. Working quickly, I add the contents of the beef-flavored packet and mix it all into a sloshy concoction which I will happily devour upon reaching my destination.

"Curling the bowl under my arm, I begin phase two of my journey. One step – stirring in Casey Parker's room. Stopping dead, in fear of being caught, I hold my breath. After what seems like enough time for hell to freeze over, I resume.

"Fourteen steps – destination reached. Forgetting everything, I throw the door open and yell, 'Get up, zit face!' He is standing in his closet and says, 'Have a seat.' Slipping on a pair of tie-dyed boxer shorts, he begins a conversation which will last long enough for us to forget our homework."

Sammy Lamba's classmate Kara Marchant submitted a carefully computer-typed piece, which she left untitled. Kara is the daughter of Blair Torrey's English department colleague Geoff Marchant.

"It was a class for all seasons. Our teacher, Miss Stone, always said, 'In this class, you learn about math *and* life.' Prep year is always confusing; we had the fourteen most confused freshmen together, in one room, for forty-five minutes, five days a week.

"Miss Stone was very organized. She never was late for our class, even when she had mono. She would check things off in her Plan Book in three different colored pens. From the start she expected a lot from us, and by the end she got it.

"First there was Renato. He sat in the back row and was always coming into class panting, twenty seconds before the bell. He would walk in, check his watch, and throw himself into his seat. One morning, just after Renato had arrived and class had begun, I heard a tearing sound. I turned just in time to see Renato dumping the contents of a small white packet into his mouth. Miss Stone looked up from her book. 'Renato, is that what I think?'

"'I didn't have time to eat breakfast.'

"'Yes, but sugar?'

"Miss Stone was not only the teacher of Math 110, but also the varsity field hockey coach and very concerned with nutrition. So the quadratic formula was forgotten for ten minutes while we discussed the importance of breakfast.

"Another boy in the class was Hobby Brown. For the first two weeks Miss Stone pronounced his name 'Hobie.' I guess they just never hit it off from the start. Maybe it was because she was so organized and he was so disorganized. We always went over our homework in class. Hobby had been on a missing-homework streak for about three days. When Miss Stone called on him to answer a homework problem, he replied, 'I didn't get that one.'

"'You mean, you didn't do your homework?'

"'No, I did my homework.'

"'Okay, what's the answer to the next problem then?'

"A pall came over the room. We all looked at each other, stifling laughs.

"'I guess I didn't get that one either.' Hobby was asked to stay after class.

"I've always attributed my lack of mathematical insight to being left-handed, and after the first marking period it was apparent that I was having serious problems. So were two other girls – Nico and Karen. The three of us began going to Miss Stone for extra help on Tuesdays, seventh period. The first day we went I said, 'Hi. Here we are, the three stooges!' Miss Stone refused to call us that at first. By December when we were going to review before the exam though, she walked in and said, 'Okay, stooges, let's roll.'

"Winter is the hardest time at Hotchkiss. Everything is dreary and gloomy, and it's so hard to get out of bed in the morning, much less get to class on time. After we had settled into our seats, Miss Stone would walk in looking absolutely stunning and incredulously say, 'What's wrong with you guys? I got up at four-thirty to correct your homework. Chitchy boom, were they well done! I also baked you some cookies. Pass 'em around.'

"At the beginning of the new semester it seemed that we were all doing badly on our quizzes (she never gave us tests), and we were very frustrated. Finally she said to us, 'Consider these quizzes as opportunities, guys, and remember that there are more important things in life besides a math quiz.' After that we started to get extra-point questions about important world events.

"In our math books we were always getting problems about Calvin Butterball and his weight-loss program, or *I Am Small* and her weight-gaining program. 'My brothers used to call me the human blimp,' Miss Stone said.

"We all looked at each other. Miss Stone probably weighed less than some of the girls in the class.

"'It gives you a bad self-image,' Miss Stone continued. 'You always think that you're fat. Right, Nico?'

"Nico, who used to be heavy, nodded.

"'Besides, that's what guys are looking for. Someone skinny as a stick.' This led us into a half-hour discussion of how men think they can have spare tires around their middles, but their women need to have hourglass figures.

"Spring suddenly appears, bringing sun, and the outdoors, and that brilliant color of green again. By that time we were all beginning to understand math. If we didn't, Miss Stone could always call on Claudia. Claudia had joined our class in January. She was a princess from El Salvador, and we never really knew why she was in our lowly class. She usually never spoke unless she was called on. When no one else knew the answer, Claudia did, and so Miss Stone could always be assured that someone understood.

"But we really did pick up the pace the last marking period. Now we weren't just getting the extra-point questions on the quizzes; we could also do the mathematical stuff. Hobby started doing his homework (or paying his roommate to do it for him – at least, that was the rumor); Renato started arriving for class two or three minutes before the bell, with a full belly of breakfast. Best of all, the stooges did well. I got a B- on the last marking period and a B+ on the exam. At the time I guess we didn't really believe we would ever learn the math, much less anything about life. But sometimes when I get dressed in the morning, I think about the fashion lessons she gave us, and I always stop to see what the headline is in the newspapers. When I see people from that class, I have a vision of Miss Stone standing there that first morning, saying, 'Son of a biscuit out of a sixteen-story window, are we going to have fun this year!'"

An addendum to Kara Marchant's word portrait of said Miss Stone: as the school's assistant athletic director and coach of the girls' field hockey team that won the eight-school Founders League championship for seven consecutive years, Kelly Stone possesses the wherewithal to offer a post-game critique which could probably make a professional football team cower with shame.

Adam Bernstein's, *What Is This Thing Called Love?* was submitted on his own initiative. A member of '92, he describes himself as "one who does not like to associate with the fast crowd."

"The incessant beckoning of savage drums and Sadie Thompson's Siren Call drove Reverend Davidson to his doom in Somerset Maugham's *Rain*. This same human yearning, this same savage call beats through the white halls of Hotchkiss.

"Any member of our small community without a date on a Saturday night cannot step fifty feet without running into two lovers talking or – uh – talking. It makes the nonparticipant feel awkward. It makes him feel like a stranger in town, like William Bendix attending a party of swells.

"Years ago, Mr. Sermersheim, the head of the music department and director of the Hotchkiss Jazz Ensemble, had hall duty on Saturday nights. In order to keep from being driven mad (like Ingrid Bergman in *Gaslight*) from boredom, he would patrol the halls with his soprano sax in hand.

"The first notes of Serm's sax would sound slowly – Moanin' Low – and only produce mood music for the unsuspecting lovers. They would bill and coo as that old black magic of the dim hallways would work its magic on them.

"The music would get a little louder, and the lovers would start to wonder where that sound was coming from. It would seem a little frightening, since the last thing (or at least one of the last things) that a comfortably ensconced couple would expect to come into contact with on a Saturday night in a dark hallway would be a peripatetic sax player – at Hotchkiss anyway.

"When the lovers and Serm finally came into contact, Serm would run wildly up and down the scales of the saxophone as they would flee, and at last the dark corners were again safe for those of us whispering a lonely melody.

"So you see, Hotchkiss did have someone to combat the creole love call. Serm has since hung up his sax, and we no longer have this intrepid interloper to safeguard our school on Saturday nights. Once again Sadie Thompson's spirit lingers in the white halls of Hotchkiss."

The final piece appeared in 1990 in the *Record*, which should in no way be viewed as the same publication that was so thoroughly panned in the 1920s by its former editor and *Time, Inc.* cofounder, Britton Hadden, for specializing in "stories like: 'Dr. Flubdub will speak at Vespers,' and 'Hadden 1916 says that journalism is a good career.'" Though no longer published with the punctilious regularity of yesteryear, the *Record* today shrinks from no controversy and has virtually put the *Whipping Post* out of existence by preempting its bark.

The article by M. Nicole Morrison '91, which she spruced up for this history, offers a heretofore unique perspective on the Hotchkiss School:

"*Moniti Meliora Sequamur.*

"Quick, who can translate that? Being an avid Latinist, I can. But the average non-Latin-loving Kissie probably has no clue what the school motto means, much less from where it was taken.

"The motto is the last three words of line 188, Book III, of *The Aeneid* by Publius Vergilius Maro, known to us as Vergil. They are usually translated as, 'Having been advised, let us follow the better ways.'

"Yet this translation, as interpreted for a hundred years by the Hotchkiss School, misrepresents the original intent of Vergil's words.

"In brief, *The Aeneid* is an epic poem about a Trojan prince, Aeneas (hence the title), and his search for a new homeland after the Greek destruction of Troy. The story chronicles his voyages as he looks for what the gods have declared is the land from which a new race will be born.

"In the forty-odd lines that precede the motto, the story is as such: Aeneas and his men want to set up their colony on Crete, an island which is now part of Greece. They interpret an omen of the gods to mean that they should go there, when, in fact, the gods mean that they should go to Italy. As they are setting up camp in Crete, another portent is sent, informing Aeneas that he has screwed up in his interpretation of the first omen. Luckily for Aeneas, he has his father, Anchises, a wise old man, to help him realize that the gods want him to go to Italy. Anchises is the one who actually says, 'Moniti meliora sequamur.' The Trojans are in the wrong place, and they now must go to the right place.

"Most people interpret the motto to mean that at Hotchkiss the students will be advised to go on to bigger and better things. Taken in the context of *The Aeneid*, the motto means that the students have come to the wrong place!

"Therefore, I would like to propose a change. This idea was actually suggested by Zaid Es-Said '90, whom most old Latin students knew as last year's *wunderkind* of the classics department. His choice is '*Dant animos plagae.*' It is found in Book VII, the first three words of line 383. It literally means, 'The blows give it life.' Now, before you start thinking about sado-masochism, or any other sort of perversions, listen to my eloquent explication:

"Aeneas has finally arrived in Italy, and it is prophesied that he will marry Lavinia, the daughter of Latinus, king of Latium, where the Trojans wish to set up their new race of men. Juno, wife of Jupiter, king of the gods, detests Aeneas and does not want him to marry her. She talks Allecto, one of the three Furies of the Underworld, into driving Lavinia's mother, Amata, insane. Amata then runs through the city and woods like a wild animal, not realizing what she is doing. Vergil compares her to a top that is spun with a whiplash by little boys. The kids try to make the top go faster and faster, which brings them great amusement. Hence the line, '*Dant animos plagae.*' In the context of Hotchkiss, the teachers are the little boys, and the students are tops. The teachers try to make the students work harder and harder, seeing just how far they can go.

"Another suitable motto, in my opinion, is '*Forsan et haec olim meminisse juvabit.*' 'Perhaps someday it will be pleasing to remember even these things.' It is early in Book I, line 203, to be exact. Aeneas and his men are shipwrecked on a beach and are quite depressed because they appear to have lost several ships en route to Carthage. (They later find the lost men.) Aeneas encourages his followers to perk up; the Trojans have lost their home, faced Scylla and Charybdis, sailed all over the Mediterranean, and outwitted the Cyclops. They are not wimps. He ends his speech by saying the above line. In the same way, maybe after graduation, one can look back on all the trials and tribulations of Hotchkiss life and laugh!

"So, please, Doctor Oden, consider changing the school motto. Okay, so it will be expensive to use up all that stockpiled stationery, and all the rugs have to be relegated to the Classics Department office as antiquities, but think of what collectors' items all the mugs, cups, and shot glasses will become!"

iv / For every student at Hotchkiss comes a moment of unique reckoning.

In 1896, of the 35 seniors graduating in the first class to have gone to Hotchkiss for four years, 25 went to Yale. In 1991, from a graduating class of 158 seniors, 11 went to Yale. If Harvard and Princeton were to be added to those bound for New Haven in 1991, chalk up 6 more. If the entire Ivy League were to be included, that total would come to 38. Thus, the great majority of graduating seniors toward the end of the school's first century were heading for colleges outside the Ivy League.

What had once been a matter of routine – getting into the college of one's choice – has become a matter of schoolwide trauma. "It's a burden that your parents put on you, that society puts on you, that you put on yourself," says Brooke Harlow, an upper mid when she was interviewed. "The acceptances come in usually in early April, and I've learned to stay away from the mailboxes. One person on the right of me last year was screaming with joy and another on the other side of me was crying. One got into Duke, the other one was rejected. I was thinking to myself, 'My God, it is going to happen to me, too.'"

One inevitable result is pressure for grades. Although some students direct their efforts exclusively to numerical results, it is probably fair to say that the majority of them enjoy at least some of their courses for the stimulation they provide. The handful of basic disciplines-by-rote offered in 1892 has burgeoned to almost two hundred courses, covering such college-level fields as anthropology, economics, and philosophy. The modest art program started under GVS by Robert Osborn and Tom Blagden (and revitalized in the latter years of the Olsen era by Blanche Hoar) has alone expanded to sixteen separate offerings, supplemented by an array of courses in dance, drama, music, and photography. "There are quite a few subjects I'm taking this year that I don't even mind doing the homework for," volunteers Brooke Harlow. "The thought of college is definitely on everyone's mind, but I don't think it's the reason most people study. Next year, I'll probably be more concerned."

The pressure on students to get into the "right" college is of special concern to the faculty. "We have many students who are eager to learn *and* to get a good grade," says Sarah Tames, who was appointed to head the English department in 1986, when Blair Torrey chose to step aside. "Unfortunately, I seem to spend much more time than I'd like talking to students about grades. I worry that perhaps I'm getting too difficult, too demanding, too harsh. A low grade can kill their chances to choose the college they want."

College placement is another of the many functions which George Van Santvoord handled virtually alone. "After I became a member of the faculty," recalls Blair Torrey, "Martha Shouse, who guarded the archives, asked me once if I would be interested in seeing the recommendation the Duke wrote to Princeton. I said, 'Sure,' and she showed it to me. It was about three sentences long. It said, 'To the Admissions Director: Torrey' – it didn't even say Blair – it said, 'Torrey is a pretty good athlete. The thing about him is he lacks any ambition at all. But take him.' And they did. I'll never understand why, except for the Duke."

Few would claim that the Duke or any earthling could have that sort of influence today. "Certainly the old-boy network as it existed decades ago has died," says John C. Virden III '64, whose father graduated from Hotchkiss in 1941 and then went on to Yale along with virtually half of his class. For several years, the younger Virden headed the college counseling staff at Hotchkiss before being appointed as the school's first provost by Rob Oden in 1991. "What happened in the past is that you were in a sort of lockstep process. If you got into the right nursery school, that would guarantee you the right grade school, which would guarantee you the right prep school, which would guarantee you the right college. Certainly there are kids on that same track, but there is no guarantee anymore. It's a lot narrower track. As recently as twenty years ago, it was not unheard of that some screw-up from prep school might get the nod over some kid who was number one in a high school in Pocatello, Idaho. Mind you, legacies are still a factor that's appreciated by a lot of the competitive colleges. A legacy alone will not make an applicant acceptable, but it is definitely one of the factors – all other things being pretty much equal – that will help a student get the nod over one who's not 'family.'

"College counseling is inevitably a series of disappointments – for us and for the kids," continues Virden. "The Yale admissions office gets approximately fourteen thousand applications for its two thousand places. Of those applicants, there are probably five hundred who aren't qualified and a like number that get accepted pretty quickly. That leaves thirteen thousand qualified kids struggling for fifteen hundred places.

"Dick Gurney used to say, 'Hotchkiss doesn't take the great kid and make him even better. Hotchkiss takes the good kid and makes him better.' Hotchkiss has traditionally done a great job in taking these middle-of-the-road kids and giving them an opportunity to succeed. And these are the kids for whom the college placement game has changed the most. They are the ones in that huge group of qualified applicants struggling for the relatively few places at Yale, Harvard, Princeton, and places of that ilk.

"Of course, the world does not revolve strictly around Yale, Harvard, and Princeton. One of the biggest frustrations we deal with is a myopia that exists on the part of many of the kids and their parents. It may be merely that the parents want the kids nearby, but their world seems to end on the other side of the Hudson River and doesn't start again until the west slope of the Sierras. One of our main jobs in college counseling is to convince students and their parents that there isn't just a big dark hole out there, but a real world of academic opportunity. There are around three thousand colleges for undergraduates, and our list extends to no more than perhaps a hundred and fifty. So we are still being selective. Our job as college counselors is to empower students to make intelligent decisions."

A Hotchkiss senior about to embark on this "empowerment" process provides a student's-eye-view. "If you know anything about choosing the right college, you know more about horse racing than you thought," wrote Walter J. Gengarelly III '91 in the *Record*. "It's all one big gamble. I look at the colleges themselves as the equivalent of horses, and what do you need to bet on horses? Bookies – that's where the college office comes in. They take your 'bets,' which in turn affect the odds of other students getting into college. What you underclassmen have to look forward to in the summer of your upper mid year is a thick letter from the college office. In it is the priceless sheet containing the odds of getting into [each one of more than a hundred colleges]."

And what do the odds average out to on that select list of colleges? "About four to one," says Virden. "It's not a buyer's market, and they can be choosy. Do they need Hotchkiss kids more than any other kids? They like good students. We have good students here, but that doesn't mean they're going to choose Hotchkiss because it is Hotchkiss. I have no doubt that any one of our students, given the opportunity, could attend any college in the country, with a very few exceptions. The frustration is that they won't be able to."

A different sort of frustration for Virden comes from not knowing how individual Hotchkiss students perform once they do get to college. In the old days, it was a matter of routine for Hotchkiss boys going through college to receive kudos from their respective headmasters for making the dean's list and other achievements – and excoriation for any shortcomings. Coy, Buehler, and especially Van Santvoord acted as virtual stand-in deans for their graduates at Yale. (I shall never forget the letter of profound disappointment from GVS in reaction to my own dismal grades at the end of my first semester at Yale. I could hardly wait for the end of the next marking period to rush up to Lakeville with a report card in hand, even before the Duke had been officially notified. How much did his exhortation to "retrieve" the situation have to do with the dramatic turnaround?)

"Because of the Buckley Amendment, the colleges can no longer release that information," explains John Virden. "So we get very little feedback. If college X decides to take boy Y, whom they consider a risky candidate, and we call up and say, 'Remember last year when you took boy Y? How is he doing?' They can't tell us, even though it would be invaluable to the admissions process vis-à-vis that college in the future."

Diminishing that symbiotic relationship, however, can have its benefits. "We're under tremendous pressure by colleges for SAT scores and test results and measurements of that sort," says Charlie Lord '52, who spent almost two decades as an international business executive before becoming headmaster of the Holton Arms School. "That's a tragedy which is neither necessary nor one we can afford. Hotchkiss certainly doesn't have to give in; it is strong enough to take risks and provide educational leadership – as is Exeter, as is Andover, as are other schools. At Holton Arms, we're asking, 'What should the educated person of the twenty-first century know? All right, let's do a profile of the United States in the year 2010 and ask, 'What do we think people should be exposed to and have knowledge of – or at least have an opportunity to learn about?' Then we should say to the colleges, 'We've got the same quality student we've always had, but if you aren't going to take them because they aren't taking an extra year of a traditional subject, we'll send them on to another college.' That's a movement I'm sensing among independent schools. I think Hotchkiss can open up more. Hotchkiss can be more innovative; not knee-jerk innovation, but thoughtful innovation. The colleges aren't changing the way they should be; so I think the strong schools have to take the lead."

v / For most of those who have graduated or otherwise departed from the school's guardian embrace, the continuing link to Hotchkiss is most directly maintained by a tall, lean, balding man named William E. Appleyard. Head of alumni/ae relations since late 1968, when Ted Cooke left to join the Yale development office, Bill has the outward calm of a Zen Buddhist but betrays the sensitivity within by a tendency to blush. What is so unusual about his holding this position is that he happens to be a graduate not of Hotchkiss, but of the nearby Salisbury School. That is about comparable to appointing a non-Catholic as the Vatican's director for the propagation of the faith. Yet it is precisely this extramural dimension, combined with his two decades plus of inside experience, which has helped to hone Bill Appleyard's view of those who have passed through the school: "What impressed me right away was how the alumni tried to help this outsider. One in particular was Roy Wilcox from the class of 1912. I had been here all of a week or so when he came up to show me *his* campus. He hadn't been here for some time and hadn't seen the new Main. So we started by parking the car by the athletic complex, which he knew, and from there we walked through the Scoville Gate. I could see he was trying to orient himself. He seemed vaguely aware that the old yellow brick building wasn't there. Ahead of us loomed the new Main, which at that time had no windows in the front, and the big square turrets went way up. He grabbed me by the arm about halfway down the driveway and said, 'My God, when the Russians attack, we'll be ready for them.'

"I would get letters from him about once a month, and he would sound off about all sorts of things. But the most important thing about Roy Wilcox was that he loved the school. So many people mention this time and time again about how they feel about the school. They loved it as a place, and for the friends they made, but ultimately they would say it was the teachers who made the difference. When I talk to an alumnus in his living room, even someone who graduated from here around fifty years ago, I'm almost certain that if I can bring up the right teacher, he will talk about that person for an hour, sometimes with tears in his eyes."

There is also a practical dimension to this love. "The reason why alumni come back, the reason why they give money," explains Penn Hulburd '74, "is because they know that those people [like Uncle Roy Smith] are here teaching and coaching the same way they were twenty years ago. They know that for another ten or fifteen years, they'll still be here and they're hoping to get their sons and daughters in, like I am."

This sort of devotion runs both ways. Retired teachers often take up residence in the vicinity of the school; others continue to contemplate from afar their Hotchkiss days and the students they encountered over the years. Penn Hulburd's classmate Tom Cholnoky provides one such saga of this enduring Hotchkiss tie: "The one guy you didn't want to cross while on the athletic field was Nels Corey. He'd had some of the best New England lacrosse teams ever. In our senior year, we turned out to be the worst team he ever had. We had gone down to play Army one Wednesday, and we played just miserably. The next day, when we came out to practice, it was a dark afternoon with storm clouds, and Nels Corey started laying into us like there was no tomorrow. It was almost on cue that every time he swore at us, there was a clap of thunder and lightning. This lasted for about ten minutes. I can remember the day vividly because of that thunder and lightning and Nels Corey going absolutely berserk, and all of us on the team shaking in our boots. Of course, we also knew how much Nels Corey cared about each of us personally. On our tenth and fifteenth reunions, our class invited him and his wife to have dinner with us at the school. He had already retired and was living in Maine. It was about a six- or seven-hour drive for Nels, but he came down both times with his wife to spend the weekend with us."

"The other aspect I always hear about," says Bill Appleyard, "is the lifelong friendships that Hotchkiss engendered. I remember Lew Lapham, the older Lew Lapham from the class of 1927, telling me about meeting for the first time his roommate, Bob Heurtematte, who was from Panama. They became such good friends that they roomed together all four years here and all four years at Yale. You had in that class also Gaylord Donnelley from Chicago and the senior Fay Vincent. Fay had been a scholarship boy recruited from Torrington by Otto Monahan. More diversified people you couldn't have possibly put together, but they began to bind together and form a friendship. Fay Vincent would have been the first to say he was not a student. Lew Lapham told me each one of them – Bob Heurtematte, Gay Donnelley, and Lew – would take turns tutoring Fay, and he finally graduated from Hotchkiss. They all went to Yale together, and the same thing happened there. Lew Lapham, Gay Donnelley, and Bob Huertematte became very successful businessmen each in his own field. Fay wouldn't be particularly successful in terms of business, but he had been an incredible athlete and the most popular person probably in that whole decade. He was captain of the baseball and the football teams at Hotchkiss and at Yale, and he was voted in as their class agent and class representative year after year. Fay would never ask his friends for a dime. He'd just drop them a note along about September or October, and say, 'Gee, I was up at Hotchkiss, and it's that time of the year.' And they'd send in their checks. This was before his son came to national prominence, although young Fay was a wonderful athlete here and had already established himself on the board of trustees at Williams and on the Hotchkiss board. No one could have been more proud than his father. And none of this which I'm telling you about Fay Vincent and the class of '27 escaped young Fay's ears. When it was time for big Fay's fiftieth reunion at Yale, Fay, Sr., was no longer alive. Fay, Jr., came to the Yale reunion with Gay Donnelley, Lew Lapham, and Bob Heurtematte, and because of their friendship with his father, he presented them and their class and Yale with a $100,000 scholarship in his father's name. Fay didn't even go to Yale; it was because of that friendship which had been first formed between his father and his three friends at Hotchkiss. And Fay made an identical gift to Hotchkiss in his father's name."

Giving by Hotchkiss alumni and alumnae has hovered around the 50 percent mark in recent years, with the women holding a slight percentage edge over the men. Though this places Hotchkiss in the top rank of private educational institutions, the school has not given up on those who year after year fail to participate. "I'm always sensitive about those people who for one reason or another are disenchanted," says Bill Appleyard. "It may be because they didn't have a happy experience here, or because they had been kicked out, or because their child or grandchild had been rejected by the admissions office, or for any number of reasons. This may be a person who has never come back for a reunion, never given to the annual fund, and then suddenly for some reason you'll get a letter in the mail or they are on the phone talking to you. Hotchkiss probably has more of those people who left or were expelled than any other school, but who still come back to reunions and still give a gift to the annual fund and, perhaps most important, consider themselves a part of the school.

"One of the biggest surprises was when we decided to take in girls. We thought we would get more 'Why are you guys going coed?' mail. But instead of being beleaguered, suddenly we heard from all those alumni who had daughters and granddaughters and now saw a chance for them to share their Hotchkiss experience. As for those who did express disenchantment, I can say fifteen years later that they may not agree with the whole process as enthusiastically as those of us do here, but they cannot deny that it has been successful."

Among that first group of girls entering the school in the fall of 1974 was Caroline Kenny Burchfield '77. Until recently the director of the annual fund,* she first returned in 1986 as a member of the admissions staff and, not surprisingly, echoes Bill in many respects: "As a student, I'd had trouble in certain subjects, and there were times when I thought I'd never get through here. The support of some of the teachers is what made the difference, particularly Mr. Marchant. The way he teaches is the way he lives his life. Robert Burns is a hero to him, and he has traveled to Scotland to visit his grave. He teaches Thoreau and Emerson, and those two people are his personal guides. He conveys that en-

---

*Her involvement is now limited by growing family responsibilities. Irene C. "Rena" Longstreth '82 is the annual fund director. She is the granddaughter of Tom Blagden '29.

thusiasm to the students, and you can't help but become a believer. You want to do well for him. Because he believed in me, I wanted to do well for him. I wanted to prove him right. In coming back to Hotchkiss, I wanted to have that sort of impact on somebody else."

Being on the front line of fund raising for the school has often exposed Caroline Kenny Burchfield to a variety of forthright views: "Van Santvoord generates some very powerful emotions. There are people out there who wouldn't give a dime to the school because of him. People either loved him or hated him. Interestingly, Bill Olsen is another one people feel either very fondly about or the exact opposite. I had a conversation with Jerry Sprole, chairman of the annual fund, recently about Olsen. [Frank Jared Sprole '65, son of the former board president.] He said this man was larger than life and whatever he said, you accepted, no questions asked. And that's how we felt in my time. He was a towering presence and aloof. I think that's how Hotchkiss developed the reputation of being a cold and uncaring place. I used to hear that over and over again when I was an admissions officer. And it was true. We had been insensitive in so many ways. It used to be that scholarship students would have special work programs here. I can remember on Sunday mornings heading off to brunch with friends; if one of them was on scholarship she would have to go and sweep the main hallway of the building. And that stays with you. Fortunately, we're not like that now. We are finally becoming a caring place. One of my joys is that I'm living at the school and experiencing the Hotchkiss connection every day. When I walk out of this office into the corridors, I'm a part of the energy the students create, and I'm able to remind myself what it is that I'm raising money for. If I can convey that to the alumni, then I've succeeded."

That Hotchkiss connection – maintained over distance and time – has instilled in large numbers of the school's alumni/ae a spirit marked by a fervor approximating that of a religion. When they return for a visit and pass through those gracious Georgian gates, they are likely to feel this spirit almost as a palpable presence, enveloping them and even overwhelming them with memories of their days on the hill. Many feel the same spirit as they gather annually from coast to coast for dinners marked by good fellowship and, at the end, an emotional rendering of "Fair Hotchkiss." And this spirit is evoked whenever classmates happen to meet, whether by design or by chance, somewhere in the United States or in one of the more than fifty countries around the world where Hotchkiss men and women reside. The clock is unconsciously turned back, and they are again together in class, sweating it out for a final exam or on the playing field cheering on good old Blue. Even if they did not consider themselves particularly close in those days, they will suddenly realize how much they really shared.

A notable contemporary drama involving the Hotchkiss connection revolves around Howard C. "Smoky" Bissell '55 (recently elected vice president of the trustees) and his role in the building of Garland Hall, the latest addition to the school's facilities. In no way related to the Bissells involved in the founding of the school, Smoky had been a jolly, gregarious prep from Florida, and lanky Bill Garland had been his soft-spoken classmate from California, who seemed imbued with an almost spiritual elegance. The two met on the first day of school in Buehler, where they were on the same corridor. Bill Appleyard picks up the story: "Like Lew Lapham and Bob Heurtematte more than thirty-five years earlier, Smoky Bissell and Bill Garland remained close friends through Hotchkiss. They both went to Yale, and roomed together all through Yale. They both went into the navy, and afterward Smoky came out to California for a couple of years. They both married and continued to keep in close touch until Bill was killed in an airplane crash in 1967. Smoky Bissell by then was a very close friend of the family. A few years ago, Smoky told the trustees, 'I've had a certain amount of success in business but I've never given more than sixty thousand dollars as a personal gift to any institution. I've been thinking what I want to do for Hotchkiss for its centennial, and I want to give a million dollars of my own. But what I want to do with that is to go to Bill Garland's mother and sister and ask them each to consider a gift of one million dollars to build Garland Hall.' He had kept up the relationship over the years since Bill died, and within a week's time, they had each committed a million dollars to the dorm. The Garland Foundation doesn't like to put its name on anything, but in this case agreed to do just that. At the dedication of the dorm, Smoky read an emotional tribute to his roommate. Edgar Cullman spoke, Rob Oden spoke, but the day belonged to Smoky and the friend he had made on his first day at Hotchkiss some forty years ago."

8   Approaching Year 2000

O f the approximately 150 Hotchkiss graduates, teachers, and staff interviewed for this centennial history, two followed up spontaneously with letters relating to the future of the school.

Thomas S. Quinn, Jr. '35, retired chairman of the Lebanon Steel Foundry in Lebanon, Pennsylvania, and a lifelong fund raiser for the school wrote in part, "There is a fundamental question at the heart of our educational system which demands to be answered: what can we do to avoid or lessen the tragedy of each generation's repeating the moral errors of the past? Does wisdom have to come only through our own bitter experience?

"All of my heroes in history have turned out to be flawed. I have to conclude that all of us just plainly have clay in our feet, limitations we cannot overcome. The irony of life is that while we think and try to control our destiny, events unravel quite differently. Great artists and sensitive people have been inclined to view the human situation as one great tragedy. A little comedy makes it more digestible, but not especially hopeful.

"I learned early in life that the greatest asset we have is the human spirit. George Van Santvoord engraved that on me, and I have since felt that there is nothing more worthwhile. His was the driving force awakening the intellect of each and every student to the wonders of the world and the ways we should seek to approach them. We learned from him the importance of curiosity and a good sense of humor. He taught us to love diversity. He taught us to be individuals dedicated to service and the public good.

"Our national tradition is to emphasize a pluralistic approach, combining public and private efforts. In education, this implies not only competition, but the freedom to experiment and to evolve. Hotchkiss must continually seek the best ways to prepare our youth for whatever lies ahead. The school's only justification – and claim to elitism – will rest in producing future generations of graduates who will strive to rise above the sort of moral failings which we, as human beings, eternally seem to inherit."

A curiously complementary perspective on the long-range role of Hotchkiss is implicit in the letter from Marcellus B. "Gus" Winston '55, the first black student at the school. Gus Winston offers as a model of excellence a school which appears to be just about as different from Hotchkiss as can be:

"When my daughter approached high school age, I wanted her to consider boarding somewhere – if not Hotchkiss, then maybe at Andover, say, or St. Paul's. My arguments had to do with the presumed superior quality of teaching, as such, green fields and sports, quasi-independence, and simply being off the streets (on her way to school one morning, she had a close call when she was shoved from a subway platform into the path of an oncoming train) – though what I meant incommunicably was that she might come across a George Van Santvoord, which I knew was hardly likely.

"But she refused to leave the city. So I obliged her, against fierce initial resistance, to accept admission to Stuyvesant High School. ('But, Dad, a public school?') Stuyvesant and its sister school, Bronx Science, consider themselves to be the best science and math high schools in the world. For several decades, Bronx Science was the slightly more prestigious of the two, presumably because it was ensconced in a middle-class Jewish neighborhood. Stuyvesant has been slightly ascendant since the late seventies, allegedly because it's closer to Chinatown. Enrollment at both is now about 40 percent Asian. Each class at each school comprises seven hundred students. Admission is solely by exam in a system of a million pupils. When my daughter took it, fifteen thousand kids competed for three hundred places.

"I don't know what goes on inside the school. It's an ancient, four-story building on East 15th Street, with sparse indoor athletic space; no pool, no fields, and decrepit labs, etc. In some spaces it gives a distinct feeling of being ramshackle, as rickety as old Main. But the couple of times I was there the place throbbed with almost flaunted high energy. The students I met didn't doubt they constituted the best school in the world.

"I don't think I've had many experiences as moving as her graduation ceremony in Avery Fisher Hall. There they were, seven hundred of them, in boisterous high energy that mocked anybody's afterlife creed, in virtually every size, shape, shade, and class of American human being imaginable. A young lady named Christine Hinkley was valedictorian and won the biology and English prizes. A young man named Sanjoy Dasgupta won the physics prize and the second mathematics prize. The language prize for Hebrew went to a tiny Vietnamese girl named Celia Ng, and the Japanese prize to a splay-footed, six-foot-six fellow named Goldhammer. Michael Hutchings won the math prize and was noted for having won a couple of computer science competitions. He was officially handed his Air Force Academy appointment by the commencement speaker, Col. Ron Grabe, Stuyvesant '62, who had just commanded the first shuttle flight (his third) following the *Challenger* accident. The school principal whimsically had looked for currently 'newsworthy' eminence and came up with Robert Moses, S'52, the SNCC philosopher-saint of the civil rights movement of the sixties, and Eric Lander, S'74, who'd been first in his class at Stuyvesant, then at Princeton, and is now a Harvard mathematician and geneticist, and a MacArthur Fellow.

"Not much Roman in any of that (there was a Latin, but no Greek, prize), but T. Jefferson – who, for that matter, had little respect for classical or any other authorities – would have delighted in it. And so, too, would G. Van Santvoord, whom, not unusually, I found sitting with me there."

ii / **P**laying on the school football team with Gus Winston during his senior year was an upper mid who would one day leave his mark on the school and on the world beyond. Not only his position on the Hotchkiss board and his public visibility as baseball commissioner, but also his lively memories of his days at the school make Fay Vincent's account of particular interest: "In my first year we had a Latin teacher named Russ Edwards. We used to call him rather ungraciously Fat Russ. He was a very heavy, sort of glandular fellow, and a wonderful teacher. One day in Latin Ib, which was the beginning Latin course, he decided to go around the room and predict how people would do. Being a brand-new prep, I was very intimidated by the school, and I wasn't sure whether he was predicting for just Hotchkiss or for life. He may have meant well by it, but it was a rather ruthless exercise. Some people he summarily wrote off; others he sort of anointed. When he got to me – he used to call me Vinchente – he said, 'As for you, Vinchente, you could go either way.' I took that very seriously to heart.

"In my lower mid year, when I came back from summer vacation, the Duke met me virtually on the steps of old Main, and said, 'Mr. Vincent, you're going to take Greek this year.' It never occurred to me to ask why, but I later learned that what the Duke did was to pick the top twenty students in each class and send them to study Greek. I must have been the twentieth, and that's the way Alan Hoey got his Greek class. It was, therefore, a very good class, and classics have been a part of my life ever since.

"In my upper mid year the Duke wrote a letter to my parents saying that Fay was a very good boy, he had done well, but he doesn't yet think of himself as a leader. 'He ought to do so quickly,' the Duke said. 'Other people will follow.' And that was the first time in my life that I ever thought that maybe there was something other than a routine existence ahead. I think the Duke really did point me toward trying to exert myself a bit more, and that was significant.

"The last turning point in growing up was when I broke my back at Williams and was in very bad shape. I found myself thinking a lot about the fact that I couldn't be a jock anymore, that I couldn't play sports anymore. It had been a big part of my life. The thing I remember falling back on was the Hotchkiss focus on the primacy of the mind. As long as you could think and read and enjoy the pleasures of the mind, everything else was in place.

"I think Hotchkiss had an enormous effect on me. I remember when Dan Lufkin [Dan W. Lufkin '49, founding partner of Donaldson, Lufkin and Jenrette, Inc.] and others hired me to run Columbia Pictures, I put a photo of the Duke on my desk. Dan came in to see me and said, 'What the hell is that doing there?' I said, 'Let me ask you a question, Lufkin. Other than your parents, what adult has had a greater impact on you?'

"When I was president of the board, I ran into some criticism up at the school. The faculty said, 'Fay's trying to bring back the Duke, and the Duke wouldn't be successful.' I said, 'You're absolutely wrong. The Duke would have been successful.' He would have adjusted, even to coeducation, though that would have been the most difficult part. After he retired in Vermont, I used to go see him up there. He reminded me of a Civil War general on horseback. I asked him once what he thought about the prospect of girls at the school. He said, 'Twice the trouble and half the fun.'

"My ideal headmaster has always been the Duke, but there aren't many Dukes. I've met only one in my life. I didn't meet a close second. We were walking around the farm another time, when I asked the Duke, 'What's the critical element in being a great headmaster? What's the key?' He said, 'Picking the faculty.'

"My view of the Olsen tenure – and I said this to him, and he really didn't disagree – is that he did a number of things terrifically well. The major negative mark I gave him was he didn't build a great faculty and he didn't replace the Duke's major figures with figures of equal standing or stature. I asked Bill Olsen after he left, 'Who are the major figures you put there who are going to lead the place to higher and greater excellence? Where are they?'

"Tim Callard was in the wrong place at the wrong time. I headed the search committee for his successor, and we felt compelled by circumstances to give the nod to Arthur White. I think Arthur was in many ways successful. He was successful because people liked him. He was warm. He created a sense of family and good feeling. Unfortunately, in my book that doesn't count for enough. My view of Hotchkiss is a very intellectually oriented one, and Arthur was not the man to take Hotchkiss in that direction. I wanted to focus on the school's deficiencies, but I couldn't make progress without a strong headmaster, and Arthur was not a strong headmaster in my sense. I believe the quality of the school and of the faculty deteriorated in those years. It was particularly painful for me with a daughter going through the place having a bad experience, not getting a terrific education, not getting any social or developmental sense. Although I could have intervened, I didn't until the very end on the theory that it would have been wrong for me to give her a different experience just because I was head of the board.

"If I did one thing for Hotchkiss as a trustee, as chairman, it was to force the school to think what it was, to define itself. This came from the process of the strategic planning study that I started. There again, I probably shouldn't have done that because the premise of a good strategic study is a strong administration that can stand the process of sort of pulling up everything by the roots, taking a look, and then replanting those that belong. I made a mistake, and the board made a mistake in doing that study while Arthur was headmaster. The faculty went crazy. They thought there were all sorts of threats to their existence. The faculty came out and said they didn't want to be 'the best.' The best connoted competition. The idea of being better than Taft, better than Andover to them sounded too much like a businessman. They just had a kind of soporific concept, 'We want to do our thing.' I told them I thought it was Plato who had something to do with the concept of excellence. In the end, they wouldn't let me say that Hotchkiss wanted to be the best. It was a trade-off. The phrase is, 'Hotchkiss is to continue to enhance its standing as a great independent secondary school.' That really symbolized the level of leadership.

"The school's mission is basically to educate people for their next stage in life. It's not necessarily preparing you for Yale or Harvard or Princeton – as it used to do almost exclusively – but for more eclectic activities. What Hotchkiss is trying to make people do is to enjoy, utilize, and benefit from their own abilities. The world to some extent is really beyond Hotchkiss's planning, but the students' own capacities and talents and abilities are clear enough. I'm with Pascal, the philosopher who said, 'The greatest challenge is to spend time in a room by yourself.' Hotchkiss succeeds to the extent that it increases a person's ability to live at peace with himself or herself, to be able to sort through and think clearly about his or her own objectives – not only as a decent citizen, a little atom in society, but ultimately to be relevant to the larger molecule.''

The interview with Fay Vincent took place early in the morning, before regular hours, at the New York office of the Major Leagues' baseball commissioner during the hectic days of the preseason baseball lockout in 1990. As his Hotchkiss visitor was about to leave, Fay offered an afterthought: "I don't want to sound like the enfant terrible of the board. On the other hand, that's the role I've played, and somebody has to be there in that role." He paused, then added, "Dick Gurney said an interesting thing to me once that you might want to use. He said, 'Look, if you stay at Hotchkiss or any place like Hotchkiss long enough, every single facet of human behavior and experience will come through. Everything – good, bad, and indifferent – takes place within Hotchkiss.' And that certainly is true. All of the miseries of life, the suicides, the sort of convoluted psychology you have up there, all show up – and all of the greatness shows up as well.''

Fay Vincent received the Alumni Award for 1991.

iii /   Is the glass half full or half empty?
No one is in a better position to supplement Fay Vincent's view of the school from the outside with a view from within than Blair Torrey; his perspective in terms of years is even longer than Fay's. As a student, Blair had admired the Duke and kept up with him to the end; he had been hired to teach at Hotchkiss by Tom Chappell, whom Blair considered "a dear, sweet person"; he had worked for twenty-one years for Bill Olsen and "couldn't understand why the alumni worshipped him"; he had known Tim Callard's

family long before Tim's arrival at Hotchkiss and thought him to be "perhaps too godly in some ways"; he voluntarily relinquished the chairmanship of the English department during Arthur White's tenure because he wanted to have more time for just teaching and coaching; as for his assessment of Arthur White, his long-time colleague and friend, Blair differed with Fay primarily on the matter of potential: "If Arthur had been headmaster as long as Bill Olsen, Arthur would have become a great headmaster. People respected Bill, but it took Arthur to do the human things. People loved Arthur, and I think he would have come into his own intellectually."

Blair Torrey's observations, it should be noted, came after Rob Oden's appointment, but before Arthur White had stepped down: "This is a small world, this little fishbowl world we live in. It exaggerates our faults, and it exaggerates the gripes people have about the place. Take, for instance, the fact that we no longer have the stiff, stilted family-style sit-down meals in the dining room. I don't like standing in line, but I think the idea of cafeteria-style is more suited to our times. I don't revere the old-fashioned ways because they were old-fashioned. I think people who do often don't remember how awkward those meals were in many ways, and how little real communication passed between the teacher and the students at that table, and how students used to fill in at the far end and would do anything to avoid the suck seat next to the teacher.

"Then there's the chapel controversy. I believe and have felt for most of my life that religion has been the cause of more serious problems in this world than about any other factor. Religious people who profess to be devout, especially Christians, turn out to be so un-Christian. Some of the most devoted churchgoers on the faculty have a noted lack of charity. Dick Gurney used to say, 'I go to the town dump at eleven o'clock on Sunday morning because I meet the best people in town there.' I guess I imbibed some of his opinions about organized religion, hypocrisy, and so forth.

"Dick Gurney always gave me lots of good tips. I remember thinking once I ought to fail a kid on an exam. He allowed as how I probably ought to give him a D-minus or something like that, which would encourage him, rather than just straight out fail him. Dick and I shared an office, and I got a lot from him by osmosis. But there are some things I picked up on my own. I have a very strong belief in teaching ways of observation that I don't think Dick would ever mention literally. I believe in teaching ways of seeing, or teaching people to see better than they do – and to be able to put it into words. They can then take the same way of seeing into art class. Dick taught observation instinctively; I came to it consciously and made it deeply a part of my pedagogy.

"The one thing Dick and I disagreed on from the beginning was coeducation. Unlike Dick, I had daughters, and I believed, I guess instinctively, that coeducation would make the place more humane, more natural. When I was a kid here, we were merciless in many ways. Now, I think there's perhaps too great an emphasis on how people interact socially. Maybe to some degree it detracts from academics. But I enjoy the classroom work no more and no less than I did when I had all boys, and I hope I don't favor either side. I think it might be easier to favor the girls because they tend to be more responsive, more careful, better workers, more meticulous and detailed. A boy may try to fake it and bluff his way along. Not so with girls. Girls are also likely to be intimidated. They can hang back and be reticent because they're afraid of a domineering boy. Whether he happens to be right or wrong isn't important, but he can shout them down and so forth – the way I do with my wife, probably. When I yell, she hates it.

"The world is changing, and it's going to change even more. I received a phone call recently from a young woman. I've had a very close relationship with her for years, starting when she was a prep or lower mid here. She said, 'It's Father's Day, and for some reason I just wanted to call you and wish you a happy Father's Day.' And we got to talking, and because I know her well enough to be able to say things like this, I said, 'How's your love life?' She said, 'To be truthful with you, I'm in love and we're living together,' and so forth. I told her that was wonderful, and again joking, said, 'Do you mean you're living in sin? What about the old traditional ethics and morals we tried to teach you here?' She said, 'Well, to be really truthful with you, the person

I'm living with is a woman, someone I'm deeply in love with.' I took it as a compliment that she told me. That kind of thing used to be shoved under the rug. I'm sure that I've had colleagues who have been gay, but they never talk about it. They don't flaunt it. I don't want to say it should be swept under the rug, but I think it's nobody's business. It's there, and we should be tolerant.

"My other interest has been coaching. For a long while I was the head coach of hockey, and there was a period when I was the head coach of football. I tried to have fun with coaching, but it's gotten so there's so much pressure on the kids now. A faculty wife was telling me this morning that the present coach here is angry with her daughter because this girl is not going to go to field hockey camp this summer. The mother said, 'Gee, there's enough pressure here during the year. We don't need to feel it during the summer.' Well, I told her I didn't approve of any of these summer camps for increasing athletic talent. I know they've got them in football. The kids who go to them learn extra skills, but a lot of the game flavor is gone. It's no longer a game.

"It's all part of the pressures of our times, whether it's the pace of life that's accelerating all the time, as *Future Shock* described, whether it's part of the demographic influences within the academic world, whether we're all in some way caught up in the imperative for excellence. Take the whole pressure of college and what's happened to that. How is it possible for a school like Hotchkiss to be what it used to be when it automatically sent kids to Yale, Harvard, and Princeton? I sometimes ask myself, 'Am I good enough to teach here, as a teacher of English?' I don't knock myself. I am what I am. I think the trustees expect Oden to come in here and change the faculty structure in such a way that there are fewer dead ends and fewer deadbeats, if there are any, and more people who will raise Hotchkiss to the eminence and prominence that it once had. I'm not sure that's even going to be possible in this day and age, in this world. We still think of the school as the be-all and end-all, and ten miles away people don't know who Hotchkiss is. If you go away to school, they figure, you must be strange, a problem child.

"What I'd love to see is that people would be interested in a boarding school such as Hotchkiss not as a strange, exclusive place, but as a community in which lots of good and not-so-good people, normal people, live and fill out their lives – working with young people and influencing them. I like to think that we can make a difference in encouraging them to be decent, moral, and sound in whatever they do."

The longest tenured woman teaching at Hotchkiss is Marilyn Coughlin, who was appointed in 1985 as dean of faculty – a position she held until the end of the school's first century: "When I first began to teach, my husband [David Coughlin] and I used to vote on opposite sides of issues in faculty meetings. Dave was known as the archconservative. I was the bleeding-heart liberal. It got to be a source of amusement to our colleagues. 'The Coughlins have canceled one another out again.' Fortunately, we never discussed these votes outside of faculty meetings. We never carried the arguments home.

"Today, we still have the license plate, ROCK '78, given to Dave by the swimming team he coached that year. But I haven't heard anyone call him 'Rock' in over a decade, and it's unusual now for us not to vote alike. When I mentioned to him how much he had changed, he said, 'Goodness, I hope we all grow and become more sensitive to the needs of the people around us. We have a very different world, a very different school population. If we're to continue to get the very best out of kids, we have to adjust to who they are.' David still has very high expectations in the classroom and in coaching sports, but he has become much more nurturing. If we were living in Buehler again today, there's no way we would have a little boy [before coeducation] named Franklin down our hall crying himself to sleep at night. I know David would be down there talking to that boy. I know he would be trying to hook him up with help. It was almost a source of faculty amusement in my early days here when some kid couldn't make it. We're very different now, and with us, the school.

"Coeducation vastly accelerated this transformation. The dialogue we need to continue now is over what diversity really means in terms of sex, in terms of race, in terms of ethnic background. Feminism in its purest form is a philosophy of inclusiveness. I didn't initially realize how very threatened male constituencies are by these questions. Asking these questions doesn't mean that women are seeking to be on top at the expense of men. It means there's a place for all of us. The young white male who is not an athlete often gets lost in the old-boy game as well. As we begin to hear the girls' voices, we will also hear the voices of the unempowered males and find a place for them. The minorities will no longer feel they have to be transformed into white Europeans, and they will find their niche.

"I don't think we are in danger if we let go of some of the things we have thought and done in the past. The critical thing is to start – and continue – a dialogue about what is valid and valuable. There's a passage I like toward the end of *Pilgrim's Progress*, a book which nobody reads anymore because it is considered rather dry and moralistic. Evangelist and Pilgrim are talking, and Evangelist says to Pilgrim, 'Do you see yonder gate?' And Pilgrim says, 'No, I don't.' Then Evangelist says, 'Do you see yonder shining light?' Pilgrim this time says, 'Yes, I do.' So Evangelist says, 'If you keep that light in your eye, you'll also find the gate.' That image has stayed with me all my life. If you hold onto those truths about human beings that aren't relative – those shining, unchanging truths about what is good and right and just in life, then somehow or other you'll find your way."

iv /   "To this day, as I drive up the hill from Millerton and pass through the school gate," says the Hotchkiss board president, Edgar Cullman, "I can feel the queasy emptiness I always experienced as a boy when coming back from vacations."

In sharing this observation with his audiences of Hotchkiss students over the past several years, the school's avuncular benefactor invariably evokes a sympathetic response. They understand only too well this tension, which is often a concomitant to their own love for the school.

Edgar Cullman's greatest anxiety-churning moment as a student also led to his most singular triumph in life: "At the age of sixteen, I was very much in love with a girl. The next year she came to visit me at Hotchkiss with another boyfriend. He had a car, and we all drove to Mount Riga, just a few miles away. That was against the rules to begin with. But then it turned out that this boyfriend couldn't maneuver the car around the mountain road. I finally said, 'Let me drive it for you. I know how to get around here.' So, breaking the Hotchkiss rule for which I could have been kicked out, I took the wheel and drove the car around Mount Riga. I was terribly worried I might be found out; yet, I felt wonderful about my ability to negotiate the roads, with the girl looking on and the boy sitting there more or less helplessly. I subsequently married the girl – and am still married to her fifty-two years later."

Conflicting emotions characterized young Edgar's four years at the school, where he followed his older brother, Joe: "When I got to Hotchkiss I felt pretty secure about my physical well-being. I was bigger than most of my classmates and faster than any of my classmates had been at Fessenden. My shoe size at age fourteen was nine. Still is. My classes were something else. I was reasonably good in math, and I guess I liked history, but the work was generally hard, and I felt put down. English courses were just pure drudgery. I left out words, I spelled badly, and my expression was poor. My mind was always racing ahead of my hand. That cost me a lot of points because my penmanship was so terrible. I always envied people who were able to do their written homework rather easily. In French I didn't understand a word; and biology, as far as I was concerned, might as well have been in French. I guess Jack Bodel was the most difficult teacher I had. We did get along, however, because I was a swimmer and he was my coach.

"I decided early on that the best way to get along with teachers was to make them feel good about me. I knew I couldn't do it with marks; so I did it with my seeming eagerness to learn. They gradually became quite sympathetic, though they still gave me terrible marks. In reality, I didn't work half as hard as they thought. I was bluffing, and I got away with it.

"I wasn't unhappy being at Hotchkiss, and I was never homesick; but I worried a lot. I always wanted to be the best in sports. I wanted to be the best football player, the best swimmer, fastest at track. I wasn't best at any of those things, but I liked to think I could be. I worried whether I could make the team, I worried about my friends, about how they might react to what I said. Learning how to get along, how to make people respond was probably the most valuable thing I learned.

"I finally graduated after having to leave Hotchkiss twice. The first time I got yellow jaundice; the second time I got an ulcer. Doc Wieler was wonderful to me. He was a special friend. I ended up with a really warm feeling for the school. I must have been sort of moronic to have liked it so much, but it was my life. I made a lot of very good friends. The skiing and the woods squad were fun, trekking all over the countryside on holidays was pure joy, and the play on the football field had been exciting. I just enjoyed it all."

What profoundly influenced Edgar Cullman in his positive view of the school was his relationship with GVS: "I don't think the Duke particularly cared for me to begin with. He was always wonderful to the boy who was the worst in the school, and he loved to be in touch with the brightest. So there was Edgar Cullman in the middle. But he always made me feel he was ready to listen. I just liked his way, and I loved to listen to him in chapel. What he had to say inspired me to want to do something more, and with every report my parents got, he had written, 'Great effort.' I used to think, 'Isn't that wonderful, I've managed to fool the Duke, too.' I'm sure the reason he came to like me was because I represented in the Hotchkiss structure what was good – a determined young man, who seemed to work hard and participated in every aspect of school life. I had a great friend in my class, Judd Pollock. We'd hunt grouse, and I went to have dinner with Judd at the Duke's house because he shot the birds and I was his friend. I had more of a relationship with the Duke after Hotchkiss. We had a correspondence about his philosophy, about his thinking, about the world we were living in. One time the Duke went fishing with Arthur and [his brother] Doc Howe on the Upsalquitch River. I fished on the Ristigouche. It was one of the great things I was always jealous of. They had him up there fishing, and I didn't. They said that seeing the Duke in the rustic camp carry on as he did – it was just spellbinding to listen to his stories. As a young person, you always put somebody on a pedestal. The Duke was on a high pedestal for me because I always thought of him as the man with the forehead that started here [Edgar points to below his eyes] and then went straight up. I didn't know what was in-between – and that kept me always in awe.

"When I got to be head of the board, my top priority became to find a headmaster of the caliber of a Van Santvoord. I wanted a person who would lift the school up both intellectually and personally and have even something more than the Duke had – a way with young people, to be able to relate to them and have them feel comfortable."

To celebrate the school's 100th anniversary, Edgar Cullman has set in motion the largest fund-raising drive of any prep school in history: "My job is to ensure that there is the wherewithal to meet the requirements of a school such as Hotchkiss as it looks to the twenty-first century. The number-one consideration is for us to be in a position to attract the very best teachers there are; to have them want to teach at Hotchkiss because of the type of student body that's here and the excitement of being here. The reality is that teachers no longer are willing to live at the end of a corridor in just one room or a tiny apartment. There are lots of young marrieds, and women teachers with husbands and children, and we can't expect them to come at a sacrifice to their families. Then, too, Lakeville is still an isolated spot, a small community without a great diversity. How do you attract single women teachers? How do you attract enough black and other minority teachers? We want to do something special to make it worthwhile for them to come here and be in the kind of frame of mind where they can be most effective in what they do. The reality is that today that takes money.

"There are other material needs. Hotchkiss perhaps looks like a plush place, but it really isn't. What's plush about it? Girls want to play ice hockey, and we need a rink for them just as there's one for the boys. Right now the students are practicing taking turns till 9 : 30 at night. The girls also need locker rooms of their own, and other facilities to make the school truly coeducational. Hotchkiss must continually upgrade its plant. It's always more expensive if you fall behind. That's what Yale has done, and it's going to cost a billion and a half dollars to get Yale back up to speed.

"If Hotchkiss is to be known as an institution of the elite, this elitism has to be purely in the realm of the mind and spirit rather than of any petty snobbery. The ultimate purpose of Hotchkiss is to teach people how to be responsive to the feelings of others."

It is perhaps ironic that after all the years of making Hotchkiss feel good about him, this member of the class of 1936 is still gripped by that same momentary boyhood queasiness whenever he visits the school. But that may now change. As we went to press, word came that Edgar M. Cullman had won the Alumni Award for 1992 – making him, in effect, the Hotchkiss Centennial Man of the Year.

v /   **O**ne crisp Saturday afternoon as the September foliage was just beginning to show its first seasonal hues, a black Bentley Corniche glided around the Hotchkiss circle and headed down Millerton Road toward Baker Field. The tan convertible top was down, and Edgar Cullman was sitting next to Dr. Robert A. Oden, Jr., who was at the wheel. In his white shirtsleeves and characteristic bow tie, the sandy-haired ninth headmaster of the school radiated a boyish delight, while the elegantly attired president of the board with his silvery halo had the benevolent air of a wealthy uncle bestowing on his protégé a well-earned privilege – and demonstrating his implicit trust.

If Tim Callard as an outsider belatedly regretted his lack of political astuteness in failing to cultivate the board, Rob Oden's involvement has gone considerably beyond taking the wheel of Edgar Cullman's favorite car or puffing on his cigars or accompanying him at the annual clash between their respective colleges, the Yale–Harvard football game. "Rob has worked very closely with the board, keeping us informed," says Edgar, "though I do want to make it clear that I'm the one who

Headmaster Rob Oden at installation ceremonies with board president, Edgar M. Cullman '36

has taken the initiative in the social sphere. I've done that not only for the school, but because I have great fun doing it."

For those who have never seen him, one way to portray Rob Oden is to say that he looks like a young Arthur Schlesinger, Jr., without the scowl – making him seem incomparably more approachable even while projecting an implicit preeminence of intellect. A Phi Beta Kappa, magna cum laude graduate of Harvard College in 1969, he took first class honors in the history of religion at Cambridge University and then returned to Harvard to earn a Ph.D. in Near and Middle Eastern studies. He is familiar with most of the languages that have ever been spoken in the Near and Middle East and would probably have been comfortable negotiating his way through that region at the time of the Nazarene (perhaps a less daunting task than trying to penetrate the Byzantine machinations confronting a neophyte headmaster at the Hotchkiss

School). For many years the director of the Humanities Institute and chairman of the religion department at Dartmouth, Rob Oden received a rousing student endorsement by being voted the college's first Distinguished Teaching Award in 1979. He is married to his South Dakota high school sweetheart, Teresa, who graduated with honors from Brandeis. She has retained the lithe presence of her youth and could grace the cover of a woman's magazine. At the ceaseless array of functions she organizes and attends, Teresa J. Oden is likely to be thought of more as an individual than a headmaster's wife. She is also a professional researcher, and in that capacity made a vital contribution to this book. Her ongoing project is to create an archive that is worthy of the school. The Odens have two children, a son at Harvard and a daughter who will be old enough to enter Hotchkiss with the class of 1998.

What kind of a school will Hotchkiss be then? Early in the fall term of his first year as headmaster, Rob Oden instituted a subtle yet symbolic elaboration on the school's most popular tradition, the holiday. In Arthur White's time, when the students thought that one of these longed-for announcements was overdue, they gathered in front of the headmaster's house on the eve of a promising day and serenaded him with "Fair Hotchkiss." Rob Oden put out the word that he would be convinced to grant his first holiday if he received letters explaining to him in as many foreign languages as possible the meaning of this strange Hotchkiss tradition. The letters, in a half-dozen languages, quickly piled up on the headmaster's desk, and the holiday was promptly declared.

This raises an interesting question, one with more than theoretical implications: would Edgar Cullman, who had found French to be right out of the Tower of Babel, have felt at least temperamentally more comfortable offering the school song? "Edgar and I should have reversed," says Fay Vincent, only half in jest. "I should have waited another ten years to head the board."

"Rob Oden has already made a tremendous difference for the school," notes Edgar Cullman. "He's beginning to put his imprint on the faculty, he's earned the confidence of the alumni, and he's great with the students. I believe he's well on his way to raising Hotchkiss to a new level of excellence."

How adeptly Rob Oden continues to implement the board's mandate to be an intellectual headmaster will depend on how he chooses to utilize the sensitivities and perceptions he brings to the task. As with virtually everything else in this time of unprecedented change, little can be taken for granted about the open-ended road ahead. The journey has to be taken up anew each day.

"We are here to learn together, and to share with one another the joy that is learning," Robert Oden said at his installation in the fall of 1989. "Learning, knowing, is joyful; life is the more enjoyable to the extent that we are more widely knowledgeable. And about almost anything. Thus . . . when I am thigh-deep in a trout stream, it makes a positive difference if I can identify properly and by their Latin names the insects hovering over my stream. . . . When I drive down the Hudson or Connecticut River valleys, through southern Pennsylvania, or from Charlottesville to Staunton, Virginia, my pleasure is enhanced to the extent that I can correlate these bits of geography with events in the glorious history of this splendid country."

When Rob Oden was interviewed for this centennial history in the middle of the fall term of his second year, he was already in a position to look back: "Among my outstanding memories of the first year will always be the graduation. I wanted to hold it outside because I think there's nothing more uniquely Hotchkiss than our location. It happened to be raining that morning, and everybody said, 'Please don't have graduation outside.' Well, I did. We got a little bit wet; but when it concluded, the sun came out. Either the foolishness or the braveness of it made it all worthwhile. At one point the president of the senior class, Natalie Coggeshall, who is now at Dartmouth, stood up and asked other seniors to stand, and they gave me a diploma that they sort of invented and put together and welcomed me as a member of their class.

"I find that we are enormously blessed at Hotchkiss in having very few of the problems that other institutions have – whether with our students, the faculty, or finances. Yet it is also a small rural community. That can mean a tendency to see that the sun rises and sets on Lakeville, a tendency to feel smug. It's a part of the self-definition of a place, implying, 'Hey, we do what we do well.' Well, I don't think anybody does something so well that they can't benefit from outside help. From the very beginning, I've recognized the need for all of us in the community to get out more often. There needs to be a greater connectedness with other boarding schools and with nonboarding schools and with colleges and universities. If faculty members aren't up on what's going on in their curriculum in other schools, I don't think they're doing the job I'd like them to be doing.

"Within a broader framework, it is self-evident to me that the wide world is our world. The school has to become more international by making the curriculum more international. I would very much like to investigate expanding our language offerings so that they include perhaps Arabic, perhaps Chinese, perhaps Japanese. And along with those language offerings would go history, art, whatever. That's not an easy task for a secondary school. This is a school that prepares for going off to college, and there are a certain number of things which one simply has to do; so tempering the curriculum at a secondary school is harder than it is at an upper level.

"My chief curricular impetus has been with regard to the natural sciences. Along with many others, I regret that so few graduates of American secondary schools continue their interest in the sciences. In my mind there is a need for special emphasis on environmental matters. I am a lover of woods and waters, a trout and salmon fisherman. Another way of looking at that is to ask what is most important in the hearts and minds of elementary and middle school students, because they're the ones who will be our students by the time these curricular changes will be fully in place. What do they care about? It's the environment. They may know little about the reunification of Germany or the politics of the Persian Gulf, but they do know about the industrial pollution in Eastern Europe and the ecological disaster from the Iraqi war.

"I know the Hotchkiss world is different from the one I've come from.

Rob and Teresa Oden with children Kate and Rob, Jr.

My colleagues all said, 'Do you have any idea of what you're getting into in terms of the hours?' It is an enormously all-encompassing, relentless, and, happily, energizing task. Because of the way most of my predecessors functioned in the past, there is an expectation that the Hotchkiss headmaster should spend all of his time at the school. People have occasionally said to me, 'Though you appear to show up a lot on athletic fields and elsewhere around here, where were you Tuesday and Wednesday of last week?' Well, I was doing things for the school, doing things that I wanted to, but not all those things are in Lakeville.

A large part of the headmaster's job is development, especially in connection with the school's centennial – getting to know alumni, and in turn, giving them the opportunity to know and, ideally, trust and respect the new headmaster. I do that not out of a sense of necessity, but because I really find it honest-to-goodness fun. At Dartmouth I was known as one person on the faculty on whom the alumni office could call to fly off to Florida, San Francisco, Boise, or wherever. The other aspect is that as a continuing scholar, it's vitally important for me to participate in the wider world. I give lectures, I attend conferences, I am a member of several academic boards. These are activities which, in turn, enable me to bring a lot back to the school. So I have to define carefully where I can make the best impact and put my time and energy there. We do best what we do best and where our interests lie."

And what are his personal long-range plans? Here is how Rob Oden concluded his state of the school address at the end of his first year: "I do not view my time at Hotchkiss as a brief, betwixt and between period, as a transition from one place before to another later, as a time when what most matters is what precedes and what follows. Nor do I imagine looking back from some future vantage point upon but eight or ten years at the school. When I have spoken this year of the love which so many feel for Hotchkiss, this has required from me no imaginative leap. No leap is needed, because this love I have come to feel already. As long as I feel there are tasks to complete at Hotchkiss which I feel able to complete, I am here to stay."

vi / The critical observations of student leaders are no less pertinent than those of their overseers in seeking to assess the future course of the school.

What impresses so many visitors to Hotchkiss in its centennial year is the almost idyllic accord and community of purpose which they encounter. Whether in the classrooms, in the corridors, or on the playing fields, there are neatly turned out boys and girls who seem to share the same energetic, purposeful look as they go about their tasks. It is almost as if they had all passed an attitudinal test as part of the admissions process.

The most astonishing discovery for this alumnus from the 1950s was that not a single student out of more than a score who were interviewed knew the meaning of *baiting*. To be sure, they offered contemporary equivalents such as *harshing, ragging,* and *dissing*. But these carry far more subtle implications and reflect how controversies of any sort have become muted or rarified. At a meeting of a consciousness-raising group, one of the examples given of unintentional sexism to guard against was, "Fill 'er up!" And one of the leading issues at the school was whether or not the boys' traditional dress code of coat and tie (or the less traditional turtleneck instead of a shirt) should be relaxed to be no more restrictive than that for the girls. Though the standards spelled out for girls in the school's Blue Book of rules appear to be comparably rigid – a dress or a skirt or nonjeans pants and appropriate tops – the enforcement is more lax. The still predominantly male faculty members do not seem prepared to assess female apparel as readily as that of the boys – at least not in terms of the rules.

"The faculty finally voted to relax the rules a bit after Wednesday athletics, but otherwise did not change the code," says Amit K. Basak '91, president of the school and head of the student-faculty council. "I've received a lot of letters from male students who are against any further relaxation. They feel the present requirements contribute to the educational atmosphere and distinguish Hotchkiss from other schools."

To watch Amit Basak chair a meeting of the student-faculty council is to see in action the quintessential Hotchkiss student of today. Sitting in a straightback chair in front of the fireplace in the Alumni Room, he projects the physicality of a three-letter football player and wrestler as he deftly mediates the discussion among the dozen or so members of the stu-fac council, lounging in a semicircle of sofas and armchairs around him. When a procedural question comes to a vote and Rob Oden, who is attending as an observer, puts up his hand, Amit says, with the right blend of joviality and firmness, "Hey, you don't have a vote. Put your hand down."

Amit Basak, who periodically visits his parents' native India, seems to be everywhere around the school at the same time and seemingly running everything. His analysis of what goes on beneath the apparent concordance at Hotchkiss comes from being perhaps better attuned to the heartbeat of student life than anyone else at the school: "Among the fundamental principles Hotchkiss tries to uphold, none is more important – or more emphasized by Dr. Oden – than respect for others. That means not only refraining from any harassment, but also respecting people's feelings. With our wide variety of kids comes a wide variety of values. There are students who feel that smearing shaving cream on somebody's door is a joke, that it's funny, that it's something that kids do – while others respond with outrage; not only the administration and faculty, but other students. There have even been extreme cases of kids urinating in a trash can in somebody's room. Lots of people have laughed about it. The crux of the matter is really who it is that you do it to. If you do it to a friend, it isn't likely to hurt. But if you do it to someone you're distant from, that's another matter.

"The overwhelming majority of kids here at the school are what you could call 'sensitive'; even so, there are tensions. Last fall, the Black and Hispanic Student Alliance invited kids from other schools for a Kwanzaa weekend, which is an African holiday. This happened to coincide with the Christmas formal, which is the one time the whole school comes together. Practically all of the invited students who came were Hispanic or black. You had this influx of minority students almost invading the campus, and it created a lot of static. One black student told me she's never gone to a formal dance here because she doesn't like the music that's played. That's why the black students invited their own DJ to play rap music, while the regular band played more popular numbers. So there are black students here on campus who do feel awfully segregated. Some white students have a tendency to view it as a majority versus minority issue, which gives them certain rights. There's just not enough communication, and I think the white students as well as the black students need to be a lot more open with each other.

"Hotchkiss is not at all an activist place. College campuses, by comparison, are electrified. But there is a minuscule minority here who are single-mindedly committed to certain causes. There's now a women's group on campus, and tensions from issues of sexism come up in spurts. Right now, we've got the Blue and White Society, the Pythians and the Olympians, in charge of school spirit. It just so turned out that all the heads are males. Some females have been protesting, but the fact is that they've been elected to other top offices. We've had several female class vice presidents, and the next school president may be female.* It just isn't correct to say that the women aren't listened to. There was a video game in the snack bar, and one female student complained to Dr. Oden that it portrayed women in a sexist way and showed white men fighting against people of color. The game was promptly banned by Dr. Oden. I think the school is beginning to be a lot more thoughtful and looking inward at its flaws – particularly the students.

"I see a more serious problem concerning the faculty. There are not enough teachers who are fun to learn with, and too many teachers who are simply boring. I don't hold these teachers responsible for making sure the students are curious. But I do hold them responsible for not being able to communicate and express themselves in a way that's going to say something to the audience. I understand the administration is working on this problem, and I hope they'll go as far as is necessary.

"The school's disciplinary system also needs attention. Although there's a tremendous amount of individual understanding and compassion, the official policies sometimes seem not only harsh, but ridiculous. For example, a kid who broke his leg on the football field was given a golf cart to get around the long corridors. On the way back from the snack bar every night, he would give other kids rides – a typical thing for a teenager to do. Yet because of this, the golf cart was taken away from him.

"In trying to keep us out of trouble, in acting *in loco parentis*, the school needs to find a balance which respects the maturity of the older students. I've been here for four years, and I've had the same check-in for four years. If the faculty imposes virtually the same restrictions on the seniors as on the preps, what's it saying about the growth of those

* On May 1, 1991, Jessica Hanley '92 was elected school president.

seniors? Between June and September after their senior year, students go from all rules to no rules in college. What has the faculty done to prepare us for this critical step?

"I don't want to sound negative, because I love Hotchkiss. I get personally offended when I see a few individuals lacking the proper respect for the school – leaving empty cups in the snack bar or newspapers lying in the corridor, or even spitting on the floor. I am proud of what Hotchkiss is – and grateful for what it has done for me. When I first came here, I had a lot of c's and d's and really had to struggle. Luckily, Hotchkiss offers an incredible amount of support from other students, senior proctors, corridor masters, and many teachers. Without them I wouldn't have been able to get through. There aren't many other schools in the country that offer you the diversity that Hotchkiss does, considering its size. I've got friends whose parents are millionaires. I also have friends who are on financial aid. Then there are the dormitory relationships I've formed. I walk into a person's room at 10:00 P.M., and the next time I look up it's like 3:00 or 4:00 A.M., and we've talked all night. These are the sort of things I'll take away with me to college and hold onto for the rest of my life."

Amit Basak was one of six students in his class who received early admission to Yale.

vii /   The election of Amit Basak as school president had been contested by numerous candidates and required a runoff. His opponent was Andrea L. Dodge, a member of the stu-fac council for the previous three years and vice president of the class. Though seven of her uncles had graduated from Hotchkiss, Andy had at one time regarded the school as an aristocratic, snobby place: "Several of my uncles then convinced me to send away for the catalogue, and I can remember being very surprised by the language, which was really friendly. When I saw the facility in comparison to several other places I visited, I applied, and I got a good scholarship.

"I was very naive when I first came. I had never seen anything like this. I had never seen so many people who were smarter than I. I had never had teachers who cared so much. I had never made friends so fast. After two weeks, I felt as if I knew my friends here as well as those I had known at home since I was two years old.

"Then lower middle year, it all sort of came together. After watching the younger students go through what I had gone through and seeing the older students crying over college rejection letters, I realized that Hotchkiss – although it's warm and it will do anything for you – it's really kind of a live-or-die place. I'd venture to say that almost 90 percent of those who graduate from Hotchkiss come out happy. It may be not quite as many, because I'm seeing it through my eyes, and my view has been predominantly positive. Yet the people who are unhappy here are really unhappy. You certainly don't read anything about them in the admissions literature.

"The admissions literature which helped to bring me here doesn't portray the school in an entirely open way. For example, you read about the great success of coeducation and nothing about sexism. Yet there's a lot of latent hostility, which only comes out when people jab at it. A couple of guys on the social committee recently put out a poster for a Saturday dance, which had women dressed in bikinis and miniskirts and their blouses open. Girls were told to look sexy, wear tight skirts, and boys were told to wear ripped jeans. This was very offensive to women. Some of the girls vented their feelings by writing things on the poster. One of the girls later had second thoughts and wrote a letter of apology to the two boys who had made the poster. It was a very calm, mature letter. She explained why she felt the way she did when she saw the poster, but she realized now that defacing the poster by writing on it had not been the proper way to protest. Well, pretty soon there was an unsigned note to her on the headmaster's board, which later turned out to have come from the two boys. They refused to accept her apology and berated her for defacing the poster. It was very harsh in its tone. They said some women enjoyed being sexy and called her ugly.

"I don't think that sexism is a problem that is ruining the spirit of the school, but one that people need to recognize. Some of us are tired of hearing sexist comments on the part of teachers. If someone were to say to the teacher, 'I think you're being sexist,' I think he would listen. Right now, he doesn't even know it hurts. I feel sometimes that this is still a boys' school. When the older alumni come back, they give us looks when they see a group of us girls sitting together in the dining room, as if to say, 'What're you doing here?'

"In a way these have been the best times that I've had so far, but in a way I also feel robbed – of my childhood, of a carefree adolescence. How many kids on the outside get sick over a deadline for a newspaper? I see my friends who are going nuts – myself included – going crazy over papers and work. I feel robbed of being with my family and being a normal kid with a dog and my own room at home. So, in a way I get angry at Hotchkiss for doing that to me; at the same time, I know I'm getting an incredible education. I've already grown in confidence. When I first came, I didn't want anyone to know I was on a scholarship. Now, I think the differences between myself and other students are kind of neat. I know what I want. I know the kind of people I want to spend my time with.

"Ultimately, it's a trade-off. Knowing what I know now, what scares me the most is thinking how robbed I'd feel if I hadn't come."

An alternate perspective is provided by Andy Dodge's classmate Ann T. Sprole '91. A corridor proctor and a member of the school's soccer and tennis teams, she is the daughter of Jerry Sprole '65, who heads the annual fund, and granddaughter of Frank Sprole, the former president of the board: "Looking back to when my grandfather and dad were here, it's so different; it's changed so much. My dad thinks he definitely learned a lot here, but he also remembers what rough times he went through. He's always saying, 'You have it so easy!' I don't know if that's the case, but I can't imagine going to a single-sex school. I like it because the guys and girls are living in a much more realistic setting. You see them all the time. It's not just the public school Friday and Saturday night dating. It's morning, breakfast, lunch, dinner; when you're crying, when you're happy; when you look horrible, when you're sick, as well as when you're at your best. There's nothing to hide, and that's nice. People say there's a lot of tension beneath the surface when there really isn't. Some girls' feelings may get hurt, but that can happen anywhere; and a girl can do it to a girl just as easily as a guy can.

"The students in general get along well. There are definitely groups here, but I've seen that everywhere. You're obviously more likely to hang out with people whose personalities are the same as yours. Sports teams always hang out together. There are people who're interested in the arts and drama, who have play rehearsal every night together. How can you not become closer? You see a lot of black people in the cafeteria eating together. It's not because we don't want them sitting with us or wouldn't want to sit with them on account of color. My roommate's black, and this is the second year we're rooming together; so we obviously spend a lot of time together, including in the cafeteria. But I think the black kids just like being with each other. Many of them come from New York, and they're just friends the same way I'd be friends with somebody from my area. And at dances, also. They're a lot better dancers, and that's fun, and a bunch of kids try it and dance with them.

"I'd hope the faculty and students could relate more. The relationships can be good, and I think definitely are better with some of the younger faculty at this point. But it's hard because of all the DC [Disciplinary Committee] issues. When people get into trouble, who can they really trust? The faculty is on the other side, and they hate it just as much as we do. So you can really *like* individuals on the faculty, but can you ever completely trust them?

"The DC keeps changing how they apply the rules. The Blue Book says that you'll be kicked out for stealing, cheating, drinking, drugs, and that sort of thing, the first time. Well, for drinking and drugs, you do get kicked out, but for stealing, cheating, and plagiarism, people often get a second chance. In my view, these things are actually more serious than drinking. It's scary to think that if you have one beer and get caught, you're kicked out of school. If you're caught with one beer at home in your teenage years, your parents might ground you – or maybe do nothing. When my aunt and uncle were here [Sarah Sprole '78 and Jonathan K. Sprole '73], they partied frequently. When my brother came here in eighty-five, they still had two chances. Then they changed that. It seems that the school doesn't want to deal with any drinking or drug problem as much as the infirmary and the counselors say they want to. It seems that they would rather kick the person out than work with them and help them get over their problem.

"In a way I think Hotchkiss is overprotecting people from the real world. Recently what got three proctors in Coy into trouble was when they made the guys on their floors do wall-sits. That's when you're up against the wall with your back, in a sitting position without a chair, and some books on your lap. You hold it for about a minute or two, and it's a little uncomfortable for your legs. The proctors would give them a choice – wall-sits, or miss going to the snack bar between 9:30 and 10:00 before bedtime. In this case, it wasn't even a punishment. The proctors did it with the rest of the floor; sort of like, let's do it all together and see what it feels like. The faculty were watching, and at some point decided it wasn't fun and reported the proctors to the Discipline Committee.

"This sort of thing snowballs at the school. A boy on the floor always asked to sharpen his pencil every night at 7:30 just when study hall started. Finally, the proctor said, 'Here, sharpen these, too,' and gave him a packet of ten pencils. That was also considered hazing. What made it all the sillier was that the faculty member didn't just take the proctor aside and discuss it with him. He turned him in to 'higher authorities' – to the DC – and made a big thing out of it.

"My brother is at Yale now, and he laughed when he heard what's going on. In the past it had been done one way, and now all of a sudden it's changed completely. Why, when it happens in life? People have become so overly touchy about everything. The real radical people want to stick out always, and make a big deal about things. We had a meeting on homophobia, and a few people decided to write signs, 'I'm proud to be gay.' They put them up all over the school, and they weren't even signing them. I guess I didn't really care. But why do you need to do that? Is that necessary? Is that a stage we have to go through in building a better school?"

viii / "**W**e've been somewhat adrift for the last few years, and depending on the time of the year or people's biorhythms or what have you, that gets exaggerated," says the school's chaplain and teacher of philosophy and religion, Louis H. Pressman. "There will always be those who say, 'Oh, my God, we're just arranging deck chairs on the *Titanic*. We're all going down.' Well, we aren't. In fact, in terms of the kids' basic experience, it's been a pretty good voyage."

Lou Pressman, an alumnus of Exeter with an M.A. from Yale who has been on the faculty since 1980, does not exactly fit the traditional chaplain mold. "I'm a Christian who was born and raised a Jew, and I'm convinced there can be rich conversation between the two traditions – and with a number of other religions as well." He feels comfortable in leading the services in the school's chapel, which, after all, was built through the generosity of a donor with comparably eclectic views.

Lou Pressman: "If one asks, 'How central is membership in a religious community in defining the identity of most of the kids at the school?' the answer would be, 'Not that central, for most of them.' Now, if you were to ask, 'To what extent are kids concerned with religious questions?' I might then want to say, 'More than you think.' Adolescence is a time when you're testing, to see what you want to hold onto and what you might want to let go from what you've gotten from your parents. Some of the most fundamental questions that are starting to percolate are the very questions that religious traditions speak to: 'What can I hope for? How should I aim to live? What's ultimately worth pursuing in life? Is there anything of ultimate value or worth?' Those kinds of questions a lot of our kids wrestle with, sometimes in articulate, sometimes in inarticulate, ways.

"The lines of social demarcation at Hotchkiss aren't religious. If one asks about prejudice or discrimination, there are occasionally hints of that. But I don't think it runs very deep or is institutionalized in any way. I've probably heard of no more than a couple of episodes of religious baiting in the years I've been here. A lot of our kids would be deeply angered at somebody going after another kid with remarks about Catholicism or Jewishness or being a Muslim.

"It's probably about the same in terms of race. I'd be lying if I said openly racist views never pop up. They do, usually in oblique, stupid ways. Kids who don't think. Adults who don't think. If you're the thirteen- or fourteen-year-old prep who bumps into that, it can be hard. But again, the kids do a pretty good job in hauling one another up on that.

"The single hardest thing at Hotchkiss, in some ways, is if you're poor. An affluent kid from Hong Kong or Saudi Arabia has more in common with the kid from Greenwich than does the blue collar kid from Torrington. What does it mean to a kid who can't afford to spend a lot of money on weekends, when some of your buddies can go to New York and stay in expensive hotels? What does it mean when you come and your clothes aren't right because you just didn't know? When some of the youngsters from inner cities first arrive, they're decked out in suits and dresses which you know their parents worked hard to get so that they could send them off with pride. Suddenly these kids come up against the fact that there's a subtle dressing down. It's khakis and Bean topsiders with holes in them that are actually what you're supposed to wear. It's not that the other kids will make fun of you; but when you're fourteen years old, you don't want to stand out in that way.

"One response is to become more royal than the king. In no time at all, some of these kids are preppier than the lifelong preppies. The other response is to resist and try to hold onto yourself and who you are. This ultimately goes beyond any class issue; it is an issue with which every student has to grapple to some extent. How can you best negotiate a critical engagement between yourself and what the school is or represents? The best thing that can often happen to students who come here is to develop a lovers' quarrel with the school. Instead of merely adopting what Hotchkiss has to offer, these kids ask some hard questions about things that aren't as they should be – while abiding by certain standards and remaining loyal to those things that are of value in this community. It's a kind of a creative dialectic between alienation and involvement, and those youngsters who negotiate their own path here are the greatest success stories we can have. When they go on from Hotchkiss and become involved inevitably in structures larger than themselves – whether in business, government, or even the creative arts – they will know how to pursue a path of integrity rather than follow one of least resistance. And those kids are the ones who're going to make a difference.

"Hotchkiss is not some kind of a paradisiacal state that was created in its final perfect form. We're going to have to fashion what Hotchkiss should become. It's not just waiting out there. What Hotchkiss should become is more nearly an invention than a discovery – the result, still ahead, of an open-ended process that builds from day to day."

ix /   On the red brick wall just beyond the sofas in the spacious entry hall of new Main Building hang portraits of several masters who have attained Hotchkiss renown. There is grizzly Dick Gurney, sitting on a snow-covered log; George Stone with his wife, Jodie, looking like a royal couple on a commemorative stamp; and John McChesney displaying the equivalent of a Mona Lisa smile.

The latest portrait is of Bob Hawkins, unveiled at a champagne ceremony for a small group of colleagues and friends during the summer vacation months. It shows him sitting in a plush red armchair, with his loyal companion of many years, a shy whippet called Brie, lounging on Bob's lap. The reaction of those present on this special occasion was that the painting was a marvelous likeness of the man who had taught prep English for most of his forty-three years at the school – and was indeed a fitting reminder to future generations of their heritage. In keeping with good form, Bob Hawkins duly protested that the artist's rendition was far too flattering, but in no way hid his delight.

In the forthright estimation of this amateur critic, it was a painting which should have pleased only the whippet and the manufacturer of that red chair. The expression around the subject's taut lips imparts to him a humorless, almost vicious look which would be far more appropriate for a prison guard than the humane, cherubic bon vivant I have known for so many years. But then Bob had never been my teacher, and it was not until after I had interviewed numerous former students of his that I realized why neither he nor his Hotchkiss colleagues had anything but praise for the artist's rendition. That intimidating look was his classroom alter ego, which had the power to make generations of preps cower about putting a comma in the wrong place. "Before I came here, my uncle used to try to intimidate me with Mr. Hawkins's first quiz," says Ann Sprole. "Fortunately for my class, Mr. Hawkins seemed to soften up because it was his last year of teaching."

It was also a new situation. "You simply can't frighten or bully kids into learning anymore," says the dean of the faculty, Marilyn Coughlin. "In that sense the school is a very different place from what it was before. I'm not opposed, mind you, to very firm standards or to making kids measure up. But there are ways of being very firm and sometimes even punitive in a caring way. Both the law of men and the maternal kind of love are needed here."

Some faculty traditionalists contend there has already been far too much maternal love, far too much softening of standards and abandonment of values. "If the school continues going in the present direction," says Steve Bolmer, whose views remain as unchanged after forty-four years on the faculty as his remarkably boyish face, "the very people who are bringing this situation about won't want to teach here in another fifteen years."

This controversy reflects the increasingly spirited questioning of the standards and values in all educational institutions – perhaps most notably articulated by Allan Bloom in *The Closing of the American Mind*. What has lent the debate a special dimension at Hotchkiss has been the changeover to coeducation, which, in effect, cut the school loose from its original mooring. "The fun is pushing off from the dock sometimes without even knowing exactly where you're going, but committing yourself to the voyage anyway," says Marilyn Coughlin. "The joy of being in an educational institution like this today is knowing that the search for what is right and good and true is ongoing – and that you've never arrived."

The original rationale for schools such as Hotchkiss was to provide boys with college preparation in a setting removed from the normal evils and temptations of the world, especially those prevalent in the big cities. Yet there was another, implicit rationale which may have played an even greater role. This becomes inescapably clear when one considers that at the end of the last century, teaching was one of the very few legitimate careers open to women. Yet, it was exclusively men who were sought out to teach at these schools. The only conclusion which can be drawn is that Hotchkiss and similar schools were founded also to remove boys from the influence of women – to wit, of mothers, who just as preponderantly did the childraising in those days. By placing the sons in a country environment together with other pubescent males, under the supervision of masters who were either unmarried or whose wives had the knack of staying discreetly in the background, these fortunate boys would be able to experience what has since come to be known as "male bonding." The traditional hazing of preps by upperclassmen created the first bonds, which were then constantly reenforced by interaction in the classrooms, in the dormitories, and especially on the playing fields.* Though the school started out with the lofty ideal of trusting the boys, the battle lines were quickly drawn. The ever-present threat of expulsion and academic failure created a unity of purpose within the student body not unlike that in an ancient city-state under siege. Whether deliberately or unconsciously, that was

---

* It may well be that the common characteristic of all the boys who continued to be "baited" by their peers was the victim's failure to "bond" and become fully one of the group, one of the boys.

all a part of the script, and by the end of this play, the boys were expected to develop a certain toughness, resiliency, and, above all, a reliance on each other that would serve them well throughout life. For many graduates of yesteryear, male bonding and its totality of shared experiences form the basis for their fondest memories of the school.

George Van Santvoord was the last headmaster who tried to stifle whatever undesirable influences threatened the status quo in this boys' enclave, be it a movie like *The Love Parade* or those dithering mothers seeking to visit their sons too often. Vacations were an unavoidable risk, but weekends and any other departures from the school were to be held to a minimum. The two or three dances a year provided a strictly controlled amount of social interaction as a pre-preparation for family life, but sexuality in any form was taboo. As late as my senior year in 1952, I heard one of the Duke's faculty disciples in class list a man's virginity prior to marriage as a prerequisite for being a gentleman.

Of all the relaxations of ingress and egress permitted by Bill Olsen, the Duke most determinedly opposed the introduction and integration of women into this enclave. To GVS, coeducation represented nothing short of the end of the Hotchkiss School in terms of its fundamental purpose and role. That is what he undoubtedly meant when he noted in his diary several months before his death that he "wished the school *bon voyage* and waved goodbye."

This is not by any means to imply that going coed was an unfortunate step, but rather to recognize, as Bill Olsen did in a report to alumni in 1970, that "to become coeducational, Hotchkiss would in essence have to become a brand-new school." (Interestingly, Bill Olsen at that time used this as a rationale *against* the school's going coed.)

Almost twenty years after taking in girls, the school finds itself divided by arguments centering on the fact that it is neither brand-new nor of the old brand, but a still undefined in-between. An uneasy truce exists between those who would have Hotchkiss continue turning out a sort of elite corps of educated Spartans ready to sally forth into a contentious world and those who would nurture the gentler human qualities which are necessary to meet the cooperative longings of an interdependent world.

Perhaps the greatest success of coeducation has provided its most formidable challenge; for while the nobler aspects of traditional male friendships have indeed extended to create similar boy-girl friendships, there has also been bonding of the kind which is totally antithetical to the Hotchkiss tradition. Although the Blue Book states that "Hotchkiss is not the appropriate place for sexual intercourse between students . . . [and] can lead to dismissal from school [in] . . . extreme or repeated cases," this is considered more an advisory than an enforceable rule. Typical of the measures taken by the school at one point was to wire the lights in the Alumni Room into a permanent "on" position — and thus discourage the use of the several couches there as an inviting trysting place.

In searching for a new mooring — or, as Bill Olsen phrased it, becoming a brand-new school — some brand-new harbors need to be explored. If only for the sake of argument as a gradual, long-term option, what if sixteen were to become the minimum Hotchkiss age? A sixteen- or seventeen-year-old does not require — and often does not welcome — the kind of supervised nurturing needed by a thirteen- or fourteen-year-old. The boys and girls thus admitted would be close enough to adulthood so that the school could focus on providing general guidance instead of trying to prescribe what kind of relationships they should have. Some of the other rigidities which create distrust between students and teachers might also disappear. And Hotchkiss would not need to become a three-year school — one of the options, in fact, explored prior to coeducation. Among the exciting alternatives would be to have the students fan out throughout the world for their third year, taking up tasks ranging from being an aide to a British member of Parliament to working in a rural community in China or as a runner at a Wall Street brokerage firm. They would then return to Hotchkiss for a sort of super fourth year, teaching each other what they had learned from their work. As for the next step, the chances are that colleges would soon be courting these twenty-year-old Hotchkiss graduates with accelerated programs. In deciding what to study and how to spend the rest of their lives, these young men and women would have incomparably broader perspectives than the eighteen-year-old lockstep students of today.

A pilot program of twenty to thirty volunteers could likely be immediately filled by students currently at the school – if they are truly the enterprising and ingenious boys and girls they appear to be. The communal togetherness of the Hotchkiss facilities would be virtually a prerequisite for such a think tank endeavor; students would hardly be able to engage in such a close and constant interaction if they were living at home and going to a day school or high school. And that is only one scenario of an almost open-ended variety that need to be examined to provide the Hotchkiss School with the sort of powerful rationale it once had.

There is an overriding irony inherent in the present situation, in the way things stand. Now that the original raison d'être for keeping out the outside world no longer exists, the Hotchkiss School nevertheless remains an isolated community in the northwest corner of Connecticut. Although the isolation would be lessened in a more centrally located spot, geography is *not* the main reason for the school's inadequate contact with the outside world. The main reason rests in the fact that the teachers and administrators rarely have a chance to overcome the mindset of their profession. Though the faculty now includes a considerable number of women and is drawn from a markedly more diverse milieu than in the past, their training is not unlike that of acolytes in a church, who return to serve the church as soon as they are ordained. Whether graduates of Hotchkiss or the South Dakota public schools, whether they attended Yale or Arizona State, whether they were Rhodes scholars at Oxford or dilettantes at Grenoble, Perugia, or Salamanca, the knowledge they bring to the classroom is overwhelmingly a repetition of what they themselves had been taught rather than based on any extensive life-experience outside of the walls of academe. Taking sabbaticals abroad, attending professional meetings, and otherwise keeping up with their disciplines is indeed broadening for the faculty. But this amounts to merely becoming more ecumenical and by no means represents stepping out of the fold.

How much more would Hotchkiss be able to experience the outside world if a small number of faculty members were to take two- or three-year leaves of absence to work in private enterprise or government? Hotchkiss alumni/ae could surely provide an enviable choice of employment slots. Another possibility – personally less wrenching but undoubtedly more challenging institutionally – would be to draw a modest number of faculty recruits from outside the scholastic milieu: a former United Nations official, an advertising executive, a lawyer, a businessman. Even if these outsiders were making several hundred thousand dollars in New York, they might find more money in their pockets at the end of each month in their new careers. Others might be drawn from those who have already retired, and still others might even be able to continue their careers, as did John Hersey when he became master of Pierson College and a member of the faculty at Yale. The ideal candidates would again be Hotchkiss graduates, who would embody a unique combination of understanding the school and having experienced the outside world. What a lasting influence just a few of these people could have on the students and the faculty! And not only within their areas of expertise. Now that headmasters can probably never again become involved in personally guiding every young life at the school, these seasoned individuals-of-the-world could share that role by each becoming a mentor for his or her small group.

In assuming the reins of the Hotchkiss School at the end of its first century, Rob Oden's intellectual mandate from the trustees has been to promote the kind of excellence symbolized by George Van Santvoord in his time. I remember the Duke quoting Lao Tse in Bible class, with a measure of empathy, to the effect that mere mastery of facts is no guarantee of wisdom and that the intellectual can be as far removed from this wisdom as the moon is from the earth. The Duke had probably as great a mastery of an encyclopaedic array of information as anyone and openly admired the brilliance of a retentive mind, yet he repeatedly extolled wisdom and common sense over anything too abstractly learned. "Unless you can explain your thinking to a child of ten," he often said, "then you really are not thinking clearly." Whether talking about something that happened five thousand years ago or five thousand miles away, the Duke gave not only clarity to the subject, but made it of personal consequence to the students in class in a way they would never forget.

This is not to imply that the Duke's approach was prevalent among his faculty contemporaries or that his wisdom was appreciated by every boy. "What we acquired at Hotchkiss in our time was merely a *veneer* of culture," says *Harper's Magazine* editor, Lewis Lapham '52, whose criticism of the school has not changed over the years. "As a country, as a society, we're still very ambivalent about the purpose of the supposedly higher education. A boy arrives in Lakeville, age thirteen, in the autumn of his prep year, knowing little or nothing of the world. What do we want him to know four years later, in the spring of his senior year? What kind of a person do we – and I say we not only as a school but also as parents and as a society – want? And what do we expect four years after that, when the same child emerges from the university? Whom do we hope to meet on the afternoon of the last commencement? Do we look for a man or a woman who has learned to trust the unique and specific value of his or her own mind? Do we hope for an individual capable of wisdom and accustomed to submitting his or her life to the questions of conscience? Do we mean to discover individuals on the order of Thomas Paine or Thomas Jefferson or Archibald MacLeish, or do we want somebody who thinks that the sum and zenith of all human experience is a killing in the bond market and a house in Palm Beach? What are the desiderata of an American upper-class education? I don't think we've answered that question. Hotchkiss, like Yale, like Harvard, is about setting wealth to music. You can make all kinds of good arguments in favor of a Hotchkiss education, but few of them have much of anything to do with what the old Greeks admired as the glittering play of 'wind-swift thought.'"

One prima facie argument is that Hotchkiss has produced the bankers and the lawyers – as well as Archibald MacLeish. "I've heard it said that even the grass stands at attention at Hotchkiss," observes Roy Smith, who has taught English for more than twenty years and enjoys being addressed by students as "Uncle Roy." "Well, there are different blades of grass. They aren't all cut to the same length, and they bend in different directions. Hotchkiss is a better school for that." Hotchkiss is also undergoing a historic but so far unheralded transformation. "The emphasis in many disciplines is beginning to shift from answer to process," explains Marilyn Coughlin, "even to celebrating ingenious explorations of what may turn out to be blind alleys. Our goal is to teach kids to trust their own minds, to think for themselves rather than defer to authorities without critical questioning." Whether this will produce a new generation of Thomas Paines and Thomas Jeffersons can no more be answered than how many such intellects our society needs to function best.

As for the undeniable wealth of these schools, they should not be stereotyped. "One of the things to say about Hotchkiss and a number of prep schools," points out Zeph Stewart '39, "is that they are not nearly as snooty and stuffy as they appear when you look at them physically. They look like country clubs, sort of preserves for the very elite – and elite not in the best sense. Well they're really not like that. They take people from as diverse a cross section as they can who have the ability to affect the world, and they make them a little better at it."

These people almost routinely belie that other common stereotype: "being preppy." "The school does not encourage a sense of entitlement," says Katha Diddel Warren '75, who became a trustee while still in her twenties. "The students have to work to be who they want to be. If you are arrogant at Hotchkiss, you don't meet with a good response from anybody. You can't really get away with being a jerk on a regular basis at the school – as can so many people in other areas of life today. I don't mind admitting that Hotchkiss students are select, that they're the best students we can find. But what counts in the end is that they be real contributors to society."

Elaborates eighty-eight-year-old Robert Osborn, the school's first art teacher, who took great pleasure in creating the cartoon for the back cover of this book, "Hotchkiss must train and turn out young leaders who will, with genuine moral and ethical sense, undertake public service rather than being sucked into the funnel of greed."

As the Hotchkiss school embarks on its second century, there is an ever more acute awareness – beginning with the president of the board and the trustees and going on through the headmaster and pervading the faculty and the student body – of the need to pursue higher goals that will move society at large forward. "You don't move it forward simply by making a quarter of a million dollars a year and being the paddle ball champion at the New Canaan Country Club," says Kip Armstrong '63, the seasoned observer of boarding schools and an active fund raiser as a class agent. "Whether you're in a democracy, an aristocracy, or an autocracy, there's only one legitimation for privilege. You must set a better example for others either by showing greater wisdom and more self-restraint or self-discipline than others. If you can't set an example that will encourage people to take greater responsibility in the society – with a vision of a better world – then perhaps the privilege of a Hotchkiss education should be given to one who can."

9   Fair Hotchkiss

From the perspective of a century, what has it meant to have been a student at the Hotchkiss School? No one expressed it with more feeling in the hundred years than Jonathan Bush '49, whom I interviewed as much for the generosity of spirit he had displayed when he was a senior and I was a prep as for his family connection, which could not be ignored in an account of this sort: "Hotchkiss was *my* place. My two older brothers had been to the grade school I attended before Hotchkiss, and they had excelled at Andover when they were there. That's where I was supposed to go. But a friend of the family who had gone to Hotchkiss, Challen R. Parker, ['28] drove my mother and me to the school in April 1944. It was a spring day. You know what a sparkling spring day is like at Hotchkiss. I loved the old Main Building and the hallway, and all of the students going by. I looked down over the lake, and I just didn't think there was a more lovely view ever created on earth. I fell in love with it instantly, and all I wanted was to go there.

"The beauty of the school was something I never took for granted the whole time I was there. Even on the most slimy, muddy winter days it still was spectacular. I was always in awe of the place. The feeling of camaraderie and the fun of seeing good friends all day long is something I'll never forget. And of course, the Duke was an awesome person. To be in a school where he was headmaster was without *pareil*. It was always a challenge to walk past the Duke. Stand up straighter, look better! He was wonderful, that glint in his eye. The questions he would ask you – oh, gosh, you'd be terrified before he talked, and feel uplifted each time you got through it. Each talk with the Duke was like a final examination, it seemed. You always had to be your best. It was said that the two worst weeks at Hotchkiss were the two weeks that one had to sit at the Duke's table in the dining room as a prep, and that the two best weeks at Hotchkiss were the two weeks one sat at the Duke's table as a senior. That's certainly true for me. I was terrified the two prep weeks and had a fabulous time the two senior weeks.

"Right through upper mid year, I sweated it out scholastically every spring term and most mid terms. I developed the ability to cram for exams that got me through. There wasn't a time in the first three years when I wasn't in doubt on at least two, occasionally three subjects. Flunking the exam would mean flunking the course, and passing the exam would mean passing the course. When I'd see on the bulletin board that I passed the exam, I'd get the greatest thrill. I think it was even a greater thrill than getting a ninety or a hundred, when you're up against the wall, just seeing that you passed, which, somehow, I always did.

"A vital factor in all of this was the affection and concern in that wonderful body of men who were the Hotchkiss faculty. Any young person who had a chance to participate and grow in that environment was fortunate. They cared for the students as much as parents would. There was freedom, but there was also control. I remember looking forward to returning from vacations to Hotchkiss. My classmates and I would talk about this strange phenomenon that existed at few other schools. Can you imagine being on vacation and looking forward to returning to school? But that's the way we felt about it, and I still have that feeling when I look forward to seeing my classmates again."

As for the final word, that was written by Monique Thomas '93, in an essay for Blair Torrey's lower mid English class: "I flipped through the Blue Book, trying to find a topic. I chose the Blue Book because it *is* Hotchkiss. By the time I got to the last page, several possibilities came to mind – but none that I really wanted to write about. So I turned the Blue Book over to see if I would get a different perspective from reading it backward. And there, on the back cover, I found my answer:

FAIR HOTCHKISS

Fair Hotchkiss! Hear our song of praise,
Through joyful and endearing days
We'll cherish all the mem'ries dear
That cluster round our sojourn here.

Fair Hotchkiss, tho' we come and go
While o'er thy walls our ivies grow,
We still shall love, shall love thee and be true
To dear, to dear old Hotchkiss and the blue.

"We learn Fair Hotchkiss on the first day we arrive, and we sing it on the day we graduate. The school song rings true for me because I shall never forget the memories that I have gathered during my sojourn here. While they may not all be joyful or endearing, I 'still shall love, shall love thee and be true to dear, to dear old Hotchkiss and the blue.'"

Hotchkiss class of 1992

Acknowledgments

To an unusual extent, this book has been a cooperative endeavor. More than one hundred and fifty members of the Hotchkiss community participated by being interviewed, and the manuscript was read and commented upon in its various stages by some two dozen individuals, including the three noted authors who contributed pieces of their own.

Through announcements in the *Hotchkiss Magazine*, at faculty meetings, and in school assembly everyone associated with Hotchkiss was invited to participate. About a half-dozen people came forth; the rest of the interviewees had to be approached. The process of singling out these individuals involved such criteria as their obvious prominence in the affairs of the school or in public life; others were approached because of their unique involvement in – or memories of – the school's past; still others because they were easily accessible at class reunions. Many of those interviewed became part of a lengthening Hotchkiss chain by suggesting somebody who had an unusual, lively, or contrasting perspective; and that person in turn suggesting still someone else. The frustrating aspect was that there were many more people in each of these categories than could be interviewed (the school's living graduates alone numbered about 7,500), though I did contact a disproportionate number of my contemporaries at the school and faculty members whom I had known. It was reassuring to realize gradually that all of the people interviewed, no matter how disparate their perspectives, were obviously talking about the same school.

In recognition of the limitations of the foregoing process, the first bow goes to those in the Hotchkiss community, present and past, who should have been but are not mentioned in this book – alumni/ae, faculty members, trustees, parents, and friends of the school; a particularly notable bow to those unmentioned Hotchkiss families who span several generations and have done so much for the school.

Thanks are next due to those who provided background or corroborating information but have not been specifically quoted. They include

Elisabeth D. Barbiero '93, Caroline P. Barlerin '92, Mrs. Milton F. Barlow, wife '22, Frank E. Bell '64, William Merriam B. Berger '44, Nancy D. Bird, director of health services, Blair M. Black '92, Robert H. Bork '44, Archibald J. Brooks '29, Judson J. Brooks '27, Barbara Brown, assistant admissions director, 1986–88, Patricia "Pam" Callard, Frederick C. Copeland, trustee 1957–1974, George R. DelPrete, director of athletics and history instructor, Carolyn F. and David Demaray, instructors in French, Luis de Yturbi '64, Michael S. Dinger '92, Mrs. Halliwell L. Duell, wife '30, James G. Gidwitz '64, Lyttleton B. Gould, Jr. '39, George S. Greene '39, Jessica L. Hanley '92, Wendy C. Helm, instructor in English, George M. D. Lewis, Jr. '39, Alexandra Loeb '79, Gay P. Lord, a parent and trustee, Alexander T. Mason '69, Rona A. Mattocks '92, Thomas E. McGivern, the school's print shop staff and head, 1959–1989, Daniel J. McNally '84, Donal C. O'Brien III '76, Dayton Ogden '32, Allison M. Pell '92, Peter S. Philip '81, director of college counselling, Susanna J. Pueschel '91, Charlotte M. Reid, daughter of history teacher A. B. Hall, Robert S. Royce, business manager 1965–1991, Jared Sprole '88, Kelly Stone, assistant director of athletics and instructor in mathematics, Ellen R. Torrey, head of dance program, Guyon W. Turner '60, Tucker H. Warner '49, Gretchen White, dean of upper classes, Henry M. Woodhouse '48.

Thanks are due to those individuals interviewed whose names are attributed to quotations in this book. Sadly, some of them are no longer with us, including Jerry Bowen '42, Francis Cochrane '10, John (Hoyt) Hoysradt '22, and Dud Parker '29.

Charles E. Berry, who taught history and German for some thirty-five years – and of whom the Duke often spoke as the ideal teacher – could not be interviewed because of illness in his family.

Bill Appleyard suggested a number of the people with whom the interview process began and, as director of alumni relations, remained helpful in other ways throughout. Thanks also to Alban F. Barker, instructor in French and dean of lower classes, and to those members of the class of 1991 who helped to set up interviews with students at the school, including Amit K. Basak, Brian Coughlin, Susanna J. Pueschel, and Margaret C. Virden.

The single most useful bit of advice in doing this centennial history came from Alumni Award winner Dan Lufkin '49. While interviewing him on the phone, I had to interrupt momentarily to check if my recently acquired but temperamental tape recorder was functioning properly. "Why don't you get another one?" suggested Dan, in a persuasive tone combining logic and disbelief. No doubt, he spared me endless grief.

All interviews that were recorded have been transcribed and will be preserved in the school archives to be available when a future version of the Hotchkiss history is prepared.

The majority of the written sources have already been identified in the text, whether the trustees' minutes or headmasters' correspondence or Uncle Joe Estill's memoirs or excerpts from the *Record*, the *Mischianza*, and other school-related publications. Besides the directly attributed quotations, these sources were indispensable for rounding out the picture of the school from year to year.

Walter E. DeMelle, Jr., director of the Hotchkiss library, was the first to call my attention to the existence of GVS's final notes. Thanks also to assistant directors Beverly K. Hoffman and Richard A. Ward, who were always ready to help.

A Portrait, the seventy-fifth anniversary history by Lael Wertenbaker, served not only as a source of lively controversy within the school, but provided a most useful framework of Hotchkiss history on which to build. Wertenbaker's colorful descriptions of such characters of yesteryear as the gusty Dean Jones of Yale were utilized, as were her recreations of such incidents as the assault on Doc Rob in study hall. Stephen Birmingham's *America's Secret Society* (Little, Brown & Co., 1987) provided several anecdotes about George Van Santvoord.

Thanks are due to Kip Armstrong '63, whose works served as the source for depicting the evolution of prep schools: *"Privilege and Productivity: A Comparison of Two Private Schools (Hotchkiss and Putney) and their Graduates"* (Ph.D. dissertation, University of Pennsylvania, 1974); "On the Making of Good Men: Character Building in the New England Boarding Schools," in *The High Status Track: Studies of Elite Schools and Stratification*, edited by Paul W. Kingston and Lionell S. Lewis, 3–24 (SUNY Press, 1990). Kip Armstrong's article "The Lessons of Sport: Class Socialization in British and American Boarding Schools," *Sociology of Sport* (December 1984): 314–31, provided historical perspective on Hotchkiss athletics.

The school's archivist, Teresa Oden, was the principal researcher, uncovering many of those documents which give life and interest to the early years of the school, including the notorious Buehler file and the long-lost tape of GVS's interview with Mrs. Wertenbaker. Whether by culling the school's publications, or ensconcing herself with the official files in the steamy basement of the library, or traveling to Yale to obtain documents, Teresa helped substantially to shape many parts of the book. She also inherited from Martha R. Virden, alumni/ae coordinator for *Hotchkiss Magazine*, the school's photographic archives.

Sharing in some of the research was Bob Hawkins, who embodies a treasure trove of history with his forty-five years at or near the school. As executive director of the centennial history committee, Bob was in touch with numerous outside sources, and he wishes especially to thank Miss Adelaide Emory of the Hotchkiss Library in Sharon, Mrs. Ruth Quattlebaum of the Phillips Academy in Andover, and the staff of the Scoville Library in Salisbury. His thanks also to the headmaster's secretary, Mrs. Jeri Johnson, and to Robert Royce for their assistance.

Bob Hawkins also provided a wealth of excerpted material from the school's one hundred years of publications, though research was not exactly his métier; even his expert blue-penciling of the manuscript, as the committee's editor-in-chief, represents only the beginning of what he did. Bob's main contribution was that he, as a venerable Hotchkiss institution in his own right, implemented from the outset an open approach to the history, which constituted a distinct break with the past. By his very presence he was giving an imprimatur to the work prior to its presentation to the committee. Moreover, during my longer sojourns at the school, Bob took on the role of considerate host, and some of his culinary offerings might rate a star or two in *Guide Michelin*.

The contribution of the centennial history committee belies the adage that bodies of this sort invariably produce only camels when trying for a horse. Or is it perhaps that camels, as creatures appropriate to a particular place and set of conditions, are vastly underrated? Be that as it may, without the direction, advice, and support of the committee there would be no book. Committee members served pro bono and at their own expense.

Among the members, there were the writers: Stephen Birmingham, who had noticed my piece on GVS in the *Alumni Magazine* several years ago, and now proposed my name for the project. Though turning out two novels of his own during the time it took to write this book (*Shades of Fortune* and *The Rothman Scandal*), he was always ready to lend an understanding ear on the telephone. He also made three trips from Cincinnati to attend meetings, lugging the bulky manuscript on the final trip with his suggested cuts penciled in, which would trim it to a more manageable weight. Any remaining flab is entirely the author's fault for not fully heeding Steve's advice.

There was *Friendly Fire* author, C. D. B. "Courty" Bryan, who resorted to the ingenious device of giving me his first-, second-, and third-place votes, thus assuring my selection for the project over a number of non-Hotchkiss candidates. He then provided the inspiration which would help validate his a priori confidence. As the writer of the National Geographic Society's centennial history, Courty was able to share with the committee some comparative guidelines for this work.

There was John Hersey, whose *A Bell for Adano* I first read under the guidance of Carle Parsons as a prep. In response to the various versions of the manuscript sent to him, I was privileged to receive from John Hersey more than twenty typed, single-spaced pages of comments and suggestions, always persuasively yet sensitively phrased. His timely communications of support sounded a note not unlike that issuing from the salutary bell which introduced me to his work.

Of the trustees on the committee, there was Edgar Cullman, who was technically an observer but took such a strong lead that after the first meeting I pointed out to him that his nonvote on the committee seemed to outweigh all of the other votes combined; however, as the project progressed, Edgar's kindness, good humor, straightforward advice, and, above all, his respect for the independent process made me grateful for his strength.

There was Gay P. Lord, who made three trips from Bethesda, Maryland, to attend committee meetings, at which she articulated a woman's point of view combined with the insight of a parent of three students spanning the eras of Bill Olsen, Tim Callard, and Arthur White. Gay's perspective and support helped reenforce some key aspects of the book.

There was John Roche '53, the committee's chairman. He proposed the idea of doing a centennial history to the board, obtained the necessary funding, and recruited key members of the staff. Drawing on his legal expertise, John stood ready throughout the project to build viable bridges over any chasms that from time to time opened up. On innumerable occasions, he proved to be a wise counselor indeed.

Representing the Hotchkiss of a more recent vintage on the committee was Carolyn Wilcox Galiette '78. Sitting at the conference table in the

Warner Room next to her former teacher of prep English, she made constructive suggestions and carried out her responsibilities in a way which
again made Bob Hawkins proud. Carolyn replaced Michael J. Carroll '75,
whose other commitments prevented him from taking part after the committee's initial meeting.

Of the administrators on the committee, there was Rusty Chandler '53,
who had at one time lived two rooms down from me as a prep in Buehler
Hall. In the intervening years, Rusty had spent another quarter of a century at the school in various posts on his way to becoming assistant headmaster. He was in a unique position to serve as a firsthand reference source
for evaluating the evenhandedness of the material in the manuscript covering those years, as well as for checking the facts.

There was Kristina "Tina" S. Chandler, the school's director of development and Rusty's wife. As a relative newcomer to the school, she was
able to offer a lively outside view and encouragement for a human approach with its multiplicity of dimensions. Tina also fulfilled the indispensable task of keeping the project fiscally sound and on schedule.

The headmaster and his wife acted as genuine observers, and their comments and attitude enhanced the committee's enthusiasm as a group. Rob
Oden's presence assumed an added dimension in that he, as the ultimate
master of ceremonies for the various centennial goings on, would stand in
a unique position vis-à-vis the forthcoming book.

The recording secretary was Virginia "Ginny" Vollet, who undoubtedly qualifies as the second most involved person in producing this book.
Because of her regular fulltime duties as alumni secretary, Ginny often
started her day at 4 A.M., either transcribing interviews or entering into
the computer at least a half-dozen different versions of the manuscript,
each time adding to the original 156-page outline and incorporating countless changes. She acted as an irreplaceable sounding board and performed a
whole array of other tasks, which, combined with her ever-helpful outlook, lightened my work.

It was perhaps inevitable that an unfettered approach to the school's past
would bring other interested members of the Hotchkiss community into
the editorial process – most notably David Luke and Zeph Stewart. While
Dave Luke took the initiative in becoming involved, Zeph Stewart was in
effect drafted into the fray to act as a sort of ombudsman. Their respective
contributions have resulted primarily in the clarification, elaboration, and

fine-tuning of some sensitive points – making it in parts a fuller, gentler book. At the same time, Zeph polished up a number of my attempted Latinisms and helped remove similar bits of tarnish previously overlooked.

The following have also read the manuscript and provided constructive comments: Woods McCahill, Archibald Coolidge, Fay Vincent, and Sylvia DeSantis, my neighbor and head librarian in Monson, Massachusetts. Thanks to Larry Becker for his comments on the portion covering the Olsen, Callard, and White administrations; to Bill Elfers and Frank Sprole for commenting on the material on Bill Olsen; and Bill Olsen for commenting on that material, too. Jane Hughes read the main chapter on Jean Olsen and offered her comments and suggestions.

The committee retained Kitty Benedict as a freelance editor, and she contributed numerous suggestions, among them several of considerable consequence. Lawrence Kenney of Cheshire, Connecticut, was the very able copyeditor. Barbara Griggs, whose husband Van taught French at Hotchkiss in the 1930s, did the proofreading and helped to improve the manuscript still further.

Mentioning names of people who commented or made suggestions about any aspect of the book does not imply that they necessarily approve of the final result. The degree of suasion involved in putting forward their views obviously varied but never exceeded the limits implicit in the school motto, *Moniti Meliora Sequamur*. Within that context, the final decisions were left to the author to make.

I would like to thank the following members of the Hotchkiss staff for their various courtesies and help: Deborah M. Fogel, Ellen T. Fontaine, William E. Gordon, Betty A. Logan, Janet Manko, Heminway Merriman 2nd, Margaret Morgan, Lucille Nelson, Joseph O'Connor, Joseph O'Loughlin, Robert Powell, Norma P. Redmond, Rosina R. Rossire, Kevin Rueger, Carolyn F. Runge, Elizabeth S. Tyburski, Gerald Wheeler, and Ken Wiseman. A special thank you to Margot W. Hooker.

I feel fortunate to have been able to count on the day-to-day counsel of Barbara W. Newell in this work. Her experience in academia and diplomacy provided just the right combination of talents to draw on for surviving a process that has been akin to going through four years of Hotchkiss again.

THE HOTCHKISS
ALUMNI AWARD
PRESENTED EACH YEAR TO
AN ALUMNUS WHO THROUGH
PERSONAL ACHIEVEMENT
HAS BROUGHT HONOR AND
DISTINCTION TO HIMSELF
AND TO THE SCHOOL
1931 HENRY KNOX SHERRILL 1907
ARTHUR HOWE 1908
LAWRENCE MC CULLY JUDD 1906
GEORGE VAN SANTVOORD 1908
HENRY ROBINSON LUCE 1916
HAROLD STANLEY 1904
CHARLES EDISON 1909
WILLIAM MANSFIELD CLARK 1903
ARTHUR LEHMAN GOODHART 1908
1940 ALLEN LAWRENCE CHICKERING 1894
HENRY LOCKWOOD DE FOREST
ARCHIBALD MAC LEISH
ARTHUR MORRIS
ARTEMUS LAMB GATES
DOUGLAS STUART
ERDMAN HARRIS 1916
EDWIN FOSTER BLAIR
EVERETT NEEDHAM
ALFRED
JOHN
WALTER

Appendix

Note: Buell served the first year of his tenure as acting headmaster, and Buehler and White started out briefly in that capacity. Joe Estill served as acting headmaster from 1902 to 1903 during Coy's illness, and again in 1912 and in 1916 during Buehler's European trips. George D. Kellogg, Jr. '35 served as acting headmaster during Olsen's around the world sabbatical.

BOARD OF TRUSTEES PRESIDENTS

Frederick J. Kingsbury	1891 – 1899
Andrew W. Phillips	1899 – 1914
Morris W. Seymour	1915 – 1920
Frederick S. Jones	1920 – 1942
Arthur M. Collens '99	1942 – 1946
John E. Bierwirth '13	1946 – 1962
James A. Linen III '30	1962 – 1967
Arthur K. Watson '38	1967 – 1970
Woods McCahill '33	1970 – 1975
David L. Luke III '41	1975 – 1980
Frank A. Sprole '38	1980 – 1985
Francis T. Vincent '56	1985 – 1987
Edgar M. Cullman '36	1987 –

Note: Collens was president of Phoenix Mutual Life Insurance; Bierwirth was president of National Distillers; Watson was chairman of IBM International and served as ambassador to Great Britain during part of the Nixon administration. Professional careers of other board presidents are detailed in the text.

THE HOTCHKISS ALUMNI AWARD

1931 Henry Knox Sherrill '07
    Arthur Howe '08
    Lawrence McCully Judd '06
    George Van Santvoord '08
    Henry Robinson Luce '16
    Harold Stanley '04
    Charles Edison '09
    William Mansfield Clark '03
    Arthur Lehman Goodhart '08

1940 Allen Lawrence Chickering '94
    Henry Lockwood de Forest '93
    Archibald MacLeish '11
    Arthur Morris Collens '99
    Artemus Lamb Gates '14

1945 No Award
 Douglas Stuart Moore '11
 Erdman Harris '16
 Edwin Foster Blair '20
 Everett Needham Case '18

1950 Alfred Whitney Griswold '25
 John Edward Bierwirth '13
 Walter Phelps Hall '01
 Henry Ford II '36
 Richard Lyon Bowditch '19
 Dickinson Woodruff Richards, Jr. '13
 Livingston Talmadge Merchant '22
 James Alexander Linen III '30
 Robert Chapman Sprague '18
 Potter Stewart '33

1960 Ernest Gruening '03
 John Hersey '32
 Roswell Leavitt Gilpatric '24
 William Warren Scranton '35
 Albert William Olsen, Jr. '39
 Arthur Kittredge Watson '38
 Charles Woodruff Yost '24
 Paul Henry Nitze '24
 Atholl McBean '00
 Arthur Howe, Jr. '38

1970 Thomas P. F. Hoving '49
 William G. McKnight, Jr. '30
 Dan Wende Lufkin '49
 Joseph Frederick Cullman 3rd '31
 Peter Matthiessen '45
 Gaylord Donnelley '27
 John Miller Musser '26
 Frank Arnott Sprole '38
 John Henry Hammond, Jr. '29
 William Elfers '37

1980 Jon Ormand Newman '49
 David L. Luke III '41
 William Block '32
 Michael MacCracken Stewart '53
 Eli Whitney Debevoise '17
 Malcolm Baldrige '40
 Robert A. Bryan '49
 Woods McCahill '33
 C. S. Harding Mott '25
 Winston Lord '55

1990 George F. Cahill, Jr. '44
 Francis T. Vincent, Jr. '56
 Edgar M. Cullman '36

Index*

*Names of people generally appear in the same format as in the text. Hotchkiss alumni/ae have been identified by the year of their graduating class.